STREET ATLAS
West Kent

First published in 1989

Philip's, a division of
Octopus Publishing Group Ltd
2–4 Heron Quays, London E14 4JP

Second colour edition 2002
First impression 2002

ISBN 0-540-07980-4 (hardback)
ISBN 0-540-07981-2 (spiral)

© Philip's 2002

To the best of the Publishers' knowledge, the
information in this atlas was correct at the time
of going to press. No responsibility can be
accepted for any errors or their consequences.

The representation in this atlas of a road, track
or path is no evidence of the existence of a right
of way.

Ordnance Survey and the OS Symbol are
registered trademarks of Ordnance Survey, the
national mapping agency of Great Britain

Printed and bound in Spain
by Cayfosa-Quebecor

Contents

III	**Key to map symbols**
IV	**Key to map pages**
VI	**Route planning**
VIII	**Administrative and Postcode boundaries**
1	**Street maps** at 3½ inches to 1 mile
190	**Town maps** of Ashford, Canterbury, Dover and Folkestone
192	**Index** of towns and villages
193	**Index** of streets, hospitals, industrial estates, railway stations, schools, shopping centres and universities

Digital Data

The exceptionally high-quality mapping found in this atlas is available as digital data in TIFF format, which is easily convertible to other bit mapped (raster) image formats.

The index is also available in digital form as a standard database table. It contains all the details found in the printed index together with the National Grid reference for the map square in which each entry is named and feature codes for places of interest in eight categories such as education and health.

For further information and to discuss your requirements, please contact Philip's on 020 7531 8440 or george.philip@philips-maps.co.uk

Motorway with junction number		**Railway station**
Primary route – dual/single carriageway		**Docklands Light Railway station**
A road – dual/single carriageway		**Private railway station**
B road – dual/single carriageway		**Bus, coach station**
Minor road – dual/single carriageway		**Ambulance station**
Other minor road – dual/single carriageway		**Coastguard station**
Road under construction		**Fire station**
Pedestrianised area		**Police station**
Postcode boundaries		**Accident and Emergency entrance to hospital**
County and unitary authority boundaries		**Hospital**
Railway		**Place of worship**
Railway under construction		**Information Centre** (open all year)
Tramway, miniature railway		**Parking**
Rural track, private road or narrow road in urban area		**Park and Ride**
Gate or obstruction to traffic (restrictions may not apply at all times or to all vehicles)		**Post Office**
Path, bridleway, byway open to all traffic, road used as a public path		**Camping site**
The representation in this atlas of a road, track or path is no evidence of the existence right of way		**Caravan site**
		Golf course
		Picnic site
Adjoining page indicators	Prim Sch	**Important buildings, schools, colleges, universities and hospitals**
	River Medway	**Water name**
		Stream
		River or canal – minor and major
		Water
		Tidal water
		Woods
		Houses
	House	**Non-Roman antiquity**
	VILLA	**Roman antiquity**

Allot Gdns	**Allotments**	Meml	**Memorial**
Acad	**Academy**	Mon	**Monument**
Cemy	**Cemetery**	Mus	**Museum**
C Ctr	**Civic Centre**	Obsy	**Observatory**
CH	**Club House**	Pal	**Royal Palace**
Coll	**College**	PH	**Public House**
Crem	**Crematorium**	Recn Gd	**Recreation Ground**
Ent	**Enterprise**	Resr	**Reservoir**
Ex H	**Exhibition Hall**	Ret Pk	**Retail Park**
Ind Est	**Industrial Estate**	Sch	**School**
Inst	**Institute**	Sh Ctr	**Shopping Centre**
Ct	**Law Court**	TH	**Town Hall/House**
L Ctr	**Leisure Centre**	Trad Est	**Trading Estate**
LC	**Level Crossing**	Univ	**University**
Liby	**Library**	Wks	**Works**
Mkt	**Market**	YH	**Youth Hostel**

■ The dark grey border on the inside edge of some pages indicates that the mapping does not continue onto the adjacent page

■ The small numbers around the edges of the maps identify the 1 kilometre National Grid lines

The scale of the maps is 5.52 cm to 1 km
3¹/₂ inches to 1 mile   1: 18103

0	¹/₄	¹/₂	³/₄	1 mile
0	250m	500m	750m	1 kilometre

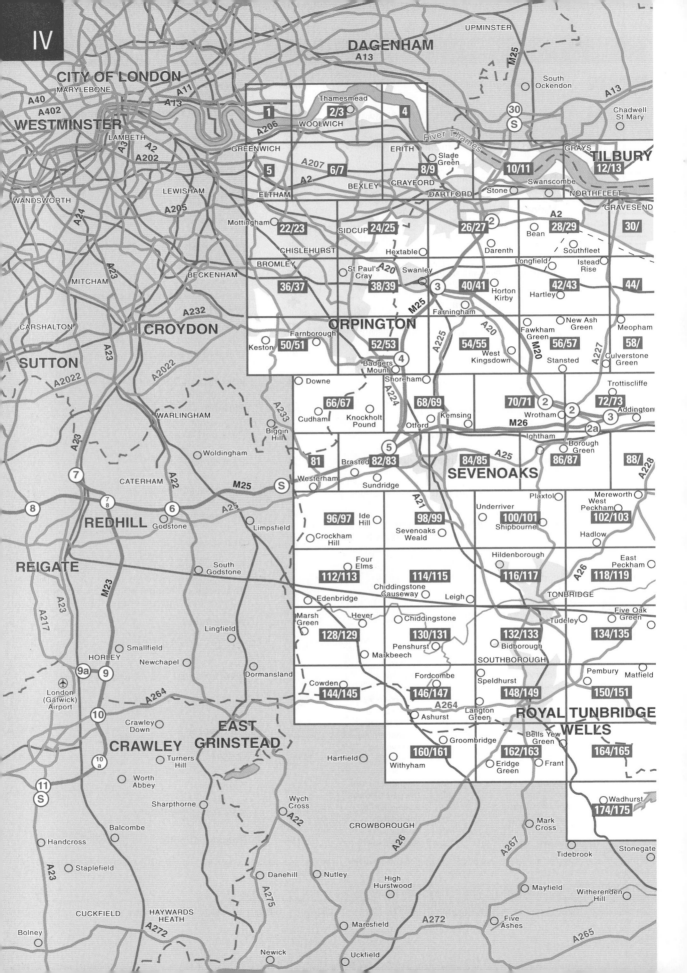

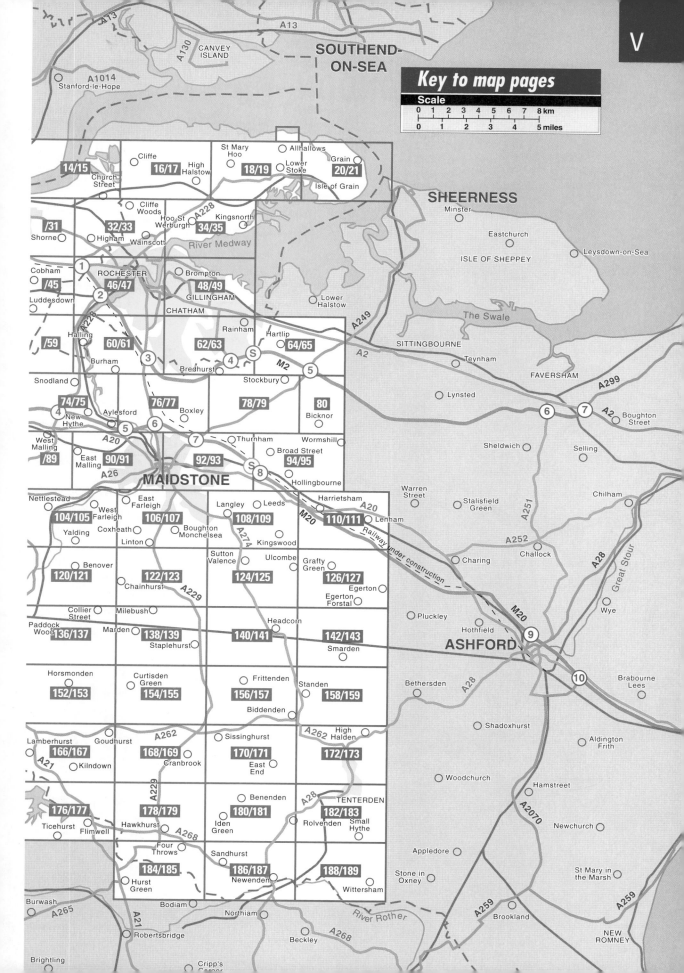

Key to map pages

Scale

0 1 2 3 4 5 6 7 8 km
0 1 2 3 4 5 miles

SOUTHEND-ON-SEA

SHEERNESS

Stanford-le-Hope

CANVEY ISLAND

A1014

A13

A130

Cliffe

14/15

16/17

High Halstow

St Mary Hoo

18/19

Allhallows

Lower Stoke

Grain

20/21

Isle of Grain

Church Street

Minster

ISLE OF SHEPPEY

Eastchurch

Leysdown-on-Sea

Cliffe Woods

Hoo St Werburgh

/31

32/33

Kingsnorth

34/35

Shorne

Higham

Wainscott

A228

River Medway

The Swale

Cobham

/45

ROCHESTER

46/47

Brompton

48/49

GILLINGHAM

Lower Halstow

SITTINGBOURNE

A249

Teynham

FAVERSHAM

A299

Luddesdown

CHATHAM

/59

Halling

60/61

62/63

Rainham

Hartlip

64/65

Burham

Bredhurst

M2

Lynsted

A2

Snodland

Stockbury

Sheldwich

Selling

Boughton Street

A251

74/75

76/77

Boxley

78/79

80

Bicknor

New Hythe

Aylesford

Thurnham

Wormshill

Warren Street

Stalisfield Green

Chilham

West Malling

/89

East Malling

90/91

A20

92/93

94/95

Broad Street

Hollingbourne

A26

MAIDSTONE

Harrietsham

A20

Charing

Challock

A252

A28

Nettlestead

West Farleigh

East Farleigh

Langley

Leeds

104/105

106/107

108/109

110/111

Lenham

Wye

Yalding

Coxheath

Boughton Monchelsea

Linton

Kingswood

A274

Railway under construction

M20

Pluckley

Hothfield

120/121

Benover

122/123

Chainhurst

A229

Sutton Valence

124/125

Ulcombe

Grafty Green

126/127

Egerton

Egerton Forstal

Collier Street

Milebush

Headcorn

136/137

Paddock Wood

Marden

138/139

Staplehurst

140/141

142/143

Smarden

ASHFORD

M20

Bethersden

A28

Horsmonden

Curtisden Green

Frittenden

Standen

152/153

154/155

156/157

Biddenden

158/159

Shadoxhurst

Aldington Frith

Lamberhurst

Goudhurst

A262

Sissinghurst

High Halden

A262

166/167

168/169

Cranbrook

170/171

East End

172/173

Woodchurch

Hamstreet

A2070

Kilndown

A21

Newchurch

Benenden

A28

TENTERDEN

176/177

178/179

Hawkhurst

A268

180/181

Iden Green

Rolvenden

182/183

Small Hythe

Appledore

Ticehurst

Flimwell

Four Throws

Sandhurst

St Mary in the Marsh

184/185

Hurst Green

186/187

Newenden

188/189

Wittersham

Stone in Oxney

Burwash

Bodiam

Northiam

A265

A21

Robertsbridge

Beckley

A268

River Rother

Brookland

A259

NEW ROMNEY

Brightling

Cripp's Corner

A259

Route planning

Scale

```
0  1  2  3  4  5  6  7  8 km
0     1     2     3     4     5 miles
```

SOUTHEND-ON-SEA

North Shoebury
Shoeburyness
Shoebury Ness

Leigh-on-Sea · Chalkwell · Southchurch
Westcliff-on-Sea · Station
Thorpe Bay

CANVEY ISLAND
Fobbing · Corringham
Coryton · Thames Haven
Mucking · Linford · East Tilbury
Chapman Sands · Leigh Beck
Blyth Sands

Halstow Matshes · St Mary's Marshes
Allhallows-on-Sea
Cliffe Fort · Cliffe · Cooling · St Mary Hoo
Church Street · High Halstow · Allhallows
Lower Stoke · Grain · Isle of Grain
Stoke · Power Station

SHEERNESS
Halfway Houses · Minster · Warden Point
Queenborough · Warden · Leysdown-on-Sea
Chetney Marshes · Eastchurch · Prison
ISLE OF SHEPPEY
Swale Station · Elmley Island · Isle of Harty · Shell Ness

Cliffe Woods · Hoo · St Werburgh · Kingsnorth
Higham · Wainscott · Chattenden · Upnor
Hoo Fort
Frindsbury · Brompton
Strood · Upchurch · Iwade · Kemsley
ROCHESTER · Borstal · GILLINGHAM · Lower Halslow
Rochester Airport · CHATHAM · Bobbing · Milton Regis
Capstone · Rainham · SITTINGBOURNE · Conyer
Halling · Wouldham · Wigmore · Hartlip · Newington · Seasalte
Blue Bell Hill · Walderslade · Borden · Uplees · Oare · Graveney
New Hythe · Burham · Bredhurst · Oad Street · Bapchild · Teynham · FAVERSHAM
Eccles · Aylesford · Stockbury · Bredgar · Tunstall · Highsted · Rodmersham · Lynsted · Ospringe · Goodnestone
Boxley · Hucking · Bicknor · Millstead · Ospringe · Hernhill · Boughton Str
West Malling · Sandling · Detling · Wormshill · Newnham · Painter's Forstal · North Street · Selling
MAIDSTONE · Thurnham · Frinsted · Doddington · Eastling · Sheldwich · Old Wi Lees
East Barming · Broad Street · Wichling · Throwley · Badlesmere · Shottenden · Chilham
Tovil · Shepway · Hollingbourne · West Street · Stalisfield Green · Leaveland · Molash
West Farleigh · Loose · Eyhorne Street · Warren Street · Godmersham
Teston · East Farleigh · Otham · Harrietsham · Challock · Bilting
Nettlestead · Langley · Leeds · Lenham · Boughton Aluph · Olantigh
Yalding · Boughton Monchelsea · Broomfield · Lenham Heath · Boughton Lees · Wye
Hunton · Kingswood · Charing Heath · Charing · Kennington
Benover · Linton · Boughton Malherbe · Westwell · Brook
Laddingford · Coxheath · Chart Sutton · Grafty Green · Little Chart · Westwell Leacon · Boughton Aluph
Chainhurst · Sutton Valence · Ulcombe · Egerton · Ram Lane · Hinxhill · Brabo
Collier Street · LOW WEALD · Egerton Forstal · Pluckley · Willesborough Lees
Milebush · Cross-at-Hand · Hawkenbury · Headcorn · Hothfield · ASHFORD
Claygate · Marden · Staplehurst · Maltman's Hill · Bethersden · Great Chart · Savington
Brenchley · Horsmonden · Curtisden Green · Smarden · Frittenden · Standen · Mersham · Cheeseman's Green
Cranbrook Common · Biddenden · High Halden · Shadoxhurst · Kingsnorth · SMEET
Goudhurst · Sissinghurst · Shirkoak · Bromley Green · Aldington Frith · Bonnington · Aldington
Kilndown · Cranbrook · East End · Woodchurch · Orlestone · Bilsington
Hartley · Benenden · TENTERDEN · Leigh Green · Hamstreet · Ruckinge
Three Leg Cross · Bedgebury Forest · Hole Park · Kenardington · Warehorne · Burma
Flimwell · Iden Green · Rolvenden · Small Hythe · Shirley Moor · Reading Street · Newchurch
Hawkhurst · Four Throws · Rolvenden Layne · Snargate · ROMNEY MARSH
The Moor · Sandhurst · Newenden · Wittersham · Appledore · Ivychurch · St Mary in the Marsh
Hurst Green · Bodiam · ISLE OF OXNEY · Stone in Oxney · Brenzett · Old Romney
Etchingham · Salehurst · Northiam · Four Oaks · Iden · Brookland · NEW

WEALD

River Medway · River Beult · The Swale · River Rother · Rother Levels · Royal Military Canal · Pilgrims Way · Railway under construction

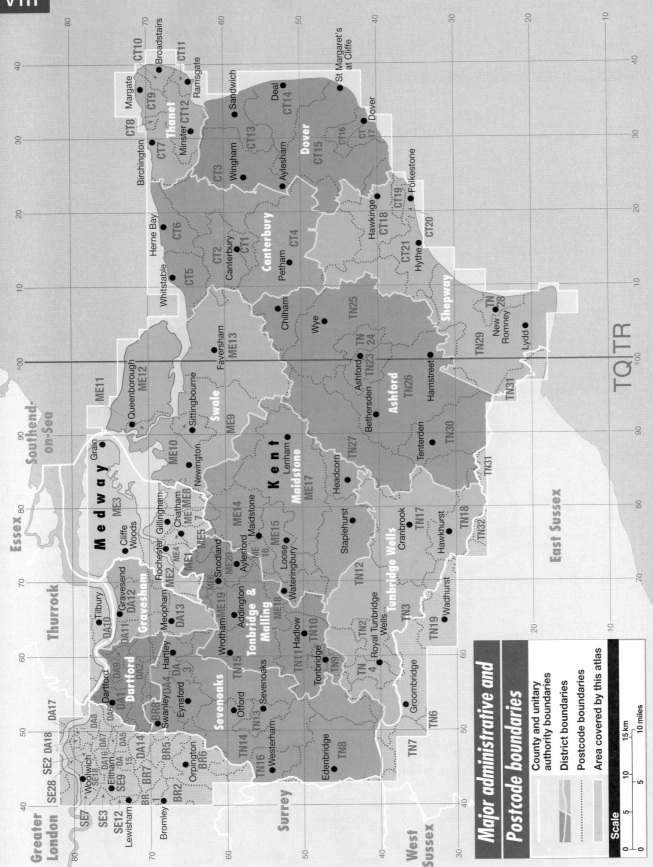

Major administrative and Postcode boundaries

	County and unitary authority boundaries
	District boundaries
	Postcode boundaries
	Area covered by this atlas

Scale

0   5   10   15 km
0   5   10 miles

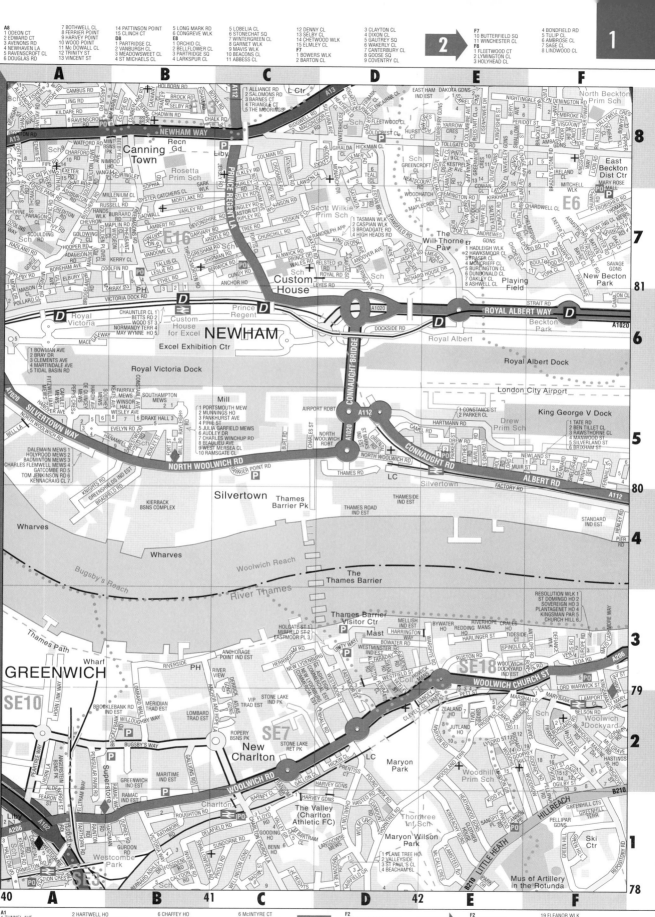

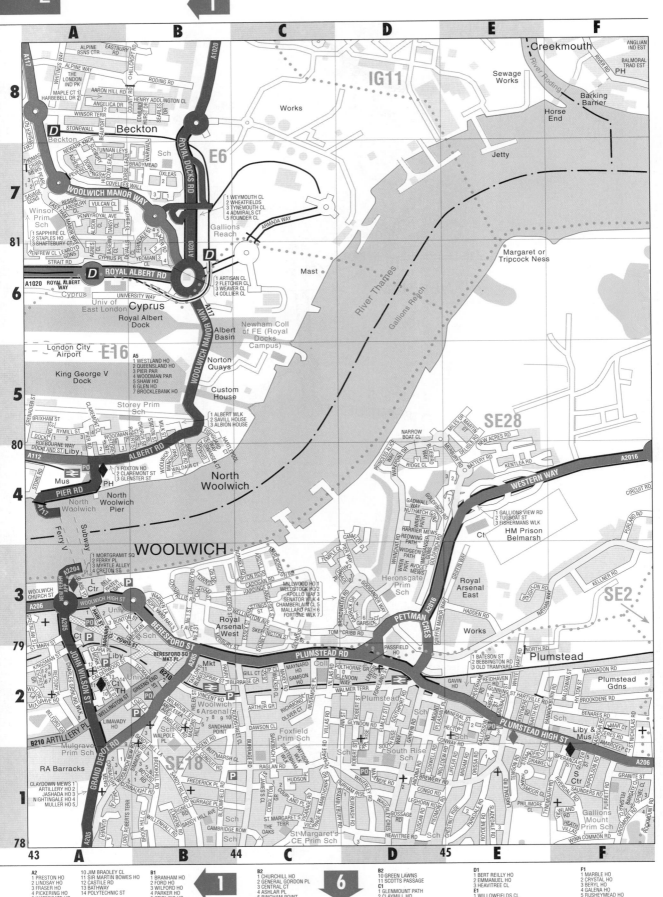

B5
1 ROWNTREE PATH
2 MACAULAY WAY
3 MANNING CT
4 CHADWICK CT
5 SIMON CT

B6
1 BEVERIDGE CT
2 HAMMOND WAY
3 LEONARD ROBBINS PATH
4 LANSBURY CT
5 RAYMOND POSTGATE CT
6 WEBB CT

7 CURTIS WAY
8 LYTTON STRACHY PATH
9 KEYNES CT
10 MARSHALL PATH
11 CROSS CT
12 OCTAVIA WAY
13 PASSFIELD PATH

14 MILL CT
15 BESANT CT
C5
1 KINGSLEY CT
2 WILBERFORCE CT
3 SHAFTESBURY CT
4 HAZLITT CT

5 RICARDO PATH
6 NASSAU PATH
7 MALTHUS PATH
8 BRIGHT CT
9 COBDEN CT

C4
1 BINSEY WLK
2 TILEHURST POINT
3 BLEWBURY HO
4 CORALLINE WLK
5 EVENLODE HO

D4
1 OAKENHOLT HO
2 TREWSBURY HO
3 PENTON HO
4 OSNEY HO
5 JACOB HO
6 MASHAM HO
7 ST HELENS RD

D4
8 CLEWER HO
9 MAPLIN HO
10 WYFOLD HO
11 HIBERNIA POINT
12 DUXFORD HO
13 RADLEY HO

E3
1 HARLEQUIN HO
2 DEXTER HO
3 ARGALL HO
4 MANGOLD WAY
5 LUCERNE CT
6 HOLSTEIN WAY
7 ABBOTSWOOD CL
8 PLYMPTON CL
9 BENEDICT CL

F1
1 SHAKESPEARE HO
2 TENNYSON HO
3 DICKENS HO
4 SCOTT HO
5 LANSBURY HO
6 SHAW HO
7 THE CHESTNUTS

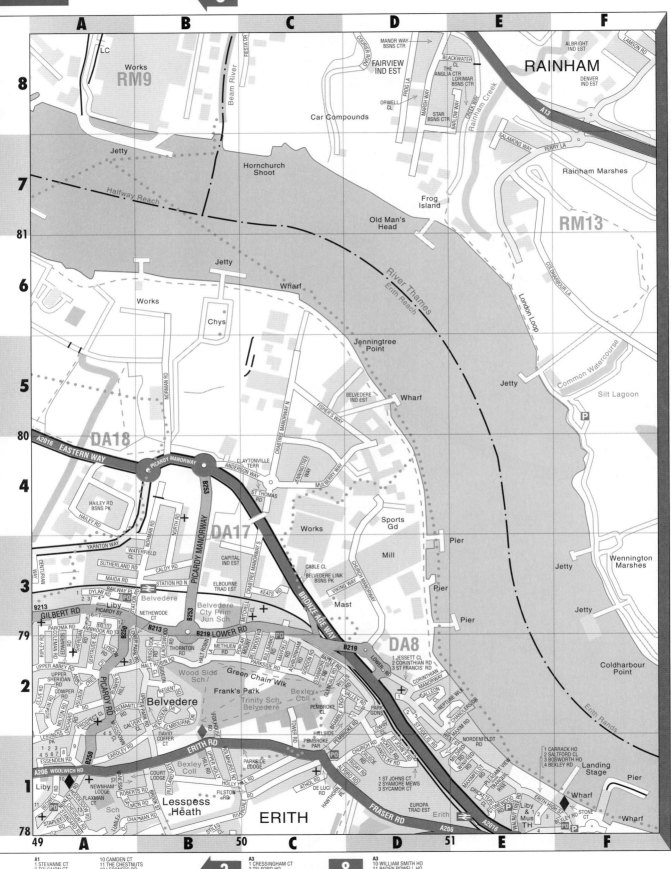

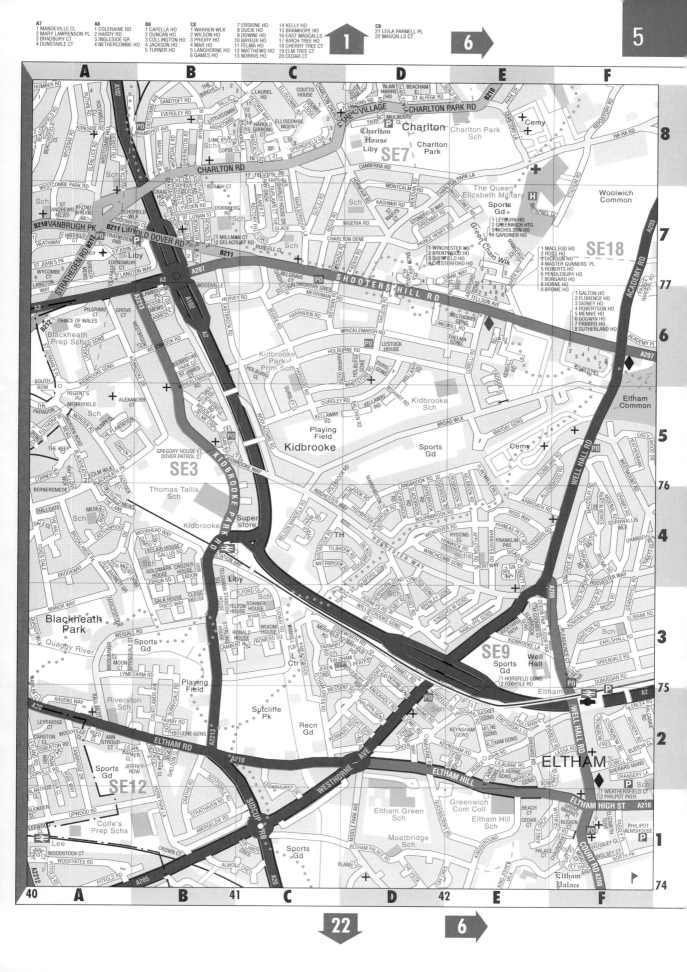

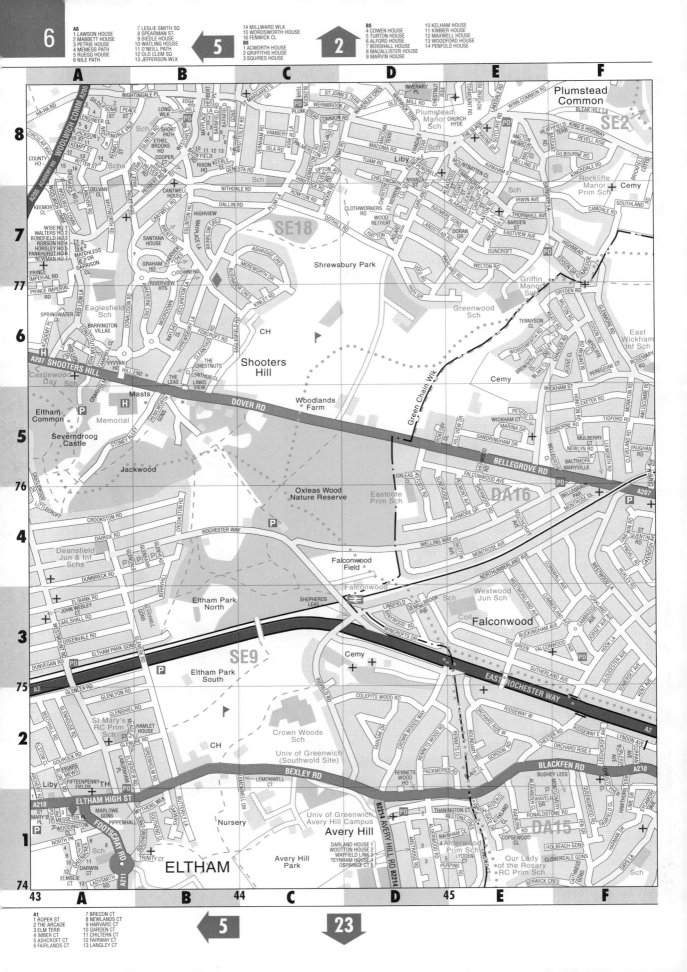

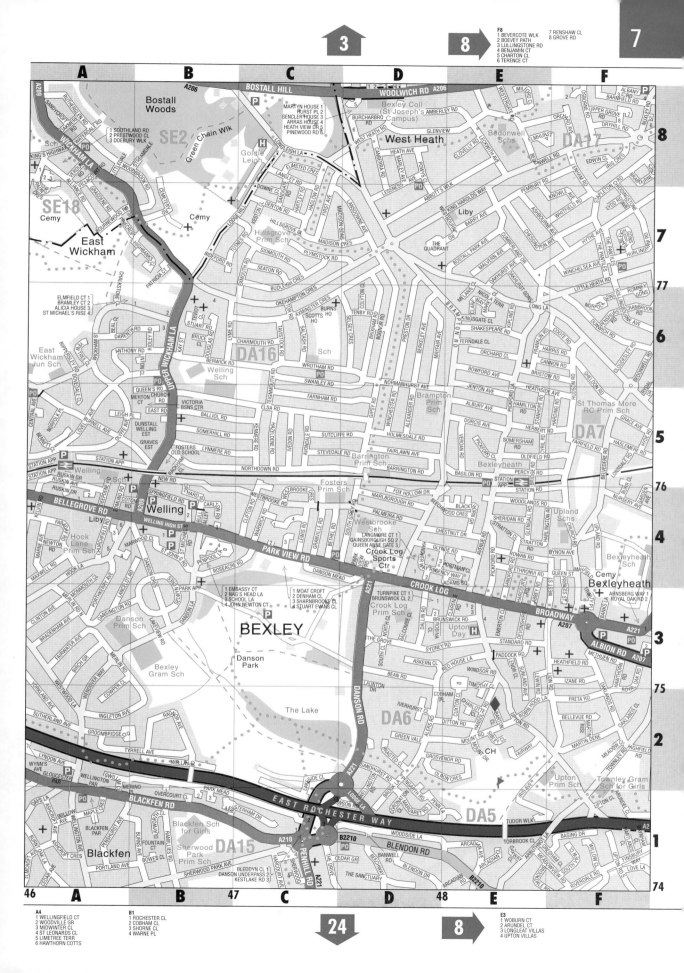

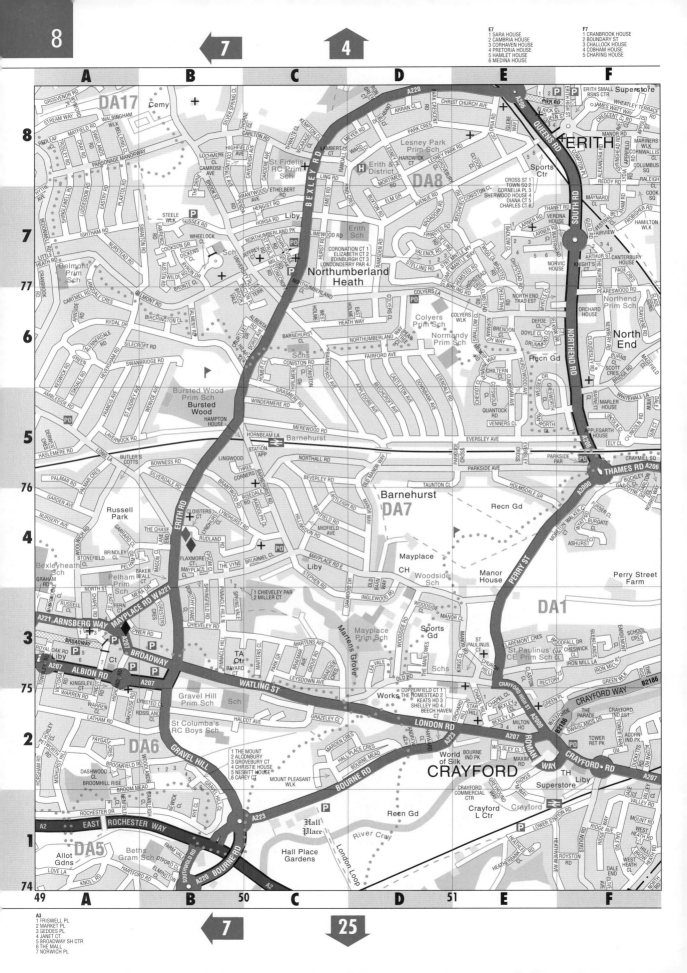

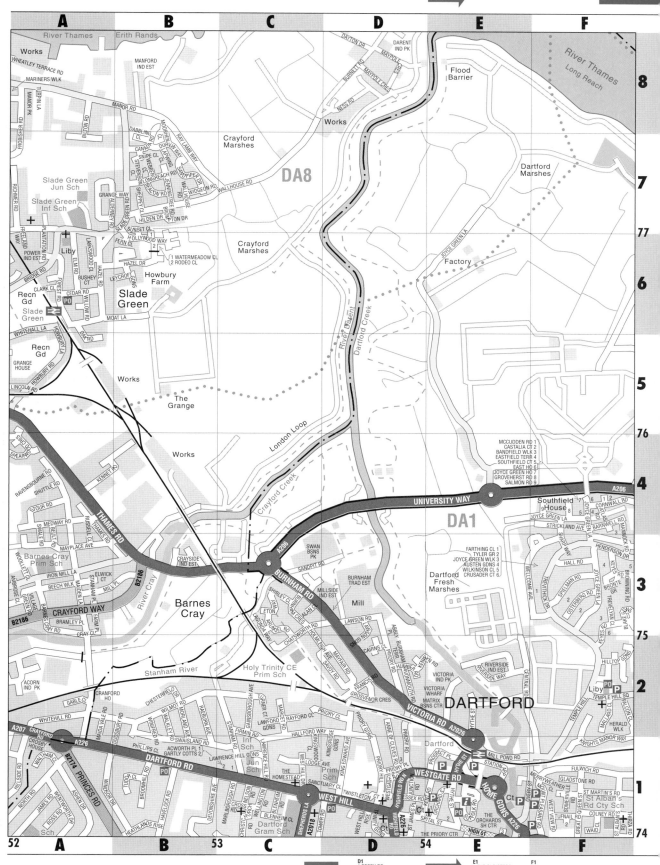

26

D1
1 ESSEX RD
2 CLEVES VIEW
3 PRIORY CT

10

E1
1 THE CLOISTERS
2 COPPERFIELDS
3 BULLACE LA

F1
1 LAVINIA RD
2 LAMPLIGHTERS CL

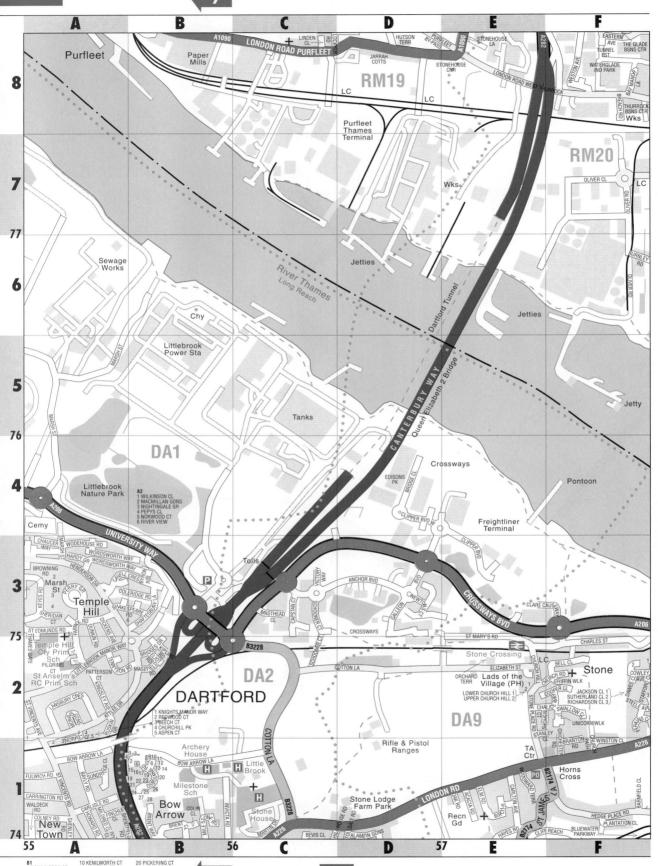

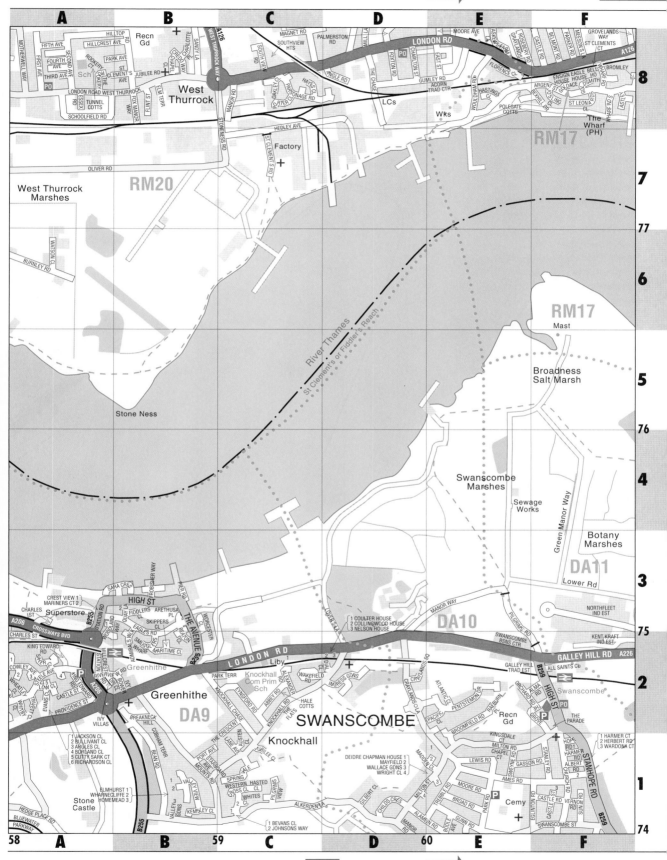

A   B   C   D   E   F

MOTHERWELL WAY
FIFTH AVE
HILLTOP
Recn Gd
MAGNET RD
MOORE AVE
LONDON RD
ASKEW GRO
GROVELANDS WAY
ST CLEMENTS CT
BELMONT RD
A126

HILLCREST AVE
FIRST AVE
FOURTH AVE
SECOND AVE
PARK AVE
SANDY LA
SOUTHVIEW HTS
PALMERSTON RD
CHARLTON RD
FOXTON RD
EAST ST
FLORENCE CT
ROSSERY RD
GRAFTON RD
CASTLE RD
PARKER RD
MEESON'S RD
BROMLEY

THIRD AVE
ROCKERY CL
CHAPEL
ST CLEMENT'S AVE
JUBILEE RD
SOUTH VIEW
OAKLEY CL
HAYES CL
PARSONAGE RD
THE CHASE
GUMLEY RD
PO
ACORN TRAD CTR
HASTINGS CL
POLEGATE COTTS
ENSIGN EAGLE BELL HOUSE HOUSE HO
ARGENT ST
JOSLING
GS PLACE
SMITH
BEXHILL DR
ST LEONA
ST LEON A
WHARF RD S
ASTL

PO
LONDON ROAD WEST THURROCK
ESSEX RD
TUNNEL COTTS
FOX MANOR WAY
FLINT ST
ELM TERR
MANOR RD
STONENESS RD
CARTER
West Thurrock
LCs
WOULDHAM RD
Wks
RM17
The Wharf (PH)

SCHOOLFIELD RD
Sch

HEDLEY AVE
ST CLEMENT S RD
Factory

OLIVER RD
RM20
West Thurrock Marshes

WATSON CL
BURNLEY RD

River Thames
St Clement's or Fiddler's Reach

Stone Ness

RM17
Mast

Broadness Salt Marsh

77
7
6
76
5
4

Swanscombe Marshes
Sewage Works

Green Manor Way
Botany Marshes
DA11
Lower Rd
3

CREST VIEW 1
MARINERS CT 2
SARA CRES
FROBISHER WAY
PIER RD
HIGH ST
CHARLES 1ST
Superstore
STATION RD
QUAY LA
FIDDLERS
ARETHUSA
WORCESTER CL
THE AVENUE
1 COULTER HOUSE
2 COLLINGWOOD HOUSE
3 NELSON HOUSE
MANOR WAY
DA10
NORTHFLEET IND EST

A206
CROSSWAYS BVD
B255
CHARLES ST
EAGLES RD
SKIPPERS
SMUGGLERS
S MAWSON WHARF
MARITIME CL
LOVERS LA
PILGRIMS RD
SWANSCOMBE BSNS CTR
KENT KRAFT IND EST
75

KING EDWARD RD
COWLEY AVE
STEELE AVE
LOW CL
SACRED
HILCREST RD
RIVERVIEW RD
GREENHITHE STATION
STATION APP
B255
London Rd
Liby
Greenhithe
PARK TERR
Knockhall Com Prim Sch
ALEXANDER RD
WAKEFIELD RD
INGRESS GDNS
CRAYLANDS LA
GALLEY HILL RD
A226
ALL SAINTS CL
B259
HIGH ST
Swanscombe
2

EVANS CL
TRIVETT CL
WHITBY
CASTLE ST
PROVIDENCE ST
KINGSMEAD
A206
IVY VILLAS
BREAKNECK HILL
COBHAM TERR
BEAN RD
Greenhithe
DA9
KNOCKHALL CHASE
EYNSFORD RD
ABBEY RD
KNOCKHALL RD
THE FLATS
HALE COTTS
SWANSCOMBE
PACIFIC CL
ATLANTIC CL
PENTSTEMON DR
ORCHARD DR
ALMA RD
RAEBURN
Recn Gd
PO
P
THE PARADE

1 JACKSON CL
2 BULLIVANT CL
3 ARGLES CL
4 BORLAND CL
5 CUTTY SARK CT
6 RICHARDSON CL
THE CRESCENT
PORT AVE
STARBOARD AVE
NELSON RD
LANE AVE
JUBILEE CL
Knockhall
BROOMFIELD RD
KINGSDALE
MILTON RD
CHAPEL
LEWIS RD
HOPE RD 1
HARMER RD
ALBERT RD
1 HARMER CT
2 HERBERT RD
3 WARDONA CT
STANHOPE RD

ELMHURST 1
WHARNECLIFFE 2
HOMEMEAD 3
Stone Castle
VALLEY VIEW
KEMSLEY CL
SPRING
WESTERN
HASTED
WHITES
CROSS CL
PILGRIMS VIEW
ALKERDEN LA
DEIDRE CHAPMAN HOUSE 1
MAYFIELD 2
WALLACE GDNS 3
WRIGHT CL 4
GILBERT CL
CHILDS CRES
MADDEN CL
MILTON ST
ALAMEIN RD
TREBLE RD
MOORE RD
BROAD RD
SWEYNE RD
GASSON RD
STANLEY RD
AMES RD
P
Cemy
EGLINTON RD
CH SC INTS
CASTLE RD
VERNON RD
SWANSCOMBE ST
B259
1

HEDGE PLACE RD
BLUEWATER PARKWAY
B255
1 BEVANS CL
2 JOHNSONS WAY
BRIDLE CL
GUNN RD
MANOR
PARK RD
CHURCH RD
74

A8
1 EASTERN WAY
2 HIGH ST
3 JETTY WLK
B8
1 DARNLEY RD
2 BRIDGE CT

3 WYVERN HOUSE
4 SEJANT HOUSE
5 LIONEL OXLEY HOUSE
6 ARTHUR TOFT HOUSE
7 GEORGE CROOKS HOUSE
8 GREENWOOD HOUSE
9 BUTLER HOUSE

B8
10 DAVALL HOUSE
C8
1 RICHMOND RD
2 SALISBURY RD
3 HARWOOD CT
4 KENSINGTON CT

5 BLOCKHOUSE RD
6 WOOD ST
7 DOUG SIDDONS CT
8 PERCY ST
9 HENRY ST
10 ST THOMAS'S PL

D8
1 CRESCENT CT
2 KEMPLEY CT
3 RECTORY RD
4 ROOKERY VIEW
5 CAMPION CT
6 MULLEIN CT

7 SORREL CT
8 SUNDEW CT
9 SYRINGA CT
10 SCILLA CT
11 CLOVER CT

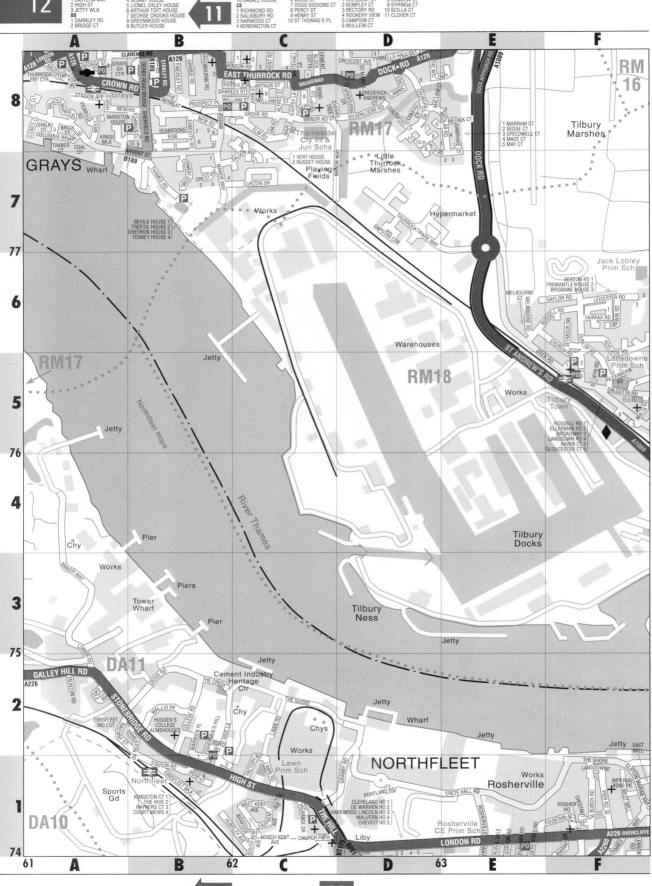

11
11
29

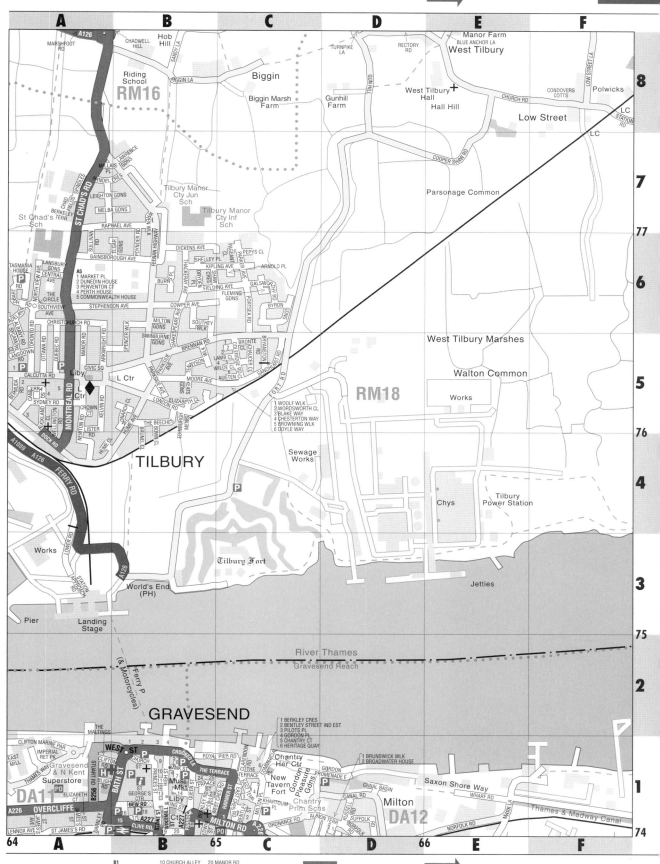

B1
1 CRAWLEY CT
2 REGENTS CT
3 MELBOURNE CT
4 TOWN PIER
5 BULL YD
6 HORN YD
7 NEW SWAN YD
8 MARKET ALLEY
9 WHITE HART YD
10 CHURCH ALLEY
11 JURY ST
12 GLOBE YD
13 CHASE SQ
14 BREWHOUSE YD
15 BARRACK ROW
16 GARRICK ST
17 ANGLESEA PL
18 ANGLESEA CTR
19 RAILWAY PL
20 MANOR RD
21 WILFRED ST
22 BERNARD ST
23 THE TERRACE
24 ST ANDREWS CT
25 CROSS ST

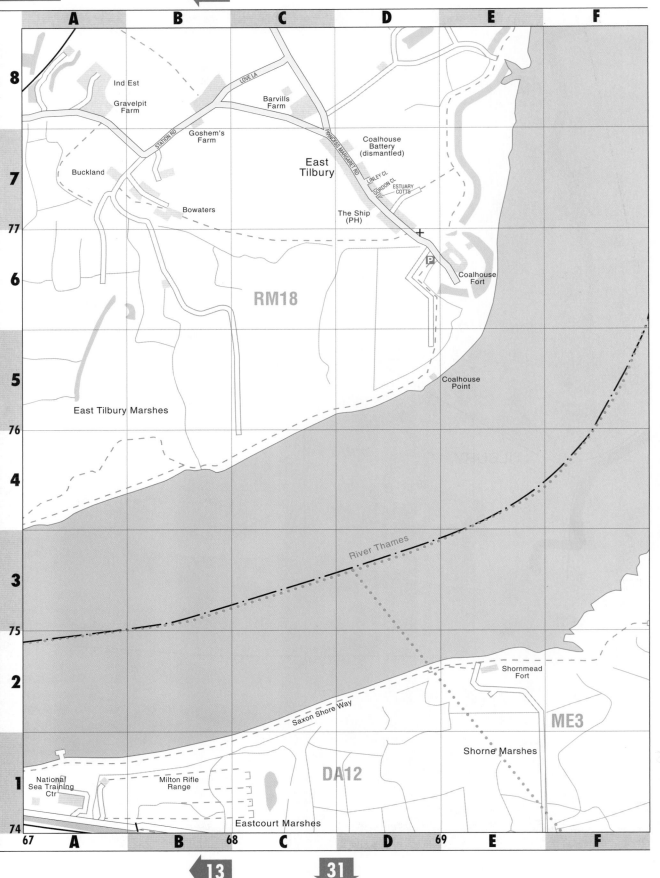

A   B   C   D   E   F

8

Ind Est

Gravelpit
Farm

LOVE LA

Barvills
Farm

STATION RD

Goshem's
Farm

PRINCESS MARGARET RD

Coalhouse
Battery
(dismantled)

East
Tilbury

7

Buckland

LINLEY CL

GORDON CL

ESTUARY
COTTS

Bowaters

The Ship
(PH)

77

P

Coalhouse
Fort

6

RM18

5

Coalhouse
Point

East Tilbury Marshes

76

4

River Thames

3

75

Saxon Shore Way

Shornmead
Fort

2

ME3

Shorne Marshes

DA12

1

National
Sea Training
Ctr

Milton Rifle
Range

Eastcourt Marshes

74

67   A   B   68   C   D   69   E   F

River Thames
The Lower Hope

COASTGUARD COTTS

Pier

Boatrick House

Cliffe Creek

RM18

Cliffe Fort (dis)

Saxon Shore Way

Jetties

Higham Creek

Conveyor

Depot

ME3

Royal Albert (PH)

CONCRETE COTTS

Quarries (dis)

SALT LA

Wks

West Court

LC

Higham Saltings

Higham Marshes

Higham Common

Barrow Hill

Beckley Hill

Oakleigh

CHURCH ST

Church Street

MEAD WALL

18

Cooling Marshes

Old Sea Wall

Decoy Fleet

The Mean

Swigshole

Buckland Marshes

Buckland Fleet

Decoy Farm

Whalebone Marshes

Masts

Eastborough Farm

Saxon Shore Way

Northward Hill

Decoy Hill Rd

Bromhey Farm

Northward Hill Nature Reserve

Clinchstreet Farm

Main Rd

Childs Farm

Eastborough Bungalow

Buckhole Farm

ME3

Marsh Cres

Lipwell Hill

Buckhole Farm Rd

Cooling Rd

Northwood Ave
Thames Ave
Longfield Ave
Medway Ave
Willowbank Dr

Harrison Dr
Eden Rd
Goodwood Cl
Drayton Cl
Valentine Dr
Topley Dr
Lemain

Dalham Farm

High Halstow Prim Sch

The Street
Ruggles Cl
Holmes Cl

High Halstow

Forge La
PH
St Margaret's Ct
Gypsy Way
Cardigan Cl
Meadow Way
PO
Christmas La

LC

Wybournes La

Hill Farm Cl

Wybournes Farm

Ducks Court

Duck Court Rd

Wybornes Wood

Solomon's Farm

Lodge Hill Wood

Ratcliffe Highway

A228

17

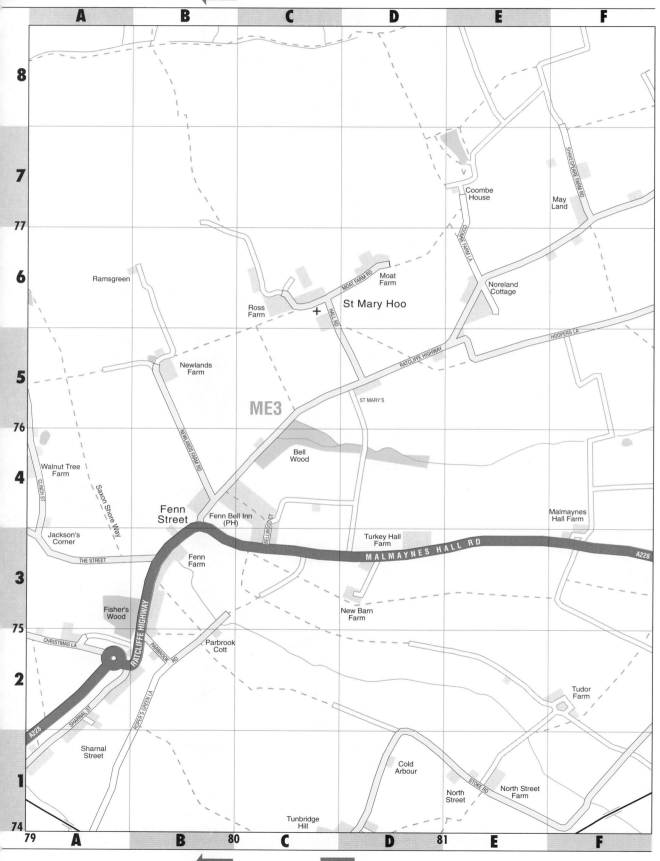

A B C D E F

8

7

77

6

5

76

4

3

75

2

1

74

79 A B 80 C D 81 E F

Ramsgreen

Coombe House

May Land

SHAKESPEARE FARM RD

COOMBE FARM LA

Moat Farm

MOAT FARM RD

St Mary Hoo

Noreland Cottage

Ross Farm

HALL RD

HOOPERS LA

RATCLIFFE HIGHWAY

Newlands Farm

ST MARY'S

ME3

NEWLANDS FARM RD

Bell Wood

Walnut Tree Farm

CLINCH ST

Saxon Shore Way

Malmaynes Hall Farm

Fenn Street

Fenn Bell Inn (PH)

BELLWOOD CT

Turkey Hall Farm

MALMAYNES HALL RD

A228

Jackson's Corner

THE STREET

Fenn Farm

Fisher's Wood

RATCLIFFE HIGHWAY

New Barn Farm

CHRISTMAS LA

Parbrook Cott

PARBROOK RD

Tudor Farm

SHARNAL ST

ROPER'S GREEN LA

A228

Sharnal Street

Cold Arbour

STOKE RD

North Street Farm

North Street

Tunbridge Hill

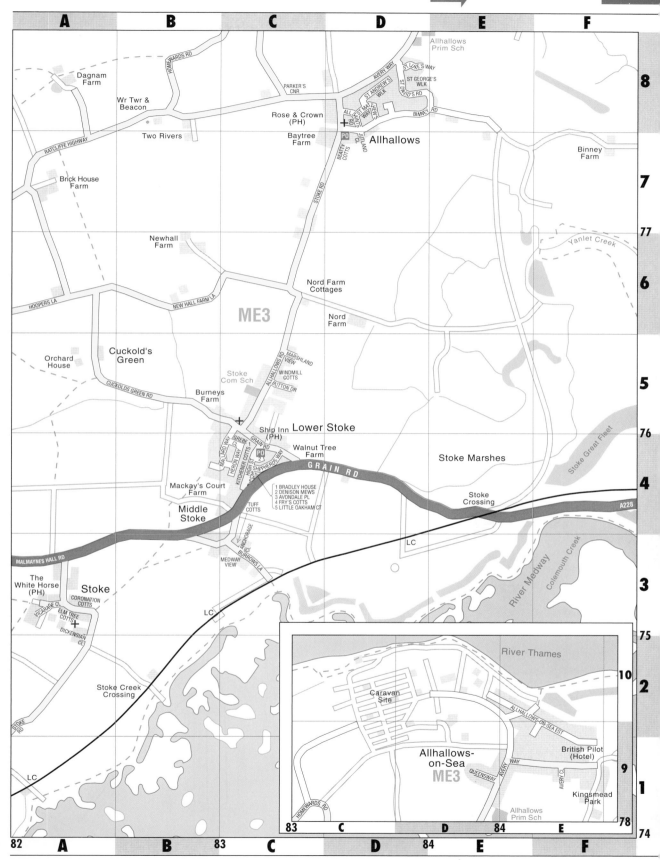

A **B** **C** **D** **E** **F**

Dagnam Farm

Wr Twr & Beacon

Two Rivers

HOMEWARDS RD

PARKER'S CNR

Rose & Crown (PH)

Baytree Farm

Allhallows

Allhallows Prim Sch

AVERY WAY

ST ANDREW'S WLK

ST LUKE'S WAY

ST GEORGE'S WLK

ST DAVID'S RD

ALL SAINTS RD

ST MATTHEW'S WAY

JUTLAND CL

BINNEY RD

PO

Binney Farm

RATCLIFFE HIGHWAY

Brick House Farm

Newhall Farm

STOKE RD

BEATTY COTTS

Yanlet Creek

77

HOOPERS LA

NEW HALL FARM LA

ME3

Nord Farm Cottages

Nord Farm

Orchard House

Cuckold's Green

CUCKOLDS GREEN RD

Burneys Farm

Stoke Com Sch

ALLHALLOWS RD

MARSHLAND VIEW

WINDMILL COTTS

BUTTON DR

Ship Inn (PH)

Lower Stoke

PO

Walnut Tree Farm

Stoke Marshes

Stoke Great Fleet

76

MALLARD WAY

GREBE

HERON WAY

GRAIN RD

HIGH ST

SHEPHERD'S WAY

GRAIN RD

Stoke Crossing

A228

Mackay's Court Farm

Middle Stoke

1 BRADLEY HOUSE
2 DENISON MEWS
3 AVONDALE PL
4 FRY'S COTTS
5 LITTLE OAKHAM CT

TUFF COTTS

LC

River Medway

Colemouth Creek

MALMAYNES HALL RD

The White Horse (PH)

Stoke

VICARAGE CL

CORONATION COTTS

ELM TREE COTTS

DICKENSIAN CL

ANCHORAGE CL

BURROWS LA

MEDWAY VIEW

LC

75

STOKE RD

Stoke Creek Crossing

LC

River Thames

Caravan Site

Allhallows-on-Sea

ME3

ALLHALLOWS-ON-SEA EST

British Pilot (Hotel)

QUEENSWAY

AVERY WAY

AVERY CL

Kingsmead Park

Allhallows Prim Sch

HOMEWARDS RD

10

9

83 **C** 84 **D** **E** 78

8
7
77
6
5
76
4
3
75
2
10
9
1
78
74

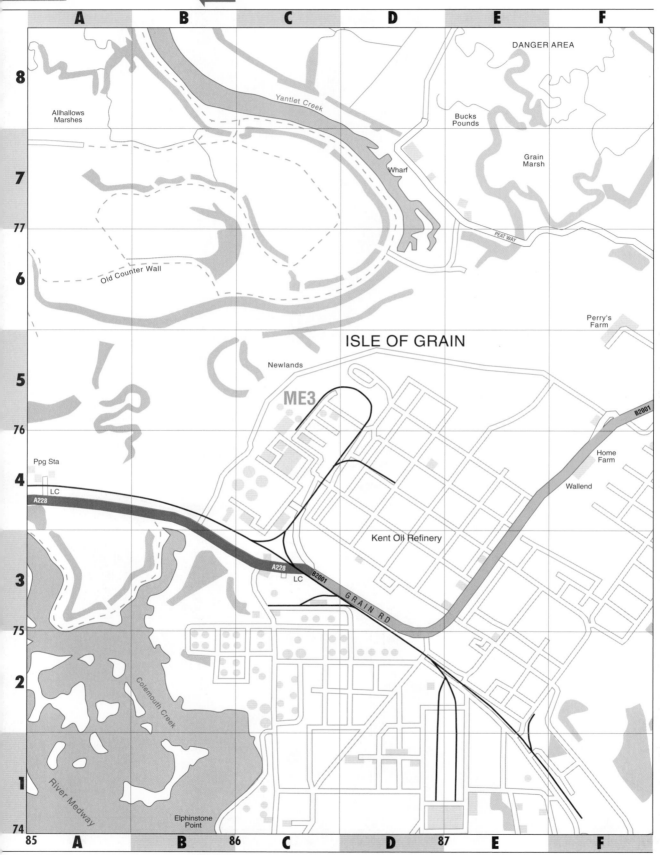

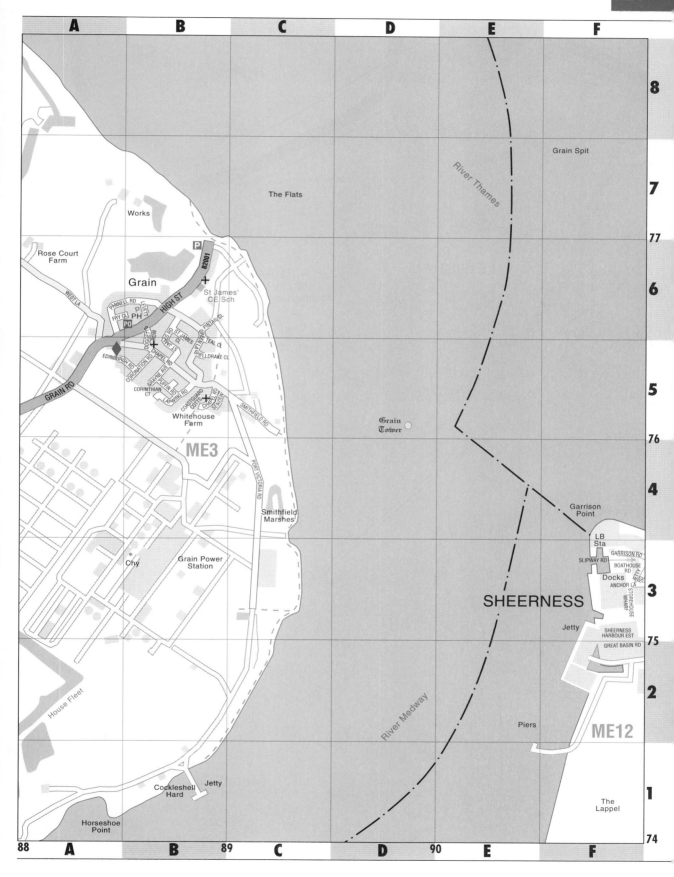

A   **B**   **C**   **D**   **E**   **F**

8

Grain Spit

7

The Flats

River Thames

77

Works

Rose Court
Farm

P

B2001

Grain

WEST LA

HIGH ST

St James'
CE Sch

6

PINNELL RD
FRY CL
PH
LEVETT
PO

DODGE ST
CHAPEL RD
ST JAMES
CL
TERBY ST
PINTAIL CL
TEAL CL

SHELLDRAKE CL

EDINBURGH RD
CORONATION RD
GRAYNE AVE
PUFFIN RD

CORINTHIAN
CT

LAPWING RD

COASTGUARD
COTT
CHAPEL CT
SEA VIEW

GRAIN RD

SMITHFIELD RD

Whitehouse
Farm

Grain
Tower

76

ME3

PORT VICTORIA RD

Smithfield
Marshes

Garrison
Point

4

LB
Sta

GARRISON RD

SLIPWAY RD
BOATHOUSE
RD
ANCHOR LA

Docks

ALL

STOREHOUSE
WHARF

SHEERNESS

3

Chy

Grain Power
Station

Jetty

SHEERNESS
HARBOUR EST

75

GREAT BASIN RD

House Fleet

River Medway

2

Piers

ME12

Cockleshell
Hard

Jetty

1

The
Lappel

Horseshoe
Point

74

5

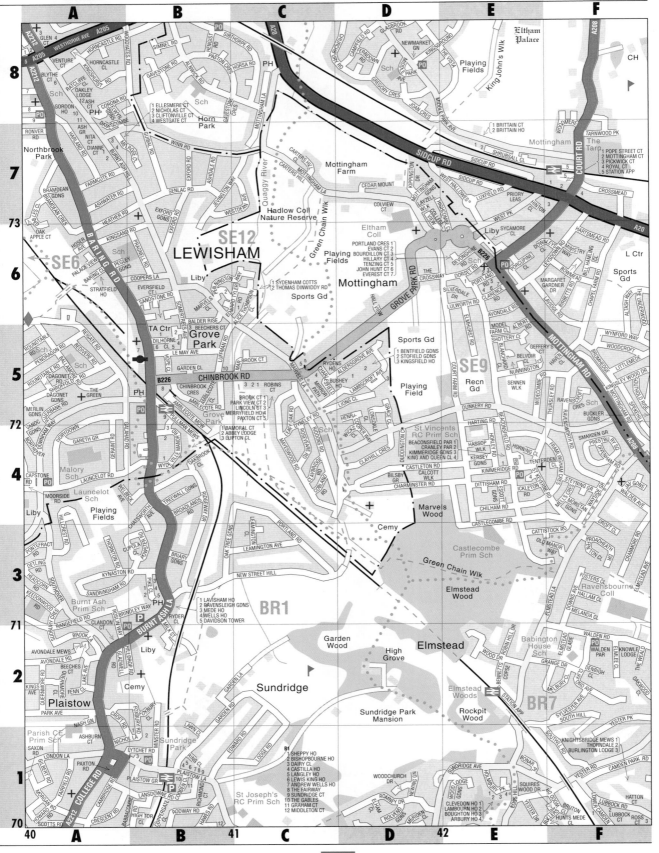

A8
1 WILDWOOD CL
2 ROWAN CT
3 SWALLOW CT
4 HONEYSUCKLE CT
5 ST WILDREDS RD
6 HARROGATE CT

7 LINCHMERE RD
8 WAITE DAVIES RD
9 SUMMERFIELD ST
10 ASKHAM LODGE
11 SYON LODGE
12 CHERITON CT

B5
1 GILLAN CT
2 NAPIER CT
3 OAKCROFT
4 ST JOSEPHS CT
5 HOLM CT
6 ROTHESAY CT

7 CANTERBURY CT
8 CHINBROOK CRES
9 BOLLON CT
10 CAMERON TERR

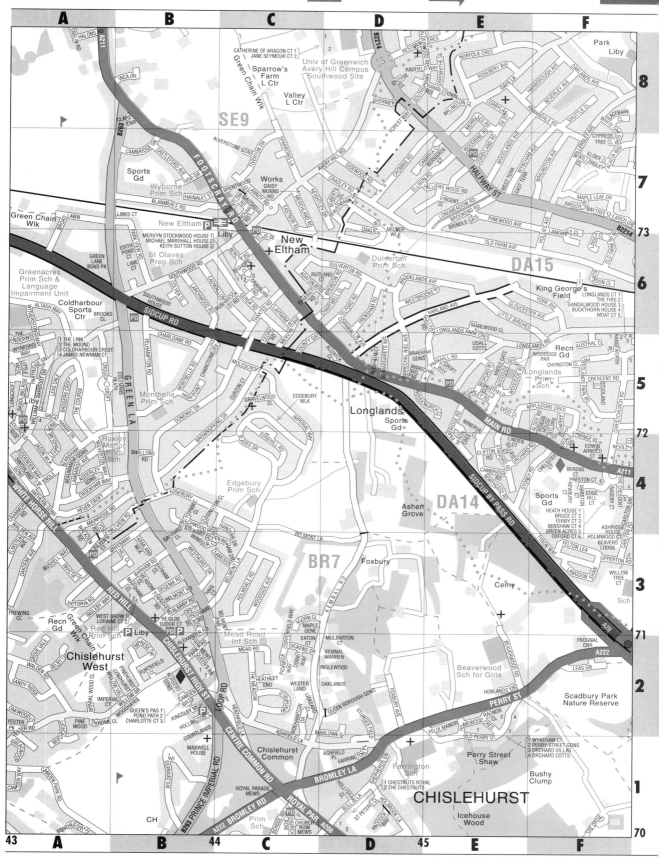

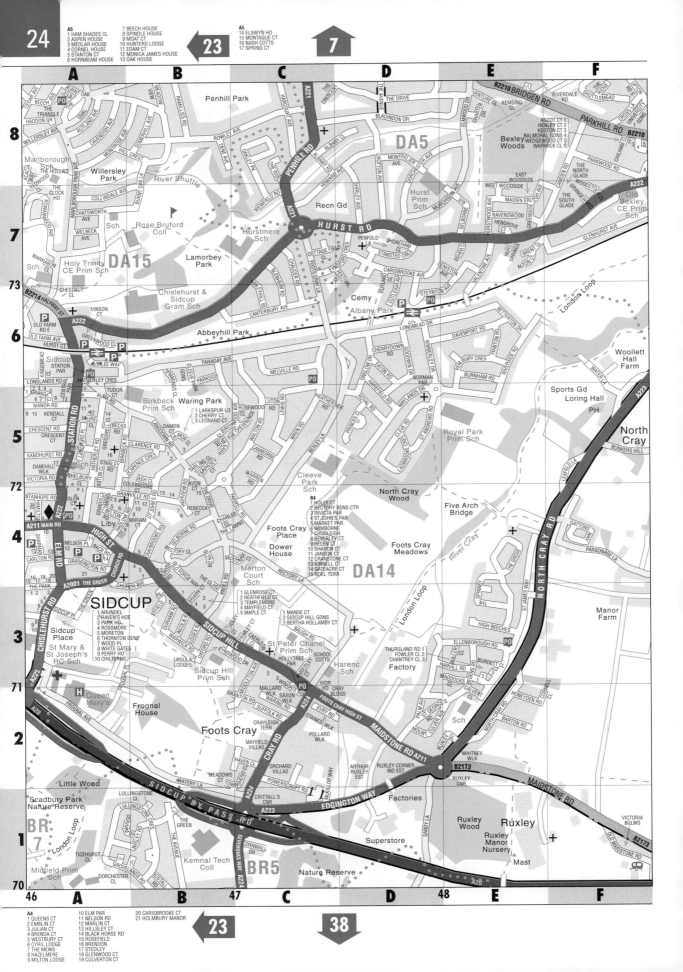

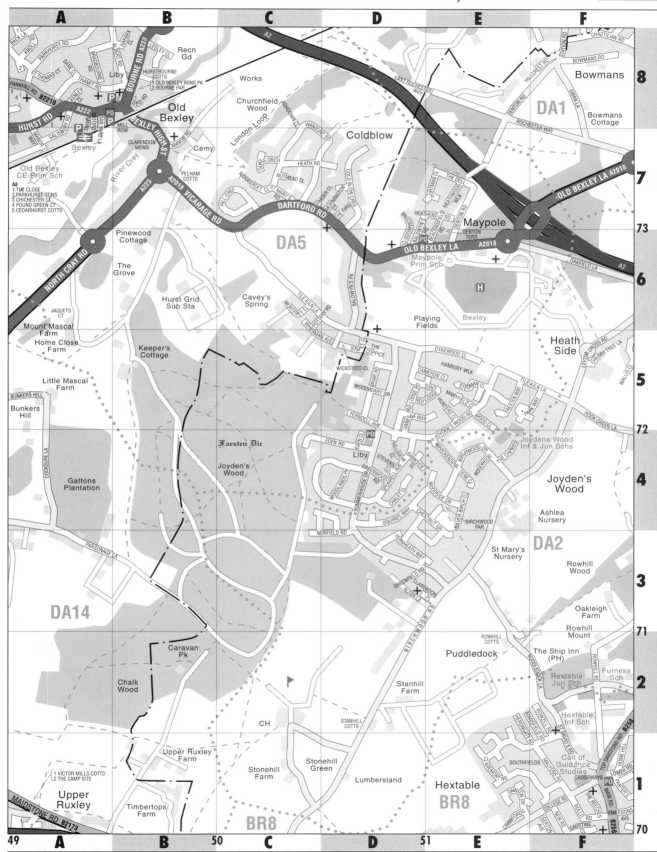

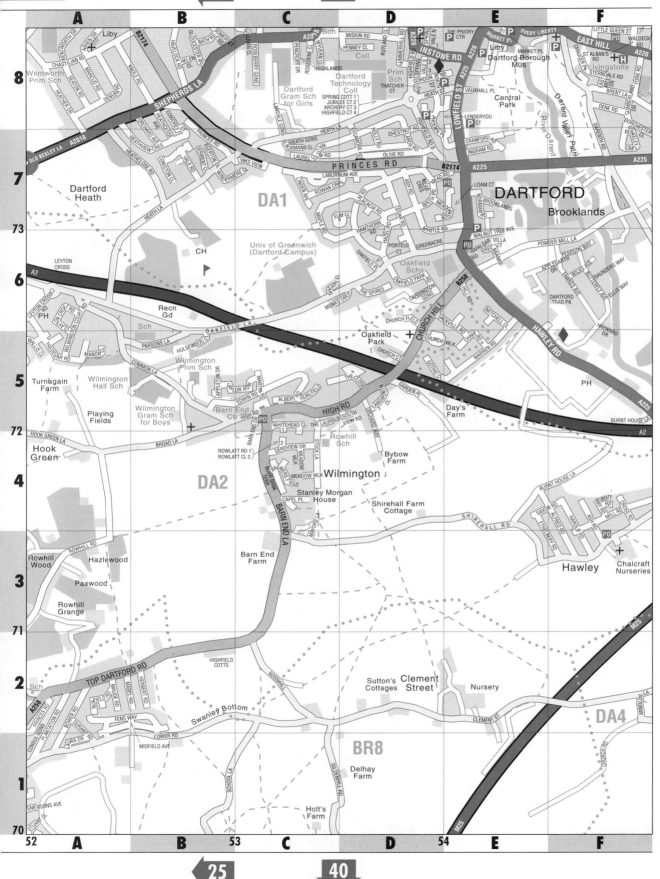

A · B · C · D · E · F

8

Liby
B2174
Wentworth Prim Sch
CHASTILIAN RD
WENTWORTH DR
MARCUS RD
SEXTON RD
HEATHER WAY
KNOLE RD
DENVER
GLOUCESTER RD
BATH RD
HAVELOCK RD
HELEN CL
SOMERSET
LILLIAN CL
ROSEBERRY GDNS
SPEN
Sch
MISKIN RD
WYVERN CL
PENCROFT DR
PENNEY CL
HIGHLANDS
Coll
RUTLAND CL
HAMMERHILL RD
MISKIN RD
A226
INSTONE RD
Prim Sch
THATCHER CT
THE PRIORY CTR
SPRING VALE N
VALE N
GORDON RD
HIGHFIELD RD S
OVERY LIBERTY
Liby
Dartford Borough Mus
LITTLE QUEEN ST
EAST HILL
ST ALBAN'S RD
WALDECK
A226
STERNDALE RD
CHAUCER RD
EAST HILL

SHEPHERDS LA
ORCHARD AVE
CONDREY
HEATHCLOSE
PRINCES RD
DERWENT CL
EGERTON RD
VALE RD
WINDERMERE CL
Dartford Gram Sch for Girls
LANSDALE GDNS
HEATH LA
SYCAMORE RD
CHESTNUT RD
HOLLY RD
Central Park
CRANFORD RD
LENDERYOU CT
INGRAM RD
River Darent
Derent Valley Path
BRENT LA
DENE RD
CUMBERLAND
DORCHESTER
BERKELEY
DARENTH RD
YORK RD

7
Old Bexley La A2018
HEATHVIEW AVE
HEATHCLOSE RD
HEATH LA
Dartford Heath
DA1
CH
Univ of Greenwich (Dartford Campus)
PRINCES RD
LABURNUM AVE
ROWAN CRES
LINDEN AVE
ELM CL
MAPLE RD
ACACIA RD
CEDAR RD
HAWTHORN
HAZEL RD
MYRTLE RD
PORTEUS CT
GREENACRE
OAKFIELD PL
OAKFIELD LA
B2174
A225
B258
BECK MEADOW
NEAD RD
ASH RD
PO
LOAM CT
NORMAN RD
WALNUT TREE AVE
TRAFALGAR RD
GREE
BROOKLANDS
DARTFORD
Brooklands
POWDER MILL LA
PEARSON WAY
APPLEGARTH DR
WM WILKS AVE
FANCES AVE
SAUNDERS WAY
BUTTERFLY AVE
ELLIS WAY
DARTFORD TRAD PK
HAYWARD DR

73

6
A2
LEYTON CROSS
Recn Gd
LEYTON CROSS RD
Sch
OAKFIELD LA
MONKS ORCH
THE SPIRES
SPINS CL
OAKFIELD PL
Oakfield Schs
OAKFIELD PARK RD
CARSINGTON GDNS
HILL RD
CHURCH FIELD
Oakfield Park
CHURCH HILL
SACKVILLE RD
MITCHELL CL
CHAVE RD
CHURCH WLK
WARREN RD
HAWLEY RD
PH

5
Turnagain Farm
PH
WHITMAN CT RD
CLAYTON CROFT RD
WALES CL
PERCGAR RD
MANOR
COMMON LA
PARSONS LA
HULSEWOOD CL
Wilmington Prim Sch
Wilmington Hall Sch
APPLETON DR
LOR ROW
EDWIN RD
MARTIN RD
ALBERT
HURLFIELD
Wilmington Gram Sch for Boys
Playing Fields
Barn End Ctr
HIGH RD
HIGH RD
PO
WHITEHEAD CL
THE LAURELS
LANGWORTH CL
ORCHARD WAY
GARDEN PL
Day's Farm
BURNT HOUSE LA
A2

72
Hook Green La
BROAD LA
Hook Green
DA2
ROWLATT RD 1
ROWLATT CL 2
BARN END LA
GERDVIEW DR
MEADOW WLK
STOCK LA
BREWERS FIELD
WEST FIELD
MEADOW WLK
Rowhill Sch
Wilmington
Bybow Farm
SHIREHALL RD
SAXON RD
ALFRED RD
ETHELBERT RD
HAROLD RD
ASH RD
MILL RD
CROSS RD
BOLT
MAY RD
PO
Burnt House La

4
Rowhill Wood
ROWHILL RD
Hazlewood
Paxwood
BOUR BANK
CAPEL PL
BARN END LA
Stanley Morgan House
MAJORS LA
Shirehall Farm Cottage
Burnt House La
Hawley
Chalcraft Nurseries

3
Rowhill Grange

71
M25

2
Sch
A258
TOP DARTFORD RD
CONSUL GDNS
PRINCES RD
PLANTATION RD
BOWER RD
LAURA DR
DURANT RD
MABEL RD
MAUDE RD
FIELD RD
HERBERT RD
FENS WAY
MIDFIELD AVE
LOWER RD
Swanley Bottom
HIGHFIELD COTTS
GOSSHILL
SCHOOL LA
GILLDERHILL RD
CLEMENT ST
Sutton's Cottages
Clement Street
Nursery
CLEMENT ST
DA4
CHURCH RD
ARNOLDS LA

1
EMERSONS AVE
STUART CL
BR8
Delhay Farm
Holt's Farm

70
M25

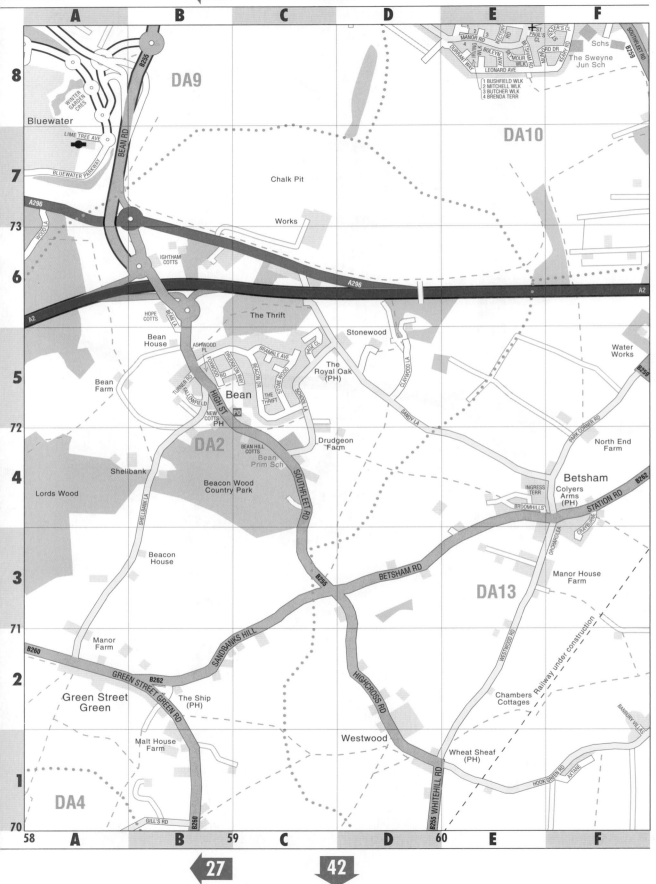

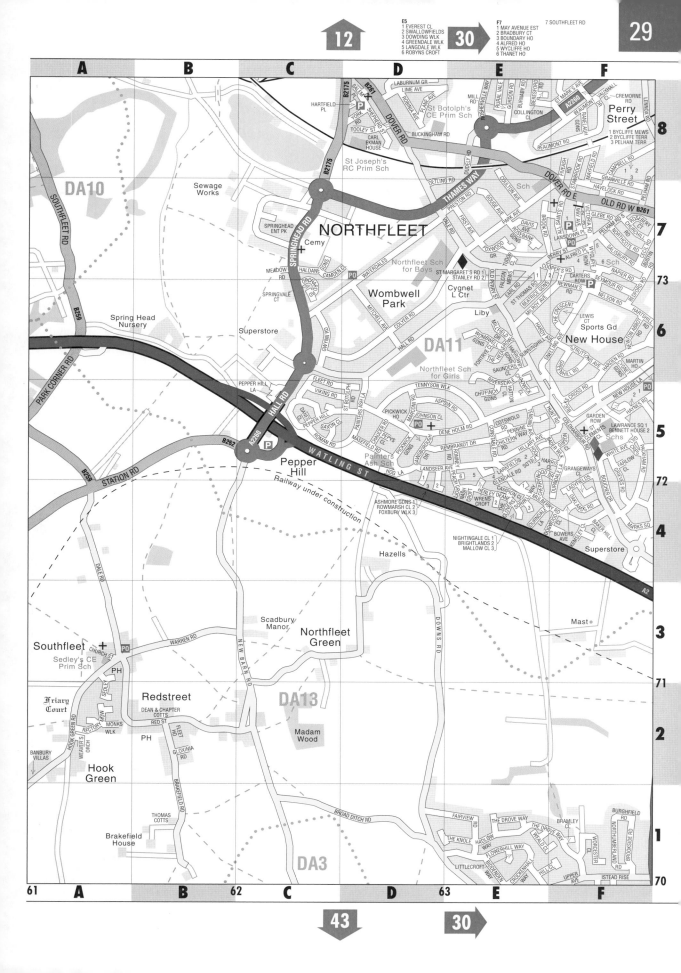

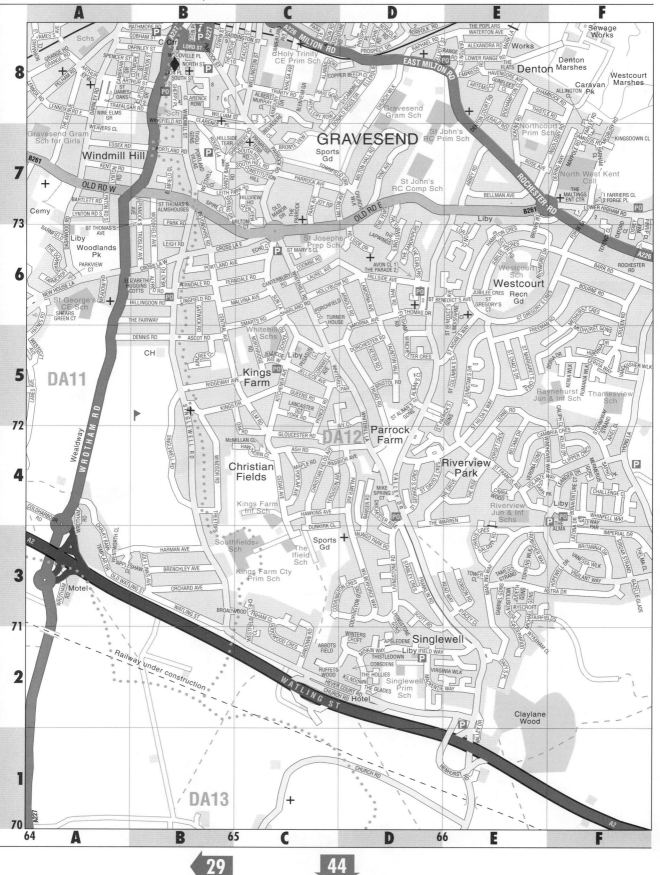

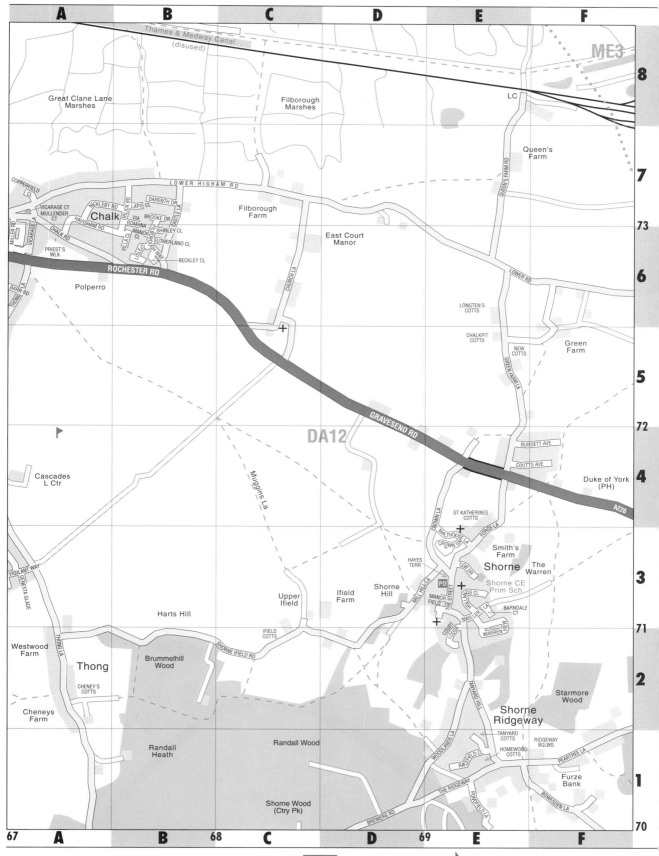

A B C D E F

8

7

73

6

5

72

4

72

3

71

2

1

70

70 A B 71 C 72 D E F

Works

Little Oakleigh

BUCKLAND RD

CANAL RD

Thames & Medway Canal (dis)

CHURCH ST

HOPE TERR
KENT TERR

GORE GREEN RD

SANDHILL LA

LILLECHURCH RD

King's Farm

Gore Green

Lillechurch

Red House

LOWER RD

MICHELE COTTS

CUCKOLD'S CNR

CHALK RD

PO

MARTINS CL

PH

Lower Higham

LOWER ROCHESTER RD

Tunbrick Cross

LAKE DR

REYNOLDS FIELDS

STEADMAN CL

THE ADELAIDE

Higham

Higham Hall Farm

LAND WAY

White House Farm

Two Gates Farm

Turks Hill

Higham Prim Sch

SCHOOL LA

ME3

Dusty Hill

TAYLOR'S LA

TWO GATES HILL

Hill Farm

The Knowle

VICARAGE ROW

HIGHWOODS CL

HIGH VIEW

Higham

OAK DR

FAIRVIEW DR

BEECH GR

MOUNTBATTEN AVE

ST JOHN'S RD

ST JOHN'S CL

HERMITAGE RD

Hillyfield

WALMERS AVE

BRIAR DALE

ASH CRES

THAMES VIEW COTTS

DA12

A226

EVERGREEN CL

HOLLYTREE DR

CARLTON RD

NORAH LA

CHILTON DR

VILLA RD

PO

THE BRACS

ELM CL

THE ARCHES

Garden Centre

A289

PEAR TREE PL

DARBY GDNS

PEGGOTY CL

DOMBEY CL

FORGE LA

HAYES CL

Liby

TELEGRAPH HILL

Telegraph Hill

Mon

Court Wood

YOUENS PL

IRVINE RD

BRIG LA

Grove Farm

Little Hermitage

Providence Cotts

PH

GRAVESEND RD

Gadshill

Gads Hill Sch

Gravesend Rd

DILLYWOOD LA

DILLYWOOD COTTS

Peartree Wood

PEARTREE LA

CHARLES DICKENS AVE

COPPERFIELD CRES

Gads Hill Farm

BEAUFORT RD

A289

ME2

Great Crabbles Wood

CRUTCHES LA

A289

FOUNTAIN RD

CONWAY RD

CROSSBROOK RD

CASSBROOK

WESTERGATE RD

HARLECH CL

HYPERION DR 1
HILLYFIELD CL 2

B2106

SANDYCROFT

ORCHARD AVE

WOODVIEW

GODFREY CL

SAXON

RISE

FARM HILL

BROMPTON FARM RD

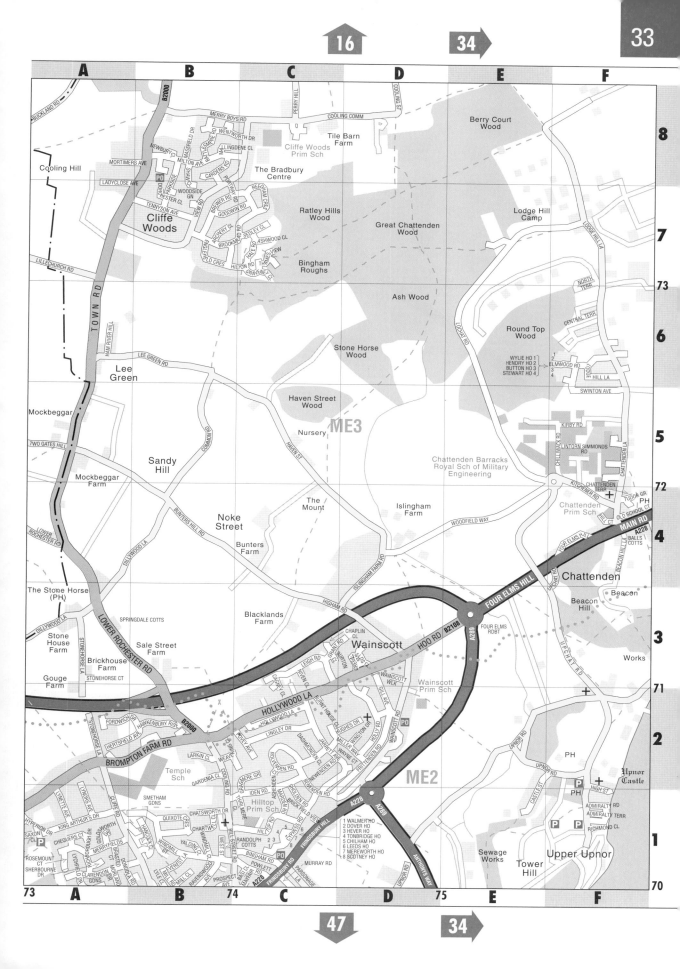

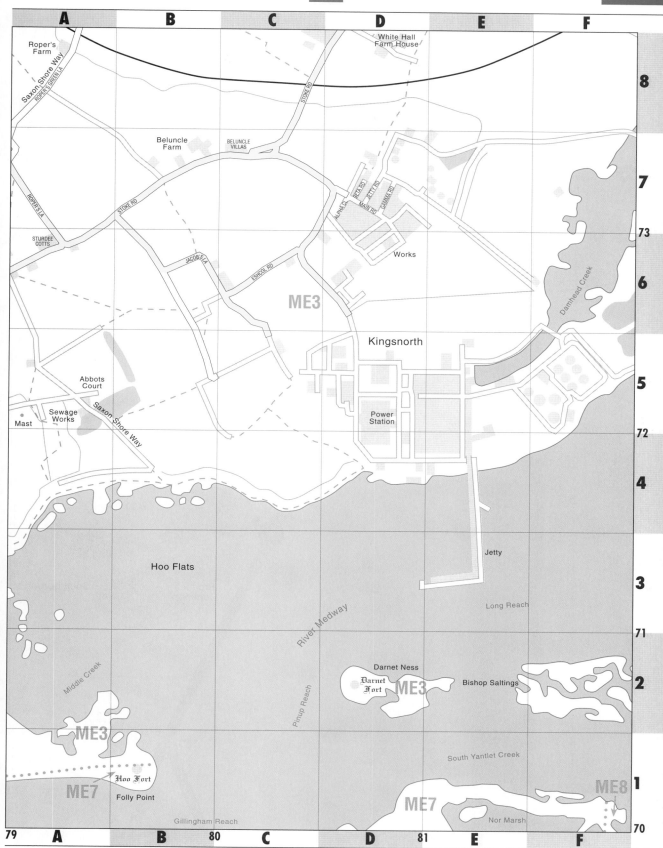

22

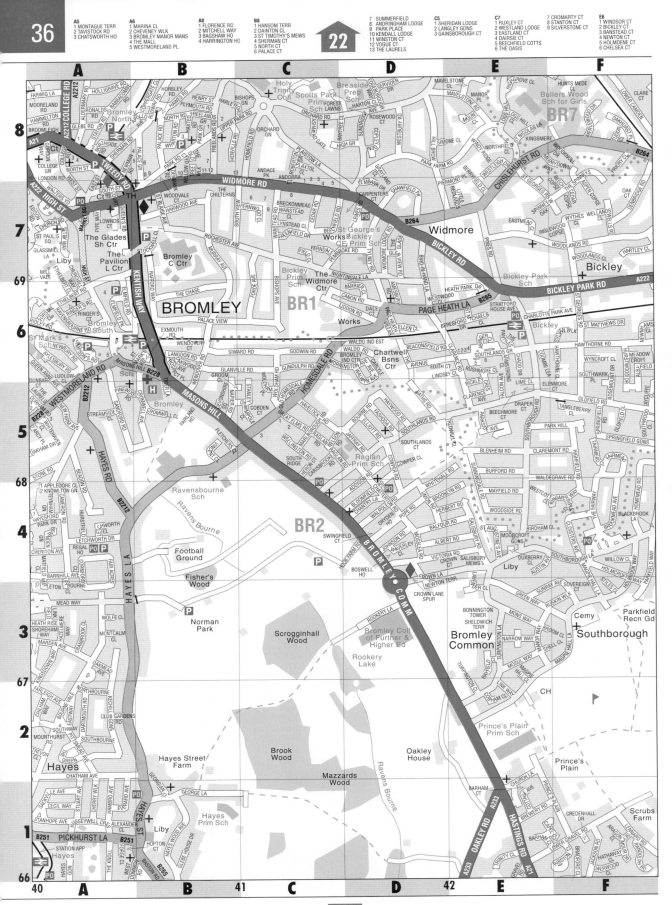

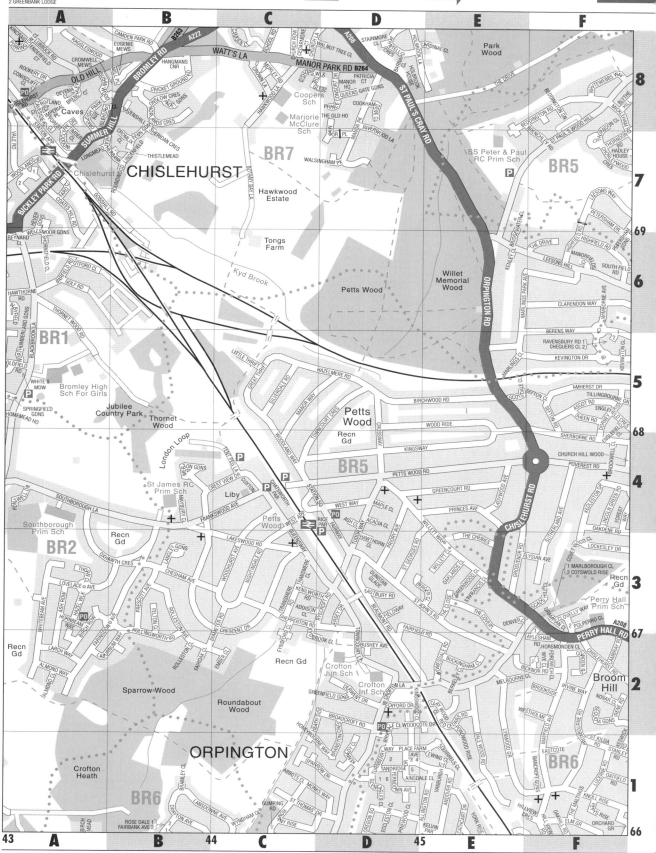

A7
1 MEREWOOD CL
2 ALPINE COPSE
A8
1 IVYBRIDGE CT
2 GREENBANK LODGE

CHISLEHURST

BR7

Hawkwood
Estate

Tongs
Farm

Kyd Brook

Petts Wood

Willet
Memorial
Wood

BR1

Bromley High
Sch For Girls

Jubilee
Country Park

Thornet
Wood

Petts
Wood

Recn
Gd

BR5

London Loop

St James RC
Prim Sch

Liby

Petts
Wood

Southborough
Prim Sch

Recn
Gd

BR2

Crofton
Jun Sch

Crofton
Inf Sch

Recn
Gd

Sparrow Wood

Roundabout
Wood

ORPINGTON

Crofton
Heath

BR6

Park
Wood

SS Peter & Paul
RC Prim Sch

BR5

Church Hill Wood

Perry Hall
Prim Sch

Broom
Hill

Recn
Gd

BR6

1 MARLBOROUGH CL
2 COTSWOLD RISE

D1
1 GLENEAGLES GN
2 TANDRIDGE PL
3 SPRINGFIELD WLK
4 PINEHURST WLK
5 CROMER PL
6 OAKMONT PL

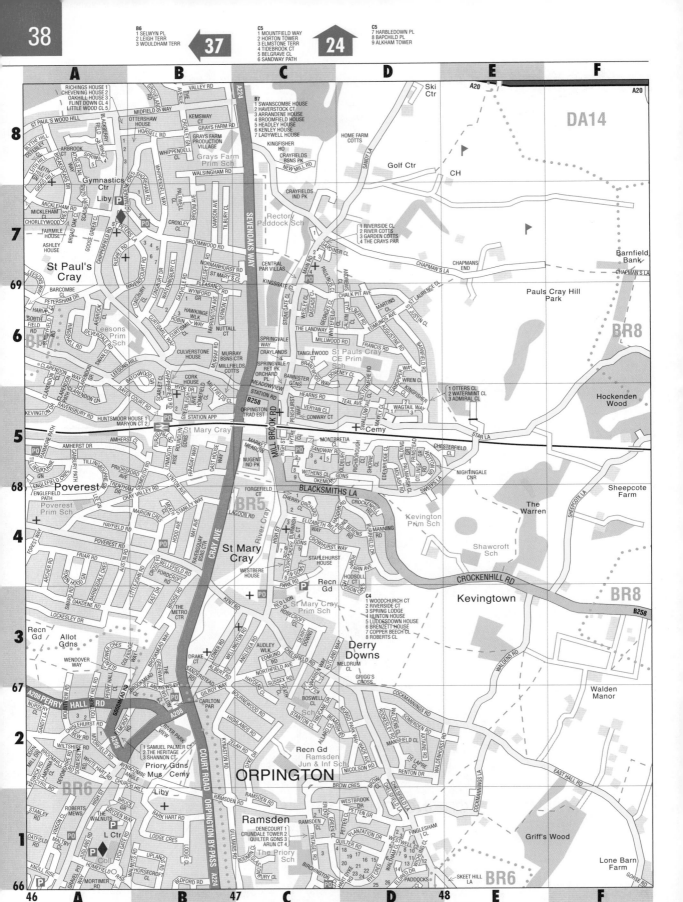

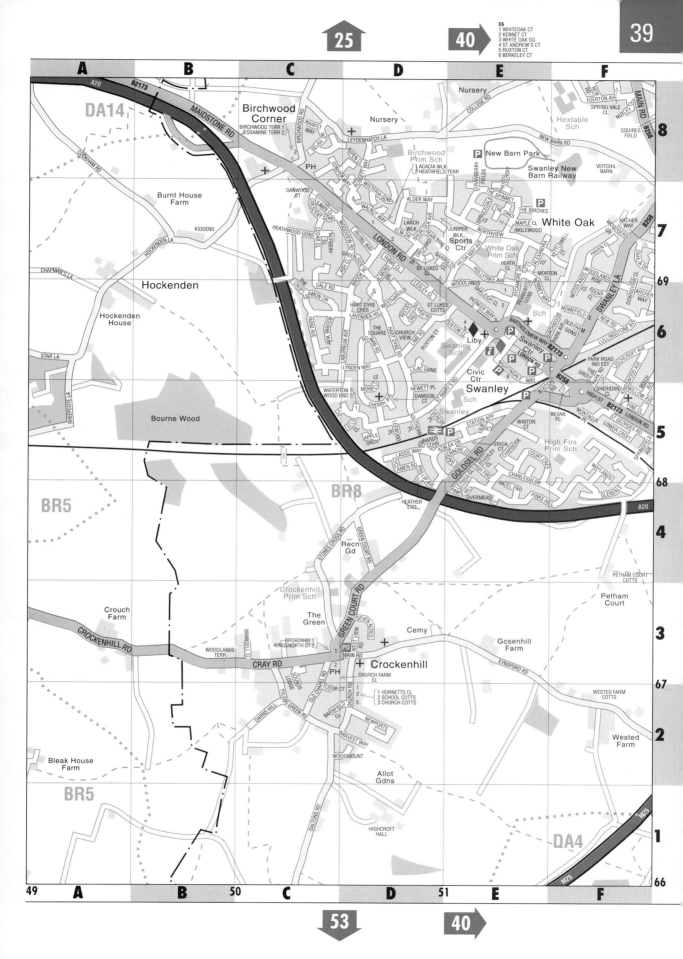

A **B** **C** **D** **E** **F**

MILLBRO

VICTORIA HILL RD

SQUIRES FIELD

B258

8

MAIN RD

Highlands Farm

HIGHLANDS HILL

HIGHLANDS HILL

SWANLEY LA

B258

THE VENTS

ANTHONY'S LA

THE STAPLES

St Paul's CE Prim Sch

HOGS ORCH

SCHOOL LA

HOTHAM CL

The Red Lion (PH)

ELM COTTS

SWANLEY VILLAGE RD

Swanley Village

GILDENHILL RD

CHURCH RD

SHIP LA

WOOD ST

SHIP LA

LC

Homefield Farm

7

PARK LA

BEECHENLEA LA

Ram's Wood

M25

69

ARCHER AVE

LEECHCROFT AVE

BEECH AVE

Downsview Prim Sch

THE ANNEX

Parkwood Hall Sch

Canada Heights

6

HILLSIDE CT

WEST VIEW RD

L Ctr

WILLOW AVE

SOUTHVIEW CL

MANSE WAY

Broom Hill

BUTTON ST

P

Farningham Wood (Nature Reserve)

P

CALFSTOCK LA

5

B2173

HIGH CROFT COTTS

ROSS CT

BRETHREN CT

ABBOTTS

MANSE PAR

BR8

DA4

SALISBURY AVE

WANSBURY WAY

MEAD

ROBINA CT

LONDON RD

MADAND TERR

68

A20

M20

3

B2173

MAIN WAY

WESTED LA

Ind Est

PEDHAM PLACE EST

A20

Hill Farm

FARNINGHAM HILL RD

The Folly

4

WESTED LA

LONDON RD

OLD DARTFORD RD

M20

DARTFORD RD

A225

3

Little Wested House

MAIN RD

LONDON RD

ELIZABETH PL

RABLUS PL

DARTFORD RD

PO

P

A20

67

EYNSFORD RD

Fort Farningham (dis)

The Mill House

HIGH ST

HORTON WAY

SOUTH HILL RD

+

Farningham

2

M25

EYNSFORD RD

CROCKENHILL LA

SPAREPENNY LA

SPAREPENNY LA

Darent Valley Path

River Darent

EYNSFORD RD

OLIVER CRES

TILL

VALLEY VIEW TERR

A225

1

Eynsford Hill

MILL HOUSE CL

OLD MILL CL

A225

PRIORY LA

EYNSFORD RD

66

MILL LA

52 **A** **B** **53** **C** **D** **54** **E** **F**

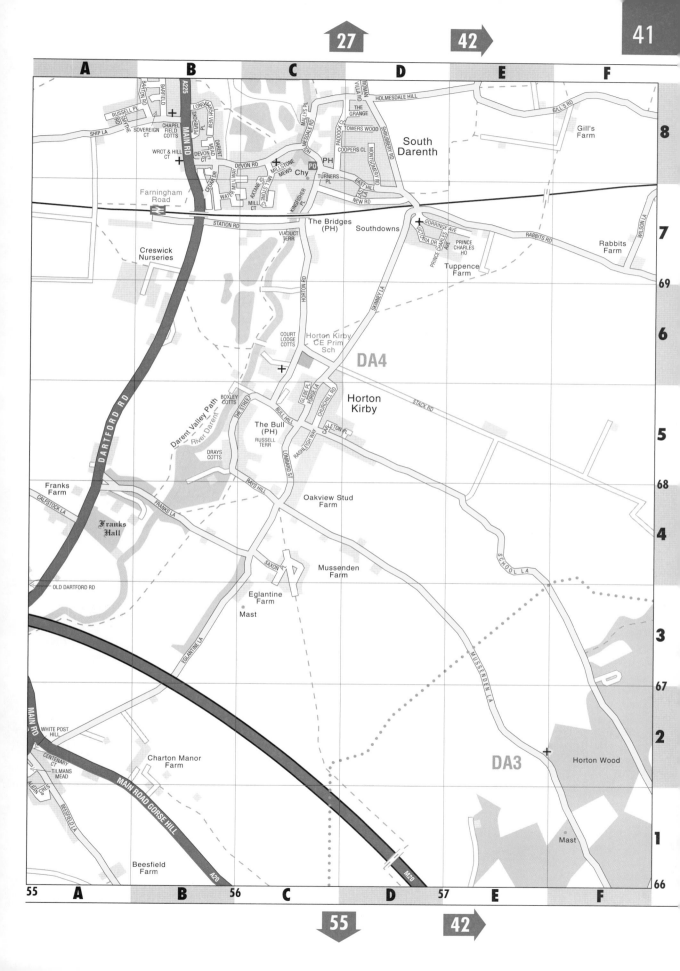

A   B   C   D   E   F

8
7
69
6
5
68
4
3
67
2
1
66

South Darenth

DA4

Horton Kirby

DA3

Gill's Farm
Rabbits Farm
Tuppence Farm
Horton Wood
Mast

Creswick Nurseries
Farningham Road
The Bridges (PH)
Southdowns

Horton Kirby CE Prim Sch
Court Lodge Cotts

The Bull (PH)
Boxley Cotts
Drays Cotts
Russell Terr

Franks Farm
Franks Hall

Oakview Stud Farm
Mussenden Farm
Eglantine Farm
Mast

Charton Manor Farm
White Post Hill
Centenary Ct
Tilmans Mead

Beesfield Farm

MAIN RD
DARTFORD RD
STATION RD
HORTON RD
FRANKS LA
CALFSTOCK LA
OLD DARTFORD RD
EGLANTINE LA
BAYS HILL
SAXON CL
LOMBARD ST
THE STREET
BULL HILL
GLEBE PL
FORGE LA
CHURCHILL RD
CARLETON PL
RASHLEIGH WAY
DARENT VALLEY PATH
River Darent

SKINNEY LA
STACK RD
SCHOOL LA
MUSSENDEN LA

GORRINGE AVE
VICTORIA DR
PRINCE CHARLES AVE
PRINCE CHARLES HO
RABBITS RD
WILSON LA
GILL'S RD

HOLMESDALE HILL
ROMAN VILLA RD
THE GRANGE
TOWERS WOOD
PADDOCK CL
COOPERS CL
SHRUBBERY RD
MONTGOMERY RD
EAST HILL
NEW RD
TURNERS PL
MALLYS PL
MEDDESDALE RD

BARFIELD
BARTON RD
RUSSELL PL
RUTH SMYTHE RD
SOVEREIGN CT
CHAPEL FIELD COTTS
WROT & HILL CT
DEVON RD
DEVON CT
CEDAR DR
MEAD CT
DARENT
WATER MILL WAY
MILLSTONE MEWS
NATALIE CL
MILL CT
KINGFISHER PL
MILLSTONE CL
LONG MEAD
MARSH VIEW PL
ENDBURGH PL
A225

MAIN RD
ALBIN CRES
BEESFIELD LA
MAIN ROAD GORSE HILL
A20
M20

VIADUCT TERR

Chy
PO
PH

41
28

A **B** **C** **D** **E** **F**

8

Grubb Street

Ryecroft
Farm

Ryecrofts
Wood

GILL'S RD

WILSON LA

B260 GREEN STREET GREEN RD

Mile End
Green

DA13

WHITEHILL RD

B255

Whitehill

DA2

Pinden

Pinden End
Farm

Longfield

B255

NORTHDOWN RD

WEST SHAW

MAIN RD

Liby

7

RABBITS RD

DA4

ESSEX RD

PH

ROWAN CL

KENT RD

PO

STATION RD

Longfield

HARTLEY RD

OAKWOOD
RISE

ST MARY'S WAY

Axton Chase
Sch

B260

69

CANADA FARM RD

Dean Bottom

Dene Bottom
Farm

FAWKHAM RD

CHEYNE WLK
CAVENDISH

RUSSELL
SQ

EATON
SQ

BRAMBLEFIELD CL

THE CRESCENT

COPSE SIDE

HOTTSFIELD

FAIRACRE
PL

QUAKERS CL

NORTHFIELD

GILCROFT

6

Churchdown
Wood

THE MEWS 1
ST JAMES SQ 2
GROSVENOR SQ 3
BEDFORD SQ 4
ST GEORGES SQ 5
SLOANE SQ 6

MERTON AVE
4 2

PITFIELD

VIEWPOINT
CT

PORCHESTER
CL

CAXTON

HAWTHORNS

BRAMBLEDOWN

WELL FIELD
3   1

1 SILVERDALE
2 MERRYFIELDS
3 EVERGLADE CL
4 FORTUNA CL

VIEW

POSELANDS

LARKWELL LA

PERRAN CL

LARKS FIELD

WOODLAND AVE

5

PARKFIELD

DIXONS VA''

GRESHAM AVE

68

Beeches
Farm

Hill Barn
Farm

CASTLE HILL

OLD DOWNS

DICKENS CL

WICKHAMS
WAY

GRESHAM RD

Canada
Farm

DA3

Hartley
Green

GREEN HATT

BROOMFIELD

STACK LA

CARMELITE WAY

CHURCH RD

GORSE WOOD RD

JOHNS
CL

Our Lady of
Hartley RC Prim
Sch

GORSE WAY

MANOR DR

4

STACK RD

Lane Oak
Farm

SCUDDERS HILL

Football
Ground

Sports
Club

Hartley Cty
Prim Prim Sch

CULVEY CL

PO

ASH RD

ROUND ASH WAY

CONIFER AVE

Liby

THE WARREN

CHERRY TREES

ST JOHN'S LA

BILLINGS HILL

HILL SHAW

Hartley

3

Nursery

VALLEY RD

Pennis
Farm

FAIRBY LA

CHANTRY AVE

GRANGE WAY

TATES ORCH

67

THREE GATES RD

The
Grove

Fawkham CE
Prim Sch

MANOR LA

Pennis
Wood

TN15

The
Black Lion
(PH)

2

SCHOOL LA

Parkfield
Wood

Fawkham
Manor

H

CH

Chapel
Wood

Mast

OLIVER MILL 1
CHAPEL WOOD 2

CHAPEL WOOD RD

CALING
CROFT

1

66

58 **A** **B** 59 **C** **D** 60 **E** **F**

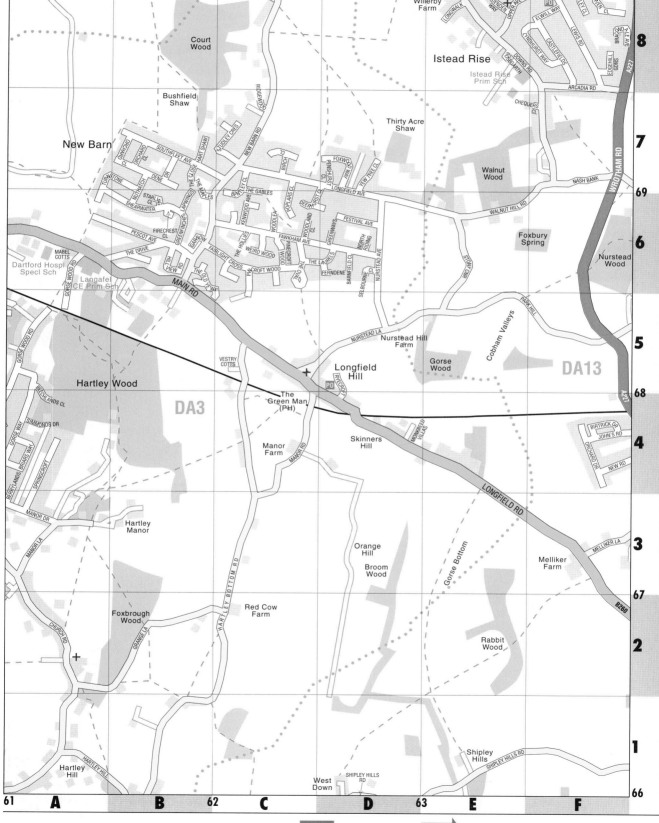

A **B** **C** **D** **E** **F**

Willerby Farm

Istead Rise

Istead Rise Prim Sch

Court Wood

Bushfield Shaw

Thirty Acre Shaw

Chequers Cl

New Barn

Walnut Wood

Nash Bank

Foxbury Spring

Nurstead Wood

Dartford Hospl Specl Sch

Langafel CE Prim Sch

Mabel Cotts

Hartley Wood

DA13

Nurstead Hill Farm

Gorse Wood

Cobham Valleys

Vestry Cotts

Longfield Hill

DA3

The Green Man (PH)

Skinners Hill

Manor Farm

Monkweed Villas

Birtrick Dr

John's Rd

Hartley Manor

Orange Hill

Broom Wood

Gorse Bottom

Melliker Farm

LONGFIELD RD

Foxbrough Wood

Red Cow Farm

Rabbit Wood

Hartley Hill

Shipley Hills

West Down

Shipley Hills Rd

61 **A** **B** 62 **C** **D** 63 **E** **F**

8
7
69
6
5
68
4
67
3
2
66
1

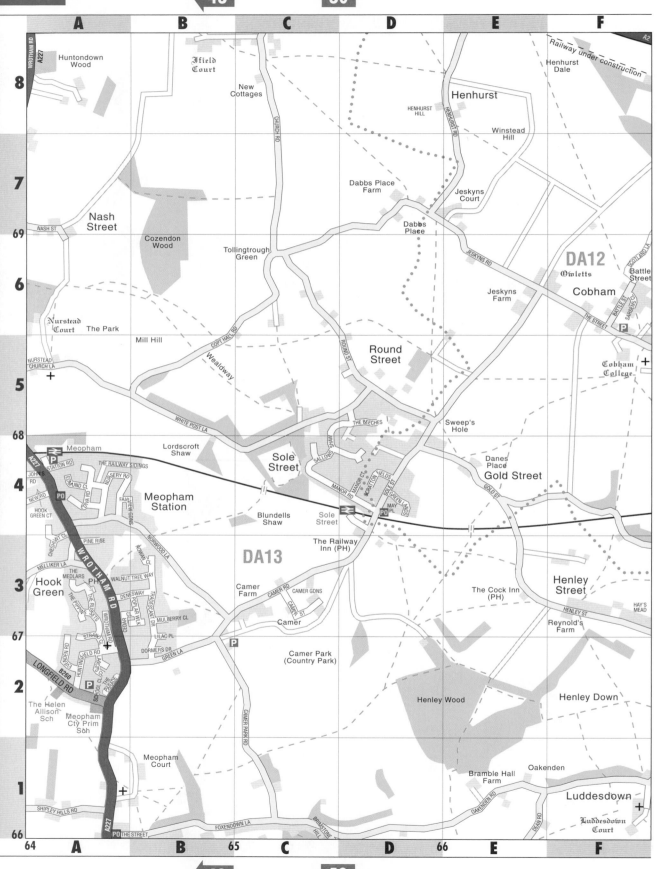

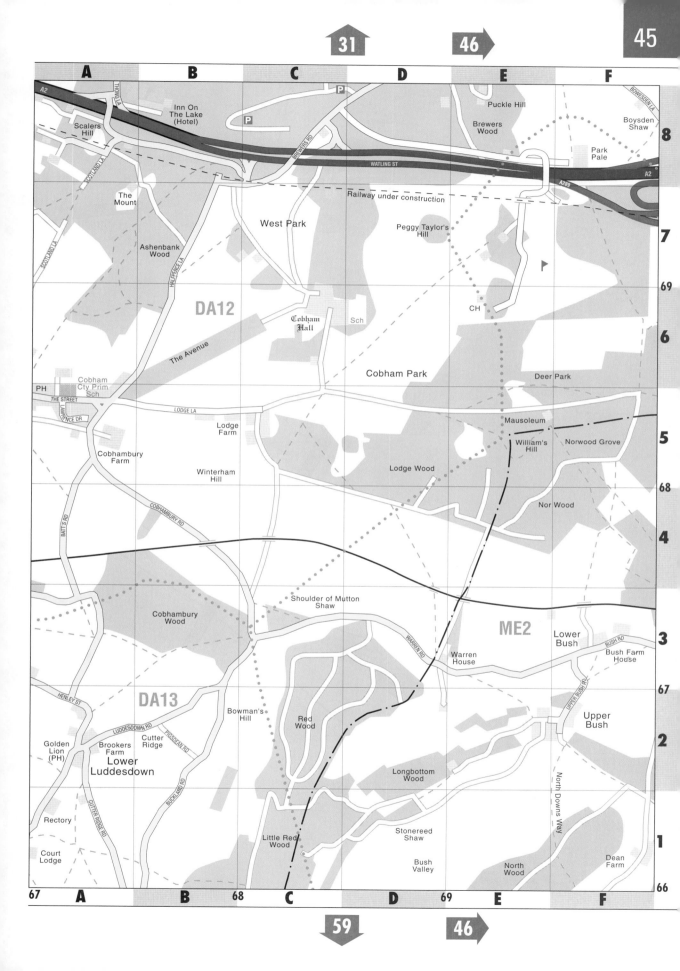

A B C D E F

DA12

8

Crutches Farm
Rose Cotts
PH
Old Watling St
Chapter Farm

Abbey Court Sch
REDE COURT RD
B2108
A26
GORSE RD
DRAKE'S AVE
BROOM HILL RD
GRAVESEND RD
A2/8

CLEWOOD DR
CRUTCHES LA
A289

BOWESDEN LA
A2
M2

ROMSEY
CLINTON AVE
CABIN
CHRISP CROSS
SUSSEX
PARADE
BRAMLEY RISE
WORCESTER
ELCOMBE RD
ABBEY RD
ROALD CT
PAPY'S WAY
DEACON

WATLING ST
B2108

THE SHADES
MILLFORDHOPE RD
STANGATE RD
PARKFIELDS
CHETNEY CL
COPPERHOUSE RD
SWALE
YANTLET
Chapter Sch
THURSTON DR

LINWOOD AVE
ALLINGTON
DAUCHESS
DEAN
COBHAM CT
GDNS
COLUMBINE
CP
DAFFODIL RD
COBHAM CL
RIVER DR
HARVEL CL
STOUR CL
HUMBER CRES
WITHAM WAY
MEWS

Strood
Sports Ctr
P

7

SEAMEW CT 1
SKUA CT 2
SNIPE CT 3
ARRAN GN 4
NIGHTINGALE CT 5

Bligh Cty Prim Inf Sch
SCHOLARS FIELD
BLIGH WAY

COLUMBINE RD
LANCELOT AVE
ELAINE AVE

CLIFTON CL
TAMAR DR
TINTAGEL GDNS
DART

CORMORANT CL
ALBATROSS AVE
SHEARWATER CL
ORCHID
PELICAN CL
CURLEW CRES
PENGUIN CL
PERI CRES

Elaine Prim Sch

69

Knights Place

CARNATION RD
HYACINTH RD
DARLEY RD
GALAHAD AVE
ELAINE CT
DARNLEY RD
MAPLE RD
WILLOW
BEECH RD
CEDAR RD

PINE RD
A28
PO

6

Broad Oak Wood
Temple Wood
Railway under construction

SOUTHWELL RD
WIDGEON RD
UPLANDS
FULMAR RD
PORTSMOUTH RD
SOUTHWARK RD
CHESTNUT RD
HAWTHORN RD
ASH RD

Clay Pond Wood

Great Wood

ME2

GUILDFORD GDNS 1
CARLISLE CL 2
PETERBOROUGH GDNS 3
WAKEFIELD CL 4
LINCOLN CL 5
ST ALBANS RD 6
NORWICH CL 7
NOTTINGHAM WLK 8

CHELMSFORD RD
HAMBOR
ST PAUL'S
BRISTOL
THE SPIRES
CHESTER CL
COVENTRY
HIGHLAND RD
WINSTON RD
WELLS CT
WELLS RD
GLAMFORD RD
LILAC CRES
LILAC RD
NORTH BANK CL

Sherwin Knight Jun & Inf Sch
HEVER CT
Cemy

5

Birch Wood

MERRALS WOOD CRES
HILLSHAW CRES
RANSCOMBE CL
LABURNUM RD
POPLAR RD
SYCAMORE RD
POPULAR CL

ELGIN GDNS
RUSHDEAN RD
BOOT

CUXTON RD
BALLARD
ESNS PK
VIKING CL
SAXON PL
NORMAN CL
ROMAN WAY

68

RANSCOMBE FARM COTTS

4

Ranscombe

Merrals Shaw

ROCHESTER RD
2

CHARIOT WAY
PH
Wickham Reach

Mill Hill

North Downs Way

Longhoes Wood

Medway Bridge

Medway Bridge Marina
CAMBRIA AVE 1
CORDELIA CRES 2
SILVER HILL 3
MANDRA LA
FARMONDE AVE

3

POPLICANS RD
HAROLD RD
REGINALD AVE
PILGRIMS WAY
Common Marsh

Kent Centenary Wlks
SILVER HILL
KENWAY

Works

NINE ACRES RD
WHITE LEAVES RD
CHARLES DR
BUSH RD
LADYWOOD RD
HAYLEY CL
JAMES DR
SUNDRIDGE HILL

LETTS CRES
WARWICK CRES
Sch
HILARY GDNS
ASSYN

67

Court Lodge
PO
1 WILLIAM RD
2 HOLLYCROFT
Cuxton
PH
STATION RD
LC
River Medway

2

Cuxton Com Jun & Inf Schs
Liby
WOOD ST
LW ST
STANFORD RD
THE GLEBE
CUXTON IND EST
BRAMBLETREE COTTS
Factory Farm

Borstal Court Farm
ME1

WOODHURST CL
HILLCROFT
Cuxton

WOULDHAM RD
BURHAM RD
Medway Valley Wlk
NASHENDER FARM LA
A2/8

Church Hill

ROCHESTER RD
A228

Wouldham Marshes

1

Bores Hole
PILGRIMS WAY

ME2
Rings Marsh

66

70 A B 71 C D 72 E F

33

48

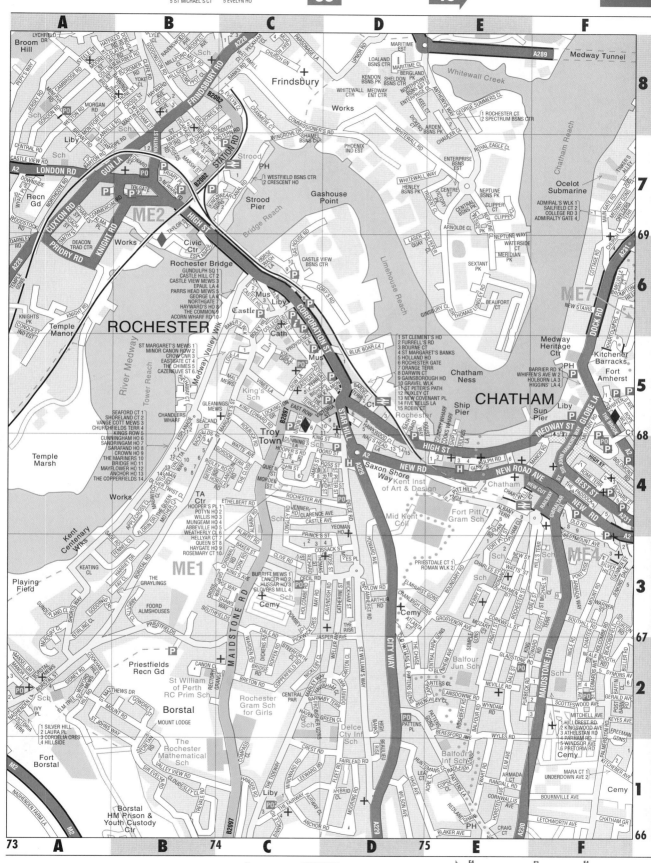

61

48

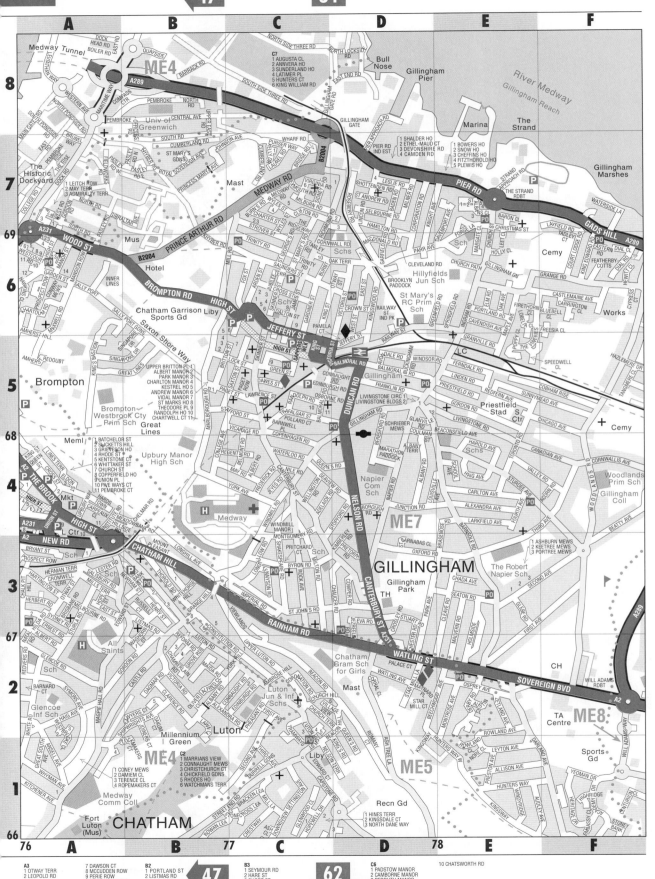

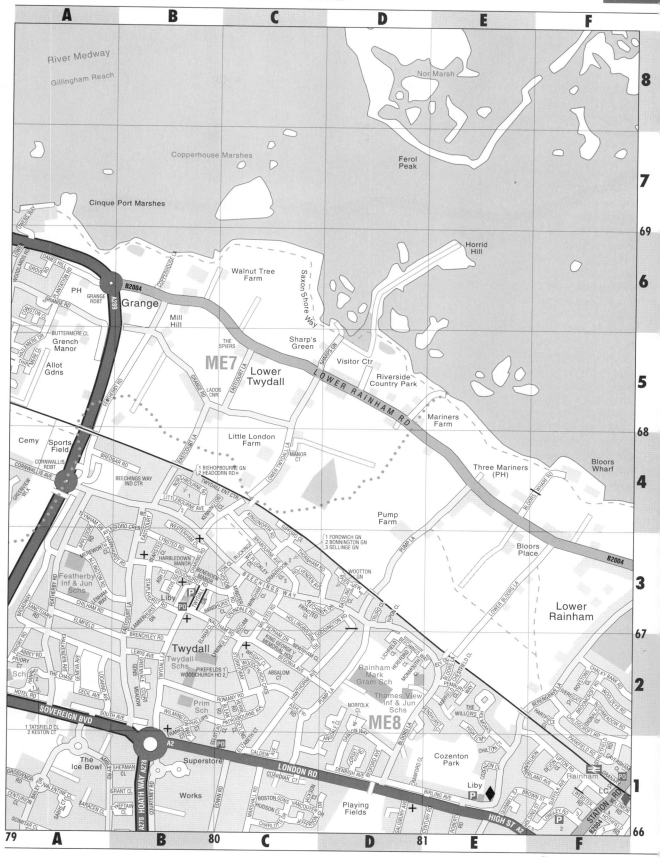

F1
1 CREVEQUER CHAMBERS
2 RAINHAM SH CTR
3 GRESHAM CL
4 HARRISON CT
5 MAPLINS CL

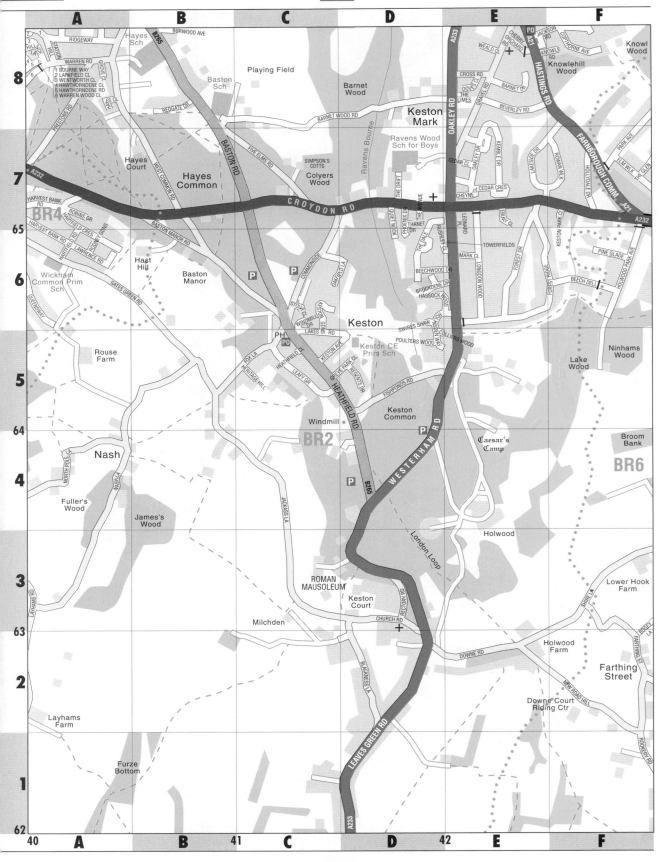

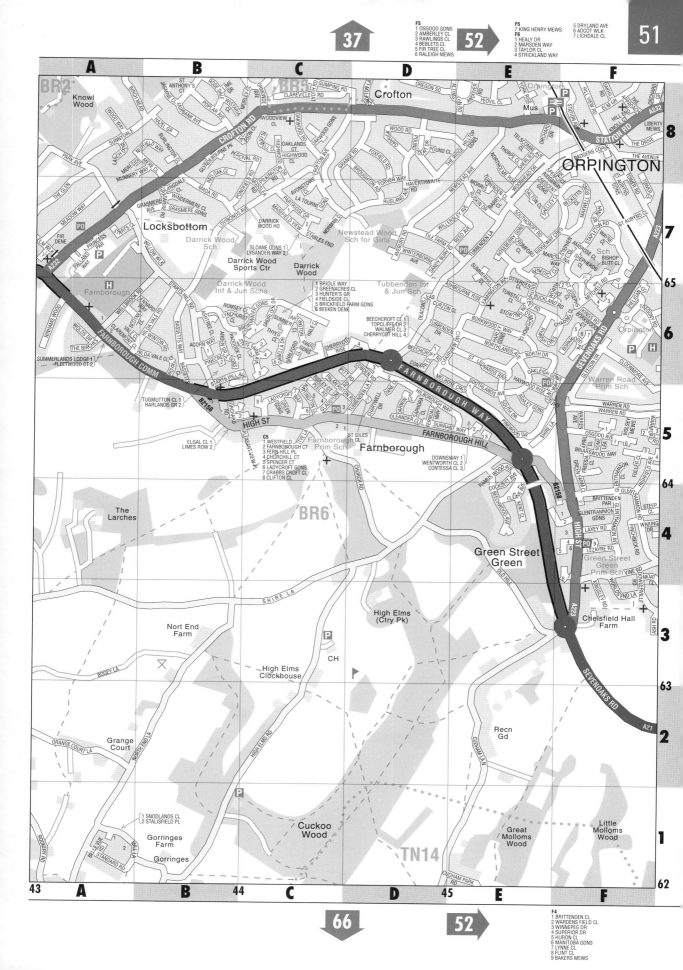

37

52

F5
1 OSGOOD GDNS
2 AMBERLEY CL
3 RAWLINGS CL
4 BEBLETS CL
5 FIR TREE CL
6 RALEIGH MEWS

F5
7 KING HENRY MEWS
F6
1 HEALY DR
2 MARSDEN WAY
3 TAYLOR CL
4 STRICKLAND WAY

5 DRYLAND AVE
6 ADCOT WLK
7 LICHDALE CL

66

52

F4
1 BRITTENDEN CL
2 WARDENS FIELD CL
3 WINNEPEG DR
4 SUPERIOR DR
5 HURON CL
6 MANITOBA GDNS
7 LYNNE CL
8 FLINT CL
9 BAKERS MEWS

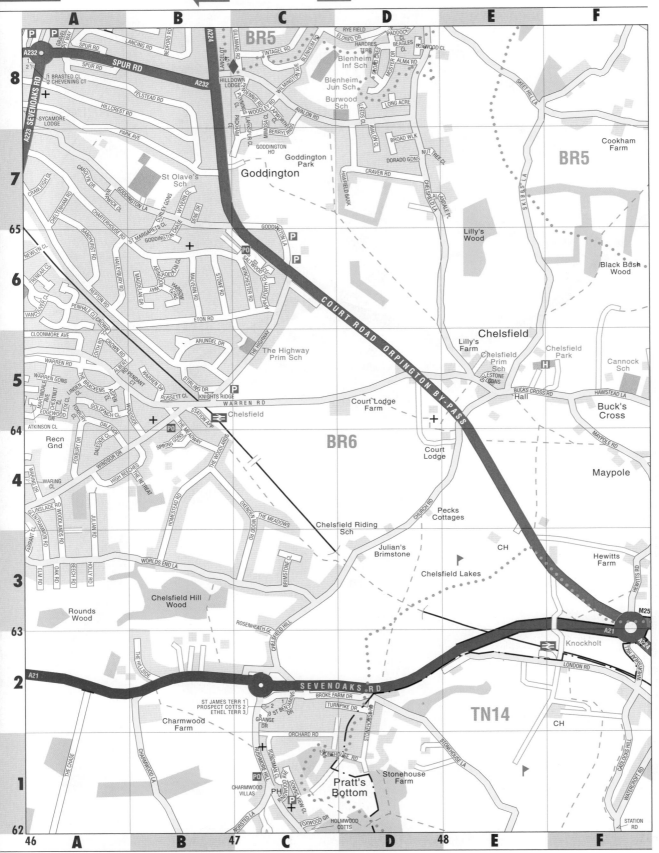

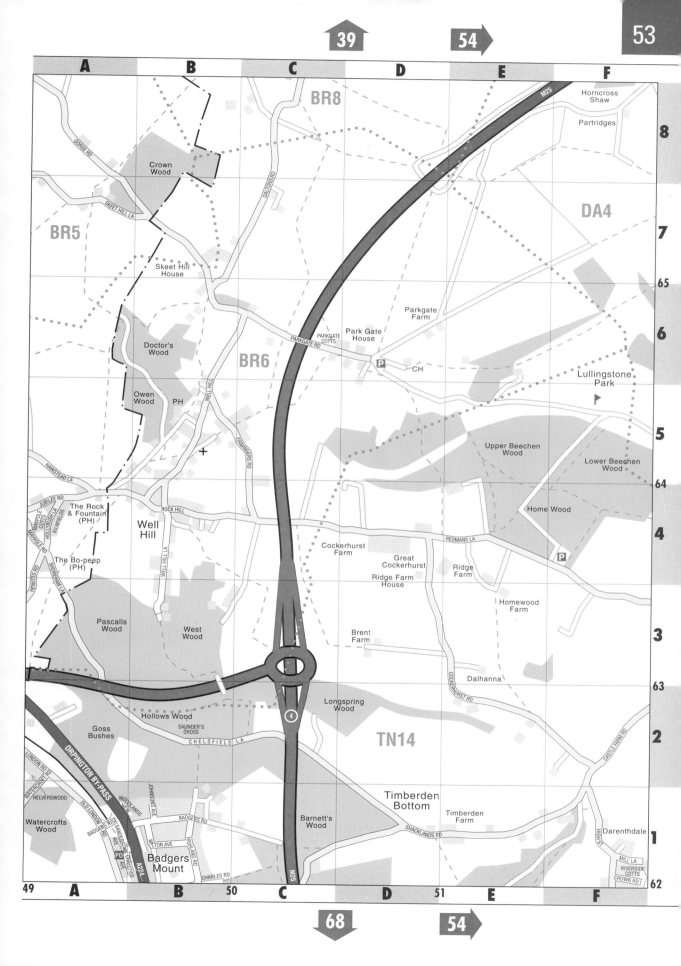

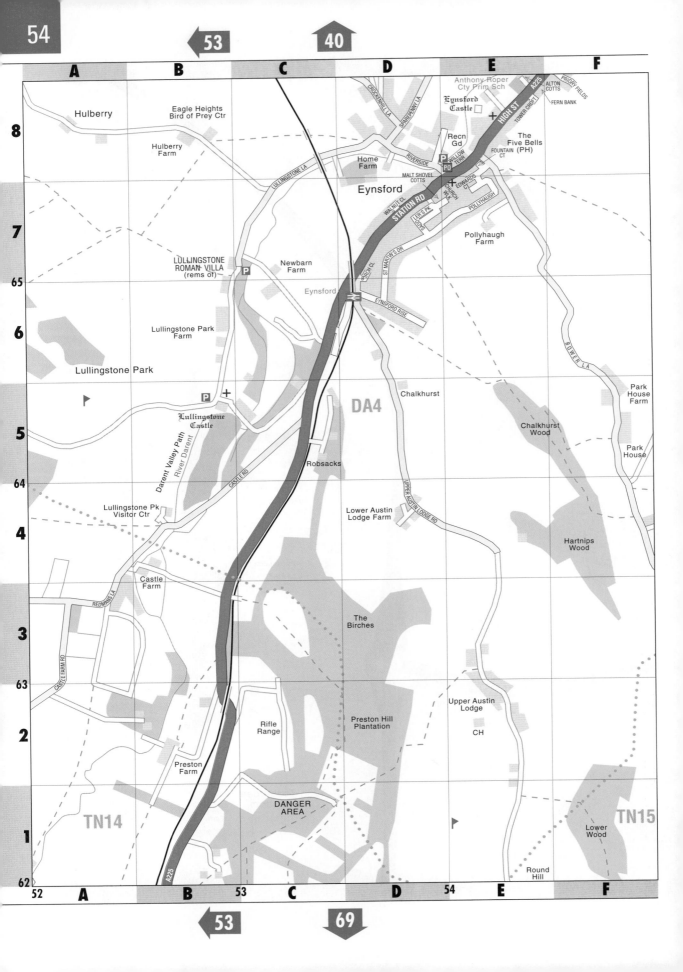

A **B** **C** **D** **E** **F**

Firpound
Shaw

Speedgate
Farm

DONKEY LA

BESSELS LA

A20

Alchin's
Wood

Lincoln
Kennels

Speed
Gate

8

GABRIEL SPRING RD

Gabrielspring
Wood

GABRIEL SPRING ROAD (EAST)

THREE GATES RD

MUSSENDEN LA

Olivers
Shaw

M20

MAIN ROAD GORSE HILL

Gorse Hill
Farm

SCRATCHERS LA

DA3

7

MAPLESCOMBE LA

65

Brands Hatch
Circuit

M20

6

DA4

COLIN CHAPMAN WAY

Lower Park
Wood

Kingsdown
Farm

Hotel

Grove
Wood

5

Adder Bank
Shaw

Maplescombe

Maplescombe
Farm

SYMONDS
CL

NEAL RD

GILLIES RD

VIKING WAY

64

Bower Park
Farm

Blue Chalet
IND PK

STACKLANDS
CL

P-E-LPS CL

SHERBO... RNE CL

OAKLANDS

LOVELACE
CL

REGE... NCY CL

HEVER AVE

WESTFIELD
COTTS

4

MILLFIELD RD

MILLFIELD RD

BOTSOM LA

Florence Farm
MOBILE HOME PK

THE BRIARS

HEVER RD

WELLS CL

HO...

WHITEGATES
AVE

MULTON RD

ASTOR RD

PENSHURST

HEVER WOOD RD

WOOD VIEW
CL

Church
Wood

Hog
Wood

Sidehilly
Wood

MITCHEM CL

LONDON RD

GLENDOWER
RD

RUSHETTS RD

CHANCEL
CL

3

KNATTS VALLEY RD

TN15

RUSHETTS RD

KINGSFISHER
CL

BAKERS
AVE

SOUTHFIELDS RD

VERNON RD

63

High Castle
Wood

The Gamecock
(PH)

Liby

KINGSINGFIELD RD

WEST
KINGSDOWN IND EST

ASH TREE DR

BLACKTHORN CL

THE GRANGE

VERNON RD

MEADOW BANK CL 1
POUND BANK CL 2
BIRCHWAY 3

West
Kingsdown

A20

2

BOWER LA

ASHEN GROVE RD

CHERRY TREE GR

EAST HILL RD

East Hill

Knatts Valley

SCHOOL LA

THE GROVE

1

Caravan
Pk

Stacklands
Wood

62

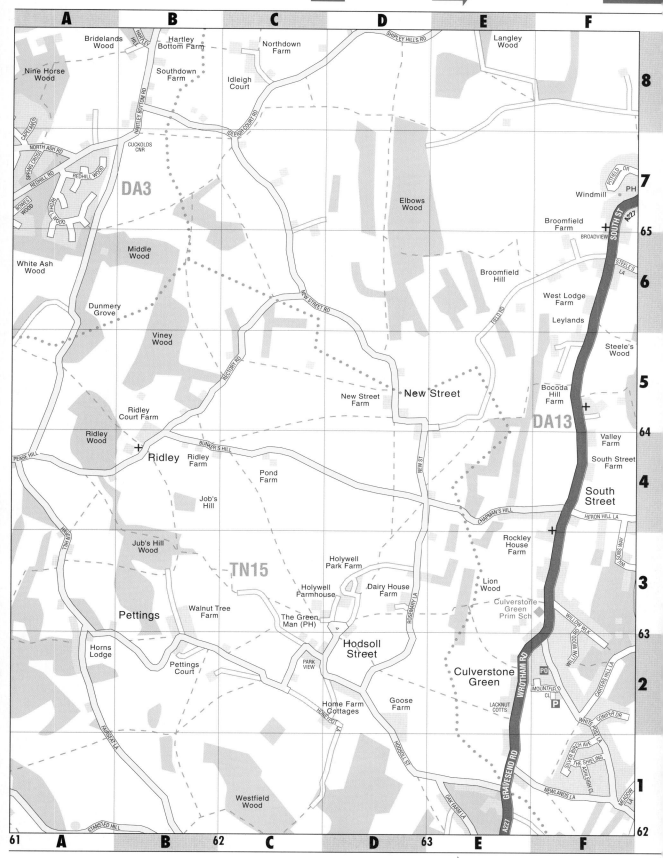

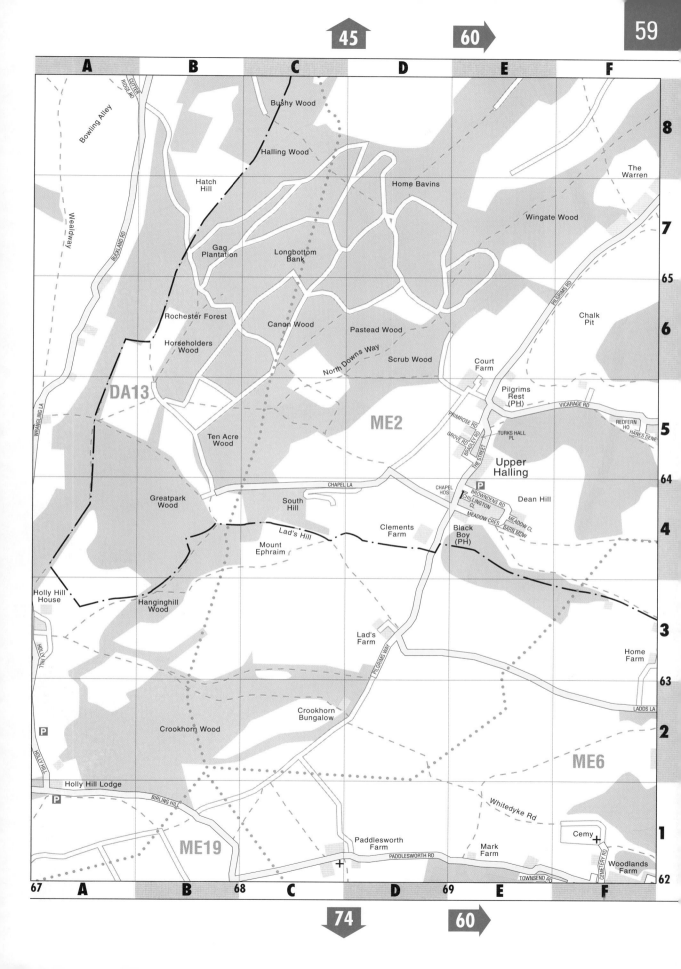

59
46

A **B** **C** **D** **E** **F**

8

May's Wood

North Halling

Ringshill Farm

Starkeys

ROCHESTER RD

A228

BURHAM RD

7

Chy

PILGRIMS RD

WOULDHAM RD

Works

Ivy Cottage

65

LC

North Downs Way

6

FORMBY RD

FORMBY TERR

LC

STAKE LA

JADE HILL

New Town

Halling Fresh Marsh

Ringshill Place

KENT RD

ESSEX RD

P

Halling Salt Marsh

School Farm

Wouldham Common

PILGRIMS WAY

ME2

5

GROVE MEWS

CHA

VICARAGE

Halling

STATION APR

MARSH RD

Halling

Medway Valley Wlk

SCHOOL LA

RECTORY CL

Wouldham CE Prim Sch

Harris's Copse

HILL RD

Cemy

Halling Common

PH

Wouldham

CEMETERY RD

LOW MEADOW

MARSHAM CL

KESTEVEN CL

WENDOVER CL

MAXIMILIAN DR

BENEDICT CL

River Medway

PO

Walter Burke Ave

64

ASHBY CL

FERRY RD

DALISON CT

HARRIS HO

TRAFALGAR RD

NELSON RD

FERRY LA

PORTLAND CL

DALES RD

ME1

LAMBARDE CL

CARROLL CL

SYLVESTRE CL

4

ACRE GRV

BRITANNIA CL

SCHOLEY CL

HERTING CL

HOLST CL

HRB

P

Recn Gd

CORNWALL CRES

RAVENS KNOWLE

KNOWLE RD

Keeper's Lodge

Whitting's Farm

HOWLSMERE CL

Halling Prim Sch

Wouldham Marshes

HALL RD

Wouldham Common

ME5

3

Scarborough

63

Holborough Marshes

ROCHESTER RD

2

LADYS LA

HOLBOROUGH RD

Works

SCARBOROUGH LA

Scarborough La

Holborough Works

ME6

MARGETTS LA

Burham

1

CLOCK TOWER MEWS 1

WARNETT CT 2

THOMSON CL

COVE HALL RD

RAYFRED CL

WILLOWSIDE

CHURCH FIELD

TILGHMAN WAY

OLD CHURCH RD

Burham Court

COURT RD

DOWNS VIEW

CHURCH ST

BAKER ST

ST MARY'S WLK

NEW RD

BRISLEY'S ROW

62

A228

70 **A** **B** **71** **C** **D** **72** **E** **F**

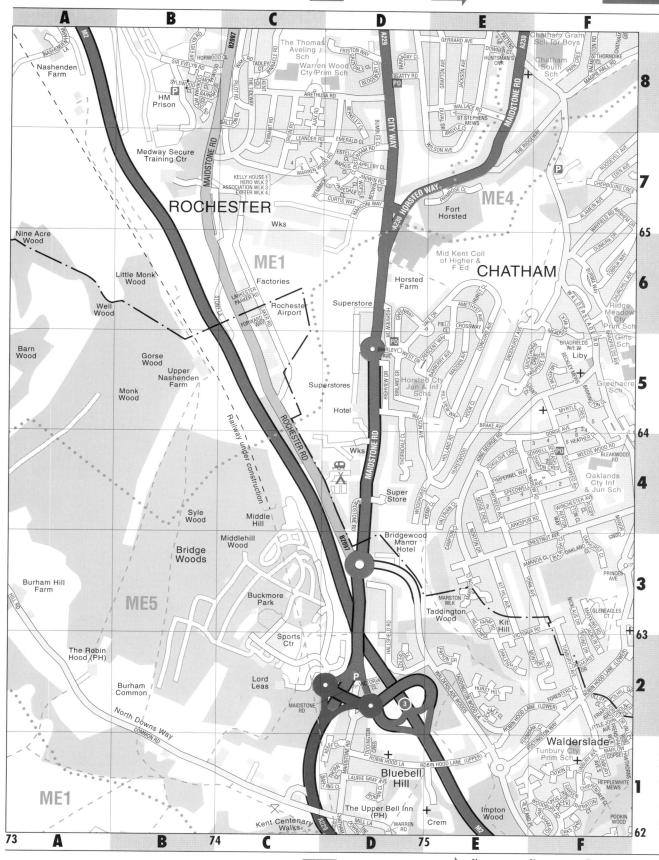

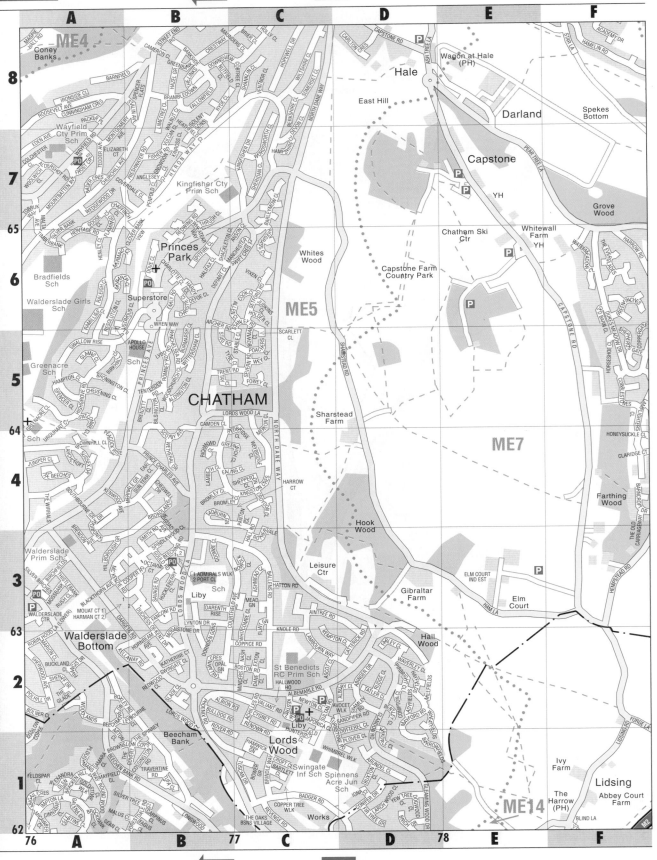

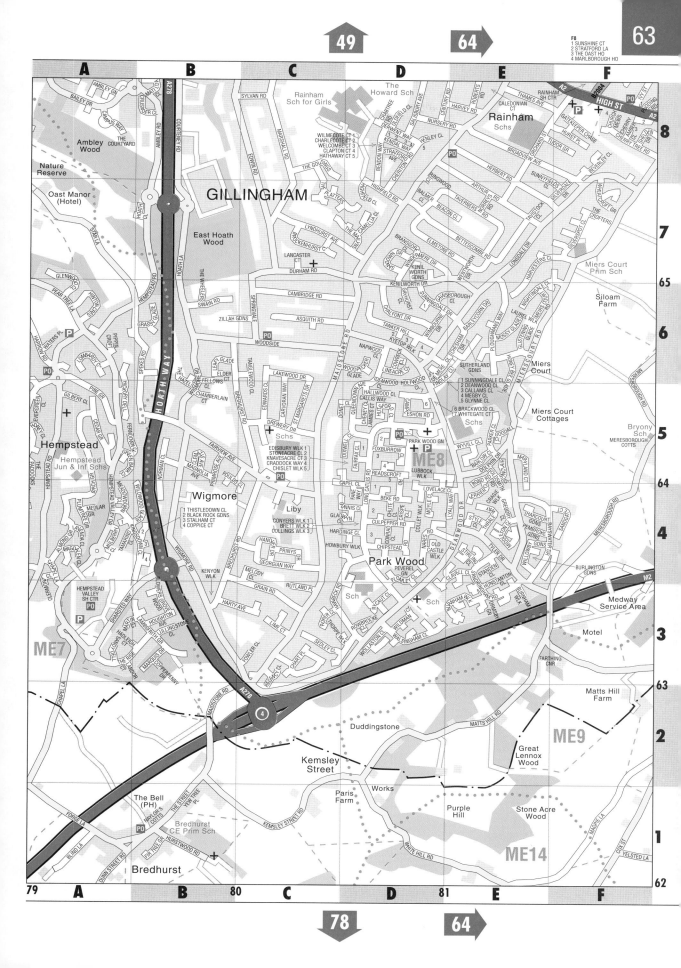

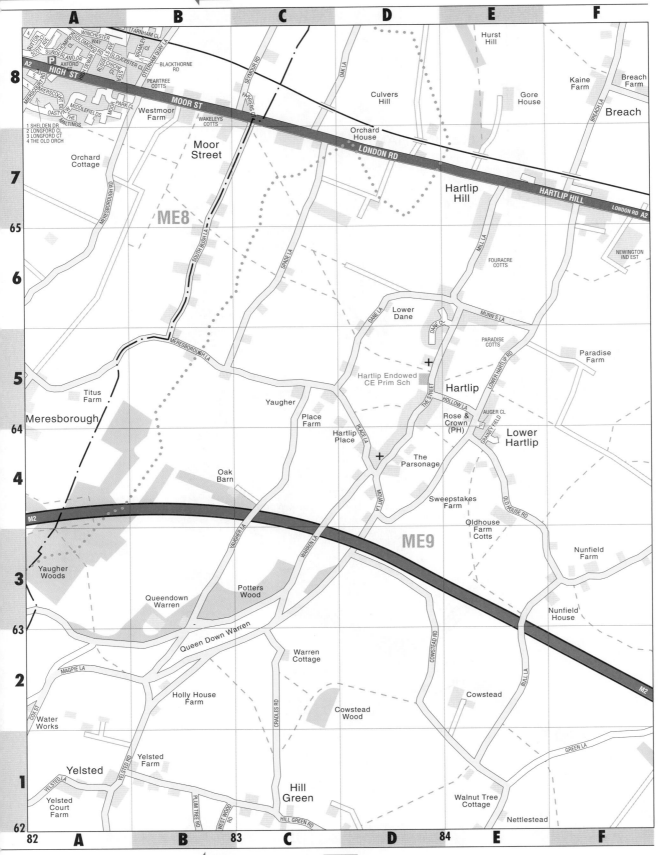

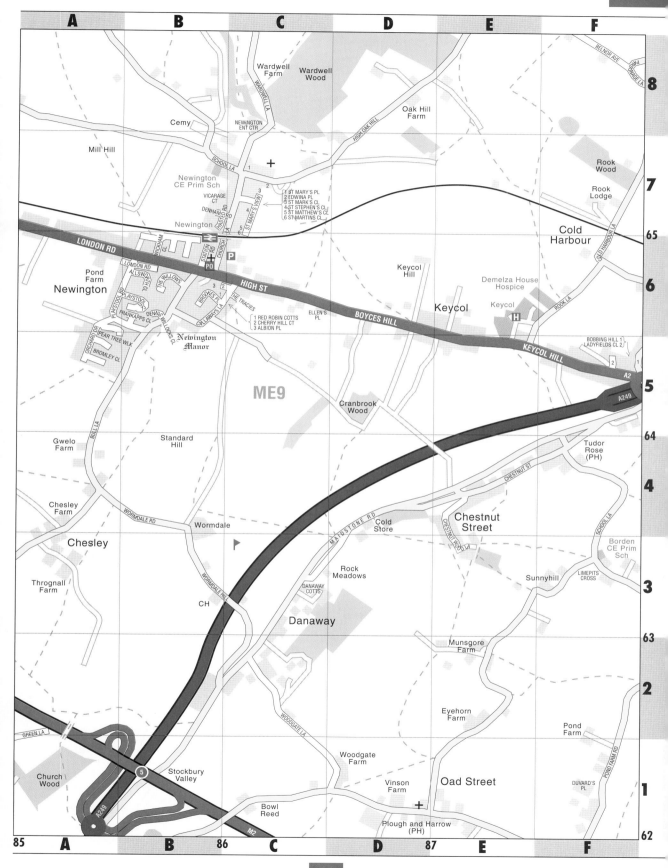

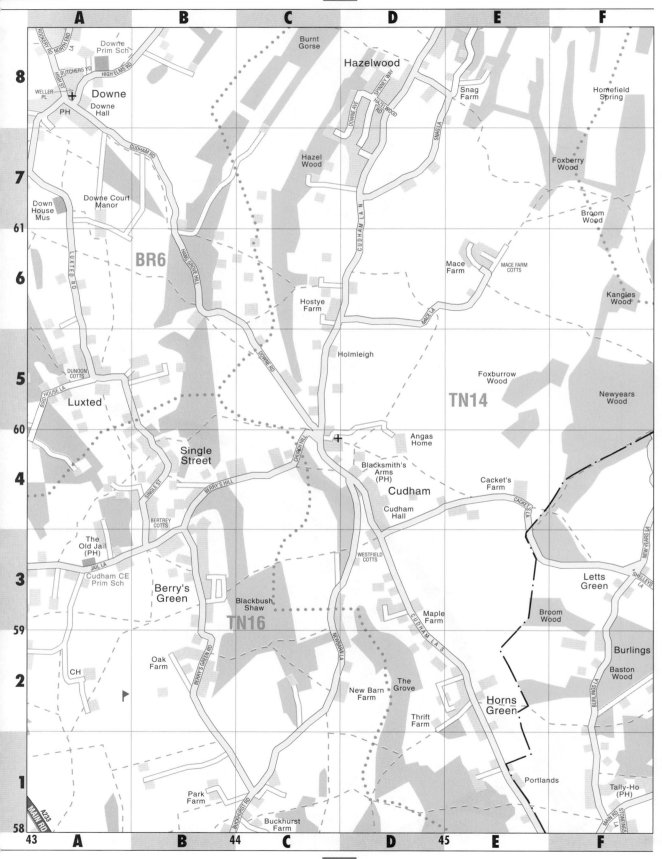

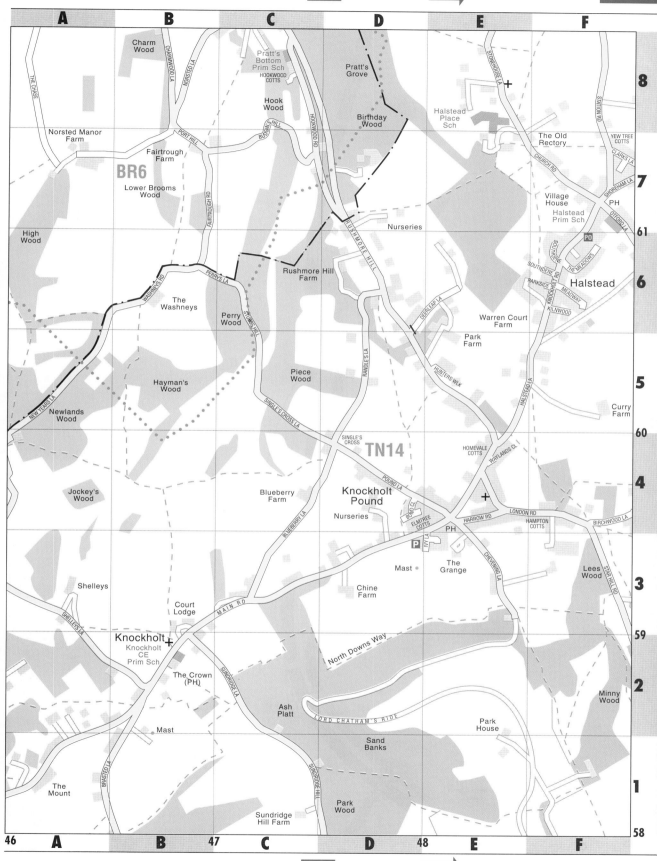

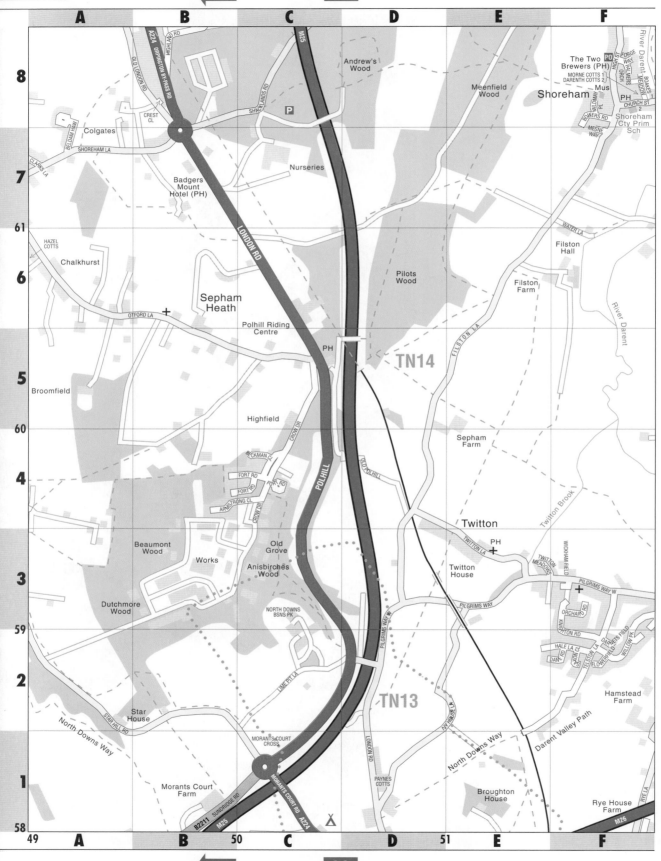

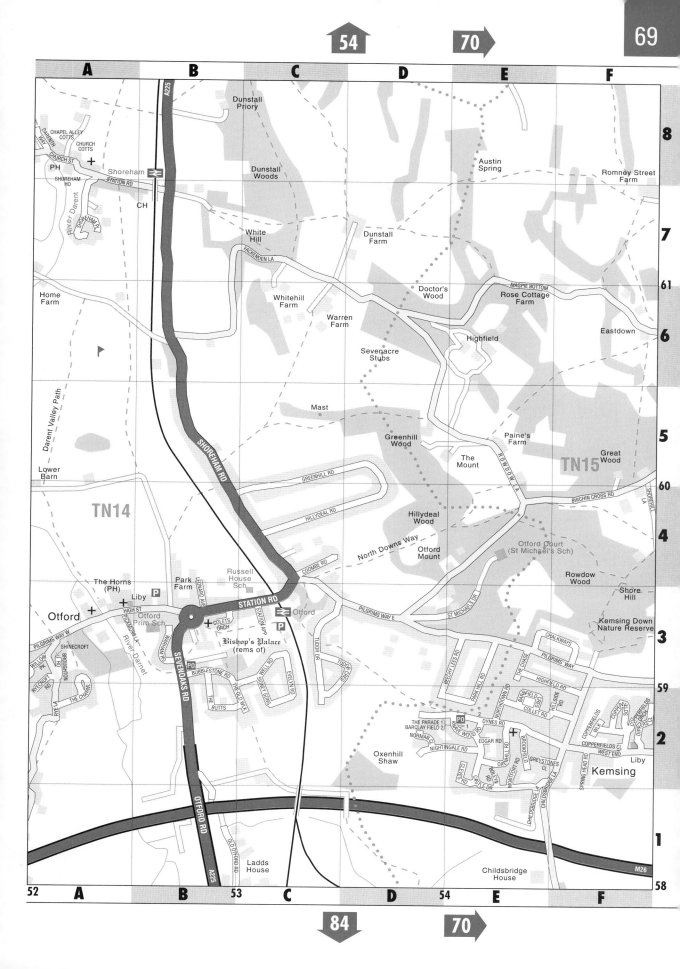

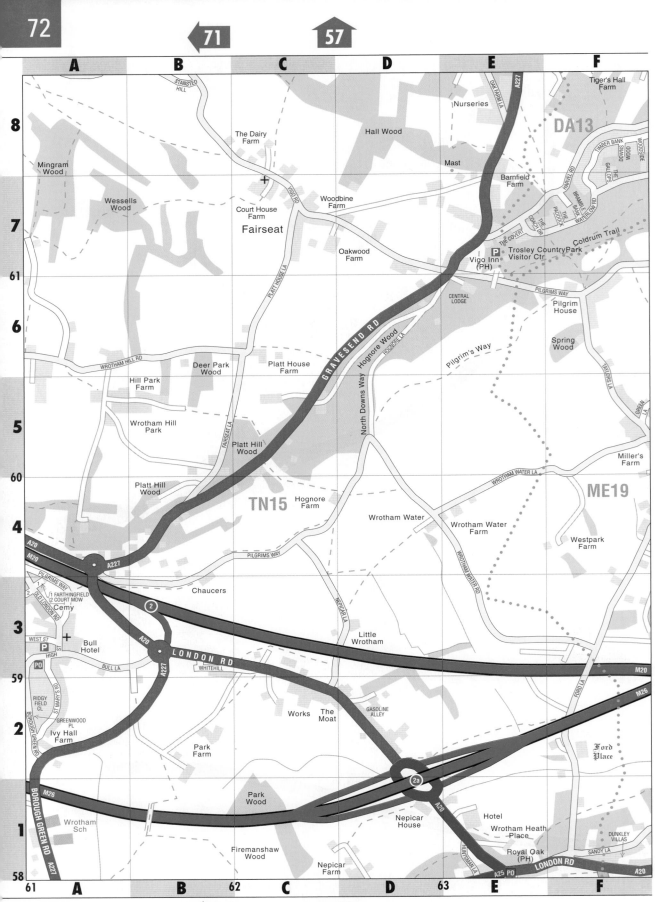

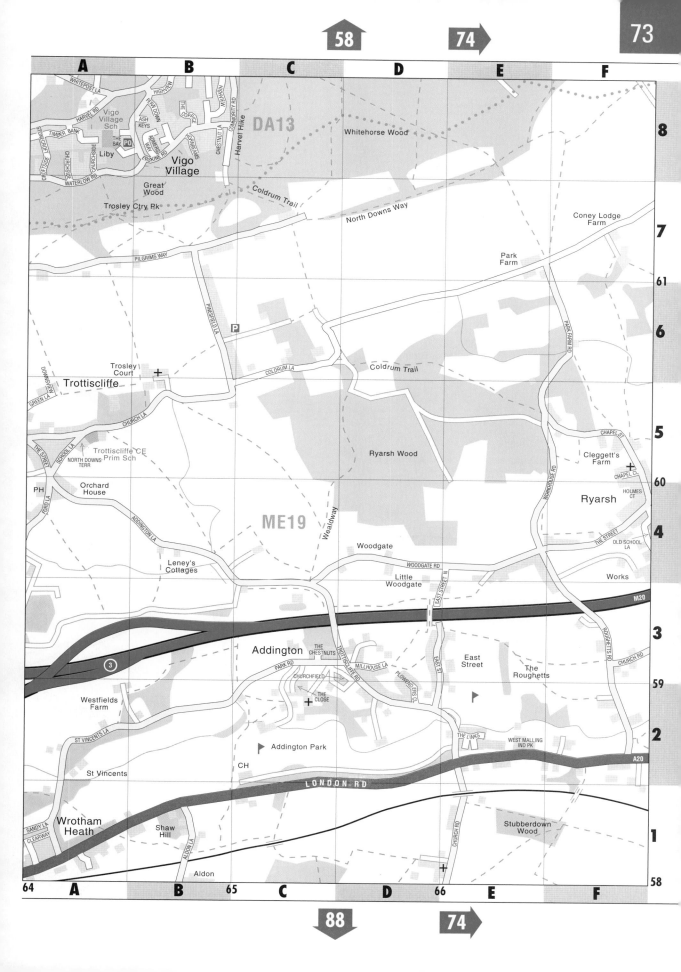

A B C D E F

8

Walnut Tree Farm

Birling Place Farm

Dyke Place

Stalks Wood

STANGATE RD

Snodland CE Prim Sch

TOWNSEND RD
HOLM RD
CONSTITUTION HILL
WOODLANDS AVE
BINGLEY CL
ROMAN RD
ROBERTS RD

MIDSUMMER HILL
ST BENEDICT RD
FREELANDS RD
DRYLAND RD
GODDEN RD
BIRLING RD
ORCHARD RD

GRASSMERE RD
DOWLING CT
GORHAM GRO
BIRLING RD
ST KATHERINE'S LA
MEADOW WLK

7

Langhold House

SNODLAND RD

LEGGE LA

Parson's Corner

Horn Street

ME6

LUCAS RD
THE GROVES
BIRLING RD
ROOKERY HILL
TAYLOR RD

St Katherine's Prim Sch

61

Austen's Farm

SANDY LA

HOLLINS LA
POUT RD
TOM JOYCE CL

Holmesdale Com Sch

EDGELER CT

Holmesdale Sch (Farm Annex)

6

Ley Farm

Birling Lodge

+ Birling

Liby

Sandhole

CH

P

ANNIE RD
SOPER RD

CORONA TERR
MALLING RD
BROOK LA

ALEX HUGHES CL

PH
BULL RD
BIRLING PK
THE CLOSE
RYARSH RD

MALLING RD

LAKESIDE

A228

5

Godfreys Farm

CLACKETTS FARM

MASTERS LA

ME19

Birling Ashes

Animal Ctr

The Vicarage

Old Place Farm

BIRLING RD

60

PH

Ryarsh Prim Sch

Birling Wood

Birling Ashes

ME20

LEYBOURNE WAY
PODEHOUSE RD

BROOK RD

LUNSFORD LA
STEVENSON WAY
SPRINGFIELD RD
GILHILL RD
PRIESTLEY DR
CHAUCER WAY

4

Stables

M20

CASTLE WAY

Leybourne Lake

AUSTEN WAY
JEROME RD
BRONTE CL

Lunsford

Lunsford Hall

HANOVER GDNS

BETJEMAN CL
CHAUCER WAY

3

Grange Park Coll

CHURCH RD

+

BIRLING RD

PARK RD

Spider's Hall

4

Hotel

Castle Lake

WILLOW RD

PARTRIDGE AVE

CARROLL GDNS
KEATS RD

M20

59

Audley House

Leybourne Pk

Leybourne Castle

+

Leybourne CE Prim Sch

CASTLE WAY

WATERSIDE CT

SCOTT WLK
WILLOW RD
OLDBY RD

ORIOLE WAY
LUNSFORD LA
SWALLOW RD
WHIMBREL GN
MERLIN AVE
PLOVER RD

2

Sports Gd

GRANGE CL

Nurseries

Wheatsheaf (PH)

Leybourne Wood

Leybourne

LITTLE MARKET ROW 1
EVERGREEN CL 2
BROADOAK 3

HAYFIELD

RECTORY LA N

THE MEADOWS
MEADOWATER

THE CROFT

LITTLE OXLEY

OLD PARK RD
OXLEY SHAW LA
RESMAN
BATWELL
HIGHBERRY

GRASSMERE

KINGFISHER RD
NIGHTINGALE CL
WOODLEA

SISKIN WLK 1
MALLARD WLK 2

SWALLOW RD
WREN CL

WOODPECKER RD

A20

1

A20

SANDY LA

BRICKFIELDS

TOWN HILL CL
TOWN HILL
NEVILL CT

LONDON RD

PUMP CL
MILLBROOK

OLD ORCHARD LA
ELLENDEN
OLD BARN RD
CROSS
RECTORY LA
WHEATFIELD
BARLEYCORN
HOP

ASHTON WAY
A228

GREBE CT 1
FALCON GN 2
BLATCHFORD CL 3
SHAFTESBURY CL 4
ADDISON CL 5
WALPOLE CL 6
COLUMBINE RD 7
COLUMBINE CL 8

HERON RD

WINTERFIELD LA
DICKENS DR
MORRIS CL
HARDIE CL
TEMPLE WAY
CARNATION CRES
ROSEMARY RD

LARKSPUR RD

58

F4
1 SOUTHEY WAY
2 CRONIN CL
3 BLAKE DR
4 COLERIDGE CL
5 CHESTERTON RD
6 BROWNING CL
7 BARRIE DR
8 CHRISTIE DR

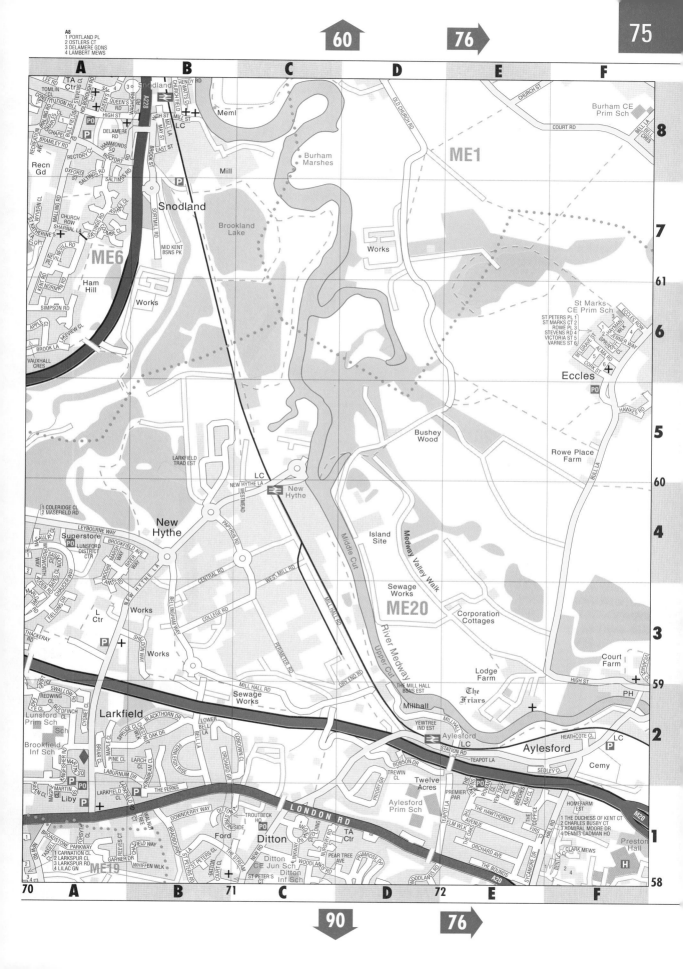

75 61

A B C D E F

ME1

ME5

ME20

ME14

ME16

Fleur de Lis (PH)

Little Culand

Hale Farm

PILGRIMS WAY

Kit's Coty Farm

Kit's Coty

Kit's Coty House

Little Kit's Coty House

The Lower Bell (PH)

North Downs Way

Wellhead

Frith Wood

Frith Wood

Masts

White Horse Stone

Railway under construction

Little Cossington Farm

Great Cossington

Pratling Street

Ind Est

Ind Est

Tyland Barn

Higham View

Pilgrims View

CH

Works

Abbey Gate

Abbey Farm

Abbey Gate Cotts

St Peter's CE Prim Sch

Sports Gd

The Deacon Est

Forstal

Superabbey Est

Forstal Cotts

Cobtree Manor

Cobtree Wharf

Crabtree Rndbt

River Medway

Medway Valley Wlk

Little Preston

Preston Hall Sports Gd

Museum of Kent Rural Life

Malta Inn (PH)

The Running Horse Rndbt

Sandling

Kent Centenary Wlks

ROCHESTER RD

CHATHAM RD

OLD CHATHAM RD

WARREN RD

KINGSWOOD RD

SALISBURY RD

VINCENT RD

BERESFORD RD

QUEENSWOOD RD

COLLINGWOOD RD

BEAUSSELL RD

LOWER WARREN RD

GREY WETHERS

CHATHAM RD

PRATLING ST

OLD MILL LA

BEDDOW WAY

POWELL CL

UNWIN CL

S MICHAELS CL

ST MICHAELS CL

FORSTAL RD

SANDLING RD

LOCK LA

CASTLE RD

FORSTAL RD

BOARLEY LA

GRANGE LA

TYLAND LA

SHRUBSOLE DR

SHENLEY GR

MOUNT PLEASANT

TRINITY CT

BUSH ROW

HIGH ST

M20

A20

The Old Oast Bsns Ctr

East Park Rd

75 91

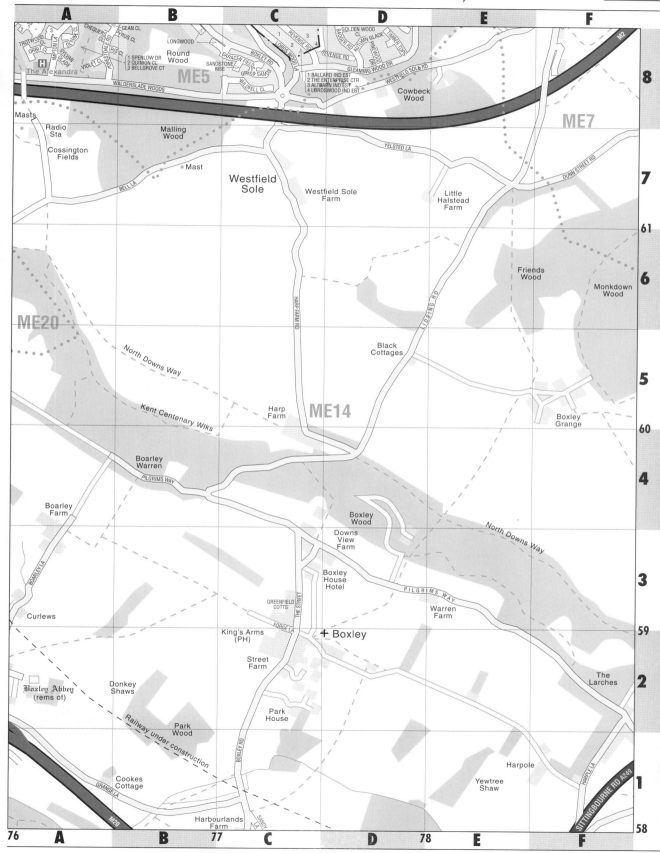

A B C D E F

8

Masts

Radio Sta

Cossington Fields

Malling Wood

Mast

Westfield Sole

Westfield Sole Farm

Little Halstead Farm

7

61

ME20

North Downs Way

Friends Wood

Monkdown Wood

6

Kent Centenary Wlks

Harp Farm

ME14

Black Cottages

Boxley Grange

5

60

Boarley Warren

PILGRIMS WAY

North Downs Way

4

Boarley Farm

Boxley Wood

Downs View Farm

3

Curlews

Boxley House Hotel

Greenfield Cotts

PILGRIMS WAY

Warren Farm

Boxley

59

King's Arms (PH)

Street Farm

The Larches

2

Boxley Abbey (rems of)

Donkey Shaws

Park House

Park Wood

Harpole

Yewtree Shaw

1

Cookes Cottage

Railway under construction

GRANGE LA

M20

BOXLEY RD

SANDY LA

Harbourlands Farm

SITTINGBOURNE RD A249

HARP LA

58

ME5

Round Wood

Longwood

WALDERSLADE WOODS

The Alexandra

1 SPENLOW DR
2 QUINION CL
3 BELLGROVE CT

SARACEN FIELD
SANDSTONE RISE
GREEN SAN
WILDFELL CL

BOXLEY RD
LORDS WOOD LA
REVENGE RD

Golden Wood CL
BADGERS RD
AUTUMN GLADE
LIMBER TOPS
LINENWOOD DR
GLEAMING WOOD DR
REVENGE RD

1 BALLARD IND EST
2 THE ENTERPRISE CTR
3 ALTBARN IND EST
4 LORDSWOOD IND EST

WESTFIELD SOLE RD

Cowbeck Wood

ME7

M2

YELSTED LA

DUNN STREET RD

BELL LA

HARP FARM RD

LIDSING RD

THE STREET

FORGE LA

BOARLEY LA

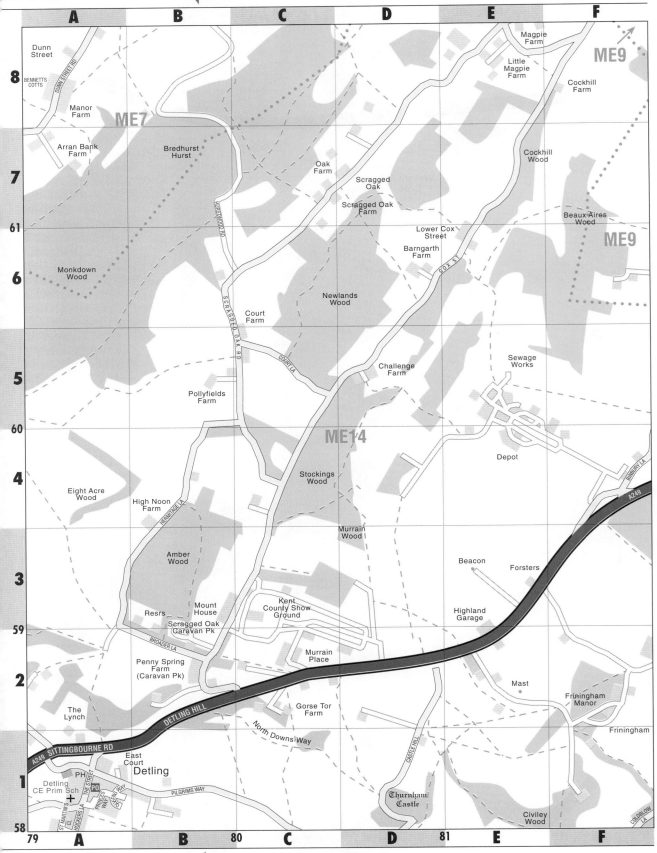

A **B** **C** **D** **E** **F**

8

Dunn
Street

BENNETTS
COTTS

Manor
Farm

ME7

Arran Bank
Farm

DUNN STREET RD

Bredhurst
Hurst

7

Oak
Farm

Scragged
Oak

Scragged Oak
Farm

Magpie
Farm

Little
Magpie
Farm

ME9

Cockhill
Farm

Cockhill
Wood

Beaux Aires
Wood

ME9

61

Monkdown
Wood

HURSTWOOD RD

Lower Cox
Street

Barngarth
Farm

COX ST

6

Court
Farm

SCRAGGED OAK RD

Newlands
Wood

Challenge
Farm

Sewage
Works

5

Pollyfields
Farm

COURT LA

Depot

60

ME14

4

Eight Acre
Wood

High Noon
Farm

HERMITAGE LA

Stockings
Wood

Murrain
Wood

Beacon

Forsters

A249

BUNBURY LA

3

Amber
Wood

Highland
Garage

Resrs

Mount
House

Kent
County Show
Ground

Murrain
Place

Mast

Friningham
Manor

Scragged Oak
Caravan Pk

BROADER LA

59

Penny Spring
Farm
(Caravan Pk)

2

Gorse Tor
Farm

Friningham

The
Lynch

DETLING HILL

North Downs Way

CASTLE HILL

1

A249

SITTINGBOURNE RD

East
Court

Detling

PH

Detling
CE Prim Sch

PO

THE STREET

PRINCES WAY

QUEENS WAY

PILGRIMS WAY

Thurnham
Castle

Civiley
Wood

COLDBLOW LA

58

ST MARTIN'S
CL

HOCKERS LA

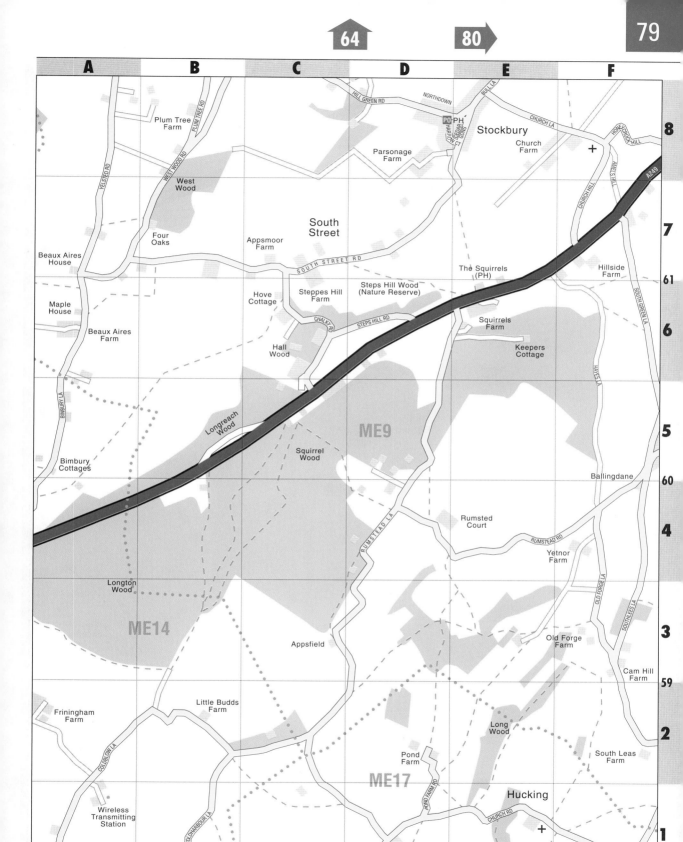

A B C D E F

8

VALE
COTTS

A249

Whipstakes
Farm

Borden
Hill

7

PETT LANE

Frid
Wood

Vigo
Farm

Stiff
Street

Stiff Street
Farm

Chantry
Farm

M2

61

Pett
Farm

Manns Place
Farm

WRENS RD

Manns
Place

Norton
Green

Little Pett
Farm

6

Gore
Wood

Deans
Hill

GORE RD

BUSH
CL

SMITHS
ORCH

TRAVERS
GDNS

BEXON LA

Magpie
Hall

Silver
Street
Farm

SILVER ST

Silver
Street

THE STREET

5

+

South
Green

Deans
Bottom

Deans
Bank
Farm

DEANS HILL RD

The Firs
Farm

Sun Inn
(PH)

PO

SOUTHGREEN LA

KENNOR BARN RD

60

ME9

BLIND MARY'S LA

4

HAZEL STREET RD

Nanjims

BICKNOR LA

BASHFORD BARN LA

Downsells

Hazel Street
Farm

Fourayes
Farm

Church
Wood

Plackett's
Hole

Swanton
Street

3

Hazel
Street

Little
Hazel Street
Farm

Trundlewood
Farm

59

SOUTHLEES LA

+

Gorham
Wood

Meadow
Farm

2

Wheatsheaf
Farm

Bicknor
Farm

Bicknor
Court

Swanton
Court

Keepers
Lodge

BICKNOR
COURT
COTTS

Bicknor

High
Wood

1

Admiral
Wood

Swanton
Farm

Bedmonton
House

58

ME17

85 A B 86 C D 87 E F

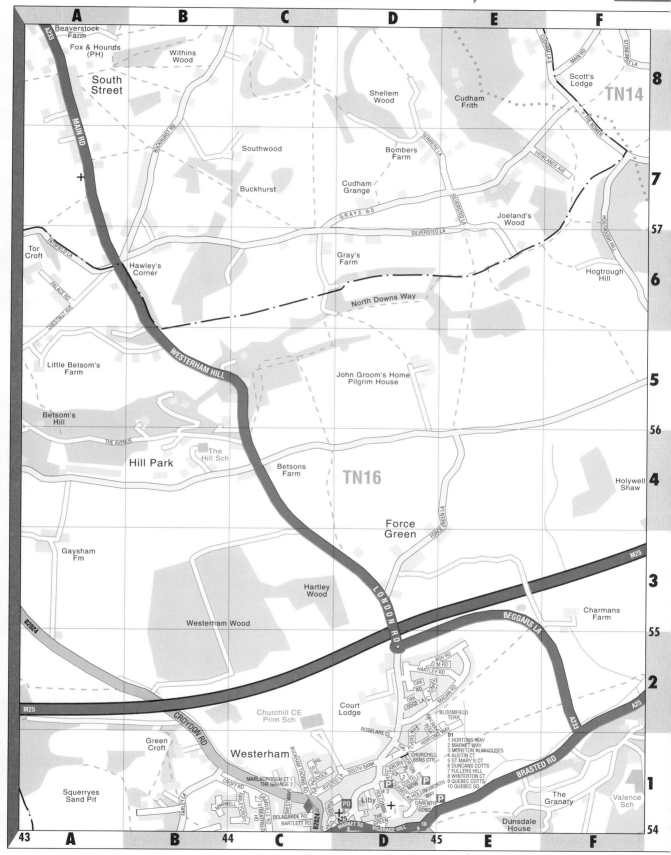

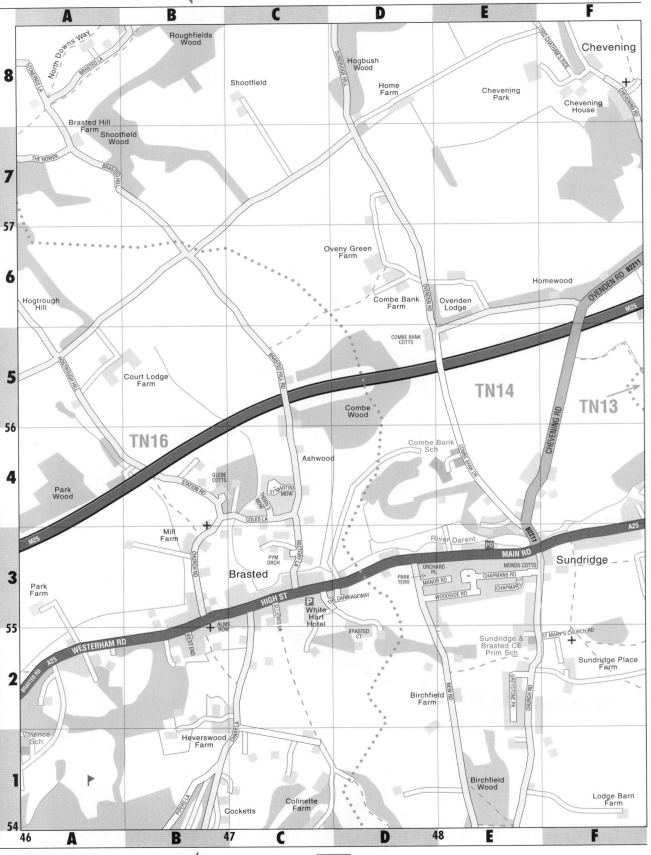

A B C D E F

8
7
57
6
5
56
4
3
55
2
1
54

North Downs Way
Roughfields Wood
Shootfield
Hogbush Wood
Home Farm
Chevening
Chevening Park
Chevening House
STONINGS LA
BRASTED LA
Brasted Hill Farm
Shootfield Wood
THE NOWER
BRASTED HILL
SUNDRIDGE HILL
LORD CHEATHAM'S RIDE
CHEVENING RD
Oveny Green Farm
Homewood
OVENDEN RD B2211
Hogtrough Hill
Combe Bank Farm
Ovenden Lodge
OVENDEN RD
M25
HOGTROUGH HILL
Court Lodge Farm
BRASTED HILL RD
COMBE BANK COTTS
TN14
CHEVENING RD
TN13
TN16
Combe Wood
Combe Bank Sch
56
Park Wood
STATION RD
GLEBE COTTS
Ashwood
COMBE BANK DR
B2211
A25
M25
Mill Farm
CHURCH RD
THORN'S MDW
ST MARTINS MDW
COLES LA
PYM ORCH
RECTORY LA
River Darent
PO
MAIN RD
Sundridge
ORCHARD PL
MONDS COTTS
Park Farm
Brasted
ELLIOTTS LA
HIGH ST
THE CARRIAGEWAY
PARK TERR
MANOR RD
CHAPMANS RD
CHAPMANS CL
CHAPMANS
WESTERHAM RD
WEST END
ALMS ROW
White Hart Hotel
BRASTED CT
WOODSIDE RD
Sundridge & Brasted CE Prim Sch
ST MARY'S CHURCH RD
BRASTED RD
A25
Sundridge Place Farm
GREYSTONE PK
CHURCH RD
Valence Sch
Heverswood Farm
CHART LA
Birchfield Farm
NEW RD
PIPERS LA
Cocketts
Colinette Farm
Birchfield Wood
Lodge Barn Farm

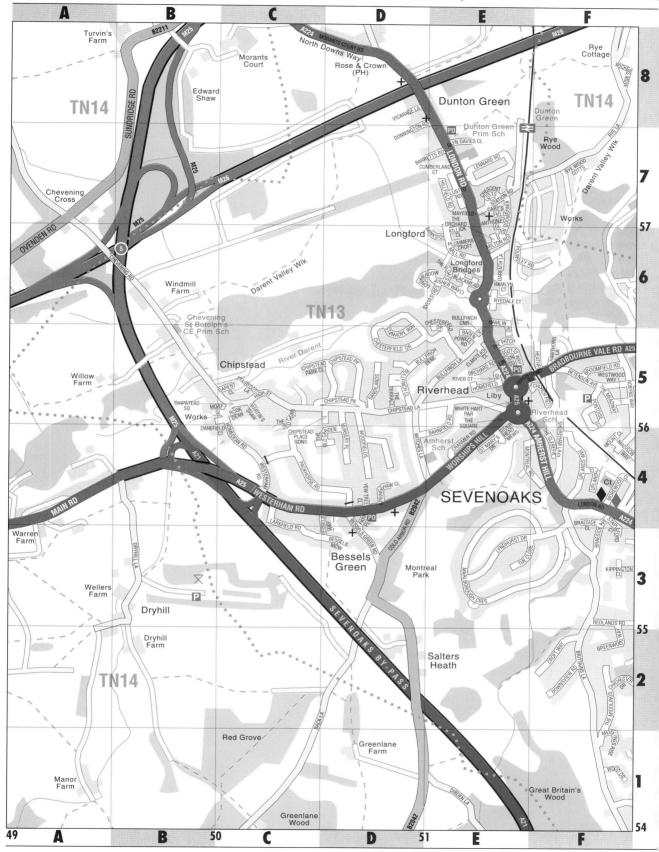

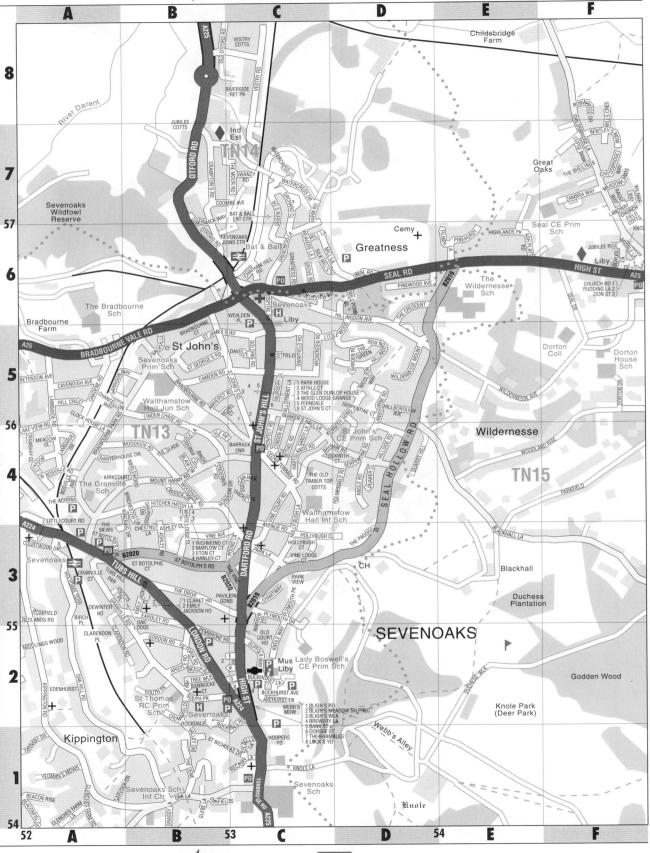

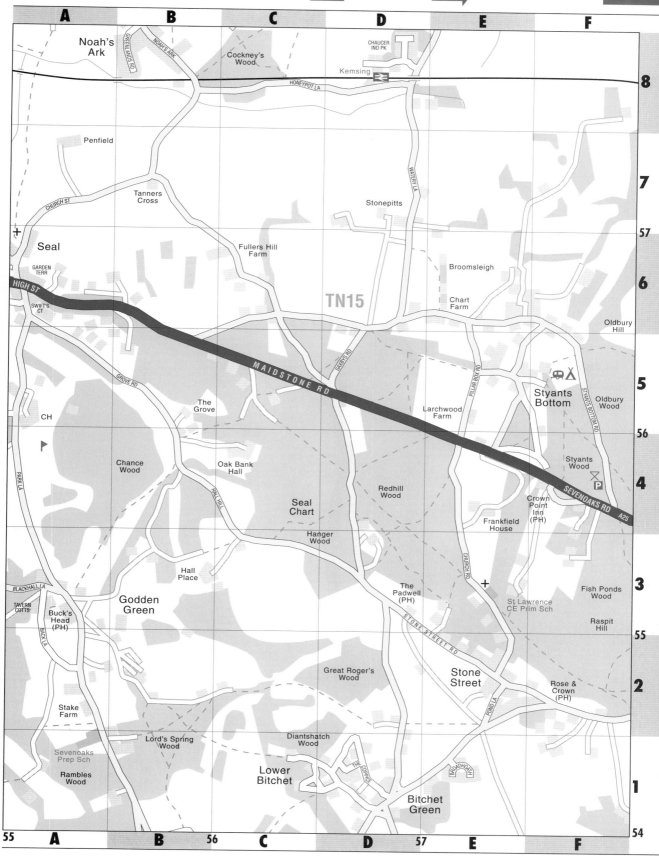

Noah's Ark

Noah's Ark

GREENLANDS RD

Cockney's Wood

CHAUCER IND PK

Kemsing

HONEYPOT LA

Penfield

CHURCH ST

Tanners Cross

WATERY LA

Stonepitts

Seal

Fullers Hill Farm

Broomsleigh

TN15

Chart Farm

GARDEN TERR

HIGH ST

SWIFT'S CT

Oldbury Hill

GROVE RD

MAIDSTONE RD

SAXBYS RD

PILLAR BOX RD

Larchwood Farm

STYANTS BOTTOM RD

Styants Bottom

Oldbury Wood

CH

The Grove

Chance Wood

Oak Bank Hall

Seal Chart

Redhill Wood

Styants Wood

SEVENOAKS RD   A25

PARK LA

HALL HILL

Hanger Wood

Frankfield House

Crown Point Inn (PH)

Fish Ponds Wood

Hall Place

CHURCH RD

Raspit Hill

BLACKHALL LA

Godden Green

The Padwell (PH)

St Lawrence CE Prim Sch

TAVERN COTTS

Buck's Head (PH)

BACK LA

STONE STREET RD

Great Roger's Wood

Stone Street

Rose & Crown (PH)

Stake Farm

POND LA

Lord's Spring Wood

Diantshatch Wood

Sevenoaks Prep Sch

THE COPPICE

BROADHOATH

Rambles Wood

Lower Bitchet

Bitchet Green

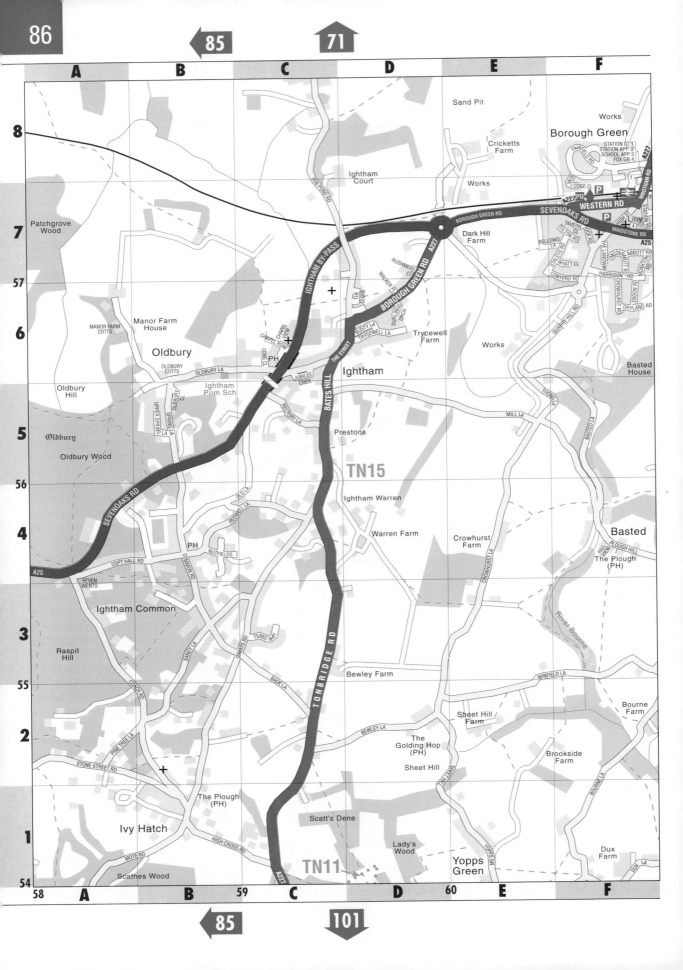

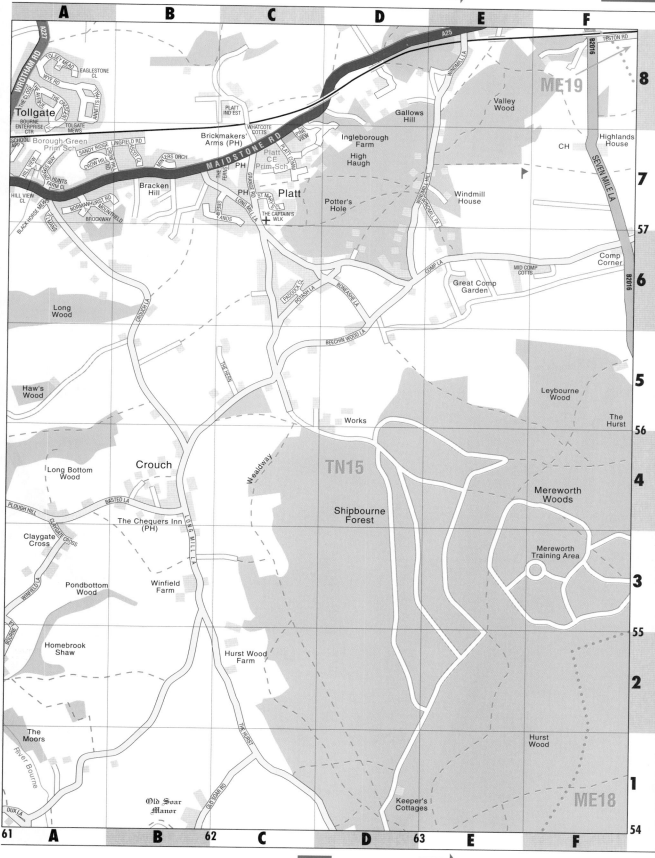

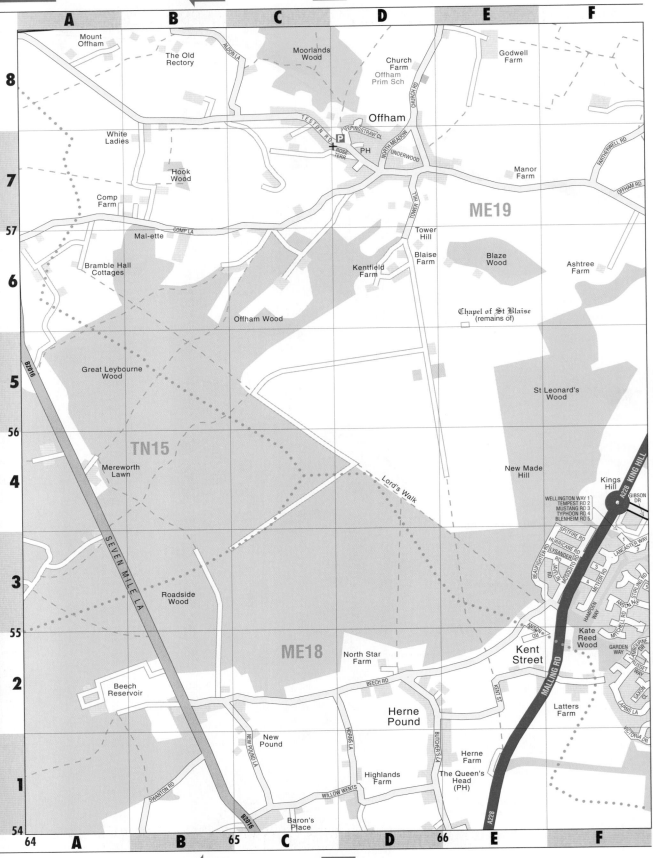

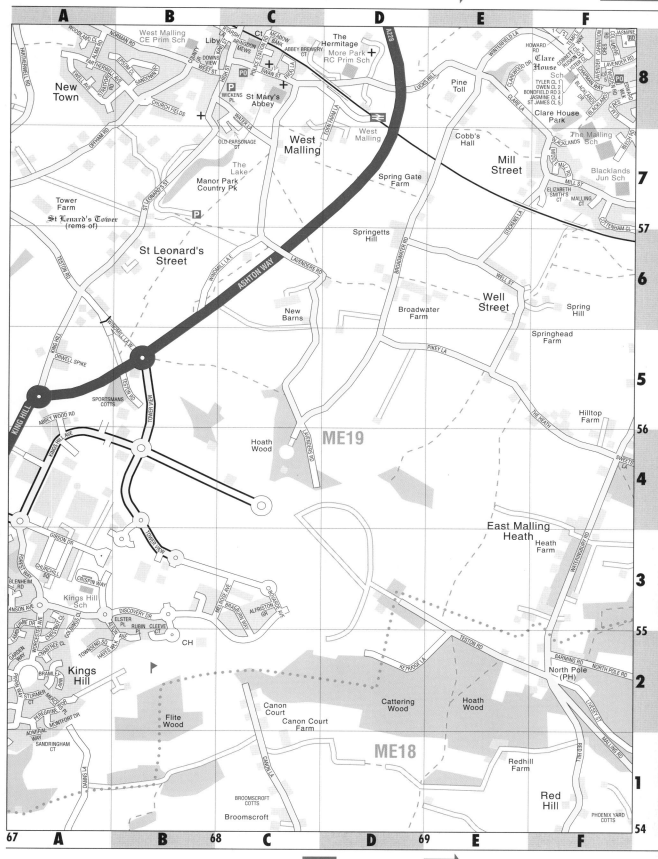

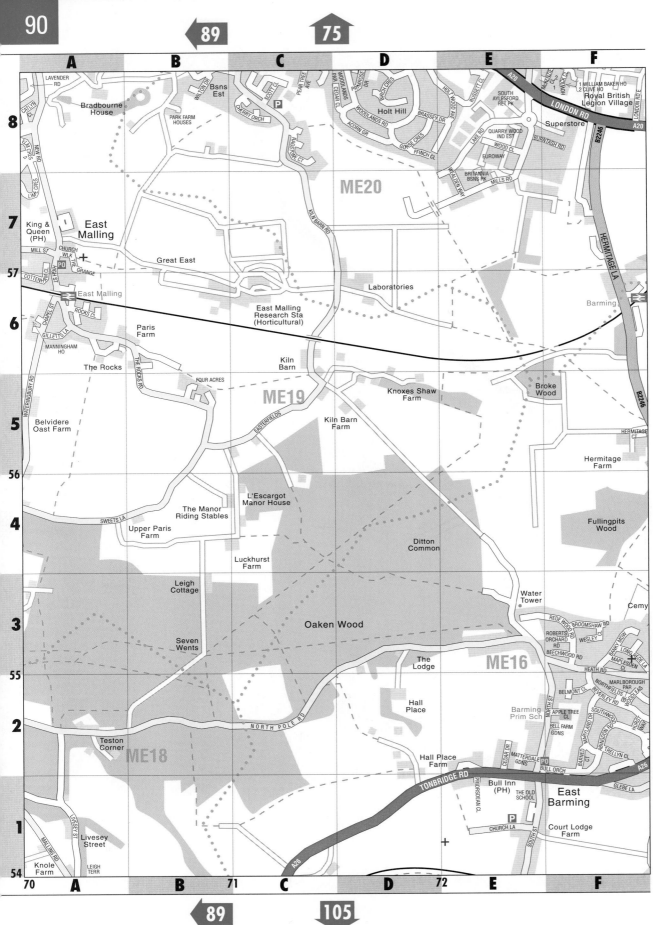

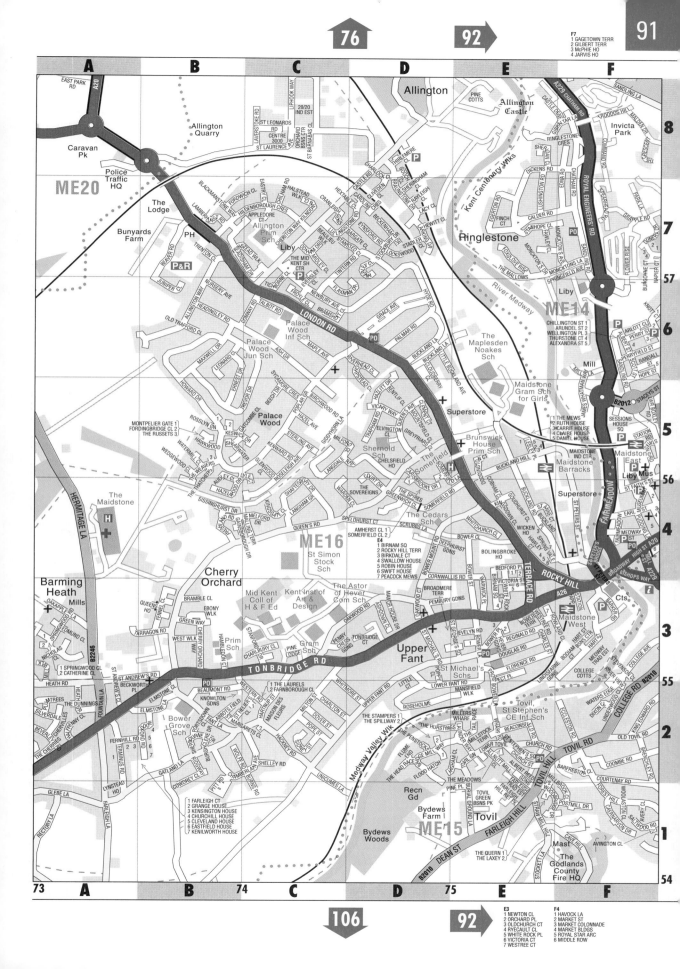

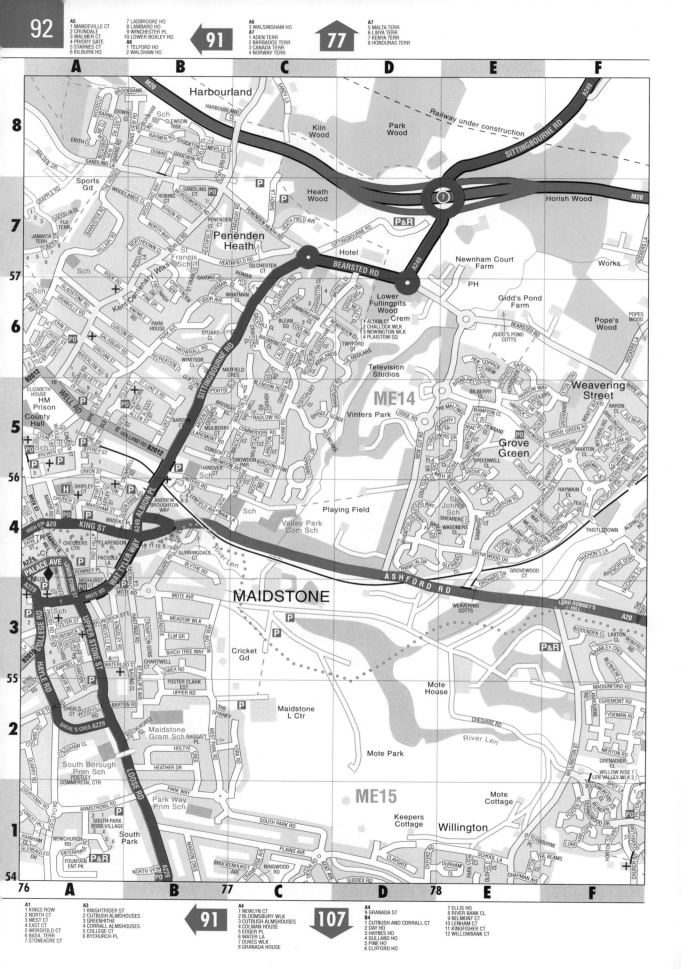

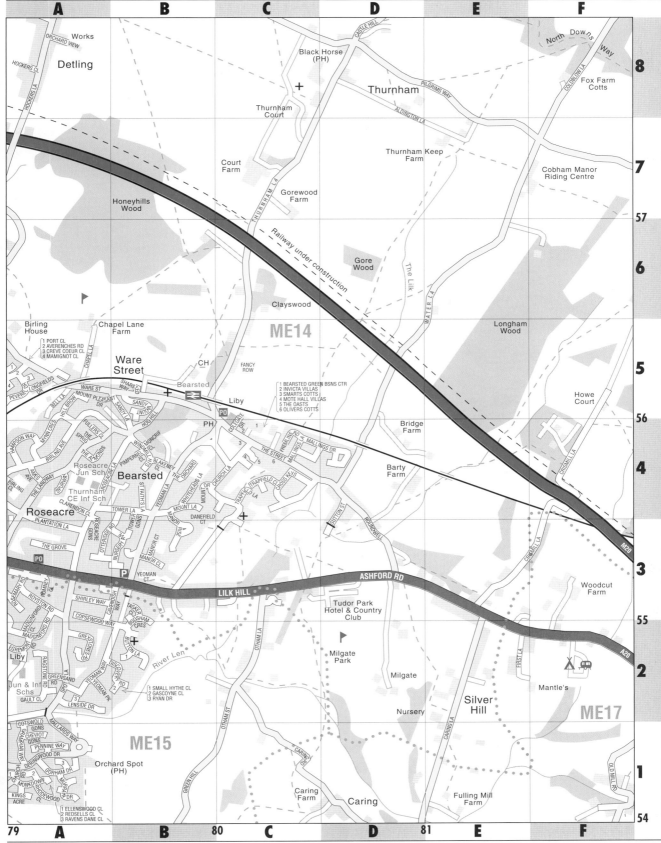

Works
ORCHARD VIEW
Detling
HOCKERS CL
HOCKERS LA

Black Horse (PH)

North Downs Way
CASTLE HILL

Thurnham
PILGRIMS WAY
ALDINGTON LA

Fox Farm Cotts
COLDBLOW LA

8

Thurnham Court

Court Farm

Thurnham Keep Farm

Cobham Manor Riding Centre

7

Honeyhills Wood

Gorewood Farm

THE LILK
WATER LA

57

Railway under construction

Gore Wood

Longham Wood

6

Chapel Lane Farm

Clayswood

ME14

Birling House
1 PORT CL
2 AVERENCHES RD
3 CREVE COEUR CL
4 MAMIGNOT CL
CHAPEL LA

Ware Street
CH
FANCY ROW

1 BEARSTED GREEN BSNS CTR
2 INVICTA VILLAS
3 SMARTS COTTS
4 MOTE HALL VILLAS
5 THE OASTS
6 OLIVERS COTTS

Howe Court

5

Bearsted
Liby
PO
WARE ST
SHARSTED WAY
SANDY MT
SANDY LA

COTECHE DR
THE STREET
FREBALINS
MALLINGS LA
MALLINGS DR

Bridge Farm

56

PH

Roseacre Jun Sch
Thurnham CE Inf Sch
Roseacre

Bearsted
THE ORCHARD
CROSS KEYS
TRAPFIELD CROSS
TRAPFIELD LA

Barty Farm

BOTTOM ST
ROUNDWELL
CRISMILL LA

M20

4

PLANTATION LA
THE GROVE
PO
P
YEOMAN CT
Danefield Ct

ASHFORD RD

Woodcut Farm

3

LILK HILL

Tudor Park Hotel & Country Club

FIRST LA
A20

55

SHIRLEY WAY
COPSEWOOD WAY
BUTTON LA

River Len
OTHAM LA

Milgate Park

Mantle's

△ ⛺

2

Liby
Jun & Inf Schs
GAULT CL

1 SMALL HYTHE CL
2 GASCOYNE CL
3 RYAN DR
OTHAM ST

Milgate

Nursery

Silver Hill

CARING LA

ME17

ME15

Orchard Spot (PH)

GREEN HILL

CARING LA

Caring Farm

Caring

Fulling Mill Farm

OLD MILL LA

1

1 ELLENSWOOD CL
2 REDSELLS CL
3 RAVENS DANE CL
KINGS ACRE

54

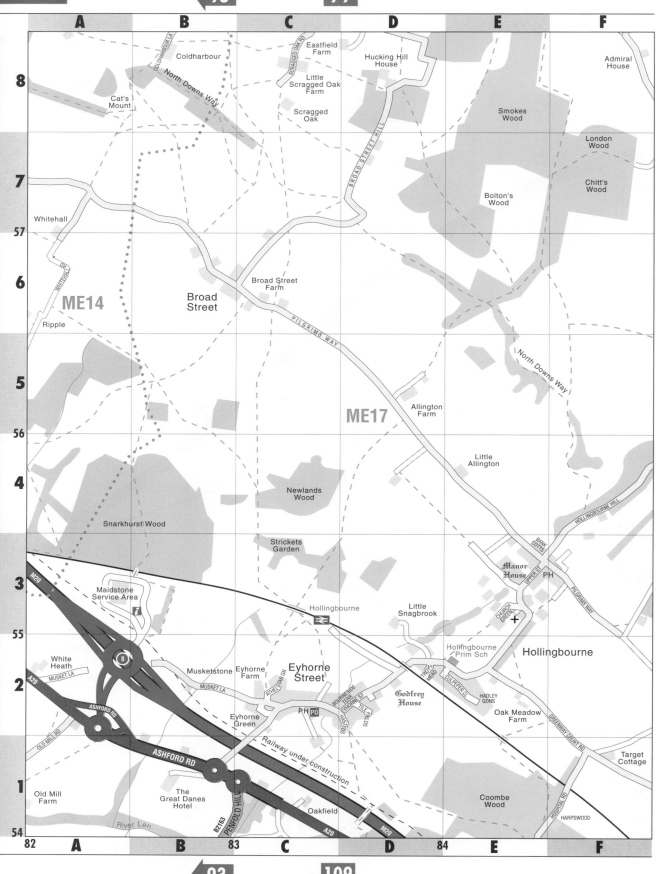

A B C D E F

8

7

57

6

56

5

4

3

55

2

1

54

82 A B 83 C D 84 E F

ME14

ME17

Coldharbour
North Downs Way
Cat's Mount
Whitehall
WHITEHALL RD
Ripple
Broad Street
Broad Street Farm
Snarkhurst Wood
M20
Maidstone Service Area
White Heath
MUSKET LA
A20
Old Mill RD
ASHFORD RD
Old Mill Farm
The Great Danes Hotel
PENFOLD HILL
B2163
River Len
ASHFORD RD
A20
Oakfield
Eyhorne Green
Musketstone
MUSKET LA
Eyhorne Farm
ATHELSTAN GN
Eyhorne Street
BOURNESIDE
EYHORNE ST
TILE FIELDS
HASTERS
PH PO
Godfrey House
CROSS MEAD
CULPEPER CL
HADLEY GDNS
Oak Meadow Farm
GREENWAY COURT RD
Coombe Wood
HOSPITAL RD
HARPSWOOD
Target Cottage
Railway under construction
Newlands Wood
Strickets Garden
PILGRIMS WAY
Allington Farm
Little Allington
North Downs Way
Hollingbourne
Little Snagbrook
Hollingbourne Prim Sch
Manor House
UPPER ST
BANK COTTS
PH
CHURCH GREEN
PILGRIMS WAY
HOLLINGBOURNE HILL
Hollingbourne
Scragged Oak
Little Scragged Oak Farm
Eastfield Farm
SCRAGGED OAK RD
Hucking Hill House
BROAD STREET HILL
Smokes Wood
Bolton's Wood
London Wood
Chitt's Wood
Admiral House
COLDHARBOUR LA

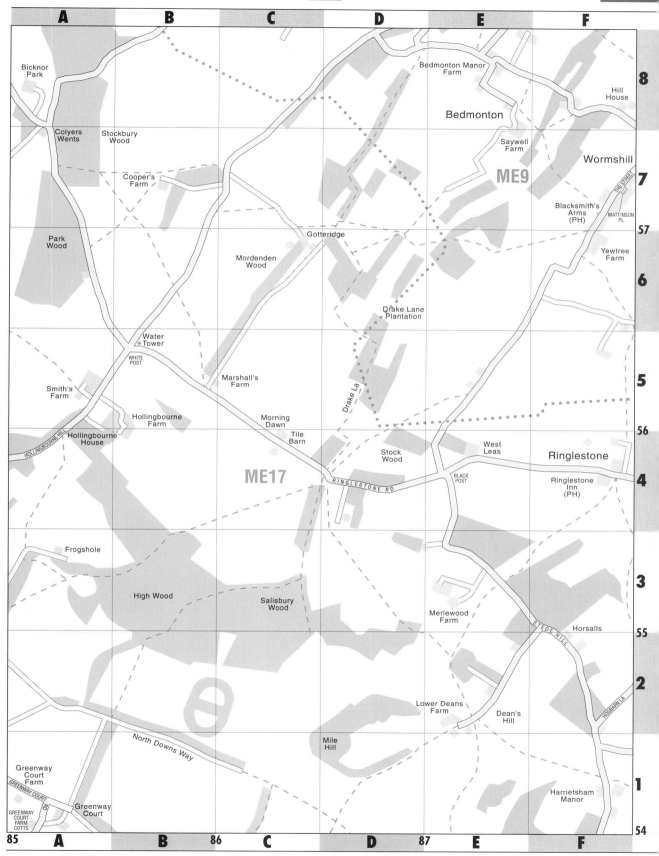

81

112

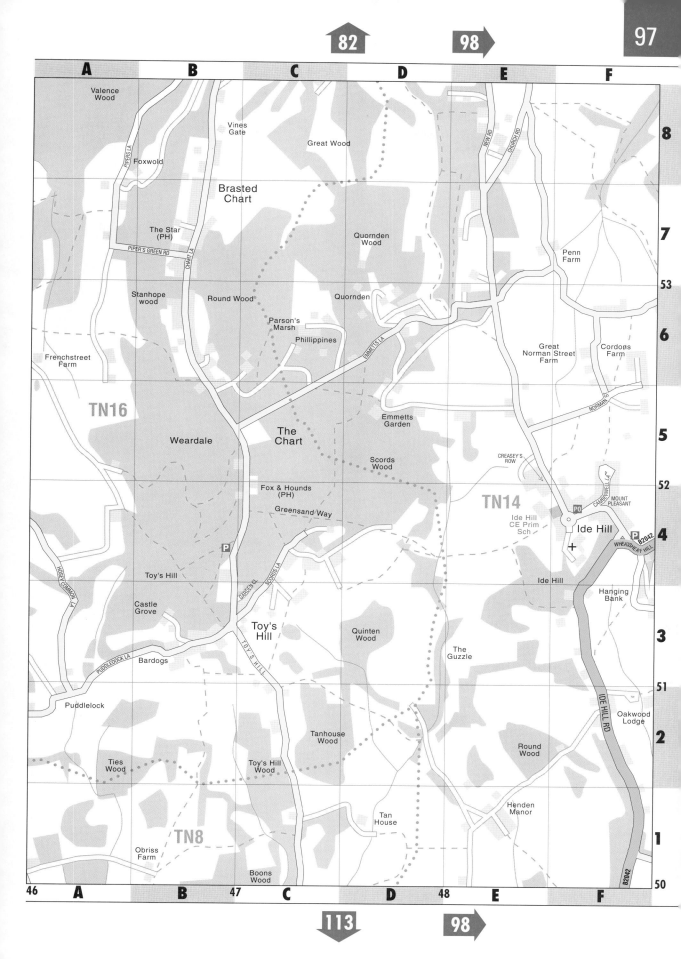

A B C D E F

8

7

53

6

TN16

5

52

4

3

51

2

1

50

Valence
Wood

Vines
Gate

Great Wood

PIPERS LA

Foxwold

The Star
(PH)

Brasted
Chart

CHART LA

PIPER'S GREEN RD

Quornden
Wood

Penn
Farm

Stanhope
wood

Round Wood

Quornden

Great
Norman Street
Farm

Cordons
Farm

Parson's
Marsh

Frenchstreet
Farm

Phillippines

EMMETTS LA

NORMAN ST

NEW RD

CHURCH RD

Weardale

The
Chart

Emmetts
Garden

Scords
Wood

TN14

CREASEY'S
ROW

Ide Hill

Fox & Hounds
(PH)

Greensand Way

P

Ide Hill
CE Prim
Sch

PO

CAMBERWELL LA

MOUNT
PLEASANT

P

WHEATSHEAF HILL

B2042

HOSEY COMMON LA

Toy's Hill

GARDEN RD

SCORDS LA

Ide Hill

Hanging
Bank

Castle
Grove

Toy's
Hill

Quinten
Wood

The
Guzzle

TOY'S HILL

PUDDLEDOCK LA

Bardogs

IDE HILL RD

Puddlelock

Tanhouse
Wood

Round
Wood

Oakwood
Lodge

Ties
Wood

Toy's Hill
Wood

TN8

Tan
House

Henden
Manor

Obriss
Farm

Boons
Wood

B2042

46 A 47 B C 47 C D 48 E F

97
83

A B C D E F

8

Willow Wood

Greenlane Wood

Whitley

Dibden

DIBDEN LA

Mildridge Wood

Beacon Sch

TN13

Hawks Wood

BACK LA

A21

SEVENOAKS BY-PASS

7

53

Brook Place

Whitley Row

Whitley Forest

Mill Bank Wood

TN13

OAK LA

6

The Woodman (PH)

Apps Hollow

Roundabout Wood

NIGHTINGALE LA

CHAPEL WLK

Dust Wood

Hyde's Forest

Pitfield Wood

GRACIOUS LANE END
WHITE HOUSE LA

5

THE PANTYLES

Goathurst Common

York's Hill

Sheephill Wood

RYCROFT LA

WHITE HOUSE RD

52

Everlands

Bayley's Hill

4

B2042

P

Stubbs Wood

Brockhill Wood

TN14

Greensand Way

BAYLEY'S HILL

WICKHURST RD

Hanging Bank

Yorkshill Farm

Hatchlands Farm

Wickhurst Manor

3

Boarhill

Harbour Hook

51

2

Bowzell Farm

BOWZELL RD

1

Bowzell Wood

Scollops Farm

Old House Farm

50

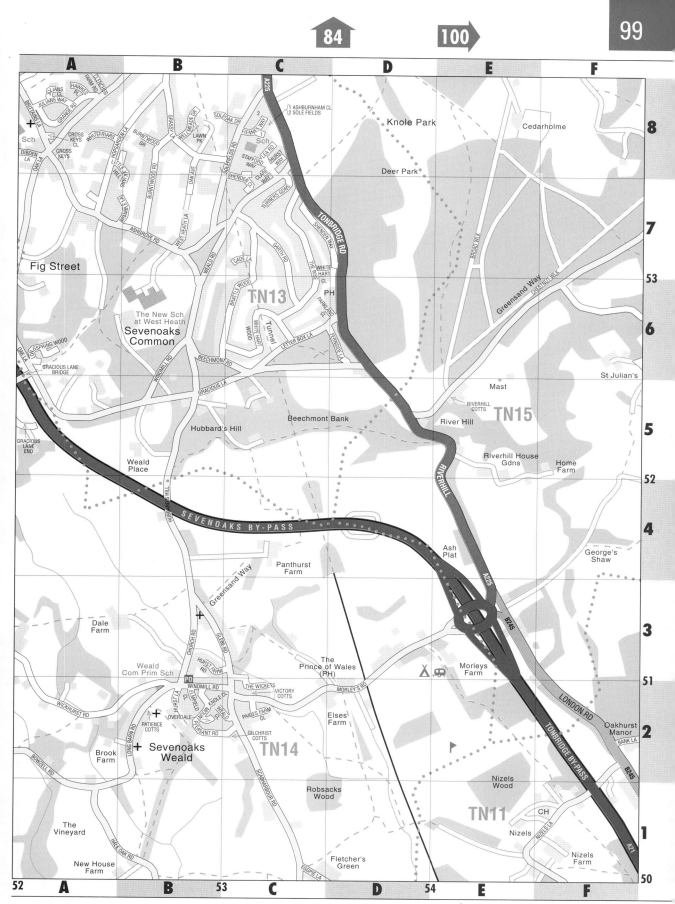

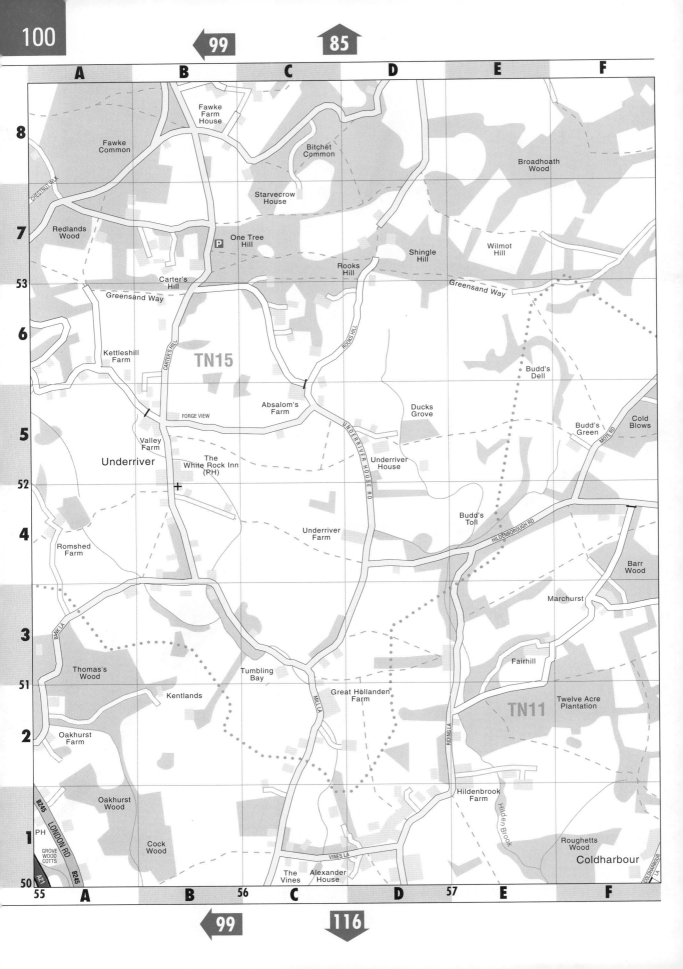

99
85

A B C D E F

8   Fawke Farm House

Fawke Common

Bitchet Common

Broadhoath Wood

CHESTNUT VLA

Starvecrow House

7   Redlands Wood

One Tree Hill

Shingle Hill

Wilmot Hill

P

Carter's Hill

Rooks Hill

53   Greensand Way

Greensand Way

6   Kettleshill Farm

TN15

CARTER'S HILL

ROOKS HILL

Budd's Dell

Budd's Green

Cold Blows

FORGE VIEW

Absalom's Farm

Ducks Grove

MOTE RD

5   Valley Farm

Underriver

The White Rock Inn (PH)

UNDERRIVER HOUSE RD

Underriver House

52   +

Budd's Toll

4   Romshed Farm

Underriver Farm

HILDENBOROUGH RD

Barr Wood

Marchurst

3   Thomas's Wood

BANK LA

Fairhill

51   Kentlands

Tumbling Bay

Great Hollanden Farm

TN11

Twelve Acre Plantation

2   Oakhurst Farm

MILL LA

RIDING LA

B245

Oakhurst Wood

Hildenbrook Farm

Hilden Brook

1   PH

LONDON RD

Cock Wood

Roughetts Wood

GROVE WOOD COTTS

Coldharbour

VINES LA

COLDHARBOUR LA

50   A21   B245

The Vines

Alexander House

55   A   B   56   C   D   57   E   F

99
116

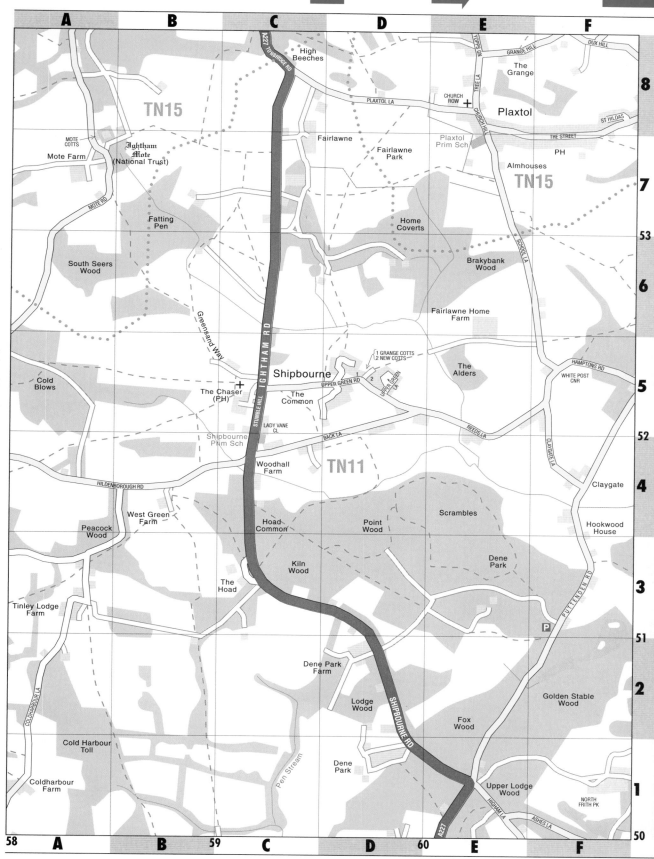

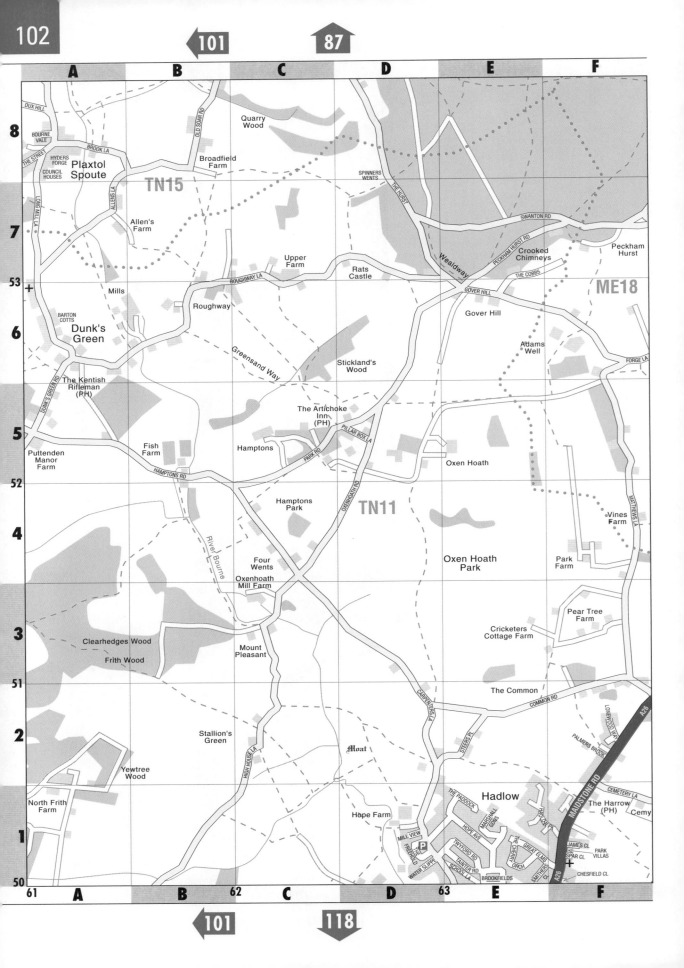

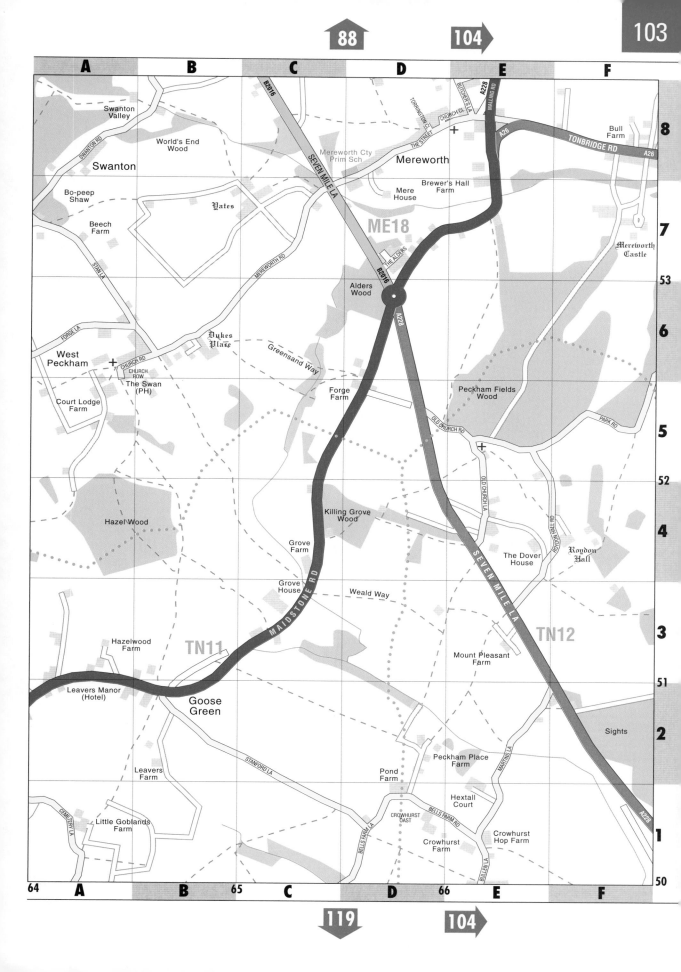

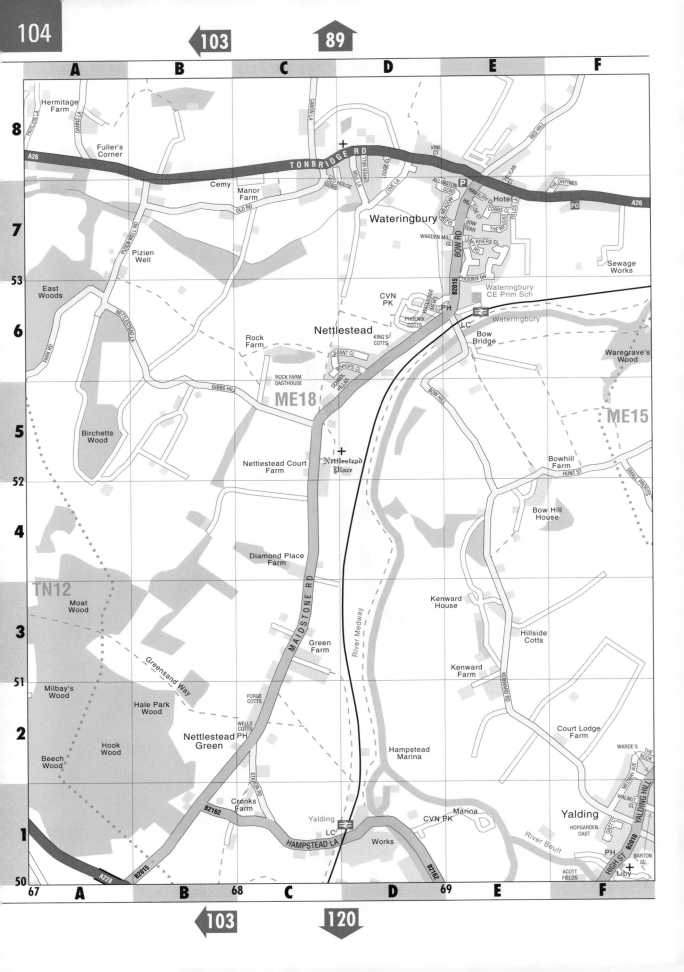

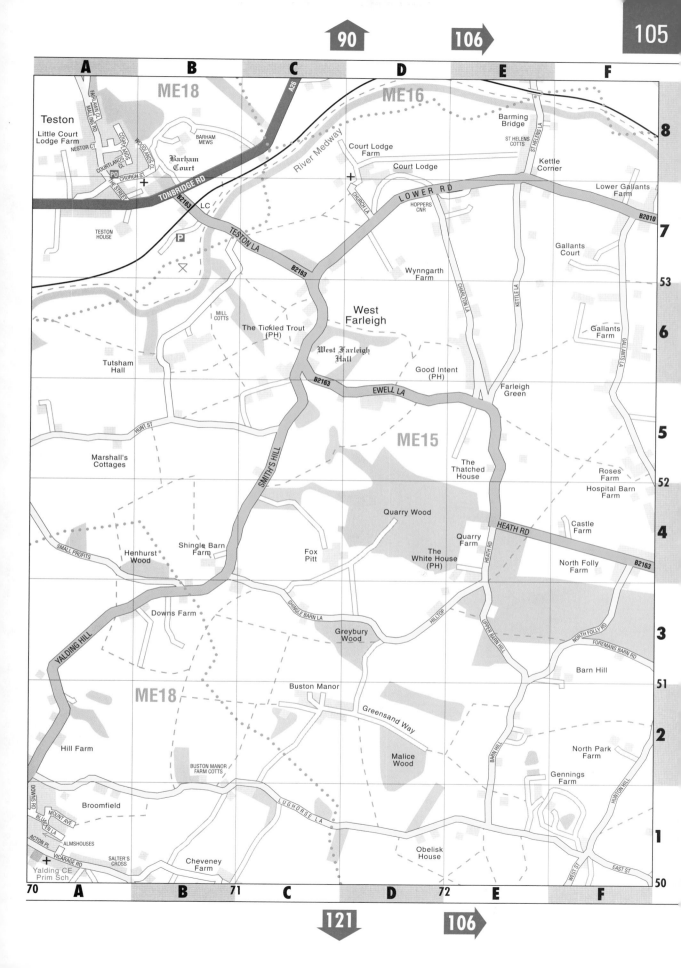

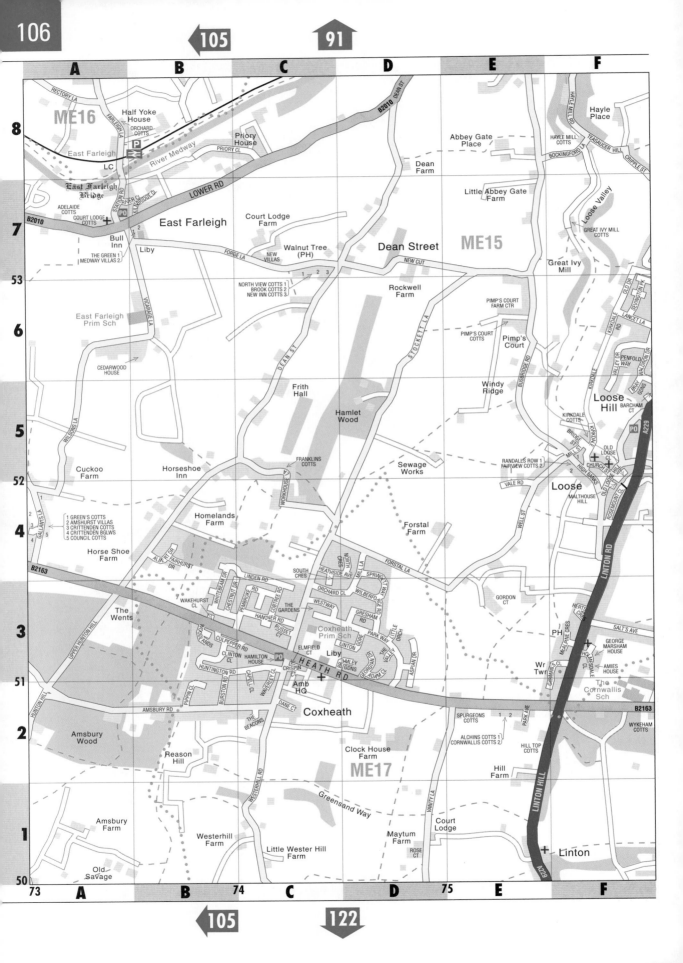

105 91

RECTORY LA

ME16

Half Yoke House

ORCHARD COTTS

Priory House

River Medway

East Farleigh

LC

FARLEIGH LA

STATION RD

KILNBRIDGE CL

PRIORY CL

DEAN ST

B2010

Abbey Gate Place

Hayle Place

HAYLE MILL RD

HAYLE MILL COTTS

TEASAUCER HILL

CRIPPLE ST

BOCKINGFORD LA

8

East Farleigh Bridge

ADELAIDE COTTS

B2010

COURT LODGE COTTS

Bull Inn

THE GREEN 1
MEDWAY VILLAS 2

Liby

LOWER RD

PO

East Farleigh

Court Lodge Farm

FORGE LA

Walnut Tree (PH)

NEW VILLAS

Dean Farm

Dean Street

Little Abbey Gate Farm

Loose Valley

GREAT IVY MILL COTTS

Great Ivy Mill

ME15

7

53

VICARAGE LA

NORTH VIEW COTTS 1
BROOK COTTS 2
NEW INN COTTS 3

1 2 3

NEW CUT

Rockwell Farm

STOCKETT LA

PIMP'S COURT FARM CTR

PIMP'S COURT COTTS

Pimp's Court

Great Ivy Mill

OLD DR

SEVINGTON PK

KIRKDALE RD

LANCET LA

VALLEY DR

PENFOLD WAY

WALNGTON DR

6

East Farleigh Prim Sch

CEDARWOOD HOUSE

WILSONS LA

DEAN ST

Frith Hall

Hamlet Wood

Windy Ridge

BUSBRIDGE RD

Loose Hill

KIRKDALE COTTS

BARCHAM CT

BRAY GDNS

A229

5

Cuckoo Farm

Horseshoe Inn

FRANKLINS COTTS

WORKHOUSE

Sewage Works

Forstal Farm

WELL ST

VALE RD

RANDALES ROW 1
FAIRVIEW COTTS 2

KIRKDALE

MILL 1

HIGH BANKS

Loose

CHURCH ST

OLD LOOSE CL

PO

BRIDGE ST 1
CT 2

MALTHOUSE HILL

ROSEMOUNT CL

OLD LOOSE HILL

52

2 4
3
5

GALLANTS LA

1 GREEN'S COTTS
2 AMSHURST VILLAS
3 CRITTENDEN COTTS
4 CRITTENDEN BGLWS
5 COUNCIL COTTS

Homelands Farm

FORSTAL LA

GORDON CT

SPRING X WAY

RICE RD

WILL LA

4

Horse Shoe Farm

ALBERT DR

FAIRHURST DR

WHITEBEAM LA

CHESTNUT DR

LINDEN RD

PEMBROKE RD

COB TREE LA

SOUTH CRES

HEATHSIDE AVE

NORTH CRES

ORCHARD CL

WILBERFORCE RD

LINTON RD

B2163

HERTS CRES

MCALPINE CRES

SALT'S AVE

George Marsham House

3

The Wents

UPPER HUNTON HILL

WOODLANDS

WAKEHURST CL

CULPEPPER RD

CLINTON CL

HUNTINGTON RD

HAMILTON HOUSE

PO

The Gardens

HANOVER RD

RUSSET CT

WESTWAY

ELMFIELD CT

GORE

GRESHAM RD

PARK WAY

Coxheath Prim Sch

Liby

THE VALLEY

BURMLEY GDNS

LITTLE ORCH

GEORDAN

STJOHN

ST ADAM

ASPIAN DR

Wr Twr

CARMAN CL

TRESDALE CL

HQ

PH

AMIES HOUSE

The Cornwallis Sch

51

HINTON HILL

B2163

CAPEL CL

CLINTON CL

BURSTON RD

PIPPIN CL

CRISPIN

WAVERLEY CL

Amb HQ

HEATH RD

DANE CT

Coxheath

SPURGEONS COTTS

1 2

ALCHINS COTTS 1
CORNWALLIS COTTS 2

PARK AVE

LINTON HILL

HILL TOP COTTS

WYKEHAM COTTS

2

Amsbury Wood

AMSBURY RD

THE BEACONS

Reason Hill

WESTERHILL RD

Clock House Farm

ME17

Hill Farm

Hill Farm

1

Amsbury Farm

Westerhill Farm

Little Wester Hill Farm

Greensand Way

VANITY LA

Maytum Farm

ROSE CT

Court Lodge

Linton

A229

Old Savage

50

73 A 74 B 74 C 75 D 75 E F

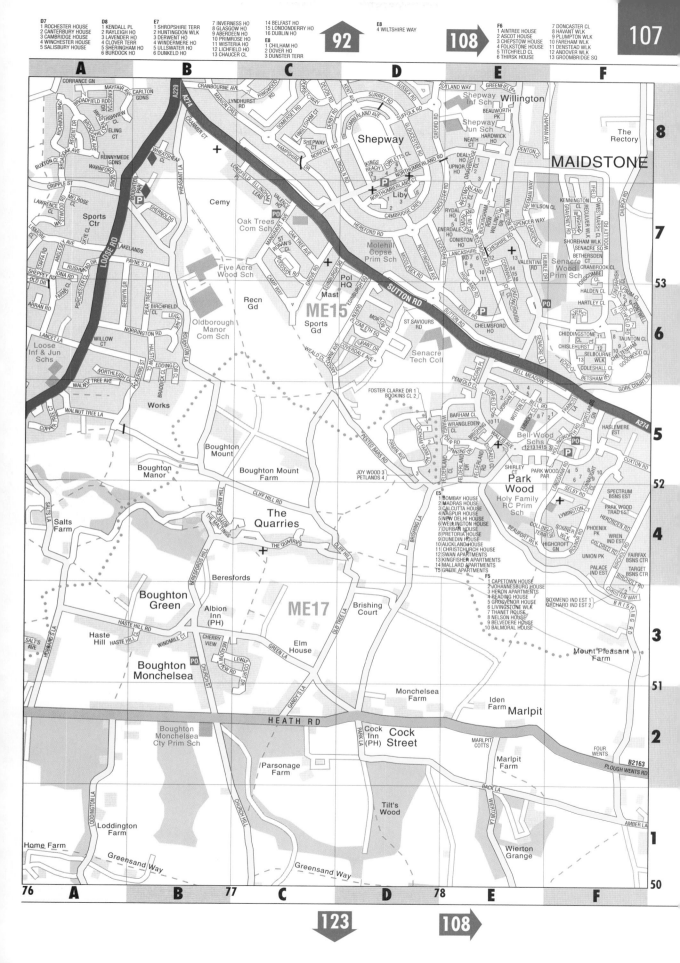

107
93

A **B** **C** **D** **E** **F**

8

Green Hill

Caring

Little Caring Farm

Merrihill

Corwainer's

Spout Farm

CARING RD

Merriams Farm

CARING LA

Otham

Stoneacre

Stoneacre Farm

OTHAM ST

ME15

Arnold Hill Farm

FORGE LA

7

Gore Court

STONEACRE LA

SIMMONS LA

Spot Farm

HOLLY FARM RD

Arnoldbrae

OLD MILL RD

53

Holly Farm

Arnold Farm

Ledian Farm

BRODGEN CRES

WHITE HORSE LA

The White Horse (PH)

HONEY LA

KINGS COTTS 1
CHURCHILL COTTS 2

B2163

6

Otham Hole

Hole Farm

AVERY LA

Lacey Farm

BACK ST

CS HALL CTR 3418

1
2

Bicknor Wood

CHAPEL COTTS

NEW RD

Burnt Barn Farm

UPPER ST

5

A274

Bicknor Farm

RUMWOOD CT

Nursery

BURBERFY LA

PEAR TREE ROW

MANOR COTTS

BIRCHOLT RD

52

THE PROGRESS EST

SUTTON RD

Pleydells Farm

Butlers Farm

Langley

HORSESHOES LA

Langley Heath

4

Golf Driving Range

Langley Park Farm

The Horseshoes (PH)

ME17

TURGIS CL
POTTERS WLK
HEATH RD
SKINNER'S WAY
DICKENS CL
COPPERFIELD DR

ASHFIELD

FORSTERS

NEPHERSON DR
ORCHARD CL

GRASSLANDS

Langley Loch

Green Lane Cotts

Green Lane Farm

GREEN LA

Four Wents

Stud Farm

LEEDS RD

ULCOMBE RD

GRAVELLY BOTTOM RD

3

Abbey Wood

PITT RD

Rectory Farm

51

PLOUGH COTTS

Plough Inn

2

Five Wents

Fir Tree Farm

COLLINGWOOD IND CTR

Oakdenne Farm

Pleasant Farm

LESTED LA

NORTON RD

WINDMILL ROW

MAIDSTONE RD

Langley Lodge

B2163

PLOUGH WENTS RD

Norton Lea Farm

Nursery

1

COBFIELD
LAXTON DR

AMBER LA

AMBER WAY
PO
CHART CNR

Chart Sutton

Buffalo's Head (PH)

CHART HILL RD
MARSH
MERCER WAY

Norton Court

CHURCH RD

WARMLAKE RD

WARMLAKE EST

A274

NORTH ST

WARMLAKE

CHARTWAY ST

Amberfield

ORCHARD BANK 1
CROSSWAYS 2

1 2

Warmlake

50

79 **A** **B** 80 **C** **D** 81 **E** **F**

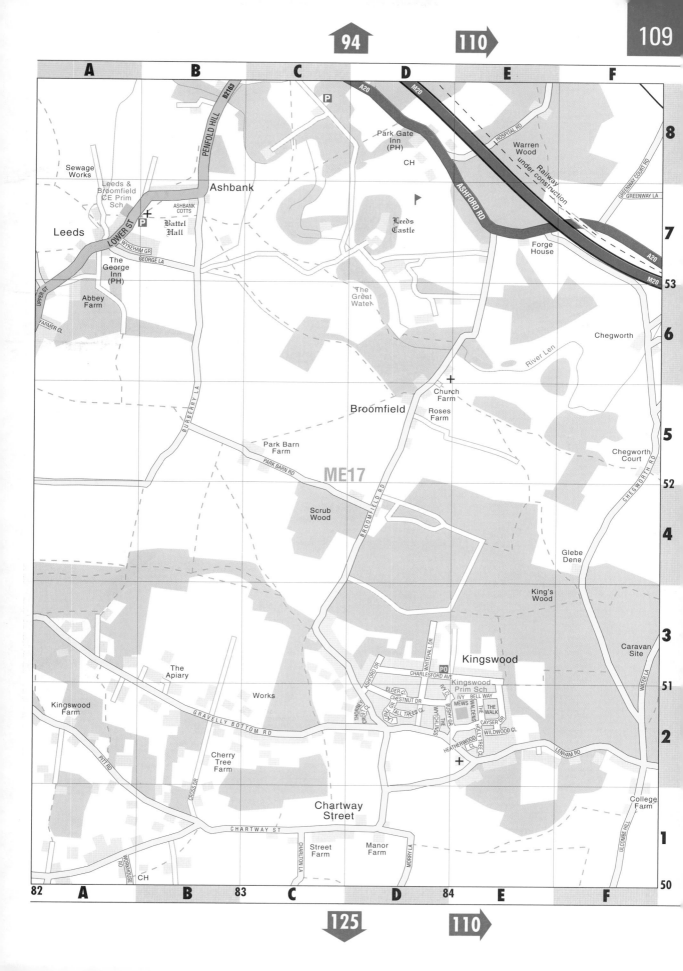

109
95

A   **B**   **C**   **D**   **E**   **F**

8

GREENWAY COURT RD

No Man's Acre

North Downs Way

Hillside Farm

Coles Dane

Stede Hill

PILGRIMS WAY

7

Mount Farm

Greenway Forstal

GREENWAY LA

GARDEN OF ENGLAND PARK (MOBILE HOME PARK)

Goddington

Ockley Mead

Court Lodge Farm

Court Lodge

PILGRIMS WAY

Kingboro Farm

53

A20

M20

Holm Mill

HOLM MILL LA

GODDINGTON LA

Trout Farm

PILGRIMS LK'S

MARLEY RD

6

CHEGWORTH LA

WEST ST

HOOK LA

QUESTED WAY

NUNS WAY

THE WHEELWRIGHTS

FORGE MEADOW

CRICKETERS CL

STATION RD

CUTBUSH RD

CHIPPENDALE DR

Harrietsham

PO

LAKELANDS

CHURCH RD

HARRISON DR

ST WILGUME'S WAY

CHURCH LA

GREY LA

CHURCH LA

OLD

DOWN THORN WAY

NEW

SUNNYWOOD

MERCER DR

A20

ASHFORD RD

Harrietsham

THE OLD BAILEY

Mayfield

5

Waterlane Farm

WATER LA

Spion Kop Farm

Pollhill

River Len

Poplar Farm

TAYLOR CL

EAST ST

CHURCH RD

RECTORY LA

The Bell Farm

Cherry Tree Farm

Stubble Hill Farm

52

Cherry Gardens

ME17

Sewage Works

Railway under construction

SANDWAY RD

4

Works

Fairbourne Mill

FAIRBOURNE LA

3

Waterlane Cottages

Fairbourne Manor Farm

RUNHAM LA

Runham Farm

The Firs

M20

51

Affers Wood

2

Mast

Heath Orchard

Gaskin Wood

Runham Wood

Wellesley House

MOUNT PLEASANT TERR

GREEN LA

SCHOOL LA

HEADCORN RD

Platt's Heath Prim Sch

Platt's Heath

1

Hill Farm

Fairbourne Heath

FAIRBOURNE HEATH COTTS

WINDMILL HILL

LENHAM RD

GREEN HILL LA

ELMSTONE HOLE RD

Liverton Street

50

Tillman Gate Farm

The Pepper Box (PH)

Greensand Way

85   **A**   **B**   **86**   **C**   **D**   **87**   **E**   **F**

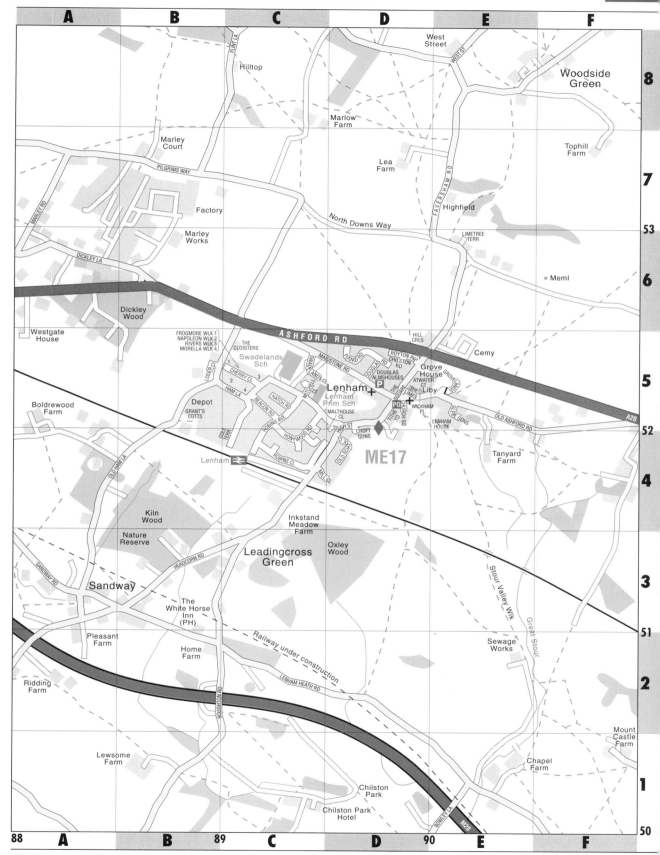

Hilltop

West
Street

Woodside
Green

Marlow
Farm

Marley
Court

Tophill
Farm

PILGRIMS WAY

Lea
Farm

Highfield

FAVERSHAM RD

Factory

North Downs Way

Marley
Works

WEST ST

MARLEY RD

DICKLEY LA

LIMETREE
TERR

Meml

Dickley
Wood

ASHFORD RD

HILL
CRES

Cemy

Westgate
House

FROGMORE WLK 1
NAPOLEON WLK 2
RIVERS WLK 3
MORELLA WLK 4

THE
CLOISTERS

Swadelands
Sch

MAIDSTONE RD

FORD RD

DOUGLAS RD

ROYTON AVE
CHILSTON
RD

DOUGLAS
ALMSHOUSES

Grove
House

ATWATER
CT

Liby

GROVE LANE

CHERRY CL

MITCHELL

LDLEY CL

HAM LA

LANDS CL

Lenham
Prim Sch

Lenham

P

THE SQUARE

THE
LIMES

WICKHAM
PL

Boldrewood
Farm

Depot

GRANT'S
COTTS

HATCH RD

BEACON RD

ROBINS AVE

HONYWOOD RD

MALTHOUSE
CL

HIGH ST

OS HORTH

CROFT
GDNS

Lenham
House

COLE
TERR

ROBINS CL

MILL CL

OLD SCH CL

GORSE GDNS

OLD ASHFORD RD

A20

Tanyard
Farm

ME17

Lenham

OLD HAM LA

Kiln
Wood

Inkstand
Meadow
Farm

Nature
Reserve

HEADCORN RD

Leadingcross
Green

Oxley
Wood

Stour Valley Wlk

Great Stour

SANDWAY RD

Sandway

The
White Horse
Inn
(PH)

Railway under construction

Sewage
Works

Pleasant
Farm

Home
Farm

BOUGHTON RD

LENHAM HEATH RD

Ridding
Farm

Mount
Castle
Farm

Lewsome
Farm

Chilston
Park

Chapel
Farm

Chilston Park
Hotel

BOWLEY LA

M20

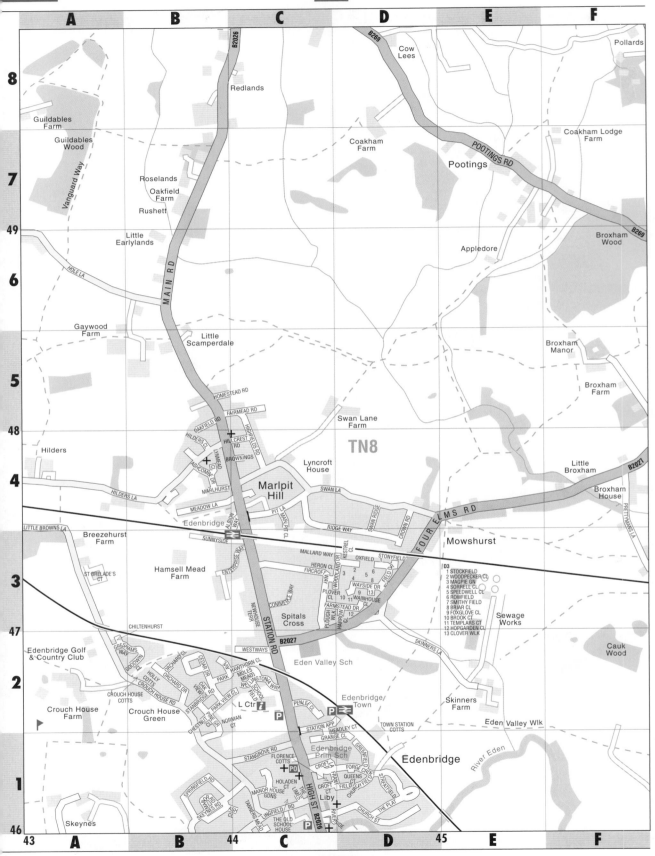

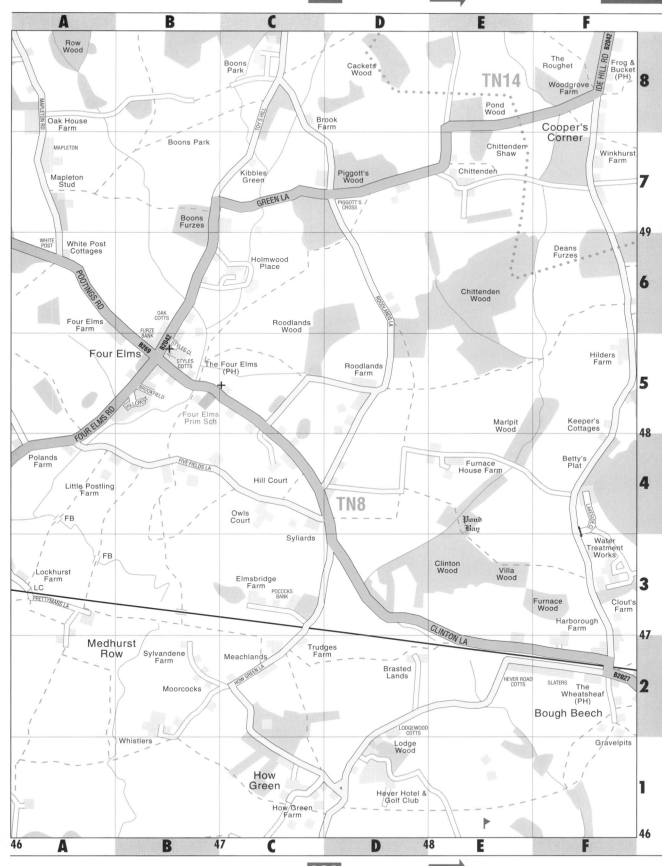

113
98

A **B** **C** **D** **E** **F**

8

Faulkners
Hill Farm

TN14

Bushes
Wood

7

Winkhurst
Green

Nature
Reserve

Bushes
Plantation

Bushes
Farm

Bough Beech Reservoir
Nature Centre

49

Deans
Wood

Field
Trail

Bore Place

Hale
Oak
Farm

6

Batfold
Wood

Sharp's
Place

Bough Beech Resr

Kilnhouse
Farm

The Old
Forge

Little
Sidcup

Hale
Farm

Little
Hale

5

Bushy
Wood

48

Damper's
Wood

Brownings
Cottage

Brownings
Farm

4

CH

Hickens

TN8

Mountjoy
Farm

HALE OAK RD

Polebrook
Farm

Birdfield
Plantation

Charcott
Farm

3

Cole's
Farm

Breeches
Wood

Waterlake

47

Waterlake
Cottage

The
Horseshoes

Chiddingstone
Causeway

Camp
Hill

CHEQUERS HILL
COTTS THE CLOSE

Somerden

Jessop's
Farm

TN11

CAMP HILL

CAMP HILL
COTTS

2

B2021

Baldocks

RICHARD'S CL

DUKES MEADOW

PO

Trad
Est

B2027

River Eden

Chested
Farm

Beckett's
Farm

Penshurst

STATION
HILL

1

Ppg
Sta

Chested

46

Mill
Farm

Sandhole

A **B** **C** **D** **E** **F**
49   50   51

113
130

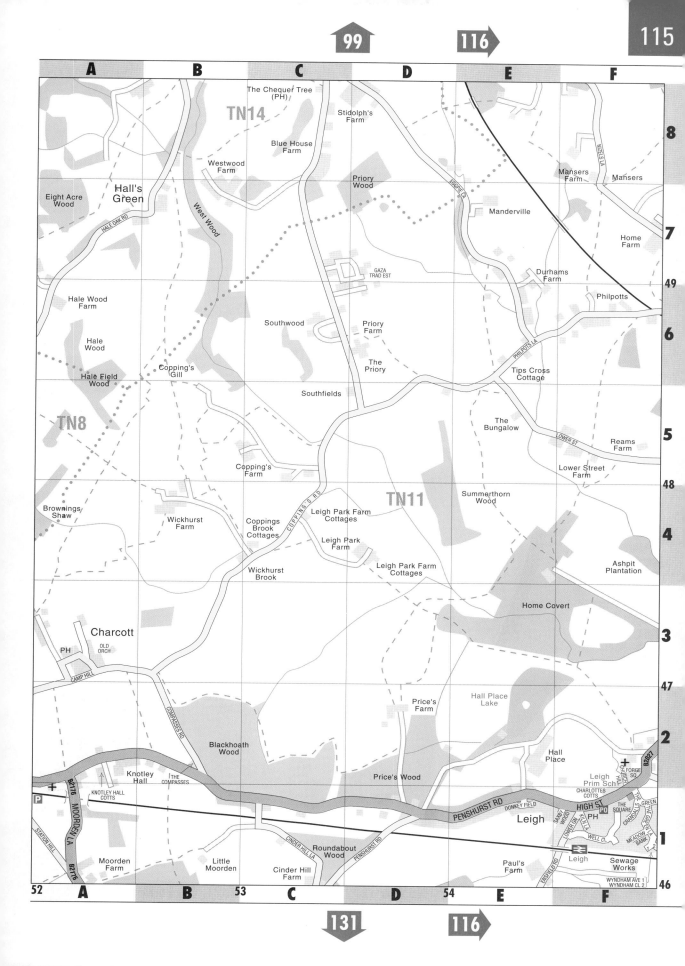

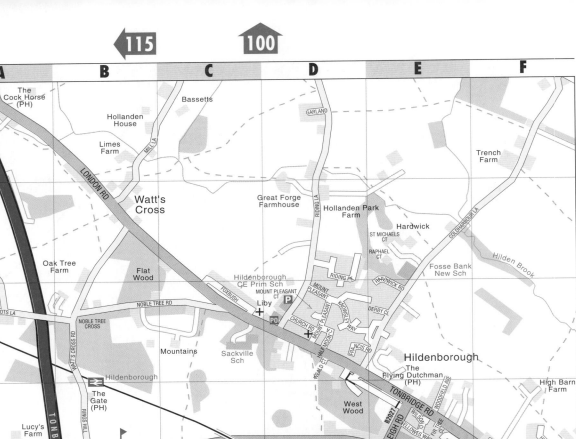

Map Labels

The Cock Horse (PH)
Hollanden House
Bassetts
Garland
Trench Farm
Limes Farm
LONDON RD
MILL LA
Watt's Cross
Great Forge Farmhouse
Hollanden Park Farm
Hardwick
ST MICHAELS CT
RIDING LA
COLDHARBOUR LA
Hilden Brook
Fosse Bank New Sch
RAPHAEL CT
NOELS LA
Oak Tree Farm
Flat Wood
NOBLE TREE RD
Hildenborough CE Prim Sch
MOUNT PLEASANT CT
Liby
RIDING PK
MOUNT PLEASANT
HARDWICK RD
DERBY CL
PHILPOTS LA
NOBLE TREE CROSS
FOXBUSH
P
Mountains
Sackville Sch
CHURCH RD
WEALD CT
MOUNT PLEASANT
FRANCIS RD
MEWSLEY WAY
Hildenborough
The Flying Dutchman (PH)
High Barn Farm
WATTS CROSS RD
RINGS HILL
Hildenborough
The Gate (PH)
West Wood
TONBRIDGE RD
WOODFIELD AVE
LEIGH RD
FELLOWES WAY
WILSON
FIR TREE
WOODLANDS
PK AVE
Lucy's Farm
STOCKS GREEN RD
CH
Stocks Green Prim Sch
FAIRFIELD WAY
MEADWAY
WEALDEN CL
HILL VIEW RD
HILDEN AVE
LOWER ST
The Old Barn
ASHLEY RD
COPSE RD
WEALDEN CRES
BRAMBLE CL
OAKLANDS WAY
TN11
BYRNESIDE
LEYBANK
B245
Stocks Green
BIRCH CL
GREENVIEW CRES
BROOKMEAD
HILDEN PARK RD
TONBRIDGE BY-PASS
Bid Bridge
Hilden Park
HAWDEN CL
STACEY RD
HANDEL LA
The Alders
Selby's Farm
Hawden Farm
Home Farm
HOME FARM CL
LEIGH RD
TN10
HILDENBOROUGH RD
The Plough (PH)
Powder Mills
B2027
Moat Farmhouse
Ramhurst Manor
Rook Wood
Works
POWDER MILL LA
Lucifer Bridge
The Fors
BARNETTS RD
Little Barnetts Farm
POWDER MILL LA
Manor Farm
ALDERS MEADOW
CHESTNUT WLK
AUDLEY AVE
CLARE AVE
Barden Park
TN9
GARDEN COTTS
HOLLOW TREES DR
Hollowtrees
LEALANDS AVE
GREEN VIEW AVE
Weald Way & Eden Valley Wlk
River Medway

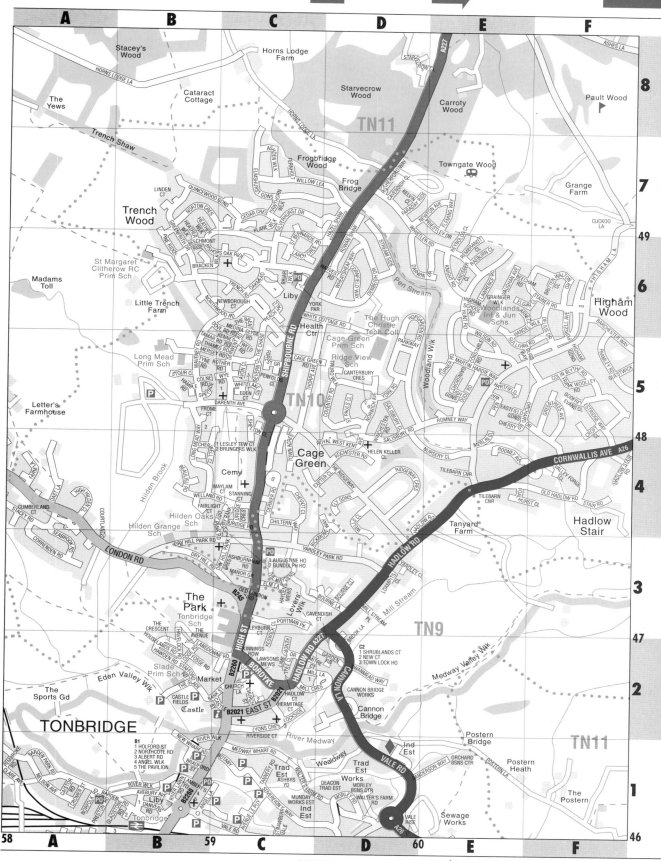

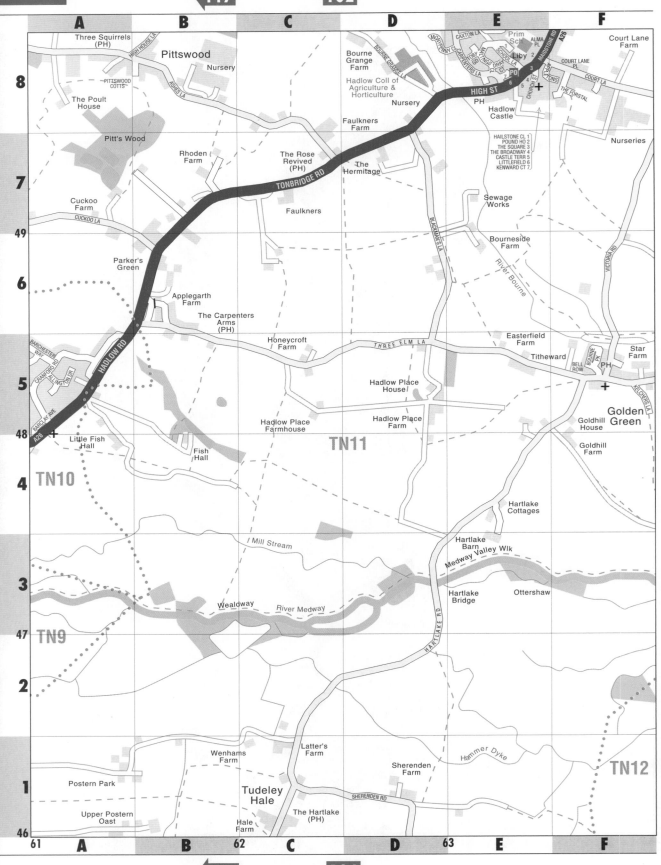

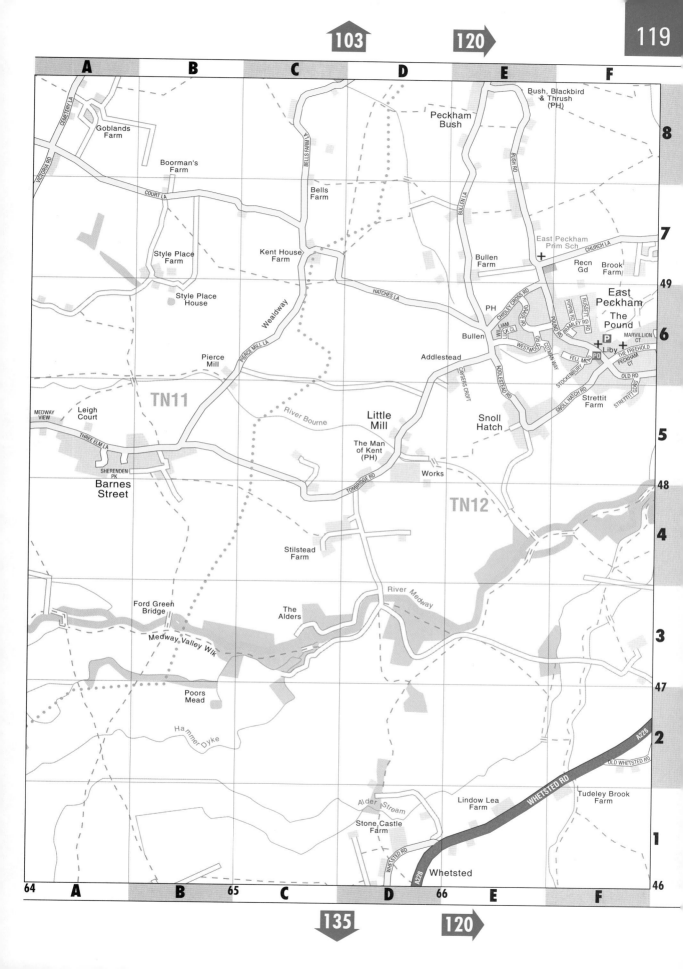

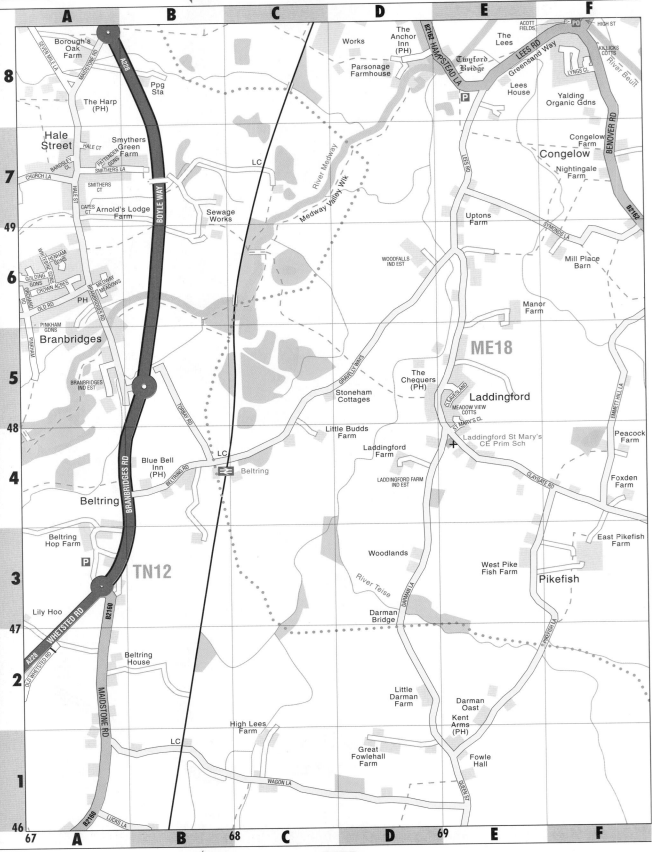

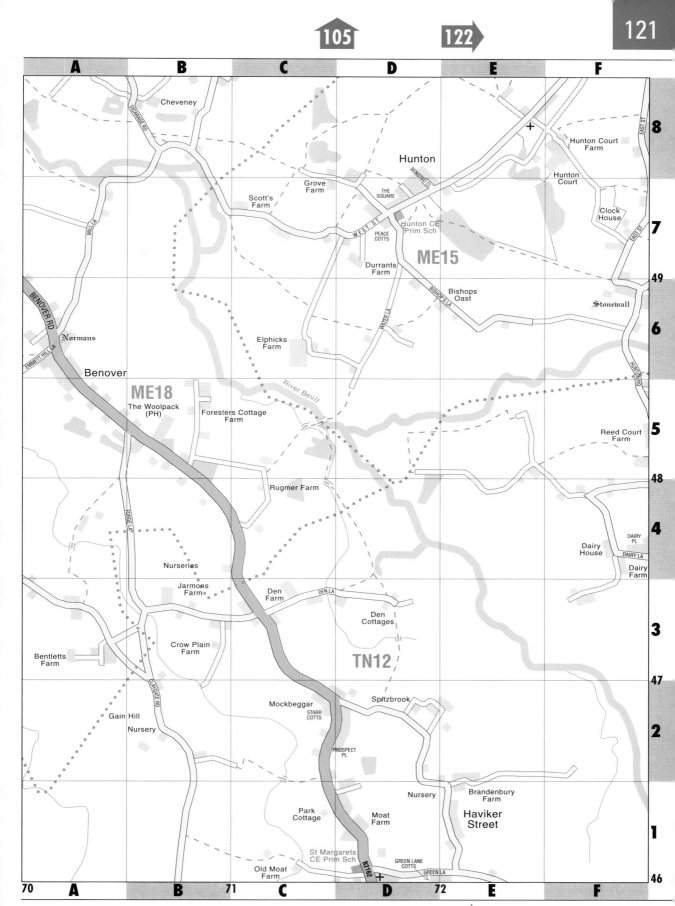

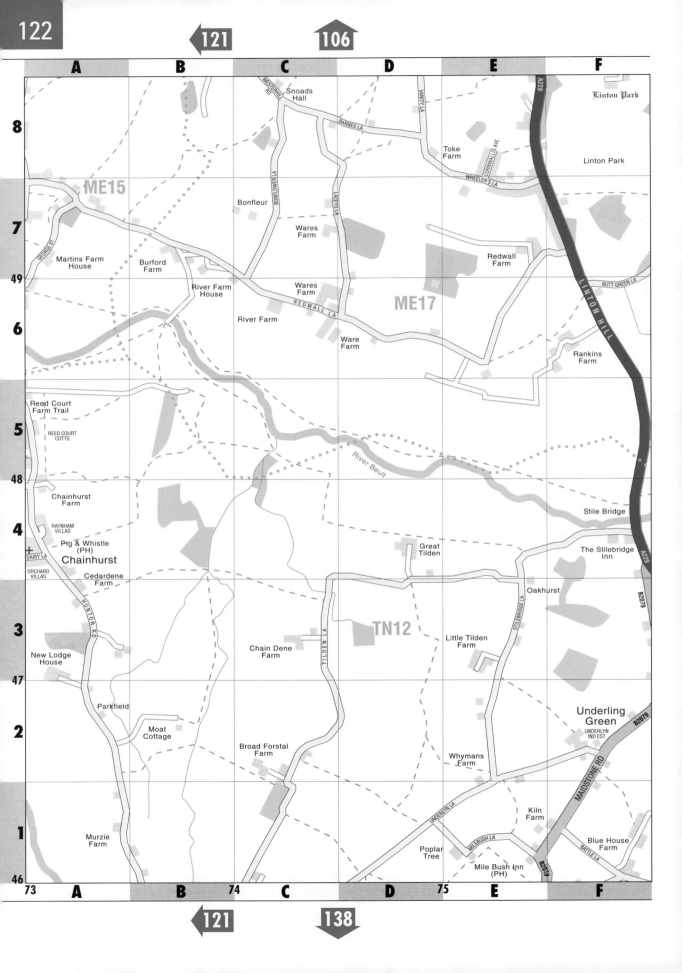

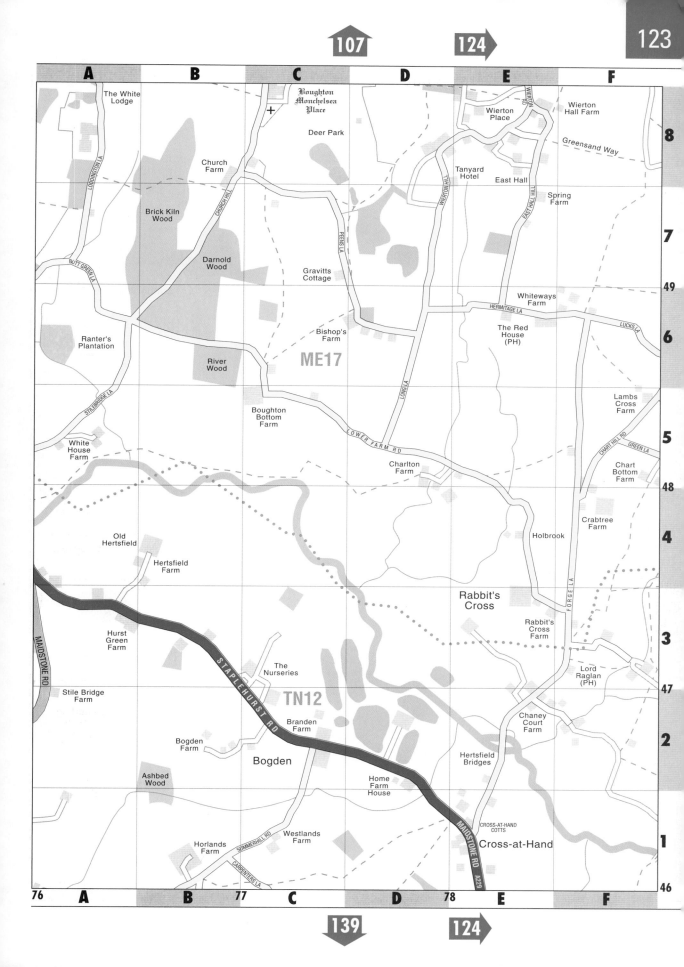

The White Lodge
LODDINGTON LA
Boughton Monchelsea Place
Deer Park
Church Farm
CHURCH HILL
Brick Kiln Wood
Darnold Wood
PEENS LA
Gravitts Cottage
Wierton Place
Wierton Hall Farm
WIERTON RD
Greensand Way
Tanyard Hotel
East Hall
WIERTON HILL
Spring Farm
EAST HILL RD
BUTT GREEN LA
Whiteways Farm
HERMITAGE LA
LUCKS LA
Ranter's Plantation
Bishop's Farm
ME17
The Red House (PH)
STILEBRIDGE LA
River Wood
LONG LA
Boughton Bottom Farm
LOWER FARM RD
Lambs Cross Farm
CHART HILL RD
GREEN LA
White House Farm
Charlton Farm
Chart Bottom Farm
Crabtree Farm
Old Hertsfield
Holbrook
Hertsfield Farm
FORGE LA
Rabbit's Cross
MAIDSTONE RD
Hurst Green Farm
Rabbit's Cross Farm
The Nurseries
STAPLEHURST RD
TN12
Lord Raglan (PH)
Stile Bridge Farm
Branden Farm
Chaney Court Farm
Bogden Farm
Bogden
Hertsfield Bridges
Ashbed Wood
Home Farm House
CROSS-AT-HAND COTTS
MAIDSTONE RD
Horlands Farm
SOMMERHALL RD
Westlands Farm
Cross-at-Hand
CARPENTERS LA
A229

76 A B 77 C D 78 E F

8 7 49 6 5 48 4 3 47 2 1 46

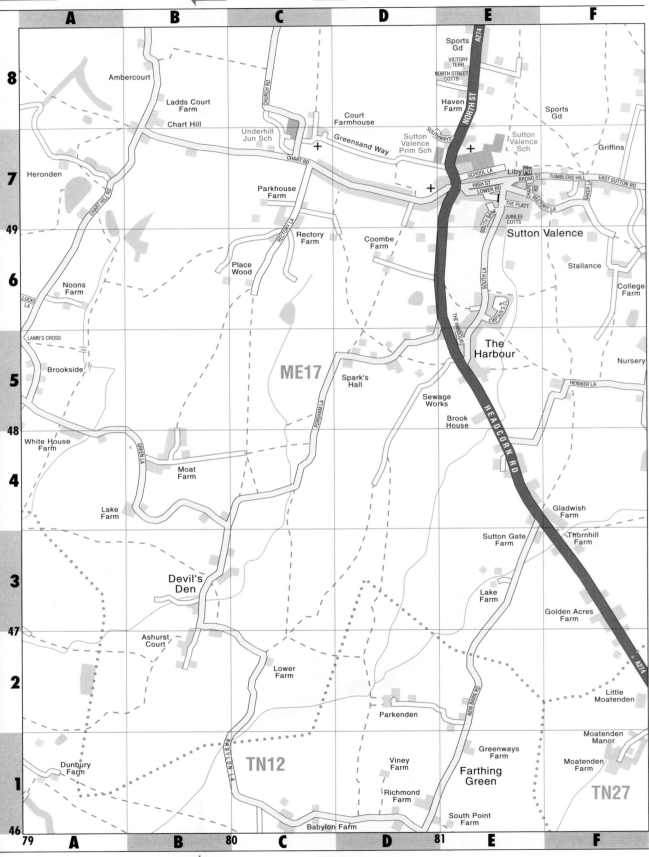

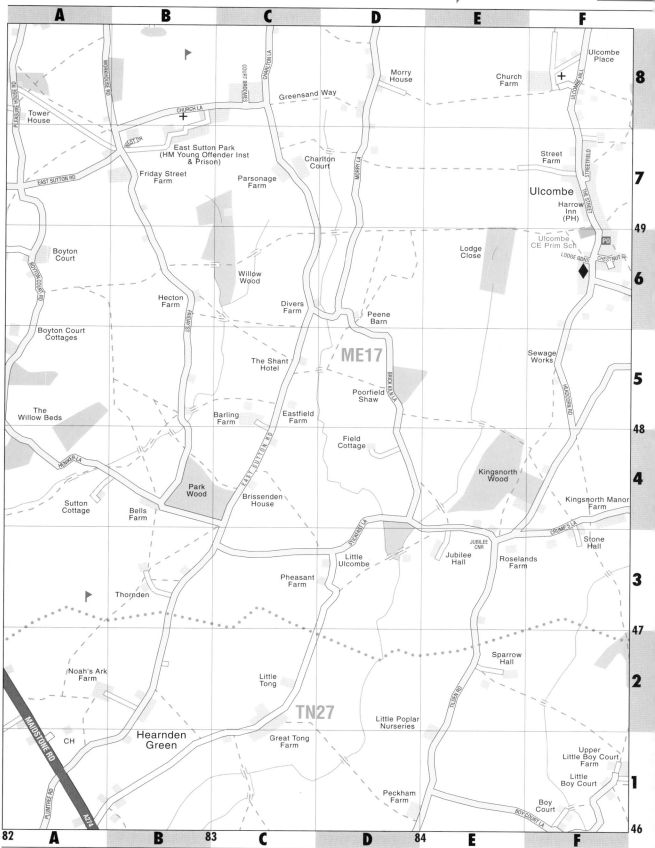

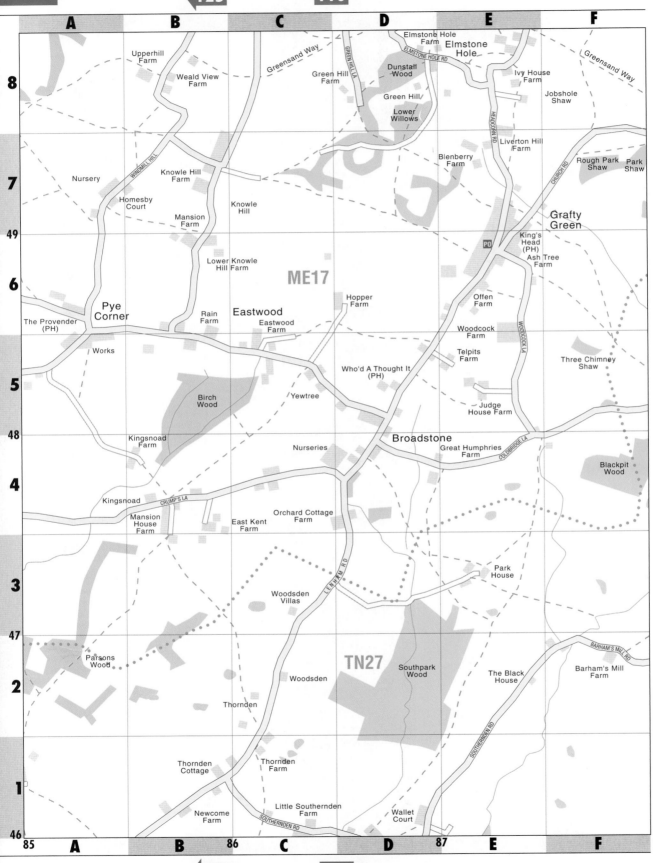

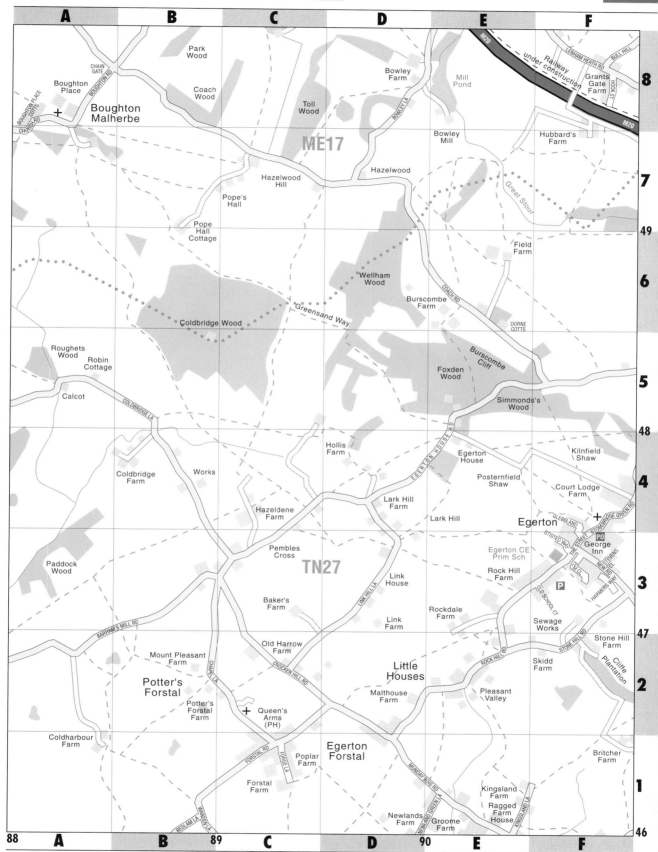

112

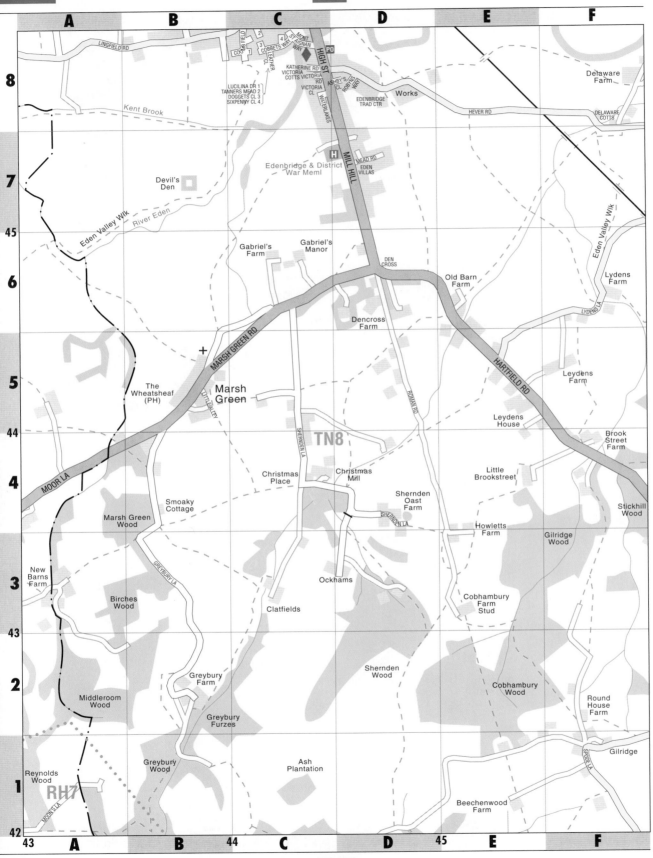

144

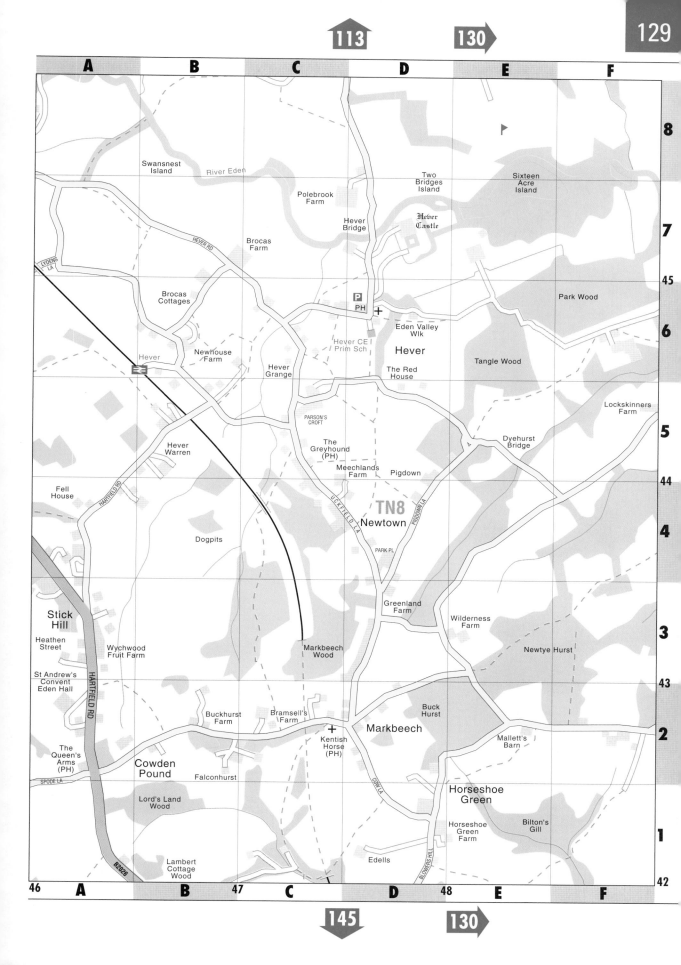

129
114

A B C D E F

8

River Eden

Mill Shaw

Somerden Green

The Grove

7

Gilwyns

Chiddingstone

Larkin's Farm

Vexour Bridge

River Eden

Hampkins Hill

Vexour

Castle Inn (PH)

PO

Chiddingstone CE Prim Sch

45

Chiddingstone Castle

Chantlers

THRESHER FIELD

6

Moor Wood

Hill Hoath

Clappers Shaw

Hill Hoath Farm

Eden Valley Wlk

BOURNE ROW

Weller's Town

Mounters

TN8

SOUTH ROW

Gillridge

Doubleton Cottage

5

The Slips

44

Sliders

Stock Wood

Lew Cross Farm

Wat Stock

TN11

Robins Land

4

Trugger's Gill

Salmans Farm

River Eden

The Warren

Russell's Wood

Harden Cottage

3

Trugger's Farm

The Rock Inn (PH)

Hoath Corner

Yewtree Wood

43

Puckden Wood

Harden Farmhouse

Penshurst Vinyard

The Grove

Oakenden Farm

Vine Cottage

2

Chiddingstone Hoath

Oakenden

Courtlands Wood

Hoath House

Stonewall Wood

South Park Wood

The Rangers

Brookers Farm House

GROVE RD

Stonewall Park

1

Bottle House (PH)

COLDHARBOUR RD

42

BOTTLE HOUSE COTTS

49 A B 50 C D 51 E F

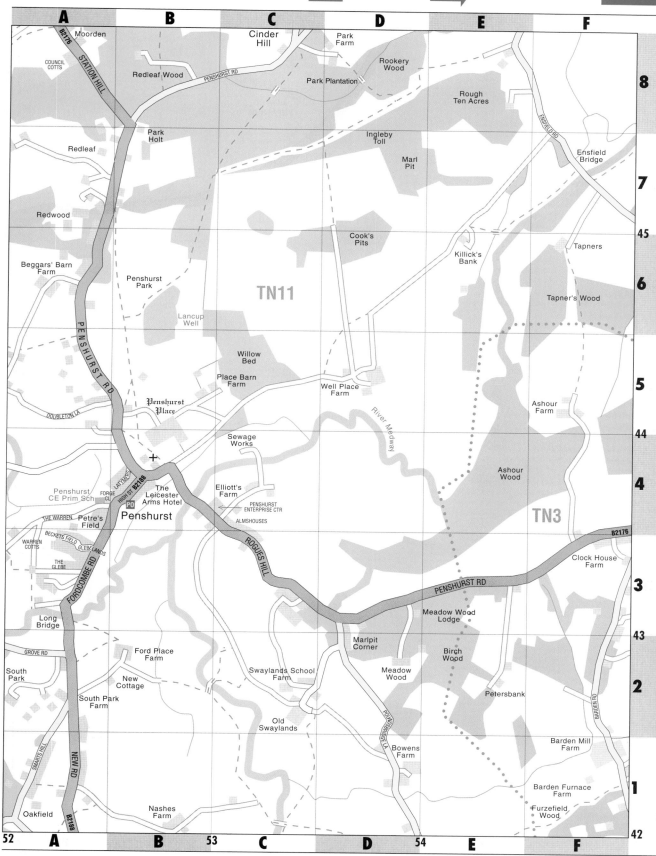

131
116

A B C D E F

8

7

TN9

Straight Mile
Haysden Water
Haysden Country Park
Lower Haysden
LOWER HAYSDEN LA
The Royal Oak (PH)
Brook Street Farm
BRANTINGHAM CL
CHAUCER CL
LECONFIELD GDNS
MASEFIELD WAY
BRIDGE CL
OLD BARN CL
BROOK ST
SHAKESPEARE RD
BEVERLEY CRES
WELTON CL
MILTON GDNS
KEYES GDNS
SWANLAND DR
LOCKINGTON CL
DRIFFIELD GDNS

TN11

Manor Farm
Chartfield

TONBRIDGE BY-PASS

A21

45

Ensfield
Great Hayesden Farm
Fosters Farm
UPPER HAYESDEN LA
Fishpond Farm

6

ENSFIELD RD
Upper Hayesden

Wealdway
Coxon Wood

A26

5

HAYESDEN LA
New Plantation
Beechy Toll
Birch Wood
Home Farm

44

Hawk's Wood
GATE FARM RD
Broadfield
Seals Wood
Waghorn's Wood
B2176
Bidborough Corner

4

Judd's Wood
Home Farm
GATEHOUSE FARM COTTS
PO
BIDBOROUGH RIDGE
THE CRESCENT
DARNLEY DR
HARLAND WAY
LONDON RD
TN4

RIDGELANDS

B2176
Printstile
PENSHURST RD
THE GLEBE
WOODLAND WAY
ST LAWRENCE AVE
GREAT BOUNDS DR
BOUNDS OAK WAY
VAUXHALL LA

3

TN3
Bidborough Court
HIGH ST
RECTORY DR
Bidborough
Birch Wood
HARDINGE AVE CRES
SMYTHE CL
LITTLE BOUNDS
JOYNER HOUSE CRES
BROADHURST GDNS
BIRCHWOOD AVE
F2
1 Pennington Manor
2 Castle St
3 Draper St
4 Sheffield Rd

Old Farmhouse
SANDS RD
SPRING LA
The Grange
Bidborough CE Prim Sch
Meadows Sch (Barnados)

43

Brock's Wood
FRANT SHALLOW RD
CHURCH RD
P
Holden House
VICTORIA RD
CONSTITUTIONAL HILL RD
PENNINGTON RD
PO

2

Sewage Works
Cemy
High Weald Wlk
MODEST CNR
Southborough Common
Holden House
SUMMERHILL AVE
HEATHVIEW

Bentham Farm

1

Speldhurst Wood
Scriventon
Birchett's Wood
Stockland Green
STOCKLAND GREEN RD
Bentham Hill
Modest Corner
The Park
SIR DAVID'S PK
KIBBLES LA
MANOR RD
CRUNDWELL RD
WOOLLEY RD
WOOLLEY CL
SPRINGFIELD RD
MEADOW RD
ELM RD

42

55 A B 56 C D 57 E F

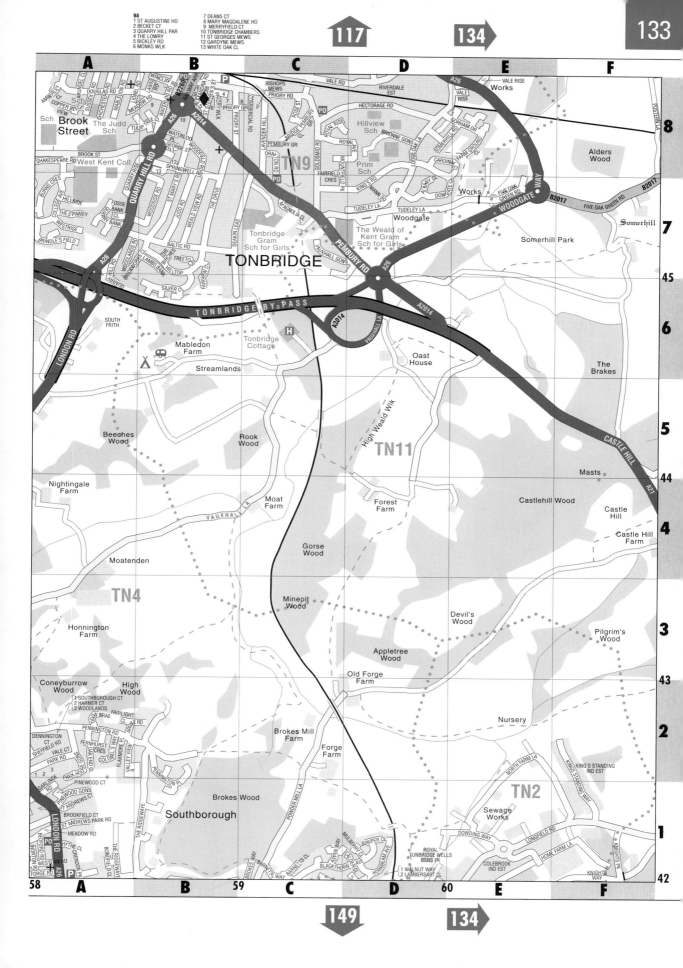

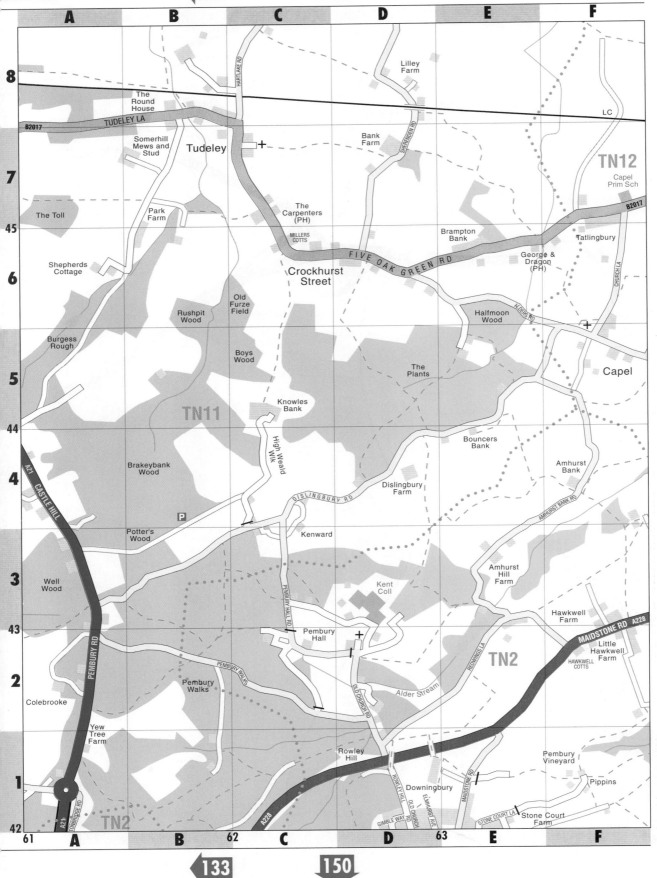

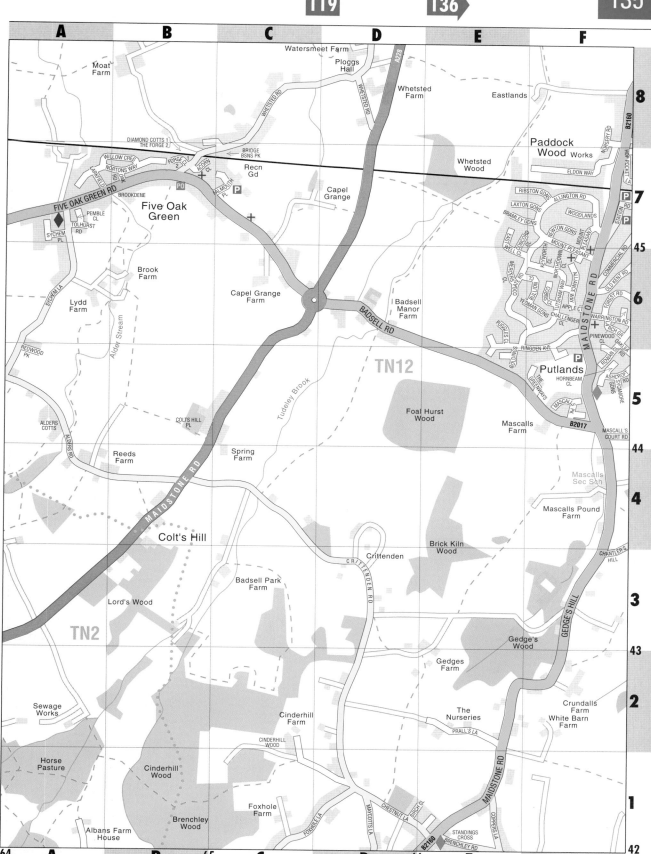

A B C D E F

8

7

45

6

5

44

4

3

43

2

1

42

67 A B 68 C D 69 E F

B2160

MAIDSTONE RD

Swatlands Farm

LC

New Barns Farm

Little Fowle Hall Farm

Upper Fowle Hall Farm

ORCHARD BSNS CTR

Depot

Works

Rhoden Farm

Queen Street

LUCKNOW RD

TRANSFESA RD

Little Rhoden Farm

Sewage Works

QUEEN ST

HENLEY RD

Paddock Wood

STATION APP

P

PO

THE CEDARS

THE SHIRES

Church Farm

Park Farm

WILLOW LA

P

45

THE RISINGS

BEECH CT

BRIDGE WAY

CHADWICK CL

Bowls

OLD KENT RD

CLENDALL RD

ST ANDREWS CL

ANCHORAGE FLATS

Recn Gd

Cemy

Ledger's Farm

GRANARY

CHURCH RD

WALNUT CL

BATTLE

MELPHAM

LE TEMPLE RD

Sch

COURTHOPE

ST ANDREWS RD

MACDONALD CT

FOREST RD

BLACKBERRY

NEW RD

WARRINGTON RD

HEATHERLEY

Knell's Farm

Great Old Hay

LINDEN CL

ASHCROFT RD

BLUEBELL WAY

THE COTGROVES

Elm Tree (PH)

TN12

Jason's Farm

HAYMAN

THE BINES

WAY

MYRTLE

CLOVER WAY

PRIMROSE WLK

BUTTERCUP

WILLETTS

GREEN LA

Oasthouse Farm

BULLFINCH

CL

CHAFFINCH WAY

LINNET AVE

SISKIN GDNS

GOLDFINCH

REDPOLL WLK

Pearsons Green Rd

L Ctr

Mascall's Court

CATTS PL

Catts Place

Greenfields Farm

MASCALL'S COURT RD

Mascalls Sec Sch

MASCALL'S COURT

Mile Oak

Three Tax Farm

CHANTLER'S HILL

MILE OAK RD

Trenches Farm

Pearson's Green

KNOWLE LA

PEARSON'S GREEN RD

Biggenden Farmhouse

Longbrooks

CHURN LA

Biggenden Barn

WATERMAN'S LA

KNOWLE RD

Moatlands Park

The Knowle

Latters Toll

Parsonage Wood

WEALD VIEW

PH

Castle Hill

Hill Top

PIXOT HILL

Crook Rd

The Crook

WINDMILL HILL

BRENCHLEY RD

BROAD OAK

PALMERS GREEN LA

Great Wood

FURNACE LA

Poulhurst

YEW TREE GREEN RD

Poulhurst Farm

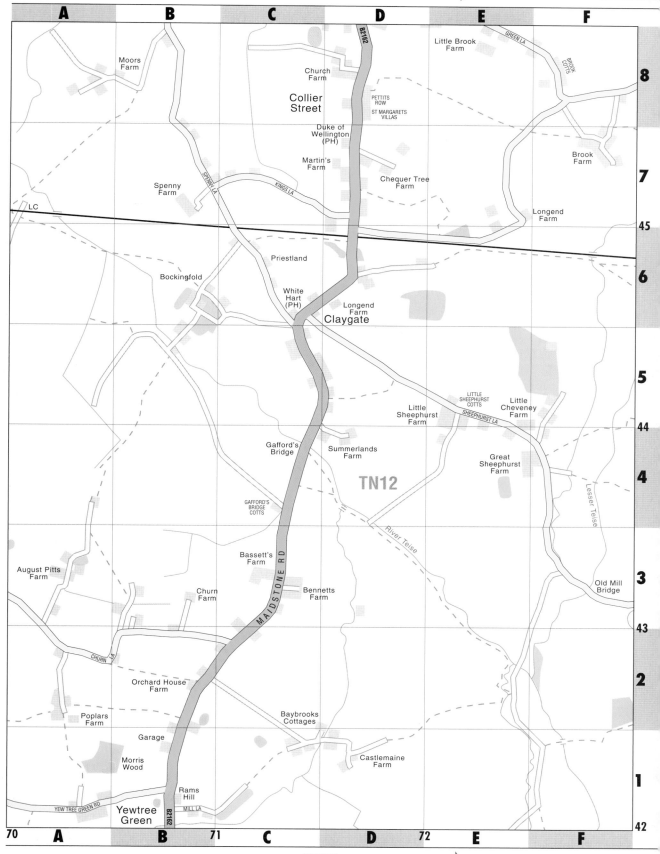

Moors Farm

Collier Street

Church Farm

Little Brook Farm

GREEN LA

BROOK COTTS

PETTITS ROW

ST MARGARETS VILLAS

Duke of Wellington (PH)

Brook Farm

Martin's Farm

Chequer Tree Farm

Spenny Farm

SPENN LA

KINGS LA

Longend Farm

LC

Priestland

Bockingfold

White Hart (PH)

Longend Farm

Claygate

LITTLE SHEEPHURST COTTS

Little Cheveney Farm

Little Sheephurst Farm

SHEEPHURST LA

Great Sheephurst Farm

Gafford's Bridge

Summerlands Farm

TN12

Lesser Teise

GAFFORD'S BRIDGE COTTS

River Teise

Old Mill Bridge

August Pitts Farm

Bassett's Farm

MAIDSTONE RD

Churn Farm

Bennetts Farm

CHURN LA

Orchard House Farm

Poplars Farm

Baybrooks Cottages

Garage

Castlemaine Farm

Morris Wood

Rams Hill

B2162

MILL LA

YEW TREE GREEN RD

Yewtree Green

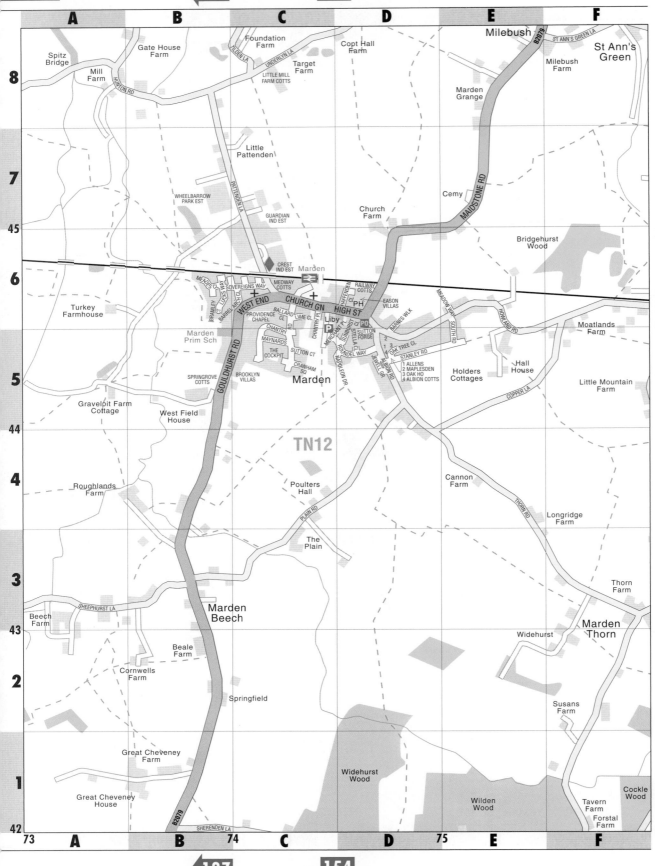

A B C D E F

8
7
45
6
5
44
4
3
43
2
1
42

Little Crew Den

BATTLE LA
SUMMERHILL RD
Allingham Farm
Summer Hill
Wanshurst Green
Manor Farm
Springfield Cottage
CARPENTERS LA
Newhaven Farm
Overbridge Farm
Sundridge Nurseries
Clapper Farm
Sweetlands Farm
CLAPPER LA
Abbotsleigh
Knowles Hill
A229
MAIDSTONE RD
COUCHMAN GREEN LA

HOWLAND RD
Duckhurst Farm
GEORGE ST
NEWTOWN COTTS
Staplehurst
Sewage Works

LINDRIDGE LA
Mountain Farmhouse
Lindridge
MARDEN RD
Limekiln Farm
LODGE RD
LARKSTONE PK
DOUGLAS BLDGS
HONEYCREST IND PK
Works
STATION APP
STATION RD
WINCH'S CL
DICKENS CT
MARKET ST
FISHERS RD
NUNNERY FIELDS
FISHERS CL
Fisher's Farm
WINCH'S GARTH
WILLIAM CRES

TN12
Fouracre
FURTHER FIELD
MARLFIELD
GREEN HILL
WATKINS CL
Baldwins Farm
CORNER FARM RD
FISHERS DR
1 BENDEN CL
2 WEAVERS CL
3 KNOWLES WLK

Park House
PARK RD
Great Pagehurst Farm
Hen & Duckhurst Farm
NORTH DOWN
BROOKS CL
CUCKOLD'S CNR
HEADCORN RD
Staplehurst
STANLEY CL
OLIVER CL
POPE DR
BUTCHER CL
FREEZES CL
BATHURST CL
BATHURST RD
THATCHER RD
CHESTNUT RD
GOWTHER CL
CHESTNUT PK
ALEN SQ
POYNTELL CL
STAPLE CNR
SLANEY RD
MARIAN SQ
CORNFORTH CL

Little Pagehurst
PAGEHURST RD
Aydhurst Farm
BOWER WLK
SURR CL
GYBBON RD
Staplehurst Sch
Liby
THE PARADE
USBORNE CL
OFFEN'S DR
FLETCHER RD
JAGGARD WAY
LIME COTTS
HIGH ST
CHAPEL LA
FIR TREE CL
VINE CT

The Wild Duck (PH)
Dourne Farm
BELL LA
VINE CL
KIRKMAN CT
SOUTH BANK
CHURCH GN
CRANBROOK RD
A229
FRITTENDEN RD

The Laurels
Clarkes Farm
FIVE OAK LA
PRISTLING LA
Saynden Farm
Brattle Farm Mus
GOUDHURST RD
PINNOCK LA
Henhurst Farm
HAMMER WAY
HALLWARDS
GARDEN CL
The Quarter
Iden Park

Ely Court
Gooseberry Wood

76 A B 77 C D 78 E F 42

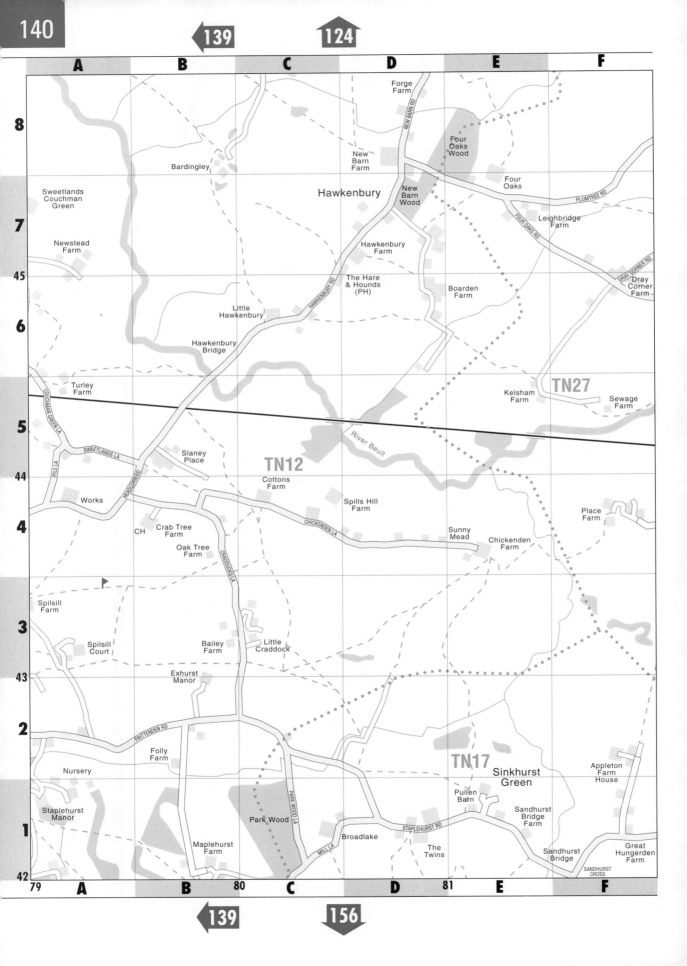

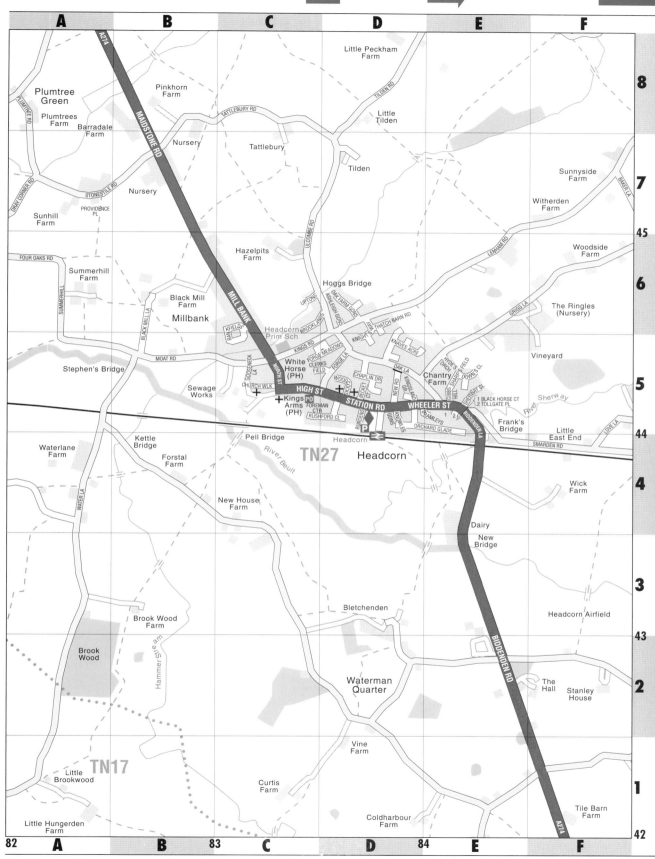

A B C D E F

8

Springfield Farm

Southernden

Southernden Farm

Little Southernden Farm

LENHAM RD

Barling Green Farm

7

Gloversbridge Farm

Glover's Bridge

Burnt House

BAKER LA

45

Little Grigg Farm

GRIGG LA

River Sherway

SHERWAY RD

Old Oak Farm

Grigg Oasts

6

Grigg Farm

Sherway Bridge

Homersham Farm

Swift's Green

Hieland Glen

Little Swift's Green Farm

BEDLAM LA

5

Homestall Farm

Luckhurst Farm

Little Luckhurst

LOVE LA

Malthouse Farm

ROSEMARY LA

Coldharbour Farm

Manor Farm

Suncrest

TN27

44

Abbotts Skreen Farm

East End

SMARDEN RD

Roland House

LC

4

Marley Farm

High Cross Wood

Hegg Hill Farm

Watch House

MARLEY LA

Hegg Hill

3

Munk's Farm

HEADCORN RD

Vane Farm

Westover Farm

Bell Farm

The Roundabout

43

Smarden Bell

The Bell (PH)

Church Farm

Ash Farm

MILL LA

2

Lashenden Air Warfare Mus

River Beult

Hadman's Place

BELL LA

Oxley Farm

WATER LA

THE OAKS

Shenley Farm

ASHENDEN

THE ACORNS

Haylands Farm

Hadman's Bridge

White House

Ebenezer Farm

Sewage Works

1

West Hoy Farm

Braid Farm

BURNTHOUSE LA

Town Bridge

PH

Snughorn Farm

CAGE LA

42

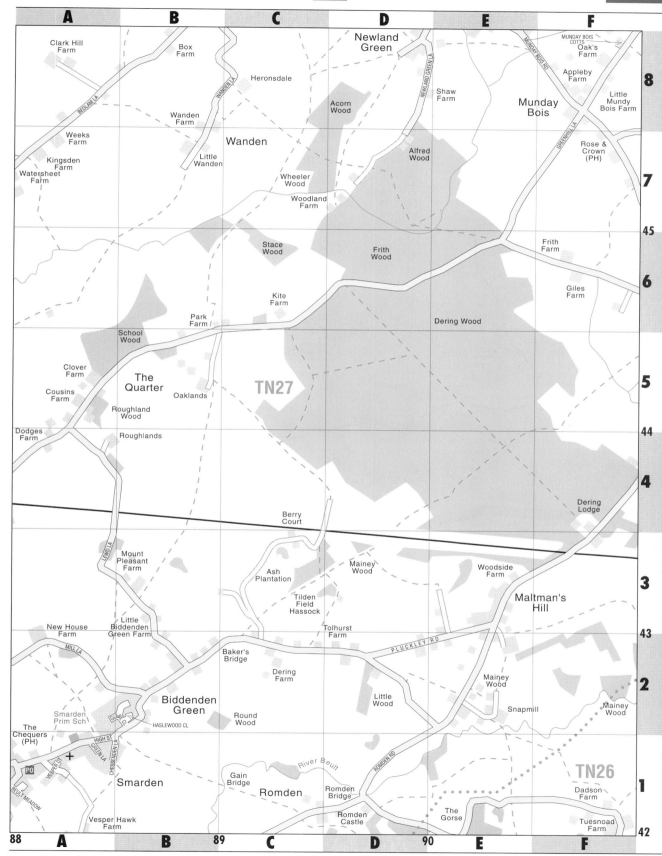

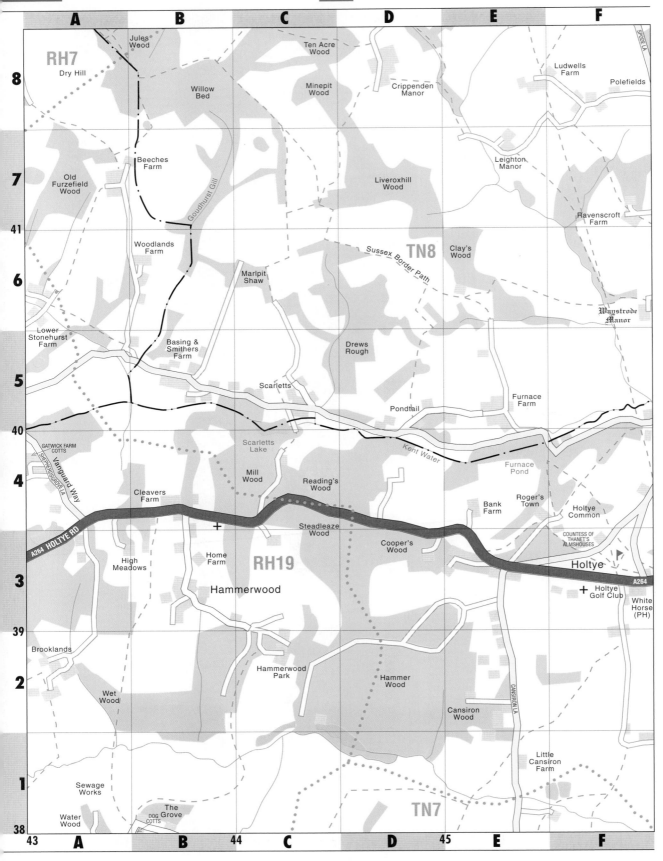

RH7

Dry Hill

Jules Wood

Ten Acre Wood

Willow Bed

Minepit Wood

Crippenden Manor

Ludwells Farm

Polefields

SPODE LA

Old Furzefield Wood

Beeches Farm

Leighton Manor

Liveroxhill Wood

Ravenscroft Farm

Woodlands Farm

Goudhurst Gill

Sussex Border Path

TN8

Clay's Wood

Marlpit Shaw

Waystrode Manor

Lower Stonehurst Farm

Basing & Smithers Farm

Drews Rough

Scarletts

Pondtail

Furnace Farm

Kent Water

Gatwick Farm Cotts

Scarletts Lake

Furnace Pond

Vanguard Way

SHEPHERDSGROVE LA

Mill Wood

Reading's Wood

Bank Farm

Roger's Town

Holtye Common

Cleavers Farm

Steadleaze Wood

Cooper's Wood

COUNTESS OF THANET'S ALMSHOUSES

A264 HOLTYE RD

High Meadows

Home Farm

RH19

Hammerwood

Holtye

A264

Holtye Golf Club

White Horse (PH)

Brooklands

Hammerwood Park

Hammer Wood

Wet Wood

Cansiron Wood

CANSIRON LA

Little Cansiron Farm

Sewage Works

The Grove

DOG COTTS

TN7

Water Wood

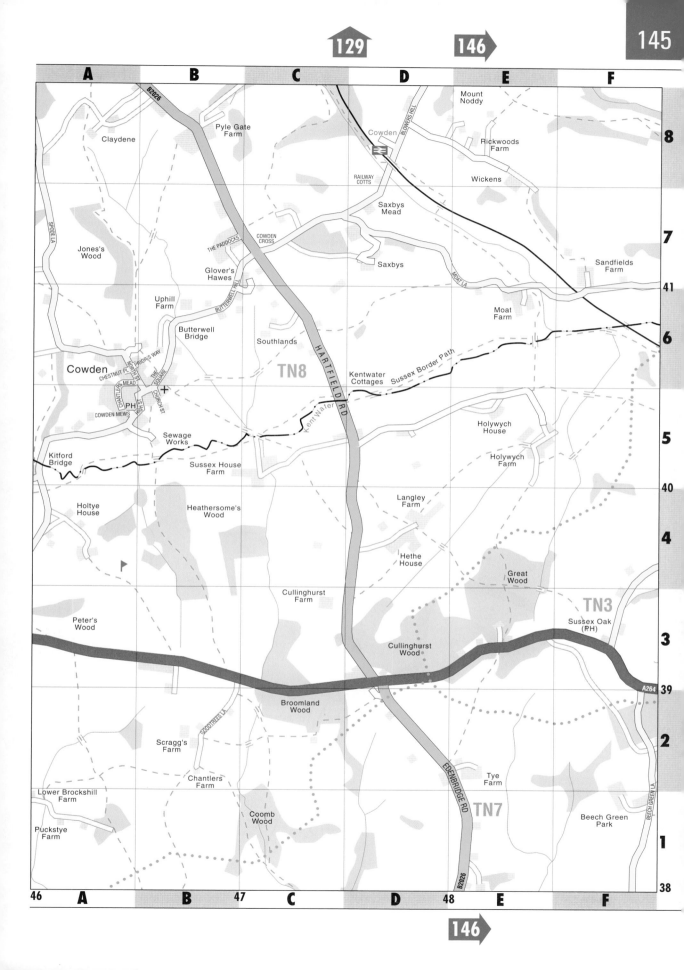

145
130

A B C D E F

8

Birchcope Shaw

Coldharbour

Westfield House

COLDHARBOUR RD

NUNNERY LA

Frienden Gill

Cook's Wood

TN8

Finch Green

White Post

Bassett's Mill

Harts

SANDFIELD RD

7

BASSETTS LA

Frienden Farm

Blacklands Wood

Hartslands Farm

Bassett's Farm

TN11

Prinkham

41

WALTERS GREEN RD

6

Kent Water

Hobbs Hill Farm

Top Hill Wood

Walter's Green

Pilbeams

BRADLEY RD

CHAFFORD LA

Nore Farm

Sussex Border Path

Chafford Bridge

CHAFFORD COTTS

5

CH

Tollhurst Farm

40

Willett's Farm

Stephnett's Farm

Salenhurst Farm

Blackham

River Medway

Chafford Park

Cousins Shaw

4

WILLETTS LA

WILLETTS COTTS

TN3

CARRIERS PL

TEASLEY MEAD

Teasley Mead

Pound Farm

Ashurst Wood

Stable Cottage

3

A264

ASHURST RD

Chafford Park

Highfields Park

ASHURST HILL

Manor Court Farm

39

Ashurst Bridge

MILLSTREAM CL

The Bald Faced Stag (PH)

2

Lodgefield Wood

Ashurst

Ashurst

CLAYTON'S LA

Lodgefield Farm

Jessup's Farm

Lords Wood

Wealdway

1

TN7

Clay Shaw

Old Woodland Wood

Minepit Wood

38

49 A B 50 C D 51 E F

145
160

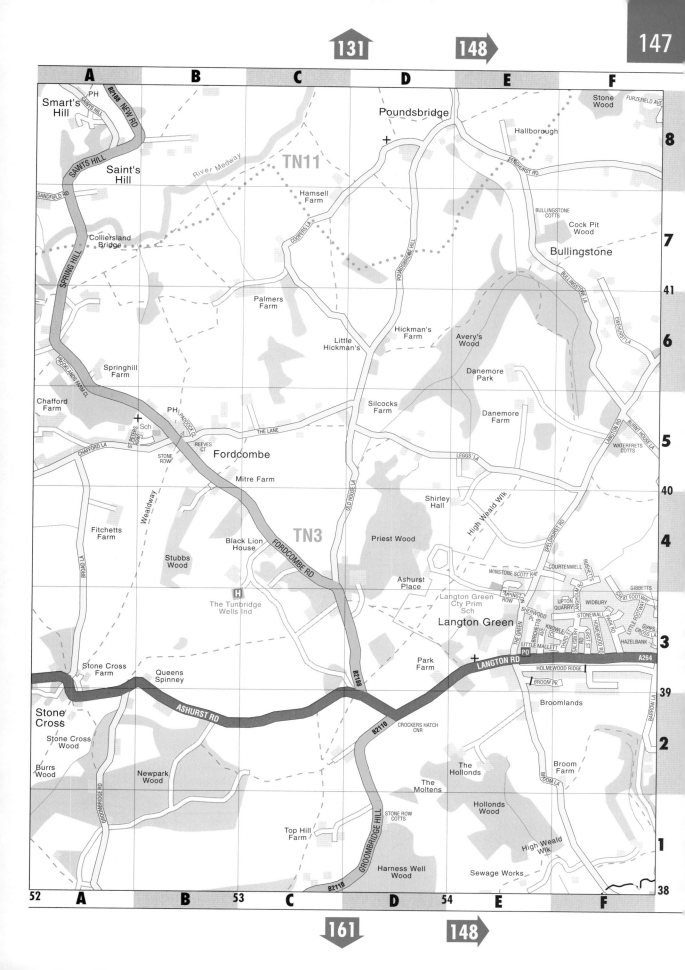

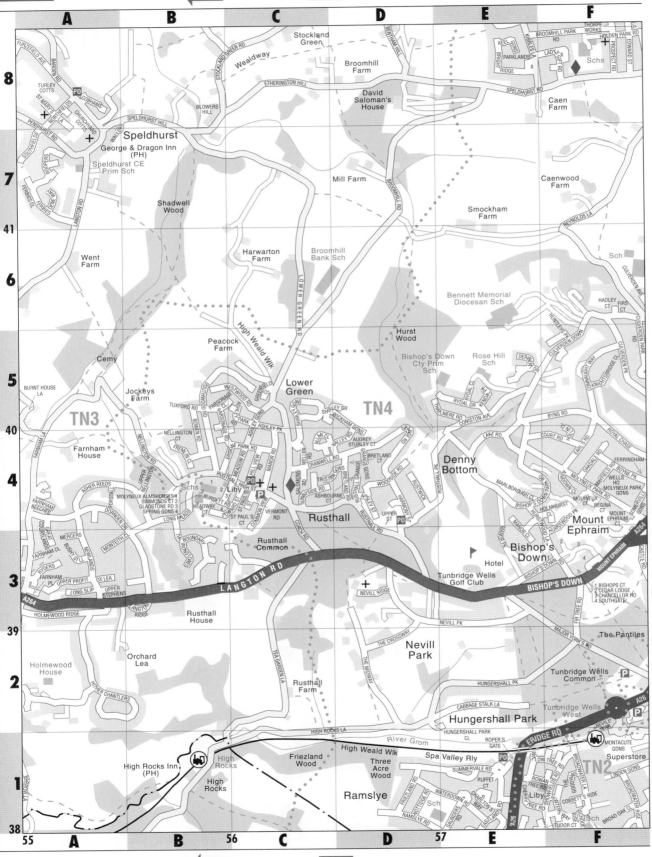

147
132

A B C D E F

8

7

41

6

5

40

4

3

39

2

1

38

55 A B 56 C D 57 E F

147
162

Stockland Green
Broomhill Farm
David Saloman's House
Wealdway
Etherington Hill
Speldhurst Hill
Blowers Hill
Speldhurst
George & Dragon Inn (PH)
Speldhurst CE Prim Sch
Shadwell Wood
Mill Farm
Caenwood Farm
Caen Farm
Smockham Farm
Sch
Went Farm
Harwarton Farm
Broomhill Bank Sch
Lower Green Rd
High Weald Wlk
Hurst Wood
Bennett Memorial Diocesan Sch
Cemy
Peacock Farm
Bishop's Down Cty Prim Sch
Rose Hill Sch
Hadley Ct
Firs Ct
Lower Green
TN4
TN3
Burnt House La
Jockeys Farm
Farnham House
Denny Bottom
Mount Ephraim
Bishop's Down
Asher Reeds
Molyneux Almshouses
Rusthall
Rusthall Common
Hotel
Tunbridge Wells Golf Club
Nevill Ridge
BISHOP'S DOWN
The Pantiles
Holmewood Ridge
LANGTON RD
Rusthall House
Nevill Pk
Nevill Park
Tunbridge Wells Common
Holmewood House
Orchard Lea
Rusthall Farm
The Crossway
The Midway
Hungershall Pk
Tunbridge Wells West
A26
Hungershall Park
High Rocks La
River Grom
High Weald Wlk
Hungershall Park Cl
Roper's Gate
Spa Valley Rly
Superstore
Montacute Gdns
TN2
High Rocks Inn (PH)
High Rocks
Friezland Wood
Three Acre Wood
Ramslye
ERIDGE RD
Liby
Sch

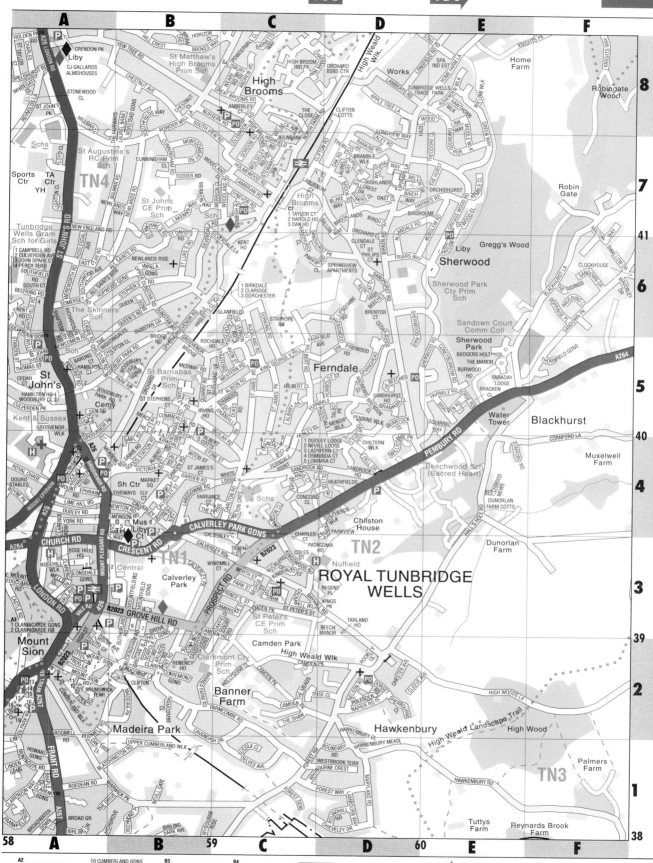

A2
1 CHRIST CHURCH AVE
2 CASTLE ST
3 WHITE BEAR PAS
4 WARWICK RD
5 BELGROVE
6 SPENCER MEWS
7 BERKELEY RD
8 CHAPEL PL
9 BEDFORD TERR

10 CUMBERLAND GDNS
11 CUMBERLAND YD
12 CUMBERLAND MEWS
13 MARKET ST
14 MARKET PL
15 COACH & HORSES PAS
16 SUSSEX MEWS
17 THE PANTILES
18 UNION SQ
19 REGENCY HALL

B3
1 CALVERLEY PARK CRES
2 MOUNT PLEASANT AVE
3 GREAT HALL ARC
4 MOUNTFIELD CT
5 THE MEWS
6 MEADOW HILL RD
7 GUILDFORD RD

B4
1 ELIZABETH GARLICK CT
2 CAMDEN CT
3 GROVER ST
4 SPENCER'S MEWS
5 MONSON WAY
6 CADOGAN GDNS
7 CATHERINE PL
8 LANSDOWNE SQ

149 134

A B C D E F

8

Sandhill Farm

TN11

Newbars Wood

A21

A228

THE GROVE
OLD CHURCH RD
ELMHURST AVE
MAIDSTONE RD
STONE COURT LA
SNIPE
MEADOW
HERONS WAY

Pembury Cty Prim Sch

PO

Lower Green

Marshleyharbour Wood

Forest Wood

BATCHELORS
BRICKFIELDS

Snipe Wood

7

Pembury

H

FOREST WAY
THE GLEBE
KNIGHTS RIDGE RD
KNIGHT'S RIDGE
RIDGEWAY
THE COPPICE
IPSWICH
LOWER GREEN RD
BEECH
POLLEY
BL PETERSFIELD
WOOD
PEMBURY CL
BERKELEY CL

Liby

Romford

BLACKHURST LA

SANDOWN PK

WESTWAY

TONBRIDGE RD

Priory Farm

WOODLANDS

ROMFORD RD

KINGS TOLL RD

41

PEMBURY GRANGE

Pembury Grange

WOODSGATE WAY

WOODHILL PK
GREENLEAS
THE VIEWS
HIGH ST
THE PADDOCK
SUNHILL CT

CORNFORD CL
CORNFORD PK
CORNFORD

Superstore

A228

AMBERLEAZE DR
TOLL
HIGH ST
BULL'S PL
BELFELD RD

HESKETT PK

Henwood Green

HENWOOD GREEN RD

WOODSIDE RD
WOODSIDE CL

RD

6

PEMBURY RD

SYCAMORE COTTS
PENN RD
CAMDEN AVE
CHALKET LA

Pembury

CAMDEN CT

STABLEDENE WAY
PO

HENWOOD CRES
CANTERBURY
STANAM RD

FIRWOODS MOUNT
SANDHURST AVE

Playing Field

Hubble's Farm

HASTINGS RD

A264

The Coach House

5

St George's Sch

A264

Larkfield Hall

CORNFORD LA

Chalket Farm

TN2

High Weald Landscape Trail

HASTINGS RD

A21

Pastheap Farm

40

Fletchers

Fletchers Farm

4

Mouseden

Little Bayhall Farm

Great Bayhall

Brickhurst Wood

TN12

3

Great Bayhall Farm

HIGH WOODS LA

Little Bayhall

Gull Rough Wood

39

2

TN3

Old Dundle

DUNDALE RD

Dodhurst

Dundale Farm

Dundale Wood

1

River Teise

Brown's Lodge

38

61 **A** 62 **B** **C** 62 **D** 63 **E** **F**

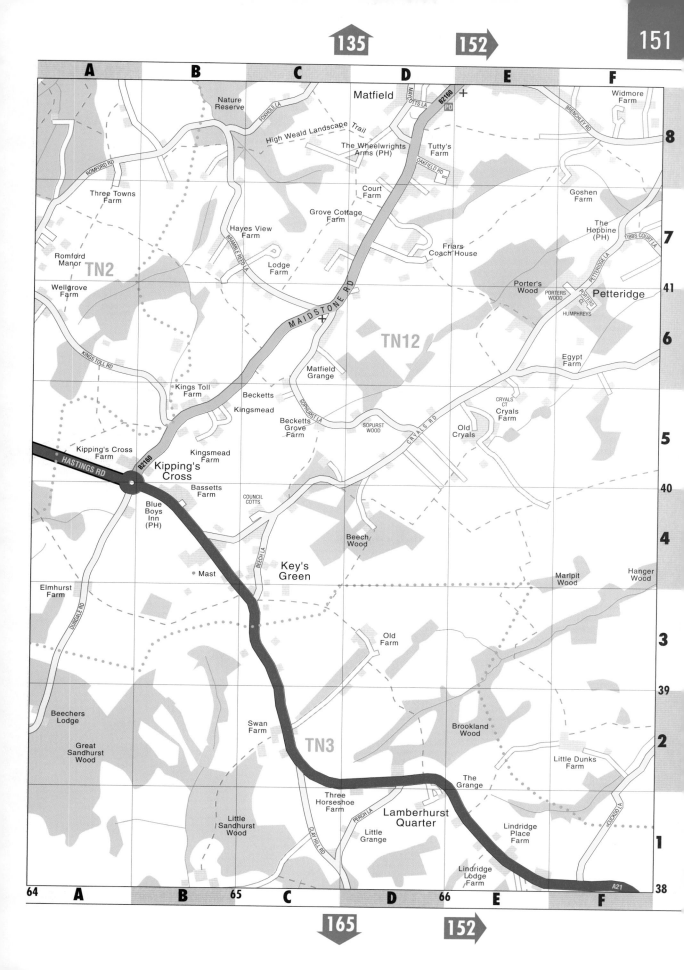

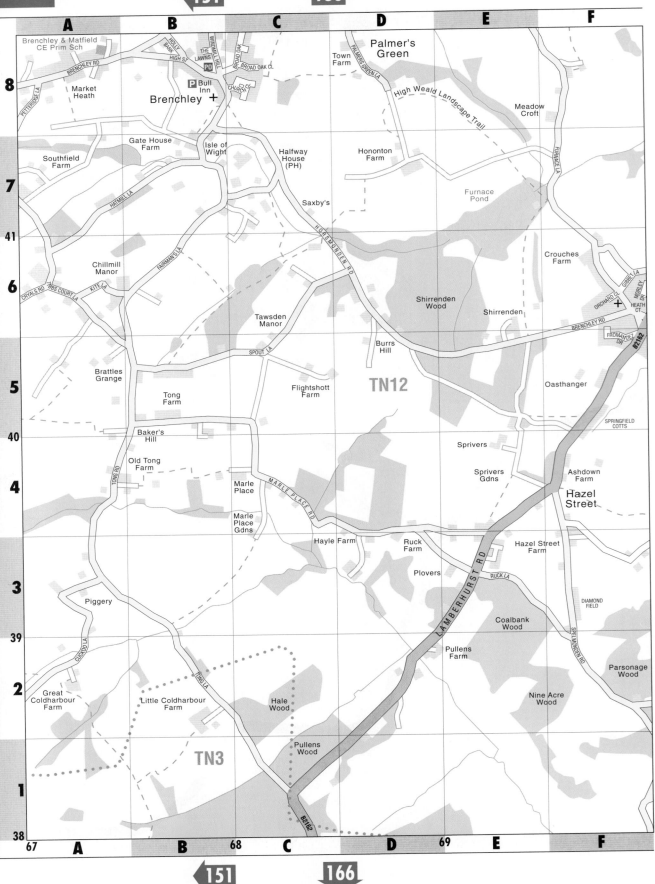

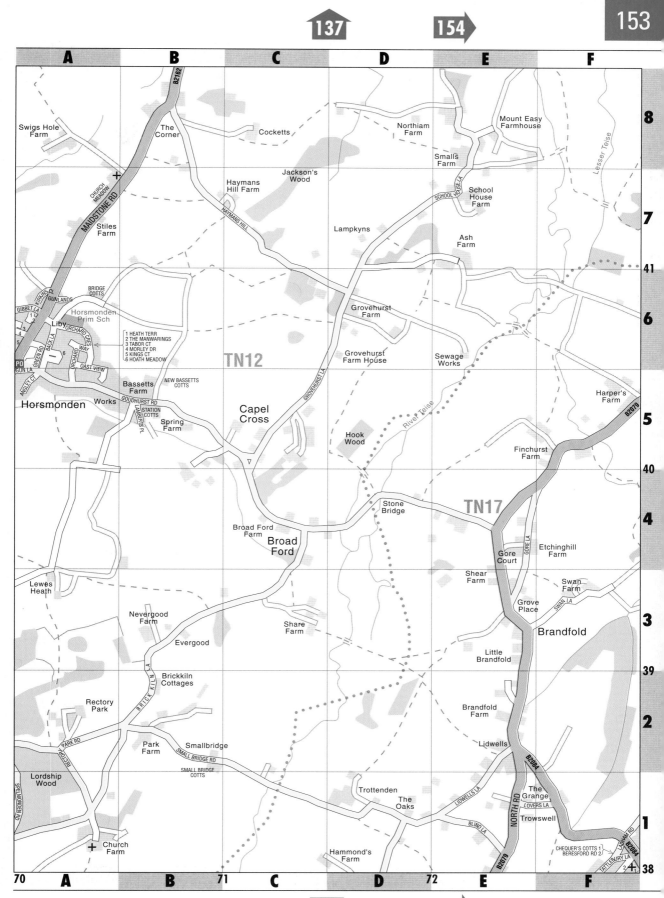

Swigs Hole Farm

The Corner

Cocketts

Northiam Farm

Mount Easy Farmhouse

8

B2162

Jackson's Wood

Smalls Farm

Lesser Teise

CHURCH MEADOW

MAIDSTONE RD

Haymans Hill Farm

SCHOOL HOUSE LA

School House Farm

Stiles Farm

HAYMANS HILL

7

Lampkyns

Ash Farm

41

KIRKINS CL

GUNLANDS

BRIDGE COTTS

Horsmonden Prim Sch

Grovehurst Farm

6

GIBBET LA

1 2 3 4

Liby

ORCHARD CRES

1 HEATH TERR
2 THE MANWARINGS
3 TABOR CT
4 MORLEY DR
5 KINGS CT
6 HOATH MEADOW

GROVEHURST LA

Grovehurst Farm House

Sewage Works

TN12

GREEN RD   BACK LA

ORCHARD   WAY

6

Harper's Farm

PO

GUN LA

OAST VIEW

B2079

ANSLEY CT

Bassetts Farm

NEW BASSETTS COTTS

Capel Cross

Hook Wood

River Teise

Finchurst Farm

5

Horsmonden

Works

GOUDHURST RD

LAMBERTS PL

STATION COTTS

Spring Farm

40

Stone Bridge

TN17

Broad Ford Farm

Broad Ford

Gore Court

GORE LA

Etchinghill Farm

4

Lewes Heath

Shear Farm

Swan Farm

SWAN LA

Nevergood Farm

Share Farm

Grove Place

Brandfold

3

Evergood

BRICK KILN LA

Brickkiln Cottages

Little Brandfold

39

Rectory Park

Brandfold Farm

2

PARK RD

BEDFORD

Park Farm

Smallbridge

SMALL BRIDGE RD

SMALL BRIDGE COTTS

Lidwells

B2084

SPELMONDEN RD

Lordship Wood

Trottenden

The Oaks

LIDWELLS LA

NORTH RD

LOVERS LA

The Grange

Trowswell

LASHAM RD

Church Farm

BLIND LA

B2079

Hammond's Farm

CHEQUER'S COTTS 1
BERESFORD RD 2

B2084

TATTLEBURY LA

1

38

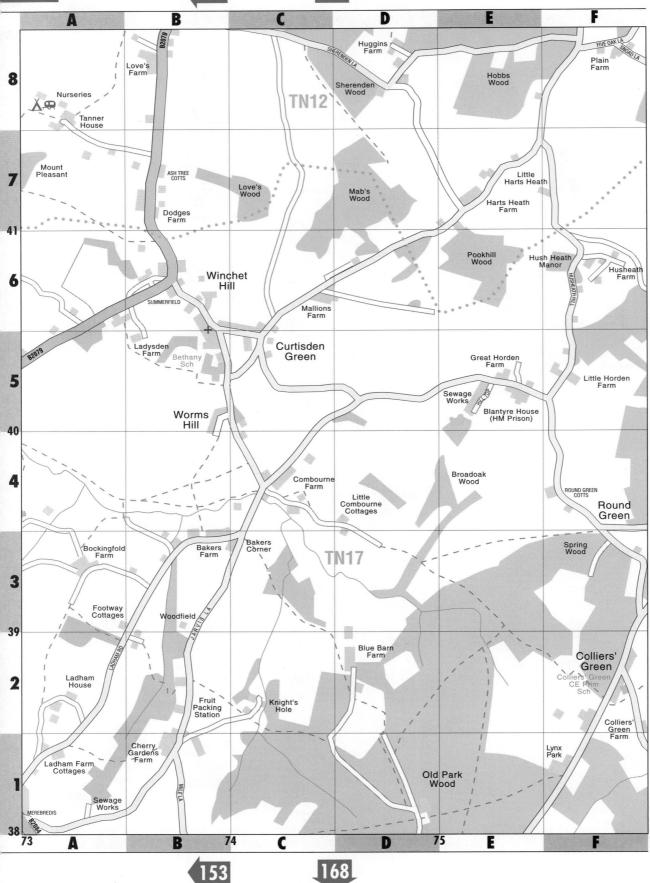

153
138
153
168

TN12

TN17

Huggins Farm

Sherenden Wood

Hobbs Wood

Plain Farm

FIVE OAK LA

SNOAD LA

SHERENDEN LA

Nurseries

Love's Farm

B2079

Tanner House

Mount Pleasant

ASH TREE COTTS

Love's Wood

Mab's Wood

Little Harts Heath

Harts Heath Farm

Dodges Farm

Winchet Hill

Pookhill Wood

Hush Heath Manor

Husheath Farm

SUMMERFIELD

Mallions Farm

HUSHEATH HILL

B2079

Ladysden Farm

Bethany Sch

Curtisden Green

Great Horden Farm

Little Horden Farm

Worms Hill

Sewage Works

Blantyre House (HM Prison)

HILL TOP

Combourne Farm

Broadoak Wood

Round Green Cotts

Round Green

Little Combourne Cottages

Bockingfold Farm

Bakers Farm

Bakers Corner

Spring Wood

Footway Cottages

Woodfield

JARVIS LA

Blue Barn Farm

Colliers' Green

Colliers' Green CE Prim Sch

Ladham House

LADHAM RD

Fruit Packing Station

Knight's Hole

Colliers' Green Farm

Cherry Gardens Farm

Lynx Park

Old Park Wood

Ladham Farm Cottages

MILE LA

Sewage Works

MEREBREDIS

B2084

155
140

A **B** **C** **D** **E** **F**

8

Iden Manor Farm

TN12

Maplehurst Wood

Cherry Tree Farm

MILL LA

Gould Farm

7

Cemy

CHARITY FARM COTTS

VALENCE VIEW

Bell & Jorrocks (PH)

Frittenden

Frittenden House

THE STREET

BAKERY CL

THE LIMES

41

Knoxbridge Farm

Little Wadd Farm

Frittenden CE Prim Sch

BRICKWELL COTTS

Hill Farm

Parsonage Farm

CHESTNUT CL

6

Great Wadd Farm

WEALD VIEW

Street Farm Oast

Tanyard

Catherine Wheel

5

Rock Farm

WALLER HILL

Leggs Wood

TN17

Beale Farm

GRANDSHORE LA

40

Eleven Acre Wood

GRANDSHORE LA

Keepers Lodge

Grayland Wood

Brissenden Farm

SAND LA

Waller Hill Farmhouse

Whitsunden

4

Vincent Wood

BOURNER COTTS

Lowland Farm

Home Wood

Foxearth Wood

Hammer Stream

3

A229

CRANBROOK RD

ROCKS HILL

Park Farm

DIGDOG LA

Works

Bettenham Manor

Mayhouse Farm

Comenden Manor

39

LONDON LA

TN27

2

A229

Cranbrook Common

Saw Lodge Wood

Satins Hill Farmhouse

Sissinghurst Castle Farm

SPONGS LA

Horse Race House

Sissinghurst Castle

Sissinghurst Castle Gardens

SISSINGHURST RD A262

1

The Manor House

38

79 **A** **B** 80 **C** **D** 81 **E** **F**

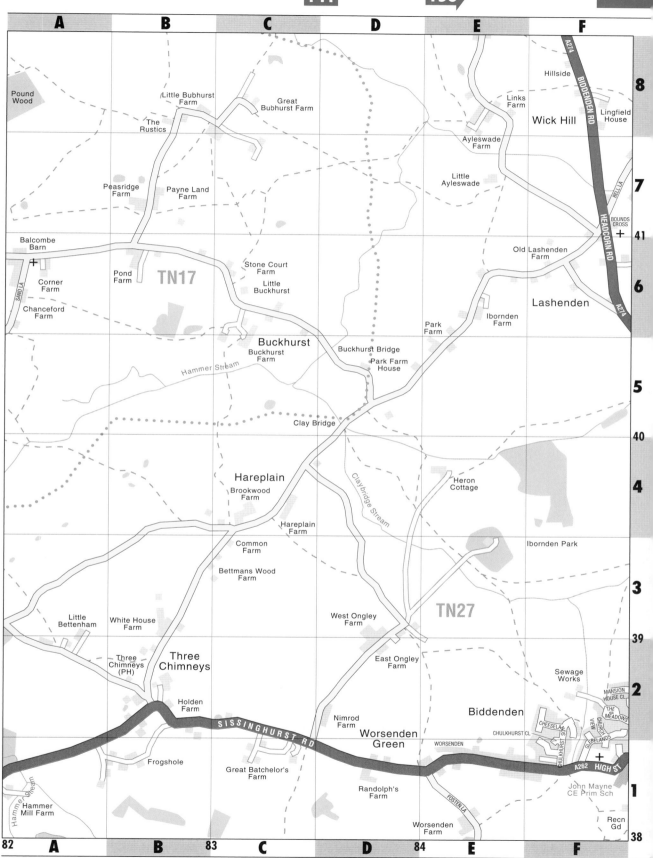

Pound Wood

Little Bubhurst Farm

Great Bubhurst Farm

Hillside

Links Farm

Wick Hill

Lingfield House

A274

BIDDENDEN RD

The Rustics

Ayleswade Farm

Peasridge Farm

Payne Land Farm

Little Ayleswade

BELL LA

HEADCORN RD

Balcombe Barn

Corner Farm

Pond Farm

TN17

Stone Court Farm

Little Buckhurst

Old Lashenden Farm

Bounds Cross

41

Chanceford Farm

SAND LA

Park Farm

Ibornden Farm

Lashenden

A274

6

Buckhurst

Buckhurst Farm

Buckhurst Bridge

Park Farm House

Hammer Stream

Clay Bridge

5

40

Hareplain

Brookwood Farm

Claybridge Stream

Heron Cottage

4

Hareplain Farm

Common Farm

Ibornden Park

Bettmans Wood Farm

TN27

3

Little Bettenham

White House Farm

West Ongley Farm

Sewage Works

39

Three Chimneys (PH)

Three Chimneys

East Ongley Farm

Biddenden

MANSION HOUSE CL.

THE MEADOWS

2

Holden Farm

Nimrod Farm

CHULKHURST CL

CHEESELANDS

CHURCH GLEBELANDS

CHULKHURST LA

VIEW

SISSINGHURST RD

Worsenden Green

WORSENDEN

A262   HIGH ST

Frogshole

Great Batchelor's Farm

Randolph's Farm

FOSTEN LA

John Mayne CE Prim Sch

1

Hammer Mill Farm

Hammer Stream

Worsenden Farm

Recn Gd

38

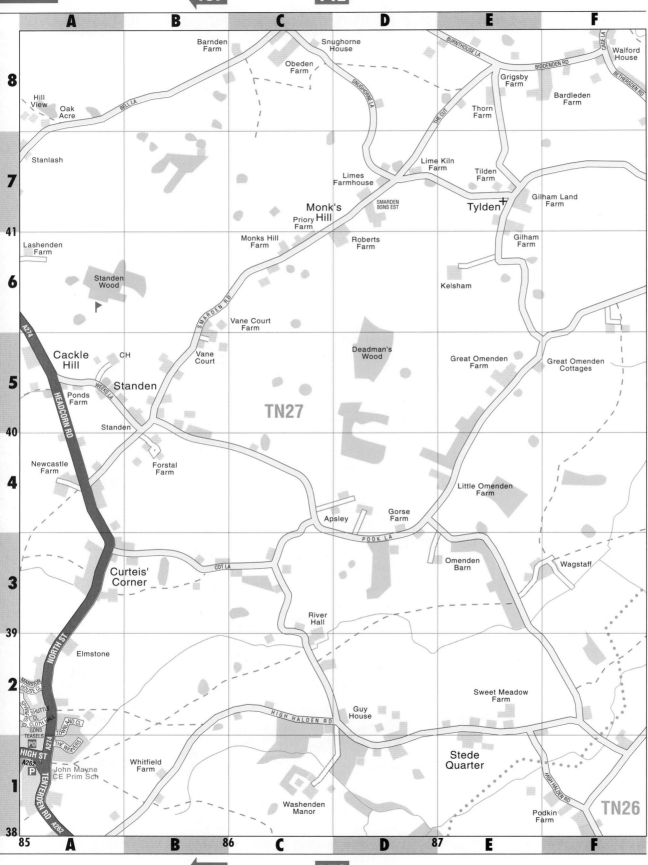

TN27

TN26

Barnden Farm
Snughorne House
Obeden Farm
Burnthouse La
Biddenden Rd
Cage La
Walford House
Bethersden Rd

Hill View
Oak Acre
Bell La
Grigsby Farm
Thorn Farm
Bardleden Farm

Stanlash
Snughorne La
The Cut
Lime Kiln Farm
Tilden Farm
Gilham Land Farm

Limes Farmhouse
Smarden Bsns Est
Tylden

Monk's Hill
Priory Farm
Gilham Farm

Lashenden Farm
Monks Hill Farm
Roberts Farm

Standen Wood
Kelsham

Smarden Rd
Vane Court Farm
Deadman's Wood
Great Omenden Farm
Great Omenden Cottages

A274
Cackle Hill
CH
Weeks La
Vane Court
Standen

Ponds Farm
Standen
Newcastle Farm
Forstal Farm

Headcorn Rd
Little Omenden Farm

Apsley
Gorse Farm
Pook La
Omenden Barn
Wagstaff

Curteis' Corner
Cot La
River Hall

North St
Elmstone

Mansion House Cl
Shuttle
Sevings Rd
Cloth Hall
Gdns
Teasels
Land Cl
The Weavers
PO
High St
A262
A274
P
John Mayne CE Prim Sch
Tenterden Rd
A262
Whitfield Farm

High Halden Rd
Guy House
Sweet Meadow Farm

Stede Quarter

Washenden Manor
Podkin Farm
High Halden Rd

143

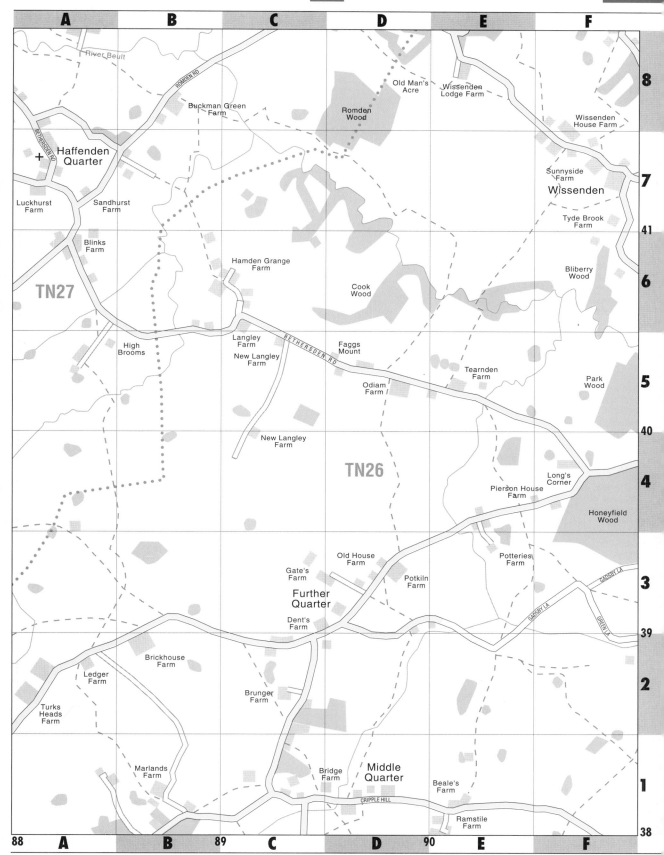

173

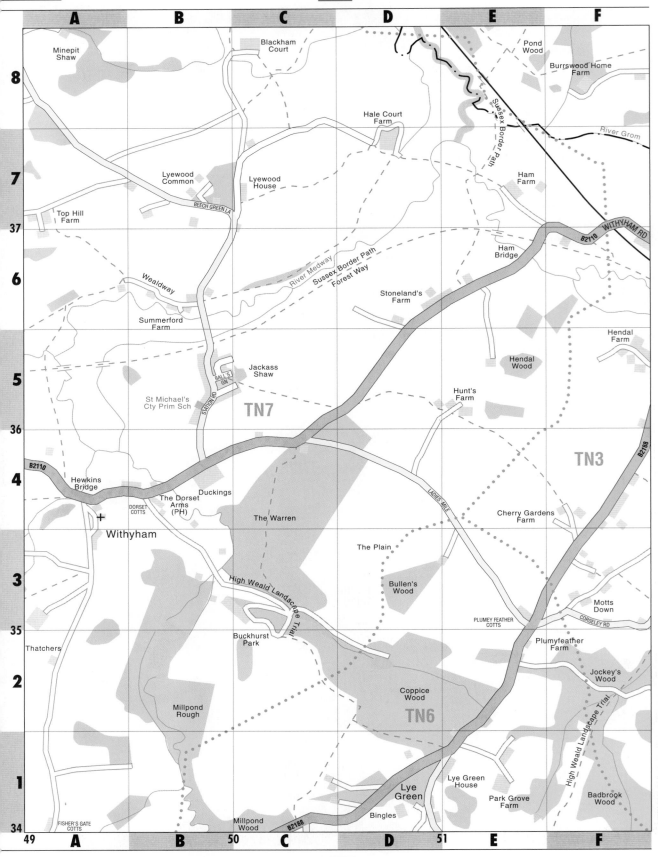

A **B** **C** **D** **E** **F**

Minepit Shaw

Blackham Court

8

Hale Court Farm

Pond Wood

Burrswood Home Farm

River Grom

7

Lyewood Common

Lyewood House

Ham Farm

Sussex Border Path

WITHYHAM RD

B2110

37

Top Hill Farm

BEECH GREEN LA

Ham Bridge

6

Wealdway

River Medway

Sussex Border Path

Forest Way

Stoneland's Farm

Hendal Farm

Summerford Farm

Hendal Wood

5

BALL'S GN

Jackass Shaw

STATION RD

Hunt's Farm

St Michael's Cty Prim Sch

TN7

36

TN3

B2110

4

Hewkins Bridge

The Dorset Arms (PH)

Duckings

The Warren

LADIES' MILE

Cherry Gardens Farm

B2188

DORSET COTTS

Withyham

The Plain

Motts Down

3

High Weald Landscape Trial

Bullen's Wood

PLUMEY FEATHER COTTS

CORSELEY RD

35

Buckhurst Park

Plumyfeather Farm

Thatchers

Jockey's Wood

2

Millpond Rough

Coppice Wood

TN6

High Weald Landscape Trial

1

Lye Green

Lye Green House

Park Grove Farm

Badbrook Wood

34

FISHER'S GATE COTTS

Millpond Wood

B2188

Bingles

49 **A** **B** **50** **C** **D** **51** **E** **F**

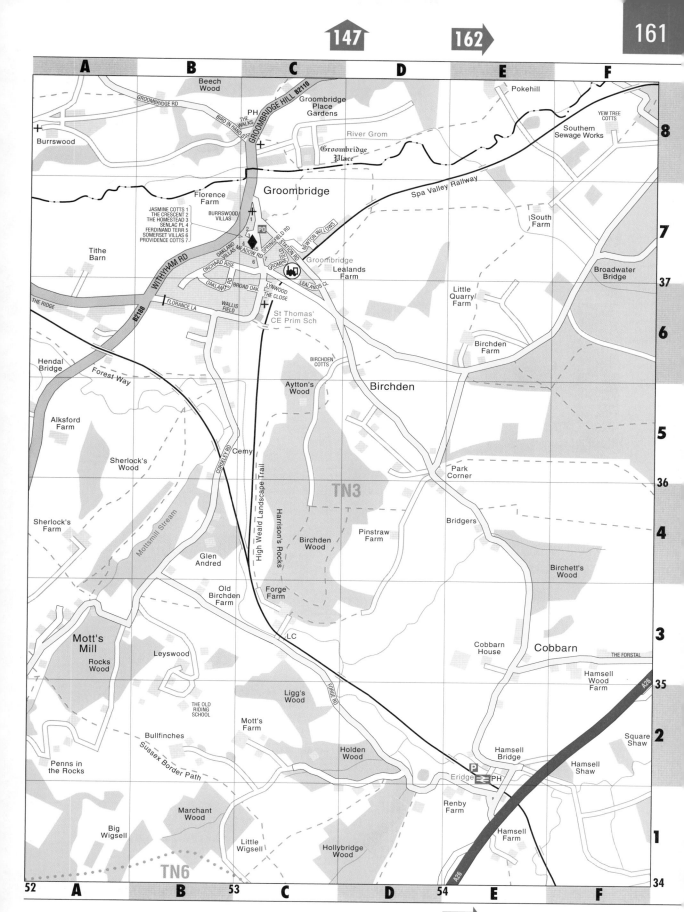

161
148

A B C D E F

Spa Valley Rly

Ramslye
Wood

TN4

RAMSLYE RD

Ramslye
Farm

EASTLANDS CL

ERIDGE RD

SCOTTS WAY

SIDNEY CL

SHOWFIELDS RD

STUART CL

FURNIVAL CT

BROADCROFT

Sch

8

Ramslye
Cotts

Strawberry
Hill

LINDEN DR

BROADMEAD

SURREY

GLENMORE PK

ST GEORGE'S PK

Ruffet
Wood

KENTISH GDNS

BROADWATER
CT

BROADWATER DOWN

ESSEX CL

1 LEICESTER DR
2 DEVONSHIRE CL
3 BROADMEAD AVE

The
Firs

STRAWBERRY CL

HARGATE CL

Broadwater
Forest

Broadwater
Down

TN2

BARNFIELD CT

ST MARK'S RD

WARESCROFT

7

Spratsbrook
Farm

Strawberry Hill
Farm

37

Broadwater
Lodge

Sprat's Brook

6

Firtree
Plantation

Hargate
Forest

The
Warren

The
Roundabouts

BUNNY LA

Bohemia

5

Eridge
Rocks

TN3

Whitehill
Wood

36

Warren
Farm

The Nevill
Crest & Gun
(PH)

Eridge
Park

Eridge
Park

4

WARREN FARM LA

Eridge
Green

3

Crown
House

Mill
Wood

A26

Steel
Bridge

Keepers
Cottages

35

High Weald Landscape Trail

2

Steel Bridge
Farm

Forge
Wood

Eridge
Old Park

Bushy
Wood

1

Bushy
Shaw

Great Robbins
Shaw

34

161

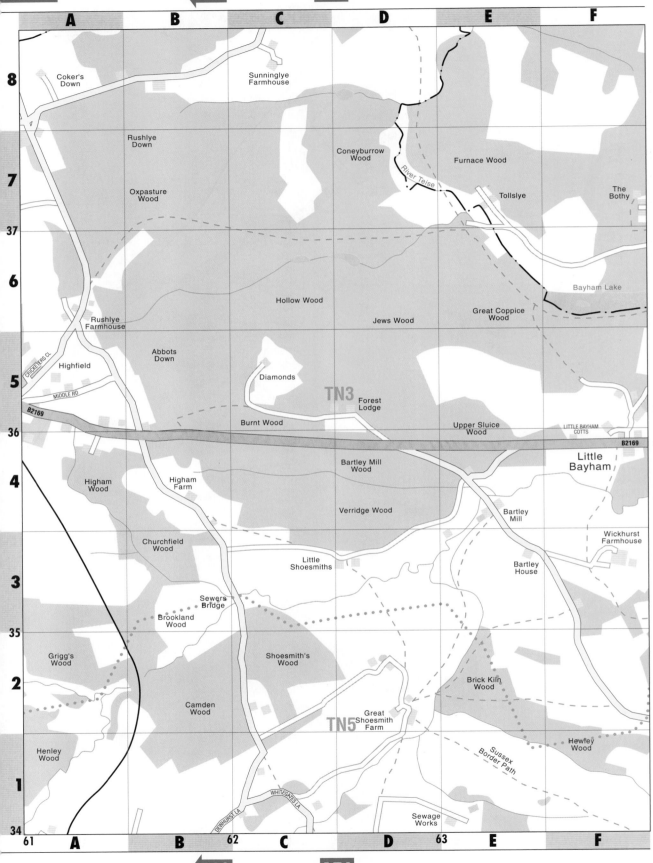

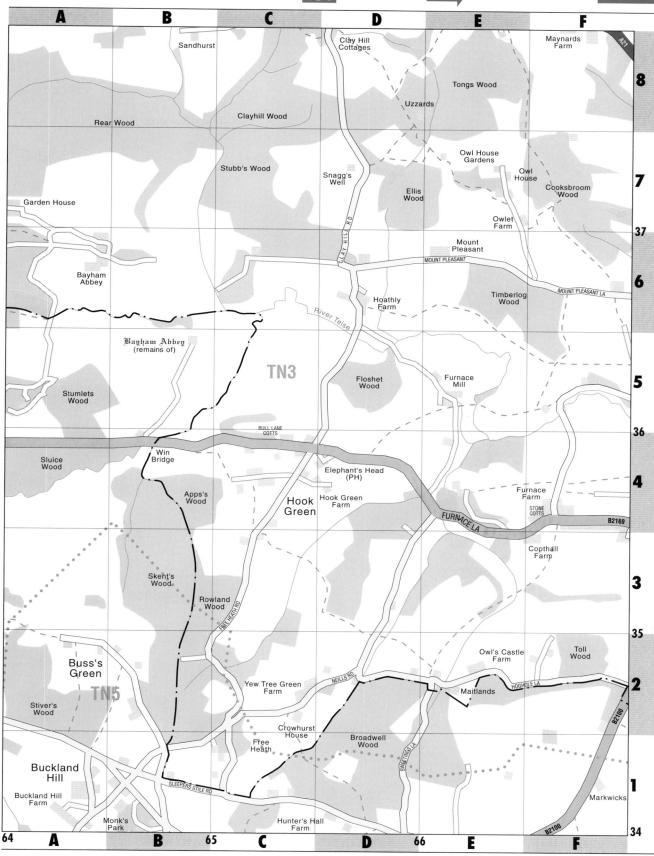

A B C D E F

Sandhurst

Clay Hill Cottages

Maynards Farm

Tongs Wood

Uzzards

Clayhill Wood

Rear Wood

Stubb's Wood

Snagg's Well

Owl House Gardens

Owl House

Cooksbroom Wood

Ellis Wood

Owlet Farm

Garden House

Mount Pleasant

MOUNT PLEASANT

MOUNT PLEASANT LA

Bayham Abbey

Hoathly Farm

Timberlog Wood

CLAY HILL RD

River Teise

Bayham Abbey (remains of)

TN3

Floshet Wood

Furnace Mill

Stumlets Wood

BULL LANE COTTS

Sluice Wood

Win Bridge

Elephant's Head (PH)

Furnace Farm

FURNACE LA

STONE COTTS

B2169

Apps's Wood

Hook Green Farm

Hook Green

Copthall Farm

Skent's Wood

Rowland Wood

FREE HEATH RD

Buss's Green

TN5

Yew Tree Green Farm

NEILLS RD

Owl's Castle Farm

Toll Wood

Stiver's Wood

Maitlands

HOGHOLE LA

Crowhurst House

Broadwell Wood

B2100

Buckland Hill

Free Heath

SNETTINGS LA

Buckland Hill Farm

SLEEPERS STILE RD

Markwicks

Monk's Park

Hunter's Hall Farm

B2100

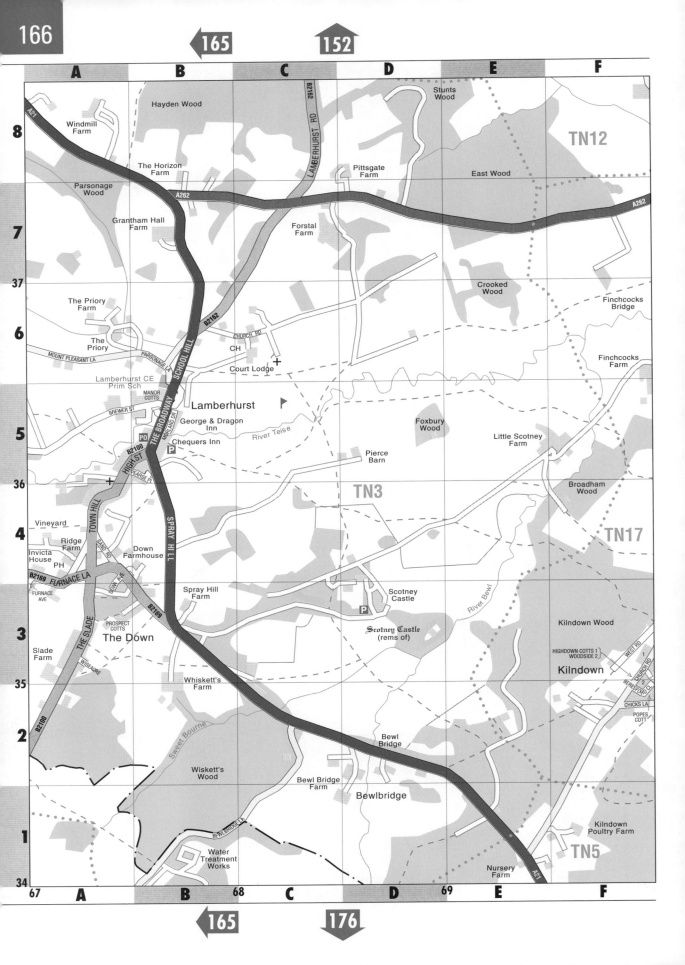

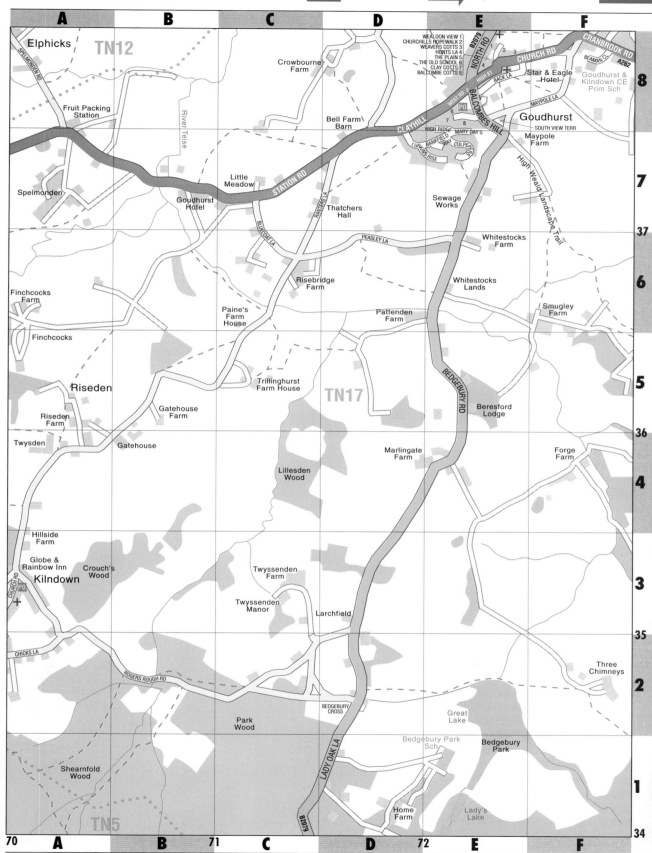

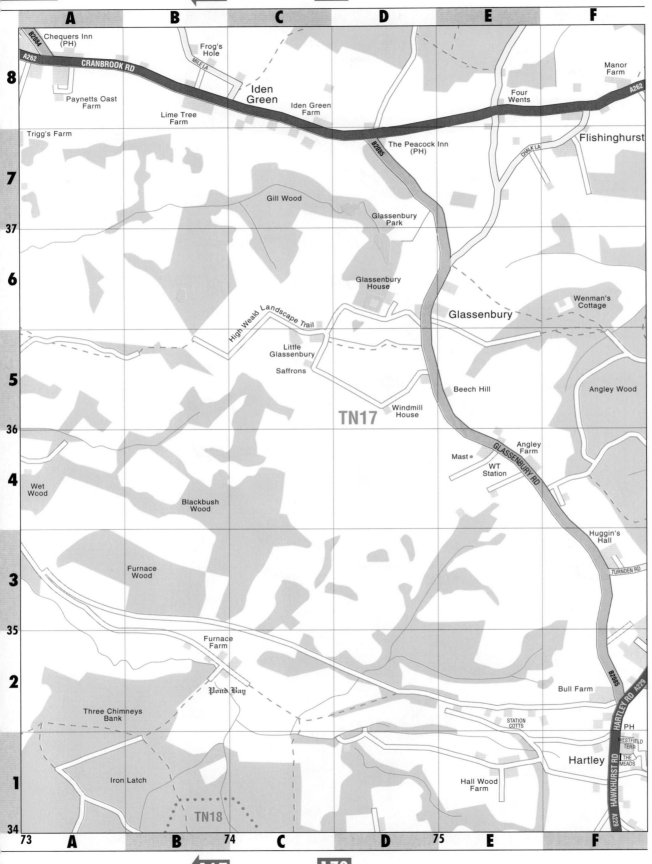

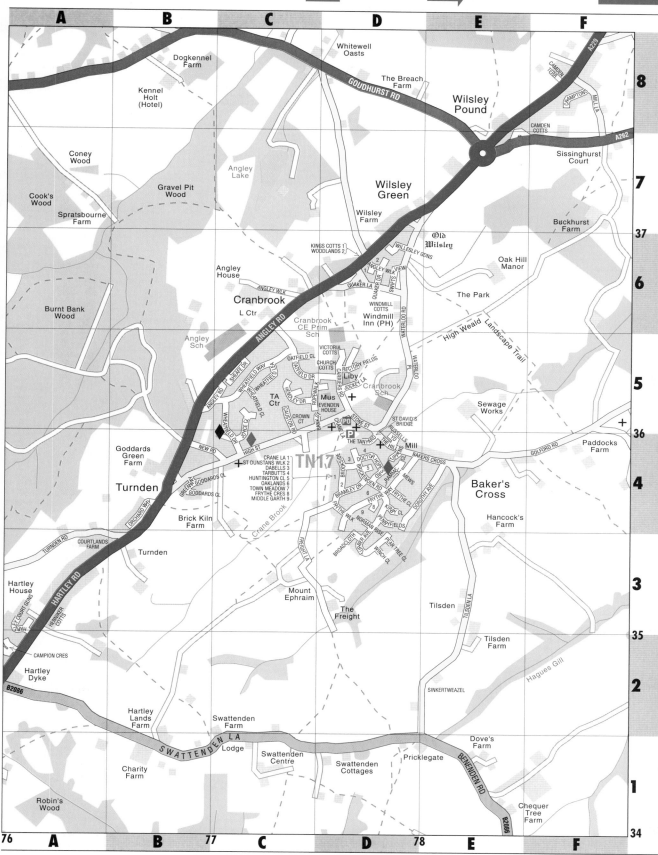

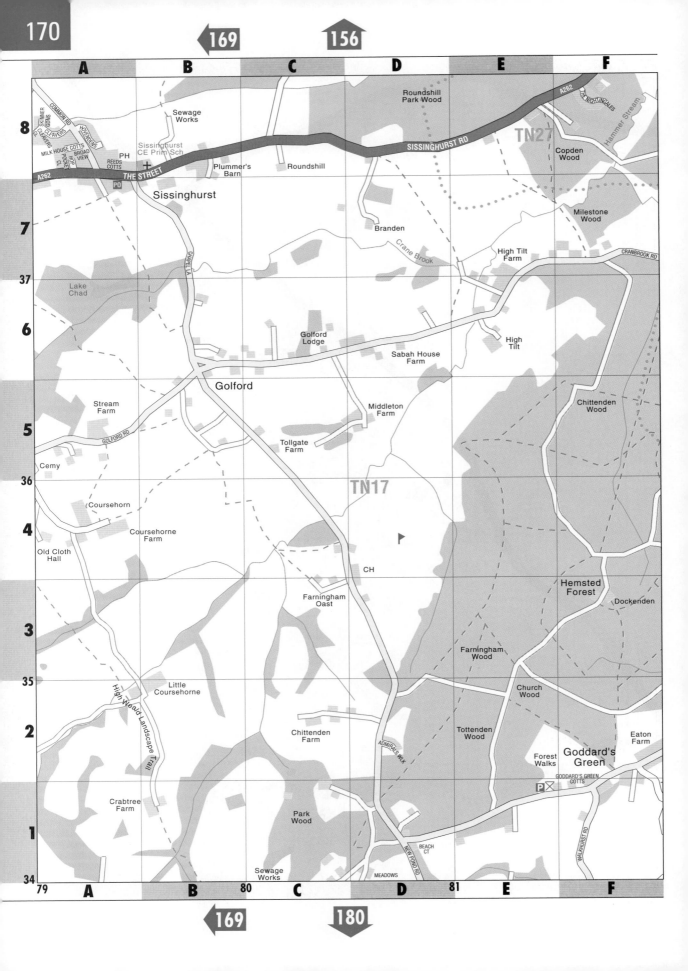

8

Hammer
Wood

Castweazel
Farm

Goose Green

7

Roger's
Wood

Castweazel
Manor

Low
Poles

Foster La

Birchley
House

Kennels

37

Forest
Walks

Medhurst

Rogley
Wood

Rogley Hill

TN27

6

Cranbrook Rd

Elmstone
Farm

Park
Farm

Bargate
Farm

Fosten Green
Nurseries

Birch
Wood

Clapper
Hill

Fosten
Green

Causton
Wood

Rogley
Farm

Birchwood
Farm House

Benenden Rd

Gribble Bridge La

Little
Whatmans

5

Pedlars
Farm

Summer
Hill

Castleton's Oak
(PH)

36

Mockbeggar La

Little
Mockbeggar

Halden
Wood

The
Brogues

Tenterden Rd

4

Trump
Farm

Brogues
Wood

Timber
Wood

East End

Wood La

P

Jackson Way

P

Bishopsden
Farm

3

+

H

Benenden

Frogs Hole La

Cleveland
Farm

35

TN17

Green La

Bexhill
Farm

Bishopsdale
Farm

Uppergate
Wood

2

Redhouse
Farm

Pympne Manor
Farm

Backtilt
Wood

Halden La

1

Tinker
Wood

Pump
Wood

Sterneyford La

Beston
Farm

34

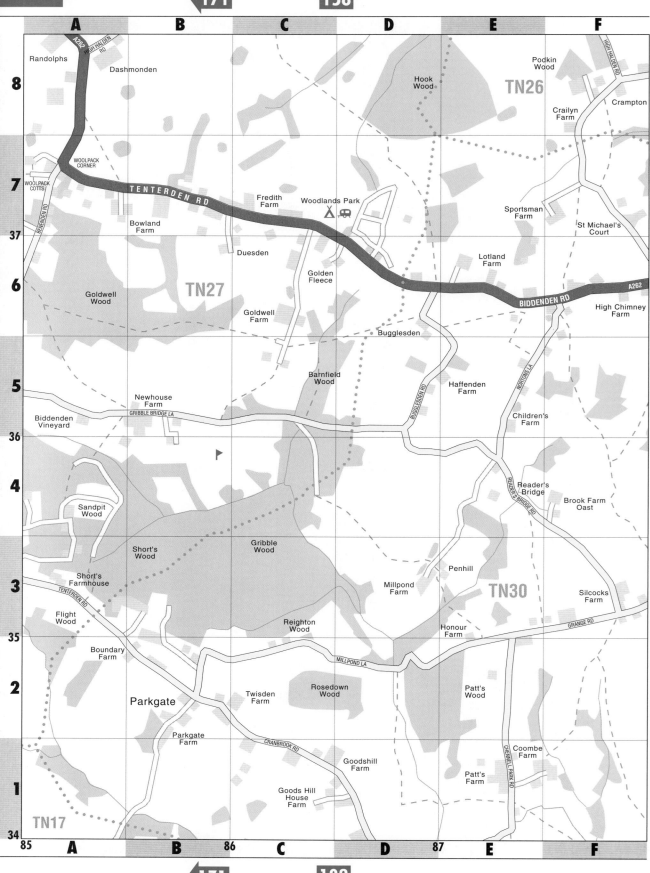

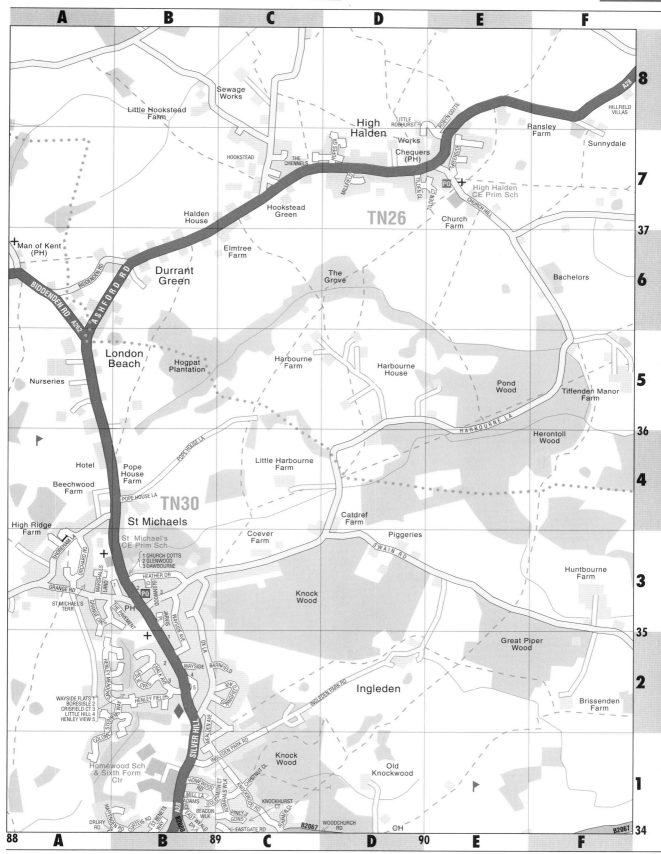

164

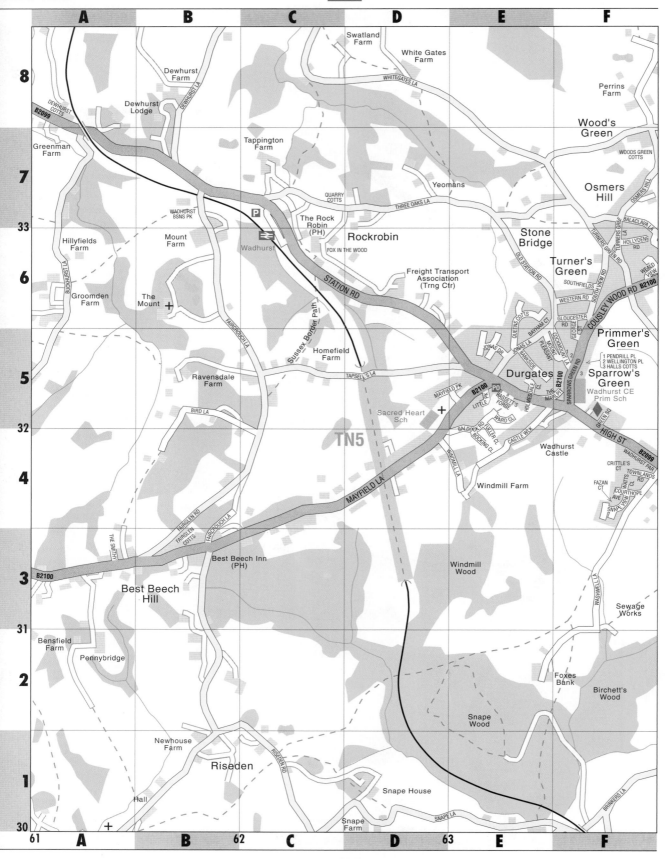

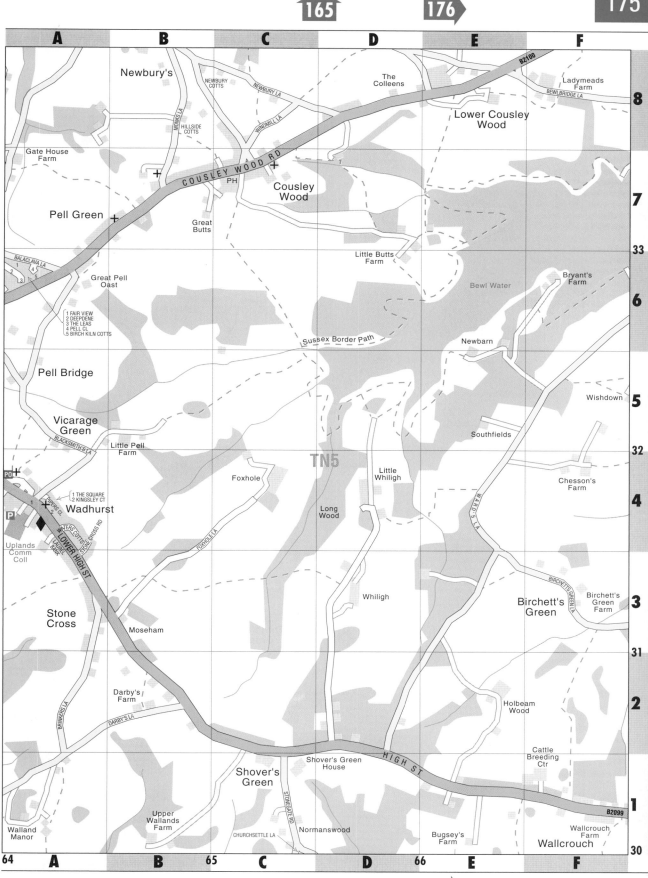

B2100

8

Newbury's

Newbury
Cotts

Newbury La

The
Colleens

Ladymeads
Farm

Bewlbridge La

Monks La

Hillside
Cotts

Windmill La

Lower Cousley
Wood

Gate House
Farm

COUSLEY WOOD RD

PH

Cousley
Wood

7

Pell Green

Great
Butts

Little Butts
Farm

33

Bryant's
Farm

Balaclava La

1
4
5
2
3

Great Pell
Oast

Bewl Water

6

1 FAIR VIEW
2 DEEPDENE
3 THE LEAS
4 PELL CL.
5 BIRCH KILN COTTS

Sussex Border Path

Newbarn

Pell Bridge

5

Wishdown

Vicarage
Green

BLACKSMITH'S LA

Little Pell
Farm

Southfields

32

TN5

Foxhole

Little
Whiligh

Chesson's
Farm

PO

WARD'S LA

1 THE SQUARE
2 KINGSLEY CT

Wadhurst

Long
Wood

4

WATER'S COTTS

STONE CROSS RD

FOXHOLE LA

P

CHURCH BANK

LOWER HIGH ST

Uplands
Comm
Coll

Whiligh

Birchett's
Green

BIRCHETTS GREEN LA

Birchett's
Green
Farm

3

Stone
Cross

Moseham

31

Darby's
Farm

Holbeam
Wood

2

BRINKERS LA

DARBY'S LA

STONEGATE RD

HIGH ST

Cattle
Breeding
Ctr

Shover's Green
House

Shover's
Green

1

Upper
Wallands
Farm

CHURCHSETTLE LA

Normanswood

Bugsey's
Farm

B2099

Wallcrouch
Farm

Wallcrouch

Walland
Manor

30

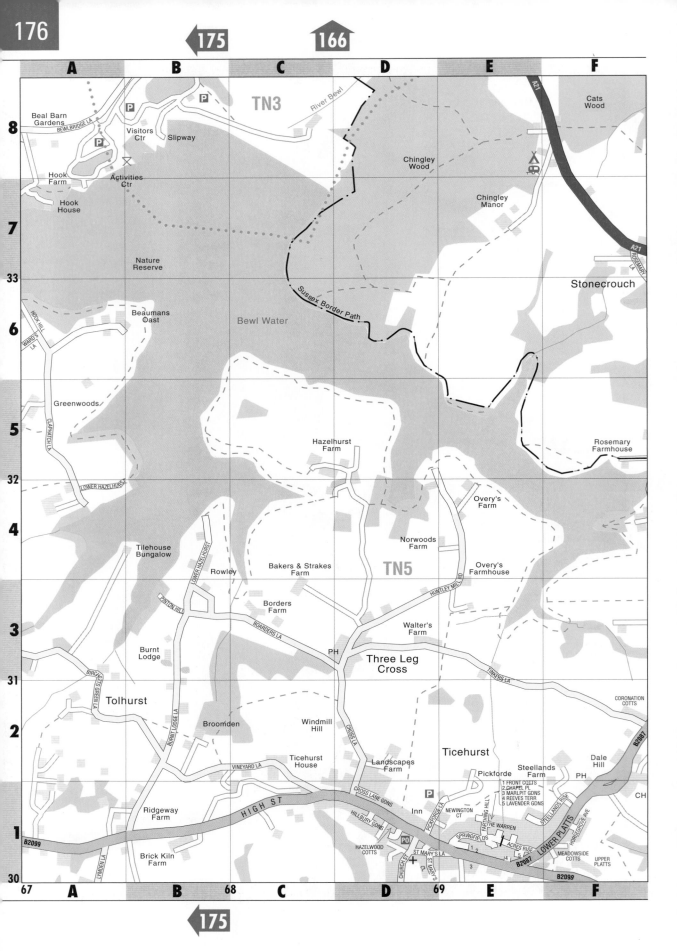

A   B   C   D   E   F

8

Beal Barn
Gardens
BEWLBRIDGE LA
Visitors
Ctr
Slipway
Hook
Farm
Hook
House
Activities
Ctr

TN3

River Bewl

Chingley Wood

Chingley
Manor

Cats
Wood

Stonecrouch

7

Nature
Reserve

Sussex Border Path

33

6

Beaumans
Oast
Bewl Water
Greenwoods

HOOK HILL LA
WARD'S LA
CLAPHATCH LA

Rosemary
Farmhouse

5

Hazelhurst
Farm

32

LOWER HAZELHURST

Overy's
Farm

4

Tilehouse
Bungalow
Rowley
Bakers & Strakes
Farm
LOWER HAZELHURST

Norwoods
Farm

Overy's
Farmhouse

TN5

HUNTLEY MILL RD

3

PINTON HILL
Borders
Farm
BOARDERS LA
Burnt
Lodge
PH

Walter's
Farm

Three Leg
Cross

TINKERS LA

31

Tolhurst

BIRCHETTS GREEN LA
BURNT LODGE LA

Broomden
Windmill
Hill

CROSS LA

Ticehurst

Pickforde
Steellands
Farm
PH
Dale
Hill

CORONATION
COTTS

B2087

2

Ridgeway
Farm
VINEYARD LA
Ticehurst
House
HIGH ST

CROSS LANE GDNS
Landscapes
Farm
HILLBURY GDNS
Inn
P
PICKFORDE LA
Newington
CT
FARTHING HILL
1 FRONT COTTS
2 CHAPEL PL
3 MARLPIT GDNS
4 REEVES TERR
5 LAVENDER GDNS
THE WARREN
SPRINGFIELDS
ACRES RISE
1 2
5
STEELLANDS RISE
LOWER PLATTS
HORSEGROVE AVE
CH

1

LYMDEN LA
Brick Kiln
Farm
B2099
PO
HAZELWOOD
COTTS
CHURCH ST
ST MARY'S LA
ST MARY'S
CL
4
3
B2087
MEADOWSIDE
COTTS
UPPER
PLATTS
B2099

30

67   A   B   68   C   D   69   E   F

A21

167
178

A **B** **C** **D** **E** **F**

8

Combwell
Wood

Bedgebury
National Pinetum

Park
House

Springwood
Lodge

Bedgebury
Park Woods

TN17

7

Combwell Priory
Farm

33

Stonecrouch
Farm House

Starvegoose
Bank

6

Windmill Down

Flimwell
Grange

Windy
Ridge

Mast

Radio
Station

5

TN5

32

TN18

Ketley
Farm

Sussex Border Path

FLIMWELL
CLI

4

LONDON RD

Downash Ho 1
Downash Ct 2

OLD WARDS DOWN

BEWL BRIDGE CL

FRUITFIELDS

RED OAST
COTTS

BLENHEIM
WAY

PO

PH

3

Union
Street

UNION
ST

Flimwell

HIGH ST
B2087

A268

PH

SUNNYBANK

Mount Pleasant
Farm

GINGERBREAD LA

31

Berner's
Hill

HAWKHURST RD

Flimwell
Bird Park

A268

2

Quedley

West
Lodge

Ringden
Wood

Seacox
Heath

Saw Mill

Keeper's
Cottage

1

TN19

Ringden
Farm

Sewage Works

A21

30

70 **A** 71 **B** **C** 72 **D** **E** **F**

ROSEMARY LA

LADY OAK LA

B2079

B2079

177
168

A   B   C   D   E   F

8 Brick Kiln Cottages

Sugarloaf Hill

WHITELIMES

TN17

Hedgingford Wood

Louisa Lodge

Foresters Cottage

TN17

Badger's Oak

Tubslake

Frith Wood

PARK LA

Osborne's

HAWKHURST RD

7

33

Louisa Lake

Rose's Farm

6 Frith Farm

Trenley Farm

Yewtree Farm

POTTER'S LA

Tanyard Farm

LIMES GR

Limes Grove Farm

STATION COTTS

5 Gill's Green

32

Siseley Farm

Gill's Green Farm

TN18

WELLING... COTTS

4 SOPER'S LA

Trewint Farm

Wellington Arms (PH)

SLIP MILL RD

CRANBROOK RD

HEARTENOAK RD

Soper's Lane Farm

3 Slip Mill

SYDNEY TERR 1
CASTLE TERR 2
SANDROOK VILLAS 3

Little Pix Hall Farm

Lightfoot GN

SPRINGFIELD IND EST

31 Elm Hill Farm

Lightfoot Green

...VALE RD

A229

2 A268

Hawkhurst Cottage

High Street

SLIP MILL LA

CH

PHILPOTT'S CROSS

Sch

OAKFIELD

HIGH ST

A268

Elm Hill House

IDDENDEN COTTS

Marlborough House Sch

WESTERN AVE

THORNCLOS

FAIRVIEW

Seacox Poultry Farm

F2
1 EDEN CT
2 DAINTONS COTTS
3 OAK TERR
4 NORMAN VILLAS
5 ARMITAGE PL
6 SCHOOL TERR
7 WESTERN AVE
8 HIGHGATE CT
9 NORTHGROVE RD
10 CRANE HOUSE GDNS
11 CRANE HOUSE
12 POST OFFICE RD

1 Delmonden Manor

DELMONDEN RD

NORTH HILL RD

LORENDEN PK

HIGHGATE HILL

A229

TN19

Sussex Border Path

Hurstwood Cottage

Hensill House

Cockshot

30

73   A   B   74   C   D   75   E   F

177
184

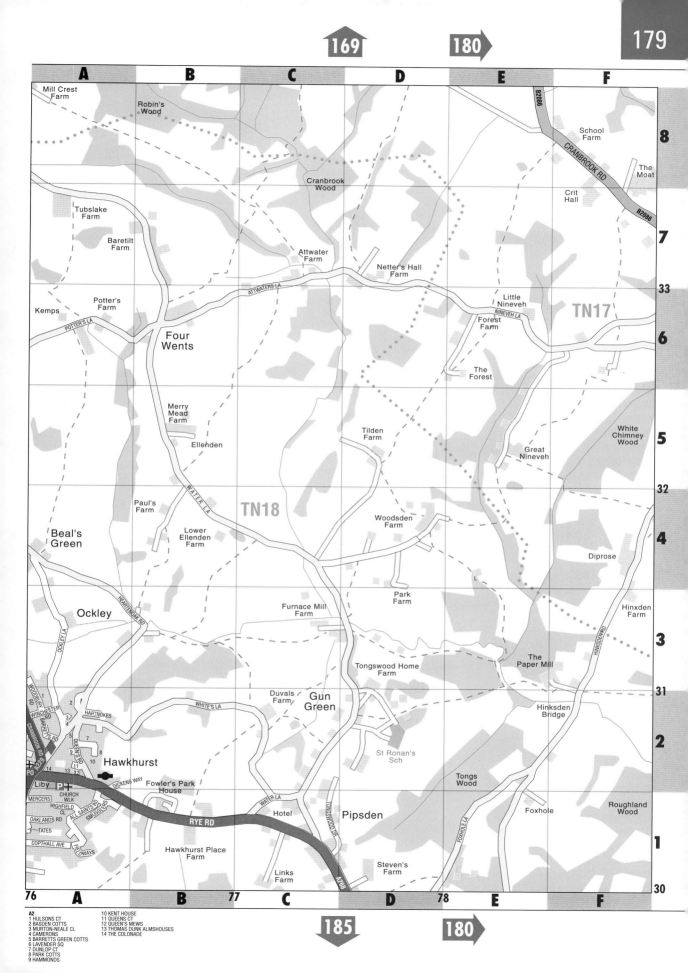

A B C D E F

8
7
33
6
5
32
4
3
31
2
1
30

Mill Crest Farm
Robin's Wood
School Farm
The Moat
Crit Hall
B2086
CRANBROOK RD
B2086

Cranbrook Wood

Tubslake Farm
Baretilt Farm
Attwater Farm
Netter's Hall Farm
Little Nineveh
NINEVEH LA
TN17
Kemps
Potter's Farm
ATTWATERS LA
Forest Farm
POTTER'S LA
Four Wents
The Forest

Merry Mead Farm
Ellenden
Tilden Farm
Great Nineveh
White Chimney Wood

WATER LA

Paul's Farm
TN18
Lower Ellenden Farm
Woodsden Farm
Diprose

Beal's Green
Hinxden Farm
HINKSDEN RD

Ockley
Park Farm
The Paper Mill
HEARTENOAK RD
OCKLEY LA
Furnace Mill Farm
Tongswood Home Farm
Hinksden Bridge

WOODBURY RD
WINCHESTER
BARRETTS RD
HARTNOKES
WHITE'S LA
Duvals Farm
Gun Green
St Ronan's Sch
Tongs Wood

QUEEN'S RD
CRANBROOK RD A229
Hawkhurst
Foxhole
Roughland Wood
Liby P
CHURCH WLK
DICKENS WAY
Fowler's Park House
WATER LA
Hotel
Pipsden
FOXHOLE LA
MERCERS
HIGHFIELD CL
ALL SAINTS RD
SMUGGLERS
RYE RD
TONGSWOOD DR
OAKLANDS RD
TATES
COPTHALL AVE
FIELDWAYS
Hawkhurst Place Farm
Links Farm
A268
Steven's Farm

A B C D E F

8

New House

Coggers

Benenden Sch

Walkhurst Farm

Sewage Works

Apple Pie Farm

Mount's Farm House

New Pond

WALKHURST RD

WALKHURST COTTS

7

CRANBROOK RD

B2086

MOUNTS HILL

33

NINEVEH LA

BABBS LA

HORTONS CL

PO

1 CHERRYFIELDS
2 BARRACK ROW

THE STREET

KINGSFORD COTTS

ROTHERMERE CL

1 CHURCHILL HOUSE
2 KENNEDY HOUSE

LEYDOUANE DELL

6

Babbes Farm

NINEVEH LA

High Weald Landscape Trail

NEW POND RD

The Green

2
1 FUGGLES CT

PH

ORCHARD CT

PULLINGTON COTTS

Collingwood Grange

Benenden CE Prim Sch

Benenden

BENENDEN RD

B2086

Scullsgate House

Pullington Farm

5

HUXSDEN RD

Iden Green Farm

Stream Farm

OLD WEAVERS COTTS

Ramsden Farm

32

COLDHARBOUR RD

TN17

Frame Farm

RAMSDEN LA

Sarnden

CLAREMONT PL

CHAPEL LA

Royal Oak (PH)

4

Yewtree Farm

OAKFIELD COTTS

Sewage Works

Broom Hill

Iden Green

Moor Wood

Nurseries

Reed Wood

VYYYAW COTTS

MEDWAY COTTS

WOODCOCK LA

Standen Wood

Dingleden

3

MILL ST

Depot

The Woodcock (PH)

DINGLEDEN LA

31

Eaglesden

STANDEN ST

Trafford Farm

2

Campion House

Cattsford

Mount Wood

Wandle Mill

Old Standen

SPONDEN LA

Standen Street

Springhill Farm

TN18

1

Bankside Farm

HOPEHOUSE LA

SANDHURST LA

30

79 A B 80 C D 81 E F

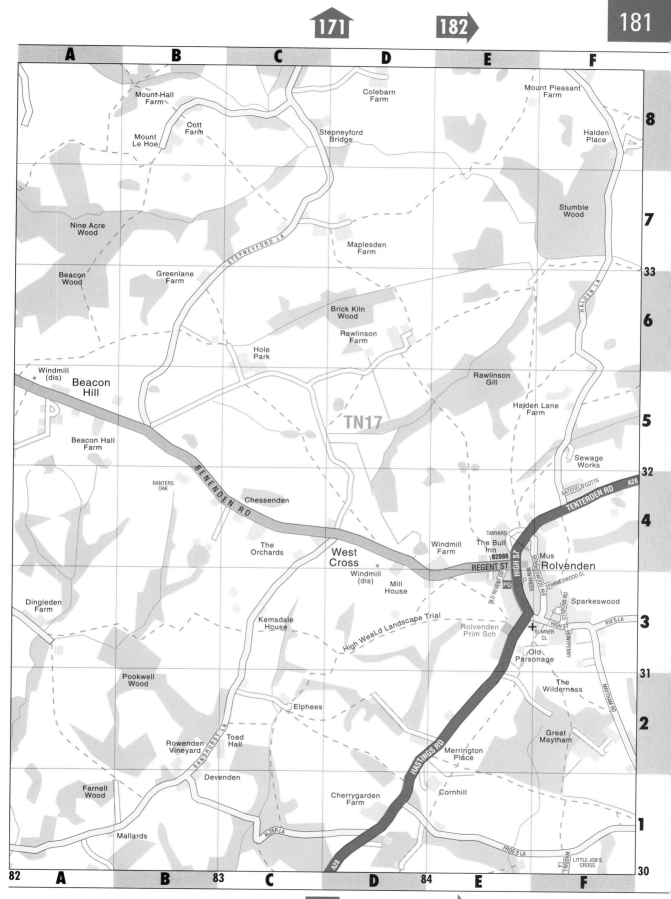

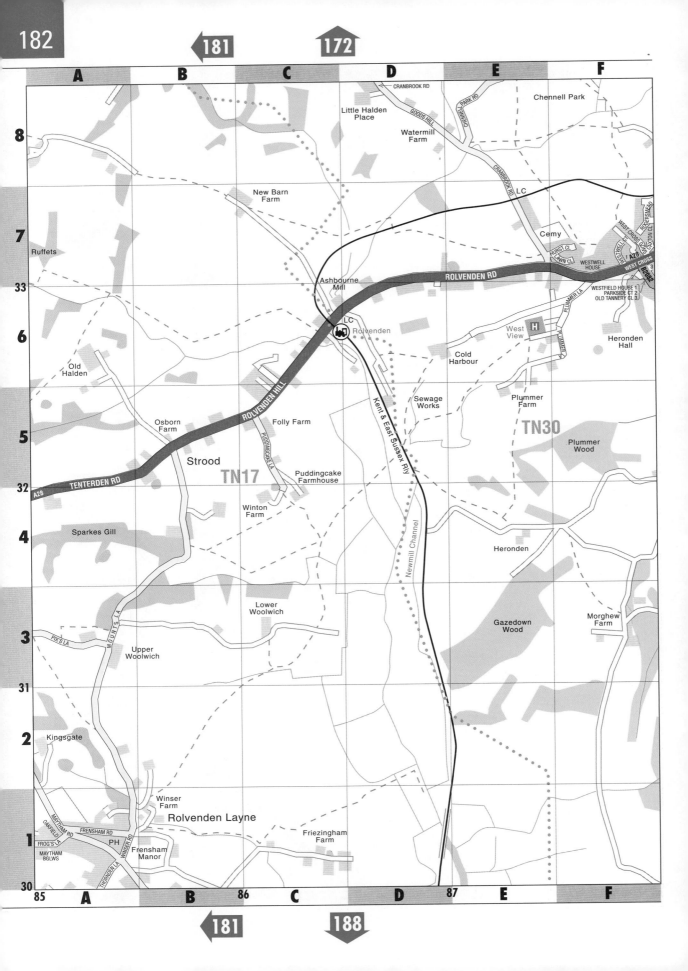

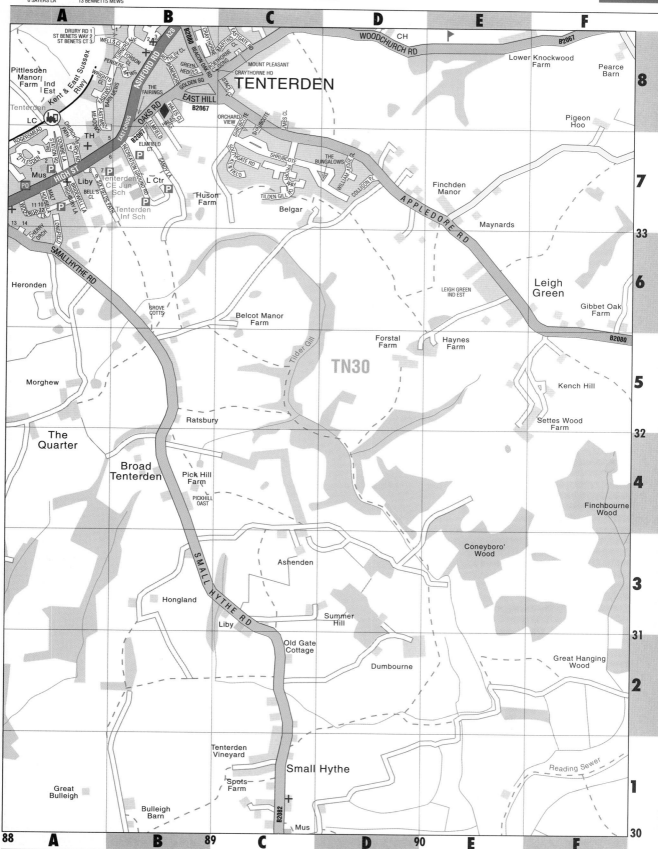

A7
1 PITTLESDEN PL
2 PARK VIEW TERR
3 STATION MEWS
4 ST MILDREDS CL
5 EASTWELL
6 SAYERS LA

7 THEATRE SQ
8 JACKSONS LA
9 BELLS LA
10 BURGESS ROW
11 MAYOR'S PL
12 CEDAR CT
13 BENNETTS MEWS

14 AUSTENS ORCH

178

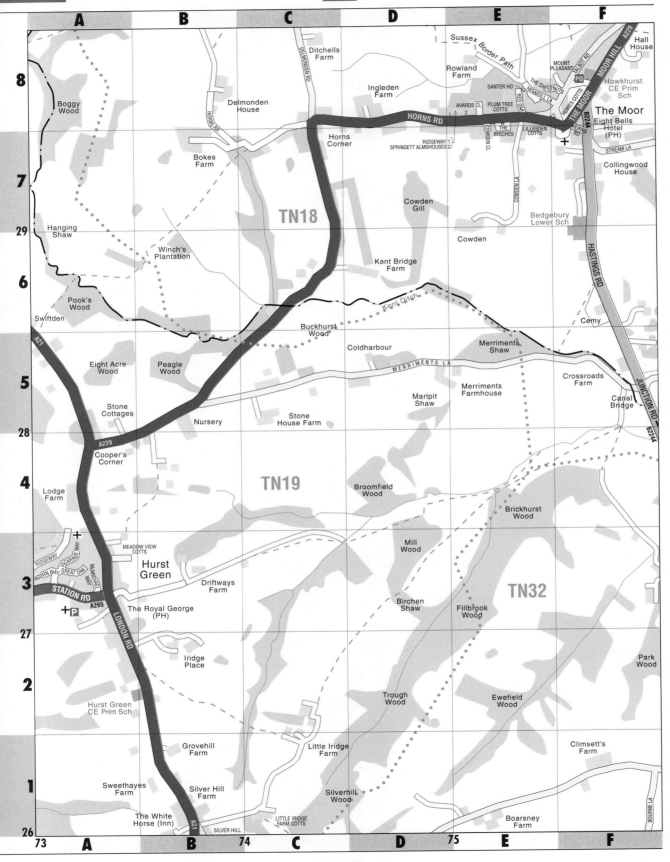

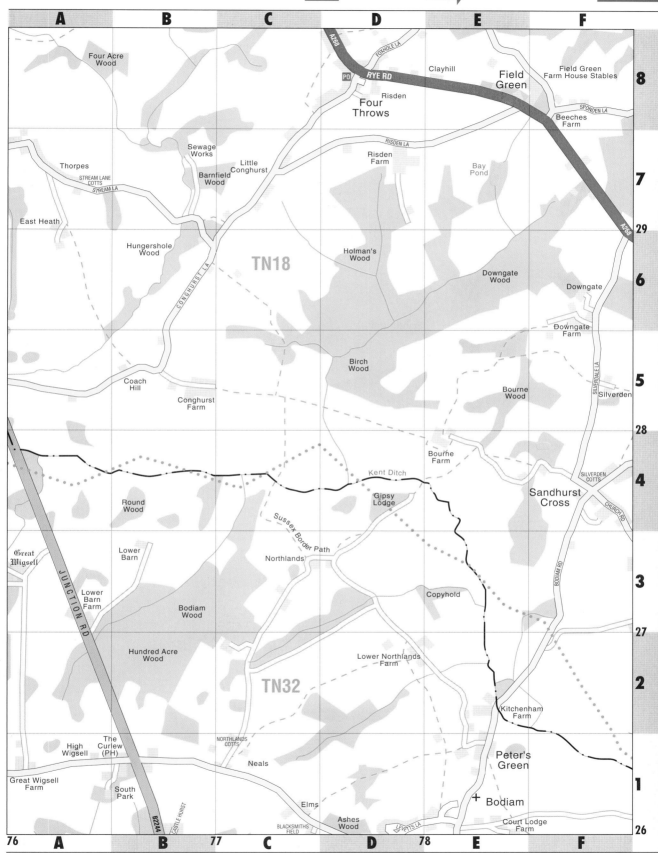

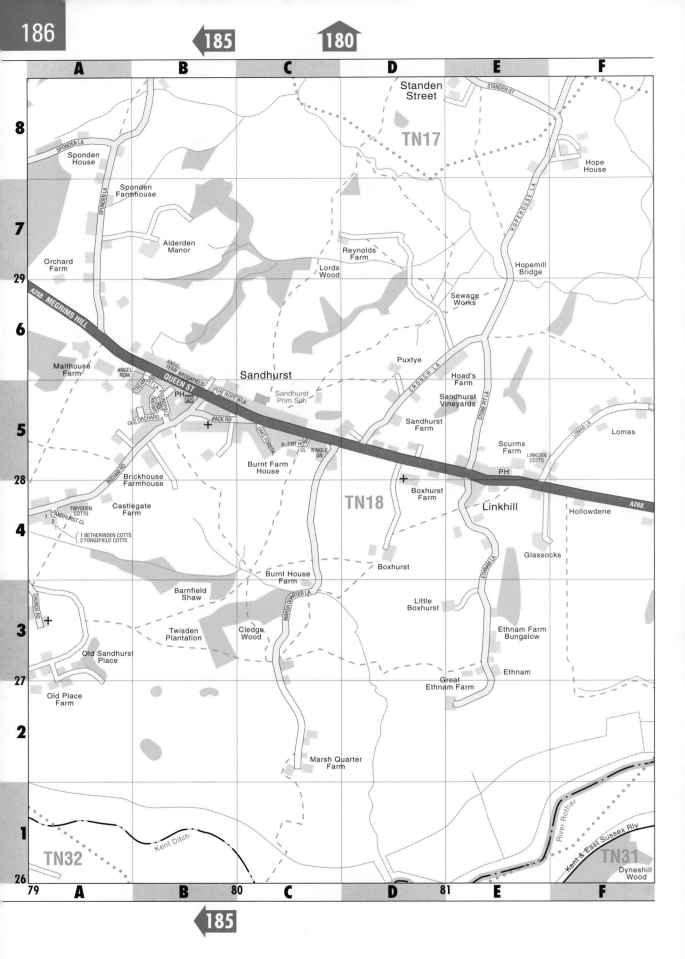

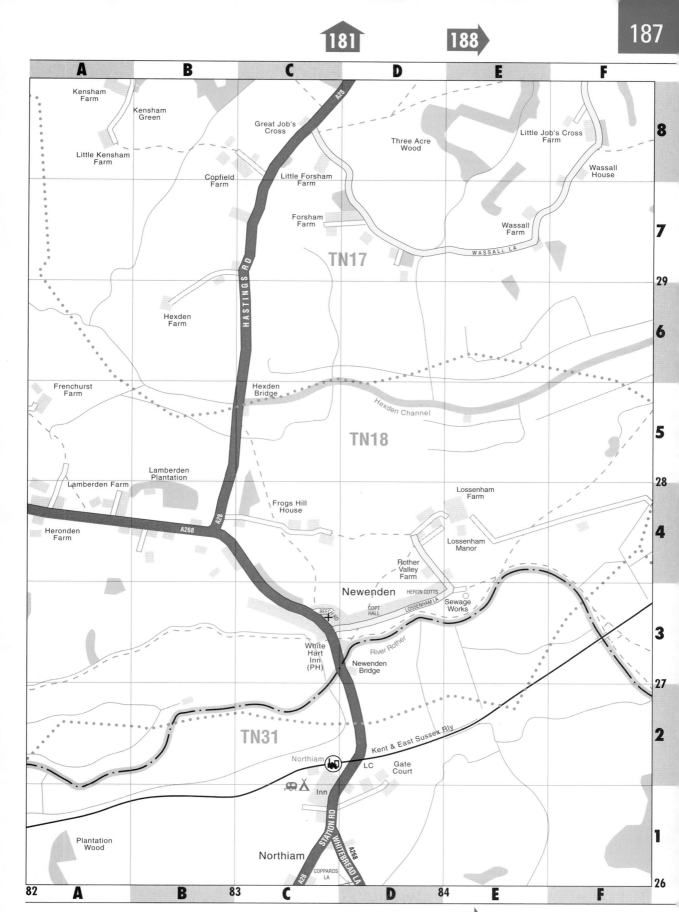

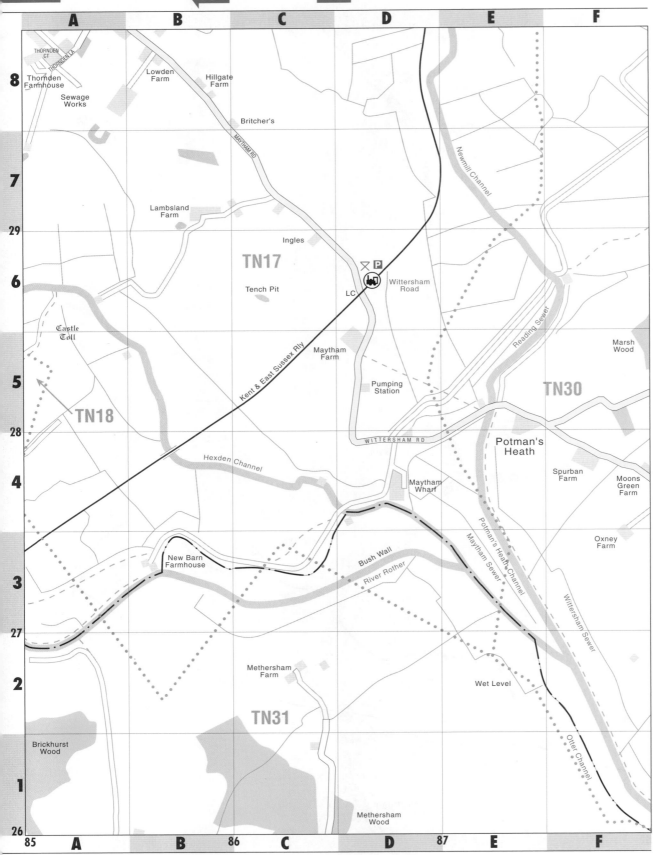

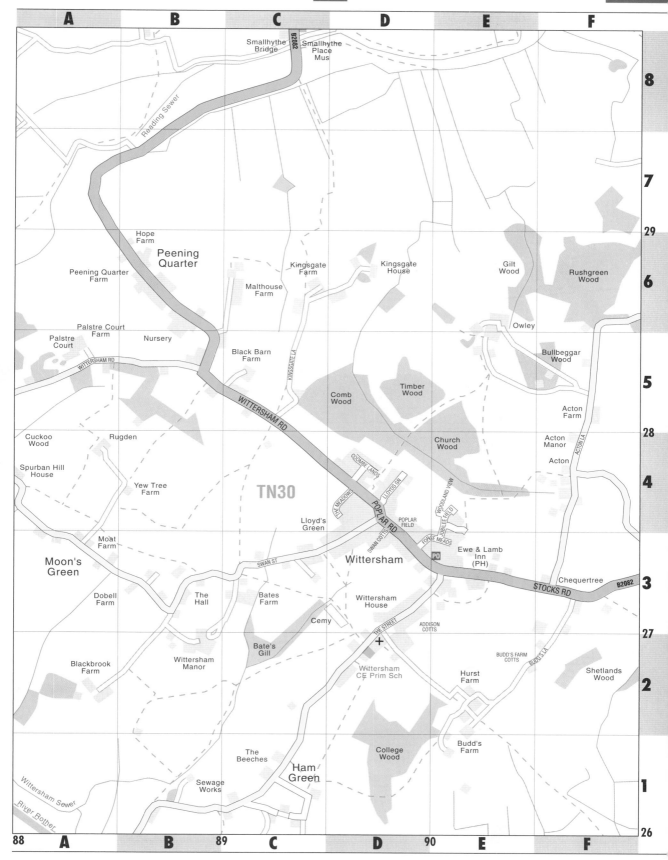

A B C D E F

8
7
29
6
5
28
4
3
27
2
1
26

Smallhythe Bridge
B2082
Smallhythe Place Mus

Reading Sewer

Hope Farm

Peening Quarter

Peening Quarter Farm

Kingsgate Farm
Kingsgate House

Gilt Wood

Rushgreen Wood

Malthouse Farm

Palstre Court Farm
Nursery
Owley

Palstre Court

Bullbeggar Wood

Black Barn Farm

KINGSGATE LA

WITTERSHAM RD

Comb Wood

Timber Wood

Acton Farm

WITTERSHAM RD

Cuckoo Wood
Rugden

Church Wood

Acton Manor
Acton

ACTON LA

Spurban Hill House

Yew Tree Farm

TN30

COOMBE LANDS

LLOYDS GN

WOODLAND VIEW
JUBILEE FIELD

Moat Farm

THE MEADOWS

POPLAR RD

Poplar Field

FORGE MEADS

Lloyd's Green

SWAN COTTS

Ewe & Lamb Inn (PH)

Moon's Green

SWAN ST

Wittersham

PO

Chequertree

STOCKS RD
B2082

Dobell Farm

The Hall

Bates Farm

Wittersham House

Cemy
ADDISON COTTS

BUDD'S FARM COTTS

BUDD'S LA

Bate's Gill

THE STREET

Blackbrook Farm

Wittersham Manor

Hurst Farm

Shetlands Wood

Wittersham CE Prim Sch

The Beeches

College Wood

Budd's Farm

Ham Green

Sewage Works

Wittersham Sewer

River Rother

88 A B 89 C D 90 E F

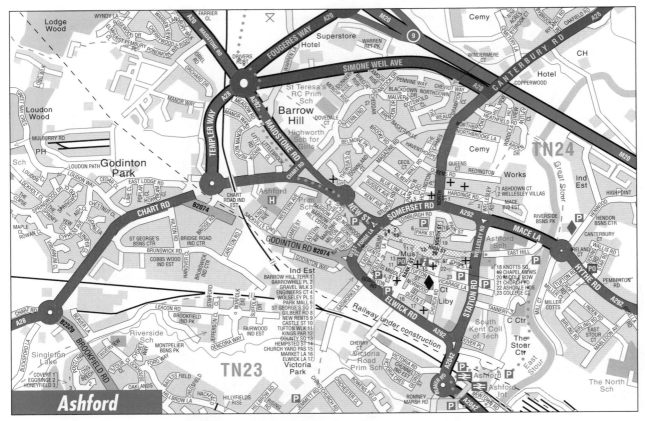

Ashford

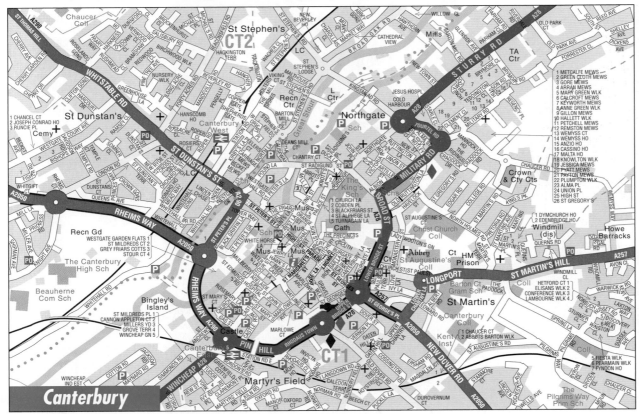

Canterbury

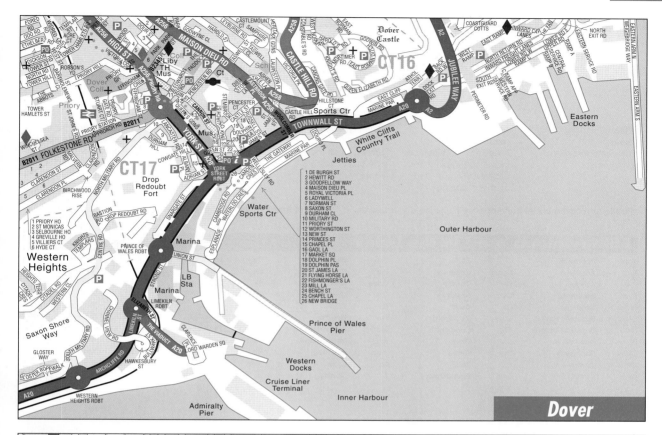

Dover

Numbered street index (Dover):
1 DE BURGH ST
2 HEWITT RD
3 GOODFELLOW WAY
4 MAISON DIEU PL
5 ROYAL VICTORIA PL
6 LADYWELL
7 NORMAN ST
8 SAXON ST
9 DURHAM CL
10 MILITARY RD
11 PRIORY ST
12 WORTHINGTON ST
13 NEW ST
14 PRINCES ST
15 CHAPEL PL
16 GAOL LA
17 MARKET SQ
18 DOLPHIN PL
19 DOLPHIN PAS
20 ST JAMES LA
21 FLYING HORSE LA
22 FISHMONGER'S LA
23 MILL LA
24 BENCH ST
25 CHAPEL LA
26 NEW BRIDGE

1 PRIORY HO
2 ST MONICAS
3 SELBOURNE HO
4 GREVILLE HO
5 VILLIERS CT
6 HYDE CT

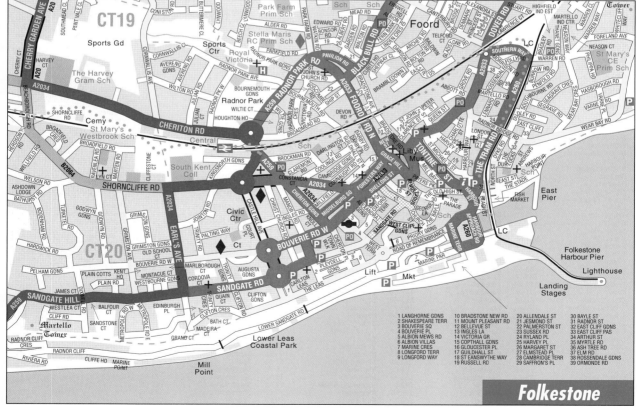

Folkestone

Numbered street index (Folkestone):
1 LANGHORNE GDNS
2 SHAKESPEARE TERR
3 BOUVERIE SQ
4 BOUVERIE PL
5 ALBION MEWS RD
6 ALBION VILLAS
7 MARINE CRES
8 LONGFORD TERR
9 LONGFORD WAY
10 BRADSTONE NEW RD
11 MOUNT PLEASANT RD
12 BELLEVUE ST
13 INGLES LA
14 VICTORIA GR
15 COPTHALL GDNS
16 GLOUCESTER PL
17 GUILDHALL ST
18 ST EANSWYTHE WAY
19 RUSSELL RD
20 ALLENDALE ST
21 JESMOND ST
22 PALMERSTON ST
23 SUSSEX RD
24 RYLAND PL
25 HARVEY PL
26 MARGARET ST
27 ELMSTEAD PL
28 CAMBRIDGE TERR
29 SAFFRON'S PL
30 BAYLE ST
31 RADNOR ST
32 EAST CLIFF GDNS
33 EAST CLIFF PAS
34 ARTHUR ST
35 MYRTLE RD
36 ASH TREE RD
37 ELM RD
38 ROSSENDALE GDNS
39 ORMONDE RD

Index

Church Rd **6** Beckenham BR2..........**53** C6

Place name	**Location number**	**Locality, town or village**	**Postcode district**	**Page and grid square**
May be abbreviated on the map	Present when a number indicates the place's position in a crowded area of mapping	Shown when more than one place has the same name	District for the indexed place	Page number and grid reference for the standard mapping

Public and commercial buildings are highlighted in **magenta**   **Places of interest** are highlighted in blue with a star★

Abbreviations used in the index

App	Approach	Cl	Close	Espl	Esplanade	Orch	Orchard	Sq	Square
Arc	Arcade	Comm	Common	Est	Estate	Par	Parade	Strs	Stairs
Ave	Avenue	Cnr	Corner	Gdns	Gardens	Pk	Park	Stps	Steps
Bvd	Boulevard	Cotts	Cottages	Gn	Green	Pas	Passage	St	Street, Saint
Bldgs	Buildings	Ct	Court	Gr	Grove	Pl	Place	Terr	Terrace
Bsns Pk	Business Park	Ctyd	Courtyard	Hts	Heights	Prec	Precinct	Trad	Trading Est
Bsns Ctr	Business Centre	Cres	Crescent	Ind Est	Industrial Estate	Prom	Promenade	Wlk	Walk
Bglws	Bungalows	Dr	Drive	Intc	Interchange	Ret Pk	Retail Park	W	West
Cswy	Causeway	Dro	Drove	Junc	Junction	Rd	Road	Yd	Yard
Ctr	Centre	E	East	La	Lane	Rdbt	Roundabout		
Cir	Circus	Emb	Embankment	N	North	S	South		

Index of localities, towns and villages

Addington 73 C2	Coldblow 25 B7	Halstead 67 F6	Nettlestead 104 B5	Sidcup 24 A3
Allhallows 19 C7	Collier Street 137 E8	Harrietsham 110 B5	Nettlestead Green ...104 C1	Silver Street 80 F5
Allhallows-on-Sea 19 D9	Colt's Hill 135 B4	Hartley 42 E4	New Ash Green 56 E7	Sissinghurst 170 A8
Ash 56 E5	Congelow 120 F8	Hartlip 64 C3	New Barn 43 A6	Snodland 75 A6
Aylesford 75 D1	Cooling 16 E4	Hawkhurst 179 A1	New Hythe 75 A4	Sole Street 44 B5
Badgers Mount 53 A1	Cowden 145 D8	Hawley 26 E4	New Street 57 D4	Speldhurst 148 B8
Barking 3 A8	Coxheath 106 A4	Hayes 36 A1	New Town 89 A8	Stansted 56 E1
Barnes Street 119 A5	Cranbrook 169 B4	Headcorn 141 A4	Newbury's 175 B8	Staplehurst 139 C5
Basted 86 E4	Cranbrook Common ..156 A2	Hever 129 B7	Newenden 187 C3	Stockbury 79 D8
Bean 28 B5	Crayford 8 D2	Hextable 25 E1	Newham 1 F5	Stone 10 E1
Bells Yew Green 163 A5	Crockenhill 39 C2	High Halden 173 E7	Newington 65 A5	Sundridge 82 D3
Beltring 120 B4	Crockham Hill 96 B1	High Halstow 17 C4	Northfleet 12 A2	Sutton at Hone 27 A2
Benenden 180 D6	Crouch 87 B3	Higham 32 B2	Northiam 187 C1	Sutton Valence 124 C6
Benover 121 A7	Cudham 66 C4	Hoo St Werburgh 34 C5	Oad Street 65 F1	Swanley 39 B8
Betsham 28 D3	Culverstone Green 57 F2	Horsmonden 153 A5	Offham 88 C7	Swanscombe 11 A3
Bexley 7 A2	Cuxton 46 B2	Horton Kirby 41 C4	Oldbury 86 B5	Tenterden 183 A6
Bidborough 132 C3	Dartford 9 C3	Hunton 121 D6	Orpington 38 A1	Teston 105 A7
Biddenden 157 C2	Detling 78 A1	Hurst Green 184 A3	Otford 69 A2	The Moor 184 E7
Biddenden Green 143 A2	Ditton 75 A1	Ide Hill 97 D6	Otham 108 B7	Thurnham 78 D1
Birling 74 B5	Downe 66 A8	Ightham 86 C5	Otham Hole 108 A6	Ticehurst 176 C1
Bitchet Green 85 D1	East End 171 C2	Istead Rise 43 F7	Paddock Wood 135 E6	Tilbury 13 A3
Bodiam 185 A3	East Farleigh 106 A7	Kemsing 70 A1	Parkgate 172 C1	Tonbridge 117 A1
Bogden 123 C1	East Malling 90 A6	Kilndown 166 F3	Pembury 150 E7	Trottiscliffe 73 A4
Borough Green 86 D6	East Peckham 119 F6	Kings Hill 89 A1	Penshurst 131 A3	Turnden 169 B4
Bough Beech 113 F4	East Tilbury 14 B7	Kingsnorth 35 C8	Platt 87 C5	Tylden 158 F8
Boxley 77 C2	Eccles 75 F5	Kingswood 109 D2	Platt's Heath 110 F1	Ulcombe 125 D5
Brandfold 153 F3	Edenbridge 112 A2	Kit's Coty 76 C7	Plaxtol 101 E6	Underling Green 122 E3
Brasted 82 A2	Egerton 127 E6	Knockmill 70 F8	Plaxtol Spoute 102 A8	Upper Halling 59 C4
Bredhurst 63 A1	Eltham 5 A2	Laddingford 120 E4	Plumtree Green 141 F7	Upper Upnor 33 E1
Brenchley 152 A6	Erith 4 A1	Lamberhurst 166 A5	Potman's Heath 188 D4	Vigo Village 73 A8
Broad Street 94 A6	Eynsford 54 B4	Langley Heath 108 E3	Potter's Forstal 127 B2	Wadhurst 175 F8
Broadstone 126 D3	Farningham 40 D3	Larkfield 75 A1	Poundsbridge 147 C7	Wateringbury 104 C7
Bromley 36 A4	Farthing Street 50 E2	Lashenden 158 B8	Pratling Street 76 B4	West Farleigh 105 B5
Burham 60 C1	Fawkham Green 56 B7	Leeds 109 A7	Pratt's Bottom 52 A1	West Kingsdown 55 E3
Capel 134 F6	Five Oak Green 135 B7	Leigh 115 E1	Purfleet 10 C8	West Malling 89 B8
Chainhurst 122 A4	Flimwell 177 C3	Lenham 111 B7	Pye Corner 126 B7	West Peckham 103 A6
Chalk 31 A6	Fordcombe 147 C4	Lewisham 22 A4	Rabbit's Cross 123 D5	West Thurrock 11 A7
Chart Sutton 108 B1	Four Elms 113 A6	Leybourne 74 C2	Rainham 4 D8	Westerham 81 B2
Chartway Street 109 A8	Frant 163 B4	Lidsing 62 F1	Rochester 47 B3	Whetsted 119 F1
Chatham 47 E4	Frittenden 156 D8	Longfield 42 D6	Rolvenden 181 E4	Withyham 160 B5
Chattenden 33 F4	Gillingham 48 F4	Lower Stoke 19 C3	Royal Tunbridge Wells .149 B4	Wittersham 189 C3
Chelsfield 52 D4	Golden Green 118 F6	Luddesdown 44 E8	Ryarsh 73 F4	Woolwich 2 A8
Chestnut Street 65 D4	Goudhurst 167 A5	Lunsford 74 F3	St Mary's Island 34 B1	Wormshill 95 F7
Chiddingstone	Grain 21 B5	Maidstone 92 B4	St Paul's Cray 38 A4	Wouldham 60 C3
Causeway 114 F2	Gravesend 13 A1	Marden 138 B6	Sandhurst 186 B5	Wrotham 71 C3
Chislehurst 37 A7	Grays 12 A8	Marlpit Hill 112 B4	Seal 85 A7	Wrotham Heath 73 D1
Cliffe 15 C8	Greenwich 1 D3	Matfield 151 C6	Sevenoaks 84 A4	Yalding 104 E2
Cliffe Woods 33 A8	Groombridge 161 A6	Meopham 58 A1	Sheerness 21 F3	Yelsted 64 A1
Cobham 161 B2	Hadlow 102 D1	Meopham Station 44 A2	Shipbourne 101 C5	
Cobham 44 F6	Hale Street 120 B7	Mereworth 103 C7	Shoreham 68 F6	
Cold Harbour 65 F8	Halling 60 A4	Mill Street 89 F7	Shorne 31 D5	

20/20 Ind Est ME16 . . . . . .91 C8

A

Aaron Hill Rd E6 . . . . .2 A8
Abbess Cl **1** E6 . . . . .1 E8
Abbet Ho SE2 . . . . .3 D1
Abbeville Ho ME1 . . . . .47 C4
Abbey Brewery Ct ME19 .89 C6
Abbey Court Sch ME2 . . . .46 E8
Abbey Cres SE2 . . . . .4 A2
Abbey Gate Cotts ME14 . .76 F2
Abbey Gr SE12 . . . . .22 B4
Abbey Lodge SE12 . . . . .22 B4
Abbey Mount DA17 . . . . .3 F1
Abbey Pl DA1 . . . . .9 D2
Abbey Prim Sch SE2 . . . . . . .3 C3
Abbey Rd Bexley DA6,DA7 . . .7 E3
   Erith DA17 . . . . .3 E3
   Gillingham ME8 . . . . .49 A2
   Gravesend DA12 . . . . .30 E7
   Rochester ME2 . . . . .46 F8
   Swanscombe DA9 . . . . . . .11 C2
Abbey Terr SE2 . . . . .3 C2
Abbey Wood Rd
   Kings Hill ME19 . . . . .89 A5
   Woolwich SE2 . . . . .3 C2
Abbey Wood Sch SE2 . . . . . .3 A3
Abbey Wood Sta SE2 . . . . . . .3 C4
Abbeyhill Rd DA15 . . . . .24 C6
Abbots Cl BR5 . . . . .37 C1
Abbots Court Rd ME3 . . . .34 F5
Abbots Field
   Gravesend DA12 . . . . .30 C2
   Maidstone ME16 . . . . .91 B2
Abbotswood Rd **7** DA17 . . .3 E3
Abbott Rd TN15 . . . . .86 F7
Abbott's Wlk DA7 . . . . .7 D7
Abbotts Cl Rochester ME1 . .47 B3
   Swanley BR8 . . . . .40 A5
   Woolwich SE28 . . . . .3 C6
Aberdeen House **9**
   ME15 . . . . .107 E7
Aberford Gdns SE18 . . . . . . .5 E6
Abergeldie Rd SE12 . . . . . . .5 B1
Abery St SE18 . . . . .2 E2
Abigail Cres ME5 . . . . .62 A1
Abingdon Mews ME19 . . . .89 C8
Abingdon Rd ME16 . . . . . . .90 F2
Abingdon Way BR6 . . . . . . .52 B6
Abinger Cl BR1 . . . . .36 E6
Abinger Dr ME5 . . . . .62 D2
Absalom Ct ME8 . . . . .49 C2
Acacia Cl BR5 . . . . .37 D4
Acacia Rd Dartford DA1 . . . .26 D7
   Stone DA9 . . . . .10 E1
Acacia Way DA15 . . . . .23 F7
Acacia Wlk BR8 . . . . .39 D7
Academy Dr ME7 . . . . .48 F1
Academy Pl SE18 . . . . .6 A6
Academy Rd SE18 . . . . .5 F7
Acer Ave TN12 . . . . .163 C8
Achilles Rd ME5 . . . . .62 C2
Acland Cl SE18 . . . . .6 D7
Acorn Cl Chislehurst BR7 . .23 C3
   Five Oak Green TN12 . . . .135 B7
Acorn Gr ME20 . . . . .90 D8
Acorn Ind Pk DA1 . . . . .9 A2
Acorn Pl ME15 . . . . .107 E6
Acorn Rd Crayford DA1 . . . . .8 F2
   Gillingham ME7 . . . . .48 F4
Acorn Trad Ctr RM20 . . . . .11 E8
Acorn Way
   Hurst Green TN19 . . . . . . .184 A3
   Orpington BR6 . . . . .51 B6
Acorn Wharf Rd ME1 . . . . . .47 C6
Acorns The
   Biddenden Green TN27 . . .142 F1
   Sevenoaks TN13 . . . . .84 A4
Acott Fields ME18 . . . . . . .120 F8
Acre Cl ME1 . . . . .47 E1
Acre Gr ME2 . . . . .60 B4
Acres Rise TN5 . . . . .176 E1
Acton La TN30 . . . . .189 F4
Acton Pl ME18 . . . . .105 A1
Acworth House **1** SE18 . . .6 B8
Acworth Pl DA1 . . . . .9 C1
Adam Cl ME17 . . . . .106 D3
Adams Cl TN30 . . . . .173 B1
Adams Sq DA6 . . . . .7 E4
Adamson Rd E16 . . . . .1 A7
Adbert Dr ME15 . . . . .106 B4
Adcot Wlk **6** BR6 . . . . . . .51 F6
Adderley Gdns SE9 . . . . . . .23 A4
Addington La ME19 . . . . . . .73 B4
Addison Cl
   East Malling ME19 . . . . . . .74 F1
   Orpington BR5 . . . . .37 C3
Addison Cotts TN30 . . . . . .189 D3
Addison Dr SE12 . . . . .5 B2
Addison Rd BR2 . . . . .36 D4
Addlestead Rd TN12 . . . . .119 E6
Adelaide Rd
   Chislehurst BR7 . . . . .23 B3
   Gillingham ME7 . . . . .48 C4
   Tilbury RM18 . . . . .12 F5
Adelaide The ME3 . . . . .32 C6
Aden Terr **1** ME14 . . . . . . .92 A7
Adisham Dr ME16 . . . . .91 B1
Admaston Rd SE18 . . . . .6 C8
Admers Way DA13 . . . . .73 B8
Admiral Cl BR5 . . . . .38 D5
Admiral Moore Dr **3**
   ME20 . . . . .75 F1

Admiral Seymour Rd SE9 . .5 F3
Admiral Way ME19 . . . . .89 A1
Admiral's Wlk ME4 . . . . .47 F7
Admirals Ct E6 . . . . .2 B7
Admirals Wlk Chatham ME5 62 B3
   Goddard's Green TN17 . . .170 D2
   Swanscombe DA9 . . . . . . .11 B2
   Tenterden TN30 . . . . .173 C1
Admiralty Rd ME4 . . . . .33 F1
Admiralty Terr
   1 Gillingham ME7 . . . . . .48 A7
   Upper Upnor ME2 . . . . . . .33 F1
Afghan Rd ME4 . . . . .47 E4
Agate Cl E16 . . . . .1 D7
Agaton Rd SE9 . . . . .23 C6
Agnes Cl E6 . . . . .2 A6
Ainsdale Cl BR6 . . . . .37 D1
Aintree Cl DA12 . . . . .30 B5
Aintree House **1** ME15 . .107 F6
Aintree Rd ME5 . . . . .62 C3
Airedale Cl DA2 . . . . .27 C7
Airport Rdbt E16 . . . . .1 D5
Aisher Rd SE28 . . . . .3 C6
Aisher Way TN13 . . . . .83 E6
Ajax Rd ME1 . . . . .61 C8
Akehurst La TN13 . . . . .84 C2
Alabama St SE18 . . . . .6 E7
Alamein Ave ME5 . . . . .61 F7
Alamein Gdns DA2 . . . . .27 D8
Alamein Rd DA10 . . . . .11 D1
Alan Cl DA1 . . . . .9 C3
Alan Marre Ho SE7 . . . . .5 D8
Alanbrooke DA12 . . . . .30 C8
Alanthus Cl SE12 . . . . .5 A1
Alban Cres DA4 . . . . .41 A1
Albany Cl Sidcup DA5 . . . . .24 D8
   Tonbridge TN9 . . . . .133 D7
Albany Hill TN2 . . . . .149 C5
Albany Rd Chatham ME4 . . .48 B4
   Chislehurst BR7 . . . . .23 B3
   Erith DA17 . . . . .7 F8
   Gillingham ME7 . . . . .48 D4
   Rochester ME1 . . . . .47 C4
   Sidcup DA5 . . . . .24 C8
   Tilbury RM18 . . . . .13 A6
Albany St ME14 . . . . .92 B5
Albany Terr Chatham ME4 . .47 E4
   Gillingham ME7 . . . . .48 D4
Albatross Ave ME2 . . . . .46 C6
Albatross St SE18 . . . . .6 E7
Albemarle Rd ME5 . . . . .62 C2
Albert Cotts TN1 . . . . .149 B4
Albert Manor ME7 . . . . .48 B5
Albert Murry Cl DA12 . . . . .30 C8
Albert Pl **2** BR7 . . . . .23 B7
Albert Rd Bromley BR2 . . . .36 D4
   Chatham ME4 . . . . .48 A3
   Chislehurst SE9 . . . . .22 E5
   Dartford DA2 . . . . .26 C5
   Erith DA17 . . . . .3 F1
   Gillingham ME7 . . . . .48 C4
   Newham E16 . . . . .1 F5
   Orpington,Chelsfield BR6 . .52 D7
   Orpington,St Mary Cray BR5 .38 B3
   Rochester ME1 . . . . .47 C3
   Sidcup DA5 . . . . .25 B8
   Swanscombe DA10 . . . . . .11 F1
   3 Tonbridge TN9 . . . . .117 B1
Albert Reed Gdns ME15 . . .91 E2
Albert St Maidstone ME14 . .91 F6
   Royal Tunbridge Wells TN1 . .149 B4
Albert Wlk E16 . . . . .2 B5
Alberta Rd DA8 . . . . .8 C6
Albion Cotts TN12 . . . . . . .138 D5
Albion Cr **2** SE18 . . . . .1 E2
Albion Ho E16 . . . . .2 B5
Albion Pl Maidstone ME14 . .92 B6
   Newington ME9 . . . . .65 B6
Albion Rd Bexley DA6 . . . . . .8 A3
   Chatham ME5 . . . . .62 B2
   Gravesend DA12 . . . . .30 C8
   Marden TN12 . . . . .138 D5
   Royal Tunbridge Wells TN1 . .149 C5
Albion Terr DA12 . . . . .13 D1
Albion Way TN8 . . . . .112 C4
Albright Ind Est RM13 . . . . . .4 F8
Albury Ave DA7 . . . . .7 E5
Albury Cl ME5 . . . . .62 D2
Albyfield BR1 . . . . .36 F6
Alchins Cotts ME17 . . . . . .106 E2
Alconbury DA6 . . . . .8 B2
Aldeburgh St SE10 . . . . .1 A1
Alder Cl TN4 . . . . .133 D1
Alder La TN17 . . . . .181 C1
Alder Rd DA14 . . . . .23 F5
Alder Way BR8 . . . . .39 D7
Aldermary Rd BR1 . . . . .36 A8
Alderney Rd DA8 . . . . .9 A7
Alders Cotts TN12 . . . . . . .135 A5
Alders Meadow TN9 . . . . .116 F2
Alders Rd TN11,TN12 . . . . .134 E6
Alders The ME18 . . . . .103 E4
Aldersgrove Ave SE9 . . . . .22 D5
Aldershot Rd ME5 . . . . .62 A7
Alderwood Prim Sch SE9 . . .6 E1
Alderwood Rd SE9 . . . . .6 D1
Aldington Cl ME5 . . . . .62 B5
Aldington La ME14 . . . . .93 D8
Aldington Rd
   Greenwich SE18 . . . . .1 D1
   Maidstone ME14 . . . . .92 D3
Aldon Cl ME14 . . . . .92 C6
Aldon Ct ME14 . . . . .92 C6
Aldon La ME19 . . . . .88 C8
Aldwick Cl SE9 . . . . .23 D5
Alen Sq TN12 . . . . .139 F4
Alers Rd DA6 . . . . .7 D2

Alestan Beck Rd E16 . . . . . . .1 D7
Alex Hughes Cl ME6 . . . . . .74 F6
Alexander Cl Hayes BR2 . . .36 A1
   Sidcup DA15 . . . . .6 E1
   1 Rochester ME2 . . . . .47 B8
Alexander McLeod
   Inf Sch SE2 . . . . .3 B1
Alexander McLeod
   Jun Sch SE2 . . . . .3 B1
Alexander Rd Bexley DA7 . . .7 D5
   Chislehurst BR7 . . . . .23 B3
   Swanscombe ME12 . . . . . .11 C2
Alexandra Ave ME7 . . . . . . .48 E4
Alexandra Cl BR8 . . . . .39 E7
Alexandra Glen 3 B2
Alexandra Hospl The ME5 .77 A8
Alexandra Rd Chatham ME4 .48 B4
   Erith DA8 . . . . .8 F8
   Gravesend DA12 . . . . .30 E8
   Tilbury RM18 . . . . .12 F5
   Tonbridge TN9 . . . . .133 B8
Alexandra St
   Maidstone ME14 . . . . .91 F6
   Newham E16 . . . . .1 A8
Alfan La DA2 . . . . .25 D3
Alford House **6** SE18 . . . . .6 B8
Alford Rd DA8 . . . . .4 C1
Alfred Cl ME4 . . . . .48 B2
Alfred Ho **4** DA11 . . . . . . .29 F7
Alfred Pl DA11 . . . . .29 F7
Alfred Rd Erith DA17 . . . . . . .3 F1
   Gravesend DA11 . . . . .30 B6
   Hawley DA2 . . . . .26 F4
Alfred St RM17 . . . . .12 C8
Alfriston Gr ME19 . . . . .89 C3
Alice Thompson Cl SE12 . .22 C6
Alicia House DA16 . . . . .7 B6
Alison Cl E6 . . . . .2 A7
Alkerden La DA9,DA10 . . . .11 C1
Alkham Rd ME14 . . . . .92 C5
Alkham Tower **9** BR5 . . . .38 C5
All Saints
   CE Prim Sch ME15 . . . . . .92 A3
All Saints Cl DA10 . . . . .11 F2
All Saints Hospl ME4 . . . . .48 A2
All Saints Rd
   Allhallows ME3 . . . . .19 D8
   Hawkhurst TN18 . . . . .179 A1
   Royal Tunbridge Wells TN4 . .149 B6
All Saints Rise TN4 . . . . . .149 A6
All Saints'
   CE Prim Sch ME4 . . . . . . .48 A3
All Saints' Rd DA11 . . . . . .29 F7
Allan Cl TN4 . . . . .148 C4
Allandale Pl BR6 . . . . .52 D7
Allandale Rd TN2 . . . . .149 D7
Allard Cl BR5 . . . . .38 C2
Allen Cl ME5 . . . . .62 C6
Allen St ME15 . . . . .92 B5
Allendale Cl DA2 . . . . .27 C5
Allens TN12 . . . . .138 D5
Allens La TN15,TN11 . . . . .102 A7
Allenswood Rd SE9 . . . . .5 F5
Allhallows Prim Sch ME3 .19 D8
Allhallows Rd
   Lower Stoke ME3 . . . . .19 C5
   Newham E6 . . . . .1 E7
Allhallows-on-Sea Est
   ME3 . . . . .19 E10
Alliance Rd Newham E13 . . . .1 D8
   Woolwich SE18 . . . . .7 A7
Alliance Way TN12 . . . . . . .135 F6
Allington Cl DA12 . . . . .30 F6
Allington Dr Rochester ME2 46 E8
   Tonbridge TN9 . . . . .118 A5
Allington Gdns ME18 . . . .104 A5
Allington Prim Sch ME16 .91 C7
Allington Rd
   Gillingham ME8 . . . . .49 A3
   Orpington BR6 . . . . .37 E1
   Paddock Wood TN12 . . . .135 F7
Allington Way ME16 . . . . . .91 B6
Allison Ave ME7 . . . . .48 E1
Allnutt Mill Cl ME15 . . . . . .91 E2
Allotment La TN13 . . . . .84 C5
Allsworth Cl ME9 . . . . .65 B6
Alma Pl Hadlow TN11 . . . . .118 E8
   Rochester ME2 . . . . .47 A7
Alma Rd Eccles ME20 . . . . .75 F6
   New Town ME19 . . . . .89 A8
   Orpington BR5 . . . . .52 D8
   Sidcup DA14 . . . . .24 A5
   Swanscombe DA10 . . . . . .11 F2
Almon Pl ME1 . . . . .47 D5
Almond Cl BR2 . . . . .37 A2
Almond Dr BR8 . . . . .39 D7
Almond Gr ME7 . . . . .63 A4
Almond Rd DA2 . . . . .27 C8
Almond Way BR2 . . . . .37 A2
Almonds The ME14 . . . . . . .93 A4
Alms Row TN16 . . . . .82 B4
Almshouses
   Penshurst TN11 . . . . .131 C4
   Yalding ME18 . . . . .105 A1
Alnwick Ct **8** DA2 . . . . . . .10 B1
Alnwick Rd Eltham SE12 . . .22 B8
   Newham E16 . . . . .1 C7
Alonso Ho **4** DA17 . . . . . . .4 A1
Alpha Cl ME3 . . . . .35 D7
Alpine Bsns Ctr E6 . . . . .2 A8
Alpine Copse **2** BR1 . . . . .37 A7
Alpine Way E6 . . . . .2 A8
Alsike Rd DA18 . . . . .3 E3
Altash Way SE9 . . . . .23 A6
Altbarn Ind Est ME5 . . . . . .77 C8
Alton Ave ME19 . . . . .89 A3
Alton Cl DA5 . . . . .24 E7

Alton Cotts DA4 . . . . .54 E8
Alverstone Gdns SE9 . . . . .23 C7
Alwold Cres SE12 . . . . .5 C1
Amanda Cl ME5 . . . . .61 F3
Amar Ct SE18 . . . . .2 F1
Amardeep Ct SE18 . . . . .2 F1
Ambassador Gdns E6 . . . . . .1 F8
Amber Cl ME17 . . . . .108 A1
Amber Way ME17 . . . . .108 B1
Amberleaze Dr TN2 . . . . . .150 D6
Amberley Cl
   2 Orpington BR6 . . . . . .51 F5
   Tonbridge TN9 . . . . .133 A8
Amberley Ct Sidcup DA14 . .24 C3
   Speldhurst TN4 . . . . .149 C8
Amberley Rd SE2 . . . . .7 D8
Amblecote Cl SE12 . . . . . . .22 B5
Amblecote Mdw SE12 . . . .22 B5
Amblecote Rd SE12 . . . . . . .22 B5
Ambleside Rd DA7 . . . . .8 A5
Ambley Gn ME8 . . . . .63 A8
Ambley Rd ME8 . . . . .63 B8
Ambrook Rd DA17 . . . . .4 A2
Ambrose Cl Crayford DA1 . . .9 A3
   6 Newham E6 . . . . .1 F8
   Orpington BR6 . . . . .51 F7
Ambrose Hill ME5 . . . . .48 C2
Amels Hill ME9 . . . . .79 F8
Ames Ave ME14 . . . . .93 A4
Ames Rd DA10 . . . . .11 E1
Amesbury Rd BR1 . . . . .36 D6
Amethyst Ave ME5 . . . . .61 E6
Amherst Cl Maidstone ME16 91 D4
   Orpington BR5 . . . . .38 A5
Amherst
   Cty Prim Sch TN13 . . . . . .83 E4
Amherst Dr BR5 . . . . .38 A5
Amherst Hill Chatham ME7 .48 A6
   Sevenoaks TN13 . . . . .83 F4
Amherst Rd ME17 . . . . .94 D3
   Royal Tunbridge Wells TN4 .149 A5
   Sevenoaks TN13 . . . . .84 B5
Amherst Redoubt ME4 . . . .48 A5
Amhurst Bank
   Rd TN2,TN11,TN12 . . . . .134 F4
Amhurst Wlk SE28 . . . . .3 A5
Amies House ME15 . . . . . .106 F3
Amsbury Rd ME15,ME17 . .106 B2
Amshurst Villas ME15 . . . .106 A4
Ancaster St **1** SE18 . . . . . .6 E7
Anchor & Hope La SE7 . . . . .1 C2
Anchor Bvd DA2 . . . . .10 D3
Anchor Ho Chatham ME1 . . .47 B4
   newham E16 . . . . .1 C7
Anchor La ME2 . . . . .21 F3
Anchor Rd ME1 . . . . .47 C1
Anchorage Cl ME5 . . . . .19 C3
Anchorage Flats TN12 . . . .136 A6
Anchorage Point
   Ind Est SE7 . . . . .1 C3
Ancona Rd SE18 . . . . .2 D1
Andace Pk BR1 . . . . .36 C8
Anderson Way DA17 . . . . . . .4 B4
Andorra Ct BR1 . . . . .36 C8
Andover Ave E16 . . . . .1 D7
Andover Rd BR6 . . . . .37 E1
Andover Wlk **12** ME15 . . .107 F6
Andrew Broughton
   Way ME14 . . . . .92 B4
Andrew Cl DA1 . . . . .8 D2
Andrew Manor ME7 . . . . . . .48 B5
Andrew Rd TN4 . . . . .149 C8
Andrew Wells Ho **7** BR1 . .22 B1
Andrewes Gdns E6 . . . . .1 E7
Andrews Cl
   Royal Tunbridge Wells TN2 .149 D5
   St Paul's Cray BR5 . . . . . . .38 D6
Andringham
   Lodge **8** BR1 . . . . .36 B8
Andwell Cl SE2 . . . . .3 B4
Anerley Rd ME16 . . . . .91 D7
Angel La TN9 . . . . .117 B1
Angel Row TN18 . . . . .186 B5
Angel Terr TN18 . . . . .186 B6
Angel Wlk **4** TN9 . . . . . . .117 B1
Angelica Dr E6 . . . . .2 B8
Angerstein Bsns Pk SE10 . .1 A2
Angle Rd RM20 . . . . .11 D8
Anglesea Ave SE18 . . . . .2 B2
Anglesea Ctr **18** DA11 . . .13 B1
Anglesea Pl **17** DA11 . . . .13 B1
Anglesea Rd Orpington BR5 38 C3
   Woolwich SE18 . . . . .2 B2
Anglesey Ave ME15 . . . . . .107 A7
Anglesey Cl ME5 . . . . .62 B7
Anglesey St SE18 . . . . .2 C3
Angley Ct TN12 . . . . .153 A5
Angley Rd TN17 . . . . .169 C6
Angley Sch TN17 . . . . .169 C5
Angley Wlk
   Cranbrook TN17 . . . . .169 C6
   Cranbrook TN17 . . . . .169 D6
Anglia Ctr The RM13 . . . . . .4 E8
Anglian Ind Est IG11 . . . . . .3 A8
Ankerdine Cres SE18 . . . . . .6 B6
Ann St SE18 . . . . .2 D2
Ann Stroud Ct SE12 . . . . . . .5 A2
Annandale Rd DA15 . . . . . .23 F8
Anne of Cleves Rd DA1 . . . .9 D1
Annesley Rd SE3 . . . . .5 B6
Annetts Hall TN15 . . . . .87 A8
Annex The BR8 . . . . .40 B6
Annie Rd ME6 . . . . .74 F6
Annvera Ho **2** ME7 . . . . . .48 C7
Ansell Ave ME4 . . . . .48 A1
Anson Ave M18,ME19 . . . . .88 F3
Anson Cl ME5 . . . . .62 C6

Anson Rd ME19 . . . . .88 E2
Anstridge Rd SE9 . . . . .6 D1
Antelope Rd SE18 . . . . .1 F3
Anthony Cl TN13 . . . . .83 E7
Anthony Rd DA16 . . . . .7 A6
Anthony Roper
   Cty Prim Sch DA4 . . . . . . .54 E8
Anthonys La BR8 . . . . .40 A8
Anthonys Way ME7 . . . . . . .47 E8
Aperfield Rd DA8 . . . . .8 F8
Apollo Ave BR1 . . . . .36 B8
Apollo House ME5 . . . . .62 A6
Apollo Way
   St Mary's Island ME4 . . . . .34 C2
   Woolwich SE28 . . . . .2 D3
Apple Cl ME6 . . . . .75 A6
Apple Ct TN12 . . . . .135 F6
Apple Orch BR8 . . . . .39 D5
Apple Tree Cl ME16 . . . . . . .90 F2
Apple Tree La TN2 . . . . . . .149 D8
Appleby Cl ME1 . . . . .61 D7
Appleby Rd E16 . . . . .1 A7
Applecross Cl ME1 . . . . . . .47 B4
Appledore Ave DA7 . . . . .8 D5
Appledore Cl BR2 . . . . .36 A4
Appledore Cres DA14 . . . . .23 F5
Appledore Ct ME16 . . . . . . .91 C7
Appledore Rd
   Gillingham ME8 . . . . .49 A3
   Tenterden TN30 . . . . .183 E7
Appleforth Cl BR6 . . . . .52 C6
Applegarth Dr DA1 . . . . . . .26 F6
Applegarth House DA8 . . . . .8 F5
Applegarth Rd SE28 . . . . . . .3 C6
Appleshaw Cl DA11 . . . . . . .30 A3
Appleton Dr DA2 . . . . .26 B5
Appleton Rd SE9 . . . . .5 E4
Appletons TN11 . . . . .118 E8
Appold St DA8 . . . . .8 F8
Approach The BR6 . . . . .51 F8
April Cl BR6 . . . . .51 F5
Apsledene DA12 . . . . .30 D2
Apsley St TN4 . . . . .148 D4
Aragon Cl BR2 . . . . .36 F1
Arbroath Rd SE9 . . . . .5 E4
Arbrook Cl BR5 . . . . .38 A6
Arbrook Cres BR5 . . . . .38 A8
Arbury Ho BR1 . . . . .22 E1
Arbuthnot La DA5 . . . . .7 E1
Arcade The **2** SE9 . . . . . . .6 A1
Arcadia Rd DA13 . . . . .43 F8
Arcadian Ave DA5 . . . . .7 E1
Arcadian Cl DA5 . . . . .7 E1
Arcadian Rd DA5 . . . . .7 E1
Archer Rd Chatham ME5 . . .62 B6
   Orpington BR5 . . . . .38 A4
Archer Way BR8 . . . . .40 A7
Archery Cl ME3 . . . . .33 B7
Archery Ct DA1 . . . . .26 D8
Archery House Hospl DA2 10 B1
Archery Rd SE9 . . . . .5 F2
Archway Ct **4** ME7 . . . . . .47 B8
Arden Bsns Pk ME2 . . . . . .47 E8
Arden Gr BR6 . . . . .51 B6
Arden Jun Sch ME7 . . . . . .48 D6
Arden St ME7 . . . . .48 C6
Ardenlee Dr ME14 . . . . .92 B5
Arethusa Pl DA9 . . . . .11 B3
Arethusa Rd ME1 . . . . .61 C8
Argall Ho **3** DA18 . . . . .3 E3
Argent St RM17 . . . . .12 B7
Argles Cl DA9 . . . . .11 A2
Argyle Cl ME1 . . . . .61 E8
Argyle Rd Newham E16 . . . . .1 B7
   Royal Tunbridge Wells TN4 .133 A2
   Sevenoaks TN13 . . . . .84 B2
Argyll Rd SE18 . . . . .2 C3
Ariel Cl DA12 . . . . .30 F4
Ariel Ct **5** DA17 . . . . .4 A1
Arkwright Rd RM18 . . . . . . .13 A5
Arlington Cl DA15 . . . . .23 E8
Arlott Cl ME14 . . . . .91 F6
Armada Ct ME4 . . . . .47 E1
Armada Way Chatham ME4 .47 F3
   Newham E6 . . . . .2 C7
Armitage Pl **5** TN18 . . . .178 F2
Armory Dr DA12 . . . . .30 C8
Armstrong Cl
   Badgers Mount TN14 . . . . .68 B4
   Bromley BR1 . . . . .36 E6
   Newham E6 . . . . .1 F7
Armstrong Rd ME15 . . . . . .92 A1
Armytage Cl ME3 . . . . .34 E4
Arne Cl TN10 . . . . .117 E6
Arne Gr BR6 . . . . .51 F7
Arnhem Dr ME5 . . . . .61 F7
Arnold Ave DA13 . . . . .58 B8
Arnold Pl RM18 . . . . .13 C6
Arnold Rd DA12 . . . . .30 D6
Arnolds Cl ME2 . . . . .47 E2
Arnolds La DA4 . . . . .27 A2
Arnott Cl SE28 . . . . .3 C5
Arnsberg Way DA6,DA7 . . . .8 A3
Arnside Rd DA7 . . . . .8 B7
Arran Cl DA8 . . . . .8 D8
Arran Gn ME2 . . . . .46 C7
Arran Rd ME15 . . . . .107 A6
Arrandene House **3** BR5 . .38 B7
Arras House SE2 . . . . .3 D1
Arras House SE2 . . . . .7 D8
Arsenal Rd SE9 . . . . .5 F4
Artemis Cl DA12 . . . . .30 E8
Arthur Gr SE18 . . . . .2 D1
Arthur Rd Gillingham ME8 . .63 E7
   Rochester ME1 . . . . .47 D3

Arthur Ruxley Est DA14 ...24 D2
Arthur St Erith DA8 ....8 F7
  Gravesend DA11 ....30 A8
  Grays RM17 ....12 C8
Arthur St W DA11 ....30 A8
Arthur Toft House **6**
  RM17 ....12 B8
Artillery Ho SE18 ....2 A1
Artillery Pl SE18 ....2 A2
Artillery Row DA12 ....30 C8
Artington Cl BR6 ....51 C6
Artisan Cl E6 ....2 B6
Arun Ct ME5 ....38 C1
Arundel DA14 ....24 A3
Arundel Cl Chatham ME5 ..62 D1
  Sidcup DA5 ....7 F1
  Tonbridge TN9 ....133 A8
Arundel Ct **2** DA6 ....7 E3
Ascot DA5 ....24 F8
Arundel Dr BR6 ....52 B5
Arundel Rd Dartford DA1 ...9 C3
  Royal Tunbridge Wells TN1 .149 B2
Arundel St ME14 ....91 F6
Ascot Cl
  Borough Green TN15 .....87 B7
  Chatham ME5 ....62 C2
Ascot Ct DA5 ....24 F8
Ascot House **2** ME15 ..107 F6
Ascot Rd Gravesend DA12 .30 B5
  Orpington BR5 ....37 F5
Ash Cl Aylesford ME20 ....75 E1
  Chatham ME5 ....48 C1
  Edenbridge TN8 ....112 B1
  Gillingham ME8 ....49 B3
  Orpington BR5 ....37 D4
  Royal Tunbridge Wells TN2 .163 D7
  Sidcup DA14 ....24 B5
  Swanley BR8 ....39 D7
Ash Cres ME3 ....32 C3
Ash Ct SE12 ....22 A8
Ash Gr Lewisham SE12 ....22 A7
  Maidstone ME16 ....91 C6
Ash Keys DA13 ....73 B8
Ash La TN15 ....56 D2
Ash Platt Rd TN15 ......84 E6
Ash Rd Dartford DA1 ....26 D7
  Gravesend DA12 ....30 C4
  Hartley DA3 ....42 F3
  Hawley DA2 ....26 F4
  New Ash Green DA3,TN15 .56 E7
  Orpington BR6 ....51 F3
  Rochester ME2 ....46 F6
  Westerham TN16 ....81 E2
Ash Row BR2 ....37 A3
Ash Tree Cl TN15 ....55 F5
Ash Tree Cotts TN12 ...154 B7
Ash Tree Dr TN15 ......55 F2
Ash Tree La ME5 ....48 C1
Ashbank Cotts ME17 ...109 B7
Ashbee Cl ME6 ....75 A7
Ashbourne Ave DA7 ....7 E7
Ashbourne Ct TN4 .....148 D4
Ashbourne Rise BR6 ....51 E6
Ashburn Cl BR1 ....22 A1
Ashburn Mews ME1 .....48 E3
Ashburnham Cl TN13 ...99 C8
Ashburnham Rd Erith DA17 .4 C2
  Maidstone ME14 ....92 B8
  Tonbridge TN10 ....117 C3
Ashburton Rd E16 ....1 A7
Ashby Cl ME2 ....60 A4
Ashby's Cl TN8 ....128 D8
Ashbys Yd TN9 ....117 C1
Ashcombe Dr TN8 .....112 B4
Ashcroft Ave DA15 ......7 A1
Ashcroft Cres DA15 ......7 A1
Ashcroft Rd Dartford DA1 .27 A8
  5 Eltham SE9 ....6 A1
Ashcroft Rd TN12 .....136 A5
Ashdale Rd SE12 ....22 B7
Ashden Wlk TN10 .....117 C2
Ashdown Cl Coldblow DA5 .25 C8
  Maidstone ME16 ....91 D3
  Royal Tunbridge Wells TN4 .148 F4
Ashen E6 ....2 A7
Ashen Dr DA1 ....9 A1
Ashen Grove Rd TN15 ...55 B1
Ashenden TN27 ....142 F2
Ashenden Cl ME2 ....33 C2
Ashenden Wlk TN2 ....149 E8
Asher Reeds TN3 ......148 A4
Ashes La TN11 ....118 B8
Ashfield La BR7 ....23 C1
Ashfield Pl BR7 ....23 D1
Ashford Dr ME17 ......109 D3
Ashford Rd
  Durrant Green TN26,TN30 .173 A6
  Harrietsham ME17 ......110 C6
  Maidstone ME14 ....93 D3
  Maidstone,Grove
  Green ME14 ....92 D4
  Tenterden TN30 ....183 B8
Ashgrove Rd TN13 ......99 B7
Ashlar Pl **4** SE18 ....2 B2
Ashleigh Cl DA13 ....57 F1
Ashleigh Commercial Est
  SE18 ....1 D3
Ashleigh Gdns TN27 ...141 D6
Ashley Cl TN13 ....84 B3
Ashley Gdns Orpington BR6 .51 E5
  Royal Tunbridge Wells TN4 .148 C5
Ashley House BR5 ....38 A7
Ashley Pk TN4 ....148 C5
Ashley Rd Gillingham ME8 .49 C2
  Sevenoaks TN13 ....84 B3

Ashley Rd continued
  Tonbridge TN11 ....116 E5
Ashmead Cl ME5 ....62 C3
Ashmead Gate BR1 .....36 C8
Ashmore Gdns DA11 ....29 D5
Ashmore Gr DA16 ....6 E4
Ashridge Cres SE18 ......6 C7
Ashton Way ME19 ......89 C6
Ashtree Cl BR6 ....51 B6
Ashurst Cl DA1 ....8 F4
Ashurst Hill TN3 ....146 D2
Ashurst Rd Maidstone ME14 92 C5
  Royal Tunbridge Wells TN3 .146 E2
Ashurst Sta TN3 ....146 D2
Ashwater Rd SE12 ......22 A7
Ashwell Cl **8** E6 ....1 E7
Ashwood Cl ME3 ....33 C7
Ashwood Pl DA2 ....28 B5
Askern Cl DA6 ....7 D3
Askews Farm La
  RM17,RM20 ....11 E8
Askham Lodge **10** SE12 ..22 A8
Aspdin Rd DA11 ....29 E5
Aspen Cl Orpington BR6 ..52 A5
  Swanley BR8 ....39 D8
Aspen Ct DA1 ....10 A3
Aspen Gn DA18 ....3 F3
Aspen House **2** DA15 ..24 A5
Aspen Way
  2 Chatham ME5 ......61 E4
  Royal Tunbridge Wells TN4 .133 C1
Aspian Dr ME17 ....106 D3
Asquith Rd ME8 ....63 D6
Association Wlk ME1 ....61 C7
Aster Rd ME3 ....34 E3
Astley RM17 ....11 F8
Astley St ME14 ....92 A4
Aston Cl Chatham ME5 ...62 A2
  Sidcup DA14 ....24 A5
Astor Ct E16 ....1 C7
Astor of Hever Com Sch
  The ME15 ....91 C3
Astor Rd TN15 ....55 E4
Astra Dr DA12 ....30 F3
Atcost Rd IG11 ....3 A8
Athelstan Gn ME17 .....94 C2
Athelstan Rd ME4 ......47 F2
Athelstan Way BR5 .....38 A8
Athill Ct TN13 ....84 C5
Athol Rd DA8 ....4 C1
Atkinson Cl BR1 ....52 A5
Atkinson Rd E16 ....1 C8
Atlanta Ct ME4 ....47 D3
Atlantic Cl DA10 ....11 E2
Atlas Gdns SE7 ....1 C2
Atlas Rd DA1 ....9 F4
Atterbury Cl TN16 ......81 D1
Attlee Dr DA1 ....10 A2
Attlee Rd SE28 ....3 B6
Attwaters La TN18 ....179 C6
Atwater Ct ME17 ......111 D5
Auckland Cl RM18 ......13 A6
Auckland House **10** ME15 107 E5
Auckland Rd TN1 ......149 C5
Auden Rd ME20 ....75 A3
Audley Ave Gillingham ME7 .48 E1
  Tonbridge TN9 ....116 F2
Audley Cl ME16 ....91 B5
Audley Dr E16 ....1 B5
Audley Rise TN9 ....116 F1
Audley Wlk BR5 ....38 C3
Audrey Sturley Ct TN4 .148 D4
Auger Cl ME9 ....64 E5
Augusta Cl **1** ME7 ......48 C7
Augustine Ho TN10 ....117 C3
Augustine Rd
  Gravesend DA12 ....30 C8
  St Paul's Cray BR5 ......38 D6
Austell Manor **5** ME7 ..48 C6
Austen Cl Swanscombe DA9 11 C1
  Tilbury RM18 ....13 C5
  Woolwich SE28 ....3 B5
Austen Gdns DA1 ....9 F3
Austen Rd DA8 ....8 B7
Austen Way ME20 ......74 F4
Austens Orch **14** TN30 .183 A7
Austin Ave BR2 ....36 E4
Austin Cl ME5 ....48 E2
Austin Ct **4** TN16 ......81 D1
Austin Rd Gravesend DA11 .29 F7
  Orpington BR5 ....38 A4
Austral Cl DA15 ....23 F5
Autumn Glade ME5 .....77 D8
Avalon Cl BR6 ....52 D7
Avalon Rd BR5,BR6 .....52 C8
Avard Gdns BR6 ....51 C6
Avards Cl TN18 ....184 E8
Aveling Cl ME3 ....34 D6
Aveling Ct **2** ME2 ......47 B7
Avenons Rd **3** E16 ......1 A8
Avenue Le Puy TN9 ....117 C1
Avenue Rd Bexley DA7,DA6 .7 E4
  Erith DA8 ....8 D7
  Sevenoaks TN13 ....84 C3
Avenue The Aylesford ME20 .75 E1
  Borough Green TN15 .....87 A8
  Bromley BR1 ....36 D6
  Gravesend DA11 ....30 A8
  Hill Park TN16 ....81 A4
  Orpington BR6 ....51 F8
  Orpington, Keston Mark BR2 .50 D8
  Sidcup DA5 ....24 D8
  St Mary's Island ME4 ...34 C2

Avenue The continued
  St Paul's Cray BR5 ......24 B1
  Swanscombe DA9 ....11 B2
  Tonbridge TN9 ....117 B2
Averenches Rd ME14 ....92 F5
Avery Cl
  Allhallows-on-Sea ME3 ...19 E9
  Maidstone ME15 ....91 F1
Avery Hill Rd SE9 ......23 D7
Avery La ME15, ME17 ..108 D6
Avery Way ME3 ....19 D8
Aviemore Gdns ME14 ...92 F4
Avington Cl ME15 ......91 F1
Avocet Mews SE28 ......2 D3
Avocet Wlk ME5 ....62 D2
Avon Cl Gravesend DA12 ..30 D6
  Tonbridge TN10 ....117 C5
Avon Ct DA14 ....24 B5
Avon St TN1 ....149 C5
Avondale Mews BR1 ....22 A2
Avondale Pl **8** ME14 ....19 C4
Avondale Rd Bexley DA16 ..7 C5
  Bromley BR1 ....22 A2
  Chislehurst SE9 ....22 E6
  Gillingham ME7 ....48 D5
Avonmouth Rd DA1 ......9 D2
Avonstowe Cl ME4 .....51 C7
Awliscombe Rd DA16 ....6 F5
Axford Ct ME8 ....64 A8
Axminster Cres DA16 ....7 C6
Axtaine Rd BR5 ....38 D2
Axtane DA13 ....28 F1
Axtane Cl DA4 ....41 C8
Axton Chase Sch DA3 ..42 F6
Aycliffe Cl BR1 ....36 F5
Ayelands DA3 ....56 E8
Ayelands La DA3 ......56 E8
Aylesbury Rd BR2 ......36 A6
Aylesford Cres ME8 ....49 B4
Aylesford Prim Sch ME20 .75 D1
Aylesford Sta ME20 ....75 E2
Aylesham Rd BR6 ......37 F2
Aynscombe Angle BR6 ..38 A4
Azalea Dr BR8 ....39 E5

B

Babb's La TN17 ....180 A6
Babbacombe Rd BR1 ...22 B1
Babington House Sch BR7 22 F2
Babylon La ME17,TN12 .124 B1
Back La Godden Green TN15 85 A2
  Goudhurst TN17 ....167 E8
  Horsmonden TN12 .....153 A6
  Ightham TN15 ....86 C2
  Maidstone ME17 ....107 E1
  Sevenoaks TN13,TN14 ..83 C1
  Shipbourne TN11 ......101 D4
  Sidcup DA5 ....25 A8
Back La Sandhurst TN18 .186 B5
  Sidcup DA14 ....24 A4
Back St ME17 ....108 A6
Backfields ME1 ....47 B4
Baden Powell Ho **11** DA17 ..4 A3
Baden Powell Rd TN3 ..83 E5
Baden Rd ME7 ....48 D7
Bader Cres ME5 ....62 A4
Bader Wlk ME3 ....29 F5
Badger Rd ME5 ....62 C1
Badgers Copse BR6 ....51 F8
Badgers Croft SE9 .....23 A5
Badgers Holt TN2 .....149 E5
Badgers Rd TN14 ......53 B1
Badgers Rise TN14 ....53 A1
Badlow Cl DA8 ....8 D6
Badminton Mews E16 ...1 A5
Badsell Park Farm TN12 .135 C3
Badsell Rd TN12 ......135 D6
Baffin Cl ME4 ....47 F2
Bagshaw Ho **3** BR1 ....36 A8
Bailey Dr ME7 ....49 A1
Baird Rd DA16 ....4 A3
Bakenham Ho **1** ME1 ..47 C1
Baker Beall Ct DA7 ......8 B4
Baker Hill Cl DA11 .....29 F4
Baker La Headcorn ME17 .141 F7
  Sutton Valence ME17 ..124 F7
Baker Rd SE18 ....5 E7
Baker St Burham ME1 ...60 F1
  Rochester ME1 ....47 C3
Baker's Wlk ME1 ....47 C6
Bakers Ave TN15 ......55 E3
Bakers Cross TN17 ....169 E4
Bakers Mews **9** BR6 ...51 F4
Bakery Cl TN17 ....156 E7
Balaclava La TN5 .....175 A6
Balcaskie Rd SE9 ....5 E1
Balchen Rd SE3 ....5 D5
Balcombe Cl DA6 ....7 D3
Balcombe Cotts TN17 .167 E8
Balcombes Hill TN17 ..167 E8
Balder Rise SE12 ......22 B6
Baldock Rd TN5 ......174 E4
Baldwin's Pk DA5 ......25 D6
Baldwyn's Rd DA5 .....25 D6
Balfour Inf Sch ME4 ...47 E1
Balfour Jun Sch ME4 ...47 E2
Balfour Rd Bromley BR2 .36 D4
  Chatham ME4 ....47 E2
Balgowan St SE18 ......2 F2
Ball's Gn TN7 ....160 B5
Ballamore Rd BR1 .....22 A5
Ballard Bsns Pk ME2 ...46 F5
Ballard Ind Est ME5 ....77 C8
Ballard Way TN12 ....136 B7
Ballens Rd ME5 ....62 C3

Balliol Rd DA16 ....7 B5
Balls Cotts ME3 ....33 F4
Balmer ME8 ....63 D7
Balmoral Ct SE12 ......22 B4
Balmoral Gdns DA5 ....24 D7
Balmoral House **10** ME15 .107 F5
Balmoral Rd
  Gillingham ME7 ....48 D5
  Sutton at Hone DA4 ....27 B1
Balmoral Trad Est E6 ....2 F8
Baltic Rd TN9 ....133 B7
Baltimore Pl DA16 ......6 F5
Banbury Villas DA13 ...28 F1
Banchory Rd SE3 ....5 B7
Banckside DA3 ....42 E5
Bancroft Gdns BR6 .....37 F1
Bancroft Rd TN15 ......71 F3
Bandfield Wlk DA1 ......9 F4
Bangor Rd ME2 ....46 D6
Bank Cotts ME17 ......94 E3
Bank La ME11,TN15 ...100 A3
Bank St Chatham ME4 ...48 B3
  Cranbrook TN17 ....169 C5
  Gravesend DA12 ....13 B1
  Maidstone ME14 ....92 A4
  Sevenoaks TN13 ....84 C2
  Tonbridge TN9 ....117 C2
Bankfield Way TN17 ...167 E7
Bankfields TN27 ......141 C6
Banks La DA6 ....7 F3
Banks Rd ME2 ....47 C8
Bankside Chatham ME5 ..62 B8
  Northfleet DA11 ....12 C1
  Sevenoaks TN13 ....83 E6
  Wadhurst TN5 ....174 E5
Bankside Cl DA5 ....25 D4
Banky Mdw ME16 ......90 F3
Banner Farm Rd TN2 .149 B2
Banning St ME2 ....47 B8
Bannister Gdns BR5 ....38 C6
Bannister Rd ME14 ....92 A7
Bannockburn Prim Sch
  SE18 ....2 F2
Bannockburn Rd SE18 ...2 F2
Banstead Ct **3** BR1 ....36 E6
Banwell Rd DA5 ....7 D1
Bapchild Pl **8** BR5 ......38 C5
Barbados Terr **2** ME14 ..92 A7
Barberry Ave ME5 ......61 C5
Barchester Way TN10 .117 F6
Barclay Ave TN10 .....118 A5
Barclay Field TN15 .....69 E2
Barcombe Cl BR5 ......38 A6
Bardell Terr ME1 ......47 D5
Barden Ct ME14 ....92 B5
Barden Park Rd TN9 ..117 A1
Barden Rd
  Bidborough TN3 ....131 F2
  Tonbridge TN9 ....117 B1
Barden St SE18 ....6 E7
Bardsley Cl TN12 .....120 A7
Barfield DA4 ....41 B8
Barfield Rd BR1,BR7 ...37 A6
Barfleur Manor **3** ME7 .48 A6
Barfreston Cl ME15 ....91 F2
Bargate Cl SE18 ....2 F1
Barge House Rd E16 ....2 A6
Bargrove Rd ME14 .....92 C5
Barham Cl
  Chislehurst BR7 ....23 B3
  Gravesend DA12 ....30 F7
  Orpington BR2 ....36 E1
Barham Ct BR2 ....36 E1
Barham Mews ME18 ..105 B8
Barham Rd
  Chislehurst BR7 ....23 B3
  Dartford DA1 ....27 A8
Barham's Mill Rd TN27 .127 B3
Baring Cl SE12 ....22 A6
Baring Prim Sch SE12 ..22 A8
Baring Rd SE12 ....22 A6
Bark Hart Rd BR6 ......38 B1
Barker Rd ME16 ....91 F3
Barking Rd E16 ....1 A8
Barkis Cl ME1 ....61 D7
Barley Fields ME14 ....92 D4
Barleycorn ME19 ......74 E1
Barleycorn Dr ME8 ....63 E6
Barleymow Cl ME5 .....62 C7
Barling Cl ME5 ....61 D1
Barlow Cl ME8 ....63 D6
Barlow Way RM13,RM9 ...4 E8
Barming Prim Sch ME16 90 F2
Barming Sta ME16 .....90 F6
Barn End Ctr DA2 .....26 C5
Barn End Dr DA2 ......26 C5
Barn End La DA2 ......26 C4
Barn Hill ME15 ....105 E2
Barn Mdw
  Staplehurst TN12 .....139 E4
  Upper Halling ME2 .....59 E4
Barnaby Terr ME1 .....47 D2
Barnard Cl Chislehurst BR7 .37 D8
  Woolwich SE18 ....3 A3
Barnard Ct Chatham ME4 .48 A3
  21 Dartford DA2 ....10 B1
Barncroft Cl ME14 .....92 A4
Barncroft Dr ME7 ......62 F4
Barndale Ct DA12 ......31 E3
Barned Ct ME4 ....47 F2
Barnehurst Ave DA7,DA8 ..8 C6
Barnehurst Cl DA8 ......8 C6
Barnehurst Inf Sch DA8 ..8 C6
Barnehurst Jun Sch DA8 ..8 C6

Barnehurst Rd DA7 ......8 C5
Barnehurst Sta DA7 .....8 C5
Barnes Cray Prim Sch DA1 .9 A3
Barnes Cray Rd DA1 ....9 A3
Barnes Ct E16 ....1 C8
Barnes La ME17 ......122 D8
Barnes Wlk TN12 .....138 D6
Barnesdale Cres BR5 ...38 A4
Barnet Dr BR2 ....50 E8
Barnet Wood Rd BR2 ..50 C8
Barnett Cl DA8 ....8 F5
Barnetts Cl TN4 ......133 C1
Barnetts Rd TN11 ....116 A2
Barnetts Way TN4 ....133 C1
Barney Cl SE7 ....1 C1
Barnfield Chatham ME5 ..62 A8
  Gravesend DA11 ....30 A6
  Royal Tunbridge Wells TN2 .162 F7
  Tenterden TN30 ....173 C2
Barnfield Cl Crockenhill BR8 39 C2
  New Barn DA3 ....43 D6
  Stone DA9 ....10 F1
Barnfield Cres TN15 ...69 E2
Barnfield Gdns SE18 ....6 B8
Barnfield Rd Erith DA17 ..7 F8
  Sevenoaks TN13 ....83 E4
  St Paul's Cray BR5 .....38 D6
  Woolwich SE18 ....6 B8
Barnhill Ave BR2 ......36 A4
Barnhurst Rd ME14 ....92 A8
Barnsole Inf Sch ME7 ..48 E4
Barnsole Jun Sch ME7 ..48 E4
Barnsole Rd ME7 ......48 E3
Barnwell Pl ME7 ....48 C5
Barnwell Rd DA1 ....9 F4
Barnwood Cl ME1 .....61 B8
Baron Cl Gillingham ME7 .48 E7
  Maidstone ME15 ....92 F5
Barons Ct TN4 ....149 A5
Barr Rd DA12 ....30 F6
Barrack Cnr TN13 .....84 C4
Barrack Rd ME4 ....48 B8
Barrack Row
  Benenden TN17 ....180 D6
  16 Gravesend DA11 ...13 B1
Barrel Arch Cl TN12 ..138 C6
Barretts Green Cotts **5**
  TN18 ....179 A2
Barretts Rd
  Hawkhurst TN18 ......179 A2
  Sevenoaks TN13 ....83 E7
Barrie Dr **7** ME20 .....74 F4
Barrier Rd ME4 ....47 F5
Barrier Point Rd E16 ....1 C5
Barrington Cl ME5 .....61 F5
Barrington Prim Sch DA7 ..7 D5
Barrington Rd DA7 .....7 D5
Barrington Villas SE18 ...6 A6
Barrow La TN3 ....147 F1
Barrowfields ME5 .....62 D1
Barry Ave DA7 ....7 E7
Barry Cl BR6 ....51 E7
Barry Rd E6 ....2 F7
Barth Rd SE18 ....2 E2
Bartholomew Way BR8 ..39 E6
Bartlett Cl ME5 ....62 C1
Bartlett Rd Gravesend DA11 30 A7
  Westerham TN16 ....81 C1
Barton Cl Bexley DA6 ....7 E2
  2 Newham E6 ....1 F7
  Yalding ME18 ....104 F1
Barton Cotts TN11 ....102 A6
Barton Rd Maidstone ME15 .92 A2
  Rochester ME2 ....47 A7
  Sidcup DA14 ....24 C2
  Sutton at Hone DA4 ....41 B8
Basden Cotts **2** TN18 .179 A2
Baseing Cl E6 ....2 A6
Bashford Barn La ME9 ..80 F4
Basi Cl ME2 ....33 C1
Basil Terr ME15 ....92 A1
Basildon Rd SE2 ....3 A1
Basilon Rd DA7 ....7 E5
Basing Cl ME15 ....92 B3
Basing Dr DA5 ....7 F1
Basket Gdns SE9 ....5 E2
Basmere Cl ME14 ......92 C6
Bassant Rd SE18 ....6 F8
Bassett's Forge TN5 ..174 E5
Bassetts BR6 ....51 B6
Bassetts La TN8,TN11 ..146 C7
Bassetts Way BR6 ....51 B6
Basted La Basted TN15 ..86 E5
  Crouch TN15 ....87 B4
Bastion Rd SE18,SE2 ...3 A1
Baston Manor Rd BR2,BR4 50 B6
Baston Rd BR2 ....50 B7
Baston Sch BR2 ....50 B8
Bat & Ball Ent Ctr TN14 .84 C7
Bat & Ball Sta TN14 ...84 C6
Batchelor St ME4 ......48 A4
Batchelors TN2 ....150 E8
Batchwood Br BR5 .....38 B6
Bates Cl ME20 ....75 A3
Bates Hill TN15 ....86 C5
Bateson St SE18 ....2 E2
Bath Hard ME1 ....47 D5
Bath Rd DA1 ....26 B8
Bath St DA11 ....13 B1
Baths Rd BR1,BR2 .....36 D5
Bathurst Cl TN12 .....139 E4
Bathurst Rd TN12 ....139 E3
Bathway **13** SE18 ......2 A2
Batt's Rd DA12 ....45 A4
Batten Cl E6 ....1 F7
Battery Rd SE28 ....2 F4
Battle La TN12 ....139 A8
Battle Rd DA8,DA17 .....4 C2

Battle St DA12 . . . . .44 F6
Battlefields TN15 . . . . . . .71 F3
Battlesmere Rd ME3 . . . .33 B8
Baugh Rd DA14 . . . . .24 C3
Baxter Rd E16 . . . . .1 C7
Bay CI ME3 . . . . .34 E3
Bay Manor La RM20 . . . . .10 F8
Bay The DA13 . . . . .73 A8
Bayard Ct DA7 . . . . .8 B3
Bayeux Ho 10 SE7 . . . . .5 C8
Bayfield Rd SE9 . . . . .5 D3
Bayhall Rd TN2 . . . . .149 C3
Bayham Abbey* TN3 . . .165 B5
Bayham Ct TN5 . . . . .174 E6
Bayham Rd Royal
  Tunbridge Wells TN2,TN3 . .163 C7
  Sevenoaks TN13 . . . . . . .84 D4
Bayley's Hill TN14 . . . . . . .98 E3
Bayliss Ave SE28 . . . . .3 D6
Bayly Rd DA1 . . . . .10 A1
Bayne CI E6 . . . . .1 F7
Baynham Ct DA5 . . . . .7 F1
Baytree CI Bromley BR1 . .36 D8
  Sidcup DA15 . . . . .23 F7
Baywell ME19 . . . . .74 E2
Bazes Shaw DA4 . . . . .56 F8
Beach CI Eltham SE9 . . . . . .5 E1
  Goddard's Green TN17 . . .170 D1
Beacham CI SE7 . . . . .5 D8
Beacon CI ME8 . . . . .63 D7
Beacon Dr DA2 . . . . .28 C5
Beacon Hill ME5 . . . . .48 D2
Beacon Hill La ME3 . . . . .33 F4
Beacon Oak Rd TN30 . . .183 B8
Beacon Rd Chatham ME5 . .48 C2
  Erith DA8 . . . . .9 B7
  Lenham ME17 . . . . .111 C5
Beacon Rise TN13 . . . . . .84 A3
Beacon Sch TN14 . . . . .98 F8
Beacon Wlk TN30 . . . . . .173 B1
Beacon Wood Ctry Pk*
  DA2 . . . . .28 B4
Beaconfields TN13 . . . . . .84 A1
Beacons The ME17 . . . . .106 C2
Beacons Wlk 10 E6 . . . . . . .1 E8
Beaconsfield Ave ME7 . . .48 E5
Beaconsfield CI SE3 . . . . . .5 A8
Beaconsfield Par SE9 . . . .22 E4
Beaconsfield Rd
  Bromley BR1 . . . . .36 B6
  Chatham ME4 . . . . .47 F3
  Chislehurst SE9 . . . . .22 E4
  Dartford DA5 . . . . .25 E6
  Greenwich SE3 . . . . .5 A7
  Maidstone ME15 . . . . . . .91 E2
Beadon Rd BR2 . . . . .36 A4
Beagles CI BR5 . . . . .52 D8
Beagles Wood Rd TN2 . .150 E7
Beal CI DA16 . . . . .7 A6
Beaman CI TN17 . . . . . . .167 F8
Beamish Rd BR5 . . . . .38 C2
Beams The ME15 . . . . . . .92 F1
Bean Hill Cotts DA2 . . . . .28 C4
Bean La DA2 . . . . .28 B6
Bean Prim Sch DA2 . . . . .28 C4
Bean Rd Bexley DA6 . . . . . .7 D3
  Swanscombe DA9 . . . . . .28 A7
Beanshaw SE9 . . . . .23 A4
Bearsted Sta
  ME14 . . . . .93 B5
Bearsted CI ME8 . . . . .49 B3
Bearsted Green Bsns Ctr
  ME14 . . . . .93 C4
Bearsted Rd ME14 . . . . . .92 E6
Beaton CI DA9 . . . . .11 B2
Beatrice Gdns DA11 . . . . .29 E6
Beatty Ave ME7 . . . . .48 F4
Beatty Cotts ME3 . . . . . . .19 D7
Beatty Rd ME1 . . . . .61 D8
Beaufighter Rd ME19 . . . .88 E3
Beaufort E6 . . . . .2 A8
Beaufort Ct ME2 . . . . .47 E6
Beaufort Rd ME2 . . . . . . .46 E8
Beaufort Wlk ME15 . . . . .107 E4
Beaulieu Ave E16 . . . . .1 B5
Beaulieu Rd TN10 . . . . . .117 B4
Beaulieu Rise ME1 . . . . . .47 D1
Beaulieu Wlk ME16 . . . . .91 C7
Beaumanor Gdns SE9 . . .23 A4
Beaumont Dr DA11 . . . . . .29 F8
Beaumont Rd
  Maidstone ME16 . . . . . . .91 B2
  Northfleet DA11 . . . . .29 E8
  Orpington BR5 . . . . .37 D3
Beauworth Pk ME15 . . . .107 E8
Beaver Rd ME16 . . . . .91 B7
Beaverbank Rd SE9 . . . . .23 D7
Beavers Lodge DA14 . . . .23 F3
Beaverwood Rd BR7 . . . .23 E2
Beaverwood Sch
  for Girls BR7 . . . . .23 E2
Bebbington Rd SE18 . . . . .2 E2
Beblets CI 4 BR6 . . . . . . .51 F5
Beckenham Dr ME16 . . . .91 D7
Becket Ct Headcorn TN27 .141 D5
  2 Tonbridge TN9 . . . . . .133 B8
Beckets Field TN11 . . . . .131 A3
Beckett CI DA17 . . . . .3 F3
Becketts CI BR6 . . . . .51 F7
Beckford Dr BR5 . . . . .37 D2
Beckley CI DA12 . . . . .31 B6
Beckley Mews ME5 . . . . . .61 F5
Beckman Rd TN14 . . . . . .68 C4
Becks Rd DA14 . . . . .24 A5
Becksbourne CI ME14 . . .92 A6
Beckton Park Sta E6 . . . . .1 F6
Beckton Rd E16 . . . . .1 A8

Beckton Spec Sch E16 . . . . .1 D8
Beckton Sta E6 . . . . .2 A8
Beckworth PI ME16 . . . . . .91 B2
Becton PI DA8 . . . . .8 C6
Bedale Wlk DA2 . . . . .27 B7
Beddington Gn BR5 . . . . . .37 F8
Beddington Rd BR5 . . . . . .37 F8
Beddow Way ME20 . . . . . .76 B3
Bedens Rd DA14 . . . . .24 E3
Bedford Ave ME8 . . . . .49 D1
Bedford PI ME1 . . . . .61 E4
Bedford Rd Dartford DA1 . .27 A8
  Northfleet DA11 . . . . .29 F6
  Orpington BR6 . . . . .38 B1
  Royal Tunbridge Wells TN4 .133 A1
  Sidcup DA15 . . . . .23 E5
Bedford Sq DA3 . . . . .42 E6
Bedford Terr 9 TN1 . . . .149 A2
Bedgebury CI
  Chatham ME1 . . . . .61 D8
  Maidstone ME14 . . . . . . .92 C6
Bedgebury Cross TN17 . .167 D2
Bedgebury Lower Sch
  TN18 . . . . .184 F7
Bedgebury National
  Pinetum* TN17 . . . . . .177 E8
Bedgebury Park Sch
  TN17 . . . . .167 E1
Bedgebury Rd Eltham SE9 . .5 D3
  Goudhurst TN17 . . . . . . .167 E5
Bedivere Rd BR1 . . . . .22 A5
Bedlam La TN27 . . . . .142 E6
Bedonwell Inf Sch SE2 . . . .7 E8
Bedonwell Jun Sch DA17 . .7 E8
Bedonwell Rd Bexley DA7 . .7 F6
  Erith DA7,DA17 . . . . .7 E8
Bedwell Rd DA17 . . . . .4 A1
Bedwin CI ME1 . . . . .61 D7
Beeby Rd E16 . . . . .1 B8
Beech Ave Sidcup DA15 . . .24 A8
  Swanley BR8 . . . . .39 F5
Beech Copse BR1 . . . . . . .36 F7
Beech Dell BR2,BR6 . . . . .50 F6
Beech Dr ME16 . . . . .91 C5
Beech Gr ME4 . . . . .32 C4
Beech Green La
  Cowden TN7 . . . . .145 F1
  Withyham TN7 . . . . .160 B7
Beech Haven Ct DA1 . . . . .8 D2
Beech House 7 DA15 . . . .24 A5
Beech Hurst TN2 . . . . . . .150 D7
Beech Hurst CI ME15 . . . .92 B2
Beech La TN12 . . . . .151 C4
Beech Manor TN2 . . . . . .149 D3
Beech Rd Dartford DA1 . . .26 D7
  East Malling ME19 . . . . . .89 F7
  Hoo St Werburgh ME3 . . .34 E3
  Kings Hill ME18 . . . . .88 D2
  Newenden TN18 . . . . . . .187 C3
  Orpington BR6 . . . . .52 A3
  Rochester ME2 . . . . .46 F6
  Sevenoaks TN13 . . . . . . .84 B2
Beech St TN1 . . . . .149 B4
Beech Wlk DA1 . . . . .9 A3
Beecham Rd TN10 . . . . . .117 C6
Beechcroft BR7 . . . . .23 A1
Beechcroft Ave DA7 . . . . . .8 D5
Beechcroft CI BR6 . . . . . . .51 D6
Beechcroft Rd BR6 . . . . . .51 D6
Beechen Bank Rd ME5 . . .62 A1
Beechenlea La BR8 . . . . . .40 B6
Beechers Ct SE12 . . . . . . .22 B5
Beeches Ct BR1 . . . . .22 A2
Beeches The
  Aylesford ME20 . . . . .75 E1
  Chatham ME5 . . . . .62 A4
  Hextable BR8 . . . . .25 F1
  Royal Tunbridge Wells TN2 .149 D6
  Sole Street DA13 . . . . . . .44 D5
  The Moor TN18 . . . . . . .184 E7
  Tilbury RM18 . . . . .13 B5
Beechfield Cotts 5 BR1 . .36 C7
Beechfield Rd Bromley BR1 .36 C7
  Erith DA8 . . . . .8 E7
Beechhill Rd SE9 . . . . .6 A2
Beeching Rd ME5 . . . . . . .62 B3
Beechings Gn ME8 . . . . . .49 C3
Beechings Way ME8 . . . . .49 C3
Beechings Way Ind Ctr
  ME8 . . . . .49 B4
Beechlands CI DA3 . . . . . .43 A4
Beechmont Rd TN13 . . . . .99 B6
Beechmont Rise TN10 . . .117 B6
Beechmore CI BR1 . . . . . .36 E5
Beechmore Dr ME5 . . . . . .62 A2
Beechway DA5 . . . . .7 D1
Beechwood Ave
  Chatham ME5 . . . . .48 D2
  Orpington BR6 . . . . .51 E4
Beechwood Cres DA7 . . . . .7 E4
Beechwood Dr
  Orpington BR2 . . . . .50 D6
  Vigo Village DA13 . . . . . .58 A1
Beechwood Gdns DA13 . . .58 A1
Beechwood Mews TN2 . .149 E4
Beechwood Rd ME16 . . . .90 F3
Beechwood Rise BR7 . . . .23 B6
Beechwood Sch
  (Sacred Heart) TN2 . . .149 E4
Beechy Lees Rd TN14 . . . .69 E3
Beeken Dene ME3 . . . . . . .51 C6
Beesfield La DA4 . . . . .41 A1
Beeston Ct 4 DA1 . . . . . . .10 B1
Begbie Rd SE3 . . . . .5 C6
Beggars La TN16 . . . . .81 E3

Begonia Ave ME8 . . . . . . .49 C2
Beke Rd ME8 . . . . .63 D4
Bekesbourne Tower 12
  BR5 . . . . .38 D1
Beldam Haw TN14 . . . . . . .68 A8
Belfast Ho 14 ME15 . . . . .107 E7
Belfield Rd ME14 . . . . . . .150 D6
Belford Gr SE18 . . . . .2 A2
Belgrave C 5 BR5 . . . . . . .38 C5
Belgrave Rd SE7 . . . . .5 C7
Belgrave Rd TN1 . . . . . . .149 B4
Belgrave St ME20 . . . . . . .75 F6
Belgrove 5 TN1 . . . . .149 A2
Bell CI DA9 . . . . .10 F2
Bell Cres ME1 . . . . .75 F8
Bell Farm Lane ME16 . . . .90 F2
Bell Gdns BR5 . . . . .38 C4
Bell Ho Erith SE18 . . . . . . .3 D1
  Grays RM17 . . . . .11 F8
Bell La Burham ME1 . . . . . .75 F8
  Chatham ME4 . . . . .77 B7
  Larkfield ME20 . . . . .75 B2
  Lashenden TN27 . . . . . . .158 B8
  Maidstone ME14 . . . . . . .93 A5
  Newham E16 . . . . .1 A5
  Staplehurst TN12 . . . . . .139 E3
Bell Meadow ME15 . . . . .107 E6
Bell Rd ME15 . . . . .107 E5
Bell Row TN11 . . . . .118 F5
Bell St SE18,SE3 . . . . .5 E6
Bell Water Gate SE18 . . . . .2 A3
Bell Way ME17 . . . . .109 E2
Bell Wood Com Sch
  ME15 . . . . .107 E5
Bell Wood Inf Sch ME15 .107 E5
Bell's CI TN30 . . . . .183 A7
Bell's La ME3 . . . . .34 E6
Belle Vue Rd BR6 . . . . . . .51 A1
Bellefield Rd BR5 . . . . . . .38 B4
Bellegrove Par DA16 . . . . . .6 F4
Bellegrove CI DA16 . . . . . . .6 F5
Bellegrove Rd DA16 . . . . . .6 E5
Bellevue Rd DA6 . . . . .7 F2
Bellflower CI 2 E6 . . . . . . .1 E8
Bellgrove St ME15 . . . . . . .77 A8
Bellingham Way ME20 . . .75 B3
Bellman Ave DA12 . . . . . . .30 E7
Bellows La TN15 . . . . .86 F7
Bellring CI DA17 . . . . .8 A8
Bells Farm La TN11 . . . . .119 C8
Bells Farm Rd TN11,TN12 103 D1
Bells La 9 TN30 . . . . .183 A7
Bellwood Ct ME3 . . . . .18 C3
Belmont Ave DA16 . . . . . . .6 E4
Belmont CI ME16 . . . . .90 F2
Belmont Ct 8 ME15 . . . . .92 B4
Belmont La BR7 . . . . .23 C3
Belmont Par BR7 . . . . .23 C3
Belmont Prim Sch DA7 . . . .8 A7
Belmont Rd Chislehurst BR7 23 B3
  Erith DA8 . . . . .8 B6
  Gillingham ME7 . . . . .48 C4
  Grays RM17 . . . . .11 F8
Belnor Ave ME9 . . . . .65 F8
Belson Rd SE18 . . . . .1 F2
Belton Rd DA14 . . . . .24 A4
Beltring Sta
  TN12 . . . . .120 B4
Beltring Hop Farm*
  TN12 . . . . .120 A3
Beltring Rd
  Beltring ME15 . . . . .120 B4
  Royal Tunbridge Wells TN4 .149 A6
Beltwood Rd DA17 . . . . . . .4 C2
Beluncle Villas ME3 . . . . .35 C7
Belvedere CI DA12 . . . . . .30 C7
Belvedere Ct DA17 . . . . . . .3 F3
Belvedere
  Cty Prim Jun Sch DA17 . . .4 B3
Belvedere House 9 ME15 107 F5
Belvedere Ind Est DA17 . . . .4 D5
Belvedere Link Bsns Pk
  DA17 . . . . .4 C3
Belvedere Rd Bexley DA7 . .7 F5
  Erith SE28 . . . . .3 D5
Belvedere Sta DA17 . . . . . .4 B3
Belvoir CI SE9 . . . . .22 E5
Ben Tillet CI E16 . . . . .1 F5
Benares Rd SE18 . . . . .2 F2
Benden CI TN17 . . . . .139 F4
Bendmore Ave SE2 . . . . . . .3 A2
Bendon Way ME8 . . . . . . .63 D8
Benedict CI 9 Erith DA17 . . .3 E3
  Halling ME2 . . . . .60 B4
  Orpington BR6 . . . . .51 E7
Benenden CE Prim Sch
  TN17 . . . . .180 D6
Benenden Gn BR2 . . . . . . .36 A4
Benenden Hospl TN17 . . .171 C3
Benenden Manor ME8 . . .49 B3
Benenden Rd
  Benenden TN17 . . . . . . .181 B4
  Cranbrook TN17 . . . . . . .169 E1
  Fosten Green TN27 . . . . .171 F5
  Rochester ME2 . . . . .33 C1
Benenden St TN17 . . . . . .180 C8
Benhall Mill Rd TN2,TN3 .163 D8
Benjamin CI 4 DA17 . . . . . .7 F8
Benn Ho SE7 . . . . .1 C1
Bennett CI DA16 . . . . .7 A5
Bennett Meml
  Diocesan Sch TN4 . . . .148 E6
Bennett Way DA2 . . . . . . .27 D3
Bennetts Ave TN15 . . . . . .71 C7
Bennetts Copse BR7 . . . . .22 E2
Bennetts Cotts ME7 . . . . . .78 A8

Bennetts Mews 13 TN30 .183 A7
Benover Rd ME18 . . . . . . .120 F7
Benson Rd RM17 . . . . .12 C8
Bensted CI ME15 . . . . . . .121 D7
Bentfield Gdns SE9 . . . . . .22 D5
Bentham Hill TN3,TN4 . . .132 C3
Bentham Rd SE28 . . . . .3 B5
Bentley CI Aylesford ME20 . .75 F1
  Chatham ME5 . . . . .62 D2
  New Barn DA3 . . . . .43 D7
Bentley St DA12 . . . . .13 C1
Bentley Street Ind Est
  DA12 . . . . .13 C1
Bentley's Mdw TN15 . . . . .84 F7
Bentlif CI ME16 . . . . .91 D5
Berber Rd ME2 . . . . .47 B8
Bercta Rd SE9 . . . . .23 C5
Berengrave La ME8 . . . . . .49 F2
Berens Ct DA14 . . . . .23 F4
Berens Rd BR5 . . . . .38 D4
Berens Way BR5 . . . . .37 F6
Beresford Ave ME1 . . . . . .47 C6
Beresford Dr BR1 . . . . .36 E6
Beresford Rd
  Gillingham ME7 . . . . .48 D5
  Goudhurst TN17 . . . . . . .153 F1
  Kit's Coty ME20 . . . . .76 D7
  Northfleet DA11 . . . . .29 E8
Beresford Square
  Market PI SE18 . . . . .2 B2
Beresford St SE18 . . . . .2 B3
Beresfords Hill ME17 . . . .107 B4
Berger CI BR5 . . . . .37 E3
Bergland Pk ME2 . . . . .47 D8
Bering Wlk E16 . . . . .1 D7
Berkeley Ave DA7 . . . . .7 D6
Berkeley CI Chatham ME1 . .61 D8
  Orpington BR5 . . . . .37 E2
  Pembury TN2 . . . . .150 E7
Berkeley Cres DA1 . . . . . .26 F7
Berkeley Ct 6 BR8 . . . . . .39 E6
Berkeley Mount ME4 . . . . .47 F4
Berkeley Rd 7 TN1 . . . . .149 A2
Berkeley Terr RM18 . . . . . .13 C1
Berkley Cres DA12 . . . . . .13 C1
Berkley Rd DA12 . . . . .13 B1
Berkshire CI ME5 . . . . .62 C8
Bermuda Rd RM18 . . . . . .13 C5
Bernal CI SE28 . . . . .3 D6
Bernard Ashley Dr SE7 . . . .1 B1
Bernard St 22 DA12 . . . . .13 B1
Bernards Ct DA15 . . . . . . .23 E7
Bernersmede SE3 . . . . .5 A4
Berry Rd ME3 . . . . .34 E3
Berry's Green Rd TN16 . . .66 E4
Berry's Hill TN16 . . . . .66 B4
Berryfield CI BR1 . . . . .36 E7
Berryhill SE9 . . . . .6 B3
Berryhill Gdns SE9 . . . . . . .6 B3
Berrylands Hartley DA3 . . .43 A3
  Orpington BR6 . . . . .52 C7
Bert Reilly Ho 1 SE18 . . . .2 D1
Bertha Hollamby Ct DA14 .24 C3
Bertrand Way SE28 . . . . . . .3 C6
Bertrey Cotts TN16 . . . . . .66 B3
Berwick Cres DA15 . . . . . . .6 E1
Berwick Ct 2 DA12 . . . . . .30 B1
Berwick Rd Bexley DA16 . . .7 B6
  Newham E16 . . . . .1 C7
Berwick Way TN14 . . . . . .84 F7
Berwyn Gr ME15 . . . . . . .107 A6
Beryl Ave E16 . . . . .1 E8
Beryl Ho 3 SE18 . . . . .2 F1
Besant Ct SE28 . . . . .3 B6
Bessels Green Rd TN13 . . .83 D3
Bessels Meadow TN13 . . .83 D3
Bessels Way TN13 . . . . . . .83 D3
Bessie Lansbury CI E6 . . . .2 A7
Best St ME4 . . . . .47 F4
Beta Rd ME3 . . . . .35 D7
Betenson St SE18 . . . . . . .83 F5
Bethany Sch TN17 . . . . . .154 B5
Bethel Bd Bexley DA16 . . . .7 C4
  Sevenoaks TN13 . . . . . . .84 C4
Betherinden Cotts TN18 .186 A4
Bethersden Ct ME15 . . . .107 F7
Bethersden Rd
  TN27,TN26 . . . . .159 C5
Beths Gram Sch DA5 . . . . .8 B1
Betjeman CI ME20 . . . . . . .74 F3
Betony Gdns ME14 . . . . . .92 F5
Betsham Rd Betsham DA13 .28 D3
  Erith DA8 . . . . .8 F7
  Maidstone ME15 . . . . . . .107 F6
  Swanscombe DA10 . . . . .28 E8
Betterton Dr DA14 . . . . . . .24 E6
Bettescombe Rd ME8 . . . .63 E7
Betts Rd E16 . . . . .1 B6
Beulah Rd TN1 . . . . .149 C4
Beult Meadow TN27 . . . .143 A1
Beult Rd DA1 . . . . .9 A3
Bevan PI BR8 . . . . .39 F5
Bevan Rd SE2 . . . . .3 B1
Bevans CI DA9 . . . . .11 C1
Bevercote Wlk 1 DA17 . . . .7 F8
Beveridge Ct 1 SE28 . . . . .3 B6
Beverley Ave DA15 . . . . . .23 F8
Beverley CI ME8 . . . . .63 F8
Beverley Cres TN9 . . . . . .132 F7
Beverley Rd Bexley DA7 . . . .8 C5
  Maidstone ME15 . . . . . . .90 F2
  Orpington BR2 . . . . .50 E8
Bevile House RM17 . . . . . .12 B7
Bevis CI DA2 . . . . .27 C8
Bewl Bridge CI TN5 . . . . .177 B3

Bewl Water* TN5 . . . . . . .176 C6
Bewl Water
  Visitors Ctr* TN5 . . . . .176 B8
Bewlbridge La
  Lamberhurst TN3,TN5 . . .166 B1
  Wadhurst TN5 . . . . .175 F8
Bewley La TN15 . . . . .86 D2
Bexhill Dr RM17 . . . . .11 F8
Bexley CI DA1 . . . . .8 E2
Bexley Coll Erith DA17 . . . . .4 B1
  DA17 . . . . .4 C2
Bexley Coll (St Joseph's
  Campus) SE2 . . . . .7 D8
Bexley Gram Sch DA16 . . . .7 B3
Bexley High St DA5 . . . . . .25 B7
Bexley Hospl DA5 . . . . . . .25 E6
Bexley La Crayford DA1 . . . .8 E2
  Sidcup DA14 . . . . .24 C5
Bexley Rd Eltham SE9 . . . . .6 C2
  Erith DA8 . . . . .4 F1
  Erith,Northumberland Heath
  DA8 . . . . .8 C8
Bexley Sta DA5 . . . . .25 A7
Bexleyheath Sch DA7 . . . . .7 F4
Bexleyheath Sta DA7 . . . . .7 F5
Bexon La ME9 . . . . .80 F5
Bickley Cres BR1 . . . . .36 E5
Bickley Ct BR1 . . . . .36 E6
Bickley Park Rd BR1 . . . . .36 F6
Bickley Park Sch BR1 . . . .36 E6
Bickley Prim Sch BR1 . . . .36 C7
Bickley Rd 2 Bromley BR1 .36 E7
  5 Tonbridge TN9 . . . . . .133 B8
Bickley Sta BR1 . . . . .36 E6
Bickmore Way TN11 . . . . .117 D3
Bicknor Court Cotts ME9 .80 C2
Bicknor La ME9 . . . . .80 D3
Bicknor Rd
  Maidstone ME15 . . . . . . .107 F4
  Orpington BR6 . . . . .51 F8
Bidborough CE Prim Sch
  TN3 . . . . .132 D3
Bidborough Ridge TN4 . .132 E4
Biddenden CI ME15 . . . . . .92 F3
Biddenden La TN27 . . . . .141 E5
Biddenden Rd
  Durrant Green TN26,TN26 .173 A6
  Headcorn TN27 . . . . . . .141 E2
  Tenterden TN30 . . . . . . .172 E6
  Tylden TN27 . . . . .158 F8
Biddenden Vineyard*
  TN27 . . . . .172 A5
Biddenden Way
  Eltham SE9 . . . . .23 A4
  Istead Rise DA13 . . . . . . .29 E1
Biddulph Ho 17 SE18 . . . . .1 F2
Bideford Rd DA16 . . . . .7 B7
Biggin La RM16 . . . . .13 B8
Bignell Rd SE18 . . . . .2 B1
Bilberry CI ME14 . . . . .92 E5
Bill Hamling CI SE9 . . . . . .22 F6
Bill Street Rd ME2 . . . . . . .33 C1
Billet Hill TN15 . . . . .56 C6
Billings DA3 . . . . .42 F3
Bilsby Gr SE9 . . . . .22 D4
Bilsington CI ME5 . . . . .62 B5
Bilton Rd DA8 . . . . .9 A8
Binbury La ME14,ME9 . . . .79 A5
Bines The TN12 . . . . .136 A5
Bingham Point 5 SE18 . . . .2 B2
Bingham Rd ME2 . . . . .33 C1
Bingley CI ME6 . . . . .74 F5
Bingley Rd 1 Chatham ME1 47 E4
  Newham E16 . . . . .1 C7
Binland Gr ME5 . . . . .61 D5
Binnacle Rd ME1 . . . . .61 C8
Binney Rd ME3 . . . . .19 D8
Binsey Wlk 1 SE2 . . . . .3 C4
Birbetts Rd SE9 . . . . .22 F6
Birch CI Eynsford DA4 . . . .54 D7
  Matfield TN12 . . . . .135 D1
  New Barn DA3 . . . . .43 C7
  Royal Tunbridge Wells TN2 .149 D7
  Sevenoaks TN13 . . . . . . .84 B4
  Tonbridge TN11 . . . . . . .116 D4
Birch Cres ME20 . . . . .90 D8
Birch Dr ME5 . . . . .62 D1
Birch Gr Bexley DA16 . . . . .7 A3
  Gillingham ME7 . . . . .48 F5
Birch Kiln Cotts TN5 . . . .175 A6
Birch Mead BR6 . . . . .51 A8
Birch PI Sevenoaks TN13 . .84 A3
  Stone DA9 . . . . .10 E1
Birch Rd
  Hoo St Werburgh ME3 . . .34 E3
  Paddock Wood TN12 . . . .136 A6
Birch Row BR2 . . . . .37 A3
Birch Tree Ho 17 SE7 . . . . .5 C8
Birch Tree Way ME15 . . . .92 B3
Birch Way TN2 . . . . .149 D7
Birchden Cotts TN3 . . . . .161 C6
Birchdene Dr SE28 . . . . . . .3 A5
Birches The Greenwich SE7 .5 B4
  Orpington BR6 . . . . .51 A6
  Swanley BR8 . . . . .39 E5
  Tonbridge TN9 . . . . .133 D2
Birchetts Ave TN3 . . . . . .147 E6
Birchetts Green La TN5 . .176 A2
Birchfield CI ME15 . . . . . .107 B6
Birchfields ME5 . . . . .62 C4
Birchin Cross Rd TN15 . . . .70 A5
Birchington CI Bexley DA7 . .8 B6
  Maidstone ME14 . . . . . . .92 A6
  Orpington BR5 . . . . .38 C1
Bircholme TN2 . . . . .149 D7

Bircholt Rd ME15 . . . . . . .107 F4
Birchway TN15 . . . . .55 F2
Birchwood Ave
  Bidborough TN4 . . . . .132 E3
  Sidcup DA14 . . . . .24 C5
Birchwood Dr DA2 . . . . . .25 E4
Birchwood La TN14 . . . . . .67 E4
Birchwood Par DA2 . . . . . .25 E4
Birchwood Park Ave BR8 .39 F6
Birchwood Prim Sch BR8 .39 D8
Birchwood Rd
  Dartford DA2,BR8 . . . . . . .25 D3
  Maidstone ME16 . . . . .91 C5
  Orpington BR5 . . . . .37 E5
Birchwood Terr BR8 . . . . .39 C8
Bird House La BR6 . . . . . . .66 A5
Bird in Hand St TN3 . . . . .161 B8
Bird La TN5 . . . . .174 B5
Bird-in-Hand La BR1 . . . . .36 D7
Birdbrook Rd SE3 . . . . . . .5 C4
Birdham Cl BR1 . . . . .36 E4
Birkbeck Prim Sch DA14 . .24 B5
Birkbeck Rd DA14 . . . . . . .24 A5
Birkdale TN1 . . . . .149 B6
Birkdale Cl BR6 . . . . .37 D2
Birkdale Ct ME16 . . . . . . .91 E4
Birkdale Rd SE2 . . . . .3 A2
Birken Rd TN2 . . . . .149 D6
Birkhall Cl ME5 . . . . .62 A1
Birling Ave Gillingham ME8 .49 E1
  Maidstone ME14 . . . . .93 A4
Birling Cl ME14 . . . . .93 A4
Birling Dr TN2 . . . . .149 A1
Birling Hill DA13,ME19,ME6 .59 B1
Birling Park Ave TN2 . . . .163 B8
Birling Pk ME19 . . . . .74 C5
Birling Rd Erith DA8 . . . . .8 E6
  Leybourne ME19 . . . . .74 C3
  Royal Tunbridge Wells TN2 .163 B8
  Ryarsh ME19 . . . . .74 A5
  Snodland ME6 . . . . .74 F7
Birnam Sq [1] ME16 . . . . . .91 E4
Birtrick Dr DA13 . . . . .43 F4
Bishop Butt Cl BR6 . . . . . .51 F7
Bishop John Robinson
  CE Prim Sch SE28 . . . . . . .3 C6
Bishop's Down TN4 . . . . .148 E5
Bishop's Down
  Cty Prim Sch TN4 . . . . . .148 E5
Bishop's Down Park Rd
  TN4 . . . . .148 F4
Bishop's Down Rd TN4 . . .148 F3
Bishop's La ME15 . . . . . . .121 D6
Bishops Ave BR1 . . . . .36 C6
Bishops Cl Eltham SE9 . . . .23 C6
  Nettlestead ME18 . . . . . . .104 D6
Bishops Ct
  Royal Tunbridge Wells TN4 .148 E3
  Stone DA9 . . . . .10 E2
Bishops Gn BR1 . . . . .36 C8
Bishops Mews TN9 . . . . . .133 C8
Bishops Oak Ride TN10 . .117 C6
Bishops Way ME15 . . . . . .91 F4
Bishops Wlk
  Chislehurst BR7 . . . . .37 C8
  Rochester ME1 . . . . .47 C5
Bishopsbourne Ho [2] BR1 .22 B1
Black Eagle Cl ME19 . . . . .96 C8
Black Horse Ct TN27 . . . .141 E5
Black Horse Mews TN15 . .87 A7
Black Horse Rd [12] DA14 . .24 A4
Black Mill La TN27 . . . . . .141 B6
Black Post ME17 . . . . .95 E4
Black Rock Gdns ME7 . . . .63 B4
Blackberry Field BR5 . . . . .38 A8
Blackberry Way TN12 . . . .136 B6
Blackbrook La BR1,BR2 . . .37 A5
Blackdale Farm Cotts DA1 27 B6
Blackfen Par DA15 . . . . . . .7 A1
Blackfen Rd DA15 . . . . . . .7 B1
Blackfen Sch for Girls DA15 7 B1
Blackhall La TN15 . . . . . . .84 E3
Blackheath Bluecoat
  CE Sec Sch SE3 . . . . .5 B7
Blackheath High Sch SE3 . .5 A7
Blackheath High Sch
  GPDST (Jun Dept) SE3 . . . .5 A5
Blackheath Pk SE3 . . . . . . .5 A5
Blackheath Prep Sch SE3 . .5 A6
Blackhurst La TN5 . . . . . .149 F6
Blacklands
  East Malling ME19 . . . . . . .89 F8
  Mill Street ME19 . . . . .89 F7
Blacklands Dr ME19 . . . . . .89 F8
Blacklands Jun Sch ME19 .89 F7
Blackman Cl ME3 . . . . . . .34 D7
Blackman's La TN11 . . . . .118 D6
Blackmans Cl DA1 . . . . . . .26 C7
Blackmanstone Way ME16 91 B7
Blackmead TN13 . . . . .83 B6
Blackness La ME7 . . . . . . .50 D2
Blacksmith Dr ME14 . . . . .92 C5
Blacksmith's La TN5 . . . . .175 A5
Blacksmiths Field TN32 . .185 C1
Blacksmiths La BR5 . . . . . .38 C4
Blacksole La TN15 . . . . . . .71 F3
Blacksole Rd TN15 . . . . . .71 F3
Blackthorn Ave
  Chatham ME5 . . . . .62 A3
  Royal Tunbridge Wells TN4 .133 C1
Blackthorn Cl TN15 . . . . . .55 F2
Blackthorn Dr ME20 . . . . .75 B2
Blackthorn Gr DA7 . . . . . . .7 E4
Blackthorne Rd ME8 . . . . .64 B8

Blackwater Cl RM13 . . . . .4 E8
Bladindon Dr DA5 . . . . . . .24 D8
Blair Cl DA15 . . . . .6 E2
Blair Dr TN13 . . . . .84 B4
Blake Cl DA16 . . . . .6 E6
Blake Dr [3] ME20 . . . . . . .74 F4
Blake Gdns DA1 . . . . .9 F3
Blake Way
  Royal Tunbridge Wells TN2 .149 D7
  Tilbury RM18 . . . . .13 C5
Blakemore Way DA17 . . . . .3 B1
Blakeney Cl ME14 . . . . . . .93 B4
Blaker Ave ME1 . . . . .47 E1
Blaker Ct SE7 . . . . .5 C7
Blanchard Cl SE9 . . . . .22 E5
Bland St SE9 . . . . .5 D3
Blanmerle Rd SE9 . . . . . . .23 B7
Blann Cl SE9 . . . . .5 D1
Blatchford Cl ME19 . . . . . .74 F1
Blatchington Rd TN1 . . . .149 B1
Bleak Hill La SE18 . . . . .6 F8
Bleakwood Rd ME5 . . . . . .61 F4
Blean Rd ME8 . . . . .49 C2
Blean Sq ME14 . . . . .92 C6
Bleddyn Cl DA15 . . . . .7 C1
Bledlow Cl SE28 . . . . .3 C6
Blendon Dr DA5 . . . . .7 D1
Blendon Rd
  Maidstone ME14 . . . . .92 C5
  Sidcup DA5 . . . . .7 D1
Blendon Terr SE18 . . . . . . .6 C8
Blenheim Cl ME4 . . . . .47 E2
Blenheim Cl Dartford DA1 . .9 C1
  Maidstone ME15 . . . . .92 F3
  Meopham MA13 . . . . .58 B8
Blenheim Ct DA15 . . . . . . .23 D5
Blenheim Dr DA16 . . . . . . .6 F6
Blenheim Gr DA12 . . . . . . .30 D8
Blenheim Inf Sch BR6 . . . .52 C8
Blenheim Jun Sch BR6 . . .52 C8
Blenheim Rd
  Bromley BR1,BR2 . . . . .36 E5
  Dartford DA1 . . . . .9 C1
  Orpington BR5,BR6 . . . . . .52 C8
  Sidcup DA15 . . . . .24 C7
Blenheim Way TN5 . . . . . .177 C3
Bletchington Ct [3] DA17 . . .4 A2
Blewbury Ho [3] SE2 . . . . . .3 C4
Bligh Prim Inf Sch ME2 . . .46 C7
Bligh Rd DA11 . . . . .13 A1
Bligh Way ME2 . . . . .46 D6
Bligh's Meadow Sh Prec
  TN13 . . . . .84 C2
Bligh's Rd TN13 . . . . .84 B2
Bligh's Wlk TN13 . . . . .84 C2
Blind La Bredhurst ME7 . . .63 A1
  Goudhurst TN17 . . . . .153 E1
  Lidsing ME7 . . . . .62 F1
Blind Mary's La ME9 . . . . .80 E4
Bliss Way TN10 . . . . .117 E5
Blithdale Rd SE2 . . . . .3 A2
Blockhouse Rd [5] RM17 . .12 C8
Blockmakers Ct ME4 . . . . .48 B1
Bloomfield Rd
  Bromley BR2 . . . . .36 D4
  Woolwich SE18 . . . . .2 B1
Bloomfield Terr TN11 . . . .81 E2
Bloomsbury Wlk [2] ME15 .92 A4
Bloors La ME8 . . . . .49 D1
Bloors Wharf Rd ME7 . . . .49 F4
Blowers Grove Wood ME7 63 B3
Blowers Hill Cowden TN8 .145 D8
  Speldhurst TN3 . . . . .148 B8
Bloxam Gdns SE9 . . . . .5 E2
Blue Anchor La RM18 . . . .13 E8
Blue Boar La ME7 . . . . . . .47 D5
Blue Chalet Ind Pk TN15 . .55 D4
Bluebell Cl Gillingham ME7 .48 F6
  Orpington BR6 . . . . .51 C8
Bluebell Wlk TN12 . . . . . .136 A5
Blueberry La TN14 . . . . . . .67 C4
Bluebird Way SE28 . . . . . . .2 D4
Bluecoat La TN17 . . . . . . .167 C6
Bluett St ME14 . . . . .92 A5
Bluewater Parkway DA9 . .27 F7
Blunden La ME18 . . . . . . .105 A1
Blunts Rd SE9 . . . . .6 A2
Blyth Rd SE28 . . . . .3 C6
Blythe Ct SE12 . . . . .22 A8
Blythe Hill BR5 . . . . .38 A8
Blythe Rd ME15 . . . . .92 B4
Boakes Meadow TN14 . . . .68 F8
Boarders La TN5 . . . . .176 C3
Boarley Ct ME14 . . . . .76 F1
Boarley La ME14 . . . . .76 F2
Boathouse Rd ME12 . . . . . .21 F3
Bobbing Hill ME9 . . . . .65 F5
Bocking Ct TN15 . . . . .174 E4
Bockingford La ME15 . . . .106 F8
Bodiam Cl ME8 . . . . .49 C3
Bodiam Ct ME16 . . . . .91 F1
Bodiam Rd RM18,TN32 . . .185 F3
Bodle Ave DA10 . . . . .11 E1
Bodmin Cl BR5 . . . . .38 C1
Bodsham Cres ME15 . . . . .93 B3
Boevey Path [2] SE2 . . . . . .7 B1
Bogey La BR6 . . . . .51 A3
Bognor Rd DA16 . . . . .7 D6
Boiler Rd ME4 . . . . .48 A8
Boley Hill ME1 . . . . .47 C5
Boleyn Rd TN15 . . . . .69 E2
Bolingbroke Ho ME16 . . . .91 E3
Bollon Ct [9] SE12 . . . . . . .22 B5
Bolner Cl ME5 . . . . .61 F2
Bombay House [1] ME15 . .107 E5
Bombers La TN16 . . . . .81 D7
Bonar Pl BR7 . . . . .22 E1

Bonaventure Ct DA12 . . . . .30 F4
Bonchester Cl BR7 . . . . . . .23 A1
Bond Cl TN14 . . . . .67 D4
Bond Rd ME8 . . . . .63 E5
Bond St RM17 . . . . .12 C8
Bondfield Cl TN4 . . . . .133 A1
Bondfield Ho SE18 . . . . .6 A7
Bondfield Rd
  East Malling ME19 . . . . . . .89 F8
  [4] Newham E6 . . . . .1 F8
Boneashe La TN15 . . . . . . .87 D6
Boneta Rd SE18 . . . . .1 F3
Bonflower La ME17 . . . . . .122 C2
Bonney Way BR8 . . . . .39 E6
Bonnington Gn ME8 . . . . .49 C3
Bonnington Rd ME14 . . . . .92 C6
Bonnington Twr BR2 . . . . .36 E3
Bookins ME17 . . . . .107 D5
Booth Cl SE28 . . . . .3 B6
Booth Rd ME4 . . . . .47 F2
Bootham Cl ME2 . . . . .46 D5
Borden CE Prim Sch ME9 . .65 F3
Bordyke TN9 . . . . .117 C2
Boreham Ave E16 . . . . .1 A7
Boresisle TN30 . . . . .173 B2
Borgard Ho SE18 . . . . .5 E6
Borgard Rd SE18 . . . . .1 F2
Borkwood Ct BR6 . . . . . . .51 F6
Borkwood Pk BR6 . . . . . . .51 F6
Borkwood Way BR6 . . . . . .51 E6
Borland Cl DA9 . . . . .11 A2
Borough Green
  & Wrotham Sta TN15 . . . . .86 F7
Borough Green Prim Sch
  TN15 . . . . .87 A7
Borough Green Rd
  Borough Green TN15 . . . . .86 E7
  Ightham TN15 . . . . .86 D6
  Wrotham TN15 . . . . .72 A1
Borough Rd ME7 . . . . .48 D4
Borstal HM Prison &
  Youth Custody Ctr ME1 . .47 B1
Borstal Manor Com Sch
  ME1 . . . . .46 F2
Borstal Mews ME1 . . . . . . .47 A2
Borstal Rd ME1 . . . . .47 B3
Borstal St ME1 . . . . .47 A2
Bostall Hill SE2 . . . . .3 B1
Bostall La SE2 . . . . .3 B1
Bostall Manorway SE2 . . . . .3 B2
Bostall Park Ave DA7 . . . . .7 E7
Bostall Rd BR5 . . . . .24 B1
Boston Gdns ME8 . . . . . . .49 C1
Boston Rd ME5 . . . . .62 C2
Bosville Ave TN13 . . . . . . .84 A4
Bosville Dr TN13 . . . . .84 A4
Bosville Rd TN13 . . . . .84 A4
Boswell Cl BR5 . . . . .38 C3
Boswell Ho BR2 . . . . .36 D4
Bosworth Rd DA8 . . . . .4 E1
Botany TN9 . . . . .117 C1
Botany Bay La BR7 . . . . . .37 C7
Botha Rd E13 . . . . .1 C8
Bothwell Cl [7] E16 . . . . . . .1 A8
Botsom La TN15 . . . . .55 D4
Bott Rd DA2 . . . . .26 F4
Bottle House Cotts TN11 .130 F1
Bottlescrew Hill ME17 . . .107 A8
Boucher Dr DA11 . . . . .29 F4
Bough Beech Reservoir
  Nature Ctr* TN14 . . . . . .114 A7
Boughton Cl ME8 . . . . . . .49 B3
Boughton Ho BR1 . . . . . . .22 E1
Boughton La ME15 . . . . . .107 B6
Boughton Monchelsea
  Cty Prim Sch ME17 . . . . .107 B2
Boughton Par ME15 . . . . .107 A7
Boughton Place Cotts
  ME17 . . . . .127 A8
Boughton Rd
  Lenham ME17 . . . . .111 B2
  Woolwich SE28 . . . . .2 E3
Boultwood Rd E6 . . . . .1 F7
Boundary Ho [3] DA11 . . . .29 F7
Boundary Rd Chatham ME4 .47 E3
  Royal Tunbridge Wells TN2 .149 D1
  Sidcup DA15 . . . . .6 E2
Boundary St [2] DA8 . . . . . .8 F7
Boundary The TN3,TN4 . . .148 B3
Bounds Cross TN27 . . . . .157 F7
Bounds Oak Way TN4 . . . .132 E3
Bounds The ME20 . . . . . . .75 E1
Bourdillon Ct SE9 . . . . . . .22 E6
Bournbrook Rd SE3,SE9 . . . .5 D4
Bourne Cl TN9 . . . . .117 D3
Bourne Ct ME1 . . . . .47 D5
Bourne Ent Ctr TN15 . . . . .87 A7
Bourne Grange La TN11 . .118 D8
Bourne Ind Pk DA1 . . . . . . .8 E2
Bourne La Bodiam TN32 . .184 F1
  Plaxtol TN15 . . . . .86 F1
  Tonbridge TN9 . . . . .117 D3
Bourne Mead DA5 . . . . . . .25 B8
Bourne Par DA5 . . . . .25 B8
Bourne Pk TN11 . . . . .118 F5
Bourne Rd
  Bexley DA1,DA5 . . . . .8 D2
  Bromley BR2 . . . . .36 D5
  Gravesend DA12 . . . . .30 F6
  Sidcup DA5 . . . . .25 B8
Bourne Row TN8 . . . . . . .130 D6
Bourne Vale Hayes BR2 . . .36 A2
  Plaxtol Spoute TN15 . . . . .102 A8
Bourne Way Hayes BR2 . . .50 A8
  Swanley BR8 . . . . .39 C6
Bourner Cotts TN17 . . . . .156 D4
Bourneside Terr ME17 . . . .94 D2
Bournewood Cl ME15 . . . . .92 F1

Bournewood Rd
  Bexley SE18,SE2 . . . . .7 A7
  Orpington BR5 . . . . .38 C2
Bournville Ave ME4 . . . . . .47 F1
Bovarde Ave ME19 . . . . . . .89 C3
Bow Arrow La DA2 . . . . . . .10 B1
Bow Hill ME18 . . . . .104 D5
Bow Rd ME18 . . . . .104 E7
Bow Terr ME18 . . . . .104 E7
Bowater Pl SE3 . . . . .5 B7
Bowater Rd SE18 . . . . .1 D3
Bowen Rd TN4 . . . . .148 B4
Bower Cl ME16 . . . . .91 E4
Bower Gr ME5 . . . . .62 C1
Bower Grove Sch ME16 . . .91 B2
Bower La Eynsford DA4 . . .54 F6
  Maidstone ME16 . . . . .91 E3
Bower Mount Rd ME16 . . .91 D4
Bower Pl ME16 . . . . .91 E3
Bower Rd BR8 . . . . .26 A2
Bower St ME16 . . . . .91 E4
Bower Terr ME16 . . . . .91 E3
Bower Wlk TN12 . . . . .139 E3
Bowers Ave DA11 . . . . .29 F4
Bowers Ho ME7 . . . . .48 E7
Bowers Rd TN14 . . . . .68 F8
Bowers Wlk [1] E6 . . . . .1 F7
Bowes Cl DA15 . . . . .7 B1
Bowes Ct [24] DA2 . . . . . . .10 B1
Bowes Rd ME2 . . . . .47 B8
Bowes Wood DA3 . . . . .56 F7
Bowesden La Shorne DA12 .31 F1
  Shorne Ridgeway ME2 . . . .46 A8
Bowford Ave DA7 . . . . .7 E6
Bowley La ME17 . . . . .127 D8
Bowling Green Row [1]
  SE18 . . . . .1 F2
Bowls Pl ME17 . . . . .136 A7
Bowman Ave E16 . . . . .1 A6
Bowman Cl ME5 . . . . .62 C5
Bowmans Rd DA1 . . . . . . .25 F8
Bowness Rd DA7 . . . . .8 B5
Bowyer Cl E6 . . . . .1 F8
Bowzell Rd TN14 . . . . .99 A2
Box Farm La ME18 . . . . . . .38 D1
Boxgrove Prim Sch SE2 . . . .3 C3
Boxgrove Rd SE2 . . . . .3 C3
Boxley Cl ME14 . . . . .92 B8
Boxley Cotts DA4 . . . . .41 C5
Boxley Rd Chatham ME5 . . .62 B2
  Maidstone ME14 . . . . .92 B7
Boxley St E16 . . . . .1 B5
Boxmend Ind Est ME15 . .107 F3
Boy Court La TN27 . . . . . .125 F1
Boyard Rd SE18 . . . . .2 B1
Boyces Hill ME9 . . . . .65 D6
Boyle Ho [12] DA17 . . . . . . .4 A3
Boyle Way TN12 . . . . .120 B7
Boyne Pk TN4 . . . . .148 F4
Boyton Court Rd ME17 . . .125 A6
Brabourne Ave ME8 . . . . . .49 C3
Brabourne Cres DA7 . . . . . .7 F8
Bracken Cl Newham E6 . . . .1 F8
  Royal Tunbridge Wells TN2 .149 E5
Bracken Hill ME5 . . . . .62 A1
Bracken Lea ME5 . . . . .48 C1
Bracken Rd TN2 . . . . .149 E5
Bracken Wlk TN10 . . . . . .117 B6
Brackendene DA2,DA5 . . . .25 E4
Brackens The ME5 . . . . . . .52 A5
Brackley Cl ME14 . . . . .92 C5
Brackwood Cl ME8 . . . . . . .63 D5
Bracondale Ave DA13 . . . . .43 F8
Bracondale Rd SE2 . . . . . . .3 A2
Bradbourne Ave ME20 . . . .75 B1
Bradbourne La ME20 . . . . .75 B1
Bradbourne Park Rd TN13 84 A4
Bradbourne Rd
  Grays RM17 . . . . .12 B8
  Sevenoaks TN13,TN14 . . . .84 B5
  Sidcup DA5 . . . . .25 A8
Bradbourne Sch The TN13 84 A6
Bradbourne Vale Rd
  TN13,TN14 . . . . .84 A5
Bradbury Ct
  [3] Greenwich SE3 . . . . . . .5 A7
  [2] Northfleet DA11 . . . . . .29 F7
Braddick Cl ME15 . . . . . . .107 B6
Bradenham Ave DA16 . . . . .7 A3
Bradfield Rd E16 . . . . .1 B4
Bradfields Ave ME5 . . . . . .61 F4
Bradfields Ave W ME5 . . . .61 F5
Bradfields Ave ME5 . . . . . .62 A6
Bradford Cl BR2 . . . . .36 F1
Bradford St TN9 . . . . .117 B1
Bradfords Cl ME4 . . . . .34 C2
Bradley House ME3 . . . . . .19 C4
Bradley Rd Penshurst TN3 .146 D5
  Upper Halling ME2 . . . . . . .59 E5
Bradley Stone Rd E6 . . . . . .1 F8
Bradymead E6 . . . . .2 B7
Braeburn Way ME19 . . . . .89 C3
Braemar Ave DA7 . . . . .8 C3
Braemar Gdns DA15 . . . . .23 D5
Braes The ME3 . . . . .32 C5
Braeside Ave TN13 . . . . . .83 F3
Braeside Cl TN13 . . . . .83 F4
Braeside Cres DA7 . . . . . . .8 C3
Braesyde Cl DA17 . . . . .3 F2
Brake Ave ME5 . . . . .61 E5
Brakefield Rd DA13 . . . . . .29 E1
Bramber Ct [9] DA2 . . . . . .10 B1
Bramble Ave DA2 . . . . .28 C5
Bramble Bank DA13 . . . . . .72 F7
Bramble Cl Maidstone ME16 91 B3

Bramble Cl continued
  Tonbridge TN11 . . . . .116 F4
Bramble Croft DA8 . . . . .4 C2
Bramble La TN13 . . . . .99 B7
Bramble Reed La TN12 . . .151 B7
Bramble Wlk TN2 . . . . . . .149 D7
Bramblebury Rd SE18 . . . . .2 C1
Brambledown
  Chatham ME5 . . . . .62 B8
  Hartley MA3 . . . . .42 A8
Bramblefield Cl DA3 . . . . . .42 E6
Brambletree Cotts ME1 . . .46 E2
Brambletree Cres ME1 . . . .46 F2
Bramdean Cres SE12 . . . . .22 A7
Bramdean Gdns SE12 . . . .22 A7
Bramhope Ho [18] SE7 . . . .5 C8
Bramhope La SE7 . . . . .5 B8
Bramley Cl Gillingham ME8 .64 B8
  Istead Rise DA13 . . . . .29 F1
  Orpington BR6 . . . . .37 B1
  Swanley BR8 . . . . .39 E5
Bramley Cres TN13 . . . . . .92 F3
Bramley Ct Bexley DA16 . . . .7 B6
  Marden TN12 . . . . .138 B6
Bramley Dr TN17 . . . . .169 D4
Bramley Gdns
  Coxheath ME17 . . . . .106 C3
  Paddock Wood TN12 . . . .135 E7
Bramley Pl DA1 . . . . .9 A3
Bramley Rd
  East Peckham TN12 . . . . .119 C6
  Snodland ME6 . . . . .75 A8
Bramley Rise ME2 . . . . . . .46 E8
Bramley Way ME19 . . . . . .89 A2
Bramleys TN27 . . . . .141 D5
Brampton Prim Sch DA7 . . .7 D5
Brampton Rd DA7 . . . . .7 E6
Bramshot Ave SE3,SE7 . . . .5 B8
Bramshott Cl ME16 . . . . . .91 C6
Branbridges Ind Est
  TN12 . . . . .120 A5
Branbridges Rd TN12 . . . .120 B4
Brandon Rd DA1 . . . . .27 A8
Brandon St DA11 . . . . .30 B8
Brandreth Rd E6 . . . . .1 F7
Brands Hatch Cotts DA3 . .56 A6
Brands Hatch Rd DA3 . . . .56 A7
Branham Ho [1] SE18 . . . . .2 B1
Bransell Cl BR8 . . . . .39 C3
Bransgore Cl ME8 . . . . . . .63 D7
Branston Cres BR5 . . . . . . .37 D1
Branstone Ct RM19 . . . . . .10 B8
Brantingham Cl TN9 . . . . .132 F2
Branton Rd DA9 . . . . .10 F1
Brantwood Ave DA8 . . . . . .8 C7
Brantwood Rd DA7 . . . . . . .8 B4
Brantwood Way BR5 . . . . .38 C6
Brasenose Rd ME7 . . . . . . .48 E4
Brassey Dr ME20 . . . . .90 D8
Brasted Cl Bexley DA6 . . . . .7 D2
  Orpington BR6 . . . . .52 A8
Brasted Ct Brasted TN16 . .82 D2
  Rochester ME2 . . . . .33 A1
Brasted Hill TN14 . . . . . . .82 A7
Brasted Hill Rd TN16 . . . . .82 C5
Brasted La TN14 . . . . .67 A1
Brasted Rd Erith DA8 . . . . .8 E7
  Westerham TN16 . . . . .81 E1
Brattle Farm Mus* TN12 .139 D1
Brattle Wood TN13 . . . . . .99 C6
Braundton Ave DA15 . . . . .23 F7
Braunstone Dr ME16 . . . . .91 D7
Bray Dr E16 . . . . .1 A6
Bray Gdns ME15 . . . . .106 F5
Braywood Rd SE9 . . . . .6 D3
Breach La ME9 . . . . .64 C5
Breach Rd RM20 . . . . .10 F8
Breakneck Hill DA9 . . . . . .11 B2
Breakspears Dr BR5 . . . . . .38 A8
Breaside Prep Sch BR1 . . .36 D8
Breckonmead BR1 . . . . . . .36 C7
Brecon Ct [7] SE9 . . . . .6 A1
Bredgar Cl ME14 . . . . .92 C5
Bredgar House [1] BR5 . . . .38 D1
Bredgar Rd ME8 . . . . .49 B4
Bredhurst CE Prim Sch
  ME7 . . . . .63 B1
Bredhurst Rd ME8 . . . . . . .63 B4
Breedon Ave TN4 . . . . .132 F1
Bremner Cl BR8 . . . . .40 A5
Brenchley & Matfield
  CE Prim Sch TN12 . . . . . .152 A8
Brenchley Ave DA11 . . . . . .30 B3
Brenchley Cl Chatham ME1 .47 C8
  Chislehurst BR7 . . . . .37 A8
Brenchley Rd
  Gillingham ME8 . . . . .49 B2
  HorsmondenZ TN12 . . . . .152 F6
  Maidstone ME15 . . . . .91 F2
  Matfield TN12 . . . . .151 F8
  St Paul's Cray BR5 . . . . . .37 F7
Brenda Ct [4] DA14 . . . . . .24 A4
Brenda Terr DA10 . . . . .28 E8
Brendon [18] DA14 . . . . . . .24 A4
Brendon Ave ME5 . . . . . . .62 A3
Brendon Cl Erith DA8 . . . . .8 E6
  Royal Tunbridge Wells TN2 .149 D5
Brendon Rd SE9 . . . . .23 D6
Brenley Gdns SE9 . . . . .5 D3
Brennan Rd RM18 . . . . . . .13 B5
Brent Cl Chatham ME5 . . . .61 E5
  Dartford DA2 . . . . .10 B1
  Sidcup DA5 . . . . .24 E7
Brent La DA1 . . . . .27 A8
Brent Prim Sch The DA2 . .27 C8
Brent Rd Newham E16 . . . . .1 B8
  Woolwich SE18 . . . . .6 B7
Brent The Dartford DA1 . . .27 B8

Brent The *continued*
Tonbridge TN10 . . . . .117 C6
Brent Way DA2 . . . . .10 B1
Brentfield Rd DA1 . . . . .27 B8
Brentlands Dr DA1 . . . . . . .27 A7
Brentor Ct TN2 . . . . .149 D6
Brentwood Cl SE9 . . . . .23 C7
Brentwood Ho SE18 . . . . .5 D7
Brenzett Cl ME5 . . . . .62 B5
Brenzett House 6 BR5 . . . .38 C4
Bretland Cl ME1 . . . . .47 B4
Bretland Rd TN4 . . . . .148 D4
Breton Rd ME1 . . . . .47 C2
Brett Wlk ME8 . . . . .63 D4
Brewer Rd ME3 . . . . .33 B7
Brewer St
Lamberhurst TN3 . . . . . . .166 A5
Maidstone ME14 . . . . .92 A5
Brewers Field DA2 . . . . .26 C4
Brewers Rd DA11 . . . . .45 C8
Brewery La TN13 . . . . .84 C2
Brewery Rd Orpington BR2 . .36 E1
Woolwich SE18 . . . . .2 D1
Brewhouse Rd SE18 . . . . . . .1 F2
Brewhouse Yd 14 DA12 . . . .13 B1
Brian Cres TN4 . . . . .149 B8
Briar Cl Larkfield ME20 . . . .75 A2
8 Marlpit Hill TN8 . . . . . .112 D3
Briar Dale ME3 . . . . .32 B4
Briar Fields ME14 . . . . .92 E5
Briar Rd DA5 . . . . .25 D3
Briar Wlk TN10 . . . . .117 C6
Briars The TN15 . . . . .55 D4
Briars Way DA3 . . . . .43 A4
Briarswood Way BR6 . . . . . .51 F5
Briary Ct DA14 . . . . .24 B3
Briary Gdns BR1 . . . . .22 B3
Brice Rd ME3 . . . . .32 B3
Brick Ct RM17 . . . . .12 A8
Brick Field View ME2 . . . . . .33 C1
Brick Kiln La
Horsmonden TN12 . . . . . .153 B2
Ulcombe ME17 . . . . .125 D5
Brickenden Rd TN17 . . . . . .169 D4
Brickfield Cotts SE18 . . . . . .6 F8
Brickfield Farm Gdns BR6 51 C6
Brickfields Pembury TN2 . .150 E8
West Malling ME19 . . . . . .74 B1
Brickwell Cotts TN17 . . . . .156 F6
Brickworks Cl TN9 . . . . . . .133 B7
Bridewell La TN30 . . . . . . .183 A7
Bridge Bsns Pk TN12 . . . . .135 C7
Bridge Cl Dartford DA2 . . . .10 D4
Tonbridge TN9 . . . . .133 C8
Bridge Cotts TN12 . . . . . . .153 A6
Bridge Ct 28 Dartford DA2 . .10 B1
2 Grays RM17 . . . . .12 B8
Bridge Ho Chatham ME1 . . .47 B4
Royal Tunbridge Wells TN4 . .149 B5
Bridge Mill Way ME15 . . . . .91 D2
Bridge Rd Bexley DA7 . . . . . .7 E5
Erith DA8 . . . . .8 F6
Gillingham ME7 . . . . .48 C7
Grays RM17 . . . . .12 B8
Orpington BR5 . . . . .38 B3
Rochester ME1 . . . . .47 C2
Bridge St ME15 . . . . .106 F5
Bridgeland Rd E16 . . . . .1 A6
Bridgen Rd DA5 . . . . .24 E8
Bridges Dr DA1 . . . . .10 B2
Bridgewater Cl BR7 . . . . . . .37 E6
Bridgewater Pl ME19 . . . . . .74 E2
Bridle Way BR6 . . . . .51 C6
Brier Cl ME5 . . . . .62 C8
Bright Cl DA17 . . . . .3 D2
Bright Ct 8 SE28 . . . . .3 C5
Bright Rd 3 ME4 . . . . .48 B4
Bright Ridge TN4 . . . . .148 E8
Brightlands DA11 . . . . .29 E4
Brigstock Rd DA17 . . . . .4 B2
Brimpsfield Cl SE2 . . . . .3 B3
Brimstone Cl BR6 . . . . .52 C3
Brimstone Hill DA13 . . . . . . .58 D8
Brindle Gate DA15 . . . . .23 E7
Brindle Way ME5 . . . . .62 C1
Brindle's Field TN9 . . . . . . .133 A7
Brindley Cl DA7 . . . . .8 A4
Brindley Way BR1 . . . . .22 A3
Brinkburn Cl SE2 . . . . .3 A2
Brinkers La TN5 . . . . .175 A2
Brinklow Cres SE18 . . . . .6 B7
Brionne Gdns TN9 . . . . . . .133 D8
Brisbane House RM18 . . . . .12 F6
Brisbane Rd ME4 . . . . .48 A3
Briset Prim Sch SE9 . . . . . . .5 D3
Briset Rd SE9 . . . . .5 D3
Brishing Cl ME15 . . . . .107 E5
Brishing La ME17 . . . . .107 D4
Brishing Rd ME15,ME17 . .107 F3
Brisley's Row ME1 . . . . .60 F1
Brissenden Cl ME2 . . . . .34 A3
Bristol Cl ME2 . . . . .46 D5
Bristol Rd DA12 . . . . .30 D5
Bristow Rd DA7 . . . . .7 E6
Britannia Bsns Pk ME20 . . . .90 E7
Britannia Cl ME2 . . . . .60 A4
Britannia Dr DA12 . . . . .30 F7
Britannia Village Sch E16 . . .1 B5
Brittain Ct SE9 . . . . .22 E7
Brittain Ho SE9 . . . . .22 E7
Brittains La TN13 . . . . .83 F2
Britten Cl TN10 . . . . .117 F6
Brittenden Cl 1 BR6 . . . . . .51 F4
Brittenden Par BR6 . . . . . . .51 F4
Britton St ME7 . . . . .48 B5
Brixham Rd DA16 . . . . .7 D6
Brixham St E16 . . . . .2 A5
Broad Bridge Cl SE3 . . . . . . .5 A7

Broad Ditch Rd DA13 . . . . .29 D1
Broad Gr TN2 . . . . .149 A1
Broad La Dartford DA2 . . . . .26 B4
Royal Tunbridge Wells TN3 . .147 A4
Broad Lawn SE9 . . . . .23 A7
Broad Oak Brenchley TN12 152 C8
Groombridge TN3 . . . . . . .161 C6
Broad Oak Cl
Brenchley TN12 . . . . .152 C8
Royal Tunbridge Wells TN2 .148 F1
St Paul's Cray BR5 . . . . . . .38 A7
Broad Rd DA10 . . . . .11 E1
Broad St ME17 . . . . .124 E7
Broad Street Hill ME17 . . . .94 D7
Broad View TN17 . . . . .170 A8
Broad Wlk Eltham SE3,SE9 . . .5 E5
Orpington BR6 . . . . .52 D7
Sevenoaks TN15 . . . . .99 F7
Broadcloth TN17 . . . . .169 D3
Broadcroft TN2 . . . . .162 F8
Broadcroft Rd BR5 . . . . .37 D2
Broader La ME14 . . . . .78 B2
Broadfield Rd ME15 . . . . . .107 A8
Broadgate Rd E16 . . . . .1 D7
Broadheath Dr BR7 . . . . . . .22 F3
Broadhoath TN15 . . . . .85 E1
Broadlands Dr ME5 . . . . . . .62 B4
Broadlands Rd BR1 . . . . . . .22 B4
Broadmead TN2 . . . . .162 F8
Broadmead Ave TN2 . . . . . .162 F8
Broadmere Terr ME16 . . . . .91 D3
Broadoak ME19 . . . . .74 E2
Broadoak Ave ME15 . . . . . .107 A8
Broadoak Cl DA4 . . . . .27 A2
Broadoak Rd DA8 . . . . .8 D7
Broadstone
Parkway ME19 . . . . .75 A1
Broadview DA13 . . . . .57 F6
Broadview Ave ME8 . . . . . . .63 E8
Broadwater Ct TN2 . . . . . . .162 E8
Broadwater Down
Cty Prim Sch TN4 . . . . . .148 F1
Broadwater Gdns BR6 . . . . .51 C6
Broadwater House DA12 . . .13 D1
Broadwater La TN2, TN4 . .148 F1
Broadwater Rd
East Malling ME19 . . . . . . .89 D6
Woolwich SE28 . . . . .2 D3
Broadwater Rise TN2 . . . . .148 F1
Broadway Bexley DA6 . . . . . .7 F3
Bexley DA6 . . . . .8 A3
Crockenhill BR8 . . . . .39 C3
Gillingham ME8 . . . . .49 A3
Grays RM17 . . . . .12 C8
Maidstone ME14 . . . . .91 F4
Tilbury RM18 . . . . .12 F5
Broadway Sh Ctr 5 DA6 . . .8 A3
Broadway The
Hadlow TN11 . . . . .118 E8
Lamberhurst TN3 . . . . . . .166 B5
Broadwood DA11 . . . . .30 B3
Broadwood Rd ME3 . . . . . . .34 A4
Brock Rd E13 . . . . .1 B8
Brockbank Cl ME5 . . . . .62 A1
Brockdene Dr BR2 . . . . .50 D6
Brockenhurst Ave ME15 . . . .92 C1
Brockenhurst Cl ME8 . . . . . .63 C7
Brocklebank Ho 7 E16 . . . . .2 A5
Brocklebank Rd SE7 . . . . . . .1 B2
Brocklebank Rd Ind Est
SE7 .1 B2
Brockway TN15 . . . . .87 A7
Brockwell Cl BR5 . . . . .37 F4
Brodrick Gr SE2 . . . . .3 B2
Brogden Cres ME17 . . . . . .108 F7
Broke Farm Dr BR6 . . . . . . .52 C2
Brokes Way TN4 . . . . .149 B8
Brome Ho SE18 . . . . .5 E6
Brome Rd SE9 . . . . .5 F4
Bromedge SE9 . . . . .22 F5
Bromholm Rd SE2 . . . . .3 B3
Bromley RM17 . . . . .12 A8
Bromley Cl Chatham ME5 . . .62 B4
Newington ME9 . . . . .65 A5
Bromley Coll of Further
& Higher Ed BR2 . . . . . . .36 D3
Bromley Comm BR2 . . . . . . .36 D3
Bromley General Hospl
BR2 . . . . .36 B5
Bromley High Sch
for Girls BR1 . . . . .37 A5
Bromley Ind Ctr BR1 . . . . . .36 D6
Bromley La BR7 . . . . .23 D1
Bromley Manor Mans 3
BR2 . . . . .36 A6
Bromley Mus * BR6 . . . . . . .38 B2
Bromley North Sta BR1 . . . .36 A8
Bromley
Public Golf Course BR2 . .36 E2
Bromley Rd BR7 . . . . .37 B8
Bromley South Sta BR1 . . . .36 A6
Bromley Valley
Gymnastics Ctr BR5 . . . . .38 A7
Brompton Dr DA8 . . . . .9 B7
Brompton Farm Rd ME2 . . .33 A2
Brompton Hill ME4 . . . . .47 F6
Brompton La ME4 . . . . .47 A8
Brompton Rd ME7 . . . . .48 B6
Brompton-Westbrook
Prim Sch ME7 . . . . .48 A5
Bronington Cl ME5 . . . . .62 A5
Bronte Cl Erith DA8 . . . . .8 B7
Lunsford ME20 . . . . .74 F3
Tilbury RM18 . . . . .13 C5
Bronte Gr DA1 . . . . .9 F3
Bronte Sch DA11 . . . . .30 A8
Bronte View DA12 . . . . .30 C7

Bronze Age Way DA8,DA17 . .4 C3
Brook Cotts
Collier Street TN12 . . . . . .137 F8
East Farleigh ME15 . . . . . .106 C7
Brook Ct Lewisham SE12 . . . .22 C5
10 Marlpit Hill TN8 . . . . . .112 D3
Brook Hill Cl SE18 . . . . .5 F1
Brook La Bexley DA5 . . . . .7 D2
Bromley BR1 . . . . .22 A2
Greenwich SE3 . . . . .5 B5
Plaxtol Spoute TN15 . . . . .102 A8
Snodland ME6 . . . . .75 A6
Tonbridge TN9 . . . . .117 D2
Brook Rd Lunsford ME20 . . .74 F5
Northfleet DA11 . . . . .29 E7
Royal Tunbridge Wells TN2 .149 B5
Swanley BR8 . . . . .39 D7
Brook St Erith DA8 . . . . .8 B7
Snodland ME6 . . . . .75 B8
Tonbridge TN9 . . . . .133 A8
Brook The ME4 . . . . .48 A4
Brook Vale DA8 . . . . .8 B6
Brookbank ME14 . . . . .92 A8
Brookdale Rd DA5 . . . . .7 E1
Brookdene TN12 . . . . .135 B7
Brookdene Rd SE18 . . . . .2 F2
Brooke Dr DA12 . . . . .31 B7
Brookend Rd DA15 . . . . .23 E7
Brookes Pl ME9 . . . . .65 B6
Brookfield Four Elms TN8 . .113 B5
Kemsing TN15 . . . . .69 E2
Sandhurst TN18 . . . . .186 B5
Brookfield Ave ME20 . . . . . .75 A4
Brookfield Cl TN4 . . . . .133 A1
Brookfield Inf Sch ME20 . . .75 A4
Brookfield Jun Sch
(Larkfield) ME20 . . . . . . .75 A4
Brookhill Cl SE18 . . . . .2 B1
Brookhill Rd SE18 . . . . .2 B1
Brookhurst Gdns TN4 . . . . .132 E3
Brooklands Dartford DA1 . . .26 C7
Headcorn TN27 . . . . .141 C6
Royal Tunbridge Wells TN2 .149 D7
Brooklands Ave DA15 . . . . . .23 D6
Brooklands Farm Cl TN3 147 A6
Brooklands Paddock ME7 . . .48 D6
Brooklands Pk SE3 . . . . .5 A4
Brooklands Prim Sch SE3 . . .5 A4
Brooklands Rd ME20 . . . . . . .75 A4
Brooklyn Paddock ME7 . . . .48 D6
Brooklyn Rd BR2 . . . . .36 D4
Brooklyn Villas TN12 . . . . .138 C5
Brookmead TN11 . . . . .116 E4
Brookmead Ave BR1 . . . . . .36 F4
Brookmead Cl BR5 . . . . .38 B3
Brookmead Rd ME3 . . . . . . .33 B7
Brookmead Way BR5 . . . . . .38 B3
Brooks Cl Eltham SE9 . . . . . .23 A6
Staplehurst TN12 . . . . . . .139 E4
Brooks Pl ME14 . . . . .92 A4
Brookside Cranbrook TN17 169 D4
Hoo St Werburgh ME3 . . . .34 E5
Orpington BR6 . . . . .37 F2
Brookside Rd DA13 . . . . . . .29 F1
Brookway SE3 . . . . .5 A4
Broom Ave BR5 . . . . .38 B7
Broom Cl BR2 . . . . .36 E3
Broom Hill Rd ME2 . . . . . . .46 F8
Broom La TN3 . . . . .147 E2
Broom Mead DA6 . . . . .8 A2
Broom Pk TN3 . . . . .147 E3
Broomcroft Rd ME8 . . . . . . .49 F2
Broomfield House 4 BR5 . . .38 A7
Broomfield Rd Bexley DA6 . . .8 A2
Kingswood ME17 . . . . . . .109 D4
Sevenoaks TN13 . . . . .83 F5
Swanscombe DA10 . . . . . . .11 E2
Broomfields DA3 . . . . .42 E4
Broomhill Bank Sch TN3 148 C6
Broomhill Park Rd TN4 . . .148 F8
Broomhill Rd
Dartford DA1 . . . . .9 B1
Orpington BR6 . . . . .38 A2
Royal Tunbridge Wells TN2 .148 D7
Broomhill Rise DA6 . . . . .8 A2
Broomhills DA13 . . . . .28 E4
Broomleigh BR1 . . . . .36 A8
Broomscroft Cotts ME18 . . .89 C1
Broomshaw Rd ME6 . . . . . . .90 F3
Broomwood Cl DA5 . . . . . . .25 D6
Broomwood Rd BR5 . . . . . . .38 B7
Brougham Ct 5 DA2 . . . . . .10 B1
Broughton Rd
Orpington BR6 . . . . .51 D8
Otford TN14 . . . . .69 A3
Brow Cl BR5 . . . . .38 D2
Brow Cres BR5 . . . . .38 D2
Brown Rd DA12 . . . . .30 E7
Brown St ME8 . . . . .49 F1
Browndens Rd ME2 . . . . . . .59 E4
Brownelow Copse ME5 . . . . .62 B1
Brownhill Cl ME5 . . . . .62 A4
Browning Cl Bexley DA16 . . . .6 E6
6 Lunsford ME20 . . . . .74 F4
Browning Rd DA1 . . . . .9 F3
Browning Wlk RM18 . . . . . .13 C5
Brownings TN8 . . . . .112 C4
Brownspring Dr SE9 . . . . . . .23 B5
Broxbourne Rd BR6 . . . . . . .37 F2
Bruce Cl DA16 . . . . .7 B6
Bruce Ct DA15 . . . . .23 F4
Bruce Gr BR6 . . . . .38 A1
Bruces Wharf Rd RM17 . . . .12 A8
Brucks The ME18 . . . . .104 E7
Brummel Cl DA7 . . . . .8 C4
Brunel Cl RM18 . . . . .13 B4
Brunel Way ME4 . . . . .48 A7
Brungers Wlk TN10 . . . . . .117 D5
Brunswick Cl DA6 . . . . .7 D3

Brunswick House
Prim Sch ME16 . . . . .91 E5
Brunswick Rd DA6 . . . . .7 D3
Brunswick St ME15 . . . . . . .92 A3
Brunswick St E ME15 . . . . . .92 A3
Brunswick Terr TN1 . . . . . .149 A2
Brunswick Wlk 1 DA12 . . . .30 D8
Brushwood Lodge 1 DA17 . .4 A2
Bruton Cl BR7 . . . . .22 F1
Bryanston Rd RM18 . . . . . . .13 C5
Bryant Cl ME18 . . . . .104 D6
Bryant Rd ME2 . . . . .47 A7
Bryant St ME4 . . . . .48 A3
Bryony Sch ME8 . . . . .63 F5
Bubblestone Rd TN14 . . . . . .69 B3
Buckden Cl SE12 . . . . .5 A1
Buckham Thorns Rd TN16 .81 C1
Buckhole Farm Rd ME23 . . .17 C4
Buckhurst Ave TN13 . . . . . . .84 C2
Buckhurst La
High Halden TN26 . . . . . . .174 A6
Sevenoaks TN13 . . . . .84 C2
Buckhurst Rd TN16 . . . . . . .81 B7
Buckingham Ave DA16 . . . . . .6 E3
Buckingham Cl BR5 . . . . . . .37 E2
Buckingham Dr BR7 . . . . . . .23 C3
Buckingham Rd
Gillingham ME7 . . . . .48 D5
Northfleet DA11 . . . . .29 D8
Royal Tunbridge Wells TN1 .149 B2
Buckingham Row ME15 . . .107 E7
Buckland Cl ME5 . . . . .62 A2
Buckland Hill ME16 . . . . . . .91 E5
Buckland La ME16 . . . . .91 E6
Buckland Pl ME16 . . . . .91 E4
Buckland Rd
Cliffe Woods ME3 . . . . .33 A8
Luddesdown DA13 . . . . . . .59 A7
Maidstone ME16 . . . . .91 E4
Orpington BR6 . . . . .51 E6
Buckler Gdns SE9 . . . . .22 F5
Bucklers Cl TN2 . . . . .149 C3
Buckles Ct SE2 . . . . .3 D2
Buckley Cl DA1 . . . . .8 F5
Bucks Cross Rd
Chelsfield BR6 . . . . .52 E5
Northfleet DA11 . . . . .29 F5
Buckthorn House DA15 . . . .23 F5
Buckwheat Ct SE2 . . . . .3 D3
Budd Ho 4 SE2 . . . . .1 C1
Budd's Farm Cotts TN30 . .189 E2
Budd's La TN30 . . . . .189 F2
Budgin's Hill BR6 . . . . .67 C8
Budleigh Cres DA16 . . . . .7 C6
Bugglesden Rd
TN27,TN30 . . . . .172 D5
Bugsby's Way SE10,SE7 . . . .1 B2
Bull Alley DA16 . . . . .7 B4
Bull Fields ME6 . . . . .75 A8
Bull Hill Egerton ME17 . . . .127 F8
Horton Kirby DA4 . . . . .41 C5
Bull La Chislehurst BR7 . . . .23 D1
Eccles ME20 . . . . .75 F5
Higham ME3 . . . . .32 D7
Stockbury ME9 . . . . .64 E2
Wrotham TN15 . . . . .72 A3
Bull Lane Cotts TN3 . . . . . .165 C4
Bull Orch ME14 . . . . .90 F2
Bull Rd ME19 . . . . .74 C5
Bull Yd 5 DA11 . . . . .13 B1
Bullace La 3 DA1 . . . . .9 E1
Bullbanks Rd DA17 . . . . .4 C2
Bulldog Rd ME5 . . . . .62 B2
Bullen La TN12 . . . . .119 E7
Buller Rd ME4 . . . . .47 F2
Bullers Cl DA14 . . . . .24 E3
Bullers Wood Dr BR7 . . . . . .22 F1
Bullers Wood Sch
for Girls BR7 . . . . .36 F8
Bullfinch Cl
Paddock Wood TN12 . . . .136 A5
Sevenoaks TN13 . . . . .83 D5
Bullfinch Cnr TN13 . . . . . . .83 E5
Bullfinch Dene TN13 . . . . . .83 D5
Bullfinch La TN13 . . . . .83 E5
Bullingstone Cotts TN3 . . .147 F6
Bullingstone La TN3 . . . . . .147 F7
Bullion Cl TN12 . . . . .135 F6
Bullivant Cl DA9 . . . . .11 A2
Bulls Pl TN2 . . . . .150 D6
Bulrush Cl ME5 . . . . .61 F3
Bumbles Cl ME1 . . . . .61 D7
Bungalows The TN30 . . . . .183 D8
Bunker's Hill Erith DA17 . . . .4 A2
New Ash Green TN15 . . . . .57 B4
Bunkers Hill DA14 . . . . .24 F5
Bunny La TN3 . . . . .162 E5
Bunters Hill Rd ME3 . . . . . . .33 B4
Bunton St SE18 . . . . .2 A3
Burberry La ME17 . . . . .109 B5
Burch Rd DA11 . . . . .12 F1
Burcharbro Rd SE2 . . . . .7 D8
Burdens TN27 . . . . .141 D5
Burdett Ave DA12 . . . . .31 F4
Burdett Cl DA14 . . . . .24 E3
Burdett Rd TN4 . . . . .148 B4
Burdock Ho 6 ME15 . . . . . .107 D8
Burford Rd BR1 . . . . .36 E5
Burgate Cl DA1 . . . . .8 F4
Burgess Hall Dr ME17 . . . .108 F6
Burgess Rd ME2 . . . . .47 B7
Burgess Row TN30 . . . . . . .183 A4
Burghclere Dr ME16 . . . . . . .91 B7
Burghfield Rd DA13 . . . . . . .29 F1
Burgoyne Ct ME14 . . . . .91 F7
Burham CE Prim Sch ME1 75 F8
Burham Rd ME1 . . . . .60 E8
Burial Ground La ME15 . . . .91 E1

Burleigh Ave DA15 . . . . .6 F2
Burleigh Cl ME2 . . . . .46 E8
Burleigh Dr ME14 . . . . .76 F1
Burley Rd E16 . . . . .1 C8
Burlings La TN14 . . . . .66 F2
Burlington Cl 5 Newham E6 .1 E7
Orpington BR6 . . . . .51 B8
Burlington Gdns ME8 . . . . . .63 E4
Burlington Lodge BR7 . . . . .22 F1
Burma Way ME5 . . . . .61 F6
Burman Cl DA2 . . . . .27 C8
Burmarsh Cl ME5 . . . . .62 B5
Burn's Rd ME7 . . . . .48 C7
Burnaby Rd DA11 . . . . .12 E1
Burnell Ave DA16 . . . . .7 A5
Burnett Rd DA8 . . . . .9 D8
Burnham Cres DA1 . . . . .9 C3
Burnham Rd Dartford DA1 . . .9 C3
Sidcup DA14 . . . . .24 E6
Burnham Terr DA1 . . . . .9 D2
Burnham Trad Est DA1 . . . . .9 D3
Burnham Wlk ME8 . . . . .63 E3
Burnley Rd RM20 . . . . .11 A6
Burns Ave DA15 . . . . .7 B1
Burns Cl Bexley DA16 . . . . . . .6 F6
Erith DA8 . . . . .8 F6
Burns Cres TN9 . . . . .133 A7
Burns Ho DA16 . . . . .7 C6
Burns Pl RM18 . . . . .13 B6
Burns Rd ME16 . . . . .91 C2
Burnt Ash Hill SE12 . . . . . . .22 A7
Burnt Ash La BR1,SE12 . . . .22 A7
Burnt Ash Prim Sch BR1 . .22 A3
Burnt House Cl ME2 . . . . . . .33 C2
Burnt House La
Dartford DA1 . . . . .26 F5
Hawley DA2 . . . . .26 F4
Royal Tunbridge Wells TN3 .148 A5
Burnt Howe Cl TN18 . . . . . .186 C5
Burnt Lodge La TN5 . . . . . .176 B2
Burnt Oak Jun Mix Sch
DA15 . . . . .24 A7
Burnt Oak La DA15 . . . . .7 A1
Burnt Oak Terr ME7 . . . . . . .48 D6
Burntash Rd ME20 . . . . .90 F8
Burnthouse La TN27 . . . . . .142 D1
Burntwood Gr TN13 . . . . . . .99 B8
Burntwood Rd TN13 . . . . . . .99 B7
Burr Bank Terr DA2 . . . . . . .26 C4
Burr Cl DA7 . . . . .7 F4
Burrage Gr SE18 . . . . .2 C2
Burrage Pl SE18 . . . . .2 B1
Burrage Rd SE18 . . . . .2 C1
Burrard Rd E16 . . . . .1 B7
Burrfield Dr BR5 . . . . .38 D4
Burritt Mews ME1 . . . . .47 C3
Burrows La ME3 . . . . .19 C3
Burrswood Villas TN3 . . . . .161 B7
Bursdon Cl DA15 . . . . .23 F6
Burslem Rd TN2 . . . . .149 E7
Bursted Wood Prim Sch
DA7 . . . . .8 B5
Burston Rd ME17 . . . . .106 B2
Burt Rd E16 . . . . .1 C5
Burton Cl ME3 . . . . .33 C3
Burton Rd ME17 . . . . .106 B2
Burwash Ct BR5 . . . . .38 C4
Burwash Rd SE18 . . . . .2 D1
Burwood Ave BR2 . . . . .50 B8
Burwood Ho TN2 . . . . .149 E5
Burwood Sch BR6 . . . . .52 D8
Busbridge Rd
Maidstone ME15 . . . . .106 E6
Snodland ME6 . . . . .74 E7
Bush Cl ME9 . . . . .80 F5
Bush Rd Cuxton ME2 . . . . . .46 B2
East Peckham TN12 . . . . . .119 E8
Bush Row ME20 . . . . .76 A3
Bushell Way BR7 . . . . .23 A3
Bushey Ave BR5 . . . . .37 D2
Bushey Ct DA8 . . . . .9 A6
Bushey Ho SE9 . . . . .22 C5
Bushey Lees DA15 . . . . .6 F1
Bushfield Wlk DA10 . . . . . . .28 E8
Bushmeadow Rd ME8 . . . . .49 F2
Bushmoor Cres SE18 . . . . . . .6 B6
Bushy Gill TN3 . . . . .148 A3
Bushy Rd TN14 . . . . .109 D2
Busty La TN15 . . . . .86 D6
Butcher Cl TN12 . . . . .139 E3
Butcher Wlk DA10 . . . . .28 E8
Butcher's La ME19 . . . . .88 D1
Butchers La TN15 . . . . .56 D8
Butchers Rd E16 . . . . .1 A7
Butchers Yd BR6 . . . . .66 A8
Butler House 9 RM17 . . . . .12 B8
Butler's Cotts DA7 . . . . .8 A5
Butler's Pl DA3 . . . . .56 E7
Butt Green La ME17 . . . . . .123 A7
Butt Haw Cl ME3 . . . . .34 E5
Buttercup Cl TN12 . . . . . . .136 A5
Butterfield Sq 10 E6 . . . . . . .1 F7
Butterfly Ave DA1 . . . . .26 F6
Butterfly La SE9 . . . . .6 B1
Buttermere Cl ME7 . . . . .49 A5
Buttermere Rd BR5 . . . . . . .38 D5
Buttmarsh Cl SE18 . . . . .2 B1
Button Dr ME3 . . . . .19 C5
Button Ho ME3 . . . . .33 F6
Button La ME15 . . . . .93 B2
Button St BR8,DA4 . . . . .40 C5
Butts The TN14 . . . . .69 B2
Buttway La ME3 . . . . .16 A6
Buxton Cl Chatham ME5 . . . .62 D1

Buxton Cl continued
Maidstone ME15 ....107 A8
Buxton Rd DA8 ....8 D7
Buzzard Creek Ind Est IG11 3 A8
Bychurch Pl 6 ME15 ....92 A3
Bycliffe Mews DA11 ....29 F8
Bycliffe Terr DA11 ......29 F8
Byland St SE2 ....3 B3
Byng Rd TN4 ....148 F5
Bynon Ave DA7 ....7 F4
Byrneside TN11 ....116 E4
Byron Cl SE28 ....3 C5
Byron Dr DA8 ....8 B7
Byron Gdns RM18 ....13 C6
Byron Prim Sch ME7 ....48 C3
Byron Rd Dartford DA1 ..10 B3
   Gillingham ME7 ....48 C3
   Maidstone ME14 ....92 B7
Bywater Ho SE18 ....1 E3

C

Cabbage Stalk La TN4 ..148 E2
Cable Cl DA8 ....4 C3
Cacket's La TN14 ....66 E4
Cade La TN13 ....99 C7
Cadlocks Hill TN14 ......52 F1
Cadnam Cl ME2 ....46 E8
Cadogan Ave DA2 ....27 D8
Cadogan Gdns 6 TN1 ..149 B4
Cadogan Rd SE18 ....2 C3
Cadwallon Rd SE9 ....23 C6
Caerleon Cl DA14 ....24 C3
Caernarvon Dr ME15 ....91 F1
Cage Green
   Prim Sch TN10 ....117 D5
Cage Green Rd TN10 ...117 C5
Cage La TN27 ....142 F1
Cagney Cl ME3 ....33 C3
Cairns Cl DA1 ....9 D7
Caistor Rd TN9 ....117 A1
Caithness Gdns DA15 ....6 F1
Calais Cotts DA3 ....56 A8
Calcott Wlk SE9 ....22 D4
Calcutta House 3 ME15 .107 E5
Calcutta Rd RM18 ....13 A5
Calder Rd ME14 ....91 E7
Calderwood DA12 ....30 E2
Calderwood St SE18 ......2 A2
Caldew Ave ME8 ....49 C1
Caldy Rd DA17 ....4 B3
Caledonian Ct ME8 ......63 E8
Calehill Cl ME14 ....92 C6
Caley Rd TN2 ....149 D7
Calfstock La DA4 ....40 F5
Caliph Cl DA12 ....30 F5
Callams Cl ME8 ....63 D6
Callaways La ME9 ....65 B6
Callis Way ME8 ....63 D5
Calshot Ct 17 DA2 ......10 B1
Calverley Ct TN1 ....149 C3
Calverley Park Cres
   1 TN1 ....149 B3
Calverley Park Gdns TN1 149 C4
Calverley Pk TN1 ....149 B3
Calverley Rd TN1 ......149 B3
Calverley St TN1 ....149 B4
Calvert Cl Erith DA17 ....4 B2
   Sidcup DA14 ....24 E2
Calverton Prim Sch E16 ..1 D7
Calvin Cl BR5 ....38 D6
Calydon Rd SE7 ....1 B1
Cambert Way SE3 ....5 B3
Camberwell La TN14 ....97 F4
Camborne Manor 2 ME7 48 C6
Camborne Rd Bexley DA16 .6 F5
   Sidcup DA14 ....24 C5
Cambray Rd BR6 ....37 F2
Cambria Ave ME1 ....46 F2
Cambria Cl DA15 ....23 E7
Cambria Cres DA12 ......30 F4
Cambria House 2 DA8 ....8 E7
Cambrian Gr DA11 ....30 A8
Cambrian Rd TN4 ....149 C7
Cambridge Ave ME9 .....6 F3
Cambridge Barracks Rd
   SE18 ....1 F2
Cambridge Cres ME15 ..107 D8
Cambridge Dr SE12 ......5 A2
Cambridge Gdns TN2 ...149 B2
Cambridge Gn SE9 ......23 B7
Cambridge Ho
   7 Greenwich SE18 ......1 F2
   3 Maidstone ME15 .....107 D7
Cambridge Rd Bromley BR1 22 A1
   Gillingham ME8 ....63 C6
   Rochester ME2 ....47 A8
   Sidcup DA14 ....23 E4
Cambridge Row SE18 ....2 B1
Cambridge St ME15 ....149 C3
Cambridge Terr 1 ME4 ..47 F4
Cambus Rd E16 ....1 A8
Camdale Rd SE18 ....6 F7
Camden Ave TN2 ....150 C6
Camden Cl Chatham ME5 62 B5
   Chislehurst BR7 ....37 C8
   Northfleet DA11 ....29 C7
Camden Cotts TN17 ....169 F8
Camden Ct 10 Erith DA17 4 A1
   Pembury TN2 ....150 D6
   2 Royal Tunbridge
   Wells TN1 ....149 B4
Camden Gr BR7 ....23 B2

Camden Hill TN2 ....149 B3
Camden Park Rd BR7 ...23 A1
Camden Pk TN2 ....149 C2
Camden Rd Gillingham ME7 48 D7
   Royal Tunbridge Wells TN1 149 B4
   Sevenoaks TN13 ....84 B5
   Sidcup DA5 ....24 F8
Camden St ME14 ....92 A5
Camden Terr TN17 .....169 F8
Camden Way BR7 ....23 A1
Camel Rd E16 ....1 D5
Camellia Cl ME8 ....63 D7
Camelot Cl SE28 ....2 D4
Camer Gdns DA13 ......44 C3
Camer Park (Ctry Pk)*
   DA13 ....44 C2
Camer Park Rd DA13 ...44 C2
Camer Rd DA13 ....44 C3
Camer St DA13 ....44 C3
Cameron Cl Chatham ME5 62 B8
   Dartford DA5 ....25 E5
Cameron Rd BR2 ....36 A4
Cameron Terr 10 SE12 ..22 B2
Camerons 4 TN18 ......179 A2
Camomile Dr ME14 .....92 F5
Camp Hill TN11 ....115 A3
Camp Hill Cotts TN11 ..114 F2
Camp Site The DA14 ....25 A1
Camp Way ME15 ....107 C6
Campbell Cl SE18 ....6 A6
Campbell Rd
   Gravesend DA11 ....29 F8
   Maidstone ME15 ....92 A3
   Royal Tunbridge Wells TN4 149 A6
Camperdown
   Manor 5 ME7 ....48 A6
Campfield Rd SE9 ......22 D8
Campion Cl Chatham ME5 61 E3
   Newham E6 ....1 F6
   Northfleet DA11 ....29 E4
Campion Cres TN17 ....169 A2
Campion Ct 6 RM17 ....12 D8
Campion Pl SE28 ....3 D5
Campleshon Rd ME8 ....63 D7
Campus Way ME8 ....63 A8
Camrose Ave DA8 ....8 B8
Camrose St SE2 ....3 A2
Canada Farm Rd DA4 ...42 A6
Canada Rd DA8 ....9 B7
Canada Terr 3 ME14 ....92 A7
Canadian Ave ME7 ......48 F4
Canal Basin ME3 ....13 D1
Canal Rd Gravesend DA12 13 D1
   Higham ME3 ....32 C8
   Rochester ME2 ....47 C7
Canal Road
   Ind Pk 2 DA12 ......30 D8
Canberra Rd Erith DA7 ..7 D8
   Greenwich SE7 ....5 D8
Canberra Sq RM18 ......13 A5
Canbury Path BR5 ......38 A5
Canning St ME14 ....92 A6
Cannock St BR6 ....52 F5
Cannon Bridge
   Works 117 D2
Cannon La TN9 ....117 D2
Cannon Pl SE7 ....1 E1
Cannon Rd DA7 ....7 F6
Canon Cl ME1 ....47 B2
Canon La ME18 ....89 C1
Canon Rd BR1 ....36 D6
Cansiron La TN7,TN8 ..144 E2
Canterbury Ave DA15 ...24 C6
Canterbury Cl Dartford DA1 27 A8
   7 Newham E6 ....1 F7
Canterbury Cres TN10 ..117 D5
Canterbury Ct 7 SE12 ..22 B5
Canterbury Ho Erith DA8 ..8 F7
   2 Maidstone ME15 .....107 D7
Canterbury Rd
   Gravesend DA12 ....30 C6
   Pembury TN2 ....150 C6
Canterbury St ME7 ......47 F5
Canterbury Way RM16,DA1 10 D5
Cantwell House SE18 ....6 B7
Cantwell Rd SE18 ....6 B7
Capel Cl Gillingham ME8 63 D4
   Orpington BR2 ....36 E1
Capel Pl DA2 ....26 C4
Capel Prim Sch TN12 ..134 F7
Capelands DA3 ....57 A8
Capell Cl ME17 ....106 C3
Capella Ho 1 SE7 ....5 B8
Capetown
   House 1 ME15 ....107 F5
Capital Ind Est DA17 ....4 B3
Capstan Ct DA2 ....10 C3
Capstan Ctr RM17 ......12 E7
Capstone Farm
   Ctry Pk* ME7 ....62 D5
Capstone Rd Chatham ME5 48 D1
   Gillingham ME7 ....62 F6
   Lewisham BR1 ....22 A4
Captain's Cl ME17 .....124 E6
Captain's Wlk The TN15 87 C7
Capulet Mews E16 ....1 A5
Caraway Cl E13 ....1 B8
Cardens Rd ME3 ....33 B8
Cardiff St SE18 ....6 E7
Cardigan Cl ME23 ......17 F3
Cardinal Ct Chislehurst BR7 37 D8
   Tonbridge TN9 ....133 D8
Cardwell Prim Sch SE18 ..1 F2
Carew Ho 5 SE18 ....1 F2
Carey Ct DA6 ....8 B2
Caring La ME14,ME17 ...93 E1
Caring Rd ME15,ME17 ...93 C1
Carisbrooke Ave DA5 ...24 D7

Carisbrooke Ct
   28 Dartford DA2 ....10 B1
   20 Sidcup DA14 ....24 A4
Carisbrooke Dr ME16 ...91 D4
Carisbrooke Rd
   Bromley BR2 ....36 C5
   Rochester ME2 ....32 E1
Carl Ekman House DA11 .29 D8
Carleton Pl DA4 ....41 C5
Carleton Rd DA1 ....27 A8
Carlisle Cl ME2 ....46 C6
Carlisle Rd DA1 ....10 A1
Carlton Ave Gillingham ME7 48 E4
   Stone DA9 ....9 A9
Carlton Cres Chatham ME5 62 D8
   Royal Tunbridge Wells TN1 149 A4
Carlton Gdns ME15 ....107 B8
Carlton Gn DA14 ....23 F4
Carlton Par BR5 ....38 B2
Carlton Rd Bexley DA16 ..7 B4
   Erith DA8 ....8 C8
   Royal Tunbridge Wells TN1 149 C4
   Sidcup DA14 ....23 F3
Carlyle Ave ME14 ......92 A3
Carlyle Rd SE28 ....3 C6
Carman's Cl ME15,ME17 106 F3
Carmelite Way DA3 .....42 F4
Carnation Cl ME19 ......75 A1
Carnation Cres ME19 ....74 F1
Carnation Rd ME2 ......46 D7
Carnation St SE2 ....3 B3
Carnbrook Rd SE3 ....5 D4
Caroline Cres ME16 ....91 D7
Carriers Pl TN3 ....146 B4
Carriers Rd TN17 ......169 D5
Carrill Way DA17 ....3 D3
Carrington Cl ME7 ......48 F6
Carrington Rd DA1 ......10 A1
Carroll Cl ME2 ....60 B4
Carroll Gdns ME20 .....74 F3
Carronade Pl SE28 ......2 D3
Carsington Gdns DA1 ....26 D6
Carson Rd E16 ....1 A8
Carston Cl SE12 ....5 A2
Carter's Hill TN15 .....100 B6
Carters Hill SE9 ....22 C7
Carters Hill Cl SE9 .....22 C7
Carters Hill La DA13 ....57 F2
Carters Row DA11 ......29 F6
Cartmel Rd DA7 ....8 A6
Carton Cl ME1 ....47 D2
Carton Rd ME3 ....32 B3
Carville Ave TN4 ....132 F1
Carvoran Way ME8 .....63 C5
Cary's Field TN13 ....83 E7
Cascade Cl BR5 ....38 B2
Cascades L Ctr DA12 ...31 A4
Caspian Wlk E16 ....1 D7
Cassilda Rd SE2 ....3 A2
Casstine Ct BR8 ....25 F1
Castalia Ct DA1 ....9 F4
Casterbridge Rd SE3 ....5 A4
Castile Rd 12 SE18 ......2 A2
Castilion Prim Sch SE28 ..3 C7
Castilla Ho 4 BR1 ......22 B1
Castle Ave ME1 ....47 C4
Castle Dene ME14 ......91 F8
Castle Dr DA15 ....69 E2
Castle Farm Rd TN14 ...54 A3
Castle Fields TN9 ......117 B2
Castle Hill Hartley DA3 ..42 E4
   Rochester ME1 ....47 C6
   Thurnham ME14 ....78 D1
   Tonbridge TN9 ....133 F5
Castle Hill Ct ME1 .....47 C6
Castle Hurst TN32 .....185 B1
Castle La DA12 ....31 B6
Castle Rd Chatham ME4 ..48 A6
   Eynsford DA4 ....54 C5
   Grays RM17 ....11 F8
   Maidstone ME16 ....91 D7
   Royal Tunbridge Wells TN4 149 A3
   Swanscombe DA10 ....11 F1
Castle St 2 Royal Tunbridge
   Wells TN1 ....149 A2
   2 Royal Tunbridge
   Wells,Southborough TN4 132 F2
   Stone DA9 ....11 A2
   Swanscombe DA10 ....11 F1
   Tonbridge TN9 ....117 C2
   Upper Upnor ME2 ....33 E1
   Wouldham ME1 ....60 C4
Castle Terr Hadlow TN11 118 E8
   Hawkhurst TN18 ....175 D8
Castle View Bsns Ctr ME1 47 C6
Castle View Mews ME1 ..47 C6
Castle View Rd ME2 ....47 A7
Castle Way ME19 ....74 D2
Castle Wlk TN5 ....174 C4
Castlecombe
   Prim Sch SE9 ....22 E3
Castlecombe Rd SE9 ....22 E4
Castlefields DA13 ....43 F8
Castleford Ave SE9 .....23 B7

Castlemaine Ave ME7 ...48 F6
Castleton Ave DA7 ......8 D5
Castleton Rd SE9 ....22 D4
Castlewood Day
   Hospl SE18 ....6 A6
Castlewood Dr SE9 ......5 F5
Cates Ct TN12 ....120 A7
Cathcart Dr BR6 ....37 E1
Catherine Cl ME16 .....91 A3
Catherine of Aragon
   Ct DA15 ....23 D8
Catherine Pl 7 TN1 ....149 B4
Catherine St ME1 ....47 D3
Catkin Cl ME5 ....61 F1
Catlyn Cl ME19 ....90 A8
Catterick Rd ME5 ......62 D2
Cattistock Rd SE9 ......22 F3
Catts Pl TN12 ....136 C4
Causton Rd TN17 ......169 C5
Cave Hill ME15 ....91 F1
Cavell Cres DA1 ....10 B3
Cavendish Ave Bexley DA16 6 F4
   Erith DA8 ....8 C8
   Gillingham ME7 ....48 E6
   Sevenoaks TN13 ....84 A5
   Sidcup DA15 ....24 A8
Cavendish Ct TN9 ......117 D3
Cavendish Dr TN2 .....149 B1
Cavendish Rd ME1 ......47 D3
Cavendish Sq DA3 ......42 D6
Cavendish Way ME15 ...93 B3
Caversham Cl ME8 ......49 F1
Caveside Cl BR7 ....37 A8
Caxton Cl Hartley DA3 ..42 F5
   Tenterden TN30 ....182 F7
Caxton La TN11 ....118 E8
Cayser Dr ME17 ....109 E2
Caysers Croft TN12 ....119 E6
Cazeneuve St ME1 ......47 C5
Cecil Ave Gillingham ME8 ..49 A2
   Rochester ME2 ....47 B8
Cecil Rd Gravesend DA11 ..29 C7
   Rochester ME1 ....47 C3
Cecil Road Prim Sch DA11 29 F7
Cecil Way BR2 ....36 A4
Cedar Ave Gravesend DA12 30 D8
   Sidcup DA15 ....24 A8
Cedar Cl Ditton ME20 ...90 D8
   Meopham Sta DA13 ......44 A3
   Orpington BR2 ....50 E7
   Swanley BR8 ....39 C7
Cedar Copse BR1 ....36 F7
Cedar Cres Orpington BR2 .50 E7
   Tonbridge TN10 ....117 C7
Cedar Ct Eltham SE9 ....5 C8
   20 Greenwich SE7 ....5 C8
   Maidstone ME14 ....92 B5
   Royal Tunbridge Wells TN4 149 A4
   12 Tenterden TN30 .....183 A7
Cedar Dr Edenbridge TN8 .112 D8
   Maidstone ME16 ....90 E2
   Sutton at Hone DA4 .....41 B7
Cedar Gdns ME9 ....79 E8
Cedar Gr Gillingham ME7 ..63 A5
   Sidcup DA5 ....7 D1
Cedar Lodge TN4 ....148 F3
Cedar Mount SE9 ....22 D7
Cedar Pl 8 SE7 ....1 C1
Cedar Rd Bromley BR1 ...36 C7
   Dartford DA1 ....26 D7
   Erith DA8 ....9 A6
   Hoo St Werburgh ME3 ..34 E3
Cedar Ridge TN2 ......149 D5
Cedar Terrace Rd TN13 ..84 C4
Cedarhurst Cotts 5 DA5 25 A8
Cedarhurst Dr SE9 ......5 C8
Cedarmore Ct BR7 ......37 C8
Cedars Sch The
   Maidstone ME16 ....91 D4
   Rochester ME1 ....47 C4
Cedars The TN12 ....136 A4
Cedarwood House ME15 106 B6
Cedric Rd SE9 ....23 C5
Celandine Dr SE28 ......3 B5
Celestine Cl ME5 ....62 A1
Cement Block Cotts RM17 12 C8
Cement Industry
   Heritage Ctr* DA11 ..12 B2
Cemetery La Hadlow TN11 103 A1
   Woolwich SE7 ....5 E8
Cemetery Rd Bexley SE2 ..7 B7
   Halling ME2 ....60 A4
   Snodland ME6 ....59 F1
Centenary Ct DA4 ......41 A2
Central Ave Bexley DA16 ..7 A5
   Gillingham ME4 ....48 B8
   Gravesend DA12 ....30 B5
   Tilbury RM18 ....13 A6
Central Bsns Pk ME2 ....47 E7
Central Ct 3 SE18 ....2 B2
Central Lodge TN15 ....72 E6
Central Par Rochester ME1 47 D2
   Sidcup DA15 ....24 A4
Central Par Villas BR5 ..38 C7
Central Park Gdns ME4 ..47 E2
Central Rd Dartford DA1 ..9 F2
   New Hythe ME20 ....75 B4
   Rochester ME2 ....47 A7
Central Sta TN1 ....149 A3
Central Terr ME2 ....33 F6
Central Way SE28 ....3 B6
Centre 2000 ME16 ......91 D7
Centre Common Rd BR7 23 C1
Centre Ct ME2 ....47 E7
Centre Rd DA3 ....56 E7
Centurian Way DA18 ....4 A3

Centurion Cl ME8 ......48 F1
Century Rd ME8 ....63 D8
Ceres Rd SE18 ....2 F2
Cerne Rd DA12 ....30 E5
Cervia Way DA12 ....30 F5
Chada Ave ME7 ....48 E3
Chadd Dr BR1 ....36 E6
Chadfields RM18 ....13 A7
Chadwell Hill RM17 .....13 A8
Chadwick Cl DA11 ......29 E5
Chadwick Ct 4 SE28 ....3 B5
Chadwick Way SE28 .....3 D6
Chadwin Rd E13 ....1 B8
Chaffey Ho 6 SE7 ....1 C1
Chaffinch Cl ME5 ....62 A7
Chaffinch Way TN12 ...136 A5
Chafford Cotts TN3 ....146 F5
Chafford La TN3 ....146 F5
Chain Gate ME17 ......127 A8
Chalcombe Rd SE2 ......3 B3
Chalet Cl DA5 ....25 D4
Chalfont Ct 3 DA17 .....4 A1
Chalfont Dr ME8 ....63 D6
Chalgrove Mews ME2 ...60 A5
Chalice Way DA9 ....10 F2
Chalk Ave TN30 ....173 B2
Chalk Ct RM17 ....12 A8
Chalk La TN17 ....168 E7
Chalk Pit Ave BR5 ......38 D6
Chalk Pit Hill ME4 ......48 A3
Chalk Rd Chalk DA12 ....31 A6
   Higham ME3 ....32 C6
   Newham E13 ....1 C8
Chalkenden Ave ME8 ....49 A2
Chalket La TN2 ....150 C5
Chalkpit Cotts DA12 ....31 E5
Chalkstone Cl DA16 .....7 A6
Chalkways TN14 ....69 F3
Chalky Bank DA11 ......30 A3
Chalky Rd ME9 ....79 C6
Challenge Cl DA12 ......30 F4
Challenger Cl TN12 ....135 F6
Challock Ho 3 Erith DA8 ..8 F7
   3 Orpington BR5 ....38 D1
Challock Wlk ME14 .....92 C6
Chamberlain Ave ME16 ..91 C2
Chamberlain Cl SE28 ....2 D3
Chamberlain Ct ME8 ....63 B5
Chamberlain Rd ME4 ....48 B2
Chancel Cl TN15 ....55 E3
Chancellor Ho TN4 ....148 F3
Chancellor Way TN13 ...84 A5
Chancelot Rd SE2 ......3 B2
Chancery Ct DA1 ....27 A7
Chancery La ME15 ......92 B3
Chancery Rd ME3 ....16 B5
Chanctonbury Cl SE9 ...23 B5
Chandler Ave E16 ....1 A8
Chandler's Hill DA13 ....58 C5
Chandler's Rd DA13 .....58 C5
Chandlers Dr DA8 ....8 F7
Chandlers Wharf ME1 ..47 B5
Chandos Rd TN1 ....149 C5
Chantler's Hill TN12 ...136 A4
Chantlers Mead TN8 ...145 A5
Chantrey Cl DA14 ......24 E3
Chantry Ave DA3 ....42 E3
Chantry Ct DA12 ....13 C1
Chantry Her Ctr* DA12 .13 C1
Chantry La BR2 ....36 D4
Chantry Pl TN12 ....138 C6
Chantry Prim Schs DA12 13 C1
Chantry Rd TN12 ......138 C5
Chapel Alley Cotts TN14 69 A8
Chapel Cl Crayford DA1 ..8 E2
   West Thurrock RM20 ....11 B8
Chapel Cotts ME17 ....108 F5
Chapel Ct DA10 ....11 E1
Chapel Farm Rd SE9 ...22 F6
Chapel Field Cotts DA4 ..41 B8
Chapel Hill DA1 ....8 E2
Chapel Hos ME2 ....59 A8
Chapel La Benenden TN17 180 C4
   Gillingham,Hempstead ME7 63 A4
   Gillingham,Lidsing ME7 ..63 A2
   Maidstone ME14 ....93 A5
   Potter's Forstal TN27 ..127 B2
   Sissinghurst TN17 ......170 B7
   Staplehurst TN12 ....139 F3
   Upper Halling ME2 ......59 C4
Chapel Pl 8 Royal Tunbridge
   Wells TN1 ....149 A2
   Ticehurst TN5 ....176 E1
Chapel Rd Bexley DA7 ...8 A3
   Grain ME3 ....21 B5
   Snodland ME6 ....75 A8
   Sutton Valence ME17 ..124 E7
Chapel Row TN15 ......56 C6
Chapel St East Malling ME19 90 A6
   Ryarsh ME19 ....73 F5
Chapel View TN15 ......86 C6
Chapel Wlk TN14 ....98 B5
Chapel Wood DA3 ......56 E8
Chapel Wood Rd DA3,TN15 56 E8
Chaplin Cl ME3 ....33 C3
Chaplin Dr TN27 ....141 D5
Chapman Ave ME15 ...107 E8
Chapman Rd DA17 ......4 B1
Chapman Way
   East Malling ME19 ......89 F8
   Speldhurst TN14 ....56 E4
Chapman's Hill DA13,TN15 57 E4
Chapman's La
   Hockenden BR8 ....39 A7
   St Paul's Cray BR5,BR8 ..38 D7
Chapmans Cl TN14 .....82 E3
Chapmans End BR5 .....38 E7

Chapmans Rd TN14 . . . . . .82 E3
Chapter Rd ME2 . . . . .46 F8
Chapter Sch ME2 . . . . .46 D7
Chardwell Cl E6 . . . . .1 F7
Charford Rd E16 . . . . .1 A8
Charing Cl BR6 . . . . .51 F6
Charing House **5** DA8 . . . . .8 F7
Charing Rd ME8 . . . . .49 B3
Chariot Way ME4 . . . . .46 E4
Charity Farm Cotts TN17 .156 F5
Charlbury Cl ME16 . . . . . . .91 C3
Charldane Rd SE9 . . . . .23 B5
Charlecote Ct ME8 . . . . . . .63 D8
Charles Busby Ct **2** ME20 .75 F1
Charles Cl Sidcup DA14 . . . .24 B4
   Snodland ME6 . . . . .75 A8
Charles Ct Erith DA8 . . . . . . .8 E8
   Royal Tunbridge Wells TN4 .149 C3
Charles Dickens Ave ME3 .32 C2
Charles Dickens Ctr
   (Mus)* ME1 . . . . .47 C5
Charles Dr ME2 . . . . .46 B2
Charles Flemwell
   Mews E16 . . . . .1 A5
Charles Grinling Wlk SE18 .2 A2
Charles Rd TN14 . . . . .53 B1
Charles St Chatham ME4 . . .47 E3
   Grays RM17 . . . . .12 C8
   Maidstone ME16 . . . . .91 E3
   Newham E16 . . . . .1 C5
   Rochester ME2 . . . . .47 A7
   Royal Tunbridge Wells TN4 .149 A8
   Stone DA9 . . . . .10 F2
Charles Winchup Rd E16 . .1 B5
Charlesfield SE9 . . . . .22 C5
Charlesford Ave ME6 . . . .109 D3
Charlieville Rd DA8 . . . . . . .8 C7
Charlock Cl ME16 . . . . .91 D8
Charlotte Cl Bexley DA6 . . . .7 E2
   Chatham ME5 . . . . .62 B6
Charlotte Ct BR7 . . . . .23 B2
Charlotte Dr ME8 . . . . .49 C1
Charlotte Park Ave BR1 . . .36 E6
Charlotte Pl RM20 . . . . . . .11 B8
Charlottes Cotts TN17 . . .115 F1
Charlton Church La SE7 . . .1 C1
Charlton Dene SE7 . . . . . . .5 D7
Charlton La
   Chartway Street ME17 . . . .125 C8
   Greenwich SE7 . . . . .1 D1
   West Farleigh ME15 . . . . .105 E6
Charlton Manor
   PrimSch SE7 . . . . .5 D7
Charlton Park La SE7 . . . . .5 E8
Charlton Park Rd SE7 . . . . .5 D8
Charlton Park Sch SE7 . . . .5 E8
Charlton Rd SE3,SE7 . . . . . .5 B8
Charlton St Grays RM20 . . .11 D8
   Maidstone ME16 . . . . .91 C2
Charlton's Way TN4 . . . . .148 E1
Charminster Rd SE9 . . . . . .22 D4
Charmouth Rd DA16 . . . . . .7 C6
Charmwood La BR6 . . . . . .52 B1
Charmwood Villas BR6 . . .52 C1
Charne The TN14 . . . . .69 A2
Charnock ME8 . . . . .39 E5
Chart Cnr ME17 . . . . .108 B1
Chart Hill Rd ME17 . . . . . .124 A7
Chart Hills Cl SE28 . . . . . . .3 E7
Chart La TN16 . . . . .97 B7
Chart Pl ME8 . . . . .63 C3
Chart Rd ME17 . . . . .124 C7
Chart View TN15 . . . . .70 B2
Charter Dr DA5 . . . . .24 E8
Charter St Chatham ME4 . . .47 F2
   Gillingham ME7 . . . . .48 C7
Charterhouse Dr TN13 . . . .84 A4
Charterhouse Rd BR6 . . . . .52 A6
Charton Cl **5** DA17 . . . . . . .7 F8
Chartway TN13 . . . . .84 C3
Chartway St ME17 . . . . . .109 C1
Chartwell (National
   Trust)* TN16 . . . . .96 F4
Chartwell Bsns Ctr BR1 . . .36 D6
Chartwell Cl Rochester ME2 33 B1
   Sidcup SE9 . . . . .23 D6
Chartwell Ct
   Maidstone ME15 . . . . .92 B3
   Rochester ME4 . . . . .47 E4
Chartwell Dr BR6 . . . . .51 D5
Chase Sq **13** DA11 . . . . . . .13 B1
Chase The Bexley DA7 . . . . .8 B4
   Bromley BR1 . . . . .36 B6
   Chatham ME4 . . . . .47 D2
   Gillingham ME8 . . . . .49 A2
   Kemsing TN15 . . . . .69 E3
   Pratt's Bottom BR6 . . . . . . .52 A1
   Tonbridge TN10 . . . . .117 C5
   West Thurrock RM20 . . . . . .11 D8
Chastilian Rd DA1 . . . . . . .26 A8
Chatfield Way ME19 . . . . . .75 B1
Chatham Ave BR2 . . . . .36 A2
Chatham Gr ME4 . . . . .47 F1
Chatham Gram Sch
   for Boys ME4 . . . . .61 F8
Chatham Gram Sch
   for Girls ME5 . . . . .48 C2
Chatham Hill ME4 . . . . . . .48 B3
Chatham Hill Rd ME4 . . . . .84 C6
Chatham Ho **16** SE18 . . . . .1 F2
Chatham Rd
   Kit's Coty ME20 . . . . .76 D6
   Maidstone ME14 . . . . .76 A4
   Maidstone,Sandling ME14 . .76 E4
Chatham Ski Ctr ME7 . . . . .62 E1
Chatham South Sch ME4 . .61 F8
Chatham St SE18 . . . . .2 B3

Chatham Sta ME4 . . . . . . .47 E4
Chatsworth Ave
   Bromley BR1 . . . . .22 B4
   Sidcup DA15 . . . . .24 A7
Chatsworth Dr ME2 . . . . . .33 B1
Chatsworth Ho **3** BR2 . . . .36 A5
Chatsworth Inf Sch DA15 . .24 A7
Chatsworth Par BR5 . . . . . .37 C4
Chatsworth Rd Dartford DA1 9 C3
   10 Gillingham ME7 . . . . . .48 C6
Chattenden Barracks
   Royal Sch of Military
   Engineering ME3 . . . . . . .33 F5
Chattenden Ct ME14 . . . . . .92 B6
Chattenden La ME3 . . . . . .33 F5
Chattenden Prim Sch ME3 33 F4
Chattenden Terr ME3 . . . . .33 F4
Chatterton Rd BR2 . . . . . . .36 A4
Chatwell Ct ME7 . . . . .48 C5
Chaucer Cl
   8 Maidstone ME15 . . . . .107 E7
   Rochester ME2 . . . . .47 E8
   Tilbury RM18 . . . . .13 C5
Chaucer Gdns TN9 . . . . . .132 F7
Chaucer Ind Pk TN15 . . . . .85 D8
Chaucer Pk DA1 . . . . .26 F8
Chaucer Rd Bexley DA16 . . . .6 F1
   Gillingham ME7 . . . . .48 D3
   Northfleet DA11 . . . . .29 D5
   Sidcup DA15 . . . . .24 C7
Chaucer Way ME20 . . . . . . .75 A3
Chaundrye Cl SE9 . . . . .5 F1
Chauntler Cl E16 . . . . .1 B6
Chauser Way DA1 . . . . . . .10 A3
Chave Rd DA1,DA2 . . . . . . .26 E5
Cheeselands TN27 . . . . . .157 F2
Cheffins Ho ME7 . . . . .48 E7
Chegwell Dr ME5 . . . . .62 B4
Chegworth La ME17 . . . . .110 A6
Chegworth Rd ME17 . . . . .109 F5
Cheldoc Rise ME4 . . . . . . .34 C2
Chelmar Rd ME7 . . . . .48 B4
Chelmsford Cl E6 . . . . .1 F7
Chelmsford Ho ME15 . . . .107 E6
Chelmsford Rd ME2 . . . . . .46 D6
Chelsea Ct **6** BR1 . . . . . . .36 E6
Chelsfield Hill BR6 . . . . . . .52 C2
Chelsfield Ho ME16 . . . . . .91 D5
Chelsfield La
   Badgers Mount BR6,TN14 . . .53 B2
   Chelsfield BR5,BR6 . . . . . .52 D7
   Orpington BR5 . . . . .38 D2
Chelsfield Lakes
   Golf Course BR6 . . . . . . .52 E3
Chelsfield Park Hospl BR6 52 F5
Chelsfield Prim Sch BR6 . .52 C5
Chelsfield Rd BR5 . . . . . . .38 C3
Chelsfield Sta BR6 . . . . . . .52 B5
Chelsiter Ct DA14 . . . . . . .23 F4
Chelsworth Dr SE18 . . . . . .6 D8
Cheltenham Cl
   Gravesend DA12 . . . . .30 C3
   Maidstone ME15 . . . . . . .107 F6
Cheltenham Rd BR6 . . . . . .52 A7
Cheney Cl ME8 . . . . .63 D5
Cheney's Cotts DA12 . . . . .31 A3
Chenies Cl ME2 . . . . .163 A8
Chenies The Dartford DA2 . .25 E4
   Orpington BR6 . . . . .51 F7
Chennell Park Rd TN30 . . .172 E1
Chennells The TN26 . . . . .173 C7
Chepstow
   House **3** ME15 . . . . . . .107 F6
Chequer's Cotts TN17 . . . .153 F1
Chequers Cl Chatham ME5 . .77 A8
   Istead Rise DA13 . . . . . . .43 F7
   St Paul's Cray BR5 . . . . . .37 F5
Chequers Dr TN9 . . . . .92 A4
Chequers Hill Cotts TN8 .114 A2
Chequers La RM9 . . . . .3 F8
Cherbourg Cres ME5 . . . . .61 F7
Cherbury Cl SE28 . . . . .3 D7
Cheriton Ave BR2 . . . . .36 A4
Cheriton Ct **12** SE12 . . . . .22 A4
Cheriton Dr SE18 . . . . .6 D8
Cheriton Rd ME8 . . . . .63 D8
Cheriton Way ME16 . . . . . .91 C7
Cherries The ME16 . . . . . . .91 A2
Cherry Amber Cl ME8 . . . . .63 F8
Cherry Ave BR8 . . . . .39 D5
Cherry Cl ME17 . . . . .111 C5
Cherry Ct DA14 . . . . .24 B5
Cherry Gr TN10 . . . . .117 E5
Cherry Hill Ct ME9 . . . . . . .65 B6
Cherry Orch Ditton ME20 . . .90 C8
   Greenwich SE7 . . . . .5 C8
   Tenterden TN30 . . . . .183 A6
Cherry Orch The TN11 . . . .102 E1
Cherry Orchard Cl BR5 . . .38 C4
Cherry Orchard Rd BR2 . . .36 C6
Cherry Orchard Way ME16 91 B3
Cherry Rd ME3 . . . . .34 E3
Cherry Tree Cl RM17 . . . . .12 C8
Cherry Tree Ct **18** SE7 . . . .5 D8
Cherry Tree Gr TN15 . . . . .55 B1
Cherry Tree La DA2 . . . . . .25 F5
Cherry Tree Rd
   Gillingham ME8 . . . . .63 F8
   Royal Tunbridge Wells TN2 .148 E1
Cherry Trees DA3 . . . . .42 F4
Cherry View ME17 . . . . . .107 B3
Cherry Wlk BR2 . . . . .36 A1
Cherrycot Hill BR6 . . . . . . .51 D6
Cherrycot Rise BR6 . . . . . .51 C6
Cherrydown Rd DA14 . . . . .24 D6
Cherryfields TN17 . . . . . .180 D6
Cherrywood Dr DA11 . . . . .29 E5

Chervil Mews SE28 . . . . . . .3 B5
Chervilles ME16 . . . . .91 A2
Cherwell Cl TN10 . . . . . . .117 B4
Chesfield Cl TN11 . . . . . . .102 F1
Chesham Ave BR5 . . . . . . .37 B3
Chesham Dr ME8 . . . . .63 C6
Cheshire Rd
   Maidstone,Shepway ME15 . .107 E7
   Maidstone,Willington ME15 . .92 E2
Cheshunt Cl DA13 . . . . . . .44 A3
Cheshunt Rd DA17 . . . . .4 A1
Chessenden La TN27 . . . . .143 A1
Chessington Ave DA7 . . . . . .7 A4
Chester Ave TN2 . . . . .149 D2
Chester Cl ME2 . . . . .46 D6
Chester Rd Gillingham ME7 .48 D2
   Sidcup DA15 . . . . .6 E2
Chesterfield Cl BR5 . . . . . .38 C5
Chesterfield Dr Dartford DA1 9 B2
   Sevenoaks TN13 . . . . .83 D5
Chesterton Rd Cliffe ME3 . .16 B5
   5 Lunsford ME20 . . . . . . .74 F4
Chesterton Way RM18 . . . .13 C5
Chestfield Cl ME8 . . . . .49 E2
Chestnut Ave Chatham ME5 .61 F3
   Hill Park TN16 . . . . .81 A6
   Speldhurst TN4 . . . . .149 B8
   Staplehurst TN12 . . . . . . .139 F4
   Stone DA9 . . . . .27 F8
Chestnut Cl
   Edenbridge TN8 . . . . .112 B2
   Frittenden TN17 . . . . .156 E6
   Kings Hill ME19 . . . . .89 A2
   Northfleet DA11 . . . . .12 F1
   Orpington BR6 . . . . .52 A8
   Royal Tunbridge Wells TN4 .149 B8
   Sidcup DA15 . . . . .24 A6
   Tenterden TN30 . . . . .173 C1
   Ulcombe ME17 . . . . .125 F6
Chestnut Dr Bexley DA7 . . . .7 A4
   Coxheath ME17 . . . . .106 B3
   Kingswood ME17 . . . . . . .109 D2
Chestnut Gr DA2 . . . . .25 E2
Chestnut La Matfield TN12 135 D1
   Sevenoaks TN13 . . . . .84 B3
   Vigo Village DA13 . . . . .73 B8
Chestnut Pl TN8 . . . . .145 A5
Chestnut Rd Dartford DA1 . .26 D7
   Rochester ME2 . . . . .46 E6
Chestnut Rise SE18 . . . . . . .2 E1
Chestnut St ME9 . . . . .65 E4
Chestnut Wlk
   Larkfield ME20 . . . . .75 B2
   Sevenoaks TN15 . . . . .99 F6
   Tonbridge TN9 . . . . .116 F2
Chestnut Wood La ME9 . . .65 E3
Chestnuts Royal BR7 . . . . .23 D1
Chestnuts The
   Addington ME19 . . . . .73 C3
   Chislehurst BR7 . . . . .23 D1
   11 Erith DA17 . . . . .4 A1
   The Moor TN18 . . . . .184 F8
   Woolwich SE18 . . . . .6 B6
Cheswick Cl DA1 . . . . .8 F3
Chesworth Cl DA8 . . . . .8 E5
Chetney Cl ME2 . . . . .46 C7
Chetwood Wlk **14** E6 . . . . . .1 E8
Cheveney Wlk **2** BR2 . . . .36 A6
Chevening
   CE Prim Sch SE10 . . . . . . .1 A1
   Sevenoaks TN13,TN14 . . . .83 B6
   Sundridge TN14 . . . . .82 F4
Chevenings The DA14 . . . . .24 C5
Cheviot Cl Erith DA7 . . . . . .8 E5
   Tonbridge TN9 . . . . .117 C4
Cheviot Gdns ME15 . . . . . .93 A1
Cheviot Ho DA11 . . . . .12 D1
Chevron Cl E16 . . . . .1 A7
Chevron House RM17 . . . . .12 B7
Cheyne Cl BR2 . . . . .50 E7
Cheyne Wlk Longfield DA3 .42 D6
   Meopham DA13 . . . . .58 A8
Chicago Ave ME7 . . . . .48 F5
Chichester Cl
   Gillingham ME8 . . . . .64 A8
   Greenwich SE3 . . . . .5 C6
   Newham E6 . . . . .1 E7
Chichester Ct **3** DA5 . . . . .25 A4
Chichester Dr TN13 . . . . . .83 F2
Chichester Rd Stone DA9 . .10 F1
   Tonbridge TN9 . . . . .133 A8
Chichester Rise DA12 . . . . .30 C4
Chickenden La NT17 . . . . .140 C4
Chickfield Gdns **4** ME5 . .48 C2
Chicks La TN17 . . . . .167 A2
Chiddingstone Ave DA7 . . . .7 F7
Chiddingstone
   Castle* TN8 . . . . .130 B7
Chiddingstone
   CE Prim Sch TN8 . . . . . .130 C7
Chiddingstone Cl ME15 . .107 F6
Chidley Cross Rd TN12 . . .119 E6
Chieftain Cl ME7 . . . . .49 B1
Chieveley Dr TN2 . . . . . . .149 D1
Chieveley Par DA7 . . . . .8 B4
Chieveley Rd DA7 . . . . .8 B3
Chiffinch Gdns DA11 . . . . .29 E5
Childs Cres DA10 . . . . .11 D1
Childs Way TN15 . . . . .71 F3
Childsbridge La TN15 . . . . .84 F7
Childsbridge Way TN15 . . .84 F7

Childscroft Rd ME8 . . . . . .49 F2
Chilham Cl Chatham ME4 . . .47 E3
   Sidcup DA15 . . . . .24 F8
Chilham Ho
   1 Maidstone ME15 . . . . .107 E8
   Rochester ME2 . . . . .33 C1
Chilham Rd Chislehurst SE9 22 E4
   Gillingham ME8 . . . . .49 A3
   Maidstone ME16 . . . . .91 C7
Chilham Way BR2 . . . . .36 A2
Chillington Cl ME2 . . . . . . .59 E4
Chillington St ME14 . . . . . .91 F6
Chilliwack Rd ME3 . . . . . . .33 F5
Chilston Cl TN4 . . . . .149 A5
Chilston Rd Lenham ME17 111 D5
   Royal Tunbridge Wells TN4 .149 A5
Chiltenhurst TN8 . . . . . . .112 A2
Chiltern Cl Erith DA7 . . . . . .8 E6
   Maidstone ME15 . . . . .92 F1
Chiltern Ct **11** SE9 . . . . . . .6 A1
Chiltern Rd DA11 . . . . .29 C5
Chiltern Way TN9 . . . . . . .117 C4
Chiltern Wlk TN2 . . . . . . .149 D4
Chilterns DA14 . . . . .24 A3
Chilterns, The BR1 . . . . . . .36 B7
Chilton Ct ME8 . . . . .49 E1
Chilton Dr ME3 . . . . .32 B3
Chimes The ME1 . . . . .47 C5
Chinbrook Cres
   8 Lewisham SE12 . . . . . .22 B5
   Lewisham SE12 . . . . .22 B5
Chinbrook Rd SE12 . . . . . .22 B5
Chippendale Cl ME5 . . . . . .61 F1
Chippendale Dr ME7 . . . . .110 D6
Chipperfield Rd BR5 . . . . . .38 A7
Chipstead Cl ME16 . . . . . . .91 D6
Chipstead La TN13 . . . . . . .83 D5
Chipstead Park Cl TN13 . . .83 C5
Chipstead Pk TN13 . . . . . . .83 D5
Chipstead Place
   Gdns TN13 . . . . .83 D5
Chipstead Rd Erith DA8 . . . .8 E7
   Gillingham ME8 . . . . .63 D4
Chipstead Sq TN13 . . . . . .83 D5
Chislehurst & Sidcup
   Gram Sch DA15 . . . . . . .24 B6
Chislehurst Caves* BR7 . . .37 A8
Chislehurst
   CE Prim Sch BR7 . . . . . .23 C1
Chislehurst Cl ME15 . . . . .107 E6
Chislehurst High St BR7 . . .23 B2
Chislehurst Rd
   Bromley BR1,BR7 . . . . . . .36 E8
   Orpington,Broom Hill BR6 . .38 A7
   Orpington,Petts Wood
   BR5,BR6 . . . . .37 E4
   Sidcup DA14 . . . . .24 A3
Chislehurst Sta BR7 . . . . . .37 A7
Chislet Wlk ME8 . . . . .63 D5
Chiswell Sq SE3 . . . . .5 B5
Chorleywood Cres BR5 . . .38 A1
Christ Church Ave Erith DA8 8 E8
   1 Royal Tunbridge
   Wells TN1 . . . . .149 A2
Christ Church CE Sch SE18 6 A6
Christ Church
   Cres **2** DA12 . . . . .30 C8
Christ Church Rd **3** DA12 .30 C8
Christchurch Ct **3** ME5 . . .48 C2
Christchurch
   House **11** ME15 . . . . . .107 E5
Christchurch Rd
   Dartford DA1 . . . . .9 C1
   Sidcup DA15 . . . . .23 F5
   Tilbury RM18 . . . . .13 A6
Christen Way ME15,ME17 .107 F3
Christian Ct **3** ME2 . . . . . .47 C8
Christian Fields Ave DA12 30 C4
Christie Cl ME5 . . . . .62 B6
Christie Dr **8** ME20 . . . . . .74 F4
Christie House DA2 . . . . . . .8 B2
Christies Ave TN14 . . . . . . .53 B1
Christmas La ME23 . . . . . . .17 F3
Christmas St ME7 . . . . .48 E7
Christopher Ct DA15 . . . . . .6 F2
Chudleigh **7** DA14 . . . . . . .24 B4
Chulkhurst TN27 . . . . .157 F1
Chulkhurst Cl TN27 . . . . . .157 F1
Church Alley **10** DA11 . . . . .13 B1
Church Ave DA14 . . . . .24 B3
Church Cl Brenchley TN12 . .152 C8
   Cliffe ME3 . . . . .16 B6
   Mereworth ME18 . . . . . . .103 D8
Church Cotts
   Cranbrook TN17 . . . . .169 D5
   Crockenhill BR8 . . . . .39 D2
   Shoreham TN14 . . . . .69 A8
   Tenterden TN30 . . . . .173 B3
Church Cres ME17 . . . . . .110 F6
Church Ct DA2 . . . . .26 D5
Church Farm Cl
   Crockenhill BR8 . . . . .39 D3
   Hoo St Werburgh ME3 . . . .34 E4
Church Field Dartford DA2 . .26 D6
   Edenbridge TN8 . . . . .112 D1
   Sevenoaks TN13 . . . . .83 F5
   Snodland ME6 . . . . .60 B1
Church Fields ME19 . . . . . .89 B8
Church Gn
   Hollingbourne ME17 . . . . . .94 E3
   Marden TN12 . . . . .138 C6
   Rochester ME2 . . . . .47 C8
   Staplehurst TN12 . . . . . . .139 D2
Church Hill Chatham ME5 . .48 C2
   Crayford DA1 . . . . .8 E1
   Cudham TN14,TN16 . . . . . .66 C4
   Dartford DA2 . . . . .26 D6

Church Hill continued
   High Halden TN26 . . . . . .173 E7
   Leigh TN11 . . . . .115 F2
   Maidstone ME17 . . . . . . .123 B7
   Orpington BR6 . . . . .38 A2
   Plaxtol TN15 . . . . .101 E8
   Stockbury ME9 . . . . .79 F7
   Stone DA9 . . . . .10 E2
   Woolwich SE18 . . . . .1 F3
Church Hill Wood BR5 . . . .37 F4
Church Hyde SE18 . . . . .6 E8
Church La Capel TN12 . . . .134 F6
   Chalk DA12 . . . . .31 C6
   Chartway Street ME17 . . . .125 B8
   Chatham ME4 . . . . .47 F6
   Chislehurst BR7 . . . . .37 C8
   East Peckham TN12 . . . . .119 C3
   Frant TN3 . . . . .163 B4
   Harrietsham ME17 . . . . . .110 E6
   Kemsing TN15 . . . . .69 F1
   Maidstone,Bearsted ME14 . .93 C4
   Maidstone, East Barming
   ME16 . . . . .90 E1
   Newington ME9 . . . . .65 B6
   Orpington BR2 . . . . .36 E1
   Stockbury ME9 . . . . .79 E8
   Tonbridge TN9 . . . . .117 C2
   Trottiscliffe ME19 . . . . .73 B5
   West Farleigh ME15 . . . . .105 D7
Church Manor Way
   SE18,SE2 . . . . .3 A2
Church Manorway DA8 . . . . .4 D3
Church Meadow TN12 . . . .153 A7
Church Mews ME8 . . . . . . .63 F8
Church Path
   Gillingham ME7 . . . . .48 C6
   Northfleet DA11 . . . . .12 C1
   Stone DA9 . . . . .10 F1
Church Rd Bexley DA7,DA6 . .7 F4
   Bexley,Welling DA16 . . . . . .7 B5
   Bitchet Green TN15 . . . . . .85 E3
   Brasted TN16 . . . . .82 B3
   Bromley BR1,BR2 . . . . . . .36 A7
   Chart Sutton ME17 . . . . . .124 C8
   Chelsfield BR6 . . . . .52 D4
   Crockenhill BR8 . . . . .39 D2
   Erith DA8 . . . . .4 D1
   Goudhurst TN17 . . . . .167 F8
   Grafty Green ME17 . . . . . .126 F7
   Gravesend DA12,DA13 . . . .30 D1
   Harrietsham ME17 . . . . . .110 E6
   Hartley DA3 . . . . .43 A2
   Henhurst DA13 . . . . .44 C8
   Hucking ME17 . . . . .79 E1
   Kilndown TN17 . . . . .166 F3
   Lamberhurst TN3 . . . . . . .166 C6
   Maidstone,Shepway ME15 . .107 F7
   Maidstone,Tovil ME15 . . . .91 E2
   Offham ME18 . . . . .88 D8
   Orpington,Farnborough BR6 .51 D3
   Orpington, Keston BR2 . . . .50 D3
   Paddock Wood TN12 . . . . .136 B6
   Royal Tunbridge Wells TN1 .149 A3
   Royal Tunbridge
   Wells,Southborough TN4 . .132 F2
   Ryarsh ME19 . . . . .74 A3
   Sandhurst TN18 . . . . .185 F4
   Seal TN15 . . . . .84 F6
   Sevenoaks Weald TN14 . . . .99 B3
   Sidcup DA14 . . . . .24 A4
   Stone DA9 . . . . .10 F2
   Sundridge TN14 . . . . .82 E2
   Sutton at Hone DA4 . . . . . .27 A2
   Swanley Village BR8 . . . . . .40 D8
   Swanscombe DA10 . . . . . . .11 F1
   Tenterden TN30 . . . . .183 A7
   Tilbury RM18 . . . . .12 F6
   Tilbury, Low Street RM18 . . .13 E8
   Tonbridge TN11 . . . . .116 D6
   West Kingsdown TN15 . . . . .55 E3
   West Peckham ME18 . . . . .103 A6
Church Row
   Chislehurst BR7 . . . . .37 C8
   Plaxtol TN15 . . . . .101 E8
   Snodland ME6 . . . . .75 A7
   West Peckham ME18 . . . . .103 B6
Church Row Mews BR7 . . .23 C1
Church Sq ME17 . . . . .111 D5
Church St Burham ME1 . . . .60 F1
   Chatham ME3 . . . . .48 A4
   Cliffe ME3 . . . . .16 B5
   Cowden TN8 . . . . .145 B5
   Edenbridge TN8 . . . . .112 D1
   Gillingham ME7 . . . . .48 E6
   Gravesend DA11 . . . . .13 B1
   Grays RM17 . . . . .12 C8
   Hadlow TN11 . . . . .118 E8
   Higham ME3 . . . . .32 D7
   Hoo St Werburgh ME3 . . . .34 E5
   Maidstone ME14 . . . . .92 A4
   Maidstone, Boughton
   Monchelsea ME17 . . . . . .107 B2
   Maidstone, Loose ME15 . . .106 F5
   Maidstone,Tovil ME15 . . . .91 E2
   Newham E16 . . . . .2 B5
   Northfleet DA13 . . . . .29 A3
   Rochester ME1 . . . . .47 D4
   Seal TN15 . . . . .85 A7
   Shoreham TN14 . . . . .69 A8
   Teston ME18 . . . . .105 A8
   Ticehurst TN5 . . . . .176 D1
   Tonbridge TN9 . . . . .117 C2
Church Terr ME5 . . . . .48 C2
Church View
   Biddenden TN27 . . . . .157 F2

Church View continued
Swanley BR8 . . . . .39 D6
Church Wlk Dartford DA2 . .26 D5
East Malling ME19 . . . . . . .90 A7
Eynsford DA4 . . . . .54 E7
Gravesend DA12 . . . . .30 D7
Gravesend DA12 . . . . .30 D8
Hawkhurst TN18 . . . . . . .179 A1
Headcorn TN27 . . . . .141 C5
Churchbury Rd SE9 . . . . . .22 D8
Churchfield ME19 . . . . . . .73 D3
Churchfield Rd DA16 . . . . .7 A4
Churchfield Sch SE2 . . . . . .3 A2
Churchfields Terr ME1 . . . .47 B4
Churchill Ave ME5 . . . . . .62 A7
Churchill Bsns Ctr TN16 .81 D1
Churchill
CE Prim Sch TN16 . . . . . .81 C2
Churchill Cl DA1 . . . . .27 B7
Churchill Cotts ME17 . . . .108 F6
Churchill Ct 4 BR6 . . . . . .51 C5
Churchill Ho
Benenden TN17 . . . . .180 E6
Maidstone ME16 . . . . .91 B2
1 Woolwich SE18 . . . . .2 B2
Churchill Pk DA1 . . . . . . .10 A2
Churchill Rd
Gravesend DA11 . . . . .29 F7
Grays RM17 . . . . .12 D8
Horton Kirby DA4 . . . . . . .41 C5
Newham E16 . . . . .1 C7
Churchill Sq ME19 . . . . . .89 A3
Churchill Way BR1 . . . . . .36 A7
Churchills
Ropewalk TN17 . . . . . . .167 E8
Churchsettle La TN5 . . . .175 C1
Churchside DA13 . . . . . . .73 A8
Churchyard Cotts TN3 . . .148 A8
Churn La TN12 . . . . .137 A2
Chute Cl ME3 . . . . .63 D4
Chyngton Cl DA15 . . . . . .23 F5
Cimba Wood DA12 . . . . . .30 E4
Cinder Hill La TN11 . . . . .115 C1
Cinderhill Wood TN12 . . .135 C2
Cinnabar Cl ME5 . . . . . . .62 A1
Circle The RM18 . . . . . . .13 A6
Circuit Rd SE28 . . . . .3 A4
Circular Way SE18 . . . . . .6 A8
Cirrus Cres DA12 . . . . . . .30 E3
City Way ME1 . . . . .47 D2
Civic Sq RM18 . . . . .13 A5
Civic Way TN1 . . . . .149 A3
CJ Gallards
Almshouses TN4 . . . . . . .149 A8
Clacket La TN16 . . . . . . .96 A8
Clacketts Farm ME19 . . . .74 B5
Claire House ME16 . . . . . .91 E5
Clandon Cl BR1 . . . . .22 A2
Clandon Rd ME5 . . . . . . .62 D2
Clanricarde Gdns 1 TN1 .149 A3
Clanricarde Rd 2 TN1 . . .149 A3
Claphatch La TN5 . . . . . .176 A5
Clapton Ct ME8 . . . . .63 D8
Clara Pl SE18 . . . . .2 A2
Clare Ave TN9 . . . . .116 F1
Clare Causeway DA9 . . . . .10 F3
Clare Cnr SE9 . . . . .23 B8
Clare Ct BR7 . . . . .36 F8
Clare La ME19 . . . . .89 E8
Clare Way Bexley DA7 . . . .7 E6
Sevenoaks TN13 . . . . .99 C8
Claremont
Cty PrimSch TN2 . . . . . .149 B2
Claremont Gdns TN2 . . . .149 B2
Claremont Pl
Benenden TN17 . . . . .180 C4
1 Gravesend DA11 . . . . . .30 B8
Claremont Rd Bromley BR1 .36 F5
Hextable BR8 . . . . .25 E1
Maidstone ME14 . . . . .92 B5
Royal Tunbridge Wells TN1 .149 B2
Claremont St E16 . . . . . . .2 A4
Claremont Way 2 ME4 . . .47 F3
Clarence Ave
Bromley BR1,BR2 . . . . . . .36 E5
Rochester ME1 . . . . .47 C4
Clarence Cres DA14 . . . . .24 B5
Clarence Ct ME14 . . . . . . .92 E4
Clarence Pl DA12 . . . . . . .30 B7
Clarence Rd Bexley DA6 . . .7 E3
Bromley BR1 . . . . .36 E6
Chatham ME4 . . . . .48 B2
Chislehurst SE9 . . . . .22 E6
Grays RM17 . . . . .12 A8
Royal Tunbridge Wells TN1 .149 A3
Sidcup DA14 . . . . .24 B5
Clarence Row
Gravesend DA12 . . . . .30 B8
Royal Tunbridge Wells TN1 .149 A3
Clarendon Cl
Maidstone ME14 . . . . .93 A4
St Paul's Cray BR5 . . . . . . .38 A6
Clarendon Gdns
Dartford DA2 . . . . .27 D8
Rochester ME2 . . . . .46 F7
Royal Tunbridge Wells TN2 .149 A1
Clarendon Gn BR5 . . . . . .38 A5
Clarendon Gr BR5 . . . . . .38 A5
Clarendon Mews DA5 . . . .25 B7
Clarendon Path BR5 . . . . .38 A6
Clarendon Pl Dartford DA2 .25 E3

Clarendon Pl continued
Maidstone ME14 . . . . .92 A4
Sevenoaks TN13 . . . . .84 A2
Clarendon Rd
Gravesend DA12 . . . . .13 C1
Sevenoaks TN13 . . . . .84 A2
Clarendon Way
Royal Tunbridge Wells TN2 .149 A1
St Paul's Cray BR5,BR7 . . . .37 F6
Claret Ho TN1 . . . . .84 B3
Clareville Rd BR5 . . . . . . .51 C8
Clarewood Dr ME19 . . . . .89 E8
Claridge TN1 . . . . .149 B6
Claridge Ct ME7 . . . . . . .62 F4
Clark Cl DA8 . . . . .9 A6
Clark Mews ME20 . . . . . . .75 F1
Clarkbourne Dr RM17 . . . .12 D8
Clarkes Green Rd TN15 . . .70 B5
Clarks La TN14 . . . . .67 F7
Claston Cl DA1 . . . . .8 E3
Clavadal Rd TN12 . . . . . .136 A7
Clavell Cl ME8 . . . . .63 E4
Clay Cotts TN17 . . . . . . .167 E8
Clay Hill Rd TN3 . . . . . . .165 D6
Clay Wood Cl BR6 . . . . . .37 E2
Claybridge Rd SE12 . . . . .22 C4
Claydown Mews SE18 . . . . .2 A1
Clayfarm Rd SE9 . . . . . . .23 C6
Claygate ME15 . . . . .92 D1
Claygate Cross TN15 . . . . .87 A3
Claygate La TN11 . . . . . .101 F4
Claygate Rd TN12 . . . . . .121 B2
Clayhill TN17 . . . . .167 D8
Clayhill Cres SE9 . . . . . . .22 D4
Claymill Ho 2 SE18 . . . . . .2 C1
Clayton Cl 3 E6 . . . . .1 F7
Clayton Croft Rd DA2 . . . .26 A6
Clayton's La TN3 . . . . . . .146 E2
Claytonville Terr DA17 . . . .4 C4
Claywood La DA2 . . . . . . .28 D5
Clayworth Cl DA15 . . . . . . .7 B1
Cleanthus Cl SE18 . . . . . . .6 B6
Cleanthus Rd SE18 . . . . . . .6 B6
Clearway ME19 . . . . .73 A1
Clearways Bsns Est TN15 .55 E3
Cleave Ave BR6 . . . . .51 E4
Cleave Rd ME7 . . . . .48 E3
Cleavers TN17 . . . . .170 A8
Cleavers Cl TN17 . . . . . . .170 A8
Cleavesland ME18 . . . . . .120 E5
Cleeve Ave TN2 . . . . . . .149 D2
Cleeve Ct ME19 . . . . .89 B3
Cleeve Park Gdns DA14 . .24 B6
Cleeve Park Sch DA14 . . . .24 C5
Clegg House SE3 . . . . .5 B3
Clematis Ave ME8 . . . . . .63 B5
Clement Ct ME16 . . . . . . .91 D5
Clement St BR8,DA4 . . . . .26 E2
Clements Ave E16 . . . . . . .1 A6
Clenches Farm La TN13 . . .84 A1
Clenches Farm Rd TN13 . . .84 A1
Clendon Way SE18 . . . . . . .2 D2
Clerks Field TN27 . . . . . .141 D5
Clermont Cl ME7 . . . . . . .63 A4
Cleve Rd DA14 . . . . .24 D5
Clevedon Ho BR1 . . . . . . .22 E1
Cleveland TN2 . . . . .149 C6
Cleveland Ho
Maidstone ME16 . . . . .91 B2
Northfleet DA11 . . . . .12 D1
Cleveland Rd
Bexley DA16 . . . . .6 F5
Gillingham ME7 . . . . .48 D6
Clevely Cl SE7 . . . . .1 D2
Cleves Rd TN15 . . . . .69 E2
Cleves View 2 DA1 . . . . . . .9 D1
Clewer Ho 8 SE2 . . . . .3 D4
Clewson Rise ME14 . . . . . .92 B8
Cliff Hill ME17 . . . . .107 D4
Cliff Hill Rd ME17 . . . . . .107 C4
Cliff Reach DA9 . . . . .10 F1
Cliffe Rd ME2 . . . . .33 A1
Cliffe Woods
Prim Sch ME3 . . . . .33 C8
Clifford Ave BR7 . . . . . . .22 F2
Clifford Ho 6 ME14 . . . . .92 B4
Clifton Cl Maidstone ME14 .92 B5
8 Orpington BR6 . . . . . . .51 C5
Rochester ME2 . . . . .46 F7
Clifton Cotts TN2 . . . . . .149 D8
Clifton Gr DA11 . . . . .30 B8
Clifton Marine Par DA11 . .12 F1
Clifton Pl TN1 . . . . .149 B2
Clifton Rd Bexley DA16 . . . .7 C4
Gillingham ME7 . . . . .48 C7
Gravesend DA11 . . . . .13 A1
Royal Tunbridge Wells TN1 .149 C7
Sidcup DA14 . . . . .23 E4
Cliftonville Ct SE12 . . . . .22 A7
Clinch Ct 15 E16 . . . . .1 A8
Clinch St ME3 . . . . .18 A4
Clinton Ave Bexley DA16 . . .7 A3
Rochester ME2 . . . . .46 E8
Clinton Cl ME17 . . . . . . .106 B3
Clinton La TN8 . . . . .113 E3
Clipper Bvd DA9 . . . . . . .10 E3
Clipper Bvd W DA2 . . . . .10 D4
Clipper Cl ME2 . . . . .47 E7
Clipper Cres DA12 . . . . . .30 F4
Clipper Ct ME2 . . . . .47 E7
Clive Ave DA1 . . . . .8 F1
Clive Ho ME20 . . . . .90 F8
Clive Rd Erith DA17 . . . . . .4 A2
Gravesend DA11 . . . . .13 B1
Rochester ME1 . . . . .47 C3
Cliveden Cl ME16 . . . . . . .91 D7
Clock Ho The DA15 . . . . .24 A7
Clock House La TN13 . . . . .84 A4

Clock Tower Mews
Snodland ME6 . . . . .60 A1
Woolwich SE28 . . . . .3 B6
Clockhouse TN2 . . . . . . .149 F6
Cloisterham Rd ME1 . . . . .61 D7
Cloisters Ave BR2 . . . . . . .36 F4
Cloisters Ct DA7 . . . . .8 B4
Cloisters The
1 Dartford DA1 . . . . .9 C1
Lenham ME17 . . . . .111 C5
Cloonmore Ave BR6 . . . . .51 F6
Close The Addington ME19 .73 C2
Birling ME19 . . . . .74 B5
Borough Green ME15 . . . . .87 A8
Bough Beech TN8 . . . . . .114 A2
Dartford DA2 . . . . .26 D5
Groombridge TN3 . . . . . .161 C6
Ightham TN15 . . . . .86 D6
New Barn DA3 . . . . .43 B7
Orpington BR5 . . . . .37 E3
Rochester ME1 . . . . .47 C4
Royal Tunbridge Wells TN2 .149 C8
Sevenoaks TN13 . . . . .83 E3
Sidcup DA14 . . . . .24 B3
Cloth Hall Gdns TN27 . . .158 A2
Clothier Ho SE7 . . . . .1 E1
Clothworkers Rd SE18 . . . . .6 D7
Cloudberry Cl ME16 . . . . .91 D6
Cloudesley Cl ME14 . . . . .47 B1
Cloudesley Rd Bexley DA7 . .7 F6
Erith DA8 . . . . .8 F6
Clovelly Rd DA7 . . . . .7 E8
Clovelly Way BR6 . . . . . . .37 F3
Clover Bank View ME5 . . .62 B6
Clover Ct 11 ME17 . . . . . .12 D8
Clover St ME4 . . . . .47 F4
Clover Terr 4 ME15 . . . . .107 D8
Clover Way TN12 . . . . . .136 A5
Clover Wlk 13 TN8 . . . . .112 D3
Cloverdale Gdns DA15 . . . .6 F1
Clovers The TN12 . . . . . .136 A5
Club Gardens Rd BR2 . . . .36 A2
Clyde Rd TN10 . . . . .117 C6
Clydesdale Ho DA18 . . . . . .3 E4
Clydon Cl DA8 . . . . .8 E8
Coach & Horses
Pas 15 TN2 . . . . .149 A2
Coach Dr The DA13 . . . . .72 E7
Coach Rd
Egerton ME17,TN27 . . . . .127 E6
Ightham TN15 . . . . .86 B2
Royal Tunbridge Wells TN4 .148 C3
Coal Ct RM17 . . . . .12 A8
Coalhouse Fort* RM18 . . . .14 E6
Coastguard Cotts
Cliffe ME3 . . . . .15 C8
Grain ME3 . . . . .21 B5
Coates Hill Rd BR1 . . . . . .37 A7
Cob Dr DA12 . . . . .31 E3
Cobb Cl ME2 . . . . .46 D8
Cobbets Way TN8 . . . . . .128 C8
Cobbett Cl ME19 . . . . . . .89 F8
Cobbett Rd SE9 . . . . .5 E4
Cobbett's Ride TN2 . . . . .148 F1
Cobblestones ME7 . . . . . .62 F5
Cobbs Cl
Paddock Wood TN12 . . . . .135 F6
Wateringbury ME18 . . . . .104 E7
Cobbs The TN11 . . . . . . .102 E6
Cobden Ct Bromley BR2 . . .36 C5
9 Woolwich SE28 . . . . . . .3 C5
Cobden Rd 4
Gillingham ME4 . . . . .48 B2
Orpington BR6 . . . . .51 D6
Sevenoaks TN13 . . . . .84 C4
Cobdown Cl ME20 . . . . . .75 C2
Cobfield ME17 . . . . .108 A1
Cobham
Cty Prim Sch DA12 . . . . . .45 A5
Cobham Hall Sch DA12 . . .45 C6
Cobham House 4 DA8 . . . . .8 F7
Cobham Pl DA6 . . . . .7 D2
Cobham Rise ME7 . . . . . . .48 F5
Cobham St DA11 . . . . .30 B8
Cobham Terr DA9 . . . . . . .11 B1
Cobhambury Rd DA12 . . . .45 B4
Cobhams TN3 . . . . .148 A8
Cobland Rd SE12 . . . . . . .22 C4
Cobs Cl TN15 . . . . .86 C6
Cobsdene DA12 . . . . .30 D2
Cobtree Cl ME5 . . . . .62 C8
Cobtree Rd ME17 . . . . . .106 C3
Cobtree Wharf ME20 . . . . .76 C2
Cockerhurst Rd TN14 . . . .53 E2
Cockmannings La BR5 . . . .38 E1
Cockmannings Rd BR5 . . . .38 D2
Cockmount La TN5 . . . . .174 F5
Cockpit The TN12 . . . . . .138 C5
Cocksett Ave BR6 . . . . . . .51 E4
Cocksure La DA14 . . . . . . .25 A4
Codington Cres DA12 . . . .30 D3
Codrington Gdns DA12 . . .30 D3
Cogate Rd TN12 . . . . . . .135 E6
Cold Arbor Rd TN13 . . . . .83 D3
Cold Blow Cres DA5 . . . . .25 D7
Cold Harbour La ME9 . . . .65 F6
Coldblow La ME14 . . . . . .79 A2
Coldbridge La TN27 . . . . .127 B5
Coldharbour Crest SE9 . . .23 A5
Coldharbour La
Aylesford ME20 . . . . .76 A1

Coldharbour La continued
Hucking ME14,ME9 . . . . . .79 B1
Rainham RM13 . . . . .4 F6
Tonbridge TN11 . . . . .116 E7
Coldharbour Rd
Benenden TN17 . . . . .180 B4
Northfleet DA11 . . . . .29 F5
Penshurst TN8, TN11 . . . .146 E8
Coldharbour
Sports Ctr SE9 . . . . .23 A6
Coldred Rd ME15 . . . . . .107 F4
Coldrum La ME19 . . . . . . .73 C6
Cole Cl SE28 . . . . .3 B5
Cole Terr ME17 . . . . .111 C4
Colebrook Ind Est TN2 . .133 E1
Colebrook Rd TN4 . . . . . .149 C8
Colebrooke Ct DA14 . . . . .24 B4
Colegate Dr ME14 . . . . . .93 C4
Coleman Rd DA17 . . . . . . .4 A2
Colemans Heath SE9 . . . . .23 B5
Colepits Wood Rd SE9 . . . .6 D2
Coleraine Rd 1 SE3 . . . . . .5 A8
Coleridge Cl 4 ME15 . . . .74 F4
Coleridge Rd Dartford DA1 .10 B3
Tilbury RM18 . . . . .13 C5
Coleridge Way BR6 . . . . . .38 A3
Coles Ct TN2 . . . . .149 C3
Coles La TN16 . . . . .82 C4
Coleshall Cl ME15 . . . . . .107 F6
Colets Orch TN14 . . . . . . .69 B3
Colewood Dr ME2 . . . . . . .46 B8
Colfe's Prep Sch SE12 . . . . .5 B1
Colin Blythe Rd TN10 . . . .117 F5
Colin Chapman Way DA3 . .55 E6
Colin Cl DA2 . . . . .10 B1
Coll of Guidance
Studies BR8 . . . . .25 F1
College Ave Gillingham ME7 .48 B4
Maidstone ME15 . . . . .91 F2
Tonbridge TN9 . . . . .133 A7
College Cotts ME16 . . . . . .91 F3
College Ct 5 ME15 . . . . . .92 A3
College Dr TN2 . . . . .149 D4
College Gn BR1 . . . . .36 A8
College Rd Bromley BR1 . . .22 A1
Chatham ME4 . . . . .48 A7
Hextable BR8 . . . . .25 F1
Maidstone ME15 . . . . .91 F2
New Hythe ME20 . . . . .75 B3
Northfleet DA11 . . . . .12 B2
College View SE9 . . . . . . .22 D7
College Yd ME1 . . . . .47 C6
Coller Cres DA12 . . . . . . .27 E3
Collet Rd TN15 . . . . .69 E2
Collet Wlk ME8 . . . . .63 D4
Collier Cl E6 . . . . .2 B1
Collier Street
CE Prim Sch TN12 . . . . . .121 D1
Colliers Wood BR2 . . . . . .50 D5
Colliers' Green
CE Prim Sch TN17 . . . . . .154 F2
Collindale Ave Erith DA8 . . .8 B8
Sidcup DA15 . . . . .24 A7
Collings Wlk ME8 . . . . . . .63 D4
Collington Cl DA11 . . . . . .29 E8
Collington Ho 3 SE7 . . . . . .5 B8
Collington Terr ME15 . . . .107 F4
Collingwood House DA9 . .11 D2
Collingwood
Ind Ctr ME17 . . . . .108 E2
Collingwood Rd ME20 . . . .76 C7
Collis St ME2 . . . . .47 A8
Collison Pl TN30 . . . . . . .183 D7
Colman House 4 ME14 . . . .92 A4
Colman Rd E16 . . . . .1 C8
Colne Rd TN10 . . . . .117 B5
Colney Rd DA1 . . . . .9 F1
Colonade The 2 TN18 . . .179 A2
Colonel Stephens
Way TN30 . . . . .173 B2
Colonel's Way TN4 . . . . .133 A2
Coltness Cres SE2 . . . . . . .3 B1
Colts Hill Pl TN12 . . . . . .135 B5
Coltsfoot Ct RM17 . . . . . .12 D8
Coltsfoot Dr ME14 . . . . . .92 F4
Coltstead DA3 . . . . .56 E7
Columbia Wharf Rd RM17 .12 A8
Columbine Ave E6 . . . . . . .1 E8
Columbine Cl
East Malling ME19 . . . . . . .74 F1
Rochester ME2 . . . . .46 E7
Columbine Rd
East Malling ME19 . . . . . . .89 F8
Rochester ME2 . . . . .46 E7
Columbus Sq DA8 . . . . . . .8 F8
Colveiw Cl SE9 . . . . .22 D7
Colyer Cl SE9 . . . . .23 B6
Colyer Ho SE2 . . . . .3 D1
Colyer Rd DA11 . . . . .29 D6
Colyers Cl DA8 . . . . .8 D6
Colyers La DA8 . . . . .8 D6
Colyers Prim Sch DA7 . . . . .8 D6
Colyers Wlk DA8 . . . . .8 D6
Colyton Cl DA16 . . . . .7 D6
Combe Bank Cotts TN14 . .82 D5
Combe Bank Dr TN14 . . . .82 E4
Combe Bank Sch TN14 . . .82 E4
Combedale Rd SE10 . . . . . .1 A1
Combeside SE18 . . . . .6 F7
Combwell Cres SE2 . . . . . .3 A3
Comfrey Ct RM17 . . . . . . .12 D8
Command Rd ME14 . . . . . .91 F8
Commerce Way TN8 . . . . .112 C3
Commercial Pl DA12 . . . . .13 C1
Commercial Rd
Paddock Wood TN12 . . . . .135 F6
Rochester ME2 . . . . .47 A7
Royal Tunbridge Wells TN1 .149 B5

Commercial Rd continued
Tonbridge TN9 . . . . .133 C8
Commissioner's Rd ME2 . .47 C8
Commodore Rd ME14 . . . .92 C5
Common La Cliffe ME3 . . . .16 C6
Dartford DA2 . . . . .26 B5
Common Rd Burham ME5 . .61 B1
Cliffe Woods ME3 . . . . . . .33 B5
Hadlow TN11 . . . . .102 E2
Ightham TN15 . . . . .86 B4
Sissinghurst TN17 . . . . . .170 A8
Common The ME1 . . . . . . .47 C6
Common View TN4 . . . . . .148 C6
Common Wall ME3 . . . . . .16 D6
Commonside BR2 . . . . . . .50 C6
Commonwealth
House RM18 . . . . .13 A5
Commonwealth Way SE2 . .3 C1
Commority Rd DA13 . . . . .73 B8
Comp La TN15 . . . . .87 E6
Compass Cl ME1 . . . . .47 C1
Compass Ctr ME4 . . . . . . .48 B8
Compasses Rd TN12 . . . . .115 B2
Compasses The TN11 . . . .115 B2
Compton Cl ME5 . . . . .62 D2
Compton Pl DA8 . . . . .8 F8
Concord Ave ME5 . . . . . . .61 C5
Concord Cl
Paddock Wood TN12 . . . . .135 E7
Royal Tunbridge Wells TN2 .149 C4
Concorde Dr E6 . . . . .1 F8
Concrete Cotts ME3 . . . . .15 E4
Condover Cres SE18 . . . . . .6 B7
Condovers Cotts RM18 . . .13 F8
Conduit Rd SE18 . . . . .2 B1
Coney Mews ME4 . . . . . . .48 A1
Coneyburrow Rd TN2 . . . .149 E5
Conference Rd SE2 . . . . . . .3 C2
Conghurst La TN18 . . . . .185 B6
Congleton Gr SE18 . . . . . . .2 C1
Congo Rd SE18 . . . . .2 D1
Congress Rd SE2 . . . . .3 C2
Congreve Rd SE9 . . . . .5 F4
Congreve Wlk 6 E16 . . . . .1 D8
Conifer Ave DA3 . . . . .42 E3
Conifer Cl BR6 . . . . .51 D6
Conifer Dr Chatham ME5 . .62 D1
Culverstone Green DA13 . . .57 F2
Conifer Way BR8 . . . . . . .39 C8
Conisborough Ct 15 DA2 . .10 B1
Coniscliffe Cl BR7 . . . . . . .37 A8
Coniston Ave Bexley DA16 . .6 E4
Royal Tunbridge Wells TN4 .148 E5
Coniston Cl Bexley DA7 . . . .8 C6
Dartford DA1 . . . . .26 B7
Erith DA8 . . . . .8 E7
Gillingham ME7 . . . . .49 A6
Coniston Rd DA7 . . . . .8 C6
Connaught Br E16 . . . . . . .1 D6
Connaught Ct ME15 . . . . .107 F4
Connaught Mews
2 Chatham ME4 . . . . .48 C2
Woolwich SE18 . . . . .2 A1
Connaught Rd
Chatham ME4 . . . . .48 C2
Gillingham ME7 . . . . .48 D5
Newham,Silvertown E16 . . . .1 D5
Woolwich SE18 . . . . .2 B1
Connaught Way TN4 . . . . .148 E5
Conquest Ind Est ME2 . . . .47 A6
Conrad Cl ME8 . . . . .63 D4
Consort Cl ME14 . . . . . . .92 D5
Constable Ave E16 . . . . . . .1 B5
Constable Rd
Northfleet DA11 . . . . .29 E5
Tonbridge TN9 . . . . .117 C5
Constance St E16 . . . . .1 E5
Constitution Hill
8 Chatham ME5 . . . . .48 B3
Gravesend DA12 . . . . .30 C7
Snodland ME6 . . . . .75 A8
Constitution Rd ME5 . . . . .48 B2
Constitution Rise SE18 . . . .6 A6
Constitutional Hill
Rd TN4 . . . . .132 F1
Consul Gdns BR8 . . . . . . .26 A1
Contessa Cl BR6 . . . . .51 E5
Convalescent La TN17 . . .155 F2
Conway Cl ME14 . . . . .32 E1
Conway Ct BR5 . . . . .38 C5
Conway Gdns RM17 . . . . .12 B7
Conway Inf & Jun Sch SE18 2 E2
Conway Mews ME7 . . . . . .48 A6
Conway Rd Maidstone ME16 91 C6
Woolwich SE18 . . . . .2 E2
Conyerd Rd TN15 . . . . . . .86 F6
Conyers Wlk ME8 . . . . . . .63 D4
Cooden Cl BR1 . . . . .22 B1
Cook Cl ME5 . . . . .62 C6
Cook Sq DA8 . . . . .8 F7
Cookham Dene Cl BR7 . . . .37 D8
Cookham Hill ME1 . . . . . . .47 A2
Cookham Rd DA14,BR8 . . .39 A8
Cookham Wood Rd ME1 . . .61 B8
Cookhill Rd SE2 . . . . .3 B3
Cooks Wharf ME1 . . . . . . .47 E4
Cookson Gr DA8 . . . . .8 B7
Coolfin Rd E16 . . . . .1 B7
Cooling Castle* ME3 . . . . .16 E4
Cooling Cl ME14 . . . . .92 C6
Cooling Comm ME3 . . . . . .33 D8
Cooling Rd Cliffe ME3 . . . .16 C4
High Halstow ME23 . . . . . .17 C4
Rochester ME2 . . . . .33 B2
Cooling St ME3 . . . . .16 D1
Coomb Field TN8 . . . . . . .128 C8
Coombe Ave TN14 . . . . . . .84 B7
Coombe Cl Chatham ME5 . .62 B3

Coombe Cl continued
Snodland ME6 ....75 A7
Coombe Farm La ME3 ....18 E6
Coombe La TN30 ....183 A7
Coombe Lands TN30 ...189 D4
Coombe Lea BR1 ....36 E6
Coombe Lodge SE7 .....5 C8
Coombe Rd
Gravesend DA12 ......30 C6
Hoo St Werburgh ME3 ...34 E5
Maidstone ME15 ......91 F2
Otford TN14 ....69 C4
Coombfield Dr DA2 .....27 D4
Cooper Cl DA9 ....10 F2
Cooper Ct SE18 ....6 B8
Cooper Rd Chatham ME5 ...62 B3
Snodland ME6 ....74 F6
Cooper Shaw Rd RM18 ...13 E7
Coopers Cl DA4 ....41 D8
Cooper's Rd DA11 .....29 F7
Coopers Cotts DA2 ....27 A4
Coopers La Lewisham SE12 ..22 B6
Poundsbridge TN11, TN3 ..147 C7
Coopers Sch BR7 ....37 C8
Coopers' Lane
Prim Sch SE12 ....22 B6
Coote Rd DA7 ....7 F6
Copenhagen Rd ME7 ...48 C4
Copley Dene BR1 ......36 D8
Copper Beech Cl
Gravesend DA12 ......30 D8
7 Orpington BR5 ......38 C4
Copper Beech View TN9 .133 A8
Copper La TN15 ....138 E5
Copper Tree Ct ME15 ..107 A5
Copper Tree Wlk ME5 ...62 C1
Copperfield Cl DA12 ...31 A7
Copperfield Cres ME3 ..32 C2
Copperfield Ct DA1 ....8 E2
Copperfield Dr ME17 ..108 E4
Copperfield Ho 6 ME4 ..47 F4
Copperfield Rd Erith SE28 ..3 C7
Rochester ME1 ....47 C2
Copperfield Way BR7 ...23 C2
Copperfields
2 Dartford DA1 ......9 E1
Kemsing TN15 ....69 F2
Copperfields Cl TN15 ..69 F2
Copperfields Orch TN15 .69 F2
Copperfields The ME1 ..47 B8
Copperfields Wlk TN15 .69 F2
Coppergate ME7 ....62 F5
Coppergate Cl BR1 ....36 B8
Copperhouse La ME7 ...49 B6
Copperhouse Rd ME2 ..46 C2
Copperpenny Dr ME7 ...63 B3
Coppers La TN12 .....135 E1
Coppice Ct ME7 ....63 B4
Coppice Rd ME5 ......62 C2
Coppice The
Aylesford ME20 ......75 C8
Bitchet Green TN15 ...85 D1
Dartford DA5 ....25 D5
Pembury TN2 ....150 D7
Vigo Village DA13 ....73 B8
Coppice View ME14 ...92 E6
Copping's Rd TN11 ...115 C4
Copse Bank TN15 .....84 F7
Copse Cl Greenwich SE7 ..5 B8
Rochester ME1 ....47 E1
Copse Rd TN11 ....116 E4
Copse Side DA3 ......42 E6
Copse The ME3 ....34 E3
Copsehill ME19 ......74 E2
Copsewood Cl DA15 ...6 E1
Copsewood Way ME15 ..93 A3
Copt Hall TN18 ....187 D3
Copt Hall Ightham TN15 ..86 A4
Sole Street DA13 .....44 B5
Coptefield Dr DA17 ...3 E3
Copthall Ave TN18 ...179 A1
Copthorne Ave BR2 ...50 F8
Coralline Wlk 4 SE2 ..3 C4
Corbyland Rd DA15 ...23 E7
Corbylands Rd DA15 ..23 E8
Cordelia Cres ME1 ...46 F2
Corelli Rd SE18,SE3 ...5 E6
Corhaven House 3 DA8 ..8 E7
Corinthian Ct ME3 ....21 B5
Corinthian Manorway DA8 .4 D2
Corinthian Rd DA8 ....4 D2
Cork House BR5 ......38 B6
Cork La TN12 ....155 D8
Cork St ME20 ....75 F6
Corkwell St ME4 .....47 E3
Cormorant Cl ME2 ....46 C7
Cornel House 4 DA15 ..24 A5
Cornelia Pl DA8 ......8 E8
Cornell Cl DA14 ......24 E2
Corner Farm Rd TN12 .139 E4
Corner Gn SE3 ....5 A5
Cornfield Way TN12 ..117 D6
Cornflower Cl ME14 ...92 E4
Cornford Cl Hayes BR2 ..36 A4
Pembury TN2 ....150 B6
Cornford La TN2 .....150 B5
Cornford Pk TN2 .....150 C5
Cornforth Cl TN12 ...139 F4
Cornwall Ave DA16 ...6 F4
Cornwall Cl ME15 ....107 E2
Cornwall Cres ME1 ...60 D4
Cornwall Dr BR5 .....24 C1
Cornwall Rd Dartford DA1 ..9 B7
Gillingham ME7 ......48 D6
Rochester ME1 ......47 C3
Cornwallis Ave
Chatham ME4 ....47 E1

Cornwallis Ave continued
Gillingham ME8 ....49 A4
Linton ME17 ....122 E8
Sidcup DA14 ....23 D6
Tonbridge TN10 ......117 F4
Cornwallis Cl DA8 ....8 F1
Cornwallis Cotts ME17 .106 E2
Cornwallis Rd
Maidstone ME16 .....91 D4
Woolwich SE18 ......2 B3
Cornwallis Rdbt ME8 ..49 A4
Cornwallis Sch
The ME15 ....106 F2
Cornwallis Wlk SE9 ...5 F4
Cornwell Ave DA12 ...30 C5
Corona Rd SE12 .....22 A8
Corona Terr ME6 .....74 F6
Coronation Cl DA5 ...7 E1
Coronation Cotts
Lower Stoke ME3 .....19 A3
Ticehurst TN5 ....176 F2
Coronation Ct DA8 ...8 D7
Coronation Flats 5 ME4 .47 F3
Coronation Rd
Chatham ME5 ....48 C2
Grain ME3 ....21 B5
Corporation Rd ME7 ..48 D7
Corporation St ME1 ..47 C6
Corral Cl ME5 ....48 D2
Corrall
Almshouses 4 ME15 ..92 A3
Corrance Gn ME15 ...107 A8
Correnden Rd TN10 ..117 A3
Corseley Rd TN3 .....161 B5
Cory's Rd ME1 ....47 D6
Cossack St ME1 .....47 D3
Cossington Rd ME5 ..62 B1
Costells Mdw TN16 ..81 D1
Cot La TN12 ....158 B3
Cotleigh Ave DA5 ...24 D6
Cotman Way TN12 ...119 E6
Cotman's Ash La TN15 .70 D4
Cotmandene Cres BR5 .38 A7
Coton Rd DA16 ......7 A4
Cotswold Cl DA7 ....8 E5
Cotswold Gdns ME15 .93 A2
Cotswold Rd ME15 ...29 E5
Cotswold Rise BR6 ...37 F3
Cottage Ave BR2 ....36 E1
Cottage Field Cl DA14 .24 C7
Cottage Rd ME4 .....47 F6
Cottall Ave ME4 .....47 F2
Cottenham Cl ME19 ..89 F7
Cotton La DA9 ....10 D3
Couchman Green
La TN12 ....139 F7
Coulman St ME7 .....48 D5
Coulter House DA9 ...11 C2
Coulters Cl ME14 ....92 D5
Coulton Ave DA11 ...29 E7
Council Ave DA11 ...12 C1
Council Cotts
Chiddingstone
Causeway TN11 ......131 A8
Coxheath ME15 ......106 A4
Key's Green TN12 ...151 C4
Council Hos TN15 ...102 A8
Countess of Thanet's
Almshouses TN30 ...144 F3
County Gate SE9 ....23 C5
County Gr ME19 .....89 B8
County Ho SE18 .....6 A8
County Rd Maidstone ME14 .92 A5
Newham E6 ....2 B8
Coupland Pl SE18 ...2 C1
Course The SE9 .....23 A5
Court Ave DA17 .....3 F1
Court Broomes ME17 .125 C8
Court Cres BR8 .....39 E5
Court Dr ME16 ......91 D4
Court Farm Rd SE9 ..22 E5
Court La Detling ME14 .78 C5
Hadlow TN11 ....119 B7
Court Lane Pl TN11 ..118 F8
Court Lodge Shorne DA12 .31 E2
DA17 ....4 A1
Court Lodge Cotts
East Farleigh ME15 ..106 A7
Horton Kirby DA4 ...41 C6
Court Lodge Rd ME7 .48 F6
Court Mdw Gillingham ME8 .49 B2
Wrotham TN15 ......71 F3
Court Mews DA11 ...12 B1
Court Rd Burham ME1 ..75 F8
Dartford DA2 ....27 E3
Eltham SE9 ....22 F7
Royal Tunbridge Wells TN4 .148 A4
Court Road (Orpington
By-Pass)
Chelsfield BR6,TN14 ..52 D5
Orpington BR6 ......38 B2
Court St BR1 ....36 A7
Court Yd SE9 ....5 F1
Courtaulds Cl SE28 ..3 A5
Courtenay Rd ME15 ..91 F2
Courteney Rd ME8 ...63 B8
Courtenwell TN3 ....147 E4
Courtfield Ave ME5 ..62 B3
Courthope TN12 .....136 A6
Courthope Ave TN5 ..174 F4
Courtland Gr SE28 ...3 D6
Courtlands Chislehurst BR7 .23 B2
Teston ME18 ....105 A8
Tonbridge TN10 ....117 A3
Courtlands Ave SE12 .5 B2
Courtlands Cl ME15 ..107 A8
Courtlands Farm TN17 .169 A3
Courtleet Dr DA8 ....8 B6

Courtwood Dr TN13 ...84 A3
Courtyard Gdns TN15 .71 F3
Courtyard The ME8 ...63 B4
Cousley Wood Rd TN5 .175 C7
Couthurst Rd SE3 ....5 B7
Coutts Ave DA12 .....31 E4
Coutts Ho SE7 ......5 C8
Covelees Wall E6 ....2 A7
Coventry Cl 9 Newham E6 .1 F7
Rochester ME2 ......46 B6
Coventry Rd ME10 ...117 D5
Coverdale Ave ME15 .107 D6
Coverdale Cl ME5 ...62 B7
Covert The Chatham ME5 .62 B1
Orpington BR6 ......37 E3
Vigo Village DA13 ...72 E7
Covet Wood Cl BR5 ..37 F3
Covey Hall Rd ME6 ...60 A1
Cow La TN8 ....129 D1
Cow Leaze ME15 ....2 A7
Cowan Cl E6 ....1 E8
Cowbeck Cl ME8 ....63 D6
Cowden Cl TN18 ....184 E8
Cowden Cross TN8 ..145 C7
Cowden La TN18 ....184 E7
Cowden Mews TN8 ..145 A5
Cowden Rd
Maidstone ME14 ....92 C5
Orpington BR6 ......37 F2
Cowden Sta TN8 ....145 D8
Cowdrey Cl
Maidstone ME16 ....91 B2
Rochester ME1 ......47 B2
Cowdrey Ct DA1 ....26 B8
Cowen House 4 SE18 .6 B8
Cowley Ave DA9 ....11 A2
Cowley Cl Bexley DA16 .7 A2
Bromley BR2 ....36 D5
Cowper Ave RM18 ...13 B6
Cowper Cl Bexley DA16 .7 A2
Bromley BR2 ....36 D5
Cowper Rd Bromley BR2 .36 D5
Erith DA17 ....4 A2
Gillingham ME7 .....48 D3
Cowstead Rd ME9 ...64 C2
Cox St ME14 ....78 E6
Cox's Cl ME9 ....74 F8
Coxheath
Prim Sch ME17 .....106 C3
Coxmount Rd SE7 ...1 D1
Coxwell Rd SE18 ....2 D1
Cozenton Cl ME8 ...49 E1
Crabbs Croft Cl 7 BR6 .51 C5
Crabtree Cl ME19 ...89 A2
Crabtree Manorway N
DA17 ....4 C5
Crabtree Manorway S DA17 .4 C3
Crabtree Rd ME8 ....63 D8
Crabtree Rndbt ME14 .76 E2
Craddock Way ME8 ...63 D5
Cradducks La TN12 ..140 B4
Cradles Rd ME9 ....64 C2
Cradley Rd SE9 .....23 D7
Cragie Wlk ME8 ....63 E4
Craig Ho Greenwich SE3 .5 B7
Rochester ME1 .....47 E1
Craigerne Rd SE3 ...5 B7
Craigholm SE18 ....6 A6
Craigton Rd SE9 ....5 F3
Crales Ho SE18 ....1 E3
Crampton's Rd TN14 .84 B7
Cramptons TN17 ....169 F8
Cranborne Ave ME15 .92 C1
Cranbourne Ave ME15 .107 B8
Cranbrook
CE Prim Sch TN17 ..169 D5
Cranbrook Cl
Gillingham ME8 .....49 C3
Hayes BR2 ....36 A3
Maidstone ME15 ...107 F7
Cranbrook House 1 DA8 .8 F7
Cranbrook Mus* TN17 .169 D5
Cranbrook Rd
Benenden TN17 .....179 F8
Erith DA7 ....7 F6
Fosten Green TN27 ..171 C6
Gill's Green TN18 ...178 F4
Goudhurst TN17 ....168 A8
Knox Bridge TN12,TN17 .155 F7
Parkgate TN30 .....172 C1
Tenterden TN30 ....182 E7
Cranbrook Sch TN17 .169 D5
Cranbrook Union
Mill* TN17 ....169 D4
Crandalls TN11 .....115 F1
Crane House 11 TN18 .178 F2
Crane House
Gdns 10 TN18 ......178 F2
Crane La TN17 .....169 D5
Cranford Cl ME8 ....49 D1
Cranford Ho DA1 ...9 A2
Cranford Rd Dartford DA1 .8 E7
Tonbridge TN10 ....118 A3
Cranham Sq TN12 ..138 C5
Cranleigh Cl Bexley DA5 .8 B1
Orpington BR6 .....52 A7
Cranleigh Dr BR8 ...39 E5
Cranleigh Gdns
Chatham ME4 ......47 D3
Maidstone ME16 ...91 C7
Cranley Par SE9 ....22 E4
Cranley Rd E13 .....1 B8
Cranmer Ct ME15 ...107 B8
Cranmer Rd TN13 ..83 E4
Cranmere Ct ME2 ...47 C8
Cranmore Rd BR7 ...22 F3
Cranstone Ct 12 DA14 .24 B4
Cranwell Rd TN4 ...148 C4
Crathie Rd SE12 ....5 B1
Craven Rd BR6 .....52 D7

Crawfords BR8 ......25 E1
Crawley Ct 1 DA11 ..13 B1
Crawshay Rd TN13 ..84 A4
Cray Ave BR5 ....38 B4
Cray Bldgs DA14 ....24 C2
Cray Cl DA1 ....9 A3
Cray Rd Crockenhill BR8 .39 C3
Erith DA17 ....8 A8
Sidcup DA14 ....24 C2
Cray Valley Rd BR5 ..38 B4
Craybrooke Rd DA14 ..24 B4
Crayburne DA13 ....28 F4
Craybury End SE9 ...23 C6
Crayford Ave DA12 ..30 C5
Crayford Rd DA1 ....8 E1
Crayfields Bsns Pk BR5 .38 C8
Crayfields Ind Pk BR5 .38 C7
Crayford
Commercial Ctr DA1 .8 E1
Crayford High St DA1 .8 E2
Crayford Ind Est DA1 .8 F2
Crayford L Ctr DA1 ..8 E1
Crayford Rd DA1 ....8 E1
Crayford Sta DA1 ...8 E1
Crayford Way DA1 ..9 A3
Craylands BR5 ......38 C6
Craylands La DA10 ..11 D2
Craylands Sq DA10 ..11 D2
Crayleigh Terr DA14 ..24 C2
Craymill Sq DA1 ....8 F5
Crays Par BR5 .....38 C7
Crayside Ind Est DA1 .9 B3
Craythorne TN30 ...183 B8
Craythorne Ho TN30 .183 B8
Creasey's Row TN14 .97 E5
Credenhall Dr BR2 ..36 F1
Crediton Rd E16 ....1 A7
Credo Way RM20 ...11 B8
Creek The DA11 ....12 B2
Creek Way RM13 ...4 E8
Cremorne Rd DA11 ..29 F7
Crescent Ave ME7 ..12 D8
Crescent Cotts TN13 .83 E7
Crescent Ct 1 Grays RM17 .12 D8
Sidcup DA15 ....24 A5
Crescent Dr BR5 ...37 C3
Crescent Gdns BR8 .39 C7
Crescent Ho ME2 ..47 C7
Crescent Rd Bromley BR1 .22 A1
Erith DA8 ....8 F8
Royal Tunbridge Wells TN1 .149 B3
Sidcup DA15 ......23 F5
Woolwich SE18 ....2 B2
Crescent The
Bidborough TN4 ...132 E4
Borough Green TN15 .87 A8
Groombridge TN3 ..161 C7
Longfield DA3 .....42 E6
Maidstone ME14 ...91 F8
Northfleet DA11 ...29 F6
Sevenoaks TN13 ...84 D6
Sidcup DA14 ......23 F4
Sidcup DA5 ....24 C8
St Mary's Island ME4 .34 B1
Swanscombe DA9 ..11 C2
Tonbridge TN9 ....117 B2
Crescent Way
Chatham ME5 .....61 D5
Orpington BR6 ....51 E5
Cressey Ct 4 ME4 ..47 E4
Cressingham Ct 1 DA17 .4 A3
Crest Ave RM17 ...12 B7
Crest Cl TN14 .....68 B8
Crest Ind Est TN12 .138 C6
Crest Rd ME1 .....47 C1
Crest View DA9 ...11 A3
Crest View Dr BR5 .37 C4
Crestway ME5 .....62 B8
Crete Hall Rd DA11 .12 E1
Creton St SE18 ....2 A3
Creve Coeur Cl ME14 .93 A5
Crevequer
Chambers 1 ME8 ..49 F1
Cricket Ground Rd BR7 .37 B8
Cricketers Cl
Bells Yew Green TN3 .164 A5
Erith DA8 ....4 E1
Harrietsham ME17 ..110 D6
Cricketers Dr DA13 ..58 A7
Cripple Hill TN26 ...159 D1
Cripple St ME15 ....107 A7
Crisfield Ct TN30 ...173 B2
Crismill La ME14,ME17 .93 F3
Crispe Ct ME8 .....63 D4
Crispin Ct ME17 ...106 C3
Crispin Rd ME2 ....46 B8
Crispin Way ME19 ..89 A3
Crittall's Cnr DA14 ..24 C1
Crittenden Bglws ME15 .106 A4
Crittenden Cotts ME15 .106 A4
Crittenden Rd TN12 .135 D3
Crocken Hill Rd TN27 .127 C2
Crockenhall Way DA13 .29 E1
Crockenhill Hill BR5 ...38 F3
Crockenhill La BR8,DA4 .40 C2
Crockenhill Prim Sch BR8 .39 C3
Crockenhill Rd BR5,BR8 .38 C4
Crockers Hatch Cnr TN3 .147 D2
Crockham Hill
CE Prim Sch TN8 ...96 C2
Crockham Way SE9 ..23 A4

Croft La TN8 ....112 C1
Croft Rd Bromley BR1 .22 A2
Westerham TN16 ...81 C1
Croft The Leybourne ME19 .74 E2
Swanley BR8 ......39 C6
Croft Way Sevenoaks TN13 .83 F7
Sidcup DA15 ......23 E5
Crofters The ME8 ..63 F7
Crofton Ave
Orpington BR5,BR6 .51 C8
Sidcup DA5 ....24 D8
Crofton Inf Sch BR5 .37 D2
Crofton Jun Sch BR5 .37 D2
Crofton La BR5,BR6 .37 D2
Crofton Rd BR6 ...51 B8
Croftside DA13 ....73 A8
Cromarty Ct 7 BR1 .36 C7
Crombie Rd DA15 ..23 D7
Cromer Pl 5 BR6 ..37 D1
Cromer Rd ME2 ...47 B8
Cromer St TN9 ....117 A1
Cromford Cl BR6 ..51 E7
Cromlix Cl BR7 ...37 B7
Crompton Gdns ME15 .92 B5
Cromwell Ave BR2 .36 B5
Cromwell Cl BR2 ..36 B5
Cromwell Mews BR7 .37 A8
Cromwell Rd
Maidstone ME14 ..92 B5
Royal Tunbridge Wells TN2 .149 C3
Cromwell Terr ME4 .48 A3
Cronin Cl 2 ME20 ..74 F4
Crook Log DA6 ....7 D3
Crook Log Prim Sch DA6 .7 D3
Crook Log Sports Ctr DA7 .7 D4
Crook Rd TN12 ...136 D1
Crooked La DA11,DA12 .13 B1
Crookston Rd SE9 ..6 A4
Croombs Rd E16 ..1 C8
Crosby House DA1 .9 A1
Crosier Cl SE3 ....5 E6
Crosley Rd ME7 ...48 D3
Cross Ct 11 SE28 ..3 B6
Cross Dr ME7 .....109 E1
Cross Keys Maidstone ME14 .93 C4
Sevenoaks TN13 ...99 A8
Cross Keys Cl TN13 .99 A8
Cross La Sidcup DA5 .24 F8
Ticehurst TN5 .....176 D2
Cross La E DA12 ...30 B6
Cross La W DA11 ...30 B6
Cross Lane Gdns TN5 .176 D1
Cross Rd Dartford DA1 .9 C1
Hawley DA2 ....26 F4
Northfleet DA11 ...12 D1
Orpington, Keston Mark BR2 .50 E8
Orpington, St Mary Cray BR5 .38 B4
Sidcup DA14 ......24 B4
Cross St Chatham ME4 .48 A4
Erith DA8 ....8 E8
Gillingham ME7 ...48 C6
25 Gravesend DA12 .13 B1
Maidstone ME14 ..92 A6
Rochester ME1 ...47 B8
Cross Way ME1 ...47 C3
Cross-at-Hand
Cotts TN12 ....123 E2
Crossbrook Rd SE3 .5 E4
Crossmead SE9 ...22 F7
Crossway Chatham ME5 .61 E6
Erith SE28 ....3 D7
Orpington BR5 ....37 D4
Crossway The
Chislehurst SE9 ...22 D6
Royal Tunbridge Wells TN4 .148 D2
Crossways
Chart Sutton ME17 .108 B1
Dartford DA2 .....10 D3
Hextable DA8 .....25 F1
Crossways Bvd DA9 .10 E3
Crouch Croft SE9 ..23 A5
Crouch House Cotts TN8 .112 B2
Crouch House Rd TN8 .112 B2
Crouch La Crouch TN15 .87 B6
Linkhill TN18 ......186 D6
Crow Cnr ME1 ....47 C5
Crow Dr TN14 ....68 C4
Crow Hill TN14 ...87 A7
Crow Hill Rd TN15 .87 A7
Crow La ME1 .....47 C5
Crowden Way SE28 .3 C6
Crowhurst La Basted TN15 .86 E4
West Kingsdown TN15 .56 B4
Crowhurst Oast TN12 .103 D1
Crowhurst Rd TN15 .86 F6
Crowhurst Way BR5 .38 C4
Crown Acres TN12 ..120 A6
Crown Cl BR6 ......52 A6
Crown Ct Bromley BR2 .36 E4
Cranbrook TN17 ...169 C5
Eltham SE12 ......5 B1
Tilbury RM18 ......13 A5
Crown Gn DA12 ...31 E3
Crown Ho ME1 ....47 B4
Crown La Bromley BR2 .36 D4
Chislehurst BR7 ...37 C8
Shorne DA12 .....31 E4
Crown Lane Spur BR2 .36 D3
Crown Rd Grays RM17 .12 A8
Marlpit Hill TN8 ...112 D4
Orpington BR6 ....52 A5
Shoreham TN14 ...53 F1
Crown St ME7 .....48 D6
Crown Woods Sch SE9 .6 C2
Crown Woods Way SE9 .6 D2

Crownfields
Maidstone ME14 . . . . **92** F4
Sevenoaks TN13 . . . .**84** B2
Crowther CI TN12 . . . .**139** E4
Croxley CI BR5 . . . .**38** B7
Croxley Gn BR5 . . . .**38** B8
Croyde CI DA15 . . . .**23** D8
Croydon CI ME5 . . . .**62** C4
Croydon Rd
Orpington BR2,BR4,BR6 . . . .**50** C7
Westerham TN16 . . . .**81** B2
Crozier House SE3 . . . .**5** B4
Cruden Rd DA12 . . . .**30** F6
Crump's La ME17 . . . .**126** B4
Crumpsall St SE2 . . . .**3** C2
Crundale **2** ME14 . . . .**92** A5
Crundale Rd ME8 . . . .**49** C3
Crundale Tower BR5 . . . . . .**38** C1
Crundwell Rd TN4 . . . .**132** F1
Crusader CI ME8 . . . .**63** B8
Crusader Ct DA1 . . . .**9** F3
Crusoe Rd SE5 . . . .**4** D1
Crutches La ME3 . . . .**32** B1
Cryals Ct TN12 . . . .**151** E5
Cryals Rd TN12 . . . .**151** D5
Crystal Ho **2** SE18 . . . .**2** F1
Cuckmere Ct **13** BR5 . . . . . .**38** D1
Cuckold's Cnr ME3 . . . .**32** C6
Cuckold's Cnr TN12 . . . . . .**139** F4
Cuckolds Cnr DA3 . . . .**57** B7
Cuckolds Green Rd ME3 . .**19** B5
Cuckoo La
Lamberhurst TN12 . . . .**152** A2
Tonbridge TN11 . . . .**118** A7
Cuckoowood Ave ME14 . . . .**76** F1
Cudham
CE Prim Sch TN16 . . . .**66** A3
Cudham CI ME14 . . . .**92** C6
Cudham La N TN14 . . . .**66** D7
Cudham La S TN14 . . . .**66** D2
Cudham Park Rd TN14 . . . .**51** E1
Cudham Rd BR6 . . . .**66** B7
Cuff Cres SE9 . . . .**5** D1
Cugley Rd DA2 . . . .**27** C8
Culcroft DA3 . . . .**42** F6
Culpeper CI
Hollingbourne ME17 . . . .**94** E2
Rochester ME2 . . . .**47** E6
Culpepers TN17 . . . .**167** E7
Culpepper Rd
Coxheath ME17 . . . .**106** B3
Gillingham ME8 . . . .**63** D4
Culverden Ave TN4 . . . . . .**149** A6
Culverden Down TN4 . . . . .**148** F5
Culverden Park Rd TN4 . . .**148** F5
Culverden Pk TN4 . . . .**148** F5
Culverden Sq TN4 . . . .**149** A5
Culverden St TN1 . . . .**149** A4
Culverstone Green
Prim Sch DA13 . . . .**57** F3
Culverstone House BR5 . . .**38** B6
Culverton Ct **19** DA14 . . . . .**24** A4
Culvey CI DA3 . . . .**42** E4
Cumberland Ave
Bexley DA16 . . . .**6** F3
Gravesend DA12 . . . .**30** C8
Maidstone ME15 . . . .**107** D8
Cumberland Comp Sch E16 **1** A8
Cumberland Dr
Dartford DA1 . . . .**26** F8
Erith DA7 . . . .**7** E7
Cumberland
Gdns **10** TN1 . . . .**149** A2
Cumberland
Mews **12** TN1 . . . .**149** A2
Cumberland Rd
Gillingham ME4,ME7 . . . . . .**48** B7
Gillingham ME7 . . . .**48** C7
Newham E13 . . . .**1** B8
Cumberland Wlk TN1 . . . .**149** A2
Cumberland Yd **11** TN1 . . .**149** A2
Cumbrian Ave DA7 . . . .**8** E5
Cundy Rd E16 . . . .**1** C7
Cunningham CI TN4 . . . . . .**149** B7
Cunningham Cres ME5 . . . .**62** A8
Cunningham Ho ME1 . . . . . .**47** B4
Cunningham Rd TN4 . . . . .**149** B7
Cupola Ct BR1 . . . .**22** B3
Curlew CI SE28 . . . .**3** D6
Curlew Cres ME4 . . . .**46** C6
Curlews The DA12 . . . .**30** C6
Curran Ave DA15 . . . .**6** F2
Currie Rd TN4 . . . .**149** A5
Curteis Rd TN30 . . . .**173** B1
Curtis Way Chatham ME1 . .**61** D7
7 Woolwich SE28 . . . .**3** B6
Curtismill CI BR5 . . . .**38** B6
Curtismill Way BR5 . . . .**38** B6
Curzon CI BR6 . . . .**51** D6
Curzon Ct SE9 . . . .**23** C5
Curzon Dr RM17 . . . .**12** C7
Curzon Rd Chatham ME4 . .**47** F3
Maidstone ME14 . . . .**92** A6
Custom House for Excel
Sta E16 . . . .**1** B6
Cut The TN27 . . . .**158** E8
Cutbush & Corrall Ct
1 ME14 . . . .**92** B4
Cutbush Almshouses
3 Maidstone ME14 . . . .**92** A4
2 Maidstone ME15 . . . .**92** A3
Cutbush Rd ME17 . . . .**110** D6

Cutmore St DA11 . . . .**30** B8
Cutter Ridge Rd DA13 . . . . .**45** A1
Cutty Sark CI DA9 . . . .**11** A2
Cuxton BR5 . . . .**37** C4
Cuxton CI DA1 . . . .**7** E2
Cuxton Com Inf Sch ME2 .**46** B2
Cuxton Com Jun Sch ME2 .**46** B2
Cuxton Ind Est ME2 . . . . . .**46** C2
Cuxton Rd
Maidstone ME15 . . . .**107** F5
Rochester ME2 . . . .**46** F5
Cuxton Sta ME2 . . . .**46** C2
Cyclamen Rd BR8 . . . .**39** D5
Cygnet CI ME20 . . . .**75** A2
Cygnet Gdns DA11 . . . .**29** F6
Cygnet L Ctr DA11 . . . .**29** E6
Cygnet Rd ME5 . . . .**62** C2
Cypress Ave ME3 . . . .**34** E3
Cypress Ct ME7 . . . .**48** F6
Cypress Gr TN2 . . . .**163** C8
Cypress Rd ME3 . . . .**33** C1
Cypress Tree CI DA15 . . . . .**23** F7
Cyprus PI E6 . . . .**2** A6
Cyprus Sta E6 . . . .**2** A6
Cyril Lodge **6** DA14 . . . . . .**24** A4
Cyril Rd Bexley DA7 . . . .**7** E5
Orpington BR6 . . . .**38** A2

D

D'arcy PI BR2 . . . .**36** A5
Dabbling CI DA8 . . . .**9** B7
Dabells TN17 . . . .**169** D4
Daerwood CI BR2 . . . .**36** F1
Daffodil Rd ME2 . . . .**46** E7
Dagmar Rd ME4 . . . .**48** B2
Dagonet Gdns BR1 . . . .**22** A5
Dagonet Rd BR1 . . . .**22** A5
Dahlia Dr BR8 . . . .**39** F7
Dahlia Rd SE2 . . . .**3** B1
Dainton CI **2** BR1 . . . .**36** B8
Daintons Cotts **2** TN18 . . .**178** F2
Dairsie Ct **4** BR1 . . . .**36** C7
Dairsie Rd SE9 . . . .**6** A4
Dairy Ct **3** Lewisham BR1 . .**22** B1
Sutton at Hone DA4 . . . .**27** B1
Dairy La Chainhurst TN12 . .**121** F4
Crockham Hill TN8 . . . .**96** B1
Woolwich SE18 . . . .**1** F2
Dairy PI TN12 . . . .**121** F4
Daisy Munns Ho SE9 . . . . . .**23** C7
Dakota Gdns E6 . . . .**1** E8
Dalberg Way SE2 . . . .**3** D3
Dale CI Crayford DA1 . . . .**8** F1
Greenwich SE3 . . . .**5** A4
Dale Ct BR1 . . . .**36** D6
Dale End DA1 . . . .**8** F1
Dale Rd Crayford DA1 . . . . . .**8** F1
Northfleet DA13 . . . .**29** A4
Rochester ME1 . . . .**47** C3
Swanley BR8 . . . .**39** C6
Dale St Chatham ME4 . . . . . .**47** E2
Royal Tunbridge Wells TN1 . .**149** B4
Dale The BR2 . . . .**50** D6
Dale View DA8 . . . .**8** F5
Dale Wlk DA2 . . . .**27** C7
Dale Wood Rd BR6 . . . .**37** E1
Dalemain Mews E16 . . . .**1** A5
Daleside BR6 . . . .**52** A5
Daleside CI BR6 . . . .**52** A4
Dalison Ct ME2 . . . .**60** A4
Dallin Rd Bexley DA6 . . . .**7** D3
Woolwich SE18 . . . .**6** B7
Dalmeny Rd DA8 . . . .**8** B6
Dalton CI BR6 . . . .**51** E7
Dalton St ME7 . . . .**48** C6
Daltons Rd BR6,BR8 . . . . . .**53** C7
Damiem CI ME4 . . . .**48** A2
Damigos Rd DA12 . . . .**30** F7
Damon CI DA14 . . . .**24** B5
Damon Ct DA14 . . . .**24** B5
Damson Ct BR8 . . . .**39** D5
Damson Dr ME3 . . . .**34** E3
Danaway Cotts ME9 . . . .**65** C3
Dando Cres SE3 . . . .**5** B4
Dandridge Ct SE10 . . . .**1** A1
Dane CI Chatham ME5 . . . . .**62** C2
Hartlip ME9 . . . .**64** D6
Orpington BR6 . . . .**51** D6
Sidcup DA15 . . . .**25** A8
Dane Ct ME17 . . . .**106** C2
Dane La ME9 . . . .**64** D6
Dane Rd TN14 . . . .**68** F2
Danecourt Sch ME8 . . . . . .**49** A2
Danefield Ct
Maidstone ME14 . . . .**93** B4
Sevenoaks TN13 . . . .**83** C4
Danehill Wlk DA14 . . . .**24** A5
Danemore TN30 . . . .**183** B8
Danes CI DA11 . . . .**29** C5
Danes Hill ME7 . . . .**49** A6
Danescombe SE12 . . . .**22** A7
Daniel Ho ME16 . . . .**91** E5
Danns La ME18,ME19 . . . . .**89** A1
Dansington Rd DA16 . . . .**7** A3
Danson Cres DA16 . . . .**7** B4
Danson La DA16 . . . .**7** B3
Danson Mead DA16 . . . .**7** C4
Danson Prim Sch DA16 . . . . .**7** A3
Danson Rd Bexley DA6 . . . . .**7** D2
Sidcup DA5 . . . .**7** D1
Danson Underpass DA5 . . . .**7** C1
Danson Way ME8 . . . .**49** D2
Danvers Rd TN9 . . . .**117** B1
Darby Gdns ME3 . . . .**32** B3
Darby's La TN5 . . . .**175** B2
Darent CI TN13 . . . .**83** C5

Darent Ind Pk DA8 . . . .**9** D8
Darent Mead DA4 . . . .**41** B8
Darent Valley Hospl DA2 . .**27** E7
Darenth
Com Prim Sch DA2 . . . .**27** E2
Darenth Cotts TN14 . . . . . .**68** F8
Darenth Ct **15** BR5 . . . .**38** D1
Darenth Dr DA12 . . . .**31** B7
Darenth Gdns TN16 . . . .**81** D1
Darenth Hill DA2 . . . .**27** C3
Darenth La TN13 . . . .**83** E6
Darenth Park Ave DA2 . . . .**27** D6
Darenth Rd Bexley DA16 . . . .**7** A6
Dartford DA1 . . . .**26** F7
Darenth Rd S DA2 . . . .**27** B4
Darenth Rise ME5 . . . .**62** B3
Darenth Way TN14 . . . .**69** A8
Darenth Wood Rd DA2 . . . .**27** D6
Dargate CI ME16 . . . .**91** D7
Dargets Rd ME5 . . . .**62** A3
Darland Ave ME7 . . . .**48** E1
Darland House SE9 . . . .**6** D1
Darlton CI DA1 . . . .**8** F4
Darman Ho TN12,ME18 . . .**120** D3
Darnets Field TN14 . . . .**68** F2
Darnley CI ME7 . . . .**46** D6
Darnley Dr TN4 . . . .**132** E4
Darnley Rd Gravesend DA11 **30** A8
1 Grays RM17 . . . .**12** B8
Rochester ME2 . . . .**46** E6
Darnley St DA11 . . . .**30** B8
Darns Hill BR8 . . . .**39** C2
Darrick Wood
Inf & Jun Schs BR6 . . . .**51** B6
Darrick Wood Rd BR6 . . . . .**51** B7
Darrick Wood Sch BR6 . . . .**51** B7
Darrick Wood
Sports Ctr BR6 . . . .**51** B7
Dart CI ME2 . . . .**46** F7
Dartford Borough
Mus* DA1 . . . .**26** E8
Dartford Gram Sch DA1 . . .**9** C1
Dartford Gram Sch
for Girls DA1 . . . .**26** C8
Dartford Hospl
Specl Sch DA3 . . . .**43** A6
Dartford Rd Coldblow DA5 .**25** C7
Dartford DA1 . . . .**9** B1
Farningham DA4 . . . .**41** A5
Sevenoaks TN13 . . . .**84** C3
Dartford Sta DA1 . . . .**9** E1
Dartford Technology
Coll DA1 . . . .**26** D8
Dartford Trad Pk DA1 . . . . .**26** F6
Dartmouth Rd BR2 . . . .**36** A2
Darwin CI BR6 . . . .**51** D5
Darwin Ct Eltham SE9 . . . . . .**6** A1
Rochester ME1 . . . .**47** D5
Darwin Dr TN10 . . . .**117** D6
Darwin Rd Bexley DA16 . . . . .**6** F4
Tilbury RM18 . . . .**12** F6
Dashmonden CI ME2 . . . . . .**33** C2
Dashwood CI DA6 . . . .**8** A2
Dashwood Rd DA11 . . . .**30** A6
Davall House **10** RM17 . . . .**12** B8
Davenport Ave ME7 . . . .**48** E7
Davenport Rd DA14 . . . .**24** E6
David Coffer Ct DA17 . . . . . .**4** B2
David Saloman's Ho*
TN3 . . . .**148** D8
Davidson Tower BR1 . . . . . .**22** B3
Davis Ave DA11 . . . .**29** E7
Davis CI TN13 . . . .**84** C5
Davy's PI DA12 . . . .**30** E2
Dawbourne TN30 . . . .**173** B3
Dawes CI DA9 . . . .**10** F2
Dawes St ME7 . . . .**48** C5
Dawson Ave BR5 . . . .**38** B7
Dawson CI SE18 . . . .**2** C1
Dawson Ct **7** ME7 . . . .**48** A6
Dawson Dr ME3 . . . .**25** E1
Day Ho **2** ME14 . . . .**92** B4
Days La DA15 . . . .**23** E8
Days Lane Prim Sch DA15 . .**6** F1
Dayton Dr DA4 . . . .**9** D8
De Lapre CI BR5 . . . .**38** D2
De Luci CI DA1 . . . .**4** C1
De Lucy Prim Sch SE2 . . . . . .**3** B4
De Lucy St SE2 . . . .**3** B2
De Mere CI ME8 . . . .**63** D6
De Quincey Mews E16 . . . . .**1** A5
De Warren Rd DA11 . . . .**12** D1
Deacon CI ME2 . . . .**46** E8
Deacon Est The ME20 . . . . .**76** A2
Deacon Trad Ctr ME2 . . . . . .**47** A6
Deacon Trad Est TN9 . . . . .**117** D1
Deacons Leas BR6 . . . .**51** D6
Deakin Leas TN9 . . . .**133** B7
Deal Ho ME15 . . . .**107** E8
Dean & Chapter
Cotts DA13 . . . .**29** B2
Dean La DA13 . . . .**58** C5
Dean Rd Luddesdown DA13 .**58** E8
Rochester ME2 . . . .**46** F8
Dean St ME15 . . . .**106** C4
Deane Ct **8** ME7 . . . .**48** C6
Deanery Rd TN **96** C1
Deangate Ridge
Sports Ground ME3 . . . . . .**34** D8
Deans Ct **7** TN9 . . . .**133** B8
Deans Hill Rd ME9 . . . .**80** D5
Deansfield Inf Sch SE9 . . . . .**6** A4
Deansfield Jun Sch SE9 . . . . .**6** A4
Deanwood CI ME8 . . . .**63** D6
Deanwood Dr ME8 . . . .**63** E4

Deanwood Prim
Education
Tech Sch ME8 . . . .**63** D3
Debrabant CI DA8 . . . .**8** D8
Decoy Hill Rd ME23 . . . .**17** F6
Deepdene TN5 . . . .**175** A6
Deepdene Rd DA16 . . . .**7** A4
Deerhurst CI DA3 . . . .**43** C6
Deerhurst Gdns ME16 . . . . .**91** D4
Deerleap La TN14 . . . .**67** E6
Defiance Wlk **1** SE18 . . . . . .**1** F3
Defiant CI ME5 . . . .**62** B6
Defoe CI Chatham ME5 . . . . .**62** B6
Erith DA8 . . . .**8** F6
Degema Rd BR7 . . . .**23** B3
Deirdre Chapman
House DA10 . . . .**11** E1
Delacourt Rd SE3 . . . .**5** B7
Delafield Rd SE7 . . . .**1** C1
Delagarde Rd TN16 . . . .**81** C1
Delamere Gdns **3** ME6 . . . .**75** A8
Delamere Rd ME6 . . . .**75** A8
Delaware Cotts TN8 . . . . . .**128** F8
Delce Inf Sch ME1 . . . .**47** D2
Delce Jun Sch ME1 . . . .**47** C2
Delce Rd ME1 . . . .**47** D4
Delisle Rd SE28 . . . .**2** E4
Delius Dr TN10 . . . .**117** F6
Dell Dr TN2 . . . .**149** D4
Dell The Dartford DA5 . . . . .**25** E7
Woolwich SE2 . . . .**3** A1
Delme Cres SE3 . . . .**5** B5
Delmonden Rd
Hawkhurst TN18 . . . .**178** B1
The Moor TN18 . . . .**184** C8
Delvan CI SE18 . . . .**6** A7
Delves Ave TN2 . . . .**149** C5
Demelza House
Hospice ME9 . . . .**65** F6
Den Cross TN8 . . . .**128** D6
Den La TN12 . . . .**121** C3
Denbigh Dr TN10 . . . .**117** D6
Denberry Dr DA14 . . . .**24** B5
Denbigh Ave ME8 . . . .**49** D1
Denbigh CI BR7 . . . .**22** F2
Denbigh Rd TN4 . . . .**149** C7
Dene Ave DA15 . . . .**24** B8
Dene CI DA2 . . . .**25** E4
Dene Dr New Barn DA3 . . . . .**43** B7
Orpington BR6 . . . .**52** B7
Dene Holm Rd DA11 . . . . . .**29** E5
Dene Lodge CI TN15 . . . . . .**86** F7
Dene Rd DA1 . . . .**26** F8
Dene The TN13 . . . .**84** B1
Dene Way TN3 . . . .**148** A7
Dene Wlk DA3 . . . .**42** E6
Denecourt BR5 . . . .**38** C1
Denesway DA13 . . . .**44** B3
Denham Rd ME9 . . . .**65** B7
Denham St **2** SE10 . . . .**1** A1
Denison Mews ME3 . . . .**19** C4
Deniston Ave DA5 . . . .**24** E7
Denmark Ho **10** SE18 . . . . . .**1** E2
Denmark Rd BR1 . . . .**36** B8
Denmark St E13 . . . .**1** B8
Dennard Way BR6 . . . .**51** A6
Denness Rd **2** ME8 . . . .**63** D6
Dennettsland Rd TN8 . . . . .**96** C1
Dennington Ct **2** ME14 . . .**133** A2
Dennis CadmanHo
4 ME20 . . . .**75** F1
Dennis Rd DA11 . . . .**30** B5
Dennis Willocks CI ME9 . . .**65** B6
Denny CI **12** E6 . . . .**1** E8
Denny Ct **3** DA2 . . . .**10** B1
Denstead Wlk **11** ME15 . . .**107** F6
Denton CI ME15 . . . .**107** E8
Denton Court Rd DA12 . . . .**30** E8
Denton Rd Bexley DA16 . . . . .**7** C4
Dartford DA1 . . . .**25** E8
Dartford DA5 . . . .**25** E7
Denton St DA12 . . . .**30** E8
Denton Terr DA5 . . . .**25** E6
Denver CI BR6 . . . .**37** E3
Denver Ind Est RM13 . . . .**4** F8
Denver Rd DA1 . . . .**26** A8
Derby CI TN11 . . . .**116** E6
Derby Rd Chatham ME5 . . . .**48** E2
Grays RM17 . . . .**12** B8
Maidstone ME15 . . . .**107** C6
Derby Road Bridge RM17 . .**12** B8
Derifall CI E6 . . . .**1** F8
Dering Way DA12 . . . .**30** F7
Deringwood Dr ME15 . . . . . .**92** F1
Dernier Rd TN10,TN9 . . . .**117** C4
Derrick Gdns SE7 . . . .**1** C3
Derry Downs BR5 . . . .**38** C3
Derwent CI DA1 . . . .**26** B7
Derwent Cres DA7 . . . .**8** A5
Derwent Dr Orpington BR5 . .**37** D2
Royal Tunbridge Wells TN4 . .**148** C5
Derwent House **3** ME15 .**107** E7
Derwent Lodge Sch TN1 . .**149** B4
Derwent Rd TN10 . . . .**117** C5
Derwent Way ME8 . . . .**63** D8
Detling
CE Prim Sch ME14 . . . .**78** A1
Detling CI ME8 . . . .**49** C2
Detling Hill ME14 . . . .**78** B2
Detling Rd Bromley BR1 . . . .**22** A3
Erith DA8 . . . .**8** D7
Northfleet DA11 . . . .**29** D7
Devalls CI E6 . . . .**2** A6
Devema CI ME2 . . . .**37** A8
Devenish Rd SE2 . . . .**3** A4
Devon CI Chatham ME5 . . . .**62** C7
Gillingham ME8 . . . .**49** F1
Devon Ct DA4 . . . .**41** B8

Devon Rd Maidstone ME15 .**107** C8
Sutton at Hone DA4 . . . .**41** C8
Devonshire Ave DA1 . . . .**9** B1
Devonshire CI TN2 . . . .**162** F8
Devonshire Rd Bexley DA6 . .**7** E3
Chislehurst SE9 . . . .**22** E6
Gillingham ME7 . . . .**48** D7
Gravesend DA12 . . . .**30** B6
Newham E16 . . . .**1** B8
Orpington BR6 . . . .**38** A2
Devonshire Sq BR2 . . . .**36** B5
Dewberry CI ME4 . . . .**34** B1
Dewberry Gdns E6 . . . .**1** E8
Dewhurst Cotts TN5 . . . . .**174** A7
Dewhurst La TN5 . . . .**174** B8
DeWinter Ho TN13 . . . .**84** A3
Dewlands Ave DA2 . . . .**27** B8
Dexter Ho **2** DA18 . . . .**3** E3
Dhekelia CI ME14 . . . .**92** A7
Dial CI Gillingham ME7 . . . . .**48** F6
Swanscombe DA9 . . . .**11** D2
Dial Rd ME7 . . . .**48** F6
Diameter Rd BR5 . . . .**37** C3
Diamond Cotts TN12 . . . . .**135** B7
Diamond Field TN12 . . . . . .**152** F3
Diana CI DA8 . . . .**8** E8
Dianne Ct SE12 . . . .**22** A7
Dianthus CI SE2 . . . .**3** B1
Dibden La TN13,TN14 . . . . .**98** E8
Dickens Ave Dartford DA1 . .**10** A3
Hartley DA3 . . . .**42** F4
Langley Heath ME17 . . . . . .**108** E4
Dickens CI Erith DA8 . . . .**8** B7
Hartley DA3 . . . .**42** F4
Langley Heath ME17 . . . . . .**108** E4
Dickens Ct Rochester ME2 . .**47** D8
Staplehurst TN12 . . . .**139** F5
Dickens Dr Chislehurst BR7 .**23** C2
East Malling ME19 . . . .**74** F1
Dickens Ho **3** DA17 . . . .**3** F1
Maidstone ME14 . . . .**91** E8
Rochester ME1 . . . .**47** C2
Dickens Rd Gravesend DA12 **30** E7
Maidstone ME14 . . . .**91** E8
Rochester ME1 . . . .**47** C2
Dickens Way TN18 . . . .**179** A2
Dickensian CI ME3 . . . .**19** A2
Dickley La ME17 . . . .**111** A6
Dickson Ho SE18 . . . .**5** E6
Dickson Rd SE9 . . . .**5** E4
Digdog La TN12,TN17 . . . . .**156** D3
Dignals CI ME8 . . . .**49** F2
Dilhorne CI SE12 . . . .**22** B5
Dillon Way TN2 . . . .**149** D6
Dillywood Cotts ME3 . . . . . .**32** F4
Dillywood La ME3 . . . .**32** F2
Dimmock CI TN12 . . . .**136** B7
Dingleden La TN17 . . . .**180** F2
Dippers CI TN15 . . . .**69** F2
Discovery Dr ME19 . . . .**89** B3
Discovery Rd ME15 . . . .**93** B2
Dislingbury Rd TN11 . . . . .**134** C4
Disraeli CI
Maidstone ME15 . . . .**107** E5
Woolwich SE28 . . . .**3** C5
Dittisham Rd SE9 . . . .**22** E4
Ditton CE Jun Sch ME20 . . .**75** C1
Ditton Court CI ME20 . . . . .**75** B1
Ditton Inf Sch ME20 . . . . . .**75** C1
Ditton PI ME20 . . . .**75** B1
Ditton Rd DA6 . . . .**7** E2
Dixon CI Maidstone ME15 . .**91** F2
4 Newham E6 . . . .**1** F7
Dixon Ho SE2 . . . .**3** C1
Dixwell CI ME8 . . . .**63** D5
Dobell Rd SE9 . . . .**5** F2
Dobson Rd DA12 . . . .**30** F8
Dock Approach Rd RM17 . .**12** E8
Dock Head Rd
Chattenden ME4 . . . .**34** A1
Gillingham ME4 . . . .**48** A4
Dock Rd Chatham ME4 . . . . .**47** F6
Gillingham ME4 . . . .**48** A7
Grays RM17 . . . .**12** D8
Grays RM17 . . . .**12** F7
Tilbury RM18 . . . .**12** F6
Dockland St E16 . . . .**2** A5
Dockside Rd E16 . . . .**1** D6
Doctor Hope's Rd TN17 . . .**169** D4
Dodd Rd TN10 . . . .**117** C5
Doddington Ct ME16 . . . . . .**91** D7
Doddington Rd ME8 . . . .**49** D3
Doebury Wlk SE18 . . . .**7** A8
Dog Cotts RH19 . . . .**144** B1
Doggets CI TN8 . . . .**128** C8
Doggetts Row ME3 . . . .**21** B6
Dogwood CI Chatham ME5 .**62** D1
Northfleet DA11 . . . .**29** F4
Dolphin CI SE28 . . . .**3** D7
Dolphin Dr ME8 . . . .**63** D6
Dombey CI Higham ME3 . . . .**32** C3
Rochester ME2 . . . .**47** C3
Domonic Dr SE9 . . . .**23** B5
Donaldson Rd SE18 . . . .**6** A6
Doncaster CI **7** ME15 . . . .**107** F6
Donet CI E16 . . . .**1** C7
Dongola Rd ME2 . . . .**33** B1
Donkey Field TN11 . . . .**115** C1
Donkey La DA4 . . . .**55** B8
Donnington Ct **11** DA2 . . . .**10** B1
Donnington Rd TN13 . . . . . .**83** D7
Doon Brae TN4 . . . .**133** A2
Dorado Gdns BR6 . . . .**52** D7
Doran Gr SE18 . . . .**6** E7
Dorchester Ave DA5 . . . . . .**24** D8
Dorchester CI
Cliffe Woods ME3 . . . .**33** B7
Dartford DA1 . . . .**26** F7
St Paul's Cray BR5 . . . .**24** B1
Dorchester Rd DA12 . . . . . .**30** D5

Dorcis Ave DA7 7 E5
Doria Dr DA12 30 F5
Doric Ave TN4 132 F1
Doric Cl TN4 132 F1
Dorin Ct TN2 149 C3
Doris Ave DA8 8 C6
Dorking Rd TN1 149 C6
Dormers Dr DA13 44 B2
Dornberg Cl SE3 5 A7
Dornberg Rd SE3 5 B7
Dornden Dr TN3 148 A4
Dornden Gdns ME5 62 B2
Dorne Cotts TN27 127 E6
Dorney Rise BR5 37 F5
Dorothy Ave TN17 169 E4
Dorothy Evans Cl DA7 8 B3
Dorrit Way Chislehurst BR7 23 C2
Rochester ME1 47 D2
Dorset Ave DA16 6 F3
Dorset Cotts TN7 160 B4
Dorset Cres DA12 30 E4
Dorset Rd Chislehurst SE9 22 E6
Royal Tunbridge Wells TN2 149 D2
Dorset Road Inf Sch SE9 22 E6
Dorset Sq ME8 49 D1
Dorset St TN13 84 C2
Dorset Way ME15 107 C8
Dorton Coll TN15 84 F5
Dorton Dr TN15 84 F5
Dorton House (Royal London Society Sch for the Blind) TN15 84 F5
Dorville Rd SE12 5 A2
Dothill Rd SE18 6 C7
Dotterel Cl ME5 62 D2
Doubleton La TN11 131 A5
Doug Siddons Ct 7 RM17 12 C8
Douglas Almshouses ME17 111 D5
Douglas Bldgs TN12 139 E5
Douglas Rd Bexley DA16 7 B6
Lenham ME17 111 D5
Maidstone ME16 91 E3
6 Newham E16 1 A8
Tonbridge TN9 133 A8
Douro Stables TN4 149 A4
Doust Way ME1 47 D5
Dove App E6 1 E8
Dove Cl ME5 62 B6
Dove Rd TN10 117 C6
Dovedale Cl DA16 7 A5
Dovedale Rd DA2 27 C7
Doveney Cl BR5 38 D6
Dover Ho 2
Maidstone ME15 107 E8
Rochester ME2 33 C1
Dover Patrol SE3 5 C5
Dover Rd Northfleet DA11 29 D8
Woolwich DA16 6 C5
Dover Rd E DA11 29 F7
Dover Road Com Prim Sch DA11 29 E7
Dover St ME16 91 C2
Doves Cl BR2 50 E8
Dowding Way TN2 133 E1
Dowding Wlk 3 DA11 29 E5
Dower House Cres TN4 132 E3
Dowgate Cl TN9 133 D7
Dowlerville Rd BR6 51 F4
Dowling Cl ME6 74 E7
Dowling Ho DA17 3 F3
Down Ave TN3 166 A4
Down House* BR6 66 A7
Down La TN3 163 B1
Down's Cl TN27 141 E5
Downage The DA11 30 A6
Downash Ct TN5 177 A3
Downash Ho TN5 177 A3
Downbank Ave DA7 8 D5
Downderry Way ME20 75 D1
Downe Ave TN14 66 D8
Downe Cl DA16 7 C7
Downe Ho 9 SE7 5 C8
Downe Prim Sch BR6 66 A8
Downe Rd
Cudham BR6,TN14 66 C5
Farthing Street BR2 50 E2
Downend SE18 6 B7
Downer Ct ME1 61 E8
Downham Way BR1 22 A4
Downings E6 2 A7
Downlands ME17 110 F6
Downleys Cl SE9 22 F6
Downman Rd SE9 5 E4
Downs Ave Chislehurst BR7 22 F3
Dartford DA1 27 A8
Downs Cl ME14 92 B8
Downs Rd Istead Rise DA13 29 D3
Maidstone ME14 92 B8
Yalding ME18 105 A1
Downs The ME5 61 D1
Downs Valley DA3 42 E5
Downs View Burham ME1 60 F1
West Malling ME19 89 B8
Downs View Cl BR6 52 C1
Downs View Rd ME14 92 B8
Downs Wood DA13 72 F8
Downside ME2 47 A7
Downsview Chatham ME5 62 C8
Trottiscliffe ME19 73 A5
Downsview Cl BR8 39 F6
Downsview Prim Sch BR8 40 A6
Downsview Rd TN13 83 F2
Downsway BR6 51 E5
Doyle Cl DA8 8 E6
Doyle Way RM18 13 C5
Drage Rd TN12 119 E6
Drake Cres SE28 3 C7
Drake Ct BR5 38 B3
Drake Hall E16 1 B5
Drake's Ave ME2 46 F8
Draper Cl DA17 3 F2
Draper Ct BR1 36 E5
Draper St 3 TN4 132 F2
Drawbridge Cl ME15 107 E8
Drawell Cl SE18 2 E1
Dray Corner Rd TN27 140 F7
Dray Ct TN11 118 E8
Drays Cotts DA4 41 B5
Drayton Ave BR6 37 B1
Drayton Cl ME23 17 E4
Drayton Rd TN9 133 C8
Drew Prim Sch E16 1 E5
Drew Rd E16 1 E5
Drewery Dr ME8 63 C5
Driffield Gdns TN9 132 F7
Drift The BR2 50 D7
Drive The Chislehurst BR7 37 E8
Erith DA8 8 B8
Gravesend DA12 30 E4
New Barn DA3 43 B6
Orpington BR6 51 F8
Royal Tunbridge Wells TN2 149 B1
Sevenoaks TN13 84 B3
Sidcup DA14 24 B4
Sidcup DA5 24 D8
St Paul's Cray BR7 37 F6
Tonbridge TN9 133 B7
Drove Way The DA13 29 E1
Drudgeon Way DA2 28 B5
Drummond Cl DA8 8 E6
Drury Rd TN30 173 B1
Dry Bank Ct TN10 117 C4
Dry Bank Rd TN10 117 C4
Dry End Rd ME20 75 D3
Dry Hill Park Cres TN10 117 C3
Dry Hill Park Rd TN10 117 B3
Dry Hill Rd TN9 117 B3
Dryden Ho BR2 36 D4
Dryden Pl RM18 13 B6
Dryden Rd DA16 6 F6
Dryden Way BR6 38 A1
Dryhill La TN14 83 B3
Dryhill Rd DA17 7 F8
Dryland Ave 5 BR6 51 F6
Dryland Rd
Borough Green TN15 86 F6
Snodland ME6 74 F8
Dublin Ho 18 ME15 107 E7
Duchess Cl ME2 46 E8
Duchess Of Kent Ct The ME20 75 F1
Duchess Of Kent Dr ME5 62 B3
Duchess' Wlk TN15 84 E2
Ducie Ho 8 SE7 5 C8
Ducketts Rd DA1 8 F2
Duddington Cl SE9 22 D4
Dudely Rd DA11 29 E8
Dudley Lodge TN2 149 C4
Dudley Rd TN1 149 A4
Dudsbury Rd DA1 9 B2
Dukes Meadow TN11 114 F2
Dukes Meadow Dr ME7 62 F6
Dukes Orch DA5 25 C7
Dukes Rd TN1 149 C5
Dukes Wlk 7 ME15 92 A4
Dulverton Prim Sch SE9 23 D6
Dulverton Rd SE9 23 D6
Dumbreck Rd SE9 6 A4
Dunbar Ct BR2 36 A6
Dunblane Rd SE9 5 E5
Duncan Ho 2 SE7 5 B8
Duncan Rd ME7 48 D5
Duncans Cotts 6 TN16 81 D1
Duncroft SE18 6 E7
Dundale Rd TN12,TN3 151 A3
Dundonald Cl 6 E6 1 E7
Dunedin Ho
9 Maidstone ME15 107 E5
2 Tilbury RM18 13 A5
Dunera Dr ME14 92 A7
Dunk's Green Rd TN11 102 A5
Dunkeld Ho 6 ME15 107 E7
Dunkery Rd SE9 22 E5
Dunkin Rd DA1 10 A3
Dunkirk Cl DA12 30 C3
Dunkirk Dr ME5 61 F6
Dunkley Villas TN15 72 F1
Dunlop Ct 7 TN18 179 A2
Dunlop Rd RM18 12 F6
Dunn Street Rd ME7 78 A8
Dunning's La ME1 47 C4
Dunnings The ME16 91 A2
Dunnock Rd E6 1 E7
Dunnose Ct RM19 10 B8
Dunoon Cotts BR6 66 A5
Dunorlan Farm Cotts TN2 149 E4
Dunstable Ct 4 SE3 5 A7
Dunstall Welling Est DA16 7 B5
Dunstan Glade BR5 37 D3
Dunstan Gr TN4 149 B6
Dunstan Rd TN4 149 B6
Dunster Ct 16 DA2 10 B1
Dunster Terr 3 ME15 107 E8
Dunton Green Cty Prim Sch TN13 83 E7
Dunton Green Sta TN13 83 E7
Dunvegan Rd SE9 5 F3
Dunwich Rd DA7 7 F6
Dupree Rd SE7 1 B1
Durant Rd BR8 26 A2
Durban House 7 ME15 107 E5
Durham Cl ME15 92 E1
Durham Rd Bromley BR2 36 A5
Gillingham ME8 63 C7
Durham Rd *continued*
Sidcup DA14 24 B3
Durham Rise SE18 2 D1
Duriun Way DA8 9 B7
Durley Gdns BR6 52 B7
Durlings Orch TN15 86 D6
Durndale La
Northfleet DA11 29 E4
Northfleet DA11 29 F5
Durrant Way
Orpington BR6 51 D5
Swanscombe DA10 28 E8
Durrell Gdns ME5 48 C1
Dursley Cl SE3 5 C5
Dursley Gdns SE3 5 D6
Dursley Rd SE3 5 C5
Duval Dr ME1 61 E8
Duvard's Pl ME9 65 F1
Dux Court Rd ME23 17 D2
Dux Hill TN15 101 F8
Dux La TN15 86 F1
Duxberry Cl BR2 36 E4
Duxford Ho 12 SE2 3 D4
Dyke Dr BR5 38 C2
Dykewood Cl DA5 25 E5
Dylan Rd DA17 4 A3
Dymchurch Cl BR6 51 E6
Dyneley Rd SE12 22 C5
Dynes Rd TN15 69 E2
Dynevor Rd TN4 149 C7

E

Eagle Cl ME20 75 A2
Eagle Heights Bird of Prey Ctr* DA4 54 B8
Eagle House RM17 11 F8
Eagle Way DA11 12 A2
Eagles Rd DA9 11 B2
Eaglesfield Rd SE18 6 B6
Eaglesfield Sch SE18 6 A6
Eaglestone Cl TN15 87 A8
Ealdham Prim Sch SE9 5 C3
Ealdham Sq SE9 5 C3
Ealing Cl ME5 62 C4
Eardemont Cl DA1 8 F3
Eardley Point 7 SE18 2 B2
Eardley Rd Erith DA17 4 A1
Sevenoaks TN13 84 B3
Earl Cl ME5 62 B4
Earl Rd DA11 29 E6
Earl Rise SE18 2 D2
Earl St ME14 91 F4
Earl's Rd TN4 148 F4
Earlshall Rd SE9 6 A3
Eason Villas TN12 138 D6
East Beckton District Ctr E16 1 F8
East Borough Prim Sch ME14 92 B5
East Cliff Rd TN4 149 A6
East Crescent Rd DA12 13 C1
East Cross TN30 183 B7
East Ct ME15 92 A1
East Dr BR5 38 B3
East End Rd ME4,ME7 48 D8
East Farleigh Prim Sch ME15 106 B6
East Farleigh Sta ME16 106 B8
East Hall Hill ME17 123 E7
East Hall Rd BR5 38 F2
East Ham Ind Est E6 1 E8
East Ham Manor Way E6 2 A7
East Hill Dartford DA1 26 F8
Sutton at Hone DA4 41 D7
Tenterden TN30 183 B8
East Hill Dr DA1 26 F8
East Hill Rd TN15 70 B7
East Ho DA1 9 F4
East Holme DA8 8 D6
East Kent Ave DA11 12 C1
East La DA4 41 D7
East Malling Research Sta (Horticultural) ME19 90 C6
East Malling Sta ME19 90 A6
East Mascalls 16 SE7 5 C8
East Mill DA11 12 F1
East Milton Rd DA12 30 D8
East Park Rd ME20 91 A8
East Peckham Prim Sch TN12 119 F6
East Rd Bexley DA16 7 B5
Chatham ME4 48 A7
Gillingham ME4 48 A8
East Rochester Way
Coldblow DA1 25 D8
Sidcup DA5,DA15 7 C1
East Row ME1 47 C5
East St Addington ME19 73 D3
Bexley DA7 8 A3
Bromley BR1 36 A7
Chatham ME4 48 A3
Gillingham ME7 48 D6
Grays RM20 11 E8
Harrietsham ME17 110 E5
Hunton ME15 121 F7
Snodland ME6 75 B8
Tonbridge TN9 117 C2
East Street N ME19 73 D3
East Sutton Park (HM Young Offender Inst & Prison) ME17 125 B7
East Sutton Rd Hearnden Green ME17,TN27 125 C4
Sutton Valence ME17 125 A7
East Terr Gravesend DA12 13 C1
Sidcup DA15 23 E7
East Thamesmead Bsns Pk DA18 3 F4
East Thurrock Rd RM17 12 C8
East Weald Dr TN30 173 B1
East Wickham Inf Sch DA16 6 F6
East Wickham Jun Sch DA16 7 A6
East Woodside DA5 24 E7
Eastbrook Rd SE3 5 B6
Eastbury Rd Newham E6 2 A8
Orpington BR5 37 D3
Eastcombe Ave SE7 5 B8
Eastcote BR6 37 F1
Eastcote Prim Sch DA16 6 D4
Eastcote Rd DA16 6 D5
Eastcourt Gn ME8 49 B4
Eastcourt La
Gillingham ME8 49 B3
Gillingham,Lower Twydall ME7,ME8 49 B4
Easterfields ME19 90 C5
Eastern Ave RM20 10 F8
Eastern Rd ME7 48 F6
Eastern Way Erith SE28 3 D5
1 Grays RM17 12 A8
Eastfield Gdns TN10 117 E5
Eastfield House ME16 91 B2
Eastfield Terr DA1 9 F4
Eastgate ME1 47 C5
Eastgate Cl SE28 3 D7
Eastgate Ct ME1 47 C5
Eastgate Rd TN30 183 C8
Eastgate Terr ME1 47 C5
Eastland Ct 3 BR1 36 C7
Eastlands Cl TN4 162 E8
Eastlands Rd TN4 148 E1
Eastleigh Rd DA7 8 C4
Eastling Cl ME8 49 D3
Eastling House 8 BR5 38 D1
Eastmead Cl BR1 36 E7
Eastmoor Pl SE7 1 D3
Eastmoor St SE7 1 D3
Eastnor Rd SE9 23 C7
Eastry Cl ME16 91 C7
Eastry Rd DA8 8 A7
Eastview Ave SE18 6 E7
Eastway BR2 36 A2
Eastwell 5 TN30 183 A7
Eastwell Barn Mews TN30 183 A8
Eastwell Cl Maidstone ME14 92 C5
Paddock Wood TN12 135 E6
Eastwell Meadows TN30 183 A8
Eaton Ct BR7 23 C2
Eaton Rd DA14 24 D6
Eaton Sq DA3 42 D6
Ebbsfleet Ind Est DA11 12 B2
Ebbsfleet Wlk DA11 12 B1
Ebdon Way SE3 5 B4
Ebony Wlk ME16 91 B3
Ebury Cl BR2 50 E7
Eccles Row ME20 75 F6
Eccleston Cl BR6 37 D1
Eccleston Rd ME15 91 F2
Echo Cl ME15 107 F6
Echo Ct DA12 30 C6
Eclipse Rd E13 1 B8
Edam Ct 11 DA14 24 A5
Eddington Cl ME15 107 B6
Eden Ave ME5 62 A7
Eden Cl DA5 25 D4
Eden Ct 1
Hawkhurst TN18 178 F2
17 Orpington BR5 38 D1
Tonbridge TN10 117 C5
Eden Farm La ME19 89 D8
Eden Pl DA12 30 B8
Eden Rd Dartford DA5 25 D4
High Halstow ME23 17 E4
Royal Tunbridge Wells TN1 149 A2
Eden Valley Sch TN8 112 C2
Eden Villas TN8 128 D7
Edenbridge & District War Meml Hospl TN8 128 D7
Edenbridge Cl BR5 38 D5
Edenbridge Golf & Country Club TN8 112 A2
Edenbridge Information Ctr* TN8 112 C2
Edenbridge Prim Sch TN8 112 D1
Edenbridge Rd TN7 145 E1
Edenbridge Sta TN8 112 C3
Edenbridge Town Sta TN8 112 D2
Edenbridge Trad Ctr TN8 128 D8
Edendale Rd DA7 8 D5
Edenhurst TN13 84 A2
Edensmuir Ct SE3 5 A7
Edgar Cl BR8 39 F6
Edgar Rd TN15 69 E2
Edge Hill SE18 6 B8
Edge Hill Ct DA14 23 F4
Edgeborough Way BR1 36 D8
Edgebury BR7,SE9 23 B4
Edgebury Prim Sch BR7 23 C4
Edgebury Wlk BR7 23 C5
Edgefield Cl DA1 27 B7
Edgehill Gdns DA13 43 F8
Edgehill Rd BR7 23 C4
Edgeler Ct ME6 74 F7
Edger Pl 5 ME15 92 A4
Edgewood Dr BR6 52 A5
Edgeworth Rd SE9 5 D3
Edgington Way DA14 24 D1
Edinburgh Ct DA8 8 D7
Edinburgh Mews RM18 13 B5
Edinburgh Rd
Chatham ME4 48 C2
Gillingham ME7 48 D5
Grain ME3 21 B5
Edinburgh Sq ME15 107 C7
Edington Rd SE2 3 B3
Edisbury Wlk ME8 63 D5
Edison Gr SE18 6 F7
Edison Rd Bexley DA16 6 F6
Bromley BR2 36 A7
Edith Ct BR1 36 D6
Edith Pond Ct SE9 23 B6
Edith Rd BR6 52 A5
Ediva Rd DA13 44 A4
Edmund Cl Maidstone ME16 91 A3
Meopham Sta DA13 44 A4
Edmund Hurst Dr E6 2 B8
Edmund Rd Bexley DA16 7 A4
Orpington BR5 38 C3
Edmunds Ave BR5 38 D6
Edna Rd ME14 91 F8
Edward Ct Chatham ME5 48 C1
2 Newham E16 1 A8
Edward Harvey Ct DA17 3 F1
Edward Rd Bromley BR1 22 C1
Chislehurst BR7 23 B3
Edward St Chatham ME4 48 A3
Rochester ME2 47 B7
Royal Tunbridge Wells, Modest Corner TN4 148 F8
Royal Tunbridge Wells, Rustall TN4 148 C4
Edward Tyler Rd SE12 22 C6
Edward Wlk ME19 89 F8
Edwards Cl ME8 63 C5
Edwards Ct DA4 54 E7
Edwards Gdns BR8 39 D5
Edwards Rd DA17 4 A2
Edwin Arnold Ct DA15 23 F4
Edwin Cl DA7 7 F8
Edwin Petty Pl DA2 27 C8
Edwin Rd Dartford DA2 26 C5
Gillingham ME8 63 C8
Edwin St Gravesend DA12 30 B8
Newham E16 1 A8
Edwina Pl ME9 65 C7
Egdean Wlk TN13 84 C4
Egerton Ave BR8 39 F8
Egerton CE Prim Sch TN27 127 F3
Egerton Cl DA1 26 B7
Egerton House Rd TN27 127 E4
Egerton Rd ME14 91 E7
Eggpie La TN11,TN14 115 E7
Egham Rd E13 1 B8
Eglantine La DA4 41 B3
Eglinton Hill SE18 6 B7
Eglinton Inf Sch SE18 6 A8
Eglinton Jun Mix Sch SE18 6 A8
Eglinton Rd
Swanscombe DA10 11 F1
Woolwich SE18 6 B8
Egremont Rd ME15 92 F2
Egret Cl ME4 34 B2
Eileen Ct BR7 23 A3
Eisenhower Dr E6 1 E8
Elaine Ave ME2 46 E7
Elaine Ct ME2 46 E6
Elaine Prim Sch ME2 46 E6
Elbourne Trad Est DA17 4 B3
Elbury Dr E16 1 A7
Elder Cl
Hoo St Werburgh ME3 34 E3
Kingswood ME17 109 D2
Sidcup DA15 23 F7
Elder Ct ME8 63 B6
Elderslie Rd SE9 6 A2
Eldon St ME4 48 A4
Eldon Way TN12 135 F7
Eldred Dr BR5 52 D8
Eleanor Wlk 19 SE18 1 F2
Elenmore Ct BR1 36 E5
Elford Cl SE3 5 C3
Elford Rd ME3 16 B5
Elgal Cl BR6 51 B5
Elgar Cl TN10 117 E6
Elgar Gdns RM18 13 B6
Elgin Gdns ME2 46 D5
Elham Cl Bromley BR1 22 D1
Gillingham ME8 49 B3
Elibank Rd SE9 6 A3
Eling Ct ME15 107 A8
Eliot Rd DA1 10 B2
Elizabeth Cl RM18 13 B5
Elizabeth Ct Chatham ME5 62 A7
Erith DA8 8 D7
Gillingham ME8 49 C1
Gravesend DA11 13 A1
Elizabeth Garlick Ct
1 TN1 149 B4
Elizabeth Garrett Anderson Ho 9 DA17 4 A3
Elizabeth House ME14 92 A6
Elizabeth Huggins Cotts DA11 30 B6
Elizabeth Pl DA4 40 E3
Elizabeth Smith's Ct ME19 89 F7
Elizabeth St DA9 10 E2
Elizabeth Terr SE9 5 F1
Elizabeth Way BR5 38 C4
Ellen Cl BR1 36 D6
Ellen Wilkinson Prim Sch E6 1 E8
Ellen's Pl ME9 65 C6
Ellenborough Rd DA14 24 E3

Ellenswood Cl ME15 . . . . . .93 A1
Ellerman Rd RM18 . . . . . . .12 F5
Ellerslie DA12 . . . . .30 D8
Ellesmere Ct SE12 . . . . .22 A7
Ellingham Leas ME15 . . . . .107 C7
Elliott Rd BR2 . . . . .36 D5
Elliott St DA12 . . . . .30 D8
Elliotts La TN16 . . . . .82 C3
Ellis Cl Sidcup SE9 . . . . . . .23 C6
    Swanley BR8 . . . . .39 D5
Ellis Ct DA1 . . . . .27 B7
Ellis Way DA1 . . . . .26 F6
Elliscombe Mount SE7 . . . . .5 C8
Elliscombe Rd SE7 . . . . .5 C8
Ellison Rd DA15 . . . . .23 D7
Elliston Ho ⑥ SE18 . . . . . . .2 A2
Elm Ave Chatham ME4 . . . .47 E1
    Chattenden ME3 . . . . . . .34 A4
Elm Cl Dartford DA1 . . . . . .26 C7
    Egerton TN27 . . . . .127 F3
    Higham ME3 . . . . .32 C3
Elm Cotts BR8 . . . . .40 B8
Elm Court Ind Est ME7 . . . .62 E3
Elm Cres ME19 . . . . .89 F8
Elm Dr BR8 . . . . .39 D7
Elm Gr Erith DA8 . . . . .8 D7
    Maidstone ME15 . . . . . . .92 B3
    Orpington BR6 . . . . .37 F1
    Tonbridge TN11 . . . . . . .116 F5
Elm La TN11 . . . . .117 C3
Elm Par ⑩ DA14 . . . . .24 A4
Elm Rd Dartford DA1 . . . . . .26 D7
    Erith DA8 . . . . .9 A6
    Gillingham ME7 . . . . .48 E6
    Gravesend DA12 . . . . . . .30 C5
    Grays RM17 . . . . .12 C8
    Hoo St Werburgh ME3 . . .34 E3
    Orpington BR6 . . . . .52 A3
    Royal Tunbridge Wells TN4 .132 F1
    Sidcup DA14 . . . . .24 A4
    Stone DA10 . . . . .11 E1
    Westerham TN16 . . . . . . .81 E2
Elm Terr ⑧ Eltham SE9 . . . .6 A1
    West Thurrock RM20 . . . . .11 B8
Elm Tree Cotts ME15 . . . . .19 A3
Elm Tree Ct ⑩ SE7 . . . . . . .5 C8
Elm Tree Dr ME1 . . . . .47 A2
Elm Wlk Aylesford ME20 . . .75 E1
    Orpington BR6 . . . . .50 F7
Elmbank Dr BR1 . . . . .36 D7
Elmbourne Dr DA17 . . . . . . .4 B2
Elmbrook Gdns SE9 . . . . . . .5 E2
Elmcroft Ave DA15 . . . . .7 A1
Elmcroft Rd BR6 . . . . .38 A2
Elmdene Rd SE18 . . . . .2 B1
Elmfield Gillingham ME8 . . .49 A3
    Tenterden TN30 . . . . . . .183 B8
Elmfield Cl Gravesend DA11 30 B7
    Sevenoaks Weald TN14 . . .99 B2
Elmfield Ct Bexley DA16 . . . .7 B6
    Coxheath ME17 . . . . . . .106 C3
    Tenterden TN30 . . . . . . .183 B8
Elmfield Pk BR1 . . . . .36 A6
Elmfield Rd BR1 . . . . .36 A6
Elmhurst DA17 . . . . .7 E8
    Swanscombe DA9 . . . . . . .11 B1
Elmhurst Ave TN2 . . . . . . .150 D8
Elmhurst Gdns ME4 . . . . . .47 E3
Elmhurst Rd SE9 . . . . .22 E5
Elmington Cl DA5 . . . . .8 B1
Elmlee Cl BR7 . . . . .22 F2
Elmley Cl ⑮ E6 . . . . .1 E8
Elmley St SE18 . . . . .2 D2
Elmshurst Gdns TN10 . . . .117 C7
Elmslie Ct SE9 . . . . .6 A1
Elmstead Ave BR7 . . . . . . .22 F3
Elmstead Cl TN13 . . . . . . .83 E5
Elmstead Glade BR7 . . . . . .22 F2
Elmstead La BR7 . . . . .22 F3
Elmstead Rd DA8 . . . . .8 E6
Elmstead Woods Sta BR7 . .22 E2
Elmsted Cres DA16 . . . . .7 C8
Elmstone Cl ME16 . . . . . . .91 B2
Elmstone Hole Rd ME17 . .126 D8
Elmstone La ME16 . . . . . . .91 B2
Elmstone Rd ME8 . . . . .63 D7
Elmstone Terr ⑧ BR5 . . . . .38 C5
Elmtree Cotts TN14 . . . . . .67 D4
Elmwood Dr DA5 . . . . .24 E8
Elmwood Rd ME3 . . . . .33 F6
Elphick's Pl TN2 . . . . .163 B8
Elrick Cl DA8 . . . . .8 E8
Elsa Rd DA16 . . . . .7 C5
Elsinore Ho ⑥ SE18 . . . . . . .1 E2
Elster Pl ME19 . . . . .89 B3
Elstow Cl Eltham SE9 . . . . . .5 F2
    Eltham SE9 . . . . .6 A2
Elstree Gdns DA17 . . . . .3 E2
Elswyn Ho ⑭ DA14 . . . . . .24 A4
Eltham CE Prim Sch SE9 . . .5 F2
Eltham Coll SE9 . . . . .22 D6
Eltham Green Rd SE9 . . . . . .5 C3
Eltham Green Rd SE9 . . . . . .5 D1
Eltham High St SE9 . . . . . . .5 F1
Eltham Hill SE9 . . . . .5 E2
Eltham Hill Sch SE9 . . . . . . .5 E1
Eltham Palace* SE9 . . . . . . .5 E1
Eltham Palace Rd SE9 . . . . . .5 D1
Eltham Park Gdns SE9 . . . . .6 D1
Eltham Rd SE12,SE9 . . . . . . .5 B2
Eltham Sta SE9 . . . . .5 F2
Elvington Cl ME16 . . . . . . .91 D5
Elwick Ct DA1 . . . . .9 A3
Elwill Way DA13 . . . . .43 F8

Elwyn Gdns SE12 . . . . .22 A8
Ely Cl Erith DA8 . . . . .8 F5
    Gillingham ME8 . . . . .49 E2
Ely Ct TN1 . . . . .149 B4
Ely Gdns TN10 . . . . .117 D4
Elysian Ave BR5 . . . . .37 F3
Embassy Ct DA14 . . . . .24 B5
Embassy Cl ME7 . . . . .48 F1
Embassy Ct DA16 . . . . .7 B4
Ember Cl BR5 . . . . .37 C2
Emblin Ct ⑧ DA14 . . . . . . .24 A4
Emerald Cl Chatham ME1 . . .61 D7
    Newham E16 . . . . .1 E7
Emersons Ave BR8 . . . . . . .25 F1
Emerton Cl DA6 . . . . .7 E3
Emes Rd DA8 . . . . .8 C7
Emily Jackson Cl TN13 . . . .84 B3
Emily Jackson Ho TN13 . . . .84 B3
Emily Rd ME5 . . . . .62 B6
Emmanuel Ho ⑧ SE18 . . . . .2 F2
Emmett Hill La ME18 . . . .120 F5
Emmetts Garden* TN14 . . .97 D5
Emmetts La TN14,TN16 . . . .97 D6
Empress Dr BR7 . . . . .23 B2
Empress Rd DA12 . . . . .30 E8
Emsworth Gr ME14 . . . . . . .92 D6
Enderfield Ct BR7 . . . . .37 A8
Engineer Cl SE18 . . . . .6 A8
Englefield Cl BR5 . . . . .37 F5
Englefield Cres
    Cliffe Woods ME3 . . . . . . .33 B7
    Orpington BR5 . . . . .38 A5
Englefield Path BR5 . . . . . .38 A5
English Martyrs'
    RC Prim Sch 47 B8
Ennerdale Rd DA7 . . . . .8 A6
Ennis Rd SE18 . . . . .6 C8
Ensfield Rd Leigh TN11 . . .115 E1
    Tonbridge TN11 . . . . . . .132 A6
Ensign House RM17 . . . . . . .11 F8
Enslin Rd SE9 . . . . .23 A8
Enterprise Bsns Est ME2 . .47 E7
Enterprise Cl ME2 . . . . .47 E7
Enterprise Ctr The ME5 . . .77 C8
Enterprise Rd ME15 . . . . . .92 A1
Enterprise Way TN8 . . . . .112 C3
Epaul La ME1 . . . . .47 C6
Eppe Cl ⑧ ME2 . . . . .47 B8
Epsom Cl Bexley DA7 . . . . . .8 B4
    Maidstone ME15 . . . . . .107 F6
    New Town ME19 . . . . . . .89 B8
Epstein Rd SE28 . . . . .3 B5
Erica Ct BR8 . . . . .39 E5
Eridge Green Cl BR5 . . . . . .38 C1
Eridge Rd TN2, TN4 . . . . . .148 E1
Eridge Sta TN3 . . . . .161 E2
Erindale SE18 . . . . .6 D8
Erindale Terr SE18 . . . . .6 D8
Erith & District Hospl DA8 . .8 D8
Erith Cl ME14 . . . . .92 A8
Erith High St DA8 . . . . .4 E1
Erith Rd Bexley DA7 . . . . . . .8 B4
    Erith DA8,DA17 . . . . .4 B1
Erith Sch DA8 . . . . .8 D7
Erith Small Bsns Ctr DA8 . . .8 F8
Erith Sta DA8 . . . . .4 E1
Ermington Rd SE9 . . . . .23 C6
Ernest Dr ME16 . . . . .91 D3
Ernest Rd ME4 . . . . .48 A3
Erskine Ho ⑦ SE7 . . . . .5 C8
Erskine Park Rd TN4 . . . . .148 C4
Erskine Rd DA13 . . . . .73 B8
Erwood Rd SE7 . . . . .1 E1
Escott Gdns SE9 . . . . .22 E4
Escreet Gr SE18 . . . . .2 A2
Eschol Rd ME3 . . . . .35 C6
Eskdale Cl DA2 . . . . .27 C7
Eskdale Rd DA7 . . . . .8 A6
Esplanade Rd DA17 . . . . . . .4 A1
Essenden Rd DA17 . . . . .4 A1
Essex Cl TN2 . . . . .162 F8
Essex Rd ⑧ Dartford DA1 . . .9 D1
    Gravesend DA11 . . . . . . .30 A7
    Halling ME2 . . . . .60 A6
    Longfield DA3 . . . . .42 D7
    Maidstone ME15 . . . . . .107 E6
    West Thurrock RM20 . . . . .11 A8
Essex St SE18 . . . . .2 C3
Estelle Cl ME1 . . . . .61 D7
Estridge Way TN10 . . . . . .117 F5
Estuary Cotts RM18 . . . . . .14 D7
Etfield Gr DA14 . . . . .24 B3
Ethel Brooks Ho SE18 . . . . .6 B8
Ethel Rd E16 . . . . .1 B7
Ethel Terr BR6 . . . . .52 C2
Ethel-Maud Ct ME7 . . . . . .48 D7
Ethelbert Cl BR1 . . . . .36 A6
Ethelbert Rd Bromley BR1 . .36 A6
    Erith DA8 . . . . .8 C7
    Rochester ME1 . . . . .47 C4
    St Paul's Cray BR5 . . . . . .38 D6
Ethelbery Rd DA2 . . . . .26 E3
Etherington Hill TN3 . . . . .148 C8
Ethnam La TN18 . . . . .186 E4
Ethronvi Rd DA7 . . . . .7 E4
Eton Cl ME5 . . . . .61 F4
Eton Ct TN13 . . . . .84 B4
Eton Rd BR6 . . . . .52 B6
Eton Way DA1 . . . . .9 C3
Eugenie Mews BR7 . . . . . . .37 B8
Europa Trad Est DA8 . . . . . .4 D1
Europe Rd SE18 . . . . .1 F3
Euroway ME20 . . . . .90 E8
Eustace Pl ⑧ SE18 . . . . .1 F2
Eva Rd ME7 . . . . .48 D3
Evans Cl DA9 . . . . .11 A2
Evans Ct SE9 . . . . .22 E6

Evelyn Cl ME2 . . . . .47 C8
Evelyn Denington Rd E6 . . . .1 F8
Evelyn Ho ⑤ ME2 . . . . .47 C8
    Otford TN14 . . . . .69 C2
Evelyn Rd Maidstone ME16 .91 E3
    Newham E16 . . . . .1 B5
Evenden House TN17 . . . .169 D5
Evenden Rd DA13 . . . . .44 A2
Evenlode Ho ⑤ SE2 . . . . . . .3 C4
Everard Ave BR2 . . . . .36 A1
Everest Cl ⑪ DA11 . . . . . . .29 E5
Everest Ct SE9 . . . . .22 E6
Everest Dr ME3 . . . . .34 E4
Everest La ME3 . . . . .34 B1
Everest Mews ME3 . . . . . . .34 E4
Everest Pl BR8 . . . . .39 D5
Everest Rd SE9 . . . . .5 F2
Everett Wlk DA17 . . . . .3 F1
Everglade Cl DA3 . . . . .42 F5
Everglades The ME7 . . . . . .62 F6
Evergreen Cl
    Gillingham ME7 . . . . .63 A5
    Higham ME3 . . . . .32 B3
    Leybourne ME19 . . . . . . .74 E2
Eversfield Ct SE12 . . . . . . .22 B6
Eversley Ave DA7,DA8 . . . . .8 E5
Eversley Cl ME16 . . . . .91 C6
Eversley Cross DA7 . . . . .8 E5
Eversley Rd SE7 . . . . .5 B8
Evesham Rd DA12 . . . . .30 D6
Evry Rd DA14 . . . . .24 C2
Ewart Rd SE4 . . . . .47 E1
Ewehurst La TN3 . . . . .147 F6
Ewell Ave ME19 . . . . .89 A8
Ewell La ME15 . . . . .105 D5
Ewins Cl TN12 . . . . .136 A6
Exedown Rd TN15 . . . . .71 C4
Exeter Ave Newham E6 . . . . .1 F7
    Tonbridge TN10 . . . . . . .117 D4
Exeter Rd Bexley DA16 . . . . .6 F5
    Gravesend DA12 . . . . . . .30 D5
    Newham E16 . . . . .1 A8
Exeter Wlk ME1 . . . . .61 C7
Exford Gdns SE12 . . . . .22 B7
Exford Rd SE12 . . . . .22 B7
Exmouth Rd Bexley DA16 . . .7 C7
    Bromley BR2 . . . . .36 B6
    Gillingham ME7 . . . . .48 C7
    Grays RM17 . . . . .12 B8
Exton Cl ME5 . . . . .62 C2
Exton Gdns ME14 . . . . .92 F5
Eyhorne St ME17 . . . . .94 D2
Eynsford Castle* DA4 . . . . .54 E8
Eynsford Cl BR5 . . . . .37 C3
Eynsford Cres DA5 . . . . . . .24 D7
Eynsford Rd Crockenhill BR8 39 E3
    Eynsford DA4 . . . . .40 F1
    Maidstone ME16 . . . . . . .91 D7
    Swanscombe DA9 . . . . . . .11 C2
Eynsford Rise DA4 . . . . . . .54 D6
Eynsford Sta DA4 . . . . .54 D6
Eynsham Dr SE2 . . . . .3 B3
Eynswood Dr DA14 . . . . . . .24 C3

F

F Ave SE18 . . . . .2 B3
Fackenden La TN14 . . . . . . .69 C7
Factory Rd Newham E16 . . . .1 E5
    Northfleet DA11 . . . . .12 C1
Faesten Way DA5 . . . . .25 E5
Fagus Cl ME5 . . . . .62 B1
Fair Acres BR2 . . . . .36 A4
Fair View TN5 . . . . .175 A6
Fair View
    Com Inf Sch ME8 . . . . . .63 C5
Fair View
    Com Jun Sch ME8 . . . . . .63 C5
Fairacre Pl DA3 . . . . .42 E6
Fairbank Ave BR6 . . . . .51 B8
Fairbourne Heath
    Cotts ME17 . . . . .110 B1
Fairbourne La ME17 . . . . .110 C4
Fairby La DA3 . . . . .42 E3
Fairby Rd SE12 . . . . .5 B2
Faircrouch La TN5 . . . . . .174 B5
Fairfax Bsns Ctr ME15 . . .107 F4
Fairfax Cl ME8 . . . . .63 D5
Fairfax Gdns SE3 . . . . .5 C6
Fairfax Mews E16 . . . . .1 B5
Fairfax Rd RM18 . . . . .12 F6
Fairfield Ave TN2 . . . . . . .149 C5
Fairfield Cl Kemsing TN15 . .70 A1
    Sidcup DA15 . . . . .6 F1
Fairfield Cres TN9 . . . . . . .133 C8
Fairfield Gr SE7 . . . . .5 D8
Fairfield Rd Bexley DA7 . . . . .7 F5
    Borough Green TN15 . . . . .86 F8
    Bromley BR1 . . . . .22 A1
    Orpington BR5 . . . . .37 D3
Fairfield Way TN11 . . . . . .116 F5
Fairfields DA12 . . . . .30 E3
Fairford Ave DA7 . . . . .8 D6
Fairglen Cotts TN5 . . . . . .174 B3
Fairglen Rd TN5 . . . . .174 B4
Fairhurst Dr ME15 . . . . . .106 B4
Fairings The TN30 . . . . . . .183 B8
Fairland Ho BR2 . . . . .36 B5
Fairlands Ct ⑥ SE9 . . . . . . .6 A1
Fairlawn SE7 . . . . .5 C8
Fairlawn Ave DA7 . . . . .7 D5
Fairlawn Cl ME18 . . . . . . .105 A8
Fairlawn Ct SE7 . . . . .5 C7
Fairlead Rd ME1 . . . . .47 D1
Fairlight Cl TN4 . . . . .133 A2
Fairlight Cross DA3 . . . . . . .43 C6
Fairlight Ct TN10 . . . . .117 B4

Fairman's La TN12 . . . . . .152 B6
Fairmead BR1 . . . . .36 F5
Fairmead Rd BR1 . . . . .36 F5
Fairmead Rd TN8 . . . . . . .112 C5
Fairmeadow ME14 . . . . . . .91 F4
Fairmile Rd TN2 . . . . .149 E5
Fairmont Cl DA17 . . . . .3 F1
Fairoak Cl BR5 . . . . .37 B2
Fairoak Dr SE9 . . . . .6 D2
Fairseat La Fairseat TN15 . .72 B5
    Stansted TN15 . . . . .57 A1
Fairthorn Rd SE7 . . . . .1 A1
Fairtrough Rd BR6 . . . . .67 B7
Fairview Erith DA8 . . . . .8 F7
    Fawkham Green DA3 . . . . .56 B7
    Hawkhurst TN18 . . . . . . .178 F2
Fairview Ave ME8 . . . . .63 B5
Fairview Cl TN9 . . . . .133 B7
Fairview Cotts ME15 . . . . .106 F5
Fairview Dr Higham ME3 . . .32 B4
    Orpington BR6 . . . . .51 D6
Fairview Gdns DA14 . . . . . .44 A4
Fairview Ind PK RM9 . . . . . .4 D8
Fairview Rd DA13 . . . . .29 E1
Fairwater Ave DA16 . . . . . . .7 A3
Fairway Bexley DA6 . . . . . . .7 E2
    Orpington BR5 . . . . .37 D4
Fairway Cl ME1 . . . . .47 C1
Fairway Ct ⑫ SE9 . . . . .6 A1
Fairway Dr Dartford DA2 . . .27 B8
    Woolwich SE28 . . . . .3 E7
Fairway The Bromley BR1 . .36 F4
    Gravesend DA11 . . . . . . .30 B6
    ⑧ Lewisham BR1 . . . . . . .22 B1
    Rochester ME1 . . . . .47 C1
Fairways The TN4 . . . . . . .149 A7
Falcon Ave Bromley BR1 . . .36 E5
    Grays RM17 . . . . .12 C7
Falcon Cl DA1 . . . . .9 F2
Falcon Gn ME20 . . . . .74 F1
Falcon Mews DA11 . . . . . . .29 E7
Falconwood Ave DA16 . . . . .6 E5
Falconwood Par DA16 . . . . . .6 F3
Falconwood Sta SE9 . . . . . . .6 D3
Falkland Pl ME5 . . . . .61 E1
Fallowfield Bean DA2 . . . . .28 B5
    Chatham ME5 . . . . .62 B8
Fallowfield Ct ME14 . . . . . .92 E4
Falmouth Pl TN12 . . . . . . .135 C7
Fanconi Rd ME5 . . . . .62 B3
Fancy Row ME14 . . . . .93 C5
Fane Way ME8 . . . . .63 D4
Fant La ME16 . . . . .91 B2
Faraday Ave DA14 . . . . . . .24 B6
Faraday Lodge ME2 . . . . .149 E5
Faraday Rd Bexley DA16 . . . .7 A4
    Maidstone ME14 . . . . . . .92 C7
Faraday Ride TN10 . . . . . .117 D7
Faraday Way
    Greenwich SE18 . . . . .1 D3
    Orpington BR5 . . . . .38 B5
Fareham Wlk ⑩ ME15 . . .107 F6
Farjeon Rd SE18,SE3 . . . . . .5 D6
Farleigh Ave BR2 . . . . .36 A2
Farleigh Ct ME16 . . . . .91 A2
Farleigh Hill ME15 . . . . . . .91 E1
Farleigh Hill Ret Pk
    ME15 . . . . .91 E1
Farleigh La ME16 . . . . .91 A1
Farleigh Trad Est ME15 . . .91 E1
Farley Cl ME5 . . . . .62 D2
Farley La TN16 . . . . .96 B8
Farley Rd DA12 . . . . .30 F7
Farleycroft TN16 . . . . .81 C1
Farlow Cl DA11 . . . . .29 F5
Farm Ave BR8 . . . . .39 C6
Farm Ground Cl TN9 . . . . .133 E8
Farm Hill Ave ME2 . . . . . . .32 F1
Farm Holt DA3 . . . . .42 F1
Farm La TN10 . . . . .117 A4
Farm Pl DA1 . . . . .9 A3
Farm Rd Chatham ME5 . . . .61 E3
    Sevenoaks TN14 . . . . . . .84 C7
Farm Vale DA5 . . . . .8 B1
Farmcombe Cl TN2 . . . . . .149 B2
Farmcombe La TN2 . . . . . .149 B2
Farmcombe Rd TN2 . . . . . .149 C2
Farmcote Rd SE12 . . . . . . .22 A7
Farmcroft DA11 . . . . .30 A6
Farmdale ME1 . . . . .46 F3
Farmdale Ave ME1 . . . . . . .46 F2
Farmdale Rd SE10 . . . . .1 A1
Farmer Cl ME17 . . . . .109 A6
Farmland Wlk BR7 . . . . . . .23 B3
Farmstead Dr TN8 . . . . . . .112 D3
Fananby Dr TN13 . . . . .84 A1
Faranby Rd SE9 . . . . .5 C3
Farnborough Cl ME16 . . . .91 C2
Farnborough Comm BR6 . .51 A6
Farnborough Ct ⑧ BR6 . . .51 D5
Farnborough Hill BR6 . . . . .51 C5
Farnborough Hospl BR6 . . .51 A6
Farnborough
    Prim Sch BR6 . . . . .51 C5
Farnborough Way BR6 . . . .51 D5
Farne Cl ME15 . . . . .107 A6
Farnham Beeches TN3 . . .148 A4
Farnham Cl Gillingham ME8 64 A8
    Royal Tunbridge Wells TN3 .148 A3
Farnham La TN3 . . . . .148 A4
Farnham Pl TN3 . . . . .148 A3
Farnham Rd DA16 . . . . .7 C5
Farningham Cl ME14 . . . . .92 C6
Farningham Hill Rd DA4 . . .40 D3
Farningham Road
    Sta DA4 . . . . .41 B7

Farningham Wood
    (Nature Reserve)*
    BR8,DA4 . . . . .40 D4
Farnol Rd DA1 . . . . .10 A3
Faro Cl BR1 . . . . .37 A7
Farraday Cl ME1 . . . . .61 D8
Farrance Ct TN1 . . . . .149 B4
Farrant Cl BR6 . . . . .52 A3
Farrier Cl Bromley BR1 . . . .36 D6
    Maidstone ME14 . . . . . . .92 E5
Farriers Cl DA12 . . . . .30 F7
Farriers Ct ME8 . . . . .64 C8
Farrington Ave BR5 . . . . . .38 B6
Farrington Pl BR7 . . . . .23 D1
Farrington Sch BR7 . . . . . .23 D1
Fartherwell Ave ME19 . . . .89 A8
Fartherwell Rd ME19 . . . . .89 A8
Farthing Cl DA1 . . . . .9 F3
Farthing Cnr ME9 . . . . .63 E3
Farthing Hill TN5 . . . . . . .176 E1
Farthing St BR6 . . . . .50 F2
Farthingfield TN15 . . . . . . .72 A3
Farthings Cotts ME14 . . . . .76 F1
Farwell Rd DA14 . . . . .24 C4
Farwig La BR1 . . . . .36 A8
Fashoda Rd BR2 . . . . .36 D5
Fauchon's Cl ME14 . . . . . . .92 F3
Fauchon's La ME14 . . . . . . .92 F4
Faversham Rd ME17 . . . . .111 E7
Fawkham Ave DA3 . . . . . . .43 C6
Fawkham
    CE Prim Sch DA3 . . . . . .42 B1
Fawkham Green Rd DA3 . . .56 B7
Fawkham House ⑧ BR5 . . .38 D1
Fawkham Manor
    Hospl DA3 . . . . .42 C1
Fawkham Rd Longfield DA3 42 D6
    West Kingsdown TN15 . . . .56 A4
Fawley Cl ME14 . . . . .91 E7
Fay Cl ME1 . . . . .47 B3
Faygate Cres DA6 . . . . .8 A2
Fazan Ct TN5 . . . . .174 F4
Fearon St SE10 . . . . .1 A1
Featherby Cotts ME7 . . . . .48 F6
Featherby Inf Sch ME8 . . . .49 A3
Featherby Jun Sch ME8 . . .49 A3
Featherby Rd
    Gillingham,Lower
    Twydall ME7 . . . . .49 A5
    Gillingham,Twydall ME8 . . .49 A3
Federation Rd SE2 . . . . .3 C2
Feenan Highway RM18 . . . .13 B6
Felderland Cl ME17 . . . . . .107 E5
Felderland Dr ME17 . . . . .107 E5
Felderland Rd ME17 . . . . .107 E5
Feldspar Ct ME5 . . . . .62 A1
Felhampton Rd SE9 . . . . . .23 B5
Felix Manor BR7 . . . . .23 E2
Felixstowe Rd SE2 . . . . .3 B3
Fell Mead TN12 . . . . .119 F6
Fellowes Way TN11 . . . . . .116 E5
Fellows Cl ME8 . . . . .63 B6
Felltram Way SE7 . . . . .1 A1
Felma Ho ⑪ SE7 . . . . .5 C8
Felspar Cl SE18 . . . . .2 F1
Felstead Rd BR6 . . . . .52 B8
Felsted Rd E16 . . . . .1 D7
Felton Cl BR5 . . . . .37 B3
Felton House SE3 . . . . .5 C3
Felton Lea DA14 . . . . .23 F3
Fen Gr DA15 . . . . .6 F1
Fen Mdw TN15 . . . . .71 C1
Fen Pond Rd TN15 . . . . . . .86 C7
Fendyke Rd DA17 . . . . .3 D3
Fenn Cl BR1 . . . . .22 A2
Fennel Cl ME16 . . . . .91 B3
Fennell Cl ME1 . . . . .47 B3
Fennell St SE18 . . . . .6 A8
Fens Way BR8 . . . . .26 A2
Fenton Cl BR7 . . . . .22 F3
Fenwick Cl ⑯ SE18 . . . . . . .6 A8
Ferbies TN3 . . . . .148 A7
Ferbies TN3 . . . . .148 A7
Ferby Ct DA15 . . . . .23 F4
Ferdinand Terr TN3 . . . . . .161 C7
Ferguson Ave DA12 . . . . . .30 C4
Fern Bank DA4 . . . . .54 E8
Fern Cl DA8 . . . . .9 B6
Fern Ct DA7 . . . . .8 A3
Fern Down DA13 . . . . .73 B8
Fern Hill Pl ⑧ BR6 . . . . . . .51 C5
Fernbank Cl ME5 . . . . .61 F2
Ferndale Bromley BR1 . . . . .36 C7
    Royal Tunbridge Wells TN2 .149 D5
    Sevenoaks TN13 . . . . . . .84 C5
Ferndale Cl Bexley DA7 . . . . .7 C6
    Royal Tunbridge Wells TN2 .149 C4
Ferndale Point TN2 . . . . . .149 C4
Ferndale Rd Gillingham ME7 48 E5
    Gravesend DA12 . . . . . . .30 B6
Ferndale St E6 . . . . .2 B7
Ferndale Way BR6 . . . . . . .51 D5
Ferndell Ave DA5 . . . . .25 D5
Ferndene DA3 . . . . .43 D6
Ferndown Ave BR6 . . . . . . .37 D1
Ferndown Cl ME7 . . . . .63 A5
Ferndown Rd SE9 . . . . .22 D8
Fernheath Way DA2 . . . . . .25 D3
Fernhill Rd ME16 . . . . .91 A2
Fernhill St E16 . . . . .1 F5
Fernholt TN10 . . . . .117 C7
Fernhurst Cres TN4 . . . . . .133 A2
Fernleigh Rise ME20 . . . . . .75 B1
Ferns The Larkfield ME20 . .75 B1
    Platt TN15 . . . . .87 C7
    Royal Tunbridge Wells TN1 .149 C4
Fernside La TN13 . . . . .99 D6
Fernwood Cl BR1 . . . . .36 C7

Ferranti Cl SE18 . . . . .1 D3
Ferrier Cl ME8 . . . . .63 E4
Ferrier Point **8** E16 . . . . . . .1 A8
Ferringham TN4 . . . . .148 F4
Ferry La Rainham RM13 . . . . .4 C8
 Wouldham ME1 . . . . .60 C4
Ferry Pl SE18 . . . . .2 A3
Ferry Rd Halling ME2 . . . . . .60 B4
 Tilbury RM18 . . . . .13 A4
Festival Ave DA3 . . . . .43 D6
Festival Cl Erith DA8 . . . . . . .8 F7
 Sidcup DA5 . . . . .24 D7
Ffinch Cl ME20 . . . . .90 D8
Fiddlers Cl DA9 . . . . .11 B3
Field Cl Bromley BR1 . . . . . .36 C7
 Chatham ME5 . . . . .61 E6
Field Dr TN8 . . . . .112 D3
Field Rd DA13,TN15 . . . . . .57 E6
Fieldfare Rd SE28 . . . . .3 C6
Fielding Ave RM18 . . . . . . .13 B6
Fielding Dr ME20 . . . . .75 A3
Fields La ME18 . . . . .104 E7
Fieldside Cl BR6 . . . . .51 C6
Fieldways TN18 . . . . .179 A1
Fieldworks Rd ME7 . . . . . . .48 A7
Fiennes Way TN13 . . . . . . .99 C8
Fiesta Dr RM9 . . . . .4 C8
Fife Rd E16 . . . . .1 A8
Fifteenpenny Fields SE9 . . . .6 A2
Fifth Ave RM20 . . . . .11 A8
Fiji Terr ME14 . . . . .92 A7
Filborough Way DA12 . . . . .31 B6
Filmer La TN14 . . . . .84 E6
Filston La TN14 . . . . .68 E5
Filston Rd DA8 . . . . .4 C1
Finch Ct ME14 . . . . .91 E7
Finchale Rd SE2 . . . . .3 A3
Finchcocks* TN17 . . . . . . .167 A5
Finchley Cl DA1 . . . . .10 A1
Finchley Rd RM17 . . . . . . .12 B8
Findlay Cl ME8 . . . . .63 D6
Finglesham Cl ME15 . . . . . .38 D1
Finglesham Ct ME15 . . . . .107 C8
Finsbury Way DA5 . . . . .7 F1
Fintonagh Dr ME14 . . . . . . .92 B6
Finucane Dr BR5 . . . . .38 C2
Fir Dene BR6 . . . . .51 A7
Fir Tree Cl
 5 Orpington BR6 . . . . . . .51 F5
 Staplehurst TN12 . . . . . .139 F3
 Tonbridge TN11 . . . . . . .116 E5
Fir Tree Gr Bredhurst ME7 . . .63 B1
 Chatham ME5 . . . . .62 D1
Fir Tree Rd TN4 . . . . .148 F3
Firbank Cl E16 . . . . .1 D8
Fircroft Way TN8 . . . . .112 C3
Firecrest Cl DA3 . . . . .43 B6
Firethorn Cl ME7 . . . . .48 E6
Firmin Ave ME17 . . . . . . .107 D5
Firmin Rd DA1 . . . . .9 C2
Firmingers Rd BR6 . . . . . . .53 C5
Firs Cl ME20 . . . . .75 E1
Firs Ct TN4 . . . . .148 F6
Firs The Coldblow DA5 . . . . .25 D7
 Sidcup DA15 . . . . .23 F5
Firside Gr DA15 . . . . .23 F7
First Ave Bexley DA7 . . . . . . .7 C7
 Chatham ME4 . . . . .48 C2
 Gillingham ME7 . . . . .48 E3
 Northfleet DA11 . . . . .29 E7
 West Thurrock RM20 . . . . .11 A8
First La ME15 . . . . .93 E2
First St TN3 . . . . .147 F3
Fisher Rd ME5 . . . . .62 B7
Fisher St Maidstone ME14 . . .92 A6
 Newham E16 . . . . .1 A8
Fisher's Gate Cotts TN7 . . .160 A1
Fisher's Way DA17 . . . . .4 C5
Fishermans Wlk SE28 . . . . . .2 E4
Fishermen's Hill DA11 . . . . .12 B2
Fishers Cl TN12 . . . . .139 F5
Fishers Rd TN12 . . . . .139 F5
Fishguard Way E16 . . . . .2 B5
Fishponds Rd BR2 . . . . . . .50 D5
Fitzroy Ct DA1 . . . . .27 B7
Fitzthorold Ho ME7 . . . . . . .48 E7
Fitzwilliam Mews E16 . . . . . .1 A5
Fitzwilliam Rd ME14 . . . . . .92 F5
Five Acre Wood
 Sch ME15 . . . . .107 B7
Five Bells La ME1 . . . . .47 D4
Five Elms Rd BR2 . . . . . . .50 C4
Five Fields La TN8 . . . . . . .113 B4
Five Oak Green Rd
 Five Oak Green TN11,TN12 .134 D6
 Tonbridge TN11 . . . . . . .133 F7
Five Oak La TN12 . . . . . . .139 B1
Five Ways Ct ME4 . . . . . . .48 A4
Five Wents BR8 . . . . .40 A4
Fiveash Rd DA11 . . . . .29 F8
Fiveways TN1 . . . . .149 A4
Fiveways L Ctr ME4 . . . . . .48 A4
Flack Gdns ME3 . . . . .34 E5
Flamingo Cl ME2 . . . . .62 A7
Flamsteed Rd SE7 . . . . .1 E1
Flats The Gravesend DA12 . . .30 E8
 Swanscombe DA9 . . . . . . .11 C2
Flaxman Ct Erith DA17 . . . . .4 A1
 13 Gillingham ME7 . . . . .48 A6
Flaxman Dr ME16 . . . . .91 C6
Flaxmore Ct DA7 . . . . .8 A4
Flaxmore Pl TN4 . . . . .133 A2
Flaxton Rd SE18 . . . . .6 E7
Fleet Ave DA2 . . . . .27 C7
Fleet Dale Par DA2 . . . . . . .27 C7
Fleet Ho DA13 . . . . .29 B2
Fleet Rd Dartford DA2 . . . . .27 C7

Fleet Rd continued
 Northfleet DA11 . . . . .29 C6
 Rochester ME1 . . . . .47 D1
Fleetdown Inf Sch DA2 . . . .27 C6
Fleetdown Jun Sch DA2 . . . .27 C6
Fleetwood Cl E16 . . . . .1 D8
Fleetwood Cl **1** Newham E6 .1 B8
 Orpington BR6 . . . . .51 A6
Fleming Gdns RM18 . . . . . .13 C6
Fleming Ho SE2 . . . . .3 C1
Fleming Way Erith SE28 . . . . .3 B7
 Tonbridge TN10 . . . . . . .117 E7
Fletcher Cl E6 . . . . .2 B6
Fletcher Rd TN12 . . . . . . .139 E3
Fletchers Cl BR2 . . . . .36 B5
Fletching Rd SE7 . . . . .5 D8
Flimwell Bird Pk* TN5 . . . .177 E2
Flimwell CI TN5 . . . . .177 D4
Flint Cl **8** BR6 . . . . .51 F4
Flint Down Cl BR5 . . . . . . .38 A8
Flint Gn ME5 . . . . .62 C3
Flint La ME17 . . . . .111 C8
Flint St ME15 . . . . .11 B8
Flintmill Cres SE3,SE9 . . . . .5 E5
Floats The TN13 . . . . .83 E6
Flood Hatch ME15 . . . . . . .91 D2
Flora St SE17 . . . . .3 F1
Florance La TN3 . . . . .161 B6
Florence Cl RM17,RM20 . . . .11 E8
Florence Cotts TN8 . . . . . .112 C1
Florence Farm Mobile
 Home Pk TN15 . . . . .55 D4
Florence House SE18 . . . . . .5 F6
Florence Rd
 1 Bromley BR1 . . . . . . .36 A8
 Erith DA8,SE2 . . . . .3 C2
 Maidstone ME16 . . . . .91 E3
Florence St **3** ME2 . . . . . .47 B8
Florin Dr ME1 . . . . .47 B4
Flower Rise ME14 . . . . .91 F7
Flowerfield TN14 . . . . .68 F2
Flowerhill Way DA13 . . . . . .29 E1
Floyd Cl TN4 . . . . .149 A8
Floyd Rd SE7 . . . . .1 C1
Flume End ME15 . . . . .91 D2
Flyers Way The TN16 . . . . . .81 D1
Foalhurst Cl TN10 . . . . . . .117 E4
Foley Cl DA1 . . . . .27 B7
Foley St ME14 . . . . .92 A5
Folkstone
 House **4** ME15 . . . . . .107 F6
Fontwell Cl ME15 . . . . . . .107 F6
Fontwell Dr BR2 . . . . .37 A4
Foord Almshouses ME1 . . . .47 B3
Foord Cl DA2 . . . . .27 E6
Foord Rd ME17 . . . . .111 D5
Foord St ME1 . . . . .47 D4
Footbury Hill Rd BR6 . . . . . .38 A2
Foots Cray High St DA14 . . .24 D2
Foots Cray La DA14 . . . . . .24 C7
Footscray Rd SE9 . . . . .23 C7
Force Green La TN16 . . . . . .81 E4
Ford Ho **2** SE18 . . . . .2 B1
Ford La Trottiscliffe ME19 . . .73 A4
 Wrotham Heath TN15,ME19 . .72 F2
Ford Rd DA11 . . . . .12 B2
Fordcombe
 CE Prim Sch TN3 . . . . . .147 B5
Fordcombe Cl ME15 . . . . .107 F7
Fordcombe Rd
 Fordcombe TN3 . . . . . . .147 C4
 Penshurst TN11 . . . . . . .131 A3
Fordcroft Rd BR5 . . . . .38 B4
Forde Ave BR1 . . . . .36 C6
Fordingbridge Cl ME19 . . . .91 B5
Fords Park Rd E16 . . . . .1 A7
Fordwich Cl
 Maidstone ME16 . . . . .91 B7
 Orpington BR6 . . . . .37 F2
Fordwich Dr ME2 . . . . .33 A2
Fordwich Gn ME8 . . . . .49 C3
Foreland St SE18 . . . . .2 D2
Foreman Ct TN12 . . . . . . .141 C5
Foremans Barn Rd ME15 . . .105 F3
Forest Cl BR7 . . . . .37 A8
Forest Dene TN2 . . . . .149 C1
Forest Dr Chatham ME5 . . . .61 F2
 Orpington BR2 . . . . .50 E6
Forest Gr TN10 . . . . .117 C5
Forest Hill ME15 . . . . .91 F1
Forest Lawns BR1 . . . . . . .36 C8
Forest Rd Erith DA8 . . . . . . .9 A6
 Paddock Wood TN12 . . . .136 A6
 Royal Tunbridge Wells TN2 .149 C1
Forest Ridge BR2 . . . . .50 F6
Forest Way Kings Hill ME19 . .89 A3
 Orpington BR5 . . . . .37 F4
 Pembury TN2 . . . . .150 D8
 Royal Tunbridge Wells TN2 .149 D1
 Sidcup DA15 . . . . .23 D8
Forestdale Rd ME5 . . . . . . .77 A8
Foresters Cl ME5 . . . . .61 F2
Foresters Cres DA7 . . . . . . .8 B3
Forge Cl
 Five Oak Green TN12 . . . .135 B7
 Hayes BR2 . . . . .36 A1
 Penshurst TN11 . . . . . . .131 B4
Forge Cotts ME18 . . . . . . .104 C2
Forge Croft TN8 . . . . .112 D1
Forge La Benover ME18 . . . .121 B4
 Boxley ME14 . . . . .77 C2
 Bredhurst ME7 . . . . .63 A1
 East Farleigh ME15 . . . . .106 C7
 Egerton Forstal TN27 . . . .127 C1
 Gillingham ME7 . . . . .48 C1
 Gravesend DA12 . . . . .30 F6
 Headcorn TN27 . . . . .141 D5
 High Halstow ME23 . . . . . .17 E3

Forge La continued
 Higham ME3 . . . . .32 C3
 Horton Kirby DA4 . . . . . . .41 C5
 Leeds ME17 . . . . .108 F7
 Rabbit's Cross ME17,TN12 .123 F3
 Shorne DA12 . . . . .31 E3
 West Kingsdown TN15 . . . .56 A1
 West Peckham ME18 . . . .103 A6
Forge Lane
 Cty Inf Sch ME7 . . . . . . .48 E6
Forge Meadow ME17 . . . . .110 D6
Forge Meadows TN27 . . . .141 D5
Forge Meads TN30 . . . . . .189 E3
Forge Pl DA12 . . . . .30 F7
Forge Rd Cobbarn TN3 . . . .161 C2
 Royal Tunbridge Wells TN4 .133 A1
Forge Sq TN11 . . . . .115 F2
Forge The TN12 . . . . .135 B7
Forge View TN15 . . . . .100 B5
Forge Way
 Paddock Wood TN12 . . . .136 A7
 Shoreham TN14 . . . . .68 F8
Forgefield Cotts TN18 . . . .186 A4
Forgefield Ct BR5 . . . . .38 C4
Formby Rd ME2 . . . . .60 A7
Formby Terr ME2 . . . . .60 A6
Forsham La ME17 . . . . . . .124 C5
Forson Cl TN30 . . . . .183 B8
Forstal Cl BR2 . . . . .36 A6
Forstal Cotts ME20 . . . . . . .76 B2
Forstal La ME17 . . . . .106 D4
Forstal Rd
 Egerton Forstal TN27 . . . .127 C1
 Pratling Street ME20 . . . . .76 C2
Forstal The Cobbarn TN3 . . .161 F3
 Hadlow TN11 . . . . .118 F8
 Pembury TN2 . . . . .150 E8
Forstall TN3 . . . . .148 A4
Forstall The TN11 . . . . . . .116 A2
Forsters ME17 . . . . .108 E4
Forsyth Cl ME19 . . . . .75 A1
Fort Amherst Heritage Pk
 & Caverns* ME4 . . . . . . .47 F5
Fort Luton (Mus)* ME4 . . . .48 A1
Fort Pitt Gram Sch ME4 . . . .47 E4
Fort Pitt Hill ME1,ME4 . . . . .47 E4
Fort Pitt St ME4 . . . . .47 E4
Fort Rd Badgers Mount TN14 .68 C4
 Tilbury RM18 . . . . .13 C5
Fort St Newham E16 . . . . . . .1 B5
 Rochester ME1 . . . . .47 D4
Fortis Cl E16 . . . . .1 C7
Fortrye Cl DA11 . . . . .29 C6
Fortuna Cl DA3 . . . . .42 F5
Fortune Wlk SE28 . . . . .2 D3
Forty Acre La E16 . . . . .1 A8
Forward Way ME1 . . . . . . .61 C6
Fossdene Prim Sch SE7 . . . .1 B1
Fossdene Rd SE7 . . . . .1 B1
Fosse Bank Cl TN9 . . . . . .133 C4
Fosse Bank
 New Sch TN11 . . . . .116 E7
Fosse Rd TN9 . . . . .117 B2
Fossington Rd DA17 . . . . . . .3 D2
Fosten La TN27 . . . . .171 E7
Foster Clark Est ME15 . . . . .92 A3
Foster Clarke Dr ME17 . . . .107 D5
Foster St ME15 . . . . .92 A3
Fosters Cl BR7 . . . . .22 F3
Fosters Old Sch DA16 . . . . . .7 B5
Fosters Prim Sch DA16 . . . . .7 C4
Fostington Way ME5 . . . . . .61 F1
Foulds Cl ME8 . . . . .63 B5
Founder Cl E6 . . . . .2 B8
Foundry Wharf ME1 . . . . . .47 E4
Fountain Ct Eynsford DA4 . . .54 E8
 Sidcup DA15 . . . . .7 B1
Fountain Ent Pk ME15 . . . . .92 A1
Fountain La ME16 . . . . .91 A2
Fountain Rd ME2 . . . . .32 C1
Fountain Wlk DA11 . . . . . . .12 F1
Four Acres ME19 . . . . .90 B5
Four Elms Hill ME3 . . . . . . .32 C1
Four Elms Prim Sch TN8 . . .113 D4
Four Elms Rd TN8 . . . . . . .112 D4
Four Elms Rdbt ME3 . . . . . .33 E3
Four Oaks Rd TN12,TN27 . .140 E7
Four Wents
 Langley Heath ME17 . . . . .108 E3
 Maidstone ME17 . . . . . . .107 F5
Fouracre Cotts ME9 . . . . . .64 E6
Fourth Ave Gillingham ME7 . .48 E4
 West Thurrock RM20 . . . . .11 A8
Fowey Cl ME5 . . . . .62 C5
Fowler Cl Gillingham ME8 . . .63 C3
 Sidcup DA14 . . . . .24 C3
Fox Cl Newham E16 . . . . . . .1 A7
 Orpington BR6 . . . . .52 A5
Fox Gr TN15 . . . . .86 F7
Fox Hollow Cl **2** SE18 . . . . .2 E1
Fox Hollow Dr DA7 . . . . .7 D4
Fox House Rd DA17 . . . . . . .4 B2
Fox in the Wood TN5 . . . .174 C6
Fox La BR2 . . . . .50 C5
Fox Manor Way RM20 . . . . .11 B8
Fox St ME7 . . . . .48 C6
Foxburrow Cl ME8 . . . . . . .63 D5
Foxbury DA3 . . . . .56 F7
Foxbury Ave BR7 . . . . .23 D2
Foxbury Cl Bromley BR1 . . . .22 B7
 Orpington BR6 . . . . .52 A5
Foxbury Dr BR6 . . . . .52 A4
Foxbury Rd BR1 . . . . .22 B2
Foxbury Wlk DA11 . . . . . . .29 C6
Foxbush TN11 . . . . .116 C6
Foxcroft Rd SE18 . . . . .6 B6
Foxden Dr ME15 . . . . .92 F1

Foxdown La DA13 . . . . . .44 B1
Foxes Dale SE3 . . . . .5 A4
Foxfield Prim Sch SE18 . . . .2 C2
Foxfield Rd BR6 . . . . .51 D8
Foxglove Cl **9** TN8 . . . . .112 D3
Foxglove Cres ME5 . . . . . .61 E4
Foxglove Rise ME14 . . . . . .91 E7
Foxgloves The TN12 . . . . .136 B5
Foxhole La
 Four Throws TN18 . . . . . .179 E1
 Matfield TN12 . . . . .151 C8
 Wadhurst TN5 . . . . .175 B4
Foxhole Rd SE9 . . . . .5 E2
Foxhome Cl BR7 . . . . .23 A2
Foxtail Cl ME4 . . . . .34 B2
Foxton Cl E16 . . . . .2 A4
Foxton Rd RM20 . . . . .11 D8
Foxwood Gr
 Northfleet DA11 . . . . .29 E7
 Pratt's Bottom BR6 . . . . . .52 C1
Foxwood Rd DA2 . . . . .28 B5
Foxwood Way DA3 . . . . . . .43 D7
Framley Rd TN10 . . . . . . .117 D5
Framlingham Cres SE9 . . . . .22 F4
Frances St SE18 . . . . .1 F7
Francis Ave DA7 . . . . .8 A5
Francis Dr ME5 . . . . .62 A2
Francis La ME15 . . . . .107 F5
Francis Rd Dartford DA1 . . . . .9 D2
 St Paul's Cray BR5 . . . . . .38 D5
 Tonbridge TN11 . . . . . . .116 D6
Frank Burton Cl **4** SE7 . . . .1 B1
Frank Woolley Rd TN10 . . . .117 F5
Frank's Hollow Rd TN3 . . . .132 C2
Frankapps Cl ME9 . . . . . . .65 B6
Frankfield Rise TN2 . . . . . .149 A1
Franklin Dr ME14 . . . . .92 A4
Franklin Pas SE9 . . . . .5 E4
Franklin Rd Bexley DA7 . . . . .7 E6
 Gillingham ME7 . . . . .48 D5
 Gravesend DA12 . . . . .30 D3
Franklins Cotts ME15 . . . . .106 C5
Franks Ct ME8 . . . . .49 B2
Franks La DA4 . . . . .41 B4
Frankswood Ave BR5 . . . . . .37 C4
Frant Field TN3 . . . . .112 C1
Frant CE Prim Sch TN3 . . . .163 B4
Frant Rd TN2,TN3 . . . . . . .163 A2
Frant Sta TN3 . . . . .163 F5
Fraser Cl Coldblow DA5 . . . .25 C7
 3 Newham E6 . . . . .1 E7
Fraser Ho **3** SE18 . . . . . . .2 A2
Fraser Rd DA8 . . . . .4 D1
Frederick Andrews
 Ct RM17 . . . . .12 D8
Frederick Ho **4** SE18 . . . . .1 B3
Frederick Pl SE18 . . . . .2 B1
Frederick Rd ME7 . . . . .48 C4
Free Heath Rd TN3,TN5 . . . .165 C3
Freehold The
 East Peckham TN12 . . . . .119 F6
 Hadlow TN11 . . . . .102 D1
Freeland Way DA8 . . . . .9 A6
Freelands Gr BR1 . . . . .36 B8
Freelands Rd Bromley BR1 . .36 B8
 Snodland ME6 . . . . .74 F8
Freeman Gdns ME4 . . . . . .47 F2
Freeman Rd DA12 . . . . . . .30 E5
Freeman Way ME15 . . . . . .107 E7
Freemasons Rd E16 . . . . . . .1 B7
Freesia Cl Gillingham ME7 . . .48 F6
 Orpington BR6 . . . . .51 F5
Freight La TN17 . . . . .169 C3
Fremantle House RM18 . . . .12 F6
Fremantle Rd DA17 . . . . . . .4 A2
Fremlin Cl TN4 . . . . .148 B4
Fremlins Rd ME14 . . . . .93 C4
Frensham
 Rolvenden TN17 . . . . . . .182 A1
 Sidcup SE9 . . . . .23 D6
Frensham Wlk ME5 . . . . . . .61 F1
Freshland Rd ME16 . . . . . . .91 B4
Freshwater Rd ME5 . . . . . . .62 B7
Freta Rd DA6 . . . . .7 F2
Frewing Cl BR7 . . . . .23 A3
Friar Rd BR5 . . . . .38 A4
Friars Ave ME5 . . . . .61 F2
Friars Mews SE9 . . . . .6 A2
Friars The* ME20 . . . . .75 E2
Friars Way TN2 . . . . .149 D6
Friars Wlk SE2 . . . . .3 D1
Friary Pl **3** ME2 . . . . .47 B7
Friary Prec ME2 . . . . .47 B7
Friday Rd DA8 . . . . .4 D1
Friday St ME17 . . . . .125 B6
Friezland Rd TN4 . . . . .148 D1
Friezley La TN17 . . . . .155 C1
Frimley Ct DA14 . . . . .24 C3
Frindsbury Hill ME2 . . . . . . .33 C1
Frindsbury Rd ME2 . . . . . . .47 B8
Frinstead Gr BR5 . . . . .38 D5
Frinstead Wlk ME16 . . . . . .91 B7
Frinsted Cl ME8 . . . . .49 C3
Frinsted Rd DA8 . . . . .8 D7
Frinton Rd DA14 . . . . .24 E6
Friston Way ME1 . . . . .61 D8
Friswell Pl **1** DA6 . . . . .8 A3
Frithwood Cl ME15 . . . . . . .92 F1
Frittenden
 CE Prim Sch TN17 . . . . . .156 E6
Frittenden Rd
 Rochester ME2 . . . . .33 D2
 Staplehurst TN12 . . . . . . .140 B2
Frobisher Gdns ME1 . . . . . .47 C2
Frobisher Rd Erith DA8 . . . . .9 A7
 Newham E6 . . . . .2 A1
Frobisher Way
 Gravesend DA12 . . . . .30 E3

Frobisher Way continued
 Swanscombe DA9 . . . . . . .11 B3
Frog La Rainham RM9 . . . . . .4 D8
 Royal Tunbridge Wells TN1 .149 A2
 West Malling ME19 . . . . . .89 C8
Frog's La TN17 . . . . .181 E1
Frogholt La TN8,TN16 . . . . . .96 D2
Frognal Ave DA14 . . . . . . .24 A2
Frognal Cnr BR7 . . . . .23 F2
Frognal Pl DA14 . . . . .24 A2
Frogs Hole La TN17,TN27 . .171 E3
Froissart Rd SE9 . . . . .5 E2
Fromandez Dr TN12 . . . . . .152 F5
Frome Ct TN10 . . . . .117 B5
Front Cotts TN5 . . . . .176 E1
Frost Cres ME5 . . . . .62 A7
Froyle Cl ME15 . . . . .91 C6
Fruitfields TN5 . . . . .177 C3
Fry Cl ME3 . . . . .21 A6
Fry's Cotts ME3 . . . . .19 C4
Frythe Cl TN17 . . . . .169 D4
Frythe Cres TN17 . . . . . . .169 D4
Frythe Way TN17 . . . . . . .169 D4
Frythe Wlk TN17 . . . . .169 D4
Fuchsia St SE2 . . . . .3 B1
Fuggles Cl TN12 . . . . .135 C6
Fuggles Ct TN17 . . . . .180 D6
Fulbert Dr ME14 . . . . .92 F5
Fuller Cl Orpington BR6 . . . .51 F5
 Wadhurst TN5 . . . . .174 E5
Fullers Cl ME14 . . . . .93 A4
Fullers Hill **7** TN16 . . . . . .81 D1
Fulmar Rd ME2 . . . . .46 D6
Fulmer Rd E16 . . . . .1 D8
Fulthorp Rd SE3 . . . . .5 A5
Fulwich Rd DA1 . . . . .9 F1
Furfield Cl ME17 . . . . .107 E5
Furnace Ave TN3 . . . . .166 A3
Furnace La
 Hook Green TN3 . . . . . . .165 E4
 Horsmonden TN12 . . . . . .152 F7
Furner Cl DA1 . . . . .8 F4
Furness Sch BR8 . . . . .25 F2
Furnival Ct TN2 . . . . .162 F8
Furrell's Rd ME1 . . . . .47 D5
Further Field TN12 . . . . . .139 E5
Furze Bank TN8 . . . . .113 B5
Furzefield Ave TN3 . . . . . .148 A8
Furzefield Cl BR7 . . . . .23 B2
Furzefield Rd SE3 . . . . .5 B7
Furzehill Sq BR5 . . . . .38 B5
Fyfe Way BR1 . . . . .36 A7

G

Gable Cl DA1 . . . . .9 A2
Gables Cl SE12 . . . . .22 A7
Gables The **10** Bromley BR1 .22 B1
 New Barn DA3 . . . . .43 C6
Gabriel Gdns DA12 . . . . . . .30 E3
Gabriel Spring Road
 (East) DA3 . . . . .55 F8
Gabriel's Hill ME15 . . . . . . .92 A4
Gabrielspring Rd DA3 . . . . .55 D8
Gads Hill ME7 . . . . .48 F6
Gads Hill Sch ME3 . . . . . . .32 C2
Gadsby La TN26 . . . . .159 F3
Gadwall Cl E16 . . . . .1 B7
Gadwall Way SE28 . . . . .2 D4
Gafford's Bridge
 Cotts TN12 . . . . .137 C4
Gagetown Terr **1** ME14 . . . .91 F7
Gainsborough Ave
 Dartford DA1 . . . . .9 C2
 Tilbury RM18 . . . . .13 B6
Gainsborough Cl ME8 . . . . .63 D6
Gainsborough Ct **3** BR2 . . . .36 C5
Gainsborough Dr
 Maidstone ME16 . . . . .91 B4
 Northfleet DA11 . . . . .29 D5
Gainsborough
 Gdns TN10 . . . . .117 C5
Gainsborough Ho ME1 . . . . .47 D5
Gainsborough Sq DA7 . . . . . .7 D4
Gaitskell Rd SE9 . . . . .23 C7
Galahad Ave ME2 . . . . .46 E6
Galahad Rd BR1 . . . . .22 A4
Galena Cl ME5 . . . . .62 A1
Galena Ho **4** SE18 . . . . . . .2 F1
Gallants La ME15 . . . . . . .105 F6
Galleon Bvd DA2 . . . . .10 D3
Galleon Cl Chatham ME1 . . .61 C8
 Erith DA8 . . . . .4 D2
Galley Hill Rd DA11,DA10 . . .11 F2
Galley Hill Trad Est DA10 . . .11 E2
Gallions Mount
 Prim Sch SE18 . . . . .2 F1
Gallions Cl E16 . . . . .2 C6
Gallions Reach Sta E6 . . . . . .2 B6
Gallions View Rd SE28 . . . . .2 E1
Gallon Cl SE7 . . . . .1 C2
Gallops The DA13 . . . . . . .72 F7
Gallosson Rd SE18 . . . . .2 E2
Gallus Sq SE3 . . . . .5 B4
Galsworthy Cl SE28 . . . . . . .3 B5
Galsworthy Cres SE3 . . . . . .5 C6
Galsworthy Rd RM18 . . . . . .13 C6
Galton House SE18 . . . . .5 F6
Games Ho **6** SE7 . . . . .5 C8
Gamma Rd ME3 . . . . .35 D7
Gandy's La ME17 . . . . . . .107 C2
Garden Ave DA7 . . . . .8 A4
Garden Cl Ide Hill TN16 . . . .97 C3

Garden Cl continued
Lewisham SE12 . . . . .22 B5
Maidstone ME15 . . . . . .107 E7
Staplehurst TN12 . . . . . . .139 F1
Garden Cotts Leigh TN11 .116 A2
St Paul's Cray BR5 . . . . . . .38 C7
Garden Ct 10 SE9 . . . . .6 A1
Garden La BR1 . . . . .22 B2
Garden of England Pk (Mobile Home Pk)
ME17 . . . . .110 B7
Garden Pl DA2 . . . . .26 D5
Garden Rd Bromley BR1 . . . .22 B2
Royal Tunbridge Wells TN1 .149 B4
Sevenoaks TN13 . . . . . . .84 D5
Tonbridge TN9 . . . . .117 D2
Garden Row DA11 . . . . . . .29 F5
Garden St Gillingham ME7 . .48 A6
Royal Tunbridge Wells TN1 .149 B4
Garden Terr TN15 . . . . .85 A6
Garden Way ME19 . . . . . . .88 F2
Gardenia Cl ME2 . . . . .33 B2
Gardens The ME17 . . . . . .106 C3
Gardiner Cl BR5 . . . . .38 C7
Gardiner Ho SE18 . . . . .5 E7
Gardiner St ME7 . . . . .48 C6
Gardyne Mews 12 TN9 .133 B8
Gareth Gr BR1 . . . . .22 A4
Garfield Rd ME7 . . . . .48 D6
Gargany Wlk SE28 . . . . .3 D6
Garibaldi St SE18 . . . . .2 E2
Garland Rd SE18 . . . . .6 D7
Garlands TN11 . . . . .116 D8
Garline Rd TN4 . . . . .133 A1
Garner Dr ME19 . . . . .75 A1
Garnet Wlk 8 E6 . . . . .1 E8
Garnett Cl SE9 . . . . .5 F4
Garrard Cl Bexley DA7 . . . . . .8 A4
Chislehurst BR7 . . . . .23 B3
Garrick Dr SE28 . . . . .2 D3
Garrick St 16 DA11 . . . . . . .13 B1
Garrington Cl ME14 . . . . . . .92 C6
Garrison Cl SE18 . . . . .6 A7
Garrison Rd ME12 . . . . .21 F3
Garrolds Cl BR8 . . . . .39 D7
Garrow DA3 . . . . .43 B6
Garside Cl SE28 . . . . .2 D3
Garth Rd TN13 . . . . .99 C7
Gartly Cotts DA1 . . . . .9 C1
Garvary Rd E16 . . . . .1 B7
Garvock Dr TN13 . . . . .84 A1
Gas House Rd ME1 . . . . . . .47 C6
Gascoyne Cl ME15 . . . . . . .93 B2
Gascoyne Dr DA1 . . . . .8 F4
Gasoline Alley TN15 . . . . . .72 D2
Gasson Rd DA10 . . . . .11 E1
Gassons Rd ME6 . . . . .74 E8
Gatcombe Cl Chatham ME5 .62 A5
Maidstone ME16 . . . . . . .91 B5
Gatcombe Rd E16 . . . . .1 A5
Gate Farm Rd TN3,TN11 . .132 C4
Gateacre Ct 14 DA14 . . . . . .24 B4
Gatefield Cotts TN17 . . . . .181 F4
Gatehouse Farm Cotts TN3 . . . . .132 C4
Gatekeeper Chase ME8 . . . .63 F8
Gates Green Rd BR2,BR4 . .50 A6
Gateway Par DA12 . . . . . . .30 F4
Gatland La ME16 . . . . .91 B2
Gatling Rd SE18,SE2 . . . . . . .3 A1
Gaton Rd SE2 . . . . .3 C3
Gattons Way DA14 . . . . . . .24 F4
Gatwick Farm Cotts RH19 . . . . .144 A4
Gatwick Rd DA12 . . . . .30 B6
Gault Cl ME15 . . . . .93 A2
Gautrey Sq 5 E6 . . . . .1 F7
Gavestone Cres SE12 . . . . . .22 B8
Gavestone Rd SE12 . . . . . . .22 B8
Gavin Ho SE18 . . . . .2 E2
Gayhurst Cl ME8 . . . . .63 D6
Gaylor Rd RM18 . . . . .12 F6
Gazelle Glade DA12 . . . . . .30 F3
Gean Cl ME5 . . . . .77 A8
Geddes Pl 3 DA6 . . . . .8 A3
Gedge's Hill TN12 . . . . . . .135 F3
Geffery's Ct SE9 . . . . .22 E5
General Gordon Pl 2 SE18 .2 B2
Genesta Glade DA12 . . . . . .31 A3
Genesta Rd SE18 . . . . .6 C8
Geneva Ave ME8 . . . . .49 A2
Gentian Cl 4 Chatham ME5 .61 E4
Maidstone ME14 . . . . . . .92 E5
George Akass Ho 3 SE18 . .2 C1
George Crooks House 7 RM17 . . . . . . .12 B8
George La Hayes BR2 . . . . . .36 B1
Leeds ME17 . . . . .109 B7
Rochester ME2 . . . . .47 C6
George Marsham House ME15 . . . . .106 F3
George St Chainhurst ME15 . . . . . . .122 A7
Grays RM17 . . . . .12 A8
Maidstone ME15 . . . . . . .92 A3
Royal Tunbridge Wells TN2 .149 C3
Staplehurst TN12 . . . . . . .139 E6
Tonbridge TN9 . . . . .133 B8
Wadhurst TN5 . . . . .174 F5
George Summers Cl ME2 .47 B8
Georges Cl BR5 . . . . .38 C6
Georgian Cl BR2 . . . . .36 B1
Georgian Dr ME17 . . . . . . .106 D3
Georgian Way ME8 . . . . . . .63 C4

Geraint Rd BR1 . . . . .22 A4
Gerald Ave ME4 . . . . .47 F2
Gerald Rd DA12 . . . . .30 E8
Gerda Rd SE9 . . . . .23 C6
Gerdview Dr DA2 . . . . .26 C4
Gerrard Ave ME1 . . . . .61 E8
Gertrude Rd DA17 . . . . .4 A2
Gibbet La TN12 . . . . .152 F6
Gibbetts TN3 . . . . .147 F3
Gibbs Hill Headcorn TN27 .141 E5
Nettlestead ME18 . . . . . .104 B5
Gibraltar Ave ME7 . . . . . . .48 B7
Gibraltar Hill ME4 . . . . . . .47 F4
Gibraltar La ME14 . . . . . . .91 F8
Gibson Cl DA11 . . . . .29 F5
Gibson Dr ME15 . . . . .6 A4
Gidd's Pond Cotts ME14 . . .92 E6
Giddyhorn La ME16 . . . . . .91 C5
Gideon Cl DA17 . . . . .4 B2
Gifford Cl ME8 . . . . .49 C3
Giggs Hill BR5 . . . . .38 A8
Gighill Rd ME20 . . . . .74 F4
Gilbert Cl Eltham SE18 . . . . . .5 F6
Gillingham ME7 . . . . .63 A5
Swanscombe DA10 . . . . . .11 D1
Gilbert Rd Bromley BR1 . . . .22 A1
Erith DA17 . . . . .4 A3
Gilbert Terr 2 ME14 . . . . . .91 F7
Gilbourne Rd SE18 . . . . .6 F8
Gilchrist Cotts TN14 . . . . . . .99 C2
Gildenhill Rd BR8 . . . . .26 C1
Gildersome St SE18 . . . . . . .6 B8
Gill Ave Newham E16 . . . . . . .1 A7
Rochester ME2 . . . . .33 D2
Gill Cres DA11 . . . . .29 F5
Gill Ct SE18 . . . . .2 C1
Gill The TN2 . . . . .150 E8
Gill's Rd Green Street Green DA2 . . .28 B1
Sutton at Hone DA4 . . . . . .41 F8
Gillan Ct 3 SE12 . . . . .22 B5
Gilletts La ME19 . . . . .90 A6
Gillies Ct DA14 . . . . .23 E4
Gillies Rd TN15 . . . . .55 E5
Gillingham Coll The ME7 . .48 C8
Gillingham Gate ME7 . . . . . .48 C8
Gillingham Gate Rd ME7 . . .48 C8
Gillingham Gn ME7 . . . . . . .48 E6
Gillingham Rd ME7 . . . . . . .48 D5
Gillingham Sta ME7 . . . . . . .48 D5
Gillmans Rd BR5 . . . . .38 B1
Gilroy Way BR5 . . . . .38 B2
Gimble Way TN2 . . . . .134 D1
Gingerbread La TN18 . . . . .177 F2
Ginsbury Cl ME2 . . . . .47 E6
Gipps Cross La TN3 . . . . . .147 F3
Gipsy La RM17 . . . . .12 C8
Gipsy Rd DA16 . . . . .7 D5
Giralda Cl E16 . . . . .1 D8
Glade Bsns Ctr The RM20 .10 F8
Glade The Bromley BR1 . . . .36 D7
Chatham ME5 . . . . .62 A2
Greenwich SE7 . . . . .5 C7
Sevenoaks TN13 . . . . . . .84 B4
Glades Sh Ctr The BR1 . . .36 A7
Glades The DA12 . . . . .30 D2
Gladeswood Rd DA17 . . . . . .4 B1
Gladstone Rd Chatham ME4 47 E2
Dartford DA1 . . . . .9 F3
Maidstone ME14 . . . . . . .92 A6
Orpington BR6 . . . . .51 C5
Royal Tunbridge Wells TN4 .148 B4
Tonbridge TN9 . . . . .117 B1
Gladwell Rd BR1 . . . . .22 A2
Gladwyn Cl ME8 . . . . .63 D4
Glamford Rd ME2 . . . . .46 D5
Glamis Cl ME5 . . . . .62 A5
Glanfield Ct TN1 . . . . .149 C2
Glanville Rd Bromley BR2 . .36 B6
Gillingham ME7 . . . . .48 D5
Rochester ME2 . . . . .47 A8
Glasbrook Rd SE9 . . . . .22 D8
Glasgow House 8 ME15 .107 E7
Glass Yd SE18 . . . . .2 A3
Glassenbury Rd TN17 . . . .168 E4
Glassmill La BR2 . . . . .36 A7
Glastonbury Cl BR5 . . . . . . .38 B5
Gleaming Wood Dr ME5 . . .77 D8
Gleaners Cl ME14 . . . . .92 E4
Gleanings Mews ME1 . . . . .47 C5
Glebe Cl TN27 . . . . .143 B2
Glebe Cotts TN16 . . . . .82 B4
Glebe Gdns ME17 . . . . . . .111 E5
Glebe Ho 7 SE18 . . . . .2 C1
Glebe House Dr BR2 . . . . . .36 B1
Glebe La Maidstone ME16 . .91 A1
Sevenoaks TN13 . . . . . . .84 B1
Glebe Meadow ME18 . . . .104 E7
Glebe Pl DA4 . . . . .41 C5
Glebe Rd Bromley BR1 . . . .36 A8
Gillingham ME7 . . . . .48 E3
Gravesend DA11 . . . . . . .29 F7
Sevenoaks Weald TN14 . . .99 B3
Glebe The Bidborough TN3 132 D3
Chislehurst BR7 . . . . .37 C8
Cuxton ME2 . . . . .46 C2
Pembury TN2 . . . . .150 D8
Penshurst TN11 . . . . . . .131 A3
Glebe Way DA8 . . . . .8 E8
Glebefield The TN13 . . . . . .83 F4
Glebeland TN27 . . . . .127 F4
Glebelands Bidborough TN3 . . . . .132 C3
Biddenden TN27 . . . . . . .157 F1
Crayford DA1 . . . . .8 F3
Penshurst TN11 . . . . . . .131 A3
Gleeson Dr BR6 . . . . .51 F6
Glen Ct Lewisham SE12 . . . .22 A8

Sidcup DA14 . . . . .24 A4
Glen Dunlop House The DA13 . . . . .84 C5
Glen Ho 6 E16 . . . . .2 A5
Glen The BR6 . . . . .51 A7
Glen View DA12 . . . . .30 C7
Glen View Rd BR1 . . . . .36 D7
Glenalvon Way 7 SE18 . . . . .1 E2
Glenbarr Cl SE9 . . . . .6 B4
Glencairne Cl E16 . . . . .1 D8
Glencoe Inf Sch ME4 . . . . .48 A2
Glencoe Jun Sch ME4 . . . . .48 A2
Glencoe Rd ME4 . . . . .48 A2
Glendale BR8 . . . . .39 F4
Glendale Cl SE9 . . . . .6 A4
Glendale Ct TN2 . . . . .149 D6
Glendale Rd Erith DA8 . . . . . .4 C2
Northfleet DA11 . . . . .29 E5
Glendale Way SE28 . . . . .3 C6
Glendower Cres BR6 . . . . . .38 A3
Glendown Rd SE2 . . . . .3 A1
Gleneagles Cl SE9 . . . . .37 D1
Gleneagles Ct ME5 . . . . . . .61 F2
Gleneagles Dr ME15 . . . . . .92 A1
Gleneagles Gn 1 BR6 . . . . .37 D1
Glenesk Rd SE9 . . . . .6 B4
Glengall Rd DA7 . . . . .7 E4
Glenhead Cl SE9 . . . . .6 B4
Glenhouse Rd SE9 . . . . .6 A2
Glenhurst Ave DA5 . . . . . . .24 F7
Glenister St E16 . . . . .2 A4
Glenlea Rd SE9 . . . . .6 A3
Glenluce Rd SE3 . . . . .5 A8
Glenlyon Rd SE9 . . . . .6 A2
Glenmore Pk TN2 . . . . . . .162 F8
Glenmore Rd DA16 . . . . .6 F6
Glenmount Path 3 SE18 . . .2 C1
Glenrosa Gdns DA12 . . . . . .30 F3
Glenrose Ct DA14 . . . . .24 B3
Glenshiel Rd SE9 . . . . .6 A2
Glentrammon Ave BR6 . . . .51 F4
Glentrammon Cl BR6 . . . . . .51 F4
Glentrammon Gdns BR6 . . .51 F4
Glentrammon Rd BR6 . . . . .51 F4
Glenure Rd SE9 . . . . .6 A2
Glenview SE7 . . . . .5 D8
Glenwood TN30 . . . . .173 B3
Glenwood Cl Chatham ME5 .48 A6
Gillingham ME7 . . . . .63 A7
Maidstone ME16 . . . . . . .91 C5
Tenterden TN30 . . . . . . .173 B3
Glenwood Ct 18 DA14 . . . .24 A4
Glimpsing Gn DA18 . . . . .3 E3
Glistening Glade ME8 . . . . .63 E6
Gload Cres BR5 . . . . .52 D8
Globe La ME4 . . . . .47 F5
Globe Yd 12 DA14 . . . . . . .13 B1
Gloucester Ave Bexley DA16 .6 F3
Sidcup DA15 . . . . .23 E6
Gloucester Ct RM18 . . . . . .12 F5
Gloucester Par DA15 . . . . . .7 A2
Gloucester Rd Dartford DA1 . . . . .26 B8
Erith DA17 . . . . .3 F1
Gravesend DA12 . . . . . . .30 C4
Maidstone ME15 . . . . . .107 D8
Wadhurst TN5 . . . . .174 F6
Glover Cl SE2 . . . . .3 C2
Glovers Mill ME4 . . . . .47 D3
Gloxinia Rd DA13 . . . . .29 B2
Glyn Davies Cl TN13 . . . . . .83 E7
Glyn Dr DA14 . . . . .24 B4
Glynde Rd DA7 . . . . .7 E4
Glyndebourne Pk BR6 . . . . .51 B8
Glyndon Rd SE18 . . . . .2 D2
Glynne Cl ME8 . . . . .63 D6
Goad Ave ME5 . . . . .62 B3
Goddard's Green Cotts TN17 . . .170 F1
Goddards Cl TN17 . . . . . . .169 B4
Godden Rd ME6 . . . . .74 F8
Goddings Dr ME1 . . . . .47 A3
Goddington Chase BR6 . . . .52 B6
Goddington Ho BR6 . . . . . . .52 C7
Goddington La Harrietsham ME17 . . . . .110 B6
Orpington BR6 . . . . .52 A7
Goddington Rd ME2 . . . . . . .47 B8
Godfrey Cl ME2 . . . . .32 F1
Godfrey Evans Cl TN10 . . .117 F5
Godfrey Hill SE18 . . . . .1 E2
Godfrey Rd SE18 . . . . .1 F2
Godstow Rd SE2 . . . . .3 C4
Godwin House SE18 . . . . . . .5 F6
Godwin Rd BR2 . . . . .36 C6
Gold St DA12,DA13 . . . . . .44 E4
Goldace RM17 . . . . .11 F8
Goldcrest Cl Newham E16 . . .1 D8
Woolwich SE28 . . . . .3 D3
Goldcrest Dr ME4 . . . . .34 C2
Golden Plover Cl E16 . . . . . .1 A7
Golden Sq TN30 . . . . .183 B8
Golden Wood Cl ME5 . . . . .77 D8
Goldfinch Cl Larkfield ME20 75 A2
Orpington BR6 . . . . .52 A5
Paddock Wood TN12 . . . .136 A5
Goldfinch Rd SE28 . . . . .2 D3
Golding Cl ME20 . . . . .75 C1
Golding Gdns TN12 . . . . . .120 A6
Golding Rd TN13 . . . . .84 C5
Goldings TN12 . . . . .135 E5
Goldings Cl ME19 . . . . .89 A3
Goldings The ME8 . . . . .63 C8
Goldmark House SE3 . . . . . .5 B4
Goldsel Rd BR8 . . . . .39 E5

Goldsmid Rd TN9 . . . . . . .133 C8
Goldsmid St 3 SE18 . . . . . . .2 E1
Goldsmith RM17 . . . . .11 F8
Goldsmith Ct TN30 . . . . . .173 B1
Goldsmith Rd ME8 . . . . . . .63 E5
Goldsworth Dr ME2 . . . . . . .33 A1
Goldthorne Cl ME14 . . . . . .92 C5
Goldwing Cl E16 . . . . .1 A7
Golf Links Ave DA11 . . . . . .30 B3
Golf Rd BR1 . . . . .37 A6
Golford Rd TN17 . . . . .169 F4
Gollogly Terr 8 SE7 . . . . . . .1 C1
Gooch Cl ME16 . . . . .91 D8
Goodall Rd ME8 . . . . .63 E5
Goodbury Rd TN15 . . . . . . .70 B6
Gooding Ho SE7 . . . . .1 C1
Goodley Stock Rd TN8,TN16 . . . . .96 B6
Goodmead Rd BR6 . . . . . . .38 A2
Goods Hill TN30 . . . . .182 D8
Goods Station Rd TN1 . . . .149 B4
Goodtrees La TN8 . . . . . . .145 B2
Goodwin Cl TN8 . . . . .112 B2
Goodwin Dr Maidstone ME14 . . . . . . .92 B8
Sidcup DA14 . . . . .24 D6
Goodwin Rd ME3 . . . . .33 B7
Goodwins The TN2 . . . . . .148 F1
Goodwood Cl High Halstow ME23 . . . . .17 E4
Maidstone ME15 . . . . . .107 F6
Goodwood Cres DA12 . . . . .30 C2
Goodworth Rd TN15 . . . . . .71 F3
Goosander Way SE28 . . . . . .2 D3
Goose Cl ME5 . . . . .62 A7
Goose Green Cl BR5 . . . . . .38 A7
Goose Sq 6 E6 . . . . .1 F7
Gooseneck La TN27 . . . . . .141 C5
Gordon Cl ME17 . . . . .106 E3
Gordon Cty Inf Sch ME2 . .47 A8
Gordon Ho SE12 . . . . .22 A8
Gordon Pl DA12 . . . . .13 C1
Gordon Prim Sch SE9 . . . . . .5 F3
Gordon Promenade E DA12 . . . . .13 D1
Gordon Rd Chatham ME4 . .48 A2
Dartford DA1 . . . . .26 B8
Erith DA17 . . . . .4 C2
Gillingham ME7 . . . . .48 E5
Gillingham,Brompton ME4 . .48 A7
Hoo St Werburgh ME3 . . . .34 D5
Northfleet DA11 . . . . .29 E8
Rochester ME2 . . . . .47 A8
Royal Tunbridge Wells TN4 .149 C2
Sevenoaks TN13 . . . . . . .84 D2
Sidcup DA15 . . . . .23 F7
Gordon Terr ME1 . . . . .47 C4
Gordon Way BR1 . . . . .36 A8
Gore Cotts DA2 . . . . .27 C4
Gore Court Rd ME15 . . . . .107 F5
Gore Farm Cotts DA2 . . . . .27 C5
Gore Green Rd ME3 . . . . . .32 E7
Gore La TN17 . . . . .153 E4
Gore Rd Dartford DA2 . . . . .27 C6
Silver Street ME9 . . . . . . .80 F5
Gorham Cl ME6 . . . . .74 F7
Gorham Dr Maidstone ME15 93 A1
Tonbridge TN9 . . . . .133 E8
Gorman Rd SE18 . . . . .1 F2
Gorringe Ave DA4 . . . . .41 D7
Gorse Ave ME5 . . . . .61 F5
Gorse Cl E16 . . . . .1 A7
Gorse Cres ME20 . . . . .90 D8
Gorse Rd Orpington BR5 . . .53 A8
Rochester ME2 . . . . .46 F8
Royal Tunbridge Wells TN2 .149 E5
Gorse Way DA3 . . . . .43 A4
Gorse Wood Rd Hartley DA3 . . . . .43 A5
New Barn DA3 . . . . .43 A6
Goss Hill BR8,DA2 . . . . . . .26 C2
Gossage Rd SE18 . . . . .2 D1
Gosshill Rd BR7 . . . . .37 A7
Gossington Cl BR7 . . . . .23 B4
Gothic Cl DA1 . . . . .26 D5
Goudhurst & Kilndown CE Prim Sch TN17 . . .167 F8
Goudhurst Cl ME16 . . . . . . .91 E4
Goudhurst Rd Cranbrook TN17 . . . . . . .169 D8
Gillingham ME8 . . . . .49 B3
Horsmonden TN12 . . . . .153 B5
Knox Bridge TN12,TN17 . .155 C6
Gouge Ave DA11 . . . . .29 E7
Gould Rd ME5 . . . . .62 B3
Gouldhurst Rd TN12 . . . . .138 B5
Gourock Rd SE9 . . . . .6 A2
Gover Hill TN11,ME18 . . . .102 E6
Grace Ave Bexley DA7 . . . . . .7 F5
Maidstone ME16 . . . . . . .91 D6
Grace Cl SE9 . . . . .22 D5
Gracious La TN13 . . . . .99 B5
Gracious Lane Bridge TN13 . . . . .99 A5
Gracious Lane End TN14 . . .98 F5
Grafton Ave ME1 . . . . .61 E8
Graham Ct 11 BR1 . . . . . . .22 B1
Graham House SE18 . . . . . . .6 B8
Graham Rd DA7 . . . . .8 A3
Grain Rd Gillingham ME8 . . .63 C3
Grain ME3 . . . . .20 D3
Grainey Hill ME9 . . . . .64 E4
Grainger Wlk TN10 . . . . . .117 E6
Gram Sch for Girls Wilmington The DA2 . . .26 B5
Grampian Cl Orpington BR6 .37 F3

Grampian Cl continued
Royal Tunbridge Wells TN2 .149 D5
Grampian Way ME15 . . . . . .93 A1
Granada House 8 ME15 . . .92 A4
Granada St 8 ME15 . . . . . . .92 A4
Granary TN12 . . . . .136 B6
Granary Cl Gillingham ME8 . .49 F1
Maidstone ME14 . . . . . . .92 E5
Granby Ho 8 SE18 . . . . .1 F2
Granby Rd Eltham SE9 . . . . . .5 F4
Northfleet DA11 . . . . .12 D1
Woolwich SE18 . . . . .2 B3
Grand Ct 7 ME7 . . . . .48 C6
Grand Depot Rd SE18 . . . . . .2 A1
Grandshore La TN17 . . . . .156 B5
Grandsire Gdns ME3 . . . . . .34 E6
Grange Cl Edenbridge TN8 .112 C1
Leybourne ME19 . . . . . . .74 C2
Sidcup DA15 . . . . .24 A5
Westerham TN16 . . . . . . .81 C1
Grange Cotts TN11 . . . . . .101 D5
Grange Cres Dartford DA2 . . . . .10 B1
Erith SE28 . . . . .3 C7
Tenterden TN30 . . . . . . .173 A3
Grange Dr Chislehurst BR7 . .22 F2
Pratt's Bottom BR6 . . . . . .52 C2
Grange Gdns TN4 . . . . . . .148 D4
Grange Hill Chatham ME5 . .48 B3
Plaxtol TN15 . . . . .101 E8
Grange Ho Erith DA8 . . . . . . .9 A5
Gravesend DA11 . . . . . . .30 A8
Grange La Hartley DA3 . . . . .43 B2
Maidstone ME16 . . . . . . .77 A1
Grange Park Coll ME19 . . . .74 B3
Grange Rd Gillingham ME7 . .49 A6
Gravesend DA11 . . . . . . .30 A8
Grays RM17 . . . . .12 B8
Orpington BR6 . . . . .51 C8
Platt TN15 . . . . .87 C7
Rochester ME2 . . . . .47 B7
Royal Tunbridge Wells TN4 .148 D4
Sevenoaks TN13 . . . . . . .99 A8
Tenterden TN30 . . . . . . .172 F3
Grange Rdbt ME7 . . . . .49 A6
Grange The East Malling ME19 . . . . . . .90 A7
Sutton at Hone DA4 . . . . . .41 D8
West Kingsdown TN15 . . . .55 F2
Westerham TN16 . . . . . . .81 C1
Grange Way Erith DA8 . . . . . .9 B7
Hartley DA3 . . . . .42 F3
Rochester ME1 . . . . .47 C3
Grangehill Pl SE9 . . . . .5 F4
Grangehill Rd SE9 . . . . .5 F4
Grangeways DA11 . . . . .29 F4
Grangewood DA5 . . . . .24 F7
Granite St SE18 . . . . .2 F1
Grant Cl ME7 . . . . .49 B1
Grant Dr ME15 . . . . .107 D6
Grant Rd ME3 . . . . .33 C3
Grant's Cotts ME17 . . . . . .111 B5
Granton Rd DA14 . . . . .24 C2
Granville Ct Erith SE2 . . . . . .3 D1
Sevenoaks TN13 . . . . . . .84 A3
Granville Mews DA14 . . . . .24 A4
Granville Rd Bexley DA16 . . .7 C4
Gillingham ME7 . . . . .48 E5
Gravesend DA11 . . . . . . .29 F7
Maidstone ME14 . . . . . . .92 A6
Royal Tunbridge Wells TN1 .149 A5
Sevenoaks TN13 . . . . . . .84 A3
Sidcup DA14 . . . . .24 B4
Westerham TN16 . . . . . . .81 C1
Granville Sch The TN13 . . .84 A4
Grapple Rd ME14 . . . . .92 A7
Grasdene Rd SE18,SE2 . . . . .7 A7
Grasmere Ave BR6 . . . . . . .51 B7
Grasmere Gdns BR6 . . . . . .51 B7
Grasmere Gr ME2 . . . . .33 C2
Grasmere Rd Bexley DA7 . . .8 C5
Orpington BR6 . . . . .51 B7
Grassington Rd DA14 . . . . .24 A4
Grasslands ME17 . . . . .108 E4
Grassmere ME19 . . . . .74 F2
Grassy Glade ME7 . . . . .63 B6
Grassy La TN13 . . . . .99 B8
Gravel Hill DA6 . . . . .8 B2
Gravel Hill Cl DA6 . . . . .8 B1
Gravel Hill Prim Sch DA6 . .8 B3
Gravel Pit Way BR6 . . . . . . .38 A1
Gravel Rd Orpington BR2 . . .50 E8
Sutton at Hone DA4 . . . . . .27 B1
Gravel Wlk ME1 . . . . .47 D5
Gravelly Bottom Rd ME17 . . . . .109 B2
Gravelly Ways TN12 . . . . . .120 D5
Gravelwood Cl BR7 . . . . . . .23 C5
Graveney Cl ME3 . . . . .33 C7
Graveney Rd ME15 . . . . . .107 F7
Graves Est DA16 . . . . .7 B5
Graves & North Kent Hospl DA11 . . . . .13 A1
Gravesend GramSch DA12 . . . . .30 D8
Gravesend Gram Sch for Girls DA11 . . . . . . .30 A7
Gravesend Rd Higham ME2,ME3,DA12 . .32 C2
Rochester ME2 . . . . .46 F8
Shorne DA12 . . . . .31 D5
Vigo Village TN15 . . . . . . .72 D6
Gravesend Sta DA11 . . . . . .13 B1
Gravesham Ct 8 DA12 . . . .30 B8
Gravesham Mus* DA11 . . .13 B1
Gray Ho SE2 . . . . .3 D1
Grayland Cl BR1 . . . . .36 D8

Graylands RM17 11 E8
Graylings The ME1 47 B3
Grayne Ave ME3 21 B5
Grays Farm Prim Sch BR5 38 B8
Grays Farm Production Village BR5 38 B8
Grays Farm Rd BR5 38 B8
Grays Rd TN16 81 D7
Grays Sh Ctr RM17 12 A8
Grays Sta RM17 12 A8
Grazeley Cl DA6 8 C2
Great Basin Rd ME12 21 F2
Great Bounds Dr TN4 132 E3
Great Brooms Rd TN4 149 C8
Great Courtlands TN3 148 A3
Great Elms TN11 102 E1
Great Elms Rd BR2 36 C5
Great Footway TN3 147 F3
Great Hall Arc 3 TN1 149 B3
Great Harry Dr SE9 23 A5
Great Ivy Mill Cotts ME15 106 F7
Great Lines ME7 48 B5
Great Maytham* TN17 181 F2
Great Oak TN19 184 A3
Great Queen St DA1 9 F1
Great South Ave ME4 48 A1
Great Thrift BR5 37 C5
Greatness La TN14 84 C6
Greatness Rd TN13,TN14 84 C6
Greatwood BR7 23 A1
Grebe Apartments 15 ME15 107 E5
Grebe Cl ME3 19 C4
Grebe Ct ME20 74 F1
Grecian Rd TN1 149 B2
Grecian St ME14 92 A6
Green Acres DA14 23 F4
Green Bank Cl ME7 63 A5
Green Cl ME1 47 D2
Green Court Rd BR8 39 D3
Green Farm Cl BR6 51 F5
Green Farm La DA12 31 E5
Green Gdns BR6 51 C5
Green Hedges TN30 183 B8
Green Hill Maidstone ME15 93 B1
Woolwich SE18 1 F1
Green Hill La ME17 110 D1
Green La
Biddenden Green TN27 143 A1
Cliffe ME3 16 B6
Collier Street TN12 137 E8
Devil's Den ME17 124 B4
East End TN17 171 C2
Eltham BR7,SE9 23 B5
Four Elms TN8 113 C7
Grain ME3 21 B5
Langley Heath ME17 108 E3
Maidstone ME17 107 C3
Meopham Sta DA13 44 B2
Paddock Wood TN12 136 A5
Platt's Heath ME17 110 F2
Stockbury ME9 64 F1
Trottiscliffe ME19 73 A5
Withyham TN26 159 F3
Green La The TN11 115 F1
Green Lands DA12 31 E4
Green Lane Bsns Pk SE9 23 A6
Green Lane Cotts
Collier Street TN12 121 D1
Langley Heath ME17 108 E3
Green Lawns 10 SE18 2 B2
Green Pl DA1 8 E2
Green Rd TN12 153 A6
Green Sands ME5 77 C8
Green Sq TN5 174 F5
Green St ME7 48 C5
Green Street Green Prim Sch BR6 51 F4
Green Street Green Rd DA1,DA2 27 D4
Green The
Bexley,Bexley Heath DA7 8 A6
Bexley,Falconwood DA16 6 E3
Dartford DA2 27 D6
East Farleigh ME15 106 B7
Frant TN3 163 B3
Hayes BR2 36 A2
Leigh TN11 115 F1
Lewisham BR1 22 A5
Royal Tunbridge Wells TN3 147 E3
Sevenoaks TN13 84 D5
Sidcup DA14 24 A4
St Paul's Cray BR5 24 B1
Westerham TN16 81 D1
Green Vale DA6 7 D2
Green View Ave TN11 116 A1
Green Way Bromley BR2 36 E3
Eltham SE9 5 D2
Hartley DA3 42 E4
Maidstone ME16 91 B3
Royal Tunbridge Wells TN2 149 E8
Green Wlk DA1 8 F3
Green's Cotts ME15 106 A4
Greenacre DA1 26 D6
Greenacre Cl Chatham ME5 62 A5
Swanley BR8 39 E5
Greenacre Sch ME5 61 F5
Greenacres SE9 6 A1
Greenacres Cl BR6 51 C6
Greenacres Prim Sch & Language Impairment Unit SE9 23 A6
Greenbank ME5 62 B8
Greenbank Lodge 2 BR7 37 A8
Greenbanks DA1 26 E6
Greenbay Rd SE7 5 D7
Greenborough Cl ME15 107 E6
Greencourt Rd BR5 37 E4
Greencroft Cl E6 1 D8
Greendale Wlk 4 DA11 29 E5
Greenfield TN8 112 D1
Greenfield Cl Eccles ME20 76 A6
Royal Tunbridge Wells TN4 148 C5
Greenfield Cotts ME14 77 A1
Greenfield Dr BR1 36 C7
Greenfield Gdns BR5 37 D2
Greenfield Rd Dartford DA2 25 D3
Gillingham ME7 48 D6
Greenfields ME15 107 E8
Greenfields Cl ME3 33 D3
Greenfinches
Gillingham ME7 62 F6
New Barn DA3 43 B6
Greenfrith Dr TN10 117 B6
Greenhaven Dr SE28 3 B7
Greenhill TN12 139 E5
Greenhill Cts SE18 1 F1
Greenhill La TN27 143 F7
Greenhill Rd
Northfleet DA11 29 F6
Otford TN14 69 C5
Greenhill Terr SE18 1 F1
Greenhithe 3 ME15 92 A3
Greenhithe Cl DA15 23 E8
Greenhithe Sta DA9 11 A2
Greenholm Rd SE9 6 B2
Greening St SE2 3 C2
Greenlands TN15 87 C7
Greenlands Rd TN15 85 B8
Greenlaw St SE18 2 A3
Greenleas TN2 150 C6
Greenleigh Ave BR5 38 B5
Greens End SE18 2 B2
Greensand Rd ME15 93 A2
Greenshields Ind Est E16 1 B5
Greenside
High Halden TN26 173 E7
Maidstone ME15 92 B3
Sidcup DA5 24 E7
Swanley BR8 39 D7
Greenslade Prim Sch SE18 6 D8
Greentrees Ave TN10 117 F5
Greenvale Gdns ME8 49 B2
Greenvale Rd SE9 6 A3
Greenview Cres TN11 116 E4
Greenview Wlk ME8 49 A4
Greenway Chatham ME5 61 D6
Chislehurst BR7 23 B3
Cranbrook TN17 169 B4
Greenway Court Farm Cotts ME17 95 A1
Greenway Court Rd ME17 95 A1
Greenway La ME17 110 A7
Greenway The BR5 38 B3
Greenways Maidstone ME14 92 F5
New Barn DA3 43 D6
Greenways The TN12 135 F5
Greenwich Cl Chatham ME5 62 B4
Maidstone ME16 91 D4
Greenwich Com Coll SE9 5 E1
Greenwich Cres E6 1 E8
Greenwich Hts SE18 5 E7
Greenwich Ind Est SE7 1 B2
Greenwood Cl
Orpington BR5 37 E3
Sidcup DA15 24 A6
Greenwood House 8 RM17 12 B8
Greenwood Pl TN15 72 A2
Greenwood Rd DA5 25 D4
Greenwood Sch SE18 6 E6
Greenwood Way TN13 83 F2
Greggs Wood Rd TN2 149 F7
Gregor Mews SE3 5 A7
Gregory Cl ME8 63 E4
Gregory Cres SE9 22 D8
Gregory House SE3 5 B5
Grenada Rd SE7 5 C7
Grenadier Cl ME15 92 F2
Grenadier St E16 2 A5
Grenville Cl DA13 58 A8
Gresham Ave DA3 42 F4
Gresham Cl 3
Gillingham ME8 49 F1
Sidcup DA5 7 F1
Gresham Rd
Coxheath ME17 106 D3
Newham E16 1 B7
Greshams Way TN8 112 A2
Gresswell Cl DA14 24 A5
Grey Wethers ME14 76 E4
Greybury La TN8 128 B3
Greyfriars Cl ME16 91 D5
Greyhound Way DA1 8 E1
Greys Park Cl BR2 50 D5
Greystone Pk TN14 82 E2
Greystones Cl TN15 69 E2
Greystones Rd ME15 93 A2
Gribble Bridge La TN27 172 B5
Grieves Rd DA11 29 F5
Grieveson Ho ME4 48 A4
Griffin Manor Sch SE18 6 E6
Griffin Manor Way SE28 2 D3
Griffin Rd SE18 2 D2
Griffin Way SE28 2 E3
Griffin Wlk DA9 10 F2
Griffiths House 2 SE18 6 B8
Grigg La TN27 142 C7
Grigg's Cross BR5 38 D3
Griggs Way TN15 87 A7
Grimsby Gr E16 2 B4
Grinling Ho 6 SE18 2 A2
Grizedale Cl ME1 61 D8
Gromenfield TN3 161 C7
Groom Cl BR2 36 B5
Groombridge Cl DA16 7 A2
Groombridge Hill TN3 147 D1
Groombridge Pl* TN3 161 C8
Groombridge Place Gdns* TN3 161 C8
Groombridge Rd TN3 147 A1
Groombridge Sq 13 ME15 107 F6
Groombridge Sta TN3 161 C7
Grosmont Rd SE18 2 F1
Grosvenor Ave ME4 47 E3
Grosvenor Bridge TN1 149 B5
Grosvenor Cres DA1 9 D2
Grosvenor House 5 ME15 107 F5
Grosvenor Pk TN1 149 A4
Grosvenor Rd Bexley DA6 7 E2
Erith DA17 8 A8
Gillingham ME7 49 A1
Orpington BR5 37 E3
Royal Tunbridge Wells TN1 149 A4
Grosvenor Sq DA3 42 E6
Grosvenor Wlk TN1 149 A4
Grove Ave TN1 149 A2
Grove Cl BR2 50 A8
Grove Cotts TN30 183 B6
Grove Ct Greenwich SE3 5 A6
4 Rochester ME2 47 B7
Grove Green La ME14 92 E5
Grove Green Rd ME14 92 F5
Grove Hill Gdns TN1 149 B2
Grove Hill Rd TN1 149 B3
Grove Market Pl SE9 5 F1
Grove Park Rd SE9 22 D6
Grove Park Sta SE12 22 B5
Grove Rd Bexley DA7 8 C3
Chatham ME4 48 B2
8 Erith DA17 7 F8
Gillingham ME7 49 A6
Grays RM17 12 C8
Maidstone ME15 107 C7
Northfleet DA11 12 B2
Penshurst TN11,TN8 130 E2
Rochester ME2 47 B8
Seal TN15 85 B5
Sevenoaks TN13,TN14 84 C6
Upper Halling ME2 59 E5
Grove The Bexley DA6 7 D3
Gravesend DA12 30 B8
Maidstone ME14 93 A3
Pembury TN2 150 D8
Sidcup DA14 24 E4
Swanley BR8 39 F6
Swanscombe DA10 11 F2
West Kingsdown TN15 55 F1
Grove Vale BR7 23 A2
Grove Wood Cotts TN11 100 A1
Grovebury Cl DA8 8 D8
Grovebury Ct DA6 8 B2
Grovebury Rd SE2 3 B4
Groveherst Rd DA1 9 F4
Grovehurst La TN12 153 C5
Grovelands ME17 111 E5
Grovelands Rd BR5 24 A1
Grovelands Way RM17 11 F8
Grover St 3 TN1 149 B4
Groves The ME6 74 F7
Grovewood Ct ME14 92 E4
Grovewood Dr ME14 92 E4
Guardian Ct ME8 49 C1
Guardian Ind Est TN12 138 C7
Guestwick TN10 117 F5
Guibal Rd SE12 22 B7
Guild Rd Erith DA8 8 F7
Greenwich SE7 5 D8
Guildhall Mus* ME1 47 C6
Guildford Gdns ME2 46 C6
Guildford Rd Newham E6 1 F7
7 Royal Tunbridge Wells TN1 149 B3
Gulland Ho 4 ME14 92 B4
Gullands ME17 108 E4
Gulliver Rd DA15 23 E6
Gumley Rd RM20 11 E8
Gumping Rd BR5,BR6 51 C8
Gun Hill RM18 13 D8
Gun La Horsmonden TN12 153 A5
Rochester ME2 47 B7
Gundulph Ho TN10 117 C3
Gundulph Rd Bromley BR2 36 C6
Chatham ME1 47 E4
Gundulph Sq ME1 47 C6
Gunfleet Cl DA12 30 E8
Gunlands TN12 153 A6
Gunn Rd DA10 11 E1
Gunner La SE18 2 A1
Gunning St SE18 2 E2
Gunnis Cl ME8 63 D4
Gurdon Rd SE7 1 B1
Guston Rd ME14 92 C6
Guy Barnett Gr SE3 5 A4
Gwillim Cl DA15 7 A2
Gwynn Rd DA11 29 C6
Gybbon Rise TN12 139 E3
Gybbons Rd TN17 181 F3
Gypsy Way ME23 17 E3

H

Ha-Ha Rd SE18 5 F8
Hackney Rd ME16 91 C2
Hadden Rd SE28 2 E3
Haddon Gr DA15 24 A8
Haddon Rd BR5 38 C4
Hadleigh Ct ME7 63 A3
Hadleigh Wlk 1 E6 1 E7
Hadley Cl DA13 58 B8
Hadley Ct TN4 148 F6
Hadley Gdns ME17 94 E2
Hadley House BR5 37 F7
Hadley Rd DA17 3 F2
Hadlow Coll Nature Reserve* SE12 22 C7
Hadlow Coll of Agriculture & Hort TN11 118 D8
Hadlow Ct TN9 117 C2
Hadlow Pk TN11 102 E1
Hadlow Prim Sch TN11 118 E8
Hadlow Rd Bexley DA16 7 C7
Maidstone ME14 92 C5
Sidcup DA14 24 A4
Tonbridge TN9 117 D3
Tonbridge,Higham Wood TN10,TN11 118 A5
Hadlow Stair Rd TN10 117 F4
Hadlow Way DA13 29 E1
Haffenden Cl TN12 138 D6
Haffenden Rd TN30 173 B1
Haig Ave Chatham ME1 47 D1
Chatham,Luton ME4 48 A2
Gillingham ME7 48 E4
Haig Ct BR7 23 B3
Haig Gdns DA12 30 C8
Haig Villas ME3 34 A5
Hailey Rd DA18 4 A4
Hailey Rd Bsns Pk DA18 4 A4
Haileybury Rd BR6 52 A6
Hailstone Cl TN11 118 E8
Haimo Prim Sch SE9 5 D2
Haimo Rd SE9 5 D2
Hainault St SE9 23 B7
Halcot Ave DA6 8 C2
Haldane Gdns DA11 29 C7
Haldane Rd SE28 3 D6
Halden Cl ME15 107 F6
Halden La TN17 181 F6
Hale Cl BR6 51 C6
Hale Cotts DA9 11 C2
Hale Ct TN12 120 A7
Hale La TN14 68 F2
Hale Oak Rd
Hall's Green TN8,TN14 114 E4
Sevenoaks Weald TN14 99 B1
Hale Rd ME3 33 C7
Hale St TN12 120 A7
Hales Cl TN30 183 B8
Hales Ct TN30 183 B8
Haleys Pl ME1 76 A8
Half Moon La TN11 116 D6
Half Moon Way ME23 17 E3
Halfpence La DA12 45 B7
Halfpenny Cl ME16 91 A2
Halfway St DA15 23 E7
Halifax Cl ME5 62 B6
Halifield Dr DA17 3 E3
Hall Hill TN15 85 C4
Hall Pl* DA5 8 C1
Hall Place Cres DA1,DA5 8 D2
Hall Rd Aylesford ME20 75 F1
Chatham ME5 62 C3
Dartford DA1 9 F3
High Halstow ME3 18 C6
Northfleet DA11 29 C5
Northfleet,Wombwell Park DA11 29 D6
Wouldham ME1 60 C3
Hall The SE3 5 A4
Hall View SE9 22 D6
Hall's Grove Rd TN2 149 D2
Hall's Hole Rd TN2 149 E4
Hallam Cl BR7 22 F3
Hallford Way DA1 9 C2
Hallgate SE3 5 A4
Halling Prim Sch ME2 60 B3
Halling Sta ME2 60 A5
Halls Cotts TN5 174 F5
Hallsfield Rd ME5 61 D2
Hallsville Prim Sch E16 1 A7
Hallwards TN12 139 E2
Hallwood Cl ME8 63 D5
Hallwood House ME5 62 C2
Hallywell Cres E6 1 F8
Halons Rd SE9 23 A8
Halsbrook Rd SE3 5 D4
Halstead La TN14 67 E5
Halstead Place Sch TN14 67 E8
Halstead Prim Sch TN14 67 F7
Halstead Rd DA8 8 E6
Halstead Wlk ME16 91 C7
Halstow Cl ME15 107 B6
Halstow Prim Sch SE10 1 A1
Halstow Rd SE10,SE3 1 A1
Halt Robin La DA17 4 B2
Halt Robin Rd DA17 4 B2
Ham La Gillingham ME7 62 E3
Lenham ME17 111 C5
Ham River Hill ME3 33 A6
Ham Shades Cl 1 DA15 24 A5
Hamble Rd TN10 117 B5
Hambledon Ct ME16 91 B3
Hambledown Rd DA15 23 E8
Hambro Ave BR2 36 A1
Hamelin Rd ME7 62 F8
Hamerton Rd DA11 12 B2
Hamilton Ct TN4 149 A5
Hamilton Ho
Coxheath ME17 106 C3
Royal Tunbridge Wells TN4 149 A5
Hamilton Rd Bexley DA7 7 E5
Gillingham ME7 48 D7
Sidcup DA15 24 A4
Hamilton Wlk DA8 8 F7
Hamlea Cl SE12 5 A2
Hamlet Ho Eltham SE9 6 A2
5 Erith DA8 8 E7
Hamlin Rd TN13 83 E6
Hamlyn Ct TN13 83 E6
Hammelton Rd BR1 36 A8
Hammerwood Pk* RH19 144 C2
Hammond Way 2 SE28 3 B6
Hammonds 9 TN18 179 A2
Hammonds Sq ME6 75 A8
Hamond Hill 6 ME4 47 E4
Hampden Way ME19 88 F3
Hampshire Cl ME5 62 C7
Hampshire Dr ME15 107 C8
Hampson Way ME14 93 A4
Hampstead Cl SE28 3 B5
Hampstead La ME18 104 C1
Hampton Cl ME5 62 A5
Hampton Cotts TN14 67 F4
Hampton Cres DA12 30 E6
Hampton House DA7 8 B5
Hampton Rd ME14 92 C6
Hamptons Rd TN11 102 B5
Hamwick Gn ME5 62 C1
Hanameel St E16 1 B5
Hanbury Cl ME18 104 E7
Hanbury Wlk DA5 25 E5
Hancock Cl ME3 33 B1
Handel Cres RM18 13 A7
Handel Wlk TN10 117 E6
Hands Wlk E16 1 A7
Hanes Dene ME2 59 F5
Hang Grove Hill BR6 66 B6
Hangmans Cnr BR7 37 B8
Hanley Ct TN13 84 B4
Hanmer Way TN12 139 E2
Hanover Ave E16 1 A5
Hanover Ct ME14 92 B5
Hanover Dr Chislehurst BR7 23 C4
Gillingham ME8 63 C4
Hanover Gn ME20 74 F3
Hanover Pl DA3 56 F8
Hanover Rd
Coxheath ME17 106 C3
Royal Tunbridge Wells TN1 149 A4
Hanover Way DA7 7 D4
Hansol Rd DA6 7 E2
Hansom Terr 1 BR1 36 B8
Hanway ME8 49 A2
Harbex Cl DA5 25 B8
Harbledown Manor ME8 49 B3
Harbledown Pl 7 BR5 38 C5
Harborough Ave DA15 23 F8
Harbour Ct 11 DA2 10 B1
Harbour The ME17 124 E5
Harbourland Cl ME14 92 B8
Harbourne La TN26,TN30 173 E5
Harcourt Ave DA15 24 C8
Harcourt Gdns ME8 63 E4
Harcourt Rd DA6,DA7 7 E3
Harden Ct 1 SE18 1 E2
Harden Rd DA11 29 F6
Hardie Cl ME19 74 F1
Harding Ho 9 SE18 1 F2
Harding Rd DA7 7 F5
Hardinge Ave TN4 132 E3
Hardinge Cl ME8 63 D4
Hardinge St SE18 2 C3
Hardman Rd SE7 1 B1
Hardres Terr BR5 52 D8
Hards Town ME4 48 A4
Hardwick Cres 2 DA2 10 B1
Hardwick Ct DA8 8 D8
Hardwick Rd TN11 116 E6
Hardy Ave Newham E16 1 A5
Northfleet DA11 29 E6
Hardy Cl ME5 62 B6
Hardy Gr DA1 10 A3
Hardy Rd 2 SE3 5 A8
Hardy St ME14 92 A6
Hare St 2 Chatham ME4 48 B3
Woolwich SE18 2 A3
Harebell Cl 3
Chatham ME5 61 F4
Maidstone ME14 92 E5
Harebell Dr E6 2 A8
Haredale Cl ME1 61 D7
Harefield Rd DA14 24 D5
Harenc Sch DA14 24 C3
Harescroft TN2 162 F7
Harewood Lincoln Ho DA11 12 D1
Harfst Way BR8 39 C8
Hargate Cl TN2 162 F8
Hargood Rd SE3 5 C6
Harland Ave DA15 23 E6
Harland Rd SE12 22 A7
Harland Way TN4 132 F4
Harlands Gr BR6 51 B6
Harlech Cl ME2 32 F1
Harlequin Ho 1 DA18 3 E3
Harley Gdns BR6 51 E6
Harleyford BR1 36 C8
Harlinger St SE18 1 E3
Harlington Rd DA7 7 E4
Harman Ave DA11 30 B3
Harman Ct ME5 62 B3
Harman Dr DA15 6 F1
Harmer Ct
Royal Tunbridge Wells TN4 133 A2
Swanscombe DA10 11 F1
Harmer Rd DA10 11 F1
Harmer St DA12 13 C1
Harmers Way TN27 127 F3
Harmony St TN4 148 D4
Harness Rd SE28 3 A4
Harold Ave Erith DA17 3 F1
Gillingham ME7 48 E4

Harold Gibbons Ct SE7 . . .5 C8
Harold Ho TN2 . . . . .149 C7
Harold Rd Cuxton ME2 . . .46 C3
  Hawley DA2 . . . . .26 F4
Harp Farm Rd ME14 . . . . .77 C6
Harper Rd E6 . . . . .1 A8
Harple La ME14 . . . . .77 F1
Harpswood ME17 . . . . .94 F1
Harptree Dr ME5 . . . . .61 F5
Harraden Rd SE3 . . . . .5 C6
Harrier Mews SE28 . . . . . .2 D4
Harrier Way E6 . . . . .1 F8
Harries Rd TN2 . . . . .149 E7
Harriestham Sta ME17 . .110 D6
Harriet Dr ME1 . . . . .47 B3
Harrington Ho 4 BR1 . . .36 A8
Harrington Way SE18 . . . .1 D3
Harris Cl DA11 . . . . .29 F5
Harris Ho ME2 . . . . .60 B4
Harris Rd DA7 . . . . .7 F6
Harrison Ct 4 ME8 . . . . .49 F1
Harrison Dr
  Harrietsham ME17 . . . . .110 E6
  High Halstow ME3 . . . . . .17 E4
Harrison Rd TN15 . . . . . . .86 F7
Harrison Way TN13 . . . . . .84 A5
Harrogate Ct 6 SE12 . . .22 A8
Harrow Cl TN8 . . . . .112 D3
Harrow Ct Chatham ME5 . .62 C4
  Stockbury ME9 . . . . .79 D8
Harrow Gdns BR6 . . . . . . .52 B6
Harrow Manor Way SE2 . .3 C3
Harrow Rd Gillingham ME7 . .62 F6
  Halstead TN14 . . . . .67 E4
Harrow Way ME14 . . . . . . .92 E5
Harrowby Gdns DA11 . . . .29 E6
Hart Dyke Cres BR8 . . . . .39 D6
Hart Dyke Rd
  Orpington BR5 . . . . .38 C1
  Swanley BR8 . . . . .39 D6
Hart Shaw DA3 . . . . .43 B7
Hart St ME1 . . . . .91 F3
Hart Street Bsns Ctr ME16 91 F3
Hartfield Cl TN10 . . . . . . .117 C5
Hartfield Cres BR4 . . . . . .50 A7
Hartfield Pl DA11 . . . . .29 D8
Hartfield Rd Hayes BR4 . .50 A6
  Hever TN8 . . . . .129 A4
Hartford Rd DA5 . . . . .8 A1
Hartford Wlk 18 DA17 . . . .4 A1
Harting Rd SE9 . . . . .22 E5
Hartington Cl BR6 . . . . . . .51 C5
Hartington Rd E16 . . . . .1 B7
Hartington St ME4 . . . . . . .48 A3
Hartlake Rd TN11 . . . . . . .118 D3
Hartlands Cl DA5 . . . . .7 F1
Hartlepool Ct E16 . . . . .2 D2
Hartley Cl Bromley BR1 . .36 F7
  Maidstone ME15 . . . . .107 F6
Hartley Court Gdns TN17 169 A3
Hartley Cty Prim Sch DA3 .42 E3
Hartley Hill DA3 . . . . .43 A1
Hartley Rd Bexley DA16 . .7 C7
  Hartley TN17 . . . . .169 A4
  Longfield DA3 . . . . .42 E7
  Westerham TN16 . . . . .81 D2
Hartlip Endowed CE
  Prim Sch ME9 . . . . .64 D5
Hartlip Hill ME9 . . . . .64 F7
Hartmann Rd E16 . . . . .1 E5
Hartnokes TN18 . . . . .179 A4
Hartnup St ME16 . . . . .91 C2
Harton Cl BR1 . . . . .36 D8
Hartpiece Cl ME8 . . . . .49 F2
Hartshill Rd TN13 . . . . . . .84 C4
Hartslands Rd TN13 . . . . .84 C4
Hartsmead Rd SE9 . . . . . . .22 F6
Hartville Rd SE18 . . . . .2 E2
Hartwell Ho 2 SE7 . . . . . . .1 B1
Harty Ave ME8 . . . . .63 B3
Harvard Ave ME2 . . . . .46 F7
Harvard Rd 9 SE9 . . . . .6 A1
Harvel Ave ME8 . . . . .63 B8
Harvel Cl BR5,BR7 . . . . . . .38 A6
Harvel Cres SE2 . . . . .3 D1
Harvel La DA13 . . . . .58 B2
Harvel Rd DA13 . . . . .73 A8
Harvel St DA13 . . . . .58 C3
Harvest Bank Rd BR4 . . . .50 A7
Harvest Rd TN10 . . . . .117 D6
Harvest Ridge ME19 . . . . .74 D2
Harvest Way BR8 . . . . .39 D2
Harvesters Cl ME8 . . . . . . .63 E7
Harvesters Way ME14 . . . .92 D4
Harvey Gdns SE7 . . . . .1 C1
Harvey Point 6 E16 . . . . . . .1 A8
Harvey Rd ME8 . . . . .63 E8
Harvill Rd DA14 . . . . .24 E3
Harwood Ave BR1 . . . . .36 B7
Harwood Ct 3 RM17 . . . . .12 C8
Haslemere Est ME15 . . . .107 F5
Haslemere Rd DA7 . . . . .8 A5
Hasler Cl SE28 . . . . .3 C6
Hasletts Cl TN1 . . . . .149 B6
Haslewood Cl TN27 . . . . .143 B2
Hassendean Rd SE3 . . . . . .5 B7
Hassock Wood BR2 . . . . . .50 E6
Hassop Wlk SE9 . . . . .22 E4
Haste Hill Cl ME17 . . . . . .107 B3
Haste Hill Rd ME17 . . . . .107 B3
Hasted Cl DA9 . . . . .11 C1
Hasted Rd Greenwich SE7 .1 C1
  Newington ME9 . . . . .65 B7
Hasteds ME17 . . . . .94 D2

Hastings Cl RM17 . . . . .11 E8
Hastings Ho SE18 . . . . .1 F2
Hastings Rd
  Kipping's Cross TN2 . . . .150 F5
  Maidstone ME15 . . . . .92 B3
  Newenden TN17,TN18 . .187 C6
  Orpington BR2 . . . . .50 E8
  Pembury TN2 . . . . .150 D6
  The Moor TN18 . . . . .184 F6
Hastings St SE18 . . . . .2 C3
Hatch Rd ME1 . . . . .111 C5
Hatches La TN11,TN12 . .119 D6
Hatfield Ct SE3 . . . . .5 A7
Hatfield Rd ME7 . . . . .47 A8
Hatham Green La TN15 . .56 D1
Hathaway Cl BR2 . . . . .36 F1
Hathaway Ct
  Gillingham ME8 . . . . .63 D8
  Rochester ME1 . . . . .47 B5
Hatherall Rd ME14 . . . . . . .92 B6
Hatherley Cres DA14 . . . .24 A4
Hatherley Rd DA14 . . . . . .24 A5
Hathern Gdns SE9 . . . . . . .23 A4
Hatmill La TN12 . . . . .152 A7
Hattersfield Cl DA17 . . . . .3 F2
Hatton Cl Northfleet DA11 .29 E5
  Woolwich SE18 . . . . .6 D7
Hatton Ct BR7 . . . . .22 F1
Hatton Rd ME5 . . . . .62 C3
Havant Wlk 8 ME15 . . . .107 F6
Havelock Rd Bromley BR2 .36 C5
  Dartford DA1 . . . . .9 B1
  Erith DA17 . . . . .3 F2
  Gravesend DA11 . . . . .29 F7
  Tonbridge TN9 . . . . .117 B2
Haven Cl Chislehurst SE9 . .22 F5
  Istead Rise DA13 . . . . .43 F8
  Rochester ME1 . . . . .47 C2
  Sidcup DA14 . . . . .24 C2
  Swanley BR8 . . . . .39 F7
Haven Hill TN15 . . . . .57 A3
Haven Lodge 9 SE18 . . . . .2 B2
Haven St ME3 . . . . .33 C5
Haven Way ME4 . . . . .34 B1
Havengore Ave DA12 . . . .30 E8
Havering Cl TN2 . . . . .149 F6
Haverstock Ct 2 BR5 . . . .38 B7
Haverthwaite Rd BR6 . . . .51 D7
Havisham Cl ME1 . . . . .47 D2
Havisham Rd DA12 . . . . . . .31 A7
Havock La 1 ME14 . . . . . . .91 F4
Hawbeck Rd ME8 . . . . .63 C3
Hawden Cl TN11 . . . . .116 F4
Hawden La TN11 . . . . .116 F4
Hawden Rd TN9 . . . . .117 B2
Hawes Rd BR1 . . . . .36 B8
Hawfield Bank BR6 . . . . . .52 D8
Hawkenbury Cl TN2 . . . . .149 D2
Hawkenbury Mead TN2 .149 D1
Hawkenbury Rd
  Hawkenbury TN12 . . . . . .140 C6
  Royal Tunbridge Wells
  TN2,TN3 . . . . .149 E1
Hawkenbury Rise ME2 . . .33 B2
Hawkes Cl RM17 . . . . .12 B8
Hawkes Pl TN13 . . . . .99 A8
Hawkes Rd ME20 . . . . .75 F5
Hawkhurst CE Prim Sch
  Hawkhurst TN18 . . . . .178 F2
  The Moor TN18 . . . . .184 F8
Hawkhurst Cottage
  Hospl TN18 . . . . .178 D2
Hawkhurst Rd
  Flimwell TN5,TN18 . . . . .177 E2
  Gillingham ME8 . . . . .49 B3
  Hartley TN17,TN18 . . . . .178 F7
Hawkinge Wlk BR5 . . . . . .38 B6
Hawkins Ave DA12 . . . . . .30 C4
Hawkins Cl ME7 . . . . .48 A6
Hawksmoor Cl
  2 Newham E6 . . . . .1 E7
  Woolwich SE18 . . . . .2 E1
Hawksmoor Prim Sch SE28 .3 B6
Hawkwell Cotts TN2 . . . .134 F2
Hawkwood ME16 . . . . .91 B5
Hawkwood Cl ME1 . . . . . . .47 D5
Hawkwood La BR7 . . . . . . .37 C8
Hawley Ct ME16 . . . . .91 E4
Hawley Rd DA1,DA2,DA4 .27 A4
Hawley Terr DA2 . . . . .27 A4
Hawley Vale DA2 . . . . .27 A4
Hawser Rd ME1 . . . . .47 C1
Hawstead La BR6 . . . . .52 F5
Hawthorn Cl
  Edenbridge TN8 . . . . .112 C2
  Gravesend DA12 . . . . .30 C4
  Orpington BR5 . . . . .37 D3
Hawthorn Cotts 6 DA16 .7 A6
Hawthorn House 5 ME5 .61 F5
Hawthorn La TN13 . . . . . . .83 F5
Hawthorn Pl DA8 . . . . .4 C1
Hawthorn Rd Bexley DA6 .7 F3
  Dartford DA1 . . . . .26 D7
  Rochester ME2 . . . . .46 E6
Hawthorn Terr DA15 . . . . .6 F8
Hawthorn Wlk
  Royal Tunbridge Wells TN2 .149 E8
  Tonbridge TN10 . . . . .117 C7
Hawthorndene Cl BR2 . . .50 A8
Hawthorndene Rd BR2 . .50 A8
Hawthorne Ave ME8 . . . . .49 C2
Hawthorne Cl BR1 . . . . . . .36 F6
Hawthorne Rd BR1 . . . . . .36 F6
Hawthorns Chatham ME5 .42 F1
  Hartley DA3 . . . . .42 F5
Hawthorns The ME20 . . . .75 E1
Haxted Rd BR1 . . . . .36 B8
Hay's Mead DA13 . . . . .44 F3

Hayday Rd E16 . . . . .1 A8
Haydens Cl BR5 . . . . .38 C3
Haydens Mews TN9 . . . . .117 C3
Haydens The TN9 . . . . . . .117 C3
Hayes Cl Hayes BR2 . . . . .50 A8
  Higham ME3 . . . . .32 C3
  West Thurrock RM20 . . . .11 C8
Hayes Gdn BR2 . . . . .36 A1
Hayes La BR2 . . . . .36 A4
  Stockbury ME9 . . . . .79 F6
Hayes Prim Sch BR2 . . . . .36 B1
Hayes Rd Hayes BR2 . . . .36 A5
  Stone DA9 . . . . .27 E8
Hayes St BR2 . . . . .36 B1
Hayes Sta BR2 . . . . .36 A1
Hayes Terr DA12 . . . . .31 E3
Hayes Wlk ME17 . . . . .89 A2
Hayes Wood Ave BR2 . . .36 B1
Hayesbrook Sch TN9 . . . .133 A8
Hayesden La TN11,TN3 .132 B5
Hayesford Park Dr BR2 .36 A4
Hayfield ME19 . . . . .74 E2
Hayfield Rd BR5 . . . . .38 A4
Hayfields ME5 . . . . .62 D2
Haygate Ho ME1 . . . . .47 C4
Hayle Mill Cotts ME15 .106 F8
Hayle Mill Rd ME15 . . . .106 F8
Hayle Rd ME15 . . . . .92 A3
Hayley Cl ME2 . . . . .46 C2
Hayman Wlk ME20 . . . . . . .75 F6
Haymans Hill TN12 . . . . .153 C7
Haymen St ME4 . . . . .47 E3
Haynes Ho 3 ME14 . . . . . .92 B4
Haynes Rd DA11 . . . . .29 F5
Hayrick Cl ME14 . . . . .92 E5
Hays Rd ME6 . . . . .74 F6
Haysden Ctry Pk* TN11 .132 D8
Haywain Cl Maidstone ME14 92 F4
  Paddock Wood TN12 . . .136 A5
Hayward Ave ME2 . . . . .47 B8
Hayward Cl DA1 . . . . .8 D2
Hayward Dr DA1 . . . . .26 F6
Hayward Rd ME20 . . . . . . .36 D5
Haywood Rd BR2 . . . . .36 D5
Haywood Rise BR6 . . . . . .51 E5
Hazel Ave
  Hoo St Werburgh ME3 . .34 E3
  Maidstone ME15 . . . . .91 C5
Hazel Cotts TN14 . . . . .68 A6
Hazel Dr DA8 . . . . .9 B6
Hazel End BR8 . . . . .39 E4
Hazel Gr Chatham ME5 . .62 B8
  Orpington BR6 . . . . .51 B8
Hazel Rd Dartford DA1 . .26 D6
  Erith DA8 . . . . .9 A6
Hazel Shaw TN10 . . . . . . .117 D7
Hazel Street Rd ME9 . . . .80 A4
Hazel Wlk BR2 . . . . .37 A3
Hazelbank ME3 . . . . .147 F3
Hazelden Cl TN15 . . . . .56 A2
Hazeldene Rd DA16 . . . . . .7 C5
Hazelmere 8 DA14 . . . . . .24 A4
Hazelmere Rd BR5 . . . . . . .37 D5
Hazelmere Way BR2 . . . .36 A3
Hazels The ME8 . . . . .63 B5
Hazelwood Cl TN2 . . . . . .149 E8
Hazelwood Cotts TN5 . .176 D1
Hazelwood Dr ME16 . . . . .91 B4
Hazelwood Rd TN14 . . . . .66 D8
Hazelmere Dr ME7 . . . . . . .49 A5
Hazlitt Ct 4 SE28 . . . . .3 C5
Hazlitt Dr ME16 . . . . .91 D5
Head Race The ME15 . . . .91 D2
Headcorn
  Prim Sch TN27 . . . . .141 C5
Headcorn Rd
  Biddenden Green TN27 .142 C3
  Bromley BR1 . . . . .22 A3
  Gillingham ME8 . . . . .49 B4
  Lashenden TN27 . . . . .158 A5
  Platt's Heath ME17 . . . .110 F1
  Staplehurst TN12 . . . . . .140 B4
  Sutton Valence ME17 . .124 E4
  Ulcombe ME17 . . . . .125 F5
Headcorn Sta TN27 . . . . .141 D4
Headingley Rd ME16 . . . . .91 B6
Headley Ct TN8 . . . . .112 C2
Headley House 5 BR5 . . .38 B7
Headway Ct TN4 . . . . .148 B4
Healy Dr 1 BR6 . . . . .51 F6
Heansill La TN18 . . . . .184 E8
Hearns Rd BR5 . . . . .38 C5
Heartenoak Rd TN18 . . . .179 B3
Heath Ave DA7 . . . . .7 D8
Heath Cl Orpington BR5 . .38 C3
  Swanley BR8 . . . . .39 E4
Heath Ct TN12 . . . . .152 F6
Heath Gdns DA1 . . . . .26 C7
Heath Gr ME16 . . . . .91 A2
Heath House DA15 . . . . . . .23 F4
Heath La Dartford DA1 . .26 C7
  Dartford,Dartford
  Heath DA1,DA2 . . . . .26 B7
Heath Park Dr BR1 . . . . . .36 E6
Heath Rd Coldblow DA5 . .25 C7
  Coxheath ME17 . . . . .106 C3
  Crayford DA1 . . . . .8 F1
  Langley Heath ME17 . . .108 A4
  Maidstone ME16 . . . . .90 F3
Heath Rise BR2 . . . . .36 A3
Heath Side BR5 . . . . .37 C2
Heath St DA1 . . . . .26 D8
Heath Terr TN12 . . . . .153 A6
Heath The ME19 . . . . .89 F5
Heath View Dr SE2 . . . . . . .7 D8
Heath Villas SE18 . . . . .2 F1
Heath Way DA7,DA8 . . . . . .8 D6

Heathclose Ave DA1 . . . . .26 B8
Heathclose Rd DA1 . . . . . .26 B7
Heathcote Cl ME20 . . . . . .75 F2
Heathdene Dr DA17 . . . . . .4 B2
Heathend Rd BR5 . . . . .25 C7
Heather Bank TN12 . . . . .136 B6
Heather Cl Chatham ME5 .61 F4
  Newham E6 . . . . .2 A7
Heather Dr Dartford DA1 .26 A8
  Maidstone ME15 . . . . .92 B2
  Tenterden TN30 . . . . .173 B3
Heather End BR2 . . . . .39 D5
Heather Rd SE12 . . . . .22 A7
Heather Wlk TN10 . . . . . .117 B6
Heatherbank
  Chislehurst BR7 . . . . .37 A7
  Eltham SE9 . . . . .5 F5
Heatherbank Cl DA1 . . . . . .8 E1
Heatherside Rd DA14 . . . .24 C5
Heatherwood Cl ME17 . .109 E2
Heathfield Chislehurst BR7 .23 C2
  Langley Heath ME17 . . .108 A4
Heathfield Ave ME14 . . . .92 C7
Heathfield Cl Chatham ME5 .62 B7
  Maidstone ME14 . . . . .92 B7
  Newham E16 . . . . .1 D8
  Orpington BR2 . . . . .50 C5
Heathfield Ct DA14 . . . . . .24 B3
Heathfield La BR7 . . . . .23 C2
Heathfield Rd Bexley DA6 .7 F3
  Maidstone ME14 . . . . .92 C7
  Orpington BR2 . . . . .50 D5
  Sevenoaks TN13 . . . . .83 F5
Heathfield Terr Bexley SE18 .6 F8
  Swanley BR8 . . . . .39 D7
Heathfields TN2 . . . . .149 D4
Heathlands Rise DA1 . . . . .9 B1
Heathlee Rd DA1 . . . . .8 E1
Heathley End BR7 . . . . .23 C2
Heathorn St ME14 . . . . . . .92 B5
Heathside Ave Bexley DA7 .7 E5
  Coxheath ME17 . . . . .106 C4
Heathview TN4 . . . . .132 F2
Heathview Ave DA1 . . . . . . .8 E1
Heathview Cres DA1 . . . . .26 B7
Heathway SE3 . . . . .5 A7
Heathwood Gdns
  Swanley BR8 . . . . .39 C7
  Woolwich SE7 . . . . .1 E1
Heathwood Wlk DA5 . . . .25 E7
Heaverham Rd TN15 . . . .70 C2
Heavitree Cl 3 SE18 . . . . . .2 D1
Heavitree Rd SE18 . . . . .2 D1
Hector St SE18 . . . . .2 E2
Hectorage Rd TN9 . . . . . .133 D8
Hedge Place Rd DA9 . . . .11 A1
Hedgerow The ME14 . . . . .92 B5
Hedgerows The DA11 . . . .29 E6
Hedges The ME14 . . . . .92 A4
Hedley Ave RM20 . . . . .11 C8
Hedley St ME14 . . . . .92 A5
Heights The SE7 . . . . .1 C1
Helen Allison Sch
  The DA13 . . . . .44 A2
Helen Cl DA1 . . . . .26 B8
Helen Ct 9 DA14 . . . . .24 B4
Helen Keller Cl TN10 . . .117 D4
Helen St SE18 . . . . .2 B1
Heligan Cl BR6 . . . . .51 F6
Hellyar Ct ME1 . . . . .47 C4
Helverswood TN14 . . . . . .53 A2
Hemmings Cl DA14 . . . . . .24 B6
Hempstead Inf Sch ME7 .63 A5
Hempstead Jun Sch ME7 .63 A5
Hempstead Rd
  Gillingham ME7,ME8 . . . .63 A6
  Gillingham,Hempstead ME7 .63 A5
Hempstead Valley Dr ME7 .63 A4
Hempstead Valley Sh
  Ctr ME7 . . . . .63 A3
Hemsted Forest
  Forest Walks* TN17 . . .170 E2
Hemsted Rd DA8 . . . . .8 E7
Henbane Cl ME14 . . . . .92 E5
Henderson Dr DA1 . . . . . . .10 A3
Hendley Dr TN17 . . . . . . .169 C5
Hendry Ho ME3 . . . . .33 F6
Hendy Rd ME6 . . . . .75 B8
Henfield Cl DA5 . . . . .8 A1
Hengist Rd Eltham SE12 .22 B8
  Erith DA8 . . . . .8 C7
Hengrove Ct DA5 . . . . .24 E7
Henham Gdns TN12 . . . .120 A6
Henhurst Rd DA11 . . . . . .44 D8
Henhurst Rd
  Gravesend DA13 . . . . .30 E1
  Henhurst DA12 . . . . .44 E8
Heniker La TN27 . . . . .125 A4
Henley Bsns Pk ME2 . . . . .47 D7
Henley Cl Chatham ME5 .62 A6
  Gillingham ME8 . . . . .63 D3
  Royal Tunbridge Wells TN2 .149 C4
Henley Ct DA5 . . . . .24 F8
Henley Deane DA11 . . . . .29 E4
Henley Fields
  Maidstone ME14 . . . . .92 E6
  Tenterden TN30 . . . . .173 B2
Henley Meadows TN30 .173 A2
Henley Rd Newham E16 . .1 F4
  Paddock Wood TN12 . . .136 A2
Henley St DA13 . . . . .44 F3
Henley View TN30 . . . . . .173 B2
Henniker Cotts TN17 . . .169 A3
Henry Addington Cl E6 . .2 A8
Henry Cooper Way SE9 .22 D4
Henry St Bromley BR1 . .36 B8
  Chatham ME4 . . . . .48 B3
  9 Grays RM17 . . . . .12 C8

Henson Cl BR6 . . . . .51 B8
Henville Rd BR1 . . . . .36 B8
Henwick Prim Sch SE9 . . .5 E4
Henwick Rd SE9 . . . . .5 E4
Henwood Green
  Rd TN12,TN2 . . . . .150 E6
Henwoods Cres TN2 . . . .150 D6
Henwoods Mount TN2 .150 E6
Herald Wlk DA1 . . . . .9 F2
Herbert Pl SE18 . . . . .6 B8
Herbert Rd Bexley DA7 . .7 E5
  Bromley BR2 . . . . .36 E4
  Chatham ME4 . . . . .48 A3
  Gillingham ME8 . . . . .63 E8
  Hextable BR8 . . . . .26 B2
  Swanscombe DA10 . . . . . .11 F1
  Woolwich SE18 . . . . .6 B8
Herdsdown ME3 . . . . .34 D5
Hereford Cl ME8 . . . . .49 D2
Hereford Rd ME15 . . . . . .107 D7
Heritage Dr ME7 . . . . .48 F1
Heritage Hill BR2 . . . . .50 C5
Heritage Quay DA12 . . . . .13 C1
Heritage Rd ME5 . . . . .62 A6
Heritage The BR6 . . . . .38 A2
Herman Terr ME4 . . . . .48 A3
Hermitage Ct
  Maidstone ME16 . . . . .90 F5
  Tonbridge TN9 . . . . .117 B5
Hermitage La Detling ME14 78 B4
  Maidstone ME16,ME20 . .90 F6
  Rabbit's Cross ME17 . . .123 E6
Hermitage Rd ME3 . . . . . . .32 E4
Hern The TN15 . . . . .87 C5
Herne Rd ME8 . . . . .49 C2
Hero Wlk ME1 . . . . .61 C7
Heron
  Apartments 8 ME15 . .107 F5
Heron Cl TN8 . . . . .112 C4
Heron Cotts TN18 . . . . . .187 D3
Heron Cres DA14 . . . . .23 E4
Heron Ct BR2 . . . . .36 C5
Heron Hill DA17 . . . . .3 F2
Heron Hill La DA13 . . . . . .58 A4
Heron Rd ME20 . . . . .74 F1
Heron Way Chatham ME5 .62 B7
  Lower Stoke ME3 . . . . . . .19 C4
Heronden Rd ME15 . . . . .107 F4
Herongate Rd BR8 . . . . . . .25 E2
Herons Way TN2 . . . . .150 E8
Heronsgate Prim Sch SE28 .2 D3
Herringham Rd SE7 . . . . . . .1 C3
Herts Cres ME15 . . . . .106 F3
Hertsfield Ave ME2 . . . . . .33 A2
Hervey Rd SE3 . . . . .5 B6
Herying Cl ME2 . . . . .60 B4
Hesketh Ave DA2 . . . . .27 B7
Heskett Pk TN2 . . . . .150 E6
Hever Ave TN15 . . . . .55 E4
Hever Castle* TN8 . . . . . .129 D7
Hever CE Prim Sch TN8 .129 D6
Hever Cl ME15 . . . . .107 F6
Hever Court Rd DA12 . . . .30 D2
Hever Croft Eltham SE9 . .23 A4
  Rochester ME2 . . . . .46 F5
Hever Gdns Bromley BR1 .37 A7
  Maidstone ME16 . . . . .91 E3
Hever Ho ME2 . . . . .33 C1
Hever Hotel &
  Golf Club TN8 . . . . .113 D1
Hever Rd Hever TN8 . . . .129 B7
  West Kingsdown TN15 . .55 E4
Hever Road Cotts TN8 . .113 E2
Hever Sta TN8 . . . . .129 B6
Hever Wood Rd TN15 . . .55 E4
Heverham Rd SE18 . . . . . . .2 E2
Heversham Rd DA7 . . . . . . .8 A6
Hewett Ho 7 SE18 . . . . .2 B1
Hewett Cl Gillingham ME7 .48 F6
  Maidstone ME16 . . . . .91 D7
Hewitts Rd BR6,TN14 . . .52 F3
Hextable BR8 . . . . .91 D7
Hextable Inf Sch BR8 . . .25 F2
Hextable Jun Sch BR8 . . .25 F2
Hextable Sch BR8 . . . . .39 F8
Hibbs Cl BR8 . . . . .39 D7
Hibernia Dr DA12 . . . . .30 F5
Hibernia Point 11 SE2 . . .3 D4
Hickin Cl SE7 . . . . .1 D2
Hickman Cl E16 . . . . .1 D8
Hickory Dell ME7 . . . . .63 A5
Hide E6 . . . . .2 A7
Higgins' La ME4 . . . . .47 F5
High Banks
  Maidstone ME15 . . . . .106 F5
  Rochester ME1 . . . . .47 D2
High Beeches
  Orpington BR6 . . . . .52 A4
  Royal Tunbridge Wells TN2 .149 D6
  Sidcup DA14 . . . . .24 E3
High Broom Ind Pk TN2 .149 C8
High Brooms Rd TN4 . . .149 C7
High Brooms Sta TN4 . .149 C7
High Croft Cotts BR8 . . .40 A5
High Cross Rd TN15 . . . . .86 B1
High Dewar Rd ME8 . . . . .64 A8
High Elms ME8 . . . . .49 E1
High Elms (Ctry Pk)* BR6 51 D3
High Elms Rd BR6 . . . . . . .51 C2
High Firs BR8 . . . . .39 E5
High Firs Prim Sch BR8 .39 F5
High Gr Bromley BR1 . . . .36 D8
  Woolwich SE18 . . . . .6 D6
High Halden
  CE Prim Sch TN26 . . . . .173 E7
High Halden
  Rd TN26,TN27 . . . . .158 C2

High Halstow
Prim Sch ME23 . . . . .17 E3
High Hilden Cl TN10 . . . .117 A4
High House La TN11 . . . .102 C2
High Meads Rd E16 . . . . .1 D7
High Oak Hill ME9 . . . . .65 D8
High Point SE9 . . . . .23 B5
High Rd DA2 . . . . .26 C5
High Ridge TN17 . . . . .167 E8
High Rocks* TN3 . . . . .148 B1
High Rocks Halt TN3 . . . . .148 B1
High Rocks La TN3, TN4 . .148 C1
High St Aylesford ME20 . . . .75 F3
Bean DA2 . . . . .28 B5
Bidborough TN3 . . . . .132 C3
Biddenden TN27 . . . . .157 F1
Biddenden Green TN27 . . .143 A1
Borough Green TN15 . . . . . .86 F7
Brasted TN14, TN16 . . . . . . .82 C3
Brenchley TN12 . . . . .152 B8
Bromley BR1 . . . . .36 A7
Chatham ME4 . . . . .48 A4
Cowden TN8 . . . . .145 B5
Cranbrook TN17 . . . . .169 C4
Dartford DA1 . . . . .9 E1
Downe BR6 . . . . .66 A8
East Malling ME19 . . . . .90 A6
Edenbridge TN8 . . . . .112 C1
Eynsford DA4 . . . . .54 E8
Farningham DA4 . . . . .40 F2
Flimwell TN5 . . . . .177 C3
Frant TN3 . . . . .163 C4
Gillingham ME7 . . . . .48 C5
Gillingham,Brompton ME7 . . .48 A6
Goudhurst TN17 . . . . .167 E8
Grain ME3 . . . . .21 B6
Gravesend DA11 . . . . .13 B1
2 Grays RM17 . . . . .12 A8
Hadlow TN11 . . . . .118 E8
Halling ME2 . . . . .60 A4
Hawkhurst TN18 . . . . .178 E2
Headcorn TN27 . . . . .141 C5
Kemsing TN15 . . . . .70 B2
Lamberhurst TN3 . . . . .166 B5
Leigh TN11 . . . . .115 F1
Lenham ME17 . . . . .111 D5
Lower Stoke ME3 . . . . .19 C4
Maidstone ME14 . . . . .91 F4
Marden TN12 . . . . .138 D6
Newington ME9 . . . . .65 C6
Northfleet DA11 . . . . .12 C1
Orpington BR6 . . . . .38 A1
Orpington,Farnborough BR6 .51 C5
Orpington,Green Street
Green BR6 . . . . .51 F4
Orpington,St Mary Cray BR5 .38 C4
Otford TN14 . . . . .69 A3
Pembury TN2 . . . . .150 C6
Penshurst TN11 . . . . .131 B4
Rainham ME8 . . . . .63 F8
Rochester ME1 . . . . .47 C6
Rochester, Strood ME2 . . . . .47 B7
Rolvenden TN17 . . . . .181 E4
Royal Tunbridge Wells TN1 .149 A2
Seal TN15 . . . . .84 F6
Sevenoaks TN13 . . . . .84 C2
Sevenoaks,Chipstead TN13 . .83 C5
Shoreham TN14 . . . . .53 F1
Sidcup DA14 . . . . .24 A4
Snodland ME6 . . . . .75 A8
Staplehurst TN12 . . . . .139 F3
Sutton Valence ME17 . . . . .124 E7
Swanley BR8 . . . . .39 F5
Swanscombe DA10 . . . . .11 F2
Swanscombe,Greenhithe DA9 11 B3
Tenterden TN30 . . . . .183 A4
Ticehurst TN5 . . . . .176 C1
Tonbridge TN9 . . . . .117 C2
Upper Upnor ME2 . . . . .33 F1
Wadhurst TN5 . . . . .174 F4
West Malling ME19 . . . . .89 C8
Westerham TN16 . . . . .96 C8
Wouldham ME1 . . . . .60 C5
Wrotham TN15 . . . . .72 A3
Yalding ME18 . . . . .104 F1
High Tor Cl BR1 . . . . .22 B1
High View ME3 . . . . .32 C4
High Woods La TN2 . . . . . .150 B3
Higham Cl ME15 . . . . .91 E2
Higham Gdns TN10 . . . . . .117 F5
Higham La TN10, TN11 . . . .117 F5
Higham Prim Sch ME3 . . . .32 C5
Higham Rd Cliffe ME3 . . . .16 A4
Rochester ME3 . . . . .33 C3
Higham School Rd TN10 .117 E6
Higham Sta ME3 . . . . .32 D6
Higham View ME14 . . . . . . .76 E4
Highbanks Cl DA16 . . . . .7 B7
Highberry ME19 . . . . .74 E2
Highbrook Rd SE3 . . . . .5 D4
Highbury La TN30 . . . . . . .183 A7
Highcombe SE7 . . . . .5 B8
Highcombe Cl SE9 . . . . .22 E7
Highcroft Gn ME15 . . . . . .107 F4
Highcroft Hall BR8 . . . . .39 D1
Highcross Rd DA13 . . . . . . .28 D2
Highdown Cotts TN17 . . . .166 F3
Highfield Ave Erith DA8 . . . .8 B8
Orpington BR6 . . . . .51 F5
Highfield Cl Gillingham ME8 63 D7
Hawkhurst TN18 . . . . .179 A1
Pembury TN2 . . . . .150 D6
Highfield Cotts DA2 . . . . . .26 B2
Highfield Ct DA1 . . . . .26 D8
Highfield Rd Bexley DA6 . . . . .7 F2
Bromley BR1 . . . . .36 F5
Dartford DA1 . . . . .26 D8
Gillingham ME8 . . . . .63 D7

Highfield Rd continued
Kemsing TN14 . . . . .69 F3
Royal Tunbridge Wells TN4 . . .149 C7
St Paul's Cray BR7 . . . . .37 F6
Highfield Rd N DA1 . . . . . . .9 D1
Highfield Rd S DA1 . . . . . .26 D7
Highfields Rd TN8 . . . . . . .112 C4
Highgate Ct **8** TN18 . . . . .178 F2
Highgate Hill TN18 . . . . . .178 F1
Highgrove TN2 . . . . .163 A8
Highgrove Cl BR7 . . . . .36 E8
Highgrove Rd ME5 . . . . .62 A5
Highland Rd
Badgers Mount TN14 . . . . . .68 A8
Bexley DA6 . . . . .8 A3
Maidstone ME15 . . . . .107 C6
Highlands Dartford DA1 . . . .26 C8
Royal Tunbridge Wells TN2 .149 D7
Highlands Cl ME2 . . . . .46 D5
Highlands Hill ME8 . . . . . . .40 A8
Highlands Pk TN15 . . . . . . .84 E6
Highlands Rd BR5 . . . . .38 C2
Highmead SE18 . . . . .6 F7
Highridge ME7 . . . . .48 F1
Highridge Cl ME14 . . . . . . .92 F5
Highstead Cres DA8 . . . . . . .8 E7
Highview Vigo Village DA13 .73 B8
Woolwich SE18 . . . . .6 B7
Highview Cl ME15 . . . . . . .107 A8
Highview Dr ME5 . . . . .61 D5
Highview Rd DA14 . . . . .24 B4
Highway Prim Sch
The BR6 . . . . .52 C5
Highway The BR6 . . . . .52 C5
Highwood BR6 . . . . .51 C8
Highwood Dr BR6 . . . . .51 C8
Highwoods Cl ME3 . . . . . . .32 C4
Hilary Cl DA8 . . . . .8 C6
Hilary Gdns ME1 . . . . .46 F1
Hilbert Cl TN2 . . . . .149 C5
Hilborough Way ME6 . . . . . .51 D5
Hilda May Ave BR8 . . . . . . .39 E7
Hilda Rd ME4 . . . . .48 A3
Hilda Vale Cl BR6 . . . . .51 A6
Hilda Vale Rd BR6 . . . . .51 B6
Hilden Ave TN11 . . . . .116 F4
Hilden Dr DA8 . . . . .9 B7
Hilden Grange Sch TN10 .117 B3
Hilden Oaks Sch TN10 . . .117 B3
Hilden Park Rd TN11 . . . .116 F4
Hildenborough
CE Prim Sch TN11 . . . . .116 D6
Hildenborough Cres ME16 91 C7
Hildenborough Rd
Leigh TN11 . . . . .116 A3
Shipbourne TN11, TN15 . . .100 A4
Hildenborough Sta TN11 .116 B6
Hilders Cl TN8 . . . . .112 B4
Hilders La TN8 . . . . .112 A4
Hill Brow Bromley BR1 . . . .36 D8
Crayford DA1 . . . . .8 F1
Maidstone ME14 . . . . .93 A5
Hill Chase ME15 . . . . .61 E3
Hill Cl Chislehurst BR7 . . . . .23 B3
Istead Rise DA13 . . . . .29 E1
Hill Cres Coldblow DA5 . . . .25 C7
Lenham ME17 . . . . .111 D5
Hill Crest
Royal Tunbridge Wells TN4 .149 B8
Sevenoaks TN13 . . . . .84 A5
Sidcup DA15 . . . . .24 B8
Hill Ct ME3 . . . . .33 F4
Hill End Orpington BR6 . . . .51 F8
Woolwich SE18 . . . . .6 A6
Hill Farm Cl ME23 . . . . . . .17 E3
Hill Green Rd ME9 . . . . .79 D8
Hill House Rd DA2 . . . . .27 C8
Hill Rd Dartford DA2 . . . . . .26 E6
Rochester ME1 . . . . .47 A2
Wouldham ME1 . . . . .60 F5
Hill Rise DA2 . . . . .27 E3
Hill Sch The ME14 . . . . . . .93 A5
Hill Shaw DA3 . . . . .42 F3
Hill St TN1 . . . . .149 B5
Hill The Cranbrook TN17 . .169 D4
Northfleet DA11 . . . . .12 C1
Hill Top TN17 . . . . .154 E5
Hill Top Cotts ME17 . . . . .106 E2
Hill View Basted TN15 . . . . .86 F4
Borough Green TN15 . . . . . .87 A7
Hill View Cl TN15 . . . . .87 A7
Hill View Dr DA16 . . . . .6 E5
Hill View Rd New Barn DA3 .43 B6
Orpington BR6 . . . . .51 F8
Royal Tunbridge Wells TN4 .148 C4
Tonbridge TN11 . . . . .116 F5
Hill View Way ME5 . . . . . . .61 E5
Hill's Terr ME4 . . . . .47 F3
Hillary Ave DA11 . . . . .29 E5
Hillary Ct SE9 . . . . .22 E6
Hillary Rd ME14 . . . . .92 A7
Hillbert Rd TN2 . . . . .149 C5
Hillborough Ave TN13 . . . . .84 D5
Hillborough Gr ME5 . . . . . . .62 A3
Hillbrow Cl DA5 . . . . .25 D4
Hillbury Gdns TN5 . . . . . . .176 D1
Hillcrest TN8 . . . . .113 B5
Hillcrest Ave RM20 . . . . . . .11 A8
Hillcrest Dr Cuxton ME2 . . . .46 C2
Royal Tunbridge Wells TN2 .149 D7
Stone DA9 . . . . .11 A2
Hillcrest Rd Bromley BR1 . .22 A4
Chatham ME4 . . . . .47 F2
Dartford DA1 . . . . .25 F8
Marlpit Hill TN8 . . . . .112 C4
Orpington BR6 . . . . .52 A8
Hillcroft Rd E6 . . . . .2 B8
Hilden Shaw ME15 . . . . . .107 A8

Hilldown Lodge BR6 . . . . . .52 B8
Hilldrop Rd BR1 . . . . .22 B2
Hillfield Rd TN13 . . . . .83 E7
Hillfield Villas TN26 . . . . . .173 F8
Hillgarth TN4 . . . . .149 A8
Hillingdon Ave TN13 . . . . . .84 D6
Hillingdon Rd Bexley DA7 . . .8 A8
Gravesend DA11 . . . . .30 B6
Hillingdon Rise TN13 . . . . .84 D5
Hillreach SE18 . . . . .1 F1
Hills La TN15 . . . . .70 C7
Hillsgrove Cl DA16 . . . . .7 C7
Hillsgrove Prim Sch DA16 .7 C7
Hillshaw Cres ME2 . . . . . . .46 D5
Hillside Dartford DA2 . . . . . .27 E3
Erith DA17 . . . . .4 C2
Farningham DA4 . . . . .40 F2
Rochester ME1 . . . . .47 A2
Tonbridge TN9 . . . . .133 A7
Hillside Ave
Gravesend DA12 . . . . .30 D6
Rochester ME2 . . . . .47 B8
Hillside Cotts TN5 . . . . . . .175 B8
Hillside Ct
2 Rochester ME2 . . . . .47 A7
Swanley BR8 . . . . .40 A5
Wateringbury ME18 . . . . . .104 E7
Hillside Dr DA12 . . . . .30 D6
Hillside La BR2 . . . . .50 A8
Hillside Rd Chatham ME4 . . .48 A4
Crayford DA1 . . . . .9 A1
Kemsing TN15 . . . . .69 F2
Sevenoaks TN13 . . . . .84 D4
Hillside Terr DA12 . . . . .30 B7
Hillside The BR6 . . . . .52 B7
Hillsley TN3 . . . . .148 B1
Hilltop Tonbridge TN9 . . . .133 B7
West Farleigh ME15 . . . . . .105 D3
Hilltop Gdns Dartford DA1 . . .9 F2
Orpington BR6 . . . . .51 E8
Hilltop Prim Sch DA1 . . . . .9 F2
Hilltop Rd Rochester ME2 . . .33 C1
West Thurrock RM20 . . . . . .11 B8
Hillview Cres BR6 . . . . .37 F1
Hillview Ho DA12 . . . . .30 C7
Hillview Rd BR7 . . . . .23 A4
Hillview
Sch forGirls TN9 . . . . . . .133 D8
Hilldeal Rd TN14 . . . . .69 C4
Hillyfield Cl ME2 . . . . .32 F1
Hillyfields Jun Sch ME7 . . .48 E6
Hilton Rd ME3 . . . . .33 B7
Hind Cres DA8 . . . . .8 D7
Hines Terr ME5 . . . . .48 C1
Hinksden Rd TN17, TN18 . .179 F3
Hinksey Path SE2 . . . . .3 C3
Hinstock Rd SE18 . . . . .6 C7
Hinton Cl SE9 . . . . .22 E7
Hinton Cres ME7 . . . . .63 A6
Historic Dockyard
The* ME4 . . . . .48 A7
Hitchen Hatch La TN13 . . . .84 B4
Hither Chantlers TN3 . . . . .148 A2
Hither Farm Rd SE3 . . . . .5 C4
Hive La DA11 . . . . .12 B2
Hive The DA11 . . . . .12 B1
Hoath Cl ME8 . . . . .63 B7
Hoath La ME8 . . . . .63 B7
Hoath Meadow TN12 . . . . .153 A6
Hoath Way ME7, ME8 . . . . . .63 B5
Hobart Rd RM18 . . . . .13 A6
Hoblands End BR7 . . . . .23 E2
Hockenden La BR8 . . . . .39 B7
Hockers Cl ME14 . . . . .93 A8
Hockers La ME14 . . . . .93 A7
Hoddesdon Rd DA17 . . . . . . .4 A1
Hodgkins Cl SE28 . . . . .3 D6
Hodgson Cres ME6 . . . . . . .60 A1
Hodsoll Ct BR5 . . . . .38 D4
Hodsoll St TN15 . . . . .57 D1
Hodson Cres BR5 . . . . .38 D3
Hog Hill ME14 . . . . .93 B5
Hog La DA11 . . . . .29 D5
Hogarth Cl E16 . . . . .1 D8
Hogben Cl ME17 . . . . .95 F2
Hoghole La TN3 . . . . .165 F2
Hognore La TN15 . . . . .72 D6
Hogs Orch BR8 . . . . .40 B8
Hogtrough Hill TN16 . . . . . .82 A5
Holaden Ct TN8 . . . . .112 C1
Holbeach Gdns DA15 . . . . . . .6 F1
Holborn La ME4 . . . . .47 F5
Holborn Rd E13 . . . . .1 B8
Holborough Rd ME6 . . . . . . .60 A1
Holbrook House BR7 . . . . . .37 D8
Holbrook La BR7 . . . . .23 D1
Holbrook Way BR2 . . . . .36 F4
Holburne Cl SE3 . . . . .5 C6
Holburne Gdns SE3 . . . . .5 D6
Holburne Rd SE3 . . . . .5 D6
Holcombe Ct TN16 . . . . . . .81 D1
Holcombe Rd
Chatham ME4 . . . . .47 F2
Rochester ME1 . . . . .47 C3
Holcote Cl DA17 . . . . .3 E3
Holden Cnr TN4 . . . . .132 F1
Holden Park Rd TN4 . . . . .149 A8
Holden Rd TN4 . . . . .132 F1
Holder Cl ME5 . . . . .62 C6
Holding St ME8 . . . . .49 F1
Hole La TN8 . . . . .112 A6
Holford St **1** TN9 . . . . . . .117 B1
Holgate St SE7 . . . . .1 D3
Holland Ho ME1 . . . . .47 D5
Hollands Cl DA12 . . . . .31 E3
Hollies Ave DA15 . . . . .23 F7

Hollies The
Gravesend DA12 . . . . .30 D2
New Barn DA3 . . . . .43 C6
Sidcup DA15 . . . . .24 A8
Holligrave Rd BR1 . . . . .36 A8
Hollin Cl TN4 . . . . .148 F4
Hollingbourne Ave DA7 . . . . .7 F6
Hollingbourne Hill ME17 .94 F4
Hollingbourne
Prim Sch ME17 . . . . .94 E2
Hollingbourne Rd ME8 . . . .49 C2
Hollingbourne Sta ME17 . .94 C3
Hollingbourne
Tower **4** ME7 . . . . .38 D1
Hollington Ct BR7 . . . . .23 B2
Hollingworth Rd
Maidstone ME15 . . . . .107 F5
Orpington BR2,BR5 . . . . . . .37 B2
Hollingworth Way TN16 . . .81 D1
Hollow La Hartlip ME9 . . . . .64 E5
Snodland ME6 . . . . .74 F6
Hollow Trees Dr TN11 . . . .116 A1
Holly Bank ME1 . . . . .152 B8
Holly Bush La TN13 . . . . . . .84 C3
Holly Cl Chatham ME5 . . . . .62 C8
Gillingham ME7 . . . . .48 E6
Holly Cotts TN18 . . . . .112 B2
Holly Ct **1** DA14 . . . . .24 B4
Holly Farm Rd ME15 . . . . .108 C6
Holly Hill DA13 . . . . .58 F3
Holly Hill Rd DA8,DA17 . . . .4 B1
Holly Rd Dartford DA1 . . . . .26 D7
Orpington BR6 . . . . .52 A3
Rochester,Strood ME2 . . . . .46 E5
Rochester,Wainscott ME2 . .33 D2
Holly Tree Cl ME17 . . . . . .109 E2
Hollybrake Cl BR7 . . . . .23 D1
Hollybush Cl TN13 . . . . . . .84 C3
Hollybush Ct TN13 . . . . . . .84 C3
Hollybush La BR6 . . . . .53 A4
Hollybush Rd DA12 . . . . . . .30 C6
Hollycroft ME2 . . . . .46 C2
Hollydale Dr BR2 . . . . .50 F7
Hollydene Rd TN5 . . . . . . .174 F6
Hollyshaw Cl TN2 . . . . . . .149 C2
Hollytree Ave BR8 . . . . .39 E7
Hollytree Dr ME3 . . . . .32 B3
Hollytree Par DA14 . . . . . . .24 C2
Hollywood La
Knockmill TN15 . . . . .70 F8
Rochester ME2 . . . . .33 C2
Hollywood Manor TN15 . . .70 F7
Hollywood Way DA8 . . . . .9 B6
Holm Ct **5** SE12 . . . . .22 B5
Holm Mill La ME17 . . . . . .110 B6
Holm Wlk SE3 . . . . .5 A5
Holmbury Manor **21** DA14 .24 A4
Holmbury Pk BR7 . . . . .22 E1
Holmcroft Way BR2 . . . . . . .36 F4
Holmdale Rd BR7 . . . . .23 C3
Holmdene Ct **5** BR1 . . . . .36 E6
Holmes Ct ME23 . . . . .17 E3
Holmes Ct ME19 . . . . .73 F4
Holmesdale Cl
Maidstone ME15 . . . . .106 F3
Wadhurst TN5 . . . . .174 E5
Holmesdale Com Sch ME6 74 F7
Holmesdale Rd Bexley DA7 .7 D5
Sevenoaks TN13 . . . . .84 D4
Sutton at Hone DA4 . . . . . . .41 C8
Holmesdale Sch
(Farm Annex) ME6 . . . . .74 F6
Holmewood Ho TN3 . . . . .148 A2
Holmewood Rd TN4 . . . . .149 C7
Holmewood Ridge TN3 . .147 F3
Holmhurst Cl TN4 . . . . . . .148 F4
Holmhurst Rd DA17 . . . . . . .4 B1
Holmleigh Ave DA1 . . . . .9 C4
Holmoaks Gillingham ME8 . .49 E2
Maidstone ME14 . . . . .92 C5
Holmside Gr DA1,DA7 . . . . . .8 E4
Holmside ME7 . . . . .48 E3
Holmwood Cotts BR6 . . . . .52 C1
Holmwood Ct DA14 . . . . . . .23 F3
Holstein Way **6** DA18 . . . . .3 E3
Holt Cl SE28 . . . . .4 D2
Holt Rd E16 . . . . .1 E5
Holt Wood Ave ME20 . . . . .90 E8
Holtwood Cl ME8 . . . . .63 D6
Holtye Cres ME15 . . . . .92 B2
Holtye Golf Club TN8 . . . .144 F3
Holtye Rd RH19 . . . . .144 A3
Holwood Park
Ave BR2,BR6 . . . . .50 F6
Holy Family RC Prim Sch
Eltham SE3 . . . . .5 C3
Maidstone ME15 . . . . .107 F4
Holy Innocents
RC Prim Sch BR6 . . . . . . .51 F7
Holy Trinity CE Prim Sch
Dartford DA1 . . . . .9 C2
Gravesend DA12 . . . . .30 C8
Holy Trinity
Coll & Prep Sch ME1 . . . .36 C8
Holy Trinity Lamorbey CE
Prim Sch DA15 . . . . .24 A7
Holyhead Cl **8** E6 . . . . .1 F8
Holyoake Terr TN13 . . . . . .84 A3
Holyrood Mews E16 . . . . . . .1 A5
Holywell Cl SE3 . . . . .5 A8
Home Farm ME17 . . . . . . .116 A3
Home Farm Cotts BR5 . . . . .38 D4
Home Farm La TN11,TN2 .133 F1
Home Gdns DA1 . . . . .9 E1
Home Hill BR8 . . . . .25 F1
Home Lea BR6 . . . . .51 F5

Home Mead Cl **6** DA12 . . .30 B8
Homedean Rd TN13 . . . . . . .83 C4
Homefarm Est ME20 . . . . . .75 F1
Homefield Cl
St Paul's Cray BR5 . . . . .38 B5
Swanley BR8 . . . . .39 F6
Homefield Rd Bromley BR1 .36 C3
Sevenoaks TN13 . . . . .83 E5
Homefield Rise BR6 . . . . . .38 A1
Homemead
7 Gravesend DA12 . . . . . . .30 B8
Swanscombe DA9 . . . . .11 B1
Homemead Rd BR2 . . . . . . .36 F4
Homer Cl DA7 . . . . .8 C6
Homesdale Rd
Bromley BR1,BR2 . . . . .36 C6
Orpington BR5 . . . . .37 E2
Homestead Rd
Marlpit Hill TN8 . . . . .112 B5
Orpington BR6 . . . . .52 B4
Homestead The
Crayford DA1 . . . . .8 E2
Dartford DA1 . . . . .9 C1
Groombridge TN3 . . . . .161 C7
Homevale Cotts TN14 . . . . .67 E4
Homewards Rd ME3 . . . . . . .19 B8
Homewood Cotts DA2 . . . . .31 E1
Homewood Cres BR7 . . . . . .23 E2
Homewood Rd
Royal Tunbridge Wells TN3 .147 F3
Tenterden TN30 . . . . .173 B1
Homewood Sch &
Sixth Form Ctr TN30 . . .173 B1
Homoeopathic Hospl TN1 .149 A3
Honduras Terr **8** ME14 . . .92 A7
Hone St ME2 . . . . .47 B8
Honey Bee Glade ME8 . . . .63 E6
Honey Cl ME7 . . . . .63 A5
Honey La ME15 . . . . .108 B6
Honeybourne Way BR7 . . . .37 D1
Honeycrest Ind Pk TN12 .139 E5
Honeycrock Hill ME9 . . . . . .79 F8
Honeyden Rd DA14 . . . . . . .24 E2
Honeypot Cl ME2 . . . . .47 B8
Honeypot La
Culverstone Green TN15 . . . .57 D2
Kemsing TN15 . . . . .85 C8
Honeysuckle Cl
3 Chatham ME5 . . . . .61 E4
Gillingham ME7 . . . . .62 F4
Honeysuckle Ct **4** SE12 . .22 A8
Honiton Rd DA16 . . . . .6 F5
Honywood Rd ME17 . . . . . .111 C4
Hoo Comm ME3 . . . . .34 A4
Hoo Rd ME2,ME3 . . . . .33 D3
Hoo St Werburgh
Mid Sch ME3 . . . . .34 C5
Hoo St Werburgh
Prim Sch ME3 . . . . .34 D5
Hood Ave BR5 . . . . .38 B4
Hook Cl ME5 . . . . .61 E5
Hook Farm Rd BR2 . . . . . . .36 D4
Hook Green Ct DA13 . . . . . .44 A4
Hook Green La DA2 . . . . . . .25 F5
Hook Green Rd DA13 . . . . . .28 E1
Hook Hill TN5 . . . . .176 A6
Hook La Bexley DA16 . . . . . . .7 A4
Harrietsham ME17 . . . . . . .110 C6
Hook Lane Prim Sch DA16 .7 A4
Hook Rd ME6 . . . . .74 F8
Hook St ME17 . . . . .127 F8
Hookfields DA11 . . . . .29 E5
Hookstead TN26 . . . . .173 C7
Hookwood Cotts TN14 . . . .67 C8
Hookwood Rd BR6,TN14 . . .67 C7
Hooper Rd E16 . . . . .1 A7
Hooper's Pl ME1 . . . . .47 C4
Hooper's Rd ME1 . . . . .47 C4
Hoopers La ME3 . . . . .18 F5
Hoopers Yd TN15 . . . . .84 C1
Hop Pocket Cl TN17 . . . . .170 A8
Hop Pocket La TN12 . . . . .135 F7
Hope Ave TN11 . . . . .102 E1
Hope Cl SE12 . . . . .22 B5
Hope Cotts DA2 . . . . .28 B6
Hope Rd DA10 . . . . .11 F1
Hope St Chatham ME4 . . . . .48 A3
Maidstone ME14 . . . . .91 F6
Hope Terr ME3 . . . . .32 D7
Hopedale Rd SE7 . . . . .5 B8
Hopehouse La TN17,TN18 186 E2
Hopes Gr TN26 . . . . .173 D7
Hopewell Dr Chatham ME5 .62 C8
Gravesend DA12 . . . . .30 F3
Hopgarden Cl **12** TN8 . . . .112 D3
Hopgarden La TN13 . . . . . . .99 A8
Hopgarden Oast ME18 . . .104 F1
Hopgarden Rd TN10 . . . . . .117 D6
Hoppers Cnr ME15 . . . . . .105 D7
Hopton Ct BR2 . . . . .36 A1
Hopton Rd SE18 . . . . .2 C3
Hopwood Gdns TN4 . . . . . .149 A6
Horizon TN4 . . . . .149 B8
Horley Cl DA6 . . . . .8 A2
Horley Rd SE9 . . . . .22 E4
Horn La SE10 . . . . .1 A2
Horn Link Way SE10 . . . . . . .1 A2
Horn Park Cl SE12 . . . . .5 B2
Horn Park La SE12 . . . . .5 B2
Horn Park Prim Sch SE12 .22 B8
Horn Yd DA11 . . . . .13 B1
Horn's Oak Rd DA13 . . . . . .58 B6
Hornbeam Ave
Chatham ME5 . . . . .62 B2
Royal Tunbridge Wells TN4 .133 D1

Hornbeam Cl
Larkfield ME20 . . . . .75 B2
Paddock Wood TN12 . . . . . .135 F5
Hornbeam House **6** DA15 .24 A5
Hornbeam La DA7 . . . . .8 C5
Hornbeam Way BR2 . . . . . . .37 A3
Hornbeams DA13 . . . . .73 B8
Horncastle Cl SE12 . . . . .22 A8
Horncastle Rd SE12 . . . . . . .22 A8
Horne Ho SE18 . . . . .5 E6
Hornetts Cl BR8 . . . . .39 D2
Hornfair Rd SE7 . . . . .5 D7
Hornfield Cotts DA13 . . . . . .58 C3
Horning Cl SE9 . . . . .22 E4
Horns La ME18 . . . . .88 D1
Horns Lodge La TN11 . . . . .117 A8
Horns Rd TN18 . . . . .184 D8
Horsa Rd Eltham SE12 . . . . .22 C8
Erith DA8 . . . . .8 C7
Horse Leaze E6 . . . . .2 A7
Horse Wash La ME1 . . . . . . .47 C6
Horsecroft Cl BR6 . . . . .38 B1
Horsegrove Ave TN5 . . . . . .176 F1
Horsell Rd BR5 . . . . .38 B8
Horseshoe Cl
Gillingham ME7 . . . . .62 F5
Maidstone ME14 . . . . .92 E5
Horseshoes La ME17 . . . . . .108 C4
Horsfeld Gdns SE9 . . . . .5 E2
Horsfeld Rd SE9 . . . . .5 D2
Horsfield Cl DA2 . . . . .27 C8
Horsham Rd DA6 . . . . .8 A2
Horsley Ho SE18 . . . . .6 A7
Horsley Rd Bromley BR1 . . . .36 B8
Rochester ME1 . . . . .47 B4
Horsmonden Cl BR6 . . . . . . .37 F2
Horsmonden
Prim Sch TN12 . . . . .153 A6
Horsmonden Rd TN12 . . . . .152 D6
Horsted Ave ME4 . . . . .47 E1
Horsted Cty Inf Sch ME4 . .61 D5
Horsted Cty Jun Sch ME5 .61 D5
Horsted Way ME1 . . . . .61 D7
Horton Downs ME15 . . . . . . .92 F1
Horton Kirby
CE Prim Sch DA4 . . . . . . .41 C6
Horton Pl TN16 . . . . .81 D1
Horton Rd DA4 . . . . .41 C6
Horton Tower **2** BR5 . . . . . .38 C5
Horton Way DA4 . . . . .40 F2
Hortons Cl TN17 . . . . .180 D7
Hortons Way **1** TN16 . . . . . .81 D1
Horwood Cl ME1 . . . . .61 B8
Hoselands View DA3 . . . . . . .42 E5
Hoser Ave SE12 . . . . .22 A6
Hosey Common La TN16 . .96 F5
Hosey Common
Rd TN8,TN16 . . . . .96 D5
Hosey Hill TN16 . . . . .96 E8
Hoskin's Cl E16 . . . . .1 C7
Hospital La **3** ME1 . . . . .47 E4
Hospital Rd
Hollingbourne ME17 . . . . .109 E8
Sevenoaks TN13 . . . . .84 C6
Hostler Cl ME2 . . . . .60 B4
Hotel Rd ME8 . . . . .49 A2
Hotham Cl
Sutton at Hone DA4 . . . . . . .27 B1
Swanley Village BR8 . . . . . . .40 B8
Hothfield Rd ME8 . . . . .49 F1
Hottsfield DA3 . . . . .42 E6
Hougham House **11** BR5 . .38 C5
Houghton Ave ME7 . . . . .63 B3
Houselands Rd TN9 . . . . . .117 B2
Hove Cl RM17 . . . . .12 A8
Hovendens TN17 . . . . .170 A8
Hoveton Rd SE28 . . . . .3 C7
How Green La TN8 . . . . . . .113 C2
Howard Ave Rochester ME1 47 C8
Sidcup DA5 . . . . .24 C8
Howard Dr ME16 . . . . .91 B5
Howard Gdns TN2 . . . . .149 A1
Howard Rd Bromley BR1 . . . .22 A1
Dartford DA1 . . . . .10 A1
East Malling ME19 . . . . .89 F8
Howard Sch The ME8 . . . . . .63 D8
Howarth Rd SE2 . . . . .3 A2
Howbury La DA8 . . . . .9 A5
Howbury Rd DA1,DA8 . . . . . . .9 A5
Howbury Wlk ME8 . . . . .63 D6
Howden Cl SE28 . . . . .3 D6
Howells Cl TN15 . . . . .55 E4
Howes Cotts TN18 . . . . . . .184 F8
Howick Cl ME20 . . . . .90 F8
Howick Mans SE18 . . . . .1 E3
Howland Rd TN12 . . . . .138 E6
Howlsmere Cl ME2 . . . . .60 B3
Hubbard's Hill TN13,TN14 .99 B4
Hubbard's La ME15 . . . . . . .107 A3
Hubble Dr ME15 . . . . .107 E7
Huckleberry Cl ME5 . . . . . . .62 B3
Hudson Cl ME8 . . . . .49 C1
Hudson Pl SE18 . . . . .2 C1
Hudson Rd DA7 . . . . .7 F6
Hugh Christie Tech Coll
The TN10 . . . . .117 D6
Hughes Dr ME2 . . . . .33 D2
Hulkes La ME1 . . . . .47 E4
Hulsewood Cl DA2 . . . . .26 B5
Hulsons Ct **1** TN18 . . . . . .179 A2
Humber Cres ME2 . . . . .46 F7
Humber Rd Dartford DA1 . . . .9 D2
Greenwich SE3 . . . . .5 A8
Humboldt Ct TN2 . . . . .149 D5
Hume Ave RM18 . . . . .13 B5

Hume Cl RM18 . . . . .13 A4
Humphreys TN12 . . . . .151 F6
Hundred of Hoo
Comp Sch The ME3 . . . . .34 C5
Hungershall Park Cl TN4 148 E1
Hungershall Pk TN4 . . . . . .148 E2
Hunsdon Dr ME13 . . . . .84 B4
Hunstanton Cl ME8 . . . . .63 E3
Hunt Rd Northfleet DA11 . . . .29 F5
Tonbridge TN10 . . . . .117 E6
Hunt St
Nettlestead ME15,ME18 . . .104 F5
West Farleigh ME15 . . . . . .105 B5
Hunter's Gr BR6 . . . . .51 C6
Hunters Cl DA5 . . . . .25 E5
Hunters Ct **5** ME7 . . . . .48 C7
Hunters Lodge **10** DA15 . . .24 A5
Hunters Way
Gillingham ME7 . . . . .48 E1
Royal Tunbridge Wells TN2 .148 F1
Hunters Way W ME5 . . . . . .48 E1
Hunters Wlk TN14 . . . . .67 E5
Huntersfield Cl ME5 . . . . . . .62 C1
Huntingdon Wlk **2** ME15 107 E7
Huntingfield Rd DA13 . . . . . .44 A2
Huntington Cl TN17 . . . . . .169 D4
Huntington Rd ME17 . . . . . .106 B3
Huntley Ave DA11 . . . . .12 C1
Huntley Mill Rd TN5 . . . . . .176 E3
Huntleys Pk TN4 . . . . .148 F5
Hunton
CE Prim Sch ME15 . . . . .121 D7
Hunton Hill ME15 . . . . .105 F1
Hunton House **4** BR5 . . . . .38 C5
Hunton Rd ME14 . . . . .122 A3
Hunts Cl SE3 . . . . .5 A5
Hunts Farm Cl TN15 . . . . . . .87 A7
Hunts La TN17 . . . . .167 E8
Hunts Mede Cl BR7 . . . . . . .22 F1
Huntsman La
Maidstone ME14 . . . . .92 B4
Wrotham Heath TN15 . . . . . .72 E1
Huntsman's Cnr ME4 . . . . . .61 E8
Huntsmans Cl ME1 . . . . .47 E1
Huntsmoor House BR5 . . . . .38 B5
Hurlfield ME2 . . . . .26 C5
Hurlingham Rd DA7 . . . . .7 F7
Huron Cl **5** BR6 . . . . .51 F4
Hurricane Rd ME19 . . . . .88 F3
Hurst Cl Chatham ME5 . . . . .61 F4
Staplehurst TN12 . . . . .139 F4
Tenterden TN30 . . . . .182 F7
Hurst Ct Newham E6 . . . . .1 D8
Sidcup DA5 . . . . .24 A6
Hurst Farm Rd TN14 . . . . . .99 B3
Hurst Green
CE Sch TN19 . . . . .184 A2
Hurst Hill ME5 . . . . .61 E2
Hurst Ho SE2 . . . . .3 D1
Hurst La Erith SE2 . . . . .3 D1
Sevenoaks Weald TN14 . . . .99 B2
Hurst Pl Erith SE2 . . . . .7 D8
Gillingham ME8 . . . . .63 F8
Woolwich SE2 . . . . .3 C1
Hurst Prim Sch DA5 . . . . . .24 D7
Hurst Rd Erith DA8 . . . . .8 C7
Sidcup DA5 . . . . .24 D7
Hurst Springs DA5 . . . . .24 E7
Hurst The Crouch TN11 . . . .102 D7
Plaxtol Spoute TN15 . . . . . . .87 C1
Royal Tunbridge Wells TN2 .149 E7
Hurst Way Maidstone ME16 .90 F2
Sevenoaks TN13 . . . . .99 C8
Hurstbourne Cotts DA5 . . . .25 B8
Hurstfield BR2 . . . . .36 A4
Hurstings The ME15 . . . . . . .91 D2
Hurstmere
Foundation Sch DA15 . .24 C7
Hurstwood ME5 . . . . .61 E4
Hurstwood Ave
Erith DA7,DA8 . . . . .8 E6
Sidcup DA5 . . . . .24 E7
Hurstwood Dr BR1 . . . . .36 F6
Hurstwood La TN4 . . . . .148 E3
Hurstwood Pk TN4 . . . . . . .148 F3
Hurstwood Rd
Bredhurst ME7 . . . . .63 B1
Detling ME14 . . . . .78 B7
Husheath Hill TN17 . . . . . . .154 F6
Hussar Ho ME1 . . . . .47 C3
Husseywell Cres BR2 . . . . . .36 A1
Hutchings Rd SE28 . . . . .3 A5
Hutsford Cl ME8 . . . . .63 D5
Hutson Terr RM19 . . . . .10 D8
Huxley Cl ME1 . . . . .47 D4
Huxley Ho SE2 . . . . .3 D1
Huxley Rd DA16 . . . . .6 F4
Hyacinth Rd ME2 . . . . .46 E6
Hybrid Cl ME1 . . . . .47 D1
Hyde Dr BR5 . . . . .38 B5
Hyde Rd Bexley DA7 . . . . .7 F5
Maidstone ME16 . . . . .91 D6
Hyde's Orch TN27 . . . . .141 E5
Hyders Forge TN15 . . . . . . .102 A8
Hylton St SE18 . . . . .2 F2
Hyperion Dr ME2 . . . . .32 F1
Hythe Ave DA7 . . . . .7 F7
Hythe Cl Orpington BR5 . . . .38 C5
Royal Tunbridge Wells TN4 .133 A1
Hythe St DA1 . . . . .9 E1

I

Ice Bowl The* ME8 . . . . .49 A1
Ickleton Rd SE9 . . . . .22 E4
Icough Ct SE3 . . . . .5 B7
Iddenden Cotts TN18 . . . . .178 D2

Ide Hill CE Prim Sch TN14 97 F4
Ide Hill Rd TN14 . . . . .97 F2
Iden Cres TN12 . . . . .139 F2
Iden Rd ME2 . . . . .33 C1
Idenwood Cl ME8 . . . . .63 D6
Idleigh Court Rd DA3,DA13 57 C8
Ifield Cl ME15 . . . . .107 F7
Ifield Cotts DA12 . . . . .31 C5
Ifield Sch The DA12 . . . . . . .30 C3
Ifield Way DA12 . . . . .30 D2
Ightham By-Pass TN15 . . . .86 C7
Ightham Cotts DA12 . . . . . . .28 B6
Ightham Mote* TN15 . . . . .101 A7
Ightham Prim Sch TN15 . . .86 B6
Ightham Rd Erith DA8 . . . . . . .8 A7
Shipbourne TN11,TN15 . . . .101 C5
Ilkley Rd E16 . . . . .1 C8
Illustrious Cl ME5 . . . . .62 A6
Imber Ct **4** SE9 . . . . .6 A1
Impala Gdns TN4 . . . . .149 B6
Imperial Bsns Pk DA11 . . . .13 B2
Imperial Ct BR7 . . . . .23 B2
Imperial Dr DA12 . . . . .30 F3
Imperial Pl BR7 . . . . .37 A8
Imperial Rd ME7 . . . . .48 C3
Imperial Ret Pk DA11 . . . . . .13 A1
Imperial Way BR7 . . . . .23 C5
Impton La ME5 . . . . .62 A1
Inca Dr SE9 . . . . .23 B8
Indus Rd SE7 . . . . .5 C7
Ingle Rd ME4 . . . . .47 F2
Ingleby Way BR7 . . . . .23 A3
Ingleden Park Rd TN30 . . . .173 C1
Ingledew Rd SE18 . . . . .2 D1
Ingleside Gr **3** SE3 . . . . .5 A8
Ingleton Ave ME16 . . . . .48 A2
Inglewood Chislehurst BR7 .23 D2
Swanley BR8 . . . . .39 E7
Inglewood Copse BR1 . . . . .36 F7
Inglewood Rd DA7 . . . . .8 D3
Ingoldsby Rd DA12 . . . . .30 F7
Ingram Rd Dartford DA1 . . . .26 E7
Gillingham ME7 . . . . .48 A6
Ingress Gdns DA9,DA10 . . . .11 D2
Ingress Terr DA13 . . . . .28 E4
Inigo Jones Rd SE7 . . . . .5 E7
Inner Lines ME7 . . . . .48 A6
Institute Rd ME4 . . . . .48 A4
Instone Rd DA1 . . . . .26 D8
Inverary Pl SE18 . . . . .6 D8
Inverine Rd SE7 . . . . .1 B1
Invermore Pl SE18 . . . . .2 C2
Inverness
House **7** ME15 . . . . . . .107 E7
Invicta Cl BR7 . . . . .23 A3
Invicta Gram Sch ME14 . .92 C4
Invicta Inf Sch SE3 . . . . .5 A7
Invicta Par **3** DA14 . . . . . . .24 B4
Invicta Rd Dartford DA2 . . . .10 B1
Greenwich SE3 . . . . .5 A8
Invicta Villas ME14 . . . . . . .93 C4
Iona Cl ME5 . . . . .62 D1
Iona Rd ME15 . . . . .107 A7
Ireland Cl E6 . . . . .1 F8
Irene Rd BR6 . . . . .37 F2
Iris Ave DA5 . . . . .7 E1
Iris Cl ME5 . . . . .77 A8
Iris Cres DA7 . . . . .7 F8
Iron Mill La DA1 . . . . .8 F3
Iron Mill Pl DA1 . . . . .8 F3
Ironside Cl ME5 . . . . .62 A8
Ironstones TN3 . . . . .148 B3
Irvine Rd ME3 . . . . .32 B3
Irvine Way ME15 . . . . .37 F2
Irving Ho TN1 . . . . .149 B5
Irving Way BR8 . . . . .39 D7
Irving Wlk DA10 . . . . .28 E8
Irwin Ave SE18 . . . . .6 E7
Isabella Dr BR6 . . . . .51 C6
Isla Rd SE18 . . . . .6 C8
Island Way East ME4 . . . . . .34 C1
Island Way West ME4 . . . . .34 B2
Islehurst Cl BR7 . . . . .37 A8
Islingham Farm Rd ME3 . . .33 D4
Ismays Rd TN15 . . . . .86 C3
Istead Rise DA13 . . . . .29 F1
Istead Rise
Prim Sch DA13 . . . . .43 E8
Ivedon Rd DA16 . . . . .7 C5
Ivens Way ME15 . . . . .110 D6
Iverhurst Cl DA6 . . . . .7 D2
Iversgate Cl ME8 . . . . .49 F2
Ives Rd TN9 . . . . .116 F1
Ivor Gr SE9 . . . . .23 B7
Ivor Ho DA14 . . . . .24 C3
Ivorydown BR1 . . . . .22 A4
Ivy Bower Cl ME2 . . . . .11 B2
Ivy Cl Dartford DA1 . . . . .27 A8
Gravesend DA12 . . . . .30 D5
Kingswood ME17 . . . . .109 D2
Ivy House La TN13,TN14 . . .68 E2
Ivy La TN14 . . . . .67 E3
Ivy Mews ME17 . . . . .109 E2
Ivy Pl ME1 . . . . .47 A2
Ivy Rd E16 . . . . .1 A7
Ivy St ME8 . . . . .63 F8
Ivy Villas DA9 . . . . .11 A2
Ivybridge Ct **1** BR7 . . . . . .37 A8
Izane Rd DA6 . . . . .7 F3

J

Jack Lobley
Prim Sch RM18 . . . . .12 F6
Jackass La BR2 . . . . .50 C4
Jacklin Cl ME5 . . . . .61 F2
Jackson Ave ME1 . . . . .61 E8

Jackson Cl Gillingham ME8 .49 C1
Stone DA9 . . . . .11 A2
Jackson Ho **4** SE7 . . . . .5 B8
Jackson Rd BR2 . . . . .50 F8
Jackson St SE18 . . . . .6 A8
Jackson Way TN17 . . . . . . .171 C3
Jacksons La **8** TN30 . . . . .183 A7
Jacob Ho **5** DA18 . . . . .3 D4
Jacob's La ME3 . . . . .35 B6
Jade Cl E16 . . . . .1 D7
Jade Hill ME2 . . . . .60 A6
Jaffray Rd BR2 . . . . .36 D5
Jaggard Way TN12 . . . . . . .139 E3
Jagger Cl DA2 . . . . .27 C8
Jago Cl SE18 . . . . .6 C8
Jail La TN16 . . . . .66 A3
Jamaica Terr ME14 . . . . .92 A7
James Cl TN11 . . . . .102 F1
James Newman Ct SE9 . . . .23 A5
James Rd Cuxton ME2 . . . . .46 C2
Dartford DA1 . . . . .26 A8
James St **5** Chatham ME4 . .47 F4
Gillingham ME7 . . . . .48 C6
Maidstone ME14 . . . . .92 A5
Rochester ME1 . . . . .47 C4
James Watt Way DA8 . . . . . . .8 F8
James Whatman
Way ME14 . . . . .91 F5
Jane Seymour Ct DA15 . . . .23 D8
Janet Ct **4** DA7 . . . . .8 A3
Janson Ct **11** DA14 . . . . . . .24 B4
Japonica Cl ME5 . . . . .62 C2
Jaquets Cl DA5 . . . . .25 A6
Jarrah Cotts RM19 . . . . .10 D8
Jarrett Ave ME2 . . . . .33 C3
Jarvis Ho **4** ME14 . . . . .91 F7
Jarvis La TN17 . . . . .154 B3
Jarvis Pl TN30 . . . . .173 B3
Jashada Ho SE18 . . . . .2 A1
Jasmine Cl **2** Chatham ME5 61 F4
East Malling ME19 . . . . .89 F8
Orpington BR6 . . . . .51 B8
Jasmine Cotts TN3 . . . . . . .161 C7
Jasmine Ct SE12 . . . . .5 A1
Jasmine Rd ME19 . . . . .89 F8
Jason Wlk SE9 . . . . .23 A4
Jasper Ave ME1 . . . . .47 D2
Jasper Rd E16 . . . . .1 D7
Javelin Rd ME19 . . . . .88 F3
Jay Gdns BR7 . . . . .22 F4
Jefferson Dr ME8 . . . . .49 C1
Jefferson Wlk **13** SE18 . . . . .6 A8
Jeffery St ME7 . . . . .48 C6
Jeffrey Cl TN12 . . . . .139 E4
Jeffrey Cl DA8 . . . . .8 C7
Jeffrey Row SE12 . . . . .5 B2
Jeffrey St ME14 . . . . .92 A5
Jeken Rd SE9 . . . . .5 C3
Jellicoe Ave DA12 . . . . .30 C5
Jellicoe Ave W DA12 . . . . . .30 C5
Jenkins Dr ME15 . . . . .107 E5
Jenkins' Dale ME4 . . . . .47 F3
Jenner Ho **4** DA17 . . . . .4 A3
Jenner Rd ME1 . . . . .47 C4
Jenner Way ME20 . . . . .75 F6
Jennifer Ct ME3 . . . . .34 F5
Jenningtree Rd DA8 . . . . .9 B7
Jenningtree Way DA17 . . . . . .4 C4
Jenton Ave DA7 . . . . .7 E5
Jerome Rd ME20 . . . . .74 F4
Jersey Dr BR5 . . . . .37 D3
Jersey Rd Newham E16 . . . . .1 B8
Rochester ME2 . . . . .47 A8
Jeskyns Rd DA12 . . . . .44 E6
Jessamine Pl DA2 . . . . .27 C8
Jessamine Terr BR8 . . . . . . .39 C8
Jessett Cl DA8 . . . . .4 D2
Jessup Cl SE18 . . . . .2 B1
Jetty Rd Kingsnorth ME3 . . .35 D7
Sheerness ME12 . . . . .21 F3
Jetty Wlk **3** ME1 . . . . .12 A8
Jevington Way SE12 . . . . . . .22 B7
Jewell Gr TN12 . . . . .138 D5
Jeyes Rd ME7 . . . . .48 C4
Jezreels Rd ME7 . . . . .48 D3
Jim Bradley Cl **10** SE18 . . . . .2 A2
Jiniwin Rd ME1 . . . . .61 D7
Joan Cres SE9 . . . . .22 D8
Jockey La TN17 . . . . .169 D5
Johannesburg
House ME15 . . . . .107 F5
John Hunt Ct SE9 . . . . .22 E6
John Mayne
CE Prim Sch TN27 . . . .157 F1
John Newton Ct DA16 . . . . . .7 B4
John Spare Ct TN4 . . . . . . .149 A6
John St Grays RM17 . . . . . . .12 C8
Maidstone ME14 . . . . .92 A6
Rochester ME1 . . . . .47 C4
Royal Tunbridge Wells TN4 .149 A5
John Wesley Ct SE9 . . . . .6 A3
John Wilson St SE18 . . . . . . .2 A2
John's Rd DA13 . . . . .43 F4
Johns Cl DA3 . . . . .42 F4
Johnson Ave ME7 . . . . .48 C7
Johnson Cl DA11 . . . . .29 D5
Johnson Rd BR2 . . . . .36 D4
Johnsons Ave TN14 . . . . . . .53 B1
Johnsons Way DA9 . . . . .11 C1
Joiners Ct ME4 . . . . .48 B2
Jonas Dr TN5 . . . . .174 E5
Jonas La TN5 . . . . .174 E5
Jordan Cl ME15 . . . . .107 E5
Josling Cl RM17 . . . . .11 F8
Joy Rd DA12 . . . . .30 C7
Joy Wood ME17 . . . . .107 D5
Joyce Cl TN17 . . . . .169 C5
Joyce Dawson Way SE28 . . .3 A6

Joyce Green Ho DA1 . . . . . . .9 F4
Joyce Green La Dartford DA1 9 E6
Dartford,Temple Hill DA1 . . . .9 F4
Joyce Green Wlk DA1 . . . . . .9 F3
Joyce Page Cl SE7 . . . . .5 D8
Joyden's Wood Rd DA5 . . . .25 E5
Joydens Wood
Inf Sch DA5 . . . . .25 E4
Joydens Wood
Jun Sch DA2 . . . . .25 E4
Jubilee Cl DA9 . . . . .11 C1
Jubilee Cnr ME17 . . . . .125 E3
Jubilee Cotts
Sevenoaks TN14 . . . . .84 B7
Sutton Valence ME17 . . . . .124 E7
Jubilee Cres
Gravesend DA12 . . . . .30 E6
Ightham TN15 . . . . .86 C6
Jubilee Ct DA1 . . . . .26 D8
Jubilee Ctry Pk* BR2 . . . . . .37 B5
Jubilee Field TN30 . . . . . . .189 E4
Jubilee Prim Sch SE28 . . . . .3 C6
Jubilee Rd Chelsfield BR6 . .53 A4
West Thurrock RM20 . . . . . .11 B8
Jubilee Rise TN15 . . . . .84 F6
Jubilee Terr ME7 . . . . .48 C6
Jubilee Way DA14 . . . . .24 A6
Judd Rd TN9 . . . . .133 B7
Judd Sch The TN9 . . . . . . .133 A8
Judeth Gdns DA12 . . . . .30 E3
Judkins Cl ME5 . . . . .62 C6
Juglans Rd BR6 . . . . .38 A1
Julia Garfield Mews E16 . . .1 B5
Julian Ct **3** DA14 . . . . .24 A4
Julian Rd BR6 . . . . .52 A4
Julians Cl TN13 . . . . .99 A8
Julians Way TN13 . . . . .99 A8
Junction Rd
Bodiam TN18, TN32 . . . . . .185 A3
Dartford DA1 . . . . .9 D1
Gillingham ME7 . . . . .48 D4
Juniper Cl Chatham ME5 . . .62 A4
Maidstone ME16 . . . . .91 B6
Royal Tunbridge Wells TN4 .133 D1
Juniper La E6 . . . . .1 E8
Juniper Wlk BR8 . . . . .39 D7
Jury St **11** DA11 . . . . .13 B1
Jutland Cl ME3 . . . . .19 D7
Jutland Ho SE18 . . . . .1 E2

K

Kale Rd DA18 . . . . .3 E4
Kashgar Rd SE18 . . . . .2 F2
Kashmir Rd SE7 . . . . .5 D7
Katherine Ct ME5 . . . . .62 B2
Katherine Gdns SE9 . . . . . . .5 D3
Katherine Rd TN8 . . . . .128 C8
Kay St DA16 . . . . .7 B6
Keary Rd DA10 . . . . .28 F8
Keating Cl ME1 . . . . .47 A3
Keats Ave E16 . . . . .1 B8
Keats Gdns RM18 . . . . .13 B5
Keats House DA1 . . . . .8 E2
Keats Rd Bexley DA16 . . . . . .6 F6
Erith DA8 . . . . .4 C3
Lunsford ME20 . . . . .74 F3
Kechill Gdns BR2 . . . . .36 A2
Kedleston Dr BR5 . . . . .37 F4
Keeble Cl SE18 . . . . .6 B8
Keedonwood Rd BR1 . . . . . .22 A3
Keefe Cl ME5 . . . . .61 D1
Keel Gdns TN4 . . . . .148 E8
Keeley Mews ME7 . . . . .48 E3
Keeling Rd SE9 . . . . .5 D3
Keemor Cl SE18 . . . . .6 A7
Keep The SE3 . . . . .5 A4
Keightley Dr SE9 . . . . .23 C7
Keir Hardy Ho **7** DA17 . . . . .4 A3
Keith Ave DA4 . . . . .27 B2
Keith Sutton House SE9 . . .23 C6
Kelbrook Rd SE3 . . . . .5 E4
Kelchers La TN11 . . . . .118 F5
Kelham House **10** ME8 . . . . .6 B8
Kellaway Rd Chatham ME5 .62 A2
Greenwich SE3 . . . . .5 D5
Kellner Rd SE28 . . . . .2 F3
Kelly Dr ME7 . . . . .48 C7
Kelly Ho **14** SE7 . . . . .5 C8
Kelly House ME1 . . . . .61 C7
Kelsall Cl SE3 . . . . .5 B7
Kelsey Rd BR5 . . . . .38 B7
Kelso Dr DA12 . . . . .30 F4
Kelvin Cl TN10 . . . . .117 D7
Kelvin Ho **3** DA17 . . . . .4 A3
Kelvin Par BR6 . . . . .37 E1
Kelvin Rd Bexley DA16 . . . . . .7 A4
Tilbury RM18 . . . . .13 A5
Kemble Cl TN2 . . . . .149 E7
Kemble Dr BR2 . . . . .50 E7
Kemnal Rd BR7 . . . . .23 D3
Kemnal Tech Coll BR5 . . . .24 E1
Kemnal Warren BR7 . . . . . . .23 D2
Kemp Cl ME5 . . . . .61 E4
Kempley Ct **2** RM17 . . . . . .12 D8
Kempt St SE18 . . . . .6 A8
Kempton Cl Chatham ME5 . .62 C2
Erith DA8 . . . . .8 C8
Kemsing Cl DA5 . . . . .24 E8
Kemsing Prim Sch TN15 . .70 A2
Kemsing Rd Greenwich SE10 .1 A1
Wrotham TN15 . . . . .71 C3
Kemsing Sta TN15 . . . . .55 D8
Kemsley Cl Northfleet DA11 .29 F4
Swanscombe DA9 . . . . .11 B1
Kemsley Street Rd ME7 . . . .63 C1
Kemsway Ct BR5 . . . . .38 B8

Kencot Cl DA18 . . . . .3 F4
Kendal Dr TN9 . . . . .117 C2
Kendal Pk TN4 . . . . .148 E5
Kendall Ct DA15 . . . . .24 A5
Kendall Lodge 10 BR1 . . . . .36 B8
Kendall Pl 1 ME15 . . . . . .107 D8
Kendall Rd SE3 . . . . .5 E6
Kendon Bsns Pk ME2 . . . . .47 D8
Kenia Wlk SE18 . . . . .30 F5
Kenilworth Ct 10 DA2 . . . . .10 B1
Kenilworth Dr ME8 . . . . . . .63 D6
Kenilworth Gdns
  Gillingham ME8 . . . . .63 D7
  Woolwich SE18 . . . . .6 B5
Kenilworth House ME16 . . .91 B2
Kenilworth Rd BR5 . . . . . . .37 C3
Kenley Cl Sidcup DA5 . . . . .25 A8
St Paul's Cray BR7 . . . . . . .37 E6
Kenley House 6 BR5 . . . . . .38 B7
Kenmere Rd DA16 . . . . .7 C5
Kennacraig Cl E16 . . . . .1 A5
Kennard Cl ME1 . . . . .46 F2
Kennard St E16 . . . . .1 F5
Kennedy Cl BR5 . . . . .37 D1
Kennedy Gdns TN13 . . . . . .84 D5
Kennedy House TN17 . . . .180 E6
Kennel Barn Rd ME9 . . . . . .80 C5
Kennet Ct 2 BR8 . . . . .39 E6
Kennet Rd Crayford DA1 . . . .9 A4
  Tonbridge TN10 . . . . .117 C5
Kennett Ct 18 BR5 . . . . . . .38 D1
Kennington Cl
  Gillingham ME8 . . . . .49 B4
  Maidstone ME15 . . . . . . .107 F7
Kensington Ct 4 RM17 . . . .12 C8
Kensington House ME16 . . .91 A4
Kent & East Sussex
  Steam Rly* TN17 . . . . . .188 C5
Kent & Sussex
  Hospl TN4 . . . . .149 A4
Kent Ave Bexley DA16 . . . . . .6 F2
  Maidstone ME15 . . . . .92 C1
Kent Cl Chatham ME1 . . . . .61 C8
  Orpington BR6 . . . . .51 E4
  Paddock Wood TN12 . . . .136 A6
Kent Coll TN2 . . . . .134 D3
Kent County Ophthalmic &
  Aural Hospl ME14 . . . . . .92 A4
Kent
  County Show Gd ME14 . . .78 C3
Kent Hatch Rd RH8,TN8 . . .96 B4
Kent Ho TN1 . . . . .149 C6
Kent House 10 TN18 . . . . .179 A2
Kent Inst of Art & Design
  Chatham ME1 . . . . .47 A6
  Maidstone ME16 . . . . .91 C3
Kent Kraft Ind Est DA11 . . .11 F2
Kent Music Sch TN9 . . . . .133 B8
Kent Rd Dartford DA1 . . . . . .9 E1
  Gravesend DA11 . . . . .30 A7
  Grays RM17 . . . . .12 C8
  Halling ME2 . . . . .60 A6
  Longfield DA3 . . . . .42 D7
  Orpington BR5 . . . . .38 B3
  Royal Tunbridge Wells TN4 .149 A6
  Snodland ME6 . . . . .75 A6
Kent St ME18 . . . . .88 E2
Kent Terr Higham ME3 . . . . .32 D7
  Meopham DA13 . . . . .58 A7
Kentish Gdns TN2 . . . . . .162 E8
Kentish Rd DA17 . . . . .4 A2
Kentish Way BR1,BR2 . . . . .36 B6
Kentlea Rd SE28 . . . . .2 E4
Kentmere Rd SE18 . . . . .2 E2
Kentstone Ct ME4 . . . . .48 A4
Kenward Ct TN11 . . . . . . .118 E8
Kenward Rd Eltham SE9 . . . .5 D2
  Maidstone ME16 . . . . .91 C5
  Yalding ME18 . . . . .104 E2
Kenwood Ave
  Chatham ME5 . . . . .62 A4
  New Barn DA3 . . . . .43 C6
Kenwyn Rd DA1 . . . . .9 D2
Kenya Rd SE7 . . . . .5 D7
Kenya Terr 7 ME14 . . . . . .92 A7
Kenyon Wlk ME8 . . . . .63 B3
Kerry Cl E16 . . . . .1 B7
Kersey Gdns SE9 . . . . .22 E4
Kesteven Cl ME2 . . . . .60 B5
Kestlake Rd DA5 . . . . .7 C1
Keston Ave BR2 . . . . .50 C5
Keston CE Prim Sch BR2 .50 D5
Keston Cl DA16 . . . . .7 C4
  Sidcup DA5 . . . . .24 F8
Keston Ct Gillingham ME8 . .49 A2
Keston Gdns BR2 . . . . .50 C6
Keston Park Cl BR2 . . . . . .50 F7
Kestrel Ave E6 . . . . .1 E8
Kestrel Cl TN8 . . . . .112 D3
Kestrel Ho 8 ME7 . . . . . . .48 B6
Kestrel Rd ME5 . . . . .62 C2
Keswick Cl TN17 . . . . .117 C2
Keswick Dr ME16 . . . . .91 B5
Keswick Rd Bexley DA7 . . . . .8 A6
  Orpington BR6 . . . . .38 A2
Ketridge La ME18 . . . . .89 D2
Kettle La ME15 . . . . .105 E6
Kettlewell Ct BR8 . . . . .39 F7
Kevington Cl BR5 . . . . .37 F5
Kevington Dr BR7 . . . . .37 F5
Kevington Prim Sch BR5 . .38 A5
Kewlands ME14 . . . . .92 C6
Keycol Hill BR6 . . . . .65 F5
Keycol Hospl ME9 . . . . . . .65 E6
Keyes Ave ME4 . . . . .47 F2
Keyes Gdns TN2 . . . . .132 F7
Keyes Rd DA1 . . . . .10 A3

Keynes Ct 9 SE28 . . . . .3 B6
Keynsham Gdns SE9 . . . . . .5 E2
Keynsham Rd SE9 . . . . .5 E2
Keyworth Cl TN12 . . . . . . .135 F6
Khalsa Ave DA12 . . . . .30 C8
Khartoum Pl DA12 . . . . . . .13 C1
Khartoum Rd Chatham ME4 .47 F6
  Gillingham ME7 . . . . .48 A6
Khyber Rd ME4,ME7 . . . . .48 B7
Kibbles La TN4 . . . . .148 E8
Kidbrooke Gr SE3 . . . . .5 A6
Kidbrooke Gr SE3 . . . . .5 B6
Kidbrooke La SE9 . . . . .5 E3
Kidbrooke Park SE3 . . . . . .5 B6
Kidbrooke Park
  Prim Sch SE3 . . . . .5 C6
Kidbrooke Park Rd
  SE12,SE3 . . . . .5 C6
Kidbrooke Sch SE3 . . . . . . .5 D5
Kidbrooke Sta SE3 . . . . . . .5 B4
Kidbrooke Way SE3 . . . . . . .5 B5
Kidd Pl SE7 . . . . .1 E1
Kiddens BR8 . . . . .39 B7
Kilburn Ho 6 ME14 . . . . . .92 A5
Kildare Rd E16 . . . . .1 A8
Killewarren Way BR5 . . . . .38 C1
Killick Cl TN13 . . . . .83 E6
Killick Rd ME3 . . . . .34 D5
Killicks Cotts ME18 . . . . .120 F8
Kiln Barn Rd ME19,ME 20 . .90 C7
Kiln Field TN30 . . . . .183 C7
Kiln La TN11 . . . . .115 F1
Kiln Way TN12 . . . . .136 A5
Kilnbank TN2 . . . . .149 C7
Kilnbridge Cl ME15 . . . . . .106 B7
Kilndown DA12 . . . . .30 D2
Kilndown Cl ME16 . . . . .91 C7
Kilnfields BR6 . . . . .53 A4
Kilnwood TN14 . . . . .67 F6
Kimball Pl SE3 . . . . .5 C3
Kimber House 11 SE18 . . . . .6 B8
Kimberley Dr DA14 . . . . . . .24 D6
Kimberley Rd ME7 . . . . . . .48 D3
Kimberly Cl DA17 . . . . .3 F2
Kimmeridge Gdns SE9 . . . .22 E4
Kimmeridge Rd SE9 . . . . . .22 E4
Kincraig BR7 . . . . .37 A8
Kincraig Dr TN13 . . . . .84 B4
Kinder Cl SE28 . . . . .3 D6
King & Queen Cl SE9 . . . . .22 E4
King Arthur's Dr ME2 . . . . .33 A1
King Edward Ave DA1 . . . . . .9 D1
King Edward Rd
  Chatham ME4 . . . . .47 F2
  Gillingham ME7 . . . . .48 F6
  Maidstone ME15 . . . . .91 F2
  Rochester ME1 . . . . .47 C5
  Stone DA9 . . . . .11 A2
King George Ave E16 . . . . . .1 D7
King George Rd ME5 . . . . . .62 A6
King George V Hill TN1 . . .149 C5
King George V
  Meml Houses ME8 . . . . . .49 C2
King Harolds Way DA7 . . . . .7 E7
King Henry Mews 7 BR6 . .51 F5
King Hill ME19 . . . . .89 A5
King John's Wlk SE9 . . . . . .5 E1
King St Chatham ME4 . . . . .48 A4
  Gillingham ME7 . . . . .48 C6
  Gravesend DA12 . . . . .13 B1
  Maidstone ME14 . . . . .92 A4
  Rochester ME1 . . . . .47 C4
  West Malling ME19 . . . . . .89 C8
King William Rd 6 ME7 . . .47 F3
King's Ave ME1 . . . . .47 C3
King's Bastion ME7 . . . . . .48 A5
King's Cotts ME18 . . . . . .104 D6
King's Highway SE18,SE2 . . .6 F8
King's Orch Eltham SE9 . . . .5 E1
  Rochester ME1 . . . . .47 C5
King's Rd Chatham ME4 . . .48 D1
  Tonbridge TN9 . . . . .133 D7
King's Sch ME1 . . . . .47 C5
King's Standing
  Ind Est TN2 . . . . .133 F2
Kingfisher
  Apartments ME15 . . . . .107 E5
Kingfisher Cl Erith SE28 . . . .3 C6
  St Paul's Cray BR5 . . . . . .38 D5
Kingfisher Ct
  11 Maidstone ME15 . . . . .92 B4
  West Kingsdown TN15 . . . .55 E3
Kingfisher
  Cty Prim Sch ME5 . . . . . .62 B7
Kingfisher Dr ME5 . . . . . . .62 C7
Kingfisher Ho BR5 . . . . . . .38 C8
Kingfisher Pl DA4 . . . . .41 C7
Kingfisher Rd ME20 . . . . . .75 A2
Kingfisher St E6 . . . . .1 E8
Kings Acre ME15 . . . . .93 A1
Kings Ave BR1 . . . . .22 A2
Kings Cl DA1 . . . . .8 E3
Kings Cotts
  Cranbrook TN17 . . . . . . .169 D6
  Leeds ME17 . . . . .108 F6
Kings Ct TN12 . . . . .153 A6
Kings Dr DA12 . . . . .30 B5
Kings Farm Inf Sch DA12 .30 C4
Kings Farm
  Prim Sch DA11 . . . . .30 C4
Kings Hill Ave ME19 . . . . . .89 A4
Kings Hill Sch ME19 . . . . . .89 A3
Kings La TN12 . . . . .137 C7
Kings Pk TN2 . . . . .149 D3
Kings Rd Headcorn TN27 . .141 C5
  Orpington BR6 . . . . .51 F6
Kings Reach ME15 . . . . . .107 D8
Kings Row Chatham ME1 . . .47 B4

Kings Row continued
  Maidstone ME15 . . . . .92 A1
Kings Standing Way TN2 133 F1
Kings Toll Rd TN2 . . . . . . .151 A6
Kings Wlk RM17 . . . . .12 A8
Kingsand Rd SE12 . . . . . . .22 A6
Kingsdale Cl Chatham ME5 .48 C1
  Swanscombe DA10 . . . . . . .11 E1
Kingsdale Rd SE18 . . . . .6 F8
Kingsdown Cl
  Gillingham ME7 . . . . .63 B4
  Gravesend DA12 . . . . .30 F7
  Maidstone ME16 . . . . .91 E4
Kingsdown Way BR2 . . . . . .36 A3
Kingsfield Ho SE9 . . . . . . .22 D5
Kingsford Cotts TN17 . . . .180 D6
Kingsford Way E6 . . . . .1 F8
Kingsgate Cl Bexley DA7 . . . .7 E6
  Maidstone ME16 . . . . .91 C4
  St Paul's Cray BR5 . . . . . .38 C6
Kingsgate La TN30 . . . . . .189 C5
Kingsground SE9 . . . . .5 E1
Kingshill Dr ME3 . . . . .34 D6
Kingsholm Gdns SE9 . . . . . .5 E3
Kingshurst Rd SE12 . . . . . .22 A8
Kingsingfield Cl TN15 . . . . .55 B8
Kingsingfield Rd TN15 . . . .55 C2
Kingsland Gr TN27 . . . . . .141 D5
Kingsland La TN27 . . . . . .127 C1
Kingsley Ave DA1 . . . . .10 A2
Kingsley Ct Bexley DA6 . . . . .8 A3
  Wadhurst TN5 . . . . .175 A4
  1 Woolwich SE28 . . . . . . .3 C5
Kingsley Mews BR7 . . . . . .23 B2
Kingsley Rd
  Maidstone ME15 . . . . .92 A3
  Orpington BR6 . . . . .51 F3
Kingsley Wood Dr SE9 . . . .22 F5
Kingsman Par SE18 . . . . . . .1 F3
Kingsman St SE18 . . . . .1 F2
Kingsmead Ct DA15 . . . . . .24 A6
Kingsmere BR7 . . . . .36 E8
Kingsnorth Ct BR8 . . . . . . .39 C3
Kingsnorth Rd ME8 . . . . . .49 C4
Kingsridge Gdns DA1 . . . . . .9 D1
Kingston Cres ME5 . . . . . . .62 C4
Kingston Ct DA11 . . . . .12 B1
Kingston Dr ME15 . . . . . . .107 A8
Kingsway Chatham ME5 . . .48 D1
  Gillingham ME8 . . . . .48 E1
  Orpington BR5 . . . . .37 D4
Kingswear Rd ME2 . . . . . . .47 C7
Kingswood Ave
  Chatham ME4 . . . . .47 F2
  Erith DA17 . . . . .3 F2
  Swanley BR8 . . . . .39 D6
Kingswood Cl Dartford DA1 . .9 C1
  Orpington BR6 . . . . .37 D4
  Royal Tunbridge Wells TN2 .149 C3
Kingswood
  Prim Sch ME17 . . . . .109 E2
Kingswood Rd
  Gillingham ME7 . . . . .48 D6
  Kit's Coty ME20 . . . . .76 D8
  Royal Tunbridge Wells TN2 .149 C3
  Sevenoaks TN13 . . . . .83 E7
Kingsworth Cl ME3 . . . . . . .34 E5
Kinlet Rd SE18 . . . . .6 C6
Kinnell Ct 18 DA14 . . . . . . .24 B4
Kinnings Row TN9 . . . . . . .117 C2
Kinross Cl ME5 . . . . .62 B7
Kinveachy Gdns SE7 . . . . . .1 E1
Kipling Ave RM18 . . . . .13 C6
Kipling Dr ME20 . . . . .74 F4
Kipling Rd Bexley DA7 . . . . .7 E6
  Dartford DA1 . . . . .10 B2
Kippington Cl TN13 . . . . . . .83 F3
Kippington Dr SE9 . . . . . . .22 D7
Kippington Rd TN13 . . . . . .84 A2
Kirby Cl TN17 . . . . .169 D4
Kirby Rd Chattenden ME3 . . .33 F5
  Dartford DA2 . . . . .27 D8
Kirk La SE18 . . . . .6 C8
Kirkcourt TN13 . . . . .84 A4
Kirkdale Cl ME5 . . . . .62 D1
Kirkdale Rd
  Maidstone ME15 . . . . . . .106 F6
  Royal Tunbridge Wells TN1 .149 B4
Kirkham Rd E6 . . . . .1 E7
Kirkham St SE18 . . . . .6 E8
Kirkins Cl TN12 . . . . .153 A6
Kirkland Cl DA15 . . . . .6 E1
Kirkman Ct TN12 . . . . .139 E3
Kirkside Rd SE3 . . . . .5 A8
Kit Hill Ave ME5 . . . . .61 C8
Kit's Coty House* ME20 . .76 C6
Kitchener Ave
  Chatham ME4 . . . . .48 A1
  Gravesend DA12 . . . . .30 C5
Kitchener Cotts ME3 . . . . .19 C4
Kitchener Rd
  Chattenden ME3 . . . . .33 F4
  Rochester ME2 . . . . .47 A8
Kite La TN12 . . . . .152 A6
Knatts La TN15 . . . . .70 C7
Knatts Valley Rd TN15 . . . .55 D2
Knave Wood Rd TN15 . . . . .69 E2
Knaves Ct ME8 . . . . .63 D5
Knaves Acre Ct ME8 . . . . .141 D5
Knee Hill SE2 . . . . .3 C1
Knee Hill Cres SE2 . . . . .3 C1
Knight Ave ME7 . . . . .48 D7
Knight Rd Rochester ME2 . .47 A6
  Tonbridge TN10 . . . . .117 E6
Knight's Ct DA3 . . . . .43 A6
Knight's Ridge TN2 . . . . . .150 D7

Knight's Way TN27 . . . . . .141 D6
Knighton Rd TN14 . . . . . . .68 F2
Knightrider Cl ME15 . . . . . .92 A3
Knightrider St 1 ME15 . . . .92 A3
Knights Cl
  Hoo St Werburgh ME3 . . . .34 E5
  Pembury TN2 . . . . .150 D7
Knights Croft DA3 . . . . .56 F7
Knights Manor Way DA1 . . . .9 F1
Knights Pk Rochester ME2 . . .47 A8
  Royal Tunbridge Wells TN11 .133 F1
Knights Rd
  Hoo St Werburgh ME3 . . . .34 D5
  Newham E16 . . . . .1 A4
Knights Ridge BR6 . . . . . . .52 B5
Knights Way TN2,TN11 . . .133 F1
Knightsbridge Cl TN4 . . . .148 F5
Knightsbridge Mews BR7 .22 F1
Knock Mill La TN15 . . . . . .71 A5
Knockhall Chase DA9 . . . . .11 C2
Knockhall
  Com Prim Sch DA9 . . . . .11 C2
Knockhall Rd DA9 . . . . . . .11 C2
Knockholt
  CE Prim Sch TN14 . . . . . .67 B2
Knockholt Rd Eltham SE9 . . .5 D2
  Halstead TN14 . . . . .67 F6
Knockholt Sta TN14 . . . . . .52 E2
Knockhurst Ct TN30 . . . . .173 C1
Knockwood Rd TN30 . . . . .173 C1
Knole* TN15 . . . . .84 D1
Knole Cl ME2 . . . . .99 B2
Knole Gate DA15 . . . . .23 E5
Knole La TN13,TN15 . . . . . .84 C1
Knole Rd Chatham ME5 . . . .62 C3
  Dartford DA1 . . . . .26 B8
  Sevenoaks TN13 . . . . .84 D4
Knole The Eltham SE9 . . . . .23 A4
  Istead Rise DA13 . . . . . . .29 E1
Knole Way TN13 . . . . .84 C2
Knoll Ct BR6 . . . . .51 F8
Knoll Rd Sidcup DA14 . . . . .24 B4
  Sidcup,Old Bexley DA5 . . . .8 A1
Knoll Rise BR6 . . . . .37 F1
Knoll The BR2 . . . . .36 C6
Knotley Hall Cotts TN11 .115 A2
Knott Ct ME7 . . . . .91 F6
Knotts Pl TN13 . . . . .84 A3
Knowle Ave DA7 . . . . .7 F7
Knowle Cl TN3 . . . . .147 E3
Knowle Cotts TN3 . . . . . . .163 E1
Knowle La TN12 . . . . .136 C3
Knowle Lodge BR7 . . . . . . .22 F2
Knowle Rd Maidstone ME14 .92 B8
  Orpington BR2 . . . . .50 E8
  Paddock Wood TN12 . . . .136 D3
  Wouldham ME1 . . . . .60 D4
Knowles Gdns TN27 . . . . .141 D5
Knowles Wlk TN12 . . . . . .139 F4
Knowlton Gdns ME16 . . . . .91 B2
Knowlton Rd BR2 . . . . .36 A4
Knowsley Way TN11 . . . . .116 D6
Knox Ct TN15 . . . . .84 F6
Kydbrook Cl BR5 . . . . .37 C2
Kyetop Wlk ME8 . . . . .63 D5
Kynaston Rd Bromley BR1 . .22 A3
  Orpington BR5 . . . . .38 B2

L

La Tourne Gdns BR6 . . . . . .51 C7
Labour-In-Vain Rd TN15 . . .71 E5
Laburnham Pl SE9 . . . . .6 A2
Laburnum Ave
  Dartford DA1 . . . . .26 D7
  Swanley BR8 . . . . .39 D6
Laburnum Cl TN2 . . . . . . .149 C7
Laburnum Dr ME20 . . . . . . .75 A2
Laburnum Gr DA11 . . . . . . .29 D8
Laburnum Rd ME2 . . . . . . .46 E5
Laburnum Way BR2 . . . . . .37 B2
Lacebark Cl DA15 . . . . .23 F8
Lacey Cl ME17 . . . . .108 E4
Laceys La ME17 . . . . .122 C7
Lacknut Cotts DA13 . . . . . .57 E2
Lacy Cl ME16 . . . . .91 D7
Ladbrooke Cres DA14 . . . . .24 D5
Ladbrooke Ho 7 ME14 . . . .92 A5
Laddington
  Ind Est ME18 . . . . .120 D4
Laddington St Mary's
  CE Prim Sch ME18 . . . . .120 E4
Ladds Cnr ME7 . . . . .49 B5
Ladds La ME6 . . . . .60 A2
Ladds Way BR8 . . . . .39 D5
Ladham Rd TN17 . . . . .154 A2
Ladies Mile TN3 . . . . .160 D4
Lady Boswell's
  CE Prim Sch TN13 . . . . . .84 D4
Lady Oak La TN5,TN17 . . .177 C2
Lady Vane Cl TN11 . . . . . .101 C5
Lady's Gift Rd TN4 . . . . . .148 F8
Ladyclose Ave ME3 . . . . . . .33 A7
Ladycroft Gdns 6 BR6 . . . .51 C5
Ladycroft Way BR6 . . . . . . .51 C5
Ladyfern Ct TN2 . . . . .149 C6
Ladyfields Chatham ME5 . . .62 D2
  Northfleet DA11 . . . . .29 F4
Ladyfields Cl ME18 . . . . . . .65 F5
Ladysmith Rd SE9 . . . . .6 A1
Ladywell House 4 BR5 . . . .38 B7
Ladywood Ave BR5 . . . . . . .37 E4
Ladywood Rd Cuxton ME2 . .46 B2
  Dartford DA2 . . . . .27 D4
Lagonda Way DA1 . . . . .9 C2
Lagoon Rd BR5 . . . . .38 B4
Lake Ave BR1 . . . . .22 A2

Lake Dr ME3 . . . . .32 C6
Lake Rd Ditton ME20 . . . . . .90 E8
  Royal Tunbridge Wells TN4 .148 A6
Lake View Rd TN13 . . . . . . .84 A4
Lakedale Rd SE18 . . . . .2 C1
Lakelands
  Harrietsham ME17 . . . . . .110 E6
  Maidstone ME15 . . . . . . .107 A7
Lakeman Way TN4 . . . . . . .149 B2
Laker Rd ME1 . . . . .61 C6
Lakes Rd BR2 . . . . .50 C5
Lakeside
  Royal Tunbridge Wells TN2 .149 E6
  Snodland ME6 . . . . .74 F6
Lakeside Ave SE28 . . . . .3 A5
Lakeside Cl
  Bough Beech TN8 . . . . . .113 F4
  Sidcup DA5,DA15 . . . . .7 C2
Lakeside Dr BR2 . . . . .50 E7
Lakeside Pk ME2 . . . . .47 E7
Lakewood Rd BR5 . . . . .37 C3
Lakeview Cl ME3 . . . . .75 A6
Lakeview Rd DA16 . . . . .7 B3
Lakewood Dr ME8 . . . . .63 C6
Lamb Cl RM18 . . . . .13 C5
Lamb's Cross ME17 . . . . . .124 A5
Lambard House 8 ME14 . . .92 A5
Lambarde Ave SE9 . . . . . . .23 A4
Lambarde Cl ME2 . . . . .60 A4
Lambarde Dr TN13 . . . . . . .84 A4
Lambarde Rd TN13 . . . . . . .84 A5
Lambardes DA3 . . . . .56 F7
Lamberhurst
  CE Prim Sch TN3 . . . . . .166 B6
Lamberhurst Ct 14 BR5 . . .38 D1
Lamberhurst Gn ME8 . . . . .49 B3
Lamberhurst Rd
  Horsmonden TN12,TN3 . . .152 E3
  Maidstone ME16 . . . . .91 B7
Lamberhurst
  Vineyard* TN3 . . . . .166 A4
Lambersart Cl TN4 . . . . . .133 D1
Lambert Ct DA8 . . . . .8 C8
Lambert Mews 4 ME6 . . . . .75 A8
Lambert Rd E16 . . . . .1 B7
Lambert's Yd TN9 . . . . . . .117 B1
Lamberts Pl TN12 . . . . . . .153 B5
Lamberts Rd TN2 . . . . . . .149 D8
Lambes Ct ME8 . . . . .63 D5
Lambeth Cl ME5 . . . . .62 B4
Lambourn Dr ME19 . . . . . . .89 A2
Lambourn Ho BR1 . . . . . . .22 E1
Lambourn Way
  Chatham ME5 . . . . .62 C2
  Royal Tunbridge Wells TN2 .149 D1
Lambourne Pl SE3 . . . . .5 B6
Lambourne Rd ME15 . . . . . .92 F2
Lambs Bank TN9 . . . . .133 B7
Lambscroft Ave SE9 . . . . . .22 D5
Lambsfrith Gr ME7 . . . . . . .63 B3
Lamorbey Cl DA15 . . . . . . .23 F6
Lamorna Ave DA12 . . . . . . .30 D6
Lamorna Cl BR6 . . . . .38 A2
Lampington Row TN3 . . . .147 E3
Lamplighters Cl
  2 Dartford DA1 . . . . .9 F1
  Gillingham ME7 . . . . .62 F5
Lamport Cl SE18 . . . . .1 F2
Lamson Rd RM13 . . . . .4 F8
Lancashire Rd ME15 . . . . .107 E7
Lancaster Ct
  Gillingham ME8 . . . . .63 C7
  Gravesend DA12 . . . . .30 C5
Lancaster Way ME19 . . . . .88 F3
Lance Croft DA3 . . . . .56 F8
Lancelot Ave ME2 . . . . .46 E7
Lancelot Cl ME2 . . . . .46 E6
Lancelot Ct BR6 . . . . .52 B8
Lancelot Rd DA16 . . . . .7 A4
Lancer Ho ME1 . . . . .47 C3
Lances Cl DA13 . . . . .44 A2
Lancet La ME15 . . . . .107 A6
Lancey Cl SE7 . . . . .1 E2
Lancing Rd BR6 . . . . .52 B8
Land Way ME3 . . . . .32 C5
Landale Gdns DA1 . . . . . . .26 C8
Landor Ct ME7 . . . . .63 A3
Landseer Ave DA11 . . . . . . .29 D5
Landseer Ho TN10 . . . . . .117 C6
Landstead Rd SE18 . . . . . . .6 D7
Landway TN15 . . . . .84 F7
Landway The
  Borough Green TN15 . . . . .86 F7
  Kemsing TN15 . . . . .70 A2
  Maidstone ME14 . . . . .93 A4
  St Paul's Cray BR5 . . . . . .38 C6
Lane Ave DA9 . . . . .11 C1
Lane End DA7 . . . . .8 B4
Lane The Fordcombe TN3 . .147 C5
  Grennwich SE3 . . . . .5 A4
Lanes Ave DA11 . . . . .30 A5
Laneside BR7 . . . . .23 D8
Langafel
  CE Prim Sch DA3 . . . . . . .43 A6
Langafel Cl DA3 . . . . .42 E7
Langdale Cl Gillingham ME8 .49 D1
  Orpington BR6 . . . . .51 B7
Langdale Cres DA7 . . . . .8 A6
Langdale Rise ME16 . . . . . .91 C5
Langdale Wlk 5 DA11 . . . . .29 C5
Langdon Rd Bromley BR2 . .36 B6
  Rochester ME1 . . . . .47 C4
Langdon Shaw DA14 . . . . .23 F3
Langford Pl DA14 . . . . .24 A5

Langham Gr ME16 ....91 C4
Langholm Rd TN3 ......147 F3
Langhorne Ho 5 SE7 .....5 C8
Langlands Dr DA2 ......27 E3
Langley Ct 18 SE9 ....6 A1
Langley Gdns
  2 Bromley BR2 ....36 C5
  Orpington BR5 ....37 B3
Langley Ho 5 BR1 ......22 B1
Langley Rd DA16 ....7 C8
Langmore Ct DA7 ....7 D4
Langton Cl ME14 ....92 C5
Langton Green
  Cty Prim Sch TN3 .....147 E4
Langton Rd Royal
  Tunbridge Wells TN3, TN4 .148 C3
  Speldhurst TN3 ....148 A7
Langton Ridge TN3 .....148 B3
Langton Way SE3 ....5 B7
Langworth Cl DA2 ....26 D5
Lankester Parker Rd ME1 .61 C6
Lannoy Rd SE9 ....23 C7
Lanridge Rd SE2 ....3 D3
Lansbury Cres DA1 ......10 A2
Lansbury Ct 4 SE28 ......3 B6
Lansbury Gdns RM18 ....13 A6
Lansbury Ho 5 DA17 .....3 F1
Lansdown Pl DA11 ......29 F7
Lansdown Rd Sidcup DA14 .24 B5
  Tilbury RM18 ....12 F5
Lansdowne Ave Bexley DA7 .7 D7
  Maidstone ME15 ....107 C6
  Orpington BR6 ....37 B1
Lansdowne Ct 9 ME4 ....47 F4
Lansdowne
  Cty Prim Sch RM18 ....12 F5
Lansdowne La SE7 ....1 D1
Lansdowne Mews SE7 ....1 D1
Lansdowne Rd
  Bromley BR1 ....22 B1
  Chatham ME4 ....47 E2
  Royal Tunbridge Wells TN1 .149 B4
  Sevenoaks TN13 ....84 D5
  Tonbridge TN9 ....117 B2
Lansdowne Sq
  Northfleet DA11 ....12 F1
  8 Royal Tunbridge
    Wells TN1 ....149 B4
Lapins La ME19 ....88 F2
Lapis Cl DA12 ....31 B7
Lapwing Cl DA8 ....9 B7
Lapwing Rd ME3 ....21 B5
Lapwings DA3 ....43 B6
Lapwings The DA12 ......30 D6
Lapworth Cl BR6 ....52 C8
Larch Cl ME20 ....75 B2
Larch Cres
  Hoo St Werburgh ME3 ...34 E3
  Tonbridge TN10 ....117 C6
Larch Dene BR6 ....51 A8
Larch Gr
  Paddock Wood TN12 ...135 F6
  Sidcup DA15 ....23 F7
Larch Rd DA1 ....26 D7
Larch Way BR2 ....37 A2
Larch Wlk BR8 ....39 D7
Larch Wood Cl ME5 .....62 D1
Larches The ME5 ....32 C3
Larchcroft ME5 ....62 A4
Larchwood Rd SE9 ......23 B6
Larkfield TN3 ....135 A7
Larkfield Ave ME7 ......48 E4
Larkfield Cl Hayes BR2 ..50 A8
  Larkfield ME20 ....75 A1
Larkfield Rd Larkfield ME20 .75 B1
  Sevenoaks TN13 ....83 C4
  Sidcup DA14 ....23 F5
Larkfield Trad Est ME20 ..75 B5
Larkfields DA11 ....29 E5
Larkin Cl ME2 ....33 B2
Larking Dr ME16 ....91 D7
Larks Field DA3 ....42 F5
Larkspur Cl
  East Malling ME19 .....75 A1
  4 Newham E6 ....1 E8
  Orpington BR6 ....52 C7
Larkspur Lodge DA14 ...24 B4
Larkspur Rd Chatham ME5 .61 E4
  East Malling ME19 .....74 F1
Larkstore Pk TN12 ......139 E5
Larkswood Cl DA8 ....9 A6
Larkwell La DA3 ....42 F5
Larner Rd DA8 ....8 E7
Laser Quay ME2 ....47 D6
Lashenden
  Air Warfare Mus* TN27 .142 A2
Lassa Rd SE9 ....5 F2
Latham Cl Dartford DA2 ..27 E6
  Newham E6 ....1 E7
Latham Rd DA6 ....8 A2
Latimer Pl 4 ME7 ....48 C7
Latona Dr DA12 ....30 F3
Latymers TN11 ....131 B4
Launcelot Prim Sch BR1 ..22 A4
Launcelot Rd BR1 ....22 A4
Launder Way ME15 ......91 E2
Launton Dr DA6 ....7 D3
Laura Dr BR8 ....26 A1
Laura Pl ME1 ....47 A2
Laurel Ave DA12 ....30 C6
Laurel Bank
  Royal Tunbridge Wells TN4 .149 B8
  Wadhurst TN5 ....175 A4
Laurel Cl Dartford DA1 ..26 C7
  Sidcup DA14 ....24 A5

Laurel Gr ME17 ....109 D2
Laurel Ho SE7 ....5 C8
Laurel Rd Gillingham ME7 .48 C7
  Royal Tunbridge Wells TN2 .149 D7
Laurel Way TN2 ....149 D7
Laurel Wlk ME8 ....63 E6
Laurels The
  18 Bromley,Widmore BR1 .36 B8
  Dartford DA2 ....26 C5
  Maidstone ME16 ....91 C2
  New Barn DA3 ....43 D6
Laurie Gray Ave ME5 ....61 D1
Lavenda Cl ME7 ....63 A4
Lavender Cl Bromley BR2 .36 E3
  1 Chatham ME5 ....61 E4
  East Malling ME19 .....89 F8
Lavender Gdns TN5 ....176 E1
Lavender Hill Swanley BR8 .39 D6
  Tonbridge TN9 ....133 C8
Lavender Ho 3 ME15 ...107 D8
Lavender Rd ME19 ......89 F8
Lavender Sq 6 TN18 ...179 A2
Lavenders ME19 ....89 C6
Lavernock Rd DA7 ....8 A5
Laverstoke Rd ME16 ....91 C8
Lavidge Rd SE9 ....22 F6
Lavinia Rd 1 DA1 ....9 F1
Lavisham Ho BR1 ....22 B3
Lawford Gdns DA1 ....9 C2
Lawn Cl Bromley BR1 ....22 B1
  Chatham ME4 ....48 B2
  Swanley BR8 ....39 C7
  Tenterden TN30 ......182 F1
Lawn Pk TN13 ....99 B8
Lawn Prim Sch DA11 ....12 C1
Lawn Rd Northfleet DA11 .12 C1
  Tonbridge TN9 ....133 B8
Lawns Cres RM17 ....12 D8
Lawns The Brenchley TN12 .152 B8
  Sidcup DA14 ....24 B4
Lawrance Sq DA11 ......29 F5
Lawrence Cl ME15 .....107 A7
Lawrence Dr DA12 ......45 A5
Lawrence Gdns RM18 ....13 B7
Lawrence Hill Gdns DA1 ..9 C1
Lawrence Hill Rd DA1 ....9 C1
Lawrence Rd Erith DA8 ...8 B7
  Hayes BR4 ....50 A6
  Tonbridge TN10 ......117 E6
Lawrence St ME7 ....48 C5
Lawson Cl E16 ....1 C8
Lawson Gdns DA1 ....9 D3
Lawson House 1 SE18 ....6 A8
Lawson Rd DA1 ....9 D3
Lawsons Mews TN9 .....117 C2
Laxey Rd BR6 ....51 F4
Laxey The ME15 ....91 E1
Laxton Cl ME15 ....92 F3
Laxton Dr ME17 ....108 A1
Laxton Gdns TN12 .....135 E7
Layfield Ho 4 SE10 ......1 A1
Layfield Rd ME7 ....48 C7
Layhams Rd BR2 ....50 A3
Laymarsh Cl DA17 ....3 F3
Layzell Wlk SE9 ....22 D7
Le May Ave SE12 ....22 B5
Le Temple Rd TN12 ....136 B6
Lea Ct ME4 ....47 E1
Lea Vale DA1 ....8 D3
Leafield La DA14 ....24 F5
Leafy Glade ME8 ....63 B6
Leafy Gr BR2 ....50 C5
Leafy La DA13 ....58 A3
Leafy Oak Rd SE12 .....22 C5
Lealands Ave TN11 .....116 A1
Lealands Cl TN3 ....161 C6
Leaman Cl ME23 ....17 E4
Leamington Ave
  Bromley BR1 ....22 C3
  Orpington BR6 ....51 E6
Leamington Cl BR1 .....22 C3
Leamouth Rd E6 ....1 E8
Leander Dr DA12 ....30 F4
Leander Rd ME1 ....61 C7
Learoyd Gdns E6 ....2 A6
Leas Dale SE9 ....23 A5
Leas Gn BR7 ....23 F2
Leas The Wadhurst TN5 .175 A6
  Woolwich SE18 ....6 B6
Leather Cl TN8 ....128 C8
Leatherbottle Gn DA18 ...3 F3
Leaves Green Rd BR2 ...50 D1
Lebrun Sq SE3 ....5 B4
Leckwith Ave DA7 ....7 E8
Leclair House SE3 ....5 B4
Leconfield Cl TN9 .....132 F7
Leda Rd SE18 ....1 F3
Lee Gn BR5 ....38 A4
Lee Green Rd ME3 ......33 B6
Lee Rd ME6 ....75 A8
Lee Sta SE12 ....5 A1
Leechcroft Ave Sidcup DA15 .6 F7
  Swanley BR8 ....39 F6
Leeds & Broomfield
  CE Prim Sch ME17 ....109 A7
Leeds Castle* ME17 ....109 D7
Leeds Cl BR6 ....52 D8
Leeds Ho ME2 ....33 C1
Leeds Rd ME17 ....108 E3
Leeds Sq ME8 ....49 B3
Leeke Ho 2 ME1 ....47 C1
Lees Rd ME18 ....120 E7
Leesons Hill BR5,BR7 ...38 A6
Leesons Prim Sch BR5 ..38 B6
Leesons Way BR5 ....37 F7
Leet Cl ME7 ....48 E6
Leeward Rd ME1 ....47 C1

Leewood Cl SE12 ....5 A1
Leewood Pl BR8 ....39 D5
Legatt Rd SE9 ....5 D2
Legge La ME19 ....74 D6
Leggs' La BR6 ....51 E5
Leghorn Rd SE18 ....2 D1
Leicester Dr TN2 ......162 F8
Leicester Rd
  Maidstone ME15 ......107 D7
  Tilbury RM18 ....12 F6
Leigh Ave ME15 ....107 B6
Leigh City Tech Coll
  The DA1 ....27 A7
Leigh Green
  Ind Est TN30 ....183 E6
Leigh Halt TN11 ....115 F1
Leigh Pl DA16 ....7 A5
Leigh Prim Sch TN11 ..115 F1
Leigh Rd Gravesend DA11 .30 B6
  Rochester ME3 ....33 C3
  Tonbridge TN11 ......116 D3
Leigh Terr
  2 St Paul's Cray BR5 ..38 B6
  Teston ME18 ....90 A1
Leighton Cl TN4 ......149 A7
Leighton Gdns RM18 ....13 A7
Leila Parnell Pl 21 SE7 ..5 C8
Leitch Row ME7 ....48 A7
Leith Hill BR5 ....38 A8
Leith Hill Gn BR5 ......38 A8
Leith Park Rd DA12 .....30 B7
Lemonwell Ct SE9 ....6 C2
Lemonwell Dr SE9 ....6 C2
Len Clifton Ho 6 SE18 ...1 F2
Len Valley Wlk ME15 ....92 F1
Lenderyou Ct DA1 ......26 E8
Lendon Rd TN15 ....86 F6
Lendrim Cl 11 ME7 .....48 A6
Leneda Dr TN2 ....162 E8
Leney Rd ME18 ....104 E7
Lenfield Ave ME14 .....92 B4
Lenham Ct 10 ME15 ....92 B4
Lenham Heath Rd ME17 .111 C2
Lenham Ho Lenham ME17 .111 E5
  18 Orpington BR5 ......38 D1
Lenham Prim Sch ME17 .111 C5
Lenham Rd
  Broadstone TN27,ME17 .126 D3
  Erith DA7 ....7 F8
  Fairbourne Heath ME17 .110 C1
  Headcorn ME17 ....141 E6
Lenham Sta ME17 .....111 C4
Lenham Way ME8 ....49 A3
Lennard Rd Orpington BR2 .36 F1
  Sevenoaks TN13 ....83 E7
Lennox Ave DA11 ....13 A1
Lennox Ho 6 DA17 ......4 A3
Lennox Rd DA11 ....29 F8
Lennox Rd E DA11 ......30 A8
Lenor Cl DA6 ....7 E3
Lensbury Way SE2 ....3 D3
Lenside Dr ME15 ....93 A2
Lenton St SE18 ....2 D2
Leonard Ave Otford TN14 .69 B3
  Swanscombe DA10 .....28 E8
Leonard Cl ME16 ....91 B6
Leonard Ct DA14 ....24 A5
Leonard Judge Ho DA2 ..27 E3
Leonard Pl BR2 ....50 E7
Leonard Rd
  7 Chatham ME4 ....48 B3
  Gillingham ME8 ....48 B3
Leonard Robbins Path 3
  SE28 ....3 B6
Leonard St E16 ....1 E5
Leopold Rd 2 ME4 ......48 A3
Lesley Cl Istead Rise DA13 .43 F8
  Sidcup DA5 ....25 B8
  Swanley BR8 ....39 D6
Lesley Pl ME16 ....91 E5
Lesley Tew Ct TN10 ...117 C5
Leslie Cres TN30 .....173 B2
Leslie Rd Gillingham ME7 .48 D7
  Newham E16 ....1 B7
Leslie Smith Sq 7 SE18 ..6 A8
Lesnes Abbey
  (remains of)* SE2 ......3 C2
Lesney Park Prim Sch DA8 .8 D8
Lesney Park Rd DA8 .....8 D8
Lesney Pk DA8 ....8 D8
Lessar Ave DA7 ....7 D7
Lessness Heath
  Prim Sch DA17 ....4 A1
Lessness Pk DA17 ....4 A1
Lessness Rd 12 DA17 ....4 A1
Lested La ME17 ....108 B2
Lester Rd ME4 ....48 A3
Lestock House SE3 ......5 D6
Letchford Ave ME4 .....47 F1
Letchford Cl BR2 ......36 A4
Letchworth Cl BR2 .....36 A4
Letter Box La TN13 .....99 C6
Leverholme Gdns SE9 ...23 A4
Levett Cl ME3 ....21 B6
Levetts La TN32 ......185 D1
Leviathan Way ME4 .....34 A1
Lewd La TN27 ....143 A3
Lewes Cl RM17 ....12 A8
Lewes Rd BR1 ....36 D7
Lewin Rd DA6 ....7 E3
Lewing Cl BR6 ....37 E1
Lewis Ave ME8 ....49 B2
Lewis Court Dr ME17 ..107 C3
Lewis Ct DA11 ....29 F6
Lewis King Ho 6 BR1 ...22 B1
Lewis Rd Bexley DA16 ....7 C4
  Istead Rise DA13 ......43 F8
  Sidcup DA14 ....24 C5

Lewis Rd continued
  Swanscombe DA10 .....11 E1
Leybank TN11 ....116 F4
Leybourne Cl Chatham ME5 62 A2
  Hayes BR2 ....36 A3
Leybourne Dell TN17 ..180 E6
Leybourne Rd ME2 ......46 F8
Leybourne Way ME20 ...74 F4
Leybourne, St Peter & St
  Paul CE Prim Sch ME19 .74 E2
Leybridge Ct SE12 ......5 A2
Leyburn Ct TN9 ....117 C3
Leyburn Ho SE18 ....5 E7
Leycroft Gdns DA8 ......9 B6
Leydenhatch La BR8 ....39 D8
Leyes Rd E16 ....1 D7
Leyhill Cl BR8 ....39 E4
Leyland Rd SE12 ....5 A2
Leysdown Ave DA7 ......8 C3
Leysdown Rd SE9 ....22 F6
Leyton Ave ME7 ....48 E1
Leyton Cross DA2 ......26 A6
Leyton Cross Rd DA2 ...25 F5
Leywood Rd DA13 ......58 D3
Lezayre Rd BR6 ....51 F4
Liberty Mews BR6 ......51 F8
Libya Terr 6 ME14 .....92 A7
Lichdale Ct SE9 ....5 A2
Lichfield Cl ME8 ....49 D2
Lichfield Ho 12 ME15 ..107 E7
Liddon Rd BR1 ....36 D6
Lidsing Rd ME14 ....77 E6
Lidwells La TN17 ......153 E1
Liffler Rd SE18 ....2 D2
Lightfoot Gn TN18 ....178 E3
Lila Pl BR8 ....39 E5
Lilac Cres ME2 ....46 E6
Lilac Gdns BR8 ....39 D6
Lilac Pl DA13 ....44 B2
Lilac Rd ME2 ....46 E5
Lilburne Gdns SE9 ......5 E2
Lilburne Rd SE9 ....5 E2
Lilian Barker Cl SE12 ...5 A2
Lilk Hill ME14 ....93 C3
Lillechurch Rd ME3 ....32 F7
Lillesden Cotts TN18 ..184 E7
Lillieburn ME19 ....74 D2
Lillieburn ME19 ....74 D2
Lima Ave DA11 ....29 D8
Lime Cl Bromley BR1 ...36 E5
  Frant TN3 ....163 B3
  Marden TN12 ....138 C6
Lime Cotts TN12 ......139 F3
Lime Cres ME19 ....90 A7
Lime Ct Eltham SE9 ....23 B6
  Gillingham ME8 ....63 C3
Lime Gr Orpington BR6 ..51 B8
  Sidcup DA15 ....6 F1
Lime Hill Rd TN1 .....149 A2
Lime Kiln Dr SE7 ....5 B8
Lime Pit La TN13,TN14 ..68 C2
Lime Rd BR8 ....39 D6
Lime Row DA18 ....3 F3
Lime Tree Ave DA9 .....28 A7
Lime Tree Cl TN9 .....117 C2
Lime Tree Wlk TN13 ....84 B2
Lime Trees TN12 ......139 E4
Limepits Cross ME9 ....65 F3
Limes Cl TN30 ....183 C6
Limes Gr TN18 ....178 F5
Limes Row BR6 ....51 B5
Limes The Edenbridge TN8 .112 C1
  Frittenden TN17 .....156 E6
  Lenham ME17 ....111 D5
  Orpington BR2 ....50 E8
Limetree Cl ME5 ....62 B8
Limetree Terr
  Lenham ME17 ....111 E6
  6 DA16 ....7 A4
Limewood Rd DA8 ......8 C7
Linchmere Rd 7 SE12 ..22 A8
Linclon Cl DA8 ....8 F5
Lincoln Cl ME2 ....46 D6
Lincoln Ct ME8 ....22 C5
Lincoln Green Rd BR5 ..37 F4
Lincoln Rd Erith DA8 ....8 F5
  Maidstone ME15 ......107 D8
  Sidcup DA14 ....24 B3
Lincolnshire Terr DA2 ..27 D4
Lincon Rd ME7 ....48 D7
Linden Ave DA1 ....26 C7
Linden Chase Rd TN13 ..84 B5
Linden Cl Orpington BR6 .52 A5
  Paddock Wood TN12 ..136 A6
  Purfleet RM19 ....10 C8
  Royal Tunbridge Wells TN4 .149 A2
Linden Ct Sidcup DA14 ..23 E4
  Tonbridge TN10 ......117 B7
Linden Gdns TN2 ......148 F1
Linden House 5 ME5 ....61 F4
Linden Park Rd TN2 ...149 A2
Linden Rd Coxheath ME17 .106 C4
  Gillingham ME7 ......48 E5
Linden Sq TN13 ....83 E5
Lindenfield BR7 ....37 B7
Lindens The ME20 ......75 E1
Lindisfarne Cl DA12 ....30 D3
Lindisfarne Gdns ME16 ..91 E3
Lindridge La TN12 ....139 C5
Lindsay Ho 2 SE18 .....2 A2
Lindsey Cl BR1 ....36 E6
Lindwood Cl 8 E6 ....1 F8
Lineacre Cl ME8 ....63 D6
Lines Terr ME4 ....48 A4
Ling Rd Erith DA8 ....8 C8
  Newham E16 ....1 A8
Lingey Cl DA15 ....23 F6

Lingfield Ave DA2 ......27 B8
Lingfield Cres SE9 ......6 D3
Lingfield Rd
  Borough Green TN15 ...87 B7
  Edenbridge TN8 ......128 A8
  Gravesend DA12 ....30 B6
Lingley Dr ME2 ....33 C2
Lingwood DA7 ....8 B5
Link Field BR2 ....36 A3
Link Hill La TN27 .....127 D3
Link The Eltham SE9 ....23 A5
  New Ash Green DA3 ....56 F8
Link Way Bromley BR2 ..36 E2
  Royal Tunbridge Wells TN2 .149 E8
Linkden Cotts TN18 ...186 E5
Links Ct SE9 ....23 B7
Links The Addington ME19 .73 E2
  Chatham ME5 ....62 B8
Links View Dartford DA1 .26 C7
  Woolwich SE18 ....6 B6
Linkway ME20 ....75 C1
Linley Cl RM18 ....14 D7
Linnet Ave TN12 ......136 A5
Linnet Cl SE28 ....3 C6
Linslade Rd BR6 ....52 A4
Linsted Ct SE9 ....6 E1
Linton Cl Bexley DA16 ...7 B6
  2 Greenwich SE7 ......1 C1
Linton Dann Cl ME3 ....34 D6
Linton Gdns E6 ....1 E7
Linton Gore ME17 ....106 D3
Linton Hill TN12 .....122 F6
Linton Mead
  Prim Sch SE28 ....3 B6
Linton Rd ME15 ....106 F4
Lintorn Symonds Rd ME3 .33 F5
Linwood Ave ME2 ......46 E8
Lion Rd Bexley DA6 .....7 F3
  Newham E6 ....1 F8
Lionel Gdns SE9 ....5 D2
Lionel Oxley
  House 5 RM17 ....12 B8
Lionel Rd Eltham SE9 ....5 D2
  Tonbridge TN9 ....133 A8
Lions Cl SE9 ....22 D5
Liphook Way ME16 .....91 D3
Lipscombe Rd TN2 ....149 D6
Lipton Cl SE28 ....3 C6
Liptraps La TN2 ......149 D7
Lipwell Hill ME23 ......17 B4
Liskeard Cl BR7 ....23 C2
Liskeard Gdns SE3 ......5 A6
Lisle Cl DA12 ....31 B6
Lismore Cl ME15 ......107 A7
Lister Cl ME19 ....89 F8
Lister Ho SE2 ....3 D1
Lister Rd RM18 ....13 A5
Lister Wlk SE28 ....3 D6
Listmas Rd ME4 ....48 B3
Little Alley TN8 ......128 B5
Little Bayham Cotts TN3 .164 F4
Little Birches DA15 ....23 E6
Little Boundes Cl TN4 ..132 F3
Little Brook Hospl DA2 ..10 C1
Little Browns La TN8 ..112 A4
Little Buckland Ave ME16 .91 D6
Little Ct E16 ....91 D2
Little Field TN12 .....139 E5
Little Footway TN3 ....147 F3
Little Heath SE7 ....1 E1
Little Heath Rd DA7 .....7 F7
Little Hill TN30 ......173 B2
Little Iridge Farm
  Cotts TN19 ....184 C1
Little Job's Cross TN17 .181 F1
Little John Ave ME5 ....61 F2
Little Julians Hill TN13 ..99 A8
Little Kit's Coty House*
  ME20 ....76 C5
Little Mallett TN3 ....147 F3
Little Market Row ME19 .74 E2
Little Mill Farm
  Cotts TN12 ....138 C8
Little Mount Sion TN1 .149 A2
Little Oakham Ct ME3 ..19 C4
Little Orch ME17 ......106 D3
Little Oxley ME19 ......74 E2
Little Pk TN5 ....174 E5
Little Queen St DA1 ....26 F8
Little Redlands BR1 ....36 E7
Little Robhurst TN26 ..173 D8
Little Sheephurst
  Cotts TN12 ....137 E5
Little Thrift BR5 ....37 C5
Little Wood TN13 ......84 D5
Little Wood Cl BR5 .....38 A8
Littlebourne Ave ME8 ..49 B4
Littlebourne Rd ME14 ..92 C6
Littlebrook Manor
  Way DA1 ....10 A2
Littlecombe SE7 ....5 B8
Littlecourt Rd TN13 ....84 A3
Littlecroft Eltham SE9 ...6 A4
  Istead Rise DA13 .....29 E1
Littledale Dartford DA2 ..27 C5
  Woolwich SE2 ....7 A8
Littlefield TN11 ......118 E8
Littlejohn Rd BR5 ......38 B4
Littlemede SE9 ....22 F5
Littlemore Rd SE2 ......3 A4
Livesey St ME18 ......90 A1
Livingstone Bldgs ME7 ..48 D5
Livingstone Circ ME7 ...48 D5
Livingstone Gdns DA12 ..30 D3
Livingstone Hospl DA1 ..26 F8
Livingstone Rd
  Gillingham ME7 ......48 E5
  Gravesend DA12 ....30 D3

Livingstone Wlk 6 ME15 .107 F5
Lizban St SE3 . . . . .5 B7
Llanover Rd DA8 . . . . .6 A7
Lloyds Gn TN30 . . . . .189 D4
Loaland Bsns Ctr ME2 . . .47 D8
Loam Ct DA1 . . . . .26 E7
Loampits Cl TN9 . . . . . . .117 D3
Lobelia Cl Gillingham ME7 .48 E6
  5 Newham E6 . . . . .1 E8
Locarno Ave ME8 . . . . . . .49 A2
Lochat Rd ME4 . . . . .33 E6
Lochmere Cl DA8 . . . . .8 B8
Lock La ME14 . . . . .76 D1
Lock St ME7 . . . . .48 C5
Lock's Yd TN13 . . . . .84 C2
Lockesley Dr BR5 . . . . . . .38 A3
Lockham Farm Ave
  ME17 . . . . .107 D5
Lockington Cl TN9 . . . . . .132 F7
Lockington Gr ME1 . . . . . .47 C5
Lockside TN9 . . . . .117 C2
Locksley Cl ME5 . . . . .61 E2
Lockwood ME16 . . . . .91 D7
Lockyer Rd RM19 . . . . . . .10 C8
Lockyers Hill DA13 . . . . . .58 F5
Lodden Cl 16 BR5 . . . . . . .38 E1
Loddington La ME17 . . . .123 A8
Loder Cl ME17 . . . . .111 B5
Lodge Ave DA1 . . . . .9 C1
Lodge Cl Orpington BR6 . . .38 B1
  Wateringbury ME18 . . . .104 D8
Lodge Cres BR6 . . . . .38 B1
Lodge Gdns ME17 . . . . . .125 F6
Lodge Hill DA16 . . . . .7 B7
Lodge Hill La ME3 . . . . . . .33 F7
Lodge La Cobham DA12 . . .45 B5
  Sidcup DA5 . . . . .7 D1
  Westerham TN16 . . . . . . .96 C8
Lodge Oak La TN9 . . . . . .133 C8
Lodge Rd Bromley BR1 . . .22 C1
  Maidstone ME14 . . . . . . .92 D5
  Staplehurst TN12 . . . . . .139 E5
  Tonbridge TN9 . . . . .117 B2
Lodgewood Cotts TN8 . .113 D2
Logs Hill BR1,BR7 . . . . . . .36 E8
Logs Hill Cl BR7 . . . . .36 E8
Lolland Ho 9 SE18 . . . . . . .1 E2
Lomaria Cl TN2 . . . . .149 C4
Lomas La TN18 . . . . .186 F5
Lombard St DA4 . . . . .41 C5
Lombard Trad Est SE7 . . . .1 B2
Lombard Wall SE7 . . . . . . .1 A3
Lombardy Cl ME7 . . . . . . .63 A6
Lombardy Dr ME14 . . . . . .92 C5
London City Airport E16 . .1 F1
London Ind Pk The E6 . . . .2 A2
London La Bromley BR1 . . .22 A1
  Cranbrook Common TN17 .156 A2
London Rd Addington ME19 73 D7
  Badgers Mount TN14 . . . .68 C6
  Bidborough TN4 . . . . . . .132 F3
  Bromley BR1 . . . . .36 A8
  Chelsfield TN14 . . . . .52 F2
  Crayford DA1 . . . . .8 D2
  Ditton ME20 . . . . .75 C1
  Farningham BR8,DA4 . . . .40 D3
  Flimwell TN5 . . . . .177 D1
  Gillingham ME8 . . . . .49 C1
  Grays RM17,RM20 . . . . . .11 E8
  Halstead TN14 . . . . .67 E4
  Hartlip ME8,ME9 . . . . . . .64 D7
  Hildenborough
  TN11,TN13,TN15 . . . . . .116 B7
  Hurst Green TN19 . . . . . .184 A3
  Maidstone ME16 . . . . . . .91 C6
  Newington ME9 . . . . .65 A6
  Northfleet DA11 . . . . .12 E1
  Otford TN13 . . . . .68 D1
  Rochester ME2 . . . . .47 A7
  Royal Tunbridge Wells TN4 .149 A8
  Royal Tunbridge
  Wells,Mount Sion TN1 . . .149 A3
  Sevenoaks TN13 . . . . . . .84 B2
  Sevenoaks,Dunton Green
  TN13 . . . . .83 E7
  Swanley BR8 . . . . .39 E6
  Swanley,White Oak BR8 . .39 D7
  Swanscombe DA9 . . . . . .11 C2
  Tilbury RM18 . . . . .13 B5
  Tonbridge TN10,TN11 . . .117 B3
  West Kingsdown TN15 . . .56 A1
  Wrotham TN15 . . . . .72 B3
  Wrotham Heath TN15,ME19 .72 F1
London Rd E ME20 . . . . . .90 F8
London Road
  Purfleet RM19 . . . . .10 C8
London Road
  West Thurrock RM20 . . . .11 A8
Londonderry Ho 15 ME15 107 E7
Londonderry Par DA8 . . . . .8 D7
Lonewood Way TN11 . . . .102 F2
Long Acre BR6 . . . . .52 D8
Long Barn Rd TN14 . . . . . . .7 E6
Long Catlis Rd ME8 . . . . . .63 D4
Long La Bexley DA7 . . . . . . .7 E6
  Rabbit's Cross ME17 . . . .123 D5
Long Mark Rd 5 E16 . . . . .1 D8
Long Mead
  Prim Sch TN10 . . . . .117 B5
Long Mead Way TN10 . . .117 B4
Long Meads TN3,TN4 . . . .148 B4
Long Mill La Crouch TN15 . .87 B3
  Platt TN15 . . . . .87 C7
Long Rede La ME16 . . . . . .90 F3
Long Slip TN3 . . . . .148 A3
Long Wlk SE18 . . . . .6 B8
Longbury Cl BR5 . . . . .38 B6
Longbury Dr BR5 . . . . .38 B7

Longcroft SE9 . . . . .23 A5
Longdon Wood BR2 . . . . .50 E6
Longfellow Rd ME7 . . . . . .48 C3
Longfield TN30 . . . . .183 A6
Longfield Ave
  High Halstow ME23 . . . . .17 E4
  New Barn DA3,DA13 . . . .43 D7
Longfield Pl ME15 . . . . . .107 C8
Longfield Rd
  Meopham Sta DA3,DA13 . . .43 E3
  Royal Tunbridge
  Wells TN1,TN2,TN11 . . . .133 E1
Longfield Sta DA3 . . . . . . .42 E6
Longfields Dr ME14 . . . . . .93 A5
Longford Cl ME8 . . . . .64 A8
Longford Ct ME8 . . . . .64 A8
Longhill Ave ME5 . . . . .48 B3
Longhurst Dr ME5 . . . . . . .61 F2
Longlands Ct DA15 . . . . . .23 F5
Longlands Park Cres
  DA15 . . . . .23 E6
Longlands Prim Sch DA15 23 E5
Longlands Rd DA15 . . . . . .23 F5
Longleat Villas 3 DA6 . . . .7 E3
Longleigh La SE2,DA7 . . . .7 C8
Longley Rd Gillingham ME8 .49 F1
  Rochester ME1 . . . . .47 C4
Longmarsh View DA4 . . . .41 B8
Longmead BR7 . . . . .37 A7
Longmead Dr DA14 . . . . . .24 D6
Longmeadow TN13 . . . . . .83 D6
Longmeadow Rd DA15 . . .23 E7
Longparish Cl ME15 . . . . .107 F6
Longreach Rd DA8 . . . . .9 B7
Longshaw Rd ME15 . . . . .107 F5
Longspring Wood TN13 . . .99 A6
Longten's Cotts ME18 . . . .31 E6
Longtown Ct 15 DA2 . . . . .10 B1
Longview Way TN2 . . . . . .149 D7
Longwalk DA13 . . . . .43 E8
Longwood ME5 . . . . .62 B1
Longworth Cl SE28 . . . . . . .3 D7
Lonsdale Cl SE9 . . . . .22 D5
Lonsdale Cres DA2 . . . . . .27 C7
Lonsdale Dr ME8 . . . . .63 E7
Lonsdale Gdns TN1 . . . . .149 A3
Lonsdale Rd DA7 . . . . .7 F5
Loop Rd BR7 . . . . .23 C2
Loose Inf & Jun Schs
  ME15 . . . . .107 A6
Loose Rd ME15 . . . . .107 A7
Loraine Ct BR7 . . . . .23 B3
Lord Chatham's Ride
  TN14 . . . . .67 D2
Lord Roberts Terr SE18 . . .2 A1
Lord Romney's Hill ME14 .92 F3
Lord St Gravesend DA12 . .30 B8
  Newham E16 . . . . .1 E5
Lord Warwick St SE18 . . . .1 F3
Lords Wood Cl ME5 . . . . . .62 B3
Lords Wood La ME5 . . . . . .62 B3
Lordswood Cl DA2 . . . . . . .27 E4
Lordswood Ind Est ME5 . . .77 C8
Lordswood Inf Sch ME5 . . .62 B3
Lordswood Jun Sch ME5 . .62 B3
Lorenden Pk TN18 . . . . . .178 F1
Lorimar Bsns Ctr RM13 . . . .4 E3
Lorton Cl DA12 . . . . .30 E6
Lossenham La TN18 . . . . .187 D3
Louisville Ave ME7 . . . . . .48 D4
Louvain Rd DA9 . . . . .27 C6
Lovage App E6 . . . . .1 E8
Love La East End TN27 . .142 B5
  East Tilbury RM18 . . . . . .14 C8
  Rochester ME1 . . . . .47 C5
  Sidcup DA5 . . . . .8 A1
  Wateringbury ME18 . . . .104 D7
  Woolwich SE18 . . . . .2 B2
Lovel Ave DA16 . . . . .7 A5
Lovelace Ave BR2 . . . . . . .37 A3
Lovelace Cl Gillingham ME8 63 D4
  West Kingsdown TN15 . . .55 E4
Lovelace Gn SE9 . . . . .5 F4
Lover's La DA9,DA10 . . . . .11 D3
Lovers La TN17 . . . . .153 F1
Lovibonds Ave BR6 . . . . . .51 B7
Low Cl DA9 . . . . .11 A2
Low Meadow ME2 . . . . . . .60 B5
Low Street La RM18 . . . . . .13 F8
Lowe Ave E16 . . . . .1 A8
Lower Bell La ME20 . . . . . .75 B2
Lower Bloors La ME8 . . . . .49 E3
Lower Boxley Rd 10 ME14 .92 A5
Lower Camden BR7 . . . . . .36 F8
Lower Church Hill DA9 . . .10 E2
Lower Croft BR8 . . . . .39 F5
Lower East Rd ME4 . . . . . .48 B8
Lower Fant Rd ME16 . . . . .91 D2
Lower Farm Rd ME17 . . . .123 D5
Lower Gn ME2 . . . . .115 F1
Lower Gravel Rd BR2 . . . .36 F1
Lower Green Rd
  Pembury TN2 . . . . .150 D7
  Royal Tunbridge Wells
  TN3, TN4 . . . . .148 C6
Lower Hartlip Rd ME9 . . . .64 E5
Lower Haysden La
  TN11,TN9 . . . . .132 D8
Lower Hazelmead ME15 . .176 A4
Lower High St TN5 . . . . . .175 A4
Lower Higham Rd DA12 . . .31 B7
Lower Park Rd DA17 . . . . . .4 A2
Lower Platts TN5 . . . . .174 F8
Lower Rainham Rd ME7 . . .49 D5
Lower Range Rd DA12 . . . .30 E8
Lower Rd Erith DA8 . . . . . . .4 D2
  Erith,Belvedere DA17 . . . .4 B3

Lower Rd continued
  Hextable BR8 . . . . .26 B1
  Higham ME3 . . . . .32 B6
  Maidstone ME15 . . . . . . .92 B3
  Northfleet DA11 . . . . .12 A3
  Orpington BR5 . . . . .38 B3
  Sutton Valence ME17 . . .124 E7
  Tilbury RM18 . . . . .13 A3
  West Farleigh ME15 . . . .105 D3
Lower Rochester Rd ME3 .32 E6
Lower St Leeds ME17 . . . .109 A7
  Tonbridge TN11 . . . . . . .115 F5
Lower Station Rd DA1 . . . . .8 E1
Lower Stone St ME15 . . . .92 A3
Lower Tovil ME15 . . . . .91 E2
Lower Twydall La
  ME7,ME8 . . . . .49 C4
Lower Warren Rd ME20 . . .76 E6
Lower Woodlands Rd
  ME7 . . . . .49 A6
Lownds Ct BR1 . . . . .36 A7
Lowry Cl DA8 . . . . .4 D2
Lowry The 4 TN9 . . . . . . .133 B8
Loxwood Cl BR5,BR6 . . . .52 D8
Lubbock Cl ME15 . . . . . . .107 E5
Lubbock Rd BR7 . . . . .22 F1
Lubbock Rd BR7 . . . . .22 F1
Lubbock Wlk ME8 . . . . . . .63 D5
Lucas Rd ME6 . . . . .74 E7
Lucerne Ct 5 DA18 . . . . . . .3 E3
Lucerne Rd BR6 . . . . .37 F1
Lucerne St ME14 . . . . .92 A5
Lucilina Dr TN8 . . . . .128 C8
Lucknow Rd TN12 . . . . . .136 A3
Lucknow St SE18 . . . . .6 E7
Lucks La
  Paddock Wood TN12 . . . .136 B3
  Rabbit's Cross ME17 . . . .123 F6
Lucks Way TN12 . . . . .138 B6
Luddenham Cl ME14 . . . . .92 C6
Luddesdon Rd DA8 . . . . . . .8 A7
Luddesdown
  House 5 BR5 . . . . .38 C4
Luddesdown Rd DA13 . . . .45 A2
Ludham Cl SE28 . . . . .3 C7
Ludlow Cl BR2 . . . . .36 A6
Luffield Rd SE2 . . . . .3 B3
Luffman Rd SE12 . . . . .5 B3
Lughorse La ME15,ME18 . .105 C1
Lullingstone Ave BR8 . . . .39 F6
Lullingstone Castle* DA4 .54 B5
Lullingstone Cl
  Gillingham ME8 . . . . .63 B3
  St Paul's Cray BR5 . . . . . .24 B1
Lullingstone Cres BR5 . . . .24 B1
Lullingstone La DA4 . . . . .54 C8
Lullingstone Pk* DA4 . . . .53 F6
Lullingstone Pk
  Visitor Ctr* DA4 . . . . . . .54 B4
Lullingstone Rd
  3 Erith DA17 . . . . .7 F8
  Maidstone ME16 . . . . . . .91 C7
Lullingstone Roman Villa
  (rems of)* DA4 . . . . .54 B7
Lulworth Rd Bexley DA16 . . .6 F5
  Chislehurst SE9 . . . . .22 E6
Lumley Cl DA17 . . . . .4 A1
Lumsden Terr 8 ME4 . . . . .47 E4
Lunedale Rd DA2 . . . . .27 C7
Lunsford District Ctr
  ME20 . . . . .75 A4
Lunsford La ME20 . . . . . . .74 F2
Lunsford Prim Sch ME20 . .75 A4
Lupton Cl SE12 . . . . .22 B4
Lurkins Rise TN17 . . . . . .167 D7
Lushington Rd ME14 . . . . .91 E7
Lusted Rd TN13 . . . . .83 E7
Luton High St ME5 . . . . . .48 C2
Luton Inf Sch ME5 . . . . . . .48 C2
Luton Jun Sch ME4 . . . . . .48 C2
Luton Rd Chatham ME4,ME5 .48 B2
  Sidcup DA14 . . . . .24 C5
Luxfield Rd SE9 . . . . .22 E7
Luxon Rd DA13 . . . . .58 E4
Luxted Rd BR6 . . . . .66 A6
Lyall Way ME8 . . . . .63 E4
Lych Gate Rd BR6 . . . . . . .38 A1
Lychfield Dr ME2 . . . . .47 A8
Lydd Cl DA14 . . . . .23 E5
Lydd Rd Chatham ME5 . . . .62 B5
  Erith DA7 . . . . .7 F7
Lydden Ct SE9 . . . . .6 E1
Lydens La TN8 . . . . .128 F6
Lydford Ct 18 DA2 . . . . . . .10 B1
Lydia Cotts 2 DA11 . . . . . .30 B8
Lydia Rd DA8 . . . . .8 F8
Lydstep Rd DA7 . . . . .23 A4
Lyford St SE18 . . . . .1 E2
Lyle Cl ME2 . . . . .47 B8
Lyle Ct ME16 . . . . .91 C5
Lyle Pk TN15 . . . . .84 B4
Lyme Farm Rd SE12 . . . . . .5 B3
Lyme Rd DA16 . . . . .7 B6
Lyminge Cl Gillingham ME8 .49 C2
  Sidcup DA14 . . . . .23 F4
Lymington Cl 2 E6 . . . . . . .1 F8
Lymington Ct ME15 . . . . .107 F4
Lyndean Ind Est SE2 . . . . . .3 C3
Lynden La TN5 . . . . .176 A1
Lynden Way ME8 . . . . .39 D6
Lyndhurst BR7 . . . . .23 B4
Lyndhurst Ave ME8 . . . . . .63 C2
Lyndhurst Cl Bexley DA7 . . .8 B4
  Orpington BR6 . . . . .51 B6
Lyndhurst Dr TN13 . . . . . .83 E3
Lyndhurst Rd Bexley DA7 . . .8 B4

Lyndhurst Rd continued
  Maidstone ME15 . . . . . . .107 C8
Lyndhurst Way DA13 . . . . .43 F8
Lyndon Ave DA15 . . . . .6 F3
Lyndon Rd DA17 . . . . .4 A2
Lynette Ave ME2 . . . . .33 A1
Lyngs Cl ME18 . . . . .120 F8
Lynmead Cl ME14 . . . . . . .112 B4
Lynmere Rd DA16 . . . . .7 B5
Lynmouth Rise BR5 . . . . . .38 B5
Lynne Cl 7 BR6 . . . . .51 F4
Lynors Ave ME2 . . . . .33 A1
Lynstead Cl BR1 . . . . .36 C7
Lynstead House ME16 . . . .91 A1
Lynsted Cl DA6 . . . . .8 B2
Lynsted Gdns SE9 . . . . .5 D4
Lynsted Rd ME8 . . . . .49 B3
Lynton Ave BR5 . . . . .38 B5
Lynton Dr ME5 . . . . .62 B3
Lynton Rd DA11 . . . . .30 A7
Lynton Rd S DA11 . . . . . . .30 A7
Lynwood TN3 . . . . .161 C6
Lynwood Gr BR6 . . . . .37 E1
Lyons Cres TN9 . . . . .117 C2
Lyoth Rd BR5 . . . . .51 C8
Lysander Rd ME19 . . . . . . .88 F3
Lysander Way BR6 . . . . . . .51 C7
Lytchet Rd BR1 . . . . .22 B1
Lytham Cl SE28 . . . . .3 E7
Lytton Strachy Path 8
  SE28 . . . . .3 B6
Lyveden Rd SE3 . . . . .5 B7

M

Mabbett House 2 SE18 . . . .6 A8
Mabel Cotts DA3 . . . . .43 A6
Mabel Rd BR8 . . . . .26 A2
Mabledon Rd TN9 . . . . . . .133 A8
Macallister House 8 SE18 .48 B4
Macaulay Cl ME20 . . . . . . .75 A4
Macaulay Way 2 SE28 . . . .3 B5
Macbean St SE18 . . . . .2 B3
Macdonald Ct TN12 . . . . .136 A6
Macdonald Rd ME7 . . . . . .48 D6
Mace Ct RM17 . . . . .12 E8
Mace Farm Cotts TN14 . . .66 E6
Mace Gateway E16 . . . . . . .1 A6
Mace La TN14 . . . . .66 D6
Macgregor Rd E16 . . . . . . .1 C8
Mackenders Cl ME20 . . . . .76 A6
Mackenders Gn ME20 . . . .76 A6
Mackenders La ME20 . . . . .76 A6
Mackenzie Way DA12 . . . .30 D2
Macleod Ho SE18 . . . . .5 E6
Macmillan Gdns 2 DA1 . . .10 A3
Macoma Rd SE18 . . . . .6 D8
Macoma Terr SE18 . . . . . . .6 D8
Mada Rd BR6 . . . . .51 B7
Madan Rd TN16 . . . . .81 E2
Madden Ave ME5 . . . . .61 E5
Madden Cl DA8 . . . . .11 E1
Maddocks Cl DA14 . . . . . .24 E3
Madeira Pk TN2 . . . . .149 B2
Madginford Cl ME15 . . . . .93 A2
Madginford Park
  Inf Sch ME15 . . . . .93 A2
Madginford Park
  Jun Sch ME15 . . . . .93 A2
Madginford Rd ME15 . . . . .92 F2
Madison Ctr DA7 . . . . .7 C7
Madison Gdns DA7 . . . . . . .7 C7
Madison Way TN13 . . . . . .83 F4
Madras House 2 ME15 . . .107 E5
Mafeking Rd ME5 . . . . .61 F3
Magdalen Cl ME7 . . . . .63 A4
Magdalen Gr BR6 . . . . . . .52 B6
Magnet Rd RM20 . . . . .11 C8
Magnolia Ave ME8 . . . . . . .63 B5
Magnolia Cl TN9 . . . . .133 C7
Magpie Cl ME20 . . . . .75 A1
Magpie Bottom TN15 . . . . .69 E6
Magpie Gn 3 TN8 . . . . . . .112 D3
Magpie Hall Cl BR2 . . . . . .36 E3
Magpie Hall La BR2 . . . . . .36 F3
Magpie Hall Rd ME4 . . . . .48 A8
Magpie La ME9,ME14 . . . . .63 F1
Magwitch Cl ME1 . . . . .47 B4
Maida Rd Chatham ME4 . . .48 B2
  Erith DA17 . . . . .4 A3
Maida Vale Rd DA1 . . . . . . .9 F2
Maiden Erlegh Ave DA5 . . .24 E7
Maiden La DA1 . . . . .9 A3
Maidstone Barracks Sta
  ME16 . . . . .91 E5
Maidstone East Sta ME14 .91 F5
Maidstone
  Gram Sch ME15 . . . . . . .92 B2
Maidstone
  Gram Sch for Girls ME16 .91 E5
Maidstone Hospl
  The ME16 . . . . .91 A4
Maidstone Ind Ctr ME14 . .91 F5
Maidstone L Ctr ME15 . . . .92 C2
Maidstone Mus & Bentlif
  Art Gallery* ME14 . . . . . .91 F5
Maidstone Rd
  Chatham ME4 . . . . .47 F2
  Chatham,Walderslade ME5 . .61 E4
  Chestnut Street ME9 . . . .65 D4
  Colt's Hill TN12,TN2 . . . .135 B4
  Five Wents ME17 . . . . . .108 B2
  Gillingham ME8 . . . . .63 C6
  ME7,ME8 . . . . .63 B2
  Goose Green ME18,TN11 .103 C3
  Grays RM17 . . . . .12 A8

Liv–Man **213**

Maidstone Rd continued
  Headcorn TN27 . . . . .141 B7
  Horsmonden TN12 . . . . .137 C3
  Lenham ME17 . . . . .111 D5
  Matfield TN12 . . . . .151 C6
  Nettlestead Green ME18 .104 C3
  Oldbury TN15 . . . . .85 C5
  Pembury TN2 . . . . .134 E1
  Platt TN15 . . . . .87 C7
  Rochester ME1 . . . . .47 C3
  Sevenoaks TN13 . . . . . . .83 E5
  Sidcup DA14 . . . . .24 F1
  Staplehurst TN12 . . . . . .139 E7
  Swanley DA14,BR8 . . . . .39 B8
  Underling Green TN12 . . .122 C3
Maidstone West Sta ME16 .91 F3
Mailyns The ME8 . . . . .63 D7
Main Gate Rd ME4 . . . . . . .47 F7
Main Rd Chattenden ME3 . .33 F4
  Cooling ME3 . . . . .16 A4
  Crockenhill BR8 . . . . .39 D3
  Cudham TN16 . . . . .81 A7
  Farningham DA4 . . . . .40 F3
  Halstead TN14 . . . . .67 C3
  Hextable BR8 . . . . .39 F8
  Hoo St Werburgh ME3 . . .34 C5
  Kingsnorth ME3 . . . . .35 D7
  Longfield DA3 . . . . .42 E7
  Marlpit Hill TN8 . . . . .112 B6
  Sidcup DA14,DA15 . . . . .23 E5
  St Paul's Cray BR5 . . . . . .38 C7
  Sundridge TN14 . . . . .82 E3
  Sutton at Hone DA4 . . . . .27 B1
Main Road Gorse Hill DA45 55 D7
Mainridge Rd BR7 . . . . . . .23 A4
Maison Des Fleurs ME16 . .91 C2
Majendie Rd SE18 . . . . .2 D1
Major York's Rd TN4 . . . .148 F2
Malden Dr ME14 . . . . .92 A8
Mall The 6 Bexley DA6 . . . .8 A3
  4 Bromley BR1 . . . . .36 A6
Mallard
  Apartments 14 ME15 . . .107 E5
Mallard Cl DA1 . . . . .9 F2
Mallard Path SE28 . . . . .2 D3
Mallard Way
  Lower Stoke ME3 . . . . . . .19 C4
  Marlpit Hill TN8 . . . . .112 C3
Mallard Wlk Larkfield ME20 74 F2
  Sidcup DA14 . . . . .24 C2
Mallards Way ME15 . . . . . .93 A1
Malling Cl ME19 . . . . .89 F7
Malling Rd
  Kings Hill M18,ME19 . . . .88 F2
  Lunsford ME6,ME20 . . . . .74 F5
  Snodland ME6 . . . . .75 A7
  Teston ME18 . . . . .90 A1
Malling Sch The ME19 . . . .89 F7
Malling Terr ME16 . . . . . . .91 C4
Mallingdene ME3 . . . . .33 B8
Mallings Dr ME14 . . . . .93 C4
Mallings La ME14 . . . . .93 C4
Mallow Cl DA11 . . . . .29 E4
Mallow Ct RM17 . . . . .12 D8
Mallow Way 1 ME5 . . . . . .61 F4
Mallows The ME14 . . . . . . .91 E7
Mallys Pl DA4 . . . . .41 C8
Malmaynes Hall Rd ME3 . .18 D3
Malory Sch BR1 . . . . .22 A4
Malt House La TN30 . . . . .183 A7
Malt Mews ME1 . . . . .47 C5
Malt Shovel Cotts DA4 . . . .54 D7
Malta Ave ME5 . . . . .62 A7
Malta Rd RM18 . . . . .12 F5
Malta Terr 5 ME14 . . . . . .92 A7
Maltby Cl BR5 . . . . .38 A1
Malthouse Cl ME17 . . . . . .111 D5
Malthouse Hill ME15 . . . .106 F4
Malthouse La DA12 . . . . . .31 E3
Malthouse Rd TN15 . . . . . .56 F2
Malthus Path 7 SE28 . . . . .3 C5
Maltings Cl TN11 . . . . . . .118 E8
Maltings Ent Ctr The DA12 30 F7
Maltings The
  Gillingham ME8 . . . . .64 A8
  Gravesend DA11 . . . . . . .13 A1
  Maidstone, Grove
  Green ME14 . . . . .92 E5
  Maidstone,The
  Quarries ME17 . . . . .107 B4
  Orpington BR6 . . . . .37 F1
Malton Mews SE18 . . . . . . .6 E8
Malton St SE18 . . . . .6 E8
Malton Way TN2 . . . . .149 F7
Malus Cl ME5 . . . . .62 B1
Malvern Ave DA7 . . . . .7 E7
Malvern Ho DA11 . . . . .12 D1
Malvern Rd Gillingham ME7 .48 B5
  Orpington BR6 . . . . .52 B6
Malvina Ave DA12 . . . . . . .30 C6
Malyons Rd BR8 . . . . .25 F1
Mamignot Cl ME14 . . . . . .93 A5
Manchester Cl ME5 . . . . . .62 C6
Mandela Rd E16 . . . . .1 A7
Mandeville Cl 1 SE3 . . . . . .5 A7
Mandeville Ct 1 ME14 . . . .92 A5
Manford Ind Est DA8 . . . . . .9 B8
Mangold Way 4 DA18 . . . . .3 E3
Mangravet Ave ME15 . . . .107 C7
Manister Rd SE2 . . . . .3 A3
Manitoba Gdns 6 BR6 . . . .51 F4
Mann Sq TN9 . . . . .133 D2
Manning Ct 3 SE28 . . . . . .3 B5
Manning Rd BR5 . . . . .38 D4
Manningham Ho ME19 . . . .90 A6

Mannock Rd DA1 .....9 F4
Manor Cl Chalk DA12 .....31 B6
  Crayford DA1 .....8 E3
  Dartford DA2 .....26 A5
  Erith SE28 .....3 C7
  Maidstone ME14 .....93 B3
  Royal Tunbridge Wells TN4 .....148 E3
Manor Cotts
  Lamberhurst TN3 .....166 B5
  Langley Heath ME17 .....108 C5
Manor Ct Gillingham ME7 .....49 C4
  Maidstone ME14 .....93 B3
  Sole Street DA13 .....44 D4
Manor Dr DA3 .....43 A3
Manor Farm Cotts TN15 .....86 A6
Manor Field DA12 .....31 E3
Manor Forstal DA3 .....56 F7
Manor Gdns ME5 .....61 F4
Manor Gr TN10 .....117 C3
Manor Ho [14] Chatham ME7 .....48 A6
  Chislehurst BR7 .....37 D8
Manor House Dr ME16 .....91 D3
Manor House Gdns TN8 .....112 C1
Manor La
  Fawkham Green DA3 .....42 C2
  Hartley DA3 .....43 A3
  Rochester ME1 .....46 F3
Manor Park Ctry Pk*
  ME19 .....89 B7
Manor Park Rd BR7 .....37 D8
Manor Pk Chislehurst BR7 .....37 D8
  Erith DA8 .....9 A8
  Royal Tunbridge Wells TN4 .....148 E3
Manor Pl Bromley BR1 .....36 E3
  Chislehurst BR7 .....37 D7
Manor Rd Chatham ME4 .....47 F4
  Crayford DA1 .....8 E3
  Edenbridge TN8 .....112 B1
  Erith DA8 .....9 B8
  [20] Gravesend DA12 .....13 B1
  Grays RM17 .....12 C8
  New Barn DA3 .....43 C4
  Royal Tunbridge Wells,
  Modest Corner TN4 .....132 E1
  Royal Tunbridge Wells,
  Rustall TN4 .....148 C4
  Sidcup DA15 .....24 A5
  Sidcup,Old Bexley DA5 .....25 B7
  Sole Street DA13 .....44 D4
  Sundridge TN14 .....82 D3
  Swanscombe DA10 .....28 E8
  Tilbury RM18 .....13 A5
  West Thurrock RM20 .....11 C8
Manor Rise ME14 .....93 B3
Manor St ME7 .....48 A6
Manor The TN2 .....149 E5
Manor Way Bexley DA7 .....8 D4
  Bromley BR2 .....36 E3
  Grays RM17 .....12 B7
  Grays RM17 .....12 D7
  Greenwich SE3 .....5 A3
  Northfleet DA11 .....12 A3
  Orpington BR5 .....37 C5
  Sidcup DA5 .....25 A7
  Swanscombe DA10 .....11 E3
Manor Way Bsns Ctr RM9 .....4 D8
Manorbrook SE3 .....5 B3
Manordene Rd SE28 .....3 D7
Manorfields Cl BR7 .....37 F6
Manorside Cl SE2 .....3 D2
Manse Ct DA14 .....24 C3
Manse Par BR8 .....40 A5
Manse Way BR8 .....40 A5
Mansel Dr ME1 .....47 A2
Mansergh Cl SE18 .....5 E7
Mansfield Cl BR5 .....38 D2
Mansfield Rd BR8 .....25 F7
Mansfield Wlk ME16 .....91 E2
Mansion House Cl TN27 .....158 A2
Mansion Row ME7 .....48 A6
Manthorpe Rd SE18 .....2 C1
Manton Rd SE2 .....3 A2
Manwarings The TN12 .....153 A6
Manwood St E16 .....1 F5
Maple Ave Gillingham ME7 .....48 E6
  Maidstone ME16 .....91 C6
Maple Cl Larkfield ME20 .....75 A2
  Orpington BR5 .....37 D4
  Royal Tunbridge Wells TN2 .....149 A1
  Swanley BR8 .....39 E7
Maple Cres 7 A1
Maple Ct Newham E6 .....2 A8
  Sidcup DA14 .....24 B3
  Stone DA9 .....27 E8
Maple Leaf Dr DA15 .....23 F7
Maple Rd Dartford DA1 .....26 C7
  Gravesend DA12 .....30 C4
  Grays RM17 .....12 C8
  Hoo St Werburgh ME3 .....34 E3
  Rochester ME2 .....46 F6
Maplecroft Cl E6 .....1 E7
Mapledene BR7 .....22 F1
Maples The DA3 .....43 B6
Maplescombe La DA4 .....55 B6
Maplesden TN12 .....138 D5
Maplesden Cl ME16 .....90 F3
Maplesden Noakes Sch
  The ME16 .....91 E6
Mapleton TN8 .....113 A7
Mapleton BR2 .....36 A3
Mapleton Rd TN8,TN16 .....96 E3
Maplin Ho [9] SE2 .....3 D4
Maplin Rd E16 .....1 B7
Maplins Cl [5] ME8 .....49 F1
Mar Ho [4] SE7 .....5 C8

Mara Ct ME4 .....47 F1
Maran Way DA18 .....3 D3
Marathon Paddock ME7 .....48 D4
Marble Ho [1] SE18 .....2 F1
Marbrook Ct SE12 .....22 C5
Marcellina Way BR6 .....51 F7
Marcet Rd DA1 .....9 C2
Marconi Ho SE2 .....3 C1
Marconi Rd DA11 .....29 D5
Marcus Rd DA1 .....26 A8
Marcus Way ME1 .....61 D7
Marden Ave BR2 .....36 A3
Marden Cres DA5 .....8 C2
Marden Prim Sch TN12 .....138 B5
Marden Rd Rochester ME1 .....33 C1
  Staplehurst TN12 .....139 C5
Marden Sta TN12 .....138 C6
Marechal Niel Ave DA15 .....23 D5
Marechal Niel Par DA15 .....23 D5
Margaret Gardner Dr SE9 .....22 F6
Margaret Rd DA5 .....7 D1
Margate Cl ME7 .....48 E6
Margetts La ME1 .....60 D1
Margetts Pl ME2 .....34 A3
Marian Sq TN12 .....139 F4
Marina Cl [1] BR2 .....36 A6
Marina Dr Bexley DA16 .....6 E5
  Dartford DA1 .....27 A7
  Northfleet DA11 .....12 F1
Marine Dr
  Hoo St Werburgh ME3 .....34 E3
  Woolwich SE18 .....1 F2
Marine View ME4 .....34 B1
Mariners Ct DA9 .....11 B3
Mariners The ME1 .....47 B4
Mariners Wlk DA8 .....8 F8
Marion Cl ME5 .....62 A2
Marion Cres
  Maidstone ME15 .....107 B8
  Orpington BR5 .....38 B4
Maritime Cl Rochester ME2 .....47 D8
  Swanscombe DA9 .....11 B2
Maritime Est ME2 .....47 D8
Maritime Ind Est SE7 .....1 B2
Maritime Way ME4 .....48 A8
Marjorie McClure Sch
  BR7 .....37 C8
Mark Cl Bexley DA7 .....7 E6
  Orpington BR2 .....50 E6
Mark La DA12 .....13 E1
Mark Way BR8 .....40 A4
Market Alley [3] DA11 .....13 B1
Market Bldgs [4] ME14 .....91 F4
Market
  Colonnade [3] ME14 .....91 F4
Market Meadow BR5 .....38 C5
Market Par [5] DA14 .....24 D4
Market Pl [2] Bexley DA6 .....8 A3
  Dartford DA1 .....26 E8
  [14] Royal Tunbridge
  Wells TN2 .....149 A2
  [1] Tilbury RM18 .....13 A5
Market Sq Bromley BR1 .....36 A7
  Royal Tunbridge Wells TN1 .....149 B4
  Westerham TN16 .....81 C1
Market St Dartford DA1 .....26 E8
  [2] Maidstone ME14 .....91 F4
  [13] Royal Tunbridge
  Wells TN2 .....149 A2
  Staplehurst TN12 .....139 F5
  Woolwich SE18 .....2 A2
Market Way [2] TN16 .....81 D1
Marks Sq DA11 .....29 F4
Marlborough Cl
  Orpington BR6 .....37 F3
  Royal Tunbridge Wells TN4 .....148 E4
Marlborough Cres TN13 .....83 E3
Marlborough Ct TN16 .....81 C1
Marlborough Ho [4] ME8 .....63 F8
Marlborough House Sch
  TN18 .....178 E2
Marlborough La SE7 .....5 C7
Marlborough Par ME9 .....90 F2
Marlborough Park Ave
  DA15 .....24 A7
Marlborough Rd Bexley DA7 .....7 D4
  Bromley BR2 .....36 C5
  Dartford DA1 .....9 C1
  Gillingham ME7 .....48 B5
  Woolwich SE18 .....2 A2
Marlborough Sch DA15 .....24 A8
Marle Place Gdns* TN12 .....152 C4
Marler House DA8 .....7 D8
Marley Ave DA7 .....7 D8
Marley La TN27 .....142 C4
Marley Rd
  Harrietsham ME17 .....110 F6
  Hoo St Werburgh ME3 .....34 D6
Marley Way ME1 .....47 C2
Marlfield TN12 .....139 E4
Marlhurst TN8 .....112 B4
Marlin Ct [12] DA14 .....24 A4
Marling Way DA12 .....30 E3
Marlings Cl BR7 .....37 B5
Marlings Park Ave BR7 .....37 E6
Marlow Copse ME5 .....61 F1
Marlow Ct TN13 .....84 B4
Marlowe Cl BR7 .....23 D2
Marlowe Gdns SE9 .....6 A1
Marlowe Rd ME20 .....75 A3
Marlowes The DA1 .....26 E8
Marlpit Cl TN8 .....112 C4
Marlpit Cotts ME17 .....107 E2
Marlpit Gdns TN5 .....176 E1
Marlpit The TN5 .....174 E5
Marlwood Cl SE18 .....23 E6
Marmadon Rd SE18 .....2 F2

Marne Ave DA16 .....7 A4
Marquis Dr ME7 .....63 B3
Marrabon Cl DA15 .....24 A7
Marram Ct RM17 .....12 E8
Marrians View [1] ME5 .....48 C2
Marriott Rd DA1 .....27 A8
Marsden Way [2] BR6 .....51 F6
Marsh Cres SE23 .....17 A4
Marsh Green Rd TN8 .....128 C5
Marsh La ME3 .....16 B6
Marsh Quarter La TN18 .....186 C3
Marsh Rd ME2 .....60 B5
Marsh St Dartford DA1 .....10 A5
  Rochester ME1 .....47 B7
Marsh Way New Hythe ME20 .....75 A4
  Rainham RM9 .....4 D8
Marshall Gdns TN11 .....102 F1
Marshall Path [10] SE28 .....3 B6
Marshall Rd ME8 .....63 C8
Marshalls Gr SE18 .....1 E2
Marshalls Land TN30 .....173 A3
Marsham Cl BR7 .....23 B3
Marsham Cres ME17 .....108 B1
Marsham St ME14 .....92 A4
Marsham Way ME2 .....60 A5
Marshbrook Cl SE3 .....5 D4
Marshland View ME3 .....19 C5
Marston Cl ME5 .....61 E3
Marston Cl DA14 .....23 F4
Marston Dr ME14 .....92 C5
Marston House RM17 .....12 A8
Marston Wlk ME5 .....61 E3
Martens Ave DA7 .....8 C3
Martens Cl DA7 .....8 C3
Martham Cl SE28 .....3 D6
Martin Bowes Rd SE9 .....5 F4
Martin Ct ME7 .....63 A3
Martin Dene DA6 .....7 F2
Martin Dr DA2 .....10 C1
Martin Hardie Way TN10 .....117 E5
Martin Ho DA2 .....27 C8
Martin House DA11 .....29 F6
Martin Rd Dartford DA2 .....26 C5
  Rochester ME2 .....47 B8
Martin Rise DA6 .....7 F2
Martin Sq ME20 .....75 A2
Martin St SE28 .....2 E5
Martin's Shaw TN13 .....83 C5
Martindale Ave Newham E16 .....1 A6
  Orpington BR6 .....52 A5
Martins Cl Higham ME3 .....32 D6
  St Paul's Cray BR5 .....38 D6
  Tenterden TN30 .....183 C8
Martins La TN12 .....103 E2
Martyn House SE2 .....7 D8
Marvels Cl SE12 .....22 B6
Marvels La SE12 .....22 C5
Marvels Lane
  Prim Sch SE12 .....22 C4
Marvillion Ct TN12 .....119 F6
Marvin House [9] SE18 .....6 B8
Marwell TN16 .....81 B1
Marwood Cl DA16 .....7 B4
Mary Burrows Gdns TN15 .....70 B2
Mary Day's TN17 .....167 E7
Mary Lawrenson Pl [2] SE3 .....5 A7
Mary Macarthur Ho [5] DA17 .....4 A3
Mary Magdalene Ho [8]
  TN9 .....133 B8
Mary Rose Mall E6 .....1 F8
Marybank SE18 .....1 F2
Maryfield Cl DA5 .....25 E5
Maryland Ct ME8 .....63 E5
Maryland Dr ME16 .....90 F2
Maryland Rd TN2 .....149 D1
Maryon Ct BR5 .....38 B5
Maryon Gr SE7 .....1 E2
Maryon Rd SE7,SE18 .....1 E2
Maryville DA16 .....6 F5
Mascall's Court La TN12 .....136 B4
Mascall's Court Rd TN12 .....136 B3
Mascalls Ct [22] SE7 .....5 C8
Mascalls Pk TN12 .....135 F5
Mascalls Rd SE7 .....5 C8
Mascalls Sec Sch TN12 .....136 A4
Masefield Cl [8] E6 .....1 F8
Masefield Dr ME8 .....63 A4
Masefield Rd Dartford DA1 .....10 B2
  Lunsford ME20 .....74 F4
  Northfleet DA11 .....29 D5
Masefield View BR6 .....51 C7
Masefield Way TN9 .....132 F7
Masham Ho [6] DA18 .....3 D4
Mason Cl Bexley DA7 .....8 B4
  Newham E16 .....1 A6
Masons Hill Bromley BR2 .....36 B5
  Woolwich SE18 .....2 B2
Master Gunners' Pl SE18 .....5 E6
Masters La ME19 .....74 B5
Masthead Cl DA2 .....10 C3
Matchless Dr SE18 .....6 A7
Matfield Cl BR2 .....36 A4
Matfield Cres ME14 .....92 C5
Matfield Rd DA17 .....8 A8
Matilda Cl ME18 .....63 B8
Matrix Bsns Ctr DA1 .....9 E2
Matterdale Gdns ME16 .....90 E2
Matthews Ho [12] SE7 .....5 C8
Matthews La TN11,ME18 .....102 F4
Mattinson Pl ME9 .....95 F7
Matts Hill Rd ME9 .....63 E2
Maud Cashmore Way SE18 .....1 F3
Maude Rd BR8 .....26 A4
Maudslay Rd SE9 .....6 A4
Maunders Cl ME5 .....62 C8
Mavelstone Cl BR1 .....36 E8
Mavelstone Rd BR1 .....36 E8

Mavis Wlk [9] E6 .....1 E8
Maxey Rd SE18 .....2 C2
Maxim Rd Crayford DA1 .....8 E2
  Erith DA8 .....4 E2
Maximfeldt Rd DA8 .....4 E1
Maxton Cl ME14 .....92 F5
Maxton Dr ME16 .....91 B6
Maxwell Gdns BR6 .....51 F7
Maxwell Ho Chislehurst BR7 .....23 B1
  [12] Woolwich SE18 .....6 B8
Maxwell Rd Bexley DA16 .....7 A4
  Gillingham ME7 .....48 A6
May Ave Northfleet DA11 .....29 F7
  Orpington BR5 .....38 B4
May Avenue Est [1] DA11 .....29 F7
May Ct RM17 .....12 E8
May Pl DA12 .....44 D4
May Rd Gillingham ME7 .....48 C5
  Hawley DA2 .....26 F4
  Rochester ME1 .....47 C3
May St Cuxton ME2 .....46 B2
  Snodland ME6 .....75 B8
May Terr [2] ME7 .....48 A7
May Wynne Ho E16 .....1 B7
Maybury Ave DA2 .....27 C7
Maybury Cl BR5 .....37 B4
Maycotts La TN12 .....135 D1
Mayday Gdns SE3 .....5 E5
Mayerne Rd SE9 .....5 D2
Mayes Cl ME8 .....40 A5
Mayeswood Rd SE12 .....22 C4
Mayfair [2] ME2 .....47 C8
Mayfair Ave Bexley DA7 .....7 D6
  Maidstone ME15 .....107 A3
Mayfair Rd DA1 .....9 D2
Mayfield Bexley DA7 .....7 F4
  Sevenoaks TN13 .....83 E7
  Swanscombe DA10 .....11 E1
Mayfield Ave BR6 .....37 F2
  [7] Chatham ME5 .....62 A1
  Gillingham ME8 .....49 E2
Mayfield Cl DA14 .....24 B3
Mayfield La TN5 .....174 D4
Mayfield Pk TN5 .....174 E5
Mayfield Rd Bromley BR1 .....36 E4
  Erith DA8 .....4 C2
  Northfleet DA11 .....29 F8
  Royal Tunbridge Wells TN4 .....148 F4
Mayfield Villas DA14 .....24 C2
Mayflower Ho ME1 .....47 B4
Mayfly Cl BR5 .....38 D6
Mayford Rd ME5 .....62 D2
Mayhill Rd SE7 .....5 B8
Maylam Ct TN10 .....117 C4
Maylands Dr DA14 .....24 D5
Maynard Cl DA8 .....8 F7
Maynard Rd SE18 .....2 C2
Maynard Pl ME5 .....48 D2
Maynards TN12 .....138 C5
Mayor's Pl [11] TN30 .....183 A7
Mayors La DA2 .....26 C3
Mayplace Ave DA1 .....9 A3
Mayplace Cl DA7 .....8 B4
Mayplace La Woolwich SE18 .....6 B7
  Woolwich SE18 .....6 B8
Mayplace Prim Sch DA7 .....8 D3
Mayplace Rd E DA7 .....8 C3
Mayplace Rd W DA7 .....8 A3
Maypole Cotts BR6 .....53 A4
Maypole Cres DA8 .....9 D8
Maypole La TN17 .....167 D8
Maypole Prim Sch DA5 .....25 E6
Maypole Rd Chelsfield BR6 .....52 F7
  Gravesend DA12 .....30 F7
Mayston Mews [6] SE10 .....1 A1
Maytham Bglws TN17 .....182 A1
Maytham Rd TN17 .....188 C2
Mayweed Ave ME5 .....61 E4
Mc Call Cres SE7 .....1 E1
Mc Dowall Cl [11] E16 .....1 A8
Mc Kenzie Rd ME5 .....62 A3
McAlpine Cres ME15 .....106 F3
McAuley Cl SE9 .....6 A2
McCabe Ct [12] E16 .....1 A7
McCudden Rd DA1 .....9 F4
McCudden Row [8] ME7 .....48 A6
McDermott Rd TN15 .....86 F7
McIntyre Ct [6] SE18 .....1 E2
McKenzie Cl ME20 .....90 F8
McKillop Way DA14 .....24 C1
McLeod Rd SE2 .....3 B2
McMichael Way TN19 .....184 A3
Mcmillan Cl DA12 .....30 C4
McPhie Ho [3] ME14 .....91 F7
Mead Cl BR8 .....40 A4
Mead Cres DA1 .....26 D7
Mead Gn ME5 .....62 C3
Mead Rd Chislehurst BR7 .....23 C2
  Dartford DA1 .....26 D7
  Edenbridge TN8 .....128 D7
  Gravesend DA11 .....30 B6
Mead Road Inf Sch BR7 .....23 C2
Mead The Leybourne ME19 .....74 D2
  New Ash Green DA3 .....56 E8
Mead Wall ME3 .....15 F8
Mead Way DA2 .....36 A3
Meades Cl TN12 .....138 B6
Meadfield Rd DA13 .....58 A8
Meadow Bank Leigh TN11 .....115 F1
  West Malling ME19 .....89 C8
Meadow Bank Cl TN15 .....55 F2
Meadow Cl Bexley DA6 .....7 F2
  Chatham ME5 .....61 F5
  Chislehurst BR7 .....23 B3
  Sevenoaks TN13 .....84 A4
  Upper Halling ME2 .....59 E4
Meadow Cres ME2 .....59 D4

Meadow Croft BR1 .....36 F6
Meadow Hill Rd [6] TN1 .....149 B3
Meadow La
  Marlpit Hill TN8 .....112 B4
  Vigo Village DA13 .....58 A1
Meadow Rd
  Gravesend DA11 .....30 A6
  Groombridge TN3 .....161 C7
  Northfleet DA11 .....29 C7
  Royal Tunbridge Wells,
  Rustall TN4 .....148 C4
  Royal Tunbridge
  Wells,Southborough TN4 .....132 F1
  Tonbridge TN9 .....133 B8
Meadow The
  Chislehurst BR7 .....23 C2
  Pembury TN2 .....150 E5
Meadow View DA15 .....24 B8
Meadow View Cotts
  Hurst Green TN19 .....184 A3
  Laddingford ME18 .....120 E5
Meadow View Rd ME17 .....107 B3
Meadow Way Dartford DA2 .....27 C8
  Marden TN12 .....138 E6
  Orpington BR6 .....51 A7
Meadow Wlk Dartford DA2 .....26 C4
  Maidstone ME15 .....92 B3
  Snodland ME6 .....74 F7
Meadowbank Rd ME4 .....48 A4
Meadowdown ME14 .....92 E4
Meadowdown Cl ME7 .....63 A4
Meadowlands TN15 .....84 F7
Meadows TN17 .....170 D1
Meadows Sch
  (Barnados) TN4 .....132 F2
Meadows The
  Biddenden TN27 .....157 F2
  Halstead TN14 .....67 F6
  Maidstone ME15 .....91 E2
  Orpington BR6 .....52 C4
  Wittersham TN30 .....189 D4
Meadowside Dartford DA1 .....26 E7
  Eltham SE3,SE9 .....5 C3
Meadowside Cotts TN5 .....176 F1
Meadowsweet Cl [3] E16 .....1 D8
Meadowsweet View ME4 .....34 B2
Meadowview BR5 .....38 C6
Meadowview Rd DA5 .....7 F1
Meads The Hartley TN17 .....168 F1
  Royal Tunbridge Wells TN2 .....149 C2
Meadside Wlk ME5 .....61 F5
Meadway Halstead TN14 .....67 F6
  Tonbridge TN9 .....116 E5
Meadway The
  Orpington BR6 .....52 B4
  Sevenoaks TN13 .....83 F5
Meath Cl BR5 .....38 B4
Medbury Rd DA12 .....30 F7
Mede Ho BR1 .....22 B3
Medebourne Cl SE3 .....5 A4
Medhurst Cres DA12 .....30 F6
Medhurst Gdns DA12 .....30 F6
Medick Ct RM17 .....12 E8
Medina House DA8 .....8 F7
Medina Rd Ditton ME20 .....75 C1
  Tonbridge TN10 .....117 C6
Medlar Gr ME7 .....63 A4
Medlar House [3] DA15 .....24 A5
Medlar Rd RM17 .....12 E8
Medlars The
  Maidstone ME14 .....92 D6
  Meopham Sta DA13 .....44 A3
Medway Ave
  High Halstow ME23 .....17 E4
  Yalding ME18 .....104 F1
Medway Com Coll ME4 .....48 A1
Medway Cotts
  Iden Green TN17 .....180 D5
  Marden TN12 .....138 C6
Medway Ct [20] BR5 .....38 D1
Medway Ent Ctr ME2 .....47 D8
Medway Gdns ME4 .....47 F7
Medway Heritage Ctr*
  ME4 .....47 F5
Medway Hts [5] ME4 .....47 F4
Medway Hospl ME7 .....48 B4
Medway Meadows TN12 .....120 A6
Medway Rd Crayford DA1 .....9 A4
  Gillingham ME7 .....48 C7
  Royal Tunbridge Wells TN1 .....149 B5
Medway St Chatham ME4 .....47 F5
  Maidstone ME14 .....91 F4
Medway Trad Est ME16 .....91 F3
Medway View
  Barnes Street TN11 .....119 A3
  Lower Stoke ME3 .....19 C3
Medway Villas ME15 .....106 B7
Medway Wharf Rd TN9 .....117 C1
Meerbrook Rd SE3 .....5 C4
Meeson's La RM17 .....11 F8
Meeting House La [2] ME4 .....47 F4
Megby Cl ME8 .....63 D6
Megrims Hill TN18 .....186 A6
Meirs Court Rd ME8 .....63 C6
Melanda Cl BR7 .....22 F3
Melanie Cl DA7 .....7 E6
Melba Gdns RM18 .....13 A7
Melbourne Cl BR6 .....37 F2
Melbourne Ct
  [3] Gravesend DA11 .....13 B1
  Tilbury RM18 .....12 E6
Melbourne Rd
  Chatham ME4 .....48 A5
  Tilbury RM18 .....12 E6
Melbury Cl BR7 .....22 F2

Meldrum Cl BR5 . . . . .38 C3
Melford Dr ME16 . . . . .91 C4
Melliker La DA13 . . . . .44 A3
Melling St SE18 . . . . .6 E8
Mellish Ind Est SE18 . . . . .1 D3
Mells Cres SE9 . . . . .22 F4
Melody Ct ME8 . . . . .63 C4
Melrose Ave ME19 . . . . .89 C3
Melrose Ct Lewisham SE12 . .22 B7
Maidstone ME15 . . . . .107 A7
Melrose Cres BR6 . . . . .51 D5
Melthorpe Gdns SE3 . . . . .5 E6
Melville Ct ME4 . . . . .47 F6
Melville Rd Maidstone ME15 92 A3
Sidcup DA14 . . . . .24 C6
Memess Path 4 SE18 . . . . . . .6 A8
Memorial Hospl SE18 . . . . .6 C4
Mendip Rd DA7 . . . . .8 E6
Mendip Wlk TN2 . . . . .149 D5
Mennie House SE18 . . . . .5 F6
Meon Ct 21 BR5 . . . . .38 D1
Meopham
    Com Prim Sch DA13 . . . . .58 A3
Meopham
    Cty Prim Sch DA13 . . . . . .44 A2
Meopham Sta DA13 . . . . .44 A4
Mera Dr DA1 . . . . .8 A3
Merbury Rd SE28 . . . . .2 E4
Merbury St SE18 . . . . .2 B3
Mercer Dr ME17 . . . . .110 F6
Mercer St TN1 . . . . .149 B5
Mercer Way ME17 . . . . .108 B1
Mercers Hawkhurst TN18 . . .179 A1
Royal Tunbridge Wells TN3 .148 A3
Mercers Cl TN12 . . . . .135 E6
Mercers Pl ME19 . . . . .89 A2
Merchant Pl TN12 . . . . .138 C5
Merchland Rd SE9 . . . . .23 C7
Mercury Rd ME1 . . . . .47 A3
Mere Cl BR6 . . . . .51 B8
Meresborough Cotts ME8 .63 F5
Meresborough La
    ME8,ME9 . . . . .64 B5
Meresborough Rd ME8 . .64 A4
Mereside BR6 . . . . .51 A8
Merewood Cl 1 BR1 . . . . . .37 A7
Merewood Rd DA7 . . . . .8 C5
Mereworth Cl ME8 . . . . .49 A3
Mereworth
    Cty Prim Sch ME18 . . . .103 C8
Mereworth Dr SE18 . . . . .6 C7
Mereworth Ho ME2 . . . . . . .33 C1
Mereworth Rd
    Mereworth ME18 . . . . . .103 C7
Royal Tunbridge Wells TN4 .149 A6
Merganser Gdns SE28 . . . . . .2 D3
Meriden Pk ME2 . . . . .47 E6
Meriden Cl BR1 . . . . .22 D1
Meridian Rd SE7 . . . . .5 D7
Meridian Trad Est SE7 . . . . . .1 B2
Merifield Rd SE9 . . . . .5 A2
Merino Pl DA15 . . . . .7 A2
Merivale Gr ME5 . . . . .62 B4
Merlewood TN13 . . . . .84 B4
Merlewood Dr BR7 . . . . .36 F8
Merlin Ave ME20 . . . . .74 F2
Merlin Cl TN10 . . . . .117 E4
Merlin Gdns BR1 . . . . .22 A5
Merlin Prim Sch BR1 . . . . . .22 A5
Merlin Rd DA16 . . . . .7 A3
Merlin Rd N DA16 . . . . .7 A3
Mermaid Cl ME5 . . . . .62 A6
Mermerus Gdns DA12 . . . . .30 F4
Merrals Wood Rd ME2 . . . . .46 D5
Merrilees Rd DA15 . . . . .23 E8
Merriman Rd SE3 . . . . .5 C6
Merriments La
    TN18,TN19 . . . . .184 D5
Merrion Cl TN4 . . . . .149 B7
Merrion Way TN4 . . . . .149 B7
Merry Boys Rd ME3 . . . . . . .33 B8
Merrydown Way BR7 . . . . . .36 F8
Merryfield SE3 . . . . .5 A5
Merryfield Ct 5 TN9 . . . . . .133 B8
Merryfield Ho SE9 . . . . .22 F4
Merryfields Longfield DA3 . . .42 F5
Rochester ME2 . . . . .33 A1
Merryweather Cl DA1 . . . . . . .9 F1
Mersey Rd TN10 . . . . .117 B5
Merton Ave DA3 . . . . .42 F5
Merton Cl ME5 . . . . .62 C5
Merton Court Sch DA14 . . .24 C4
Merton Ct DA16 . . . . .7 B5
Merton Gdns BR5 . . . . .37 B4
Merton Rd ME15 . . . . .92 F2
Mervyn Ave SE9 . . . . .23 C6
Mervyn Stockwood
    House SE9 . . . . .23 C6
Mesne Way TN14 . . . . .68 F7
Messent Rd SE9 . . . . .5 D2
Messeter Pl SE9 . . . . .6 A1
Meteor Rd ME19 . . . . .88 F3
Methuen Rd Bexley DA6 . . . . .7 F3
Erith DA17 . . . . .4 B2
Metro Ctr The BR5 . . . . .38 C7
Mews The Longfield DA3 . . . .42 E6
Maidstone ME16 . . . . .91 E5
Pembury TN2 . . . . .150 E4
Rochester ME2 . . . . .46 F7
5 Royal Tunbridge
    Wells TN1 . . . . .149 B3
Sevenoaks TN13 . . . . .84 A3
7 Sidcup DA14 . . . . .24 A4
Meyer Rd DA8 . . . . .8 D8
Micawber Cl ME5 . . . . .62 A1
Michael Gdns DA12 . . . . . . .30 E3
Michael Marshall
    House SE9 . . . . .23 C6

Michael Tetley Hall
    (Nursery Trng Coll, Dr
    Barnardo's Home) TN2 .149 D6
Michaels La DA3,TN15 . . . . .56 C8
Michele Cotts ME3 . . . . .32 C6
Mickleham Cl BR5 . . . . .38 A7
Mickleham Rd BR5 . . . . .38 A7
Mid Comp Cotts TN15 . . . . .87 E6
Mid Kent Bsns Pk ME6 . . . .75 B7
Mid Kent Coll of H & F Ed
    Chatham ME1 . . . . .47 E4
    Maidstone,Cherry
    Orchard ME16 . . . . .91 C3
Mid Kent Coll of Higher
    & F Ed ME1,ME4 . . . . . .61 C7
Mid Kent Sh Ctr The ME16 91 C7
Middle Field TN2 . . . . .150 B3
Middle Garth TN17 . . . . . . .169 D4
Middle La TN15 . . . . .84 F6
Middle Mill Rd ME19 . . . . . .89 F7
Middle Park Ave SE9 . . . . . .22 E8
Middle Park
    Inf & Jun Sch SE9 . . . . .22 D8
Middle La TN3 . . . . .164 A5
Middle Row 6 ME14 . . . . . .91 F4
Middle St 4 ME7 . . . . .48 A6
Middle Wlk TN2 . . . . .149 E8
Middlefields ME8 . . . . .64 A8
Middleham Ct 26 DA2 . . . . . .10 B1
Middlesex Rd ME15 . . . . . . .107 D7
Middleton Ave DA14 . . . . . .24 C3
Middleton Cl ME8 . . . . .63 E4
Middleton Ct 12 BR1 . . . . . .22 B1
Middlings Rise TN13 . . . . . .83 F1
Middlings The TN13 . . . . . . .83 F2
Middlings Wood TN13 . . . . . .84 A2
Midfield Ave Bexley DA7 . . . . .8 C4
Hextable BR8 . . . . .26 B2
Midfield Prim Sch BR5 . . . .24 A1
Midfield Way BR5 . . . . .38 B8
Midhurst Ct ME15 . . . . .92 A3
Midhurst Hill DA6 . . . . .8 A2
Midley Cl ME16 . . . . .91 C7
Midsummer Ct SE12 . . . . .5 A3
Midsummer Rd ME6 . . . . . . .74 E8
Midway The TN4 . . . . .148 D2
Midwinter Cl 3 DA16 . . . . . . .7 A4
Miers Court
    Prim Sch ME8 . . . . .63 F7
Mierscourt Cl ME8 . . . . .64 A8
Mierscourt Rd ME8 . . . . . . .63 E6
Mike Spring Ct DA12 . . . . . .30 F4
Milburn Rd ME7 . . . . .48 C7
Mildmay Rd TN14 . . . . .68 F8
Mildred Cl DA1 . . . . .10 A1
Mildred Rd DA8 . . . . .4 E1
Mile La TN17 . . . . .168 B8
Mile Oak Rd TN12 . . . . .136 C3
Mile Stone Rd DA2 . . . . .10 B1
Milebush La TN12 . . . . .122 E1
Miles Dr SE28 . . . . .2 E5
Miles Pl ME1 . . . . .47 D3
Milestone Sch DA2 . . . . . . .10 B1
Milford Cl Erith SE2 . . . . .7 E8
Maidstone ME16 . . . . .91 D5
Military Rd ME4 . . . . .47 F5
Milk House Cotts TN17 . . . .170 A8
Milk St Bromley BR1 . . . . . . .22 B2
Newham E16 . . . . .2 B5
Mill Bank TN27 . . . . .141 C6
Mill Brook Rd BR5 . . . . .38 C5
Mill Cl Lenham ME17 . . . . . .111 C4
Rochester ME2 . . . . .33 B1
Mill Cotts ME15 . . . . .105 B6
Mill Cres TN9 . . . . .117 C2
Mill Ct Sutton at Hone DA4 . .41 C7
14 Woolwich SE28 . . . . .3 B6
Mill Hall Bsns Est The
    ME20 . . . . .75 D2
Mill Hall Rd ME20 . . . . .75 C2
Mill Hill TN8 . . . . .128 D7
Mill Hill La DA12 . . . . .31 D3
Mill House Cl DA4 . . . . .40 E1
Mill La Benover ME18 . . . . . .121 A7
Biddenden Green TN27 . . . .143 A2
Chatham,Bluebell Hill ME5 . .61 D1
Chatham,Luton ME5 . . . . . . .48 C1
Coxheath ME17 . . . . .106 D4
Eynsford DA4 . . . . .40 E1
Farthing Street BR6 . . . . . . .51 B1
Frittenden TN17 . . . . .156 D8
Hartlip Hill ME9 . . . . .60 C2
Hildenborough TN11,TN15 . .100 C2
Horsmonden TN12 . . . . . . .137 B1
Ightham TN15 . . . . .86 D5
Maidstone ME14 . . . . .91 F6
Sevenoaks TN14 . . . . .84 D6
Shoreham TN14 . . . . .53 F1
Sissinghurst TN17 . . . . . . .169 F8
Snodland ME6 . . . . .75 B8
Tenterden TN30 . . . . .173 B1
Tonbridge TN9 . . . . .117 C2
Wateringbury ME18 . . . . . .104 D7
West Thurrock RM20 . . . . . .11 D8
Westerham TN16 . . . . .96 C8
Woolwich SE18 . . . . .2 A1
Mill Pl Chislehurst BR7 . . . . .37 B8
Crayford DA1 . . . . .9 A3
Mill Pond Cl TN14 . . . . .84 D6
Mill Pond Rd DA1 . . . . .9 E1
Mill Rd Erith DA8 . . . . .8 C7
Gillingham ME7 . . . . .48 C6
Hawley DA2 . . . . .26 F4
Newham E16 . . . . .1 B5
Northfleet DA11 . . . . .29 E8
Rochester ME2 . . . . .47 B8
Sevenoaks TN13 . . . . .83 E6
Mill Row DA5 . . . . .25 B8

Mill St
    Benenden TN17,TN18 . . .180 C3
Maidstone ME15 . . . . .91 F4
Maidstone, Loose Hill ME15 .106 F5
Mill Street ME19 . . . . .89 F7
Snodland ME6 . . . . .75 B8
Westerham TN16 . . . . .96 D8
Mill Stone Cl DA4 . . . . .41 C7
Mill Stream Pl TN9 . . . . . . .117 D3
Mill Vale BR2 . . . . .36 A7
Mill View TN11 . . . . .102 D1
Mill Wlk ME15 . . . . .91 A3
Millais Pl RM18 . . . . .13 A7
Millbank Way SE12 . . . . .5 A2
Millbro BR8 . . . . .40 A8
Millbrook Ave DA16 . . . . .6 D3
Millcroft Cl ME15 . . . . .91 F1
Millcroft Rd ME3 . . . . .16 B4
Miller Ct DA7 . . . . .8 B4
Miller Rd DA12 . . . . .31 A6
Miller Way ME7 . . . . .33 D2
Millers Cotts TN11 . . . . . . .134 C6
Millers Wharf ME15 . . . . . . .91 E2
Millers Wlk DA13 . . . . .58 A7
Millfield High Halden TN26 .173 D7
New Ash Green DA3 . . . . . . .56 E8
Millfield Dr DA11 . . . . .29 E6
Millfield La TN3 . . . . .56 E8
Millfield Rd TN15 . . . . .55 D4
Millfields ME8 . . . . .62 D2
Millfields Cl BR5 . . . . .38 B5
Millfields Cotts BR5 . . . . . . .38 B5
Millfordhope Rd ME2 . . . . . .46 C7
Millhall ME20 . . . . .75 E2
Millhouse La ME19 . . . . .73 D3
Millman Ct SE3 . . . . .5 B7
Millpond Cl ME2 . . . . .47 B8
Millpond La TN30 . . . . .172 D2
Mills Cres TN15 . . . . .84 F8
Mills Rd ME20 . . . . .90 E7
Mills Terr ME4 . . . . .48 A3
Millstock Terr ME15 . . . . . . .91 E2
Millstone Mews DA4 . . . . . .41 C8
Millstream Cl TN3 . . . . .146 D2
Millward Wlk 14 SE18 . . . . . .6 A8
Millwood Ct 4 ME4 . . . . . . .47 F4
Millwood Ho SE28 . . . . .2 D3
Millwood Rd BR5 . . . . .38 C6
Milne Gdns SE9 . . . . .5 E2
Milne Ho 11 SE18 . . . . .1 F2
Milner Rd ME7 . . . . .48 D7
Milner Wlk SE9 . . . . .23 D7
Milroy Ave DA11 . . . . .29 E6
Milstead Cl ME14 . . . . .92 C5
Milsted Rd ME8 . . . . .49 C3
Milton Ave
    Badgers Mount TN14 . . . . .53 B1
Cliffe Woods ME3 . . . . .33 B8
Gravesend DA12 . . . . .30 C7
Milton Ct DA12 . . . . .30 C6
Milton Dr TN2 . . . . .149 D7
Milton Gdns Tilbury RM18 . . .13 B6
Tonbridge TN9 . . . . .132 F7
Milton Hall Rd DA12 . . . . . .30 D7
Milton House DA1 . . . . .8 E2
Milton Lodge 9 DA14 . . . . . .24 A4
Milton Pl DA12 . . . . .13 C1
Milton Rd Bexley DA16 . . . . . .6 F6
Erith DA8 . . . . .4 A2
Gillingham ME7 . . . . .48 C3
Gravesend DA12 . . . . .30 C8
Sevenoaks TN13 . . . . .83 E6
Swanscombe DA10 . . . . . . .11 E1
Milton St Maidstone ME16 . .91 C7
Swanscombe DA10 . . . . . . .11 D1
Milverton Way SE9 . . . . .23 A4
Mimosa Cl BR6 . . . . .52 C8
Mincers Cl ME5 . . . . .62 C2
Mineral St SE18 . . . . .2 E2
Minerva Cl DA14 . . . . .23 E4
Minerva Rd ME2 . . . . .47 A8
Ministry Way SE9 . . . . .22 F6
Minshaw Ct SE9 . . . . .22 F6
Minster Rd Bromley BR1 . . . .22 B1
Gillingham ME8 . . . . .49 C3
Mint Bsns Pk E16 . . . . .1 A8
Minters Orch TN15 . . . . .87 B7
Miranda Ho 6 DA17 . . . . .4 A1
Mirfield St SE7 . . . . .1 D3
Miriam Ct DA14 . . . . .24 B4
Miriam Rd SE18 . . . . .2 E1
Mirror Path SE9 . . . . .22 C5
Miskin Cotts ME3 . . . . .16 B6
Miskin Rd Dartford DA1 . . . .26 D8
Hoo St Werburgh ME3 . . . . .34 E5
Miskin Way DA12 . . . . .30 D8
Mitchell Ave Chatham ME4 . .47 F2
Northfleet DA11 . . . . .29 D6
Mitchell Cl Dartford DA1 . . . .26 E6
Erith DA17 . . . . .4 C3
Lenham ME17 . . . . .111 C5
Woolwich SE2 . . . . .3 C2
Mitchell Rd Kings Hill ME19 .88 F2
Orpington BR6 . . . . .51 F6
Mitchell Way 2 BR1 . . . . . . .36 A8
Mitchell Wlk Newham E6 . . . .1 F8
Swanscombe DA10 . . . . . . .28 E8
Mitcham Cl TN15 . . . . .55 E3
Mitre Cl 5 Erith DA17 . . . . . .4 A2
Tonbridge TN9 . . . . .117 C2
Mitre Rd ME1 . . . . .47 B4
Moat Cl Orpington BR6 . . . . .51 F4
Sevenoaks TN13 . . . . .83 D5

Moat Croft DA16 . . . . .7 C4
Moat Ct Eltham SE9 . . . . .5 E5
Sidcup DA14 . . . . .23 F5
Moat Farm TN2 . . . . .163 A7
Moat Farm Rd ME3 . . . . . . .18 D6
Moat La Cowden TN8 . . . . .145 E7
Erith DA8 . . . . .9 A6
Moat Rd TN27 . . . . .141 B5
Moatbridge Sch SE9 . . . . . . .5 D1
Mockbeggar La
    TN17,TN27 . . . . .171 C4
Model Farm Cl SE9 . . . . . . .22 E5
Modest Cnr TN4 . . . . .132 E1
Moira Rd SE9 . . . . .5 F3
Molash Rd BR5 . . . . .38 D5
Molehill Copse
    Prim Sch ME15 . . . . . . .107 D7
Moles Mead TN8 . . . . .112 C2
Molescroft SE9 . . . . .23 C5
Molescroft Way TN9 . . . . . .132 F7
Mollison Rise DA12 . . . . . . .30 E3
Molyneux Almshouses
    TN4 . . . . .148 B4
Molyneux Ct TN4 . . . . .148 B4
Molyneux Park Gdns TN4 148 A4
Molyneux Park Rd TN4 . . .148 B4
Monarch Cl Chatham ME5 . . .62 A6
Hayes BR4 . . . . .50 A6
Tilbury RM18 . . . . .13 B5
Monarch Dr E16 . . . . .1 D8
Monarch Rd 8 DA17 . . . . .4 A3
Monckton's Ave ME14 . . . . .91 F7
Monckton's Dr ME14 . . . . . .91 E7
Moncktons La ME14 . . . . . . .91 F7
Moncrieff Cl 4 E6 . . . . .1 E7
Moncrif Cl ME14 . . . . .93 B4
Monds Cotts TN14 . . . . .82 E3
Monica James House 12
    DA14 . . . . .24 A5
Monk Dr E16 . . . . .1 A6
Monk St SE18 . . . . .2 A2
Monkdown ME15 . . . . .93 A1
Monkreed Villas DA3 . . . . . .43 D4
Monks Cl SE2 . . . . .3 D2
Monks La TN5 . . . . .175 B8
Monks Orch DA13 . . . . .26 D6
Monks Way BR5 . . . . .37 D1
Monks Wlk Northfleet DA13 .29 A4
6 Tonbridge TN9 . . . . .133 B8
Monkton Rd Bexley DA16 . . . .6 F5
Borough Green TN15 . . . . . .86 F7
Monkwood Cl ME1 . . . . .61 B8
Monmouth Cl Bexley DA16 . .7 A3
Gillingham ME8 . . . . .49 D2
Mons Way BR2 . . . . .36 E3
Monson Rd TN1 . . . . .149 B4
Monson Way 5 TN1 . . . . . .149 B4
Mont St Aignan Way TN8 128 C8
Montacute Gdns TN2 . . . . .148 F2
Montacute Rd TN2 . . . . . . .149 A1
Montague Ct 15 DA15 . . . . .24 A5
Montague Pl BR8 . . . . .39 F5
Montague Terr 1 BR2 . . . . .36 A5
Montbelle Prim Sch SE9 . .23 B5
Montbelle Rd SE9 . . . . .23 B5
Montbretia Cl BR5 . . . . .38 C5
Montcalm Cl BR2 . . . . .36 A3
Montcalm Rd SE7 . . . . .5 D7
Monteith Cl TN3 . . . . .148 A3
Monterey Cl DA5 . . . . .25 C6
Montfort Dr ME19 . . . . .89 A2
Montfort Rd Chatham ME5 . .61 F2
Kemsing TN15 . . . . .69 E2
Rochester ME2 . . . . .47 A8
Montgomery Ave ME5 . . . . .62 A7
Montgomery Cl DA15 . . . . . . .6 F1
Montgomery Rd
    Gillingham ME7 . . . . .48 C3
Royal Tunbridge Wells TN4 .149 B7
Sutton at Hone DA4 . . . . . .41 D8
Montpelier Ave DA5 . . . . . . .24 D8
Montpelier Gate ME16 . . . . .91 B5
Montreal Rd
    Sevenoaks TN13 . . . . . . .83 E4
Tilbury RM18 . . . . .13 A5
Montrose Ave Bexley DA16 . .6 E4
Chatham ME5 . . . . .48 E2
Sidcup DA15 . . . . .24 A8
Montrose Cl DA16 . . . . .6 F4
Monypenny TN17 . . . . .181 F3
Monypenny Cl TN11 . . . . . .118 D3
Moon Ct SE12 . . . . .5 A3
Moon's La RH7 . . . . .128 A1
Moonstone Dr ME5 . . . . . . .62 B2
Moor Hill TN18 . . . . .184 F8
Moor La TN8 . . . . .128 A4
Moor Park Cl ME8 . . . . .64 A8
Moor Rd The TN14 . . . . .84 C7
Moor St ME8 . . . . .64 B8
Moor The TN18 . . . . .184 F8
Moorcroft Gdns BR2 . . . . . .36 E4
Moorden La TN11 . . . . .115 A1
Moordown SE18 . . . . .6 B7
Moore Ave Grays RM20 . . . .11 B8
Tilbury RM18 . . . . .13 B5
Moore Cl DA2 . . . . .27 D6
Moore Rd DA10 . . . . .11 E1
Moore St ME8 . . . . .47 A8
Mooreland Rd BR1 . . . . .36 A5
Moorfield Rd BR6 . . . . .38 A2
Moorhead Way SE3 . . . . .5 B4
Moorhen Cl DA8 . . . . .3 B7
Moorhouse Rd RH8,TN16 . .96 A5
Mooring Rd ME1 . . . . .47 D1
Moorings The E16 . . . . .1 A7
Moorside Rd BR1 . . . . .22 A4
Morants Court Cross
    TN14 . . . . .68 C1

Morants Court Rd TN13 . .83 C1
Morden Rd SE3 . . . . .5 A5
Morden Road Mews SE3 . . .5 A5
Morden St ME1 . . . . .47 C3
More Park
    RC Prim Sch ME19 . . . . .89 D8
Morel Ct TN13 . . . . .84 B5
Morella Wlk ME17 . . . . .111 C5
Morello Ct BR6 . . . . .39 D5
Morement Rd ME3 . . . . .34 D6
Moreton DA14 . . . . .153 A6
Moreton Almhouses 3
    TN16 . . . . .81 D1
Moreton Cl DA1 . . . . .10 A6
Morewood Cl TN13 . . . . . . .83 F4
Morgan Dr DA9 . . . . .27 E8
Morgan Motor Mus*
    TN17 . . . . .181 E4
Morgan Rd Bromley BR1 . . . .22 A5
Rochester ME2 . . . . .47 A8
Morgan St E16 . . . . .1 A8
Morhen Cl ME6 . . . . .74 E7
Morland Ave DA1 . . . . .8 B2
Morland Dr
    Lamberhurst TN3 . . . . . .166 B5
Rochester ME2 . . . . .33 A1
Morley Bsns Ctr TN9 . . . . .117 C3
Morley Cl BR6 . . . . .51 B8
Morley Dr TN12 . . . . .136 A6
Morley Rd Chislehurst BR7 . .37 C8
Tonbridge TN9 . . . . .117 D1
Morley's Rd TN14 . . . . .99 D2
Morne Cotts TN14 . . . . .68 F8
Morning Cross Cotts ME3 .16 B4
Mornington Ave BR1 . . . . . .36 D6
Mornington Ct DA5 . . . . . . .25 D7
Morris Cl East Malling ME19 .74 F1
Orpington BR6 . . . . .51 E7
Morris Gdns DA1 . . . . .10 A2
Morry La ME17 . . . . .125 D7
Morstan Gdns SE9 . . . . .22 F4
Mortgramit Sq SE18 . . . . . . .2 A3
Mortimer Rd Erith DA8 . . . . . .8 B8
Orpington BR6 . . . . .38 A1
Mortimers Ave ME3 . . . . . . .33 A8
Mortlake Rd E16 . . . . .1 B7
Morton Cl
    Maidstone ME15 . . . . . .107 D6
Swanley BR8 . . . . .39 E7
Morvale Cl DA17 . . . . .3 F2
Mosquito Rd ME19 . . . . . . .88 F3
Mossbank ME5 . . . . .62 A3
Mossdown Cl DA17 . . . . .4 A2
Mosslea Rd Bromley BR2 . . .36 C4
Orpington BR6 . . . . .51 C7
Mossy Glade ME8 . . . . .63 E6
Mostyn Rd ME14 . . . . .92 C4
Mosul Way BR2 . . . . .36 E3
Mosyer Dr BR5 . . . . .52 D8
Mote Ave ME15 . . . . .92 B3
Mote Cotts TN15 . . . . .101 A7
Mote Hall Villas ME14 . . . . .93 C4
Mote Pk ME15 . . . . .92 D2
Mote Rd
    Ivy Hatch TN15,TN11 . . .101 A7
Maidstone ME15 . . . . .92 A3
Mote The DA3 . . . . .56 F8
Motherwell Way RM20 . . . . .11 A8
Mottingham Ct SE9 . . . . . . .22 F7
Mottingham Gdns SE9 . . . .22 D7
Mottingham La
    Eltham SE12 . . . . .22 C8
Lewisham SE12,SE9 . . . . . .22 C7
Mottingham Prim Sch SE9 22 F5
Mottingham Rd SE9 . . . . . .22 F5
Mottingham Sta SE9 . . . . . .22 F7
Mottisfont Rd SE2 . . . . .3 B2
Mouat Ct SE9 . . . . .62 A3
Moultain Hill BR8 . . . . .40 A5
Mound The SE9 . . . . .23 A5
Mount Ave ME18 . . . . .105 A1
Mount Cl Bromley BR1 . . . . .36 E8
Sevenoaks TN13 . . . . .83 F4
Mount Culver Ave DA14 . . .24 D2
Mount Dr Bexley DA6 . . . . . .7 E2
Maidstone ME14 . . . . .93 B4
Mount Edgcumbe Rd
    TN4 . . . . .149 A3
Mount Ephraim TN4 . . . . . .149 A4
Mount Ephraim Ct TN4 . . .148 F4
Mount Ephraim Rd TN1 . . .149 A4
Mount Harry Rd TN13 . . . . .84 B4
Mount La Hartlip ME9 . . . . .64 D4
Maidstone ME14 . . . . .93 B4
Mount Lodge ME1 . . . . .47 B2
Mount Pleasant
    Aylesford ME20 . . . . . . .76 A3
Gillingham ME8 . . . . .48 B3
Hook Green TN3 . . . . .165 E6
Ide Hill TN14 . . . . .97 F4
Paddock Wood TN12 . . . . .135 F7
Tenterden TN30 . . . . .183 C8
The Moor TN18 . . . . .184 F8
Tonbridge TN11 . . . . .116 D6
Wadhurst TN5 . . . . .174 E5
Mount Pleasant Ave 2
    TN1 . . . . .149 B3
Mount Pleasant Ct TN11 .116 D6
Mount Pleasant La ME14 . .93 A5
Mount Pleasant La TN3 . .166 A6
Mount Pleasant Pl SE18 . . .2 D2
Mount Pleasant Rd
    Dartford DA1 . . . . .9 F1
Royal Tunbridge Wells TN1 .149 A3
Sevenoaks Weald TN14 . . .99 B2

Mount Pleasant Terr
ME17 . . . .**110** E2
Mount Pleasant Wlk DA5 . .**8** C2
Mount Rd Bexley DA6 . . . .**7** E2
Chatham ME4 . . . .**47** F3
Crayford DA1 . . . .**8** F1
Rochester ME2 . . . .**47** B2
Mount Sion TN1 . . . .**149** A2
Mount The DA6 . . . .**8** B2
Mount View Ct 3 ME4 . . . . .**47** F3
Mountbatten Ave
Chatham ME5 . . . .**62** A7
Higham ME3 . . . .**32** C4
Mountbatten Cl SE18 . . . .**6** E8
Mountfield TN15 . . . .**87** A7
Mountfield Cl DA13 . . . .**57** F2
Mountfield Ct 4 TN1 . . . . .**149** B3
Mountfield Gdns TN1 . . . . .**149** B3
Mountfield Pk TN9 . . . .**133** C8
Mountfield Rd TN1 . . . .**149** B3
Mountfield Way 1 BR5 . . . .**38** C5
Mounthurst Rd BR2 . . . .**36** A2
Mountjoy Cl SE2 . . . .**3** B4
Mounts Hill TN17 . . . .**180** B7
Mounts La TN17 . . . .**182** A3
Mounts Rd DA9 . . . .**11** B1
Mountsfield Cl ME16 . . . .**91** D5
Mountview Rd BR6 . . . .**38** A2
Moyle Cl ME8 . . . .**63** D4
Mozart Ct ME4 . . . .**47** E3
Muir Rd ME15 . . . .**92** A2
Muir St E16 . . . .**1** E5
Mulbarton Ct BR7 . . . .**23** D2
Mulberry Cl Gillingham ME7 **63** A4
Greenwich SE7 . . . .**5** D8
Meopham Sta DA13 . . . .**44** B3
Royal Tunbridge Wells TN4 .**133** D1
Mulberry Ct Bexley DA16 . . . . .**6** F5
Maidstone ME14 . . . .**92** B5
Mulberry Rd DA11 . . . .**29** E4
Mulberry Way DA17 . . . .**4** C4
Mulgrave Rd 13 SE18 . . . .**1** F2
Mulgrave Prim Sch SE18 . . . .**2** A2
Mullein Ct 6 RM17 . . . .**12** D8
Mullender Ct DA12 . . . .**31** A7
Muller Ho SE18 . . . .**2** A1
Multon Rd TN15 . . . .**55** E4
Munday Bois Cotts TN27 .**143** F8
Munday Bois Rd TN27 . . . . .**127** E1
Munday Rd E16 . . . .**1** A7
Munday Works Est TN9 . . . .**117** C1
Munford Dr DA10 . . . .**28** E8
Mungeam Ho ME1 . . . .**47** C4
Mungo Park Rd DA12 . . . . . .**30** D3
Mungo Park Way BR5 . . . . . .**38** D2
Munn's La ME9 . . . .**64** E6
Munnery Way BR6 . . . .**51** B8
Munnings Ho E16 . . . .**1** C7
Murchison Ave DA5 . . . .**24** E7
Murrain Dr ME15 . . . .**93** A1
Murray Ave BR1 . . . .**36** B7
Murray Bsns Ctr BR5 . . . .**38** B6
Murray Ho 15 SE18 . . . .**1** F2
St Paul's Cray BR5 . . . .**38** B6
Murray Rd Rochester ME2 . . .**47** C8
St Paul's Cray BR5 . . . .**38** B6
Murray Sq E16 . . . .**1** B6
Murton-Neale Cl 3
TN18 . . . .**179** A2
Mus of Artillery
in the Rotunda* SE18 . . . .**1** F1
Muscovy Ho DA18 . . . .**3** E4
Mus of Kent Rural Life*
ME14 . . . .**76** D1
Museum St ME14 . . . .**91** F4
Musket La
Hollingbourne ME17 . . . .**94** B2
Maidstone ME17 . . . .**94** A2
Mussenden La DA3,DA4 . . . .**41** E3
Mustang Rd ME19 . . . .**88** F3
Mycenae Rd SE3 . . . .**5** A8
Mynn Cres ME14 . . . .**93** A4
Myra St SE2 . . . .**3** A2
Myrtle Alley SE18 . . . .**2** A3
Myrtle Cl DA8 . . . .**8** E6
Myrtle Cres ME5 . . . .**61** F5
Myrtle Pl DA2 . . . .**27** D8
Myrtle Rd DA1 . . . .**26** D6
Myrtledene Rd SE2 . . . .**3** A1

N

Nadine St SE7 . . . .**1** C1
Nag's Head La Bexley DA16 . . .**7** B4
Chatham ME1 . . . .**47** D4
Nagpur House 4 ME15 . .**107** E5
Nairn Ct RM18 . . . .**12** F5
Nansen Rd DA12 . . . .**30** D4
Napier Com Sch ME7 . . . .**48** D4
Napier Ct
2 Lewisham SE12 . . . .**22** B5
Maidstone ME14 . . . .**91** F7
Napier Rd Bromley BR2 . . . . .**36** B5
Erith DA17 . . . .**3** F2
Gillingham ME7 . . . .**48** D4
Northfleet DA11 . . . .**29** F7
Royal Tunbridge Wells TN2 .**149** D2
Napoleon Dr TN12 . . . .**138** D5
Napoleon Wlk ME17 . . . . . .**111** C5
Napwood Cl ME8 . . . .**63** D6
Nares Rd ME8 . . . .**63** D4
Narrow Boat Cl SE28 . . . .**2** D4
Narrow Way BR2 . . . .**36** E3

Naseby Ct DA14 . . . .**23** F4
Nash Bank DA13 . . . .**43** F7
Nash Cl ME5 . . . .**62** C2
Nash Cotts 16 DA14 . . . .**24** A5
Nash Croft DA11 . . . .**29** E4
Nash Gn BR1 . . . .**22** A2
Nash La BR2 . . . .**50** A4
Nash St DA13 . . . .**44** A7
Nashenden Farm La ME1 .**61** A8
Nashenden La ME1 . . . .**46** F1
Nassau Path 6 SE28 . . . .**3** C5
Natal Rd ME4 . . . .**48** A3
Nathan Way SE28,SE18 . . . . . .**2** E3
Naylor's Cotts ME7 . . . .**63** B1
Neal Rd TN15 . . . .**55** E5
Neale St ME4 . . . .**47** F2
Neatscourt Rd E6 . . . .**1** D8
Neills Rd TN3 . . . .**165** D2
Nellington Terr TN4 . . . .**148** B4
Nellington Rd TN3, TN4 . . .**148** B4
Nelson Ave TN9 . . . .**117** A1
Nelson Ho
8 Maidstone ME15 . . . . . .**107** F5
Swanscombe DA9 . . . .**11** D3
Nelson Mandela Rd SE3 . . . .**5** C4
Nelson Pl DA14 . . . .**24** A4
Dartford DA1 . . . .**9** C1
Erith DA17 . . . .**3** F1
Gillingham ME7 . . . .**48** D4
Northfleet DA11 . . . .**29** F6
Royal Tunbridge Wells TN2 .**149** D2
11 Sidcup DA14 . . . .**24** A4
Wouldham ME1 . . . .**60** C5
Nelson Terr ME5 . . . .**48** C1
Nepicar Farm* TN15 . . . . . .**72** D1
Nepicar La TN15 . . . .**72** D3
Neptune Bsns Pk ME2 . . . . . .**47** E7
Neptune Cl ME2 . . . .**47** E7
Neptune Way ME2 . . . .**47** E6
Neptune Wlk DA8 . . . .**4** D2
Nesbit Rd SE9 . . . .**5** D3
Nesbitt House DA6 . . . .**8** B2
Ness Rd DA8 . . . .**9** D8
Nestor Ct ME14 . . . .**105** A8
Nethercombe Ho 4 SE3 . . . .**5** A8
Nethewode Ct DA17 . . . .**4** B3
Netley Cl ME14 . . . .**92** D6
Nettlestead La ME18 . . . . . .**104** A6
Nevill Cl ME19 . . . .**74** C1
Nevill Gate TN2 . . . .**149** B1
Nevill Lodge TN2 . . . .**149** C4
Nevill Pk TN4 . . . .**148** E3
Nevill Pl ME6 . . . .**75** A7
Nevill Rd ME6 . . . .**75** A7
Nevill Ridge TN4 . . . .**148** D3
Nevill St TN2 . . . .**149** A2
Nevill Terr TN2 . . . .**148** F2
Neville Cl Maidstone ME14 . .**92** B8
Sidcup DA15 . . . .**23** F4
Neville Rd ME4 . . . .**47** E2
New Acres Rd SE28 . . . .**2** E4
New Ash Green
Prim Sch DA3 . . . .**56** F8
New Barn Pk BR8 . . . .**39** E8
New Barn Rd
Hawkenbury ME17, TN12 . . .**124** E2
Northfleet Green DA13 . . . . . .**29** C3
Swanley BR8 . . . .**39** F8
New Barn St E13 . . . .**1** B8
New Barns Rd ME14 . . . .**92** A8
New Bassetts Cotts TN12 **153** B5
New Cotts Bean DA2 . . . .**28** B5
Shipbourne TN11 . . . .**101** D5
Shorne DA12 . . . .**31** E5
New Covenant Pl ME1 . . . . . .**47** D4
New Ct 2 TN9 . . . .**117** C2
New Cut Chatham ME4 . . . . . .**47** F4
East Farleigh ME15 . . . .**106** D7
New Cut Rd ME14 . . . .**92** D5
New Delhi House 5
ME15 . . . .**107** E5
New Eltham Sta SE9 . . . .**23** C7
New England Rd TN4 . . . . . .**149** A4
New Farm Ave BR2 . . . .**36** A5
New Hall Farm La ME3 . . . . .**19** B6
New House La DA11 . . . .**30** A6
New Hythe La ME20 . . . .**75** B5
New Hythe Sta ME20 . . . .**75** C4
New Inn Cotts ME15 . . . . . .**106** C7
New Lydenburg
Commercial Est SE7 . . . .**1** C3
New Lydenburg St SE7 . . . . . .**1** C3
New Mill Rd BR5 . . . .**38** C8
New Pond Rd TN17 . . . .**180** D6
New Pound La ME18 . . . .**88** C1
New Rd Bexley DA16 . . . .**7** B5
Burham ME1 . . . .**60** F1
Chatham ME1 . . . .**47** D4
Chatham ME4 . . . .**47** F4
Cliffe ME3 . . . .**16** A4
Cranbrook TN17 . . . .**169** B4
Ditton ME20 . . . .**75** C1
East Malling ME19 . . . .**90** A8
Egerton TN27 . . . .**127** F3
Erith SE2 . . . .**3** D1
Fordcombe TN11 . . . .**131** A1
Gravesend DA11 . . . .**13** B1
Grays RM17 . . . .**12** A8
Grays RM17 . . . .**12** B8
Headcorn TN27 . . . .**141** D5
Hextable BR8 . . . .**25** F1
Langley Heath ME17 . . . .**108** C5
Meopham Sta DA13 . . . .**43** F4
Orpington BR6 . . . .**38** A2
Paddock Wood TN12 . . . . . .**136** A6
Sundridge TN14 . . . .**82** E2
Sutton at Hone DA4 . . . .**41** D7

New Rd continued
Swanley BR8 . . . .**39** F6
New Road Ave ME4 . . . .**47** E4
New Road
Cty Prim Sch ME4 . . . .**48** A3
New Road Hill BR2, BR6 . . . . .**50** F2
New Sch at West Heath
The TN13 . . . .**99** B6
New St Chatham ME4 . . . .**47** E3
New Street TN15 . . . .**57** D4
Westerham TN16 . . . .**96** C8
New Stairs ME4 . . . .**47** F6
New Street Hill BR1 . . . .**22** C3
New Street Rd DA13, TN15 . .**57** C6
New Swan Yd 7 DA12 . . . . . .**13** B1
New Tavern Fort* DA12 . . . . .**13** C1
New Villas ME15 . . . .**106** C7
New Wharf Rd TN9 . . . .**117** B1
New Wlk TN15 . . . .**71** F3
New Years La BR6, TN14 . . . . .**67** A5
Newark Ct 1 ME2 . . . .**47** B7
Newark Knok E6 . . . .**2** A7
Newark Yd ME2 . . . .**47** B7
Newbarn La TN14, TN16 . . . . .**66** C2
Newbery Rd DA8 . . . .**8** F6
Newborough Ct TN10 . . . . . .**117** C6
Newbury Ave ME16 . . . .**91** C6
Newbury Cl ME3 . . . .**33** B8
Newbury Cotts TN5 . . . .**175** C8
Newbury Ct DA14 . . . .**23** F4
Newbury La TN5 . . . .**175** C8
Newbury Rd BR2 . . . .**36** A6
Newchurch Rd ME15 . . . .**92** A1
Newcomen Rd TN4 . . . .**149** A5
Newenden Cl ME14 . . . .**92** D6
Newenden Rd ME2 . . . .**33** C2
Newham Coll of FE (Royal
Docks Campus) E16 . . . .**2** C5
Newham St ME4 . . . .**48** B3
Newham Way E13 . . . .**1** B8
Newhaven Gdns SE9 . . . .**5** D3
Newhaven La 4 E16 . . . .**1** A8
Newhouse Terr TN8 . . . .**112** C3
Newick Cl DA5 . . . .**8** B1
Newing Gn BR1 . . . .**22** D1
Newington
CE Prim Sch ME9 . . . .**65** B7
Newington Ct TN5 . . . .**176** E1
Newington Ent Ctr ME9 . . . .**65** C8
Newington House 9 BR5 . . .**38** D1
Newington Ind Est ME9 . . . .**64** F6
Newington Sta ME9 . . . .**65** B6
Newington Wlk ME14 . . . . . .**92** C6
Newitt Rd ME3 . . . .**34** E5
Newland Green La TN27 . . .**143** D8
Newland St E16 . . . .**1** F5
Newlands TN3 . . . .**148** A3
Newlands Ct 8 SE9 . . . .**6** A1
Newlands Farm Rd ME3 . . . .**18** B4
Newlands La DA13 . . . .**57** F2
Newlands Rd TN4 . . . .**149** B7
Newlands Rise TN4 . . . .**149** A6
Newlands Way TN4 . . . .**149** B7
Newling Cl E6 . . . .**1** F7
Newlyn Cl BR6 . . . .**52** A6
Newlyn Ct 1 ME14 . . . .**92** A4
Newlyn Dr TN12 . . . .**139** F5
Newlyn Rd DA16 . . . .**6** F5
Newman Ho SE18 . . . .**6** A7
Newman Rd BR1 . . . .**36** A8
Newman's Rd DA11 . . . .**29** F6
Newmarket Gn SE9 . . . .**22** D8
Newnham Cl ME8 . . . .**49** C2
Newnham Lodge DA17 . . . . . .**4** A1
Newnhams Cl BR1 . . . .**36** F6
Newports BR8 . . . .**39** D2
Newstead Ave BR6 . . . .**51** E8
Newstead Wood
Sch for Girls BR6 . . . .**51** D7
Newton Abbot Rd DA11 . . . .**29** F6
Newton Ave TN10 . . . .**117** E7
Newton Cl Chatham ME5 . . . .**62** C2
1 Maidstone ME16 . . . .**91** E3
Newton Ct 4 BR1 . . . .**36** E6
Newton Gdns TN12 . . . .**135** F7
Newton Ho SE2 . . . .**3** C1
Newton Rd Bexley DA16 . . . . . .**7** A5
Royal Tunbridge Wells TN1 .**149** B4
Tilbury RM18 . . . .**13** A5
Newton Terr BR2 . . . .**36** D3
Newton's Ct DA9 . . . .**10** D3
Newtown Cotts TN12 . . . . . .**139** E6
Nichol La BR1 . . . .**22** A1
Nicholas Cl ME16 . . . .**91** A3
Nicholas Ct SE28 . . . .**3** C7
Nicholas Stacey Ho 3 SE7 .**1** B1
Nicholson Ho SE18 . . . .**5** E7
Nickelby Cl SE28 . . . .**3** C7
Nickelby Cl ME1 . . . .**47** C2
Nickleby Rd DA12 . . . .**31** A7
Nicola Terr DA7 . . . .**7** E6
Nicolson Rd BR5 . . . .**38** D2
Nicolson Way TN13 . . . .**84** D5
Nigeria Rd SE7 . . . .**5** D7
Nightingale Cl
Gillingham ME8 . . . .**63** E6
Larkfield ME20 . . . .**74** F2
Northfleet DA11 . . . .**29** E4
Nightingale Cnr BR5 . . . .**38** D5
Nightingale Ct ME2 . . . .**46** F5
Nightingale Gr 3 DA1 . . . . .**10** A3
Nightingale Ho SE18 . . . .**2** A1
Nightingale La
Bromley BR1 . . . .**36** D7
Goathurst Common TN14 . . .**98** B5
Nightingale Pl SE18 . . . .**6** B8

Nightingale Prim Sch SE18 .**2** B1
Nightingale Rd
Kemsing TN15 . . . .**69** E2
Orpington BR5 . . . .**37** C3
Nightingale Vale SE18 . . . .**6** A8
Nightingale Way Newham E6 **1** E8
Swanley BR8 . . . .**39** E6
Nightingales The
Royal Tunbridge Wells TN4 .**149** A5
Sissinghurst TN27 . . . .**170** F8
Nile Path 6 SE18 . . . .**6** A8
Nile Rd ME7 . . . .**48** C4
Nimrod Ho E16 . . . .**1** B8
Nine Acres Rd ME4 . . . .**46** B3
Nine Acres Sch SE18 . . . .**2** D1
Nineveh La TN17, TN18 . . . .**179** E6
Ninhams Wood BR6 . . . .**51** A6
Nita Ct SE12 . . . .**22** A7
Nithdale Rd SE18 . . . .**6** C7
Niven Cl ME3 . . . .**33** C3
Nizels La TN11 . . . .**115** F3
No 1 St SE18 . . . .**2** B3
No 2 St SE18 . . . .**2** B3
Noah's Ark TN15 . . . .**70** B1
Noble Tree Cross TN11 . . . . .**116** B6
Noble Tree Rd TN11 . . . .**116** B6
Noel Terr 15 DA14 . . . .**24** B4
Nook The ME18 . . . .**104** F2
Norah La ME3 . . . .**32** B3
Nordenfeldt Rd DA8 . . . .**4** D1
Nore Cl ME7 . . . .**48** E1
Norfield Rd DA2 . . . .**25** D3
Norfolk Cl Chatham ME5 . . . .**62** C3
Dartford DA1 . . . .**10** A1
Gillingham ME8 . . . .**49** D2
Norfolk Cres DA15 . . . .**23** E8
Norfolk Gdns DA7 . . . .**7** F6
Norfolk Pl DA16 . . . .**7** A5
Norfolk Rd Gravesend DA12 . .**30** D8
Maidstone ME15 . . . .**107** C8
Royal Tunbridge Wells TN1 .**149** B2
Tonbridge TN9 . . . .**117** A1
Norham Ct 25 DA2 . . . .**10** B1
Norlands Cres BR7 . . . .**37** B8
Norman Cl Gillingham ME8 . .**63** B5
Kemsing TN15 . . . .**69** D2
Maidstone ME14 . . . .**92** B6
Orpington BR6 . . . .**51** C7
Rochester ME2 . . . .**46** F4
Norman Ct TN8 . . . .**112** B2
Norman Par DA14 . . . .**24** D6
Norman Rd Dartford DA1 . . . .**26** E7
Erith DA17 . . . .**4** B3
Erith DA17 . . . .**4** B5
New Town ME19 . . . .**89** B8
Royal Tunbridge Wells TN1 .**149** B5
Snodland ME6 . . . .**75** A6
Norman St TN14 . . . .**97** F5
Norman Villas 4 ME14 . . . .**178** F2
Normandy Prim Sch DA7 . . .**8** D6
Normandy Terr E16 . . . .**1** B7
Normandy Way DA8 . . . .**8** E7
Normanhurst Rd DA7 . . . .**7** D6
Normanhurst Rd
Borough Green TN15 . . . .**87** A7
St Paul's Cray BR5 . . . .**38** B7
Normans Cl DA11 . . . .**30** A8
Norreys Rd ME8 . . . .**63** E7
Norrington Rd ME15 . . . .**107** B6
Norris Ho 15 SE7 . . . .**5** C8
Norris Way DA1 . . . .**8** F4
Norstead Gdns TN4 . . . .**149** B7
Norsted La BR6 . . . .**67** B8
North Bank Cl ME2 . . . .**46** F5
North Beckton
Prim Sch E16 . . . .**1** F8
North Borough
Jun Sch ME15 . . . .**92** A6
North Cl DA6 . . . .**7** D3
North Cray Prim Sch DA14 **24** E2
North Cray Rd DA14 . . . .**24** E4
North Cres ME17 . . . .**106** D4
North Ct 5 Bromley BR1 . . . .**36** B8
Maidstone ME15 . . . .**92** A1
North Dane Way ME5 . . . .**62** C4
North Down TN12 . . . .**139** C4
North Downs Terr ME19 . . . . .**73** A5
North Downs Bsns Pk
TN13 . . . .**68** C3
North Dr BR6 . . . .**51** E6
North End La BR6 . . . .**51** B2
North End Trad Est DA8 . . . . .**8** E6
North Farm La TN2 . . . .**133** E2
North Farm Rd TN2 . . . .**149** C8
North Folly Rd ME15 . . . . . .**105** F3
North Frith Pk TN11 . . . .**101** F1
North Glade The DA5 . . . .**24** F7
North Hill Rd TN18 . . . .**178** C1
North Kent Ave DA11 . . . .**12** C1
North Lockside Rd ME4 . . . . .**48** B8
North Meadow ME19 . . . .**88** D7
North Pk SE9 . . . .**6** A1
North Pole La BR2 . . . .**50** A4
North Pole Rd ME16, ME18 . . .**90** C2
North Pondside Rd ME4 . . . .**48** A8
North Rd Bromley BR1 . . . . . .**36** B8
Chatham ME4 . . . .**48** B8
Cliffe ME3 . . . .**16** B6
Dartford DA1 . . . .**9** C1
Erith DA17 . . . .**4** B4
Gillingham ME4, ME7 . . . .**48** A7
Goudhurst TN17 . . . .**153** E1
Woolwich SE18 . . . .**2** C2
North Riding DA3 . . . .**43** D6
North Side Three Rd ME4 . . .**48** C8

North St Bexley DA7 . . . .**8** A3
Biddenden TN27 . . . .**158** A2
Bromley BR1 . . . .**36** A8
Cowden TN8 . . . .**145** A6
Dartford DA1 . . . .**26** D8
Gravesend DA12 . . . .**30** B8
Headcorn TN27 . . . .**141** C5
Maidstone ME16 . . . .**90** F2
Rochester ME2 . . . .**47** B7
Royal Tunbridge Wells TN2 .**149** C3
Sutton Valence ME17 . . . . . .**124** E8
North Street Cotts ME17 .**124** E8
North Terr ME3 . . . .**33** F6
North View ME15 . . . .**92** B1
North View Ave RM18 . . . . . .**13** A6
North View Cotts ME15 . . . .**106** C7
North View Rd TN13, TN14 . .**84** C6
North Way ME14 . . . .**92** B7
North West Kent Coll
DA12 . . . .**30** F7
North Woolwich
Old Sta Mus* E16 . . . .**2** A4
North Woolwich Rdbt E16 .**1** D5
North Woolwich Sta E16 . . .**2** A4
Northall Rd DA7 . . . .**8** C5
Northbourne BR2 . . . .**36** A2
Northbourne Rd ME8 . . . .**49** B4
Northcote Rd
Gravesend DA11 . . . .**29** F7
Rochester ME2 . . . .**47** A7
Sidcup DA14 . . . .**23** E4
2 Tonbridge TN9 . . . .**117** B1
Northcourt Prim Sch
DA12 . . . .**30** E7
Northdown ME9 . . . .**79** D8
Northdown Cl
Maidstone ME14 . . . .**92** B7
Paddock Wood TN12 . . . . . .**136** A6
Northdown Rd Bexley DA16 . . .**7** C5
Kemsing TN15 . . . .**69** C2
Longfield DA3 . . . .**42** E7
Northdown View ME17 . . .**110** F6
Northend Prim Sch DA8 . . . . .**8** F6
Northend Rd DA8 . . . .**8** F6
Northfield DA3 . . . .**42** F6
Northfield Ave BR5 . . . .**38** C3
Northfield Cl BR1, BR7 . . . .**36** E8
Northfields Maidstone ME16 .**90** F2
Speldhurst TN3 . . . .**148** A8
Northfleet Cl ME14 . . . .**92** C5
Northfleet Ind Est DA11 . . . .**11** F3
Northfleet
Sch for Boys DA11 . . . . . .**29** D7
Northfleet
Sch for Girls DA11 . . . . . .**29** D6
Northfleet Sta DA11 . . . .**12** B1
Northgate ME1 . . . .**47** C6
Northgrove Rd 19 TN18 . . .**178** F2
Northiam Sta TN31 . . . .**187** C2
Northlands Ave BR6 . . . .**51** E6
Northlands Cotts TN32 . . . .**185** C1
Northleigh Cl ME15 . . . .**107** A6
Northolme Rise BR6 . . . .**51** E8
Northover BR1 . . . .**22** A4
Northpoint Bsns Est ME2 . . .**47** D8
Northridge Rd DA12 . . . .**30** C5
Northside Rd BR1 . . . .**36** A8
Northumberland Ave
Bexley ME8 . . . .**6** A4
Gillingham ME8 . . . .**49** E1
Northumberland Cl DA8 . . . . .**8** C7
Northumberland Ct
ME15 . . . .**107** D7
Northumberland Gdns
BR1 . . . .**37** A5
Northumberland Heath
Prim Sch DA8 . . . .**8** B7
Northumberland Pk DA8 . . . .**8** C7
Northumberland Rd
Istead Rise DA13 . . . .**29** F1
Maidstone ME15 . . . .**107** D8
Newham E6 . . . .**1** E7
Northumberland Way DA8 . .**8** D6
Northview BR8 . . . .**39** F2
Northward Hill
Nature Reserve* ME23 . . . . . .**17** E5
Northwood Ave ME23 . . . .**17** E4
Northwood Pl DA18 . . . .**3** F3
Northwood Prim Sch DA18 .**3** F3
Northwood Rd TN10 . . . .**117** C6
Norton Cres TN10 . . . .**117** B7
Norton Gr ME7 . . . .**61** E3
Norton Rd
Five Wents ME17 . . . .**108** D1
Royal Tunbridge Wells TN4 .**133** A1
Nortons La TN30 . . . .**172** C5
Nortons Way TN12 . . . .**135** B7
Norvic House DA8 . . . .**8** F7
Norway Terr 4 ME14 . . . .**92** A7
Norwich Ave TN10 . . . .**117** D5
Norwich Cl ME2 . . . .**46** D6
Norwich Pl 7 DA6 . . . .**8** A3
Norwood Cl ME3 . . . .**16** B4
Norwood Ct 5 DA1 . . . .**10** A3
Norwood La DA13 . . . .**44** B3
Notre Dame
RC Prim Sch SE18 . . . .**6** B8
Nottidge Rd TN4 . . . .**148** D1
Nottingham Ave
Maidstone ME15 . . . .**107** D7
Newham E16 . . . .**1** C7
Nottingham Wlk ME2 . . . .**46** D6
Novar Cl BR6 . . . .**37** F2
Novar Rd SE9 . . . .**23** C7
Nower The TN14, TN16 . . . . . .**81** F8
Nuffield Hospl TN2 . . . .**149** C3
Nuffield Rd BR8 . . . .**26** A2
Nugent Ind Pk BR5 . . . .**38** C5

Nunnery La TN11 . . . . . . .146 F8
Nunnington Cl SE9 . . . . . . .22 E5
Nursery Ave Bexley DA7 . . . .7 F4
Maidstone ME16 . . . . .91 B6
Maidstone,Bearsted ME14 . .93 B3
Nursery Cl Dartford DA2 . . .27 C8
Flimwell TN5 . . . . .177 B3
Orpington BR6 . . . . .38 A2
Sevenoaks TN13 . . . . .84 C5
Swanley BR8 . . . . .39 C7
Tonbridge TN10 . . . . .117 E4
Nursery Gdns
Chislehurst BR7 . . . . .23 B2
Hoo St Werburgh ME3 . . . .34 E5
Nursery Pl TN13 . . . . .83 D4
Nursery Rd Ditton ME20 . . .75 C1
Gillingham ME8 . . . . .63 D8
Meopham Sta DA13 . . . . . .44 A4
Paddock Wood TN12 . . . . .135 F8
Royal Tunbridge Wells TN4 .149 B8
Nursery The Erith DA8 . . . . .8 F7
Westerham TN16 . . . . .96 C8
Nurstead Ave DA3 . . . . . . .43 D6
Nurstead Church La DA13 44 A5
Nurstead La DA3,DA13 . . . .43 D5
Nurstead Rd DA8 . . . . .8 A7
Nut Tree La ME5 . . . . .52 D7
Nutfield Cl ME5 . . . . .62 B8
Nutfield Way BR6 . . . . .51 B8
Nutfields TN15 . . . . .86 B4
Nuthatch DA3 . . . . .43 B7
Nuthatch Gdns SE28 . . . . . .2 C6
Nutley Cl BR8 . . . . .39 F8
Nutmead Cl DA5 . . . . .25 C7
Nuttall Ct BR5 . . . . .38 B6
Nutwood Cl ME14 . . . . . . .92 E4
Nuxley Rd DA17 . . . . .4 A1
NW Kent Coll DA1 . . . . . . .26 D8
Nyanza St SE18 . . . . .6 D8

O

O'Neill Path [1] SE18 . . . . . . .6 A8
Oak Apple Ct SE12 . . . . . . .22 A7
Oak Ave Gillingham ME7 . . .48 E6
Sevenoaks TN13 . . . . .99 B7
Oak Cl Crayford DA1 . . . . . .8 F3
Hoo St Werburgh ME3 . . . .34 E3
Oak Cotts TN8 . . . . .113 B6
Oak Ct BR1 . . . . .36 F7
Oak Dr Higham ME3 . . . . . .32 B4
Larkfield ME20 . . . . .75 B2
Oak End Cl TN4 . . . . .133 A2
Oak Farm Gdns TN27 . . . .141 D6
Oak Farm La TN15 . . . . . . .57 E1
Oak Hill Rd TN13 . . . . .84 A2
Oak Ho [6] Chatham ME5 . . .61 F4
Marden ME14 . . . . .138 D5
Royal Tunbridge Wells TN2 .149 C7
[13] Sidcup DA15 . . . . .24 A5
Oak La Gillingham ME8 . . . .64 D8
Headcorn TN27 . . . . .141 D5
Sevenoaks TN13 . . . . .99 A8
Oak Lodge TN3 . . . . .84 A3
Oak Lodge La TN16 . . . . . .81 D2
Oak Rd Erith,Northumberland
Heath DA8 . . . . .8 C7
Erith,Slade Green DA8 . . . . .9 A4
Five Oak Green TN12 . . . . .135 B7
Gravesend DA12 . . . . .30 C4
Grays RM17 . . . . .12 C8
Hoo St Werburgh ME3 . . . .34 E3
Orpington BR6 . . . . .52 A3
Rochester ME2 . . . . .46 E6
Royal Tunbridge Wells TN2 .149 D7
Stone DA9 . . . . .10 E1
Westerham TN16 . . . . .81 D2
Oak Terr [3] TN18 . . . . . . .178 F2
Oak Tree Ave
Maidstone ME15 . . . . . . .107 C7
Stone DA9 . . . . .27 F8
Oak Tree Cl Marden TN12 .138 D5
Royal Tunbridge Wells TN1 .149 A1
Oak Tree Gdns BR1 . . . . . .22 B3
Oak Trees Com Sch
ME15 . . . . .107 C7
Oak View TN8 . . . . .112 B2
Oakapple La ME16 . . . . . . .91 A3
Oakbrook Cl BR1 . . . . .22 B4
Oakcroft [3] SE12 . . . . .22 B4
Oakdale La TN8 . . . . .96 C2
Oakdale Rd TN4 . . . . .148 F4
Oakdene Ave
Chislehurst BR7 . . . . .23 A3
Erith DA8 . . . . .8 C8
Oakdene Rd Orpington BR5 .38 A3
Sevenoaks TN13 . . . . .84 A5
Oakenden Rd DA13 . . . . . .44 E1
Oakenholt Ho [1] SE2 . . . . . .3 D4
Oakes Cl E6 . . . . .1 F7
Oakfield Hawkhurst TN18 . .178 F2
Rolvenden TN17 . . . . .182 A1
Oakfield Cotts TN17 . . . . .180 D4
Oakfield Court Rd TN2 . . .149 C3
Oakfield Inf Sch DA1 . . . . .26 D6
Oakfield Jun Sch DA1 . . . .26 D6
Oakfield La
Dartford DA1,DA2 . . . . . . .26 B6
Orpington BR2 . . . . .50 D6
Oakfield Park Rd DA1 . . . . .26 D6
Oakfield Pl DA1 . . . . .26 D6
Oakfield Rd
Marlpit Hill TN8 . . . . .112 B5
Matfield ME14 . . . . .151 D8
Oakfields TN13 . . . . .84 B1
Oakham Dr BR2 . . . . .36 A5
Oakhill House BR5 . . . . . . .38 A8

Oakhill Rd BR6 . . . . .51 F8
Oakhouse Rd DA6 . . . . .8 A2
Oakhurst Ave DA7 . . . . .7 E7
Oakhurst Cl ME5 . . . . .61 F3
Oakhurst Gdns DA7 . . . . . . .7 E7
Oakhurst Pl BR7 . . . . .36 F8
Oakland Cl ME5 . . . . .61 F3
Oakland Villas TN3 . . . . . .161 B7
Oaklands Chislehurst BR7 . .23 D2
Cranbrook TN17 . . . . .169 D4
Oaklands Ave DA15 . . . . . .23 F8
Oaklands Cl Bexley DA6 . . . .7 E2
Orpington BR5 . . . . .37 E3
West Kingsdown TN15 . . . . .55 F4
Oaklands Ct BR6 . . . . .51 C8
Oaklands
Cty Inf & Jun Sch ME5 . .61 F4
Oaklands Rd Bexley DA6 . . . .7 E2
Dartford DA2 . . . . .27 C7
Groombridge TN3 . . . . . . .161 B6
Hawkhurst TN18 . . . . .179 A1
Northfleet DA11 . . . . .29 F4
Oaklands Way TN11 . . . . .116 F4
Oaklea Rd TN12 . . . . .135 F6
Oakleigh Cl Chatham ME5 . .61 F3
Swanley BR8 . . . . .39 E6
Oakleigh Gdns BR6 . . . . . .51 E6
Oakleigh Park Ave BR7 . . . .37 A8
Oakley Cl [7] Newham E6 . . . .1 F7
West Thurrock RM20 . . . . .11 C8
Oakley Ct DA1 . . . . .27 B7
Oakley Dr Orpington BR2 . . .50 E7
Sidcup SE9 . . . . .23 D7
Oakley Lodge SE12 . . . . . .22 A8
Oakley Pk DA5 . . . . .24 C8
Oakley Rd BR2 . . . . .36 E5
Oakmead Meopham DA13 . .58 A8
Tonbridge TN10 . . . . .117 C6
Oakmead Ave BR2 . . . . . . .36 A3
Oakmere Rd SE2 . . . . .7 A8
Oakmont Pl BR6 . . . . .37 D1
Oaks Bsns Village The
ME5 . . . . .62 C1
Oaks Dene ME5 . . . . .61 F1
Oaks Forstal TN18 . . . . . . .186 C5
Oaks Rd TN30 . . . . .183 B8
Oaks The Aylesford ME20 . . .75 E1
Biddenden Green TN27 . . . .142 F2
Swanley BR8 . . . . .39 E7
Woolwich SE18 . . . . .2 C1
Oakum Ct ME4 . . . . .48 B2
Oakway Cl DA5 . . . . .7 E1
Oakways SE9 . . . . .6 B1
Oakwood Ave BR2 . . . . . . .36 B6
Oakwood Cl
Chislehurst BR7 . . . . .23 A2
Dartford DA1 . . . . .27 B7
Oakwood Ct
Maidstone ME16 . . . . .91 D3
Swanley BR8 . . . . .39 C7
Oakwood Dr Bexley DA7 . . . .8 C3
Sevenoaks TN13 . . . . .84 B4
Oakwood Gdns BR6 . . . . . .51 C8
Oakwood Park
Gram Sch ME16 . . . . .91 C3
Oakwood Rd
Maidstone ME16 . . . . .91 D3
Orpington BR6 . . . . .51 C8
Oakwood Rise
Longfield DA3 . . . . .42 E6
Royal Tunbridge Wells TN2 .149 E7
Oasis The [6] BR1 . . . . .36 C7
Oast Cl TN2 . . . . .149 D7
Oast Ct ME18 . . . . .104 F1
Oast Ho The [3] ME8 . . . . . .63 F8
Oast House Way BR5 . . . . . .38 D5
Oast La TN10 . . . . .117 A4
Oast View TN12 . . . . .153 A6
Oast Way DA3 . . . . .42 E3
Oastfield Ct TN15 . . . . .84 C2
Oasts The ME14 . . . . .93 C4
Oastview ME8 . . . . .64 A8
Oatfield Cl TN17 . . . . .169 C5
Oatfield Dr TN17 . . . . . . .169 C5
Oatfield Rd BR6 . . . . .37 F1
Occupation La SE18 . . . . . . .6 B6
Ocelot Ct [6] ME4 . . . . .48 B3
Ockham Dr BR5 . . . . .24 A1
Ockley La TN18 . . . . .179 A3
Ockley Rd TN18 . . . . .179 A2
Octavia Ct ME5 . . . . .62 B3
Octavia Way [12] SE28 . . . . . .3 B6
Odeon Ct [1] E16 . . . . .1 A8
Odeon Par SE9 . . . . .5 E3
Odiham Dr ME16 . . . . .91 C7
Offen's Dr TN12 . . . . .139 E3
Offenham Rd SE9 . . . . .22 F4
Offham Prim Sch ME19 . . . .88 D8
Offham Rd ME19 . . . . .89 A7
Officers' Rd ME4 . . . . .48 B8
Offlcers Terr ME4 . . . . .47 F7
Ogilby St SE18 . . . . .1 F2
Okehampton Cres DA16 . . . .7 C6
Okemore Gdns BR5 . . . . . .38 C5
Old Ashford Rd ME14 . . . .111 E5
Old Bailey The ME17 . . . . .110 E6
Old Barn Cl Gillingham ME7 .62 F6
Kemsing TN15 . . . . .70 A2
Tonbridge TN9 . . . . .132 F8
Old Barn Rd ME19 . . . . . . .74 E2
Old Barn Way DA7 . . . . .8 D4
Old Bexley Bsns Pk DA5 . . .25 B8
Old Bexley
CE Prim Sch DA5 . . . . . . .24 F7
Old Bexley La DA5 . . . . . . .25 E6
Old Carriageway The
Gillingham ME7 . . . . .62 F4
Sevenoaks TN13 . . . . .83 C5

Old Castle Wlk ME8 . . . . . .63 D4
Old Chapel Rd BR8 . . . . . . .39 C2
Old Chatham Rd
Kit's Coty ME20 . . . . .76 D6
Maidstone ME5 . . . . .76 F1
Old Church La ME18 . . . . .103 E4
Old Church Rd
Burham ME1 . . . . .60 C1
Matfield ME7 . . . . .134 D2
Mereworth ME18,TN12 . . .103 D5
Pembury TN2 . . . . .150 D8
Old Clem Sq [12] SE18 . . . . . .6 A8
Old Coach Rd TN15 . . . . . .71 E5
Old Court Ho TN3 . . . . .84 C2
Old Ctyd The BR1 . . . . .36 B8
Old Dartford Rd DA4 . . . . . .40 F3
Old Dover Rd SE3 . . . . .5 B7
Old Downs DA3 . . . . .42 E4
Old Dr ME15 . . . . .106 F6
Old Farm Ave DA15 . . . . . .23 E6
Old Farm Gdns BR8 . . . . . .39 F6
Old Farm Rd E DA15 . . . . .24 A6
Old Farm Rd W DA15 . . . . .23 F6
Old Forge La ME9 . . . . .79 F3
Old Forge Way DA14 . . . . . .24 B4
Old Garden The TN13 . . . . .83 D4
Old Gardens Cl TN2 . . . . . .163 B8
Old Hadlow Rd TN10 . . . .117 F4
Old Ham La ME17 . . . . . . .111 A4
Old Hill Chislehurst BR7 . . . .37 A8
Orpington BR6 . . . . .51 E4
Old Ho The BR7 . . . . .37 D8
Old Homesdale Rd BR2 . . . .36 C5
Old House La ME3 . . . . . . .147 D4
Old House Rd ME9 . . . . . . .64 E4
Old Kent Rd TN12 . . . . . . .136 A6
Old La TN15 . . . . .86 C4
Old Lain ME17 . . . . .110 F6
Old London Rd
Badgers Mount TN14 . . . . .53 A1
Tonbridge TN10 . . . . .117 C3
Wrotham TN15 . . . . .71 F4
Old Loose Hill ME15 . . . . .106 F4
Old Maidstone Rd DA14 . . .24 F1
Old Manor Dr DA12 . . . . . .30 C7
Old Manor Way Bexley DA7 . .8 D5
Chislehurst BR7 . . . . .22 F3
Old Mill Cl DA4 . . . . .40 E1
Old Mill La ME6 . . . . .74 E5
Old Mill Rd Maidstone ME17 93 F1
Woolwich SE18 . . . . .6 D8
Old Oast Bsns Ctr The
ME20 . . . . .76 A1
Old Orch Sandhurst TN18 . .186 B5
TN11 . . . . .115 A3
Old Orch The ME8 . . . . . . .64 A8
Old Orchard La ME19 . . . . .74 D1
Old Otford Rd TN14 . . . . . .69 B1
Old Park Rd SE2 . . . . .3 A1
Old Parsonage Ct ME19 . . .89 C7
Old Pattens La ME1 . . . . . .47 D2
Old Perry St
Chislehurst BR7 . . . . .23 E1
Northfleet DA11 . . . . .29 E6
Old Polhill TN14 . . . . .68 D4
Old Rd Chatham ME4 . . . . .47 F4
Crayford DA1,DA7 . . . . .8 D3
East Peckham TN12 . . . . . .120 A6
Wateringbury ME18 . . . . . .104 C7
Old Rd E DA12 . . . . .30 D7
Old Rd W DA11 . . . . .30 A7
Old Regent Dr TN17 . . . . .181 E3
Old Riding School The
TN3 . . . . .161 B2
Old School Cl ME17 . . . . . .111 D4
Old School Ct
Chattenden ME3 . . . . .33 F4
Egerton TN27 . . . . .127 F1
Old School House The
TN8 . . . . .112 C1
Old School La ME19 . . . . . .73 F4
Old School The
Goudhurst TN17 . . . . .167 E8
Maidstone ME16 . . . . .90 E1
Old Soar Manor* TN15 . . . .87 B1
Old Station Rd TN5 . . . . . .174 E6
Old Tannery Cl TN30 . . . . .182 F7
Old Terry's Lodge Rd
TN15 . . . . .71 A4
Old Timber Top Cotts The
TN13 . . . . .84 C4
Old Tovil Rd ME15 . . . . . . .92 A2
Old Trafford Cl TN16 . . . . . .91 B6
Old Tramyard SE18 . . . . . . .2 E2
Old Tree La TN17 . . . . . . .107 D3
Old Wardsdown TN5 . . . . .177 B3
Old Watling St Cuxton ME2 . .46 B8
Gravesend DA11 . . . . .30 A3
Old Weavers Cotts TN17 . .180 D5
Old Whetsted Rd TN12 . . .120 A2
Old Wlk The TN14 . . . . . . .69 C2
Old Yews The DA3 . . . . . . .43 B6
Oldborough Manor
Com Sch ME15 . . . . .107 B6
Oldbury Cl Oldbury TN15 . . .86 B5
Orpington BR5 . . . . .38 D5
Oldbury Cotts TN15 . . . . . .86 B6
Oldbury La TN15 . . . . .86 B6
Oldchurch Ct [3] ME16 . . . . .91 E3
Oldfield Cl Bromley BR1 . . .36 F5
Gillingham ME8 . . . . .63 D8
Maidstone ME15 . . . . .92 E1
Oldfield Rd Bexley DA7 . . . . .7 E4
Bromley BR1 . . . . .36 F5
Oleander Cl BR6 . . . . .51 D5
Olive Rd DA1 . . . . .26 D7
Oliver Cl Chatham ME4 . . . .48 B2

Oliver Cl continued
West Thurrock RM20 . . . . . .10 F7
Oliver Cres DA4 . . . . .40 F2
Oliver Ct SE18 . . . . .2 C2
Oliver Gdns E6 . . . . .1 E8
Oliver Rd Staplehurst TN12 139 E4
Swanley BR8 . . . . .39 D6
West Thurrock RM20 . . . . .11 A7
Oliver Twist Cl ME1 . . . . . .47 B4
Olivers Cotts ME14 . . . . . . .93 C4
Olivers Mill DA3 . . . . .56 E8
Olivine Cl ME5 . . . . .77 A8
Olliffe Cl ME5 . . . . .61 F2
Olron Cres DA6 . . . . .7 E2
Olven Rd SE18 . . . . .6 C8
Olyffe Ave DA16 . . . . .7 A5
Onslow Cres BR7 . . . . .37 B8
Onslow Dr DA14 . . . . .24 D6
Onslow Rd ME1 . . . . .47 D3
Opal Cl E16 . . . . .1 D7
Opal Gn ME5 . . . . .62 B2
Openshaw Rd SE2 . . . . .3 B2
Orache Dr ME14 . . . . .92 E5
Orange Court La BR6 . . . . .51 A2
Orange Terr ME1 . . . . .47 D5
Orangery La SE9 . . . . .5 F2
Orbit Cl ME5 . . . . .77 A8
Orbital One DA1 . . . . .27 B6
Orchard Ave
Aylesford ME20 . . . . .75 E1
Dartford DA1 . . . . .26 B7
Erith DA17 . . . . .7 F8
Gravesend DA11 . . . . .30 B3
Rochester ME2 . . . . .32 F1
Orchard Bank ME17 . . . . .108 B1
Orchard Bsns Ctr
Maidstone ME16 . . . . .91 C8
Paddock Wood TN12 . . . .136 A8
Royal Tunbridge Wells TN2 .149 D8
Tonbridge TN9 . . . . .117 E1
Orchard Cl Bexley DA7 . . . . .7 E6
Coxheath ME17 . . . . .106 C3
Edenbridge TN8 . . . . .112 B2
Horsmonden TN12 . . . . . .152 F6
Langley Heath ME17 . . . . .108 E4
New Barn DA3 . . . . .43 B7
Royal Tunbridge Wells TN2 .149 D6
Sevenoaks TN14 . . . . .84 C7
Orchard Cotts
Chislehurst BR7 . . . . .23 E2
East Farleigh ME16 . . . . . .106 A8
Orchard Cres TN12 . . . . . .153 A6
Orchard Ct TN17 . . . . .180 D6
Orchard Dr
Edenbridge TN8 . . . . .112 B2
Maidstone ME14 . . . . .92 E4
Meopham Sta DA13 . . . . . .43 F4
Newington ME9 . . . . .65 A5
Tonbridge TN10 . . . . .117 E5
Orchard Glade TN27 . . . . .141 E5
Orchard Gn Bromley BR1 . . .36 C8
Orpington BR6 . . . . .51 E8
Orchard Gr Larkfield ME20 . .75 B2
Orpington BR6 . . . . .37 F1
Royal Tunbridge Wells TN1 .149 A1
Orchard Hill DA1 . . . . .8 E2
Orchard House ME1 . . . . . .47 D3
Orchard Ind Est ME15 . . . .107 F3
Orchard Pl
[2] Maidstone ME16 . . . . . .91 E3
St Paul's Cray BR5 . . . . . . .38 C6
Sundridge TN14 . . . . .82 D3
Orchard Rd Bexley DA16 . . . .7 B4
Bromley BR1 . . . . .36 C8
East Peckham TN12 . . . . . .120 A6
Erith DA17 . . . . .4 A2
Northfleet DA11 . . . . .29 C6
Orpington BR6 . . . . .51 B5
Otford TN14 . . . . .68 F3
Pratt's Bottom BR6 . . . . . .52 C1
Sevenoaks TN13 . . . . .83 E5
Sidcup DA14 . . . . .23 E4
Swanscombe DA10 . . . . . .11 E2
Tenterden TN30 . . . . .173 A3
Orchard Rise E DA15 . . . . . .6 F2
Orchard Rise W DA15 . . . . . .6 F2
Orchard St Dartford DA1 . . . .9 E1
Gillingham ME8 . . . . .63 E8
Maidstone ME15 . . . . .92 A3
Orchard Terr DA9 . . . . .10 E2
Orchard The
Maidstone ME14 . . . . .93 B4
Sevenoaks TN13 . . . . .83 E6
Swanley BR8 . . . . .39 D7
Orchard View TN30 . . . . . .183 C8
Orchard Villas
Chainhurst TN12 . . . . .122 A4
Chislehurst BR7 . . . . .23 E2
[1] Rochester ME4 . . . . . . .47 F3
Sidcup DA14 . . . . .24 A4
Orchard Way Dartford DA2 .26 D5
Horsmonden TN12 . . . . . .153 A6
Kemsing TN15 . . . . .70 A2
Snodland ME6 . . . . .74 F7
Turnden TN17 . . . . .169 B4
Orchardlea DA13 . . . . .41 A8
Orchards Sh Ctr The DA1 . .9 E1
Orchid Cl [1] Newham E6 . . . .1 E8
Rochester ME2 . . . . .46 C6
Orchidhurst TN2 . . . . .149 D7
Ordnance Rd
Gravesend DA12 . . . . .13 C1
Woolwich SE18 . . . . .2 B1
Ordnance St ME4 . . . . .47 E3
Ordnance Terr [4] ME4 . . . . .47 E4
Oregon Sq BR6 . . . . .37 D1
Orford Ct [7] DA2 . . . . .10 B1

Oriental Rd E16 . . . . .1 D5
Oriole Way Larkfield ME20 . .74 F2
Woolwich SE28 . . . . .3 B6
Orion Rd ME1 . . . . .61 C7
Orissa Rd SE18 . . . . .2 E1
Orlestone Gdns BR6 . . . . . .52 E5
Orlick Rd DA12 . . . . .31 B7
Ormesby Cl SE28 . . . . .3 D6
Ormiston Rd SE10 . . . . .1 A1
Ormonde Ave BR6 . . . . . . .51 C8
Ormsby Gn ME8 . . . . .63 E3
Ormsby Point [8] SE18 . . . . . .2 B2
Orpines The ME18 . . . . . . .104 F7
Orpington By-Pass TN14 . .53 A2
Orpington Coll of
Further Education BR6 . . .38 A1
Orpington Hospl BR6 . . . . .51 F6
Orpington Rd BR7 . . . . . . .37 E6
Orpington Sta BR6 . . . . . . .51 E8
Orpington Trad Est BR5 . . .38 C5
Orwell Cl Lunsford ME20 . . .74 F3
Rainham RM9 . . . . .4 D8
Orwell Spike ME19 . . . . . . .89 A5
Osberton Rd DA2 . . . . .5 A2
Osborne Rd Erith DA17 . . . .7 F8
Gillingham ME7 . . . . .48 C5
Osbourne Rd DA2 . . . . .10 B1
Osgood Ave BR6 . . . . .51 F5
Osgood Gdns [1] BR6 . . . . . .51 F5
Osmers Hill TN5 . . . . .174 F7
Osmunda Ct TN2 . . . . .149 C4
Osney Ho [4] SE2 . . . . .3 D4
Osney Way DA12 . . . . .30 F6
Osprey Ave ME5 . . . . .48 E2
Osprey Cl E6 . . . . .1 E8
Osprey Wlk ME20 . . . . .74 F1
Ospringe Ct SE9 . . . . .6 D1
Ospringe Pl TN2 . . . . .149 F6
Osterberg Rd DA1 . . . . .9 F3
Osterley Ct BR5 . . . . .38 A8
Ostlers Ct [2] ME6 . . . . .75 A8
Otford Cl Bromley BR1 . . . .37 A6
Sidcup DA5 . . . . .8 B1
Otford Court (St
Michael's Sch) TN14 . . . .69 E4
Otford La TN14 . . . . .68 B6
Otford Prim Sch TN14 . . . .69 B3
Otford Rd TN14 . . . . .84 B7
Otford Sta TN14 . . . . .69 C3
Otham La ME15 . . . . .93 C2
Otham St Maidstone ME15 . .93 C2
Otham ME15 . . . . .108 B7
Otley Rd E16 . . . . .1 F7
Otlinge Rd BR5 . . . . .38 D5
Ottawa Rd RM18 . . . . .13 A5
Otterbourne Pl ME15 . . . . .92 E1
Otterden Cl BR6 . . . . .51 E6
Otterham Quay La ME8 . . .64 B8
Otteridge Rd ME14 . . . . . . .93 A3
Otters Cl BR5 . . . . .38 B8
Ottershaw House BR5 . . . . .38 B8
Otway St Chatham ME4 . . . .48 A3
Gillingham ME7 . . . . .48 D6
Otway Terr [1] ME4 . . . . . . .48 A3
Our Lady of Grace
RC Jun Mix Sch SE7 . . . . .5 B8
Our Lady of Hartley RC
Prim Sch DA3 . . . . .42 F4
Our Lady of the Rosary RC
Prim Sch DA15 . . . . .6 E1
Our Lady's RC
Prim Sch 9 D1
Oval The New Barn DA3 . . .43 C6
Sidcup DA14 . . . . .24 A8
Ovenden Rd
Sevenoaks TN14 . . . . .82 F6
Sundridge TN14 . . . . .82 F6
Over Minnis DA3 . . . . .56 F7
Overcliffe DA11 . . . . .13 A1
Overcourt Cl DA15 . . . . .7 B1
Overdale TN14 . . . . .99 B2
Overmead Eltham DA15 . . .23 D8
Swanley BR8 . . . . .39 E4
Overton Rd DA2 . . . . .3 D3
Overy Liberty DA1 . . . . . . .26 E8
Overy St DA1 . . . . .9 E1
Owen Cl
East Malling ME19 . . . . . . .89 F8
Woolwich SE28 . . . . .3 C5
Owenite St SE2 . . . . .3 B2
Owens Way ME7 . . . . .49 A6
Owl House Gdns* TN3 . . . .165 E7
Owletts* DA12 . . . . .44 F6
Owletts ME15 . . . . .107 D8
Ox La TN30 . . . . .173 B2
Ox Lea TN3 . . . . .148 A3
Oxenden Wood Rd BR6 . . .52 C4
Oxenhill Rd TN15 . . . . .69 C2
Oxenhoath Rd TN11 . . . . .102 D4
Oxfield TN8 . . . . .112 D3
Oxford Cl DA12 . . . . .30 F6
Oxford Ct DA14 . . . . .23 F4
Oxford Mews DA5 . . . . . . .25 A7
Oxford Rd Gillingham ME7 . .48 D3
Maidstone ME15 . . . . .107 D8
Sidcup DA14 . . . . .24 B3
Oxford St ME6 . . . . .75 A8
Oxhawth Cres BR2 . . . . . . .37 B3
Oxleas E6 . . . . .2 B7
Oxleas Cl DA16 . . . . .6 D5
Oxleas Wood
Nature Reserve* SE18 . . . .6 C4
Oxley Shaw La TN11 . . . . . .74 E2
Oyster Catchers Cl E16 . . . .1 B7
Ozolins Way E16 . . . . .1 A7

P

Pacific Cl DA10 . . . . .11 E2
Pacific Rd E16 . . . . .1 A7
Packer Pl ME5 . . . . .62 A8
Packham Cl BR6 . . . . .52 C7
Packham Rd DA11 . . . . .29 F5
Packhorse Rd TN3 . . . . .83 C4
Packmores Rd SE9 . . . . .6 E2
Pad's Hill ME15 . . . . .92 A4
Paddlesworth Rd ME6 . . . . .59 D1
Paddock Cl
  Fordcombe TN3 . . . . .147 B5
  Greenwich SE3 . . . . .5 A5
  Orpington BR6 . . . . .51 B6
  Platt TN15 . . . . .87 C6
  Sutton at Hone DA4 . . . . . .41 C8
Paddock Rd DA6 . . . . .7 E3
Paddock The Chatham ME4 .47 F4
  Hadlow TN11 . . . . .102 E1
  Pembury TN2 . . . . .150 C6
  Vigo Village DA13 . . . . . . .72 F7
  Westerham TN16 . . . . .81 C1
Paddock Way BR7 . . . . .23 D1
Paddock Wood
  Prim Sch TN12 . . . . .136 A6
Paddock Wood Sta TN12 136 A7
Paddocks Cl BR5 . . . . .52 D8
Paddocks The
  Cowden TN8 . . . . .145 B7
  Gillingham ME7 . . . . .63 A5
  Sevenoaks TN13 . . . . .84 D3
Padsole La ME15 . . . . .92 A4
Padstow Manor 1 ME7 . . .48 C6
Page Cl DA2 . . . . .28 C5
Page Cres DA8 . . . . .8 F7
Page Heath La BR1 . . . . . . .36 D6
Page Heath Villas BR1 . . . . .36 D6
Pageant Cl RM18 . . . . .13 C6
Pagehurst Rd TN12 . . . . . .139 B3
Paget Gdns BR7 . . . . .37 B8
Paget Rise SE18 . . . . .6 A7
Paget Row ME7 . . . . .48 C5
Paget St ME7 . . . . .48 C5
Paget Terr SE18 . . . . .6 B7
Pagitt St ME4 . . . . .47 E3
Paiges Farm Cl TN14 . . . . . .99 C2
Painters Ash La DA11 . . . . .29 D5
Painters Ash
  Prim Sch DA11 . . . . .29 D5
Palace Ave ME15 . . . . .92 A4
Palace Ct 6 Bromley BR1 . .36 B8
  Chatham ME5 . . . . .48 D2
  Eltham SE9 . . . . .5 F1
Palace Gr BR1 . . . . .36 B8
Palace Ind Est ME15 . . . . . .107 F4
Palace Rd Bromley BR1 . . . . .36 B8
  Hill Park TN16 . . . . .81 A6
Palace View Bromley BR1 . .36 B6
  Lewisham SE12 . . . . .22 A6
Palace Wood
  Inf Sch ME16 . . . . .91 C6
Palace Wood
  Jun Sch ME16 . . . . .91 C6
Palewell Cl BR5 . . . . .38 B7
Pallant Way BR6 . . . . .51 A7
Pallet Way SE18 . . . . .5 E6
Palm Ave DA14 . . . . .24 D2
Palmar Cres DA7 . . . . .8 A5
Palmar Rd Bexley DA7 . . . . . .8 A5
  Maidstone ME16 . . . . .91 D6
Palmarsh Cl BR5 . . . . .38 D5
Palmeira Rd DA7 . . . . .7 D4
Palmer Ave DA12 . . . . .30 D4
Palmers Brook TN11 . . . . .102 F2
Palmers Green La TN12 .136 D1
Palmers Orch TN14 . . . . . . .68 F8
Palmerston Cres SE18 . . . . . .6 C8
Palmerston Rd
  Chatham ME4 . . . . .47 F1
  Grays RM20 . . . . .11 D8
  Orpington BR6 . . . . .51 C5
Pamela Ct ME7 . . . . .48 D5
Panbro House SE18 . . . . .5 F6
Panfield Rd SE28 . . . . .3 A3
Pankhurst Ave E16 . . . . .1 B5
Pankhurst Ho SE18 . . . . .6 A7
Pankhurst Rd ME3 . . . . .34 D6
Pannell Rd ME3 . . . . .21 A6
Panter's BR8 . . . . .25 F1
Pantiles The Bromley BR1 . .36 E6
  Erith DA7 . . . . .7 F7
17 Royal Tunbridge
  Wells TN2* 149 A2
Panton Cl ME5 . . . . .62 C4
Pantyles The TN14 . . . . . . .98 B5
Papillons Wlk SE3 . . . . .5 A4
Papion Gr ME5 . . . . .61 E2
Papyrus Rd ME20 . . . . .75 B4
Parade The Crayford DA1 . . . .8 F2
  Gravesend DA12 . . . . .30 D6
  Kemsing TN15 . . . . .69 D2
  Meopham DA13 . . . . .44 A2
  Rochester ME2 . . . . .46 E8
  Staplehurst TN12 . . . . . .139 F3
  Swanscombe DA10 . . . . . .11 F2
Paradise Cotts ME9 . . . . . . .64 E5
Paradise Pl 14 SE18 . . . . .1 E2
Paragon Cl E16 . . . . .1 A7
Paragon The SE3 . . . . .5 A5
Parbrook Rd ME3 . . . . .18 B2
Parham Rd ME4 . . . . .47 F2
Parish CE Prim Sch BR1 . .22 A1
Parish Gate Dr DA15 . . . . . . .6 E1

Parish Wharf 5 SE18 . . . . . . .1 E2
Park App DA16 . . . . .7 B3
Park Ave Bromley BR1 . . . . .22 A2
  Edenbridge TN8 . . . . . . .112 B2
  Gillingham ME7 . . . . .48 D3
  Gravesend DA12 . . . . .30 C7
  Maidstone, Linton ME17 . .106 C2
  Maidstone, Penenden
    Heath ME14 . . . . .92 B6
  Northfleet DA11 . . . . .29 C7
  Orpington,Goddington BR6 .32 C6
  Orpington,Locksbottom BR6 .51 A8
  Tonbridge TN11 . . . . .116 F5
  West Thurrock RM20 . . . . .11 B8
Park Barn Rd ME17 . . . . . .109 C5
Park Corner Rd DA13 . . . . .28 F4
Park Cotts 8 TN18 . . . . . . .179 A2
Park Cres Chatham ME4 . . . .61 F8
  Erith DA8 . . . . .8 D8
Park Crescent Rd DA8 . . . . .8 D8
Park Dr Longfield DA3 . . . . . .42 E6
  Woolwich SE7 . . . . .5 E8
Park Farm Houses ME7 . . .90 B8
Park Farm Rd Bromley BR1 36 D8
  Ryarsh ME19 . . . . .73 F6
Park Gdns DA8 . . . . .4 D2
Park Gr Bexley DA7 . . . . .8 C3
  Bromley BR1 . . . . .36 B8
Park Hill Bromley BR1 . . . . .36 F5
  Meopham DA13 . . . . .43 F5
Park Hill Rd ME14 . . . . .69 E2
  Sevenoaks TN13 . . . . .84 C5
Park Ho Maidstone ME14 . . .92 B6
  Sidcup DA14 . . . . .24 A3
Park House Gdns TN4 . . . .133 A2
Park La
  Gill's Green TN17,TN18 . . .178 D7
  Godden Green TN15 . . . . . .85 A4
  Kemsing TN15 . . . . .70 A1
  Maidstone, Cock
    Stone ME17 . . . . .107 D2
  Maidstone, Ringlestone ME14 91 F7
  Sevenoaks TN13 . . . . .84 C3
  Swanley Village BR8 . . . . . .40 C1
Park Manor ME7 . . . . .48 B5
Park Mead DA15 . . . . .7 B1
Park Mews ME7 . . . . .23 B2
Park Pl 9 Bromley BR1 . . . .36 B8
  Gravesend DA12 . . . . .30 C8
  Hever TN8 . . . . .129 D4
  Sevenoaks TN13 . . . . .83 D4
Park Rd Addington ME19 . . .73 C3
  Bromley BR1 . . . . .36 B8
  Chislehurst BR7 . . . . .23 B2
  Dartford DA1 . . . . .27 A8
  Dunk's Green TN11 . . . . .102 C5
  Gravesend DA11 . . . . .30 B7
  Leybourne ME19 . . . . .74 D3
  Marden Thorn TN12 . . . . .139 A4
  Mereworth ME18 . . . . . . .103 F5
  Orpington BR5 . . . . .38 C4
  Royal Tunbridge Wells TN4 .149 B5
  Royal Tunbridge
    Wells,Southborough TN4 .133 A2
  Swanley BR8 . . . . .39 F5
  Swanscombe DA10 . . . . . .11 E1
Park Road Ind Est BR8 . . . .39 F6
Park St TN2 . . . . .149 C3
Park Terr Sundridge TN14 . . .82 D3
  Swanscombe DA9 . . . . . . .11 B3
Park The DA14 . . . . .24 A3
Park View
  Culverstone Green TN15 . . .57 C2
  Sevenoaks TN13 . . . . .84 C3
Park View Cl TN8 . . . . .112 B2
Park View Ct
  Lewisham SE12 . . . . .22 C5
  Maidstone ME15 . . . . .91 D6
Park View Rd Bexley DA16 . . .7 C4
  Eltham SE9 . . . . .23 B6
Park View Terr 2 TN30 . . .183 A7
Park Villas TN11 . . . . .102 F1
Park Way Coxheath ME17 .106 D3
  Dartford DA5 . . . . .25 E5
  Maidstone ME15 . . . . .92 B1
Park Way Prim Sch ME15 .92 B1
Park Wood Gn ME8 . . . . . .63 D5
Park Wood La TN12 . . . . . .140 C1
Park Wood Par ME15 . . . . .107 F5
Park Wood Trad Est
  ME15 . . . . .107 F4
Parkdale Rd SE18 . . . . .2 E1
Parker Ave RM18 . . . . .13 C6
Parker Cl Gillingham ME8 . . .63 E5
  Newham E16 . . . . .1 E5
Parker Ho 4 SE18 . . . . .2 B1
Parker Rd RM17 . . . . .11 F8
Parker St E16 . . . . .1 F5
Parker's Cnr ME3 . . . . .19 C8
Parkfield Hartley DA3 . . . . . .42 E5
  Sevenoaks TN15 . . . . .84 F4
Parkfield Rd ME8 . . . . .49 F1
Parkfield Way BR2 . . . . .36 F4
Parkfields ME2 . . . . .46 C7
Parkgate Cotts BR6 . . . . . . .53 C6
Parkgate Rd BR6 . . . . .53 C6
Parkhill Rd
  Sidcup, Longlands DA15 . . .23 E5
  Sidcup, Old Bexley DA15 . . .7 E1
Parkhurst Gdns 2 DA5 . . .25 A8
Parkhurst Rd DA5 . . . . .25 A8
Parkland Ct TN13 . . . . .99 D6
Parklands TN4 . . . . .148 B3
Parkside Cliffe Woods ME3 . .33 B7
  Halstead TN14 . . . . .67 F6
  Sidcup DA14 . . . . .24 B6
Parkside Ave Bromley BR1 . .36 F5
  Crayford DA1,DA7 . . . . .8 E5

Parkside Ave continued
  Tilbury RM18 . . . . .13 B5
Parkside Cross DA7 . . . . .8 E5
Parkside Ct TN30 . . . . .182 F7
Parkside Lodge DA17 . . . . . .4 C1
Parkside Par DA8 . . . . .8 F5
Parkside Rd DA17 . . . . .4 C2
Parkview TN2 . . . . .149 D4
Parkview St DA11 . . . . .30 A6
Parkway Erith DA18 . . . . .3 E3
  Tonbridge TN11 . . . . .117 D5
Parkway Prim Sch DA18 . . .3 E3
Parkwood Cl TN2 . . . . .149 C6
Parkwood Rd BR8 . . . . .40 B6
Parkwood Inf Sch ME8 . . . .63 E5
Parkwood Jun Sch ME8 . . .63 E5
Parkwood Rd DA5 . . . . .24 C8
Paroma Rd DA7 . . . . .4 A3
Parr Ave ME7 . . . . .48 D6
Parrock Ave DA12 . . . . .30 C7
Parrock Rd DA12 . . . . .30 C7
Parrock St DA12 . . . . .30 B8
Parrock The DA12 . . . . .30 C7
Parrs Head Mews ME1 . . . .47 C6
Parry Ave E6 . . . . .1 F7
Parry Pl SE18 . . . . .2 B2
Parson's Croft TN8 . . . . . .129 C5
Parsonage Cl TN4 . . . . . . .148 B5
Parsonage La
  Cold Harbour ME9 . . . . . . .65 F8
  Lamberhurst TN3 . . . . . . .166 B6
  Rochester ME2 . . . . .47 C8
  Sidcup DA14 . . . . .24 F4
  Sutton at Hone DA4 . . . . . .27 B2
Parsonage
  Manor Way DA8,DA17 . . . .8 A8
Parsonage Rd
  Royal Tunbridge Wells TN4 .148 B5
  West Thurrock RM20 . . . . .11 C8
Parsons La DA2 . . . . .26 B5
  Stansted TN15 . . . . .56 E1
Partridge Ave ME20 . . . . . .74 F3
Partridge Cl 1 E16 . . . . .1 D8
Partridge Dr Orpington BR6 51 C7
  St Mary's Island ME4 . . . . .34 B1
Partridge Gn SE9 . . . . .23 A5
Partridge Rd DA14 . . . . . . .23 E4
Partridge Sq 3 E6 . . . . .1 E8
Pasley Rd ME4,ME7 . . . . . .48 A7
Pasley Rd E ME7 . . . . .48 B7
Pasley Rd N ME4 . . . . .48 B7
Pasley Rd W ME7 . . . . .48 A7
Passey Pl SE9 . . . . .5 F1
Passfield Ho SE18 . . . . .5 E6
Passfield Path 18 SE28 . . . . .3 B6
Paston Cres SE12 . . . . .22 B8
Patagonia Ho TN2 . . . . . . .149 C3
Patch The TN15 . . . . .83 E5
Patience Cotts TN14 . . . . . .99 B2
Patricia Ct Bexley SE2 . . . . . .7 B7
  Chislehurst BR7 . . . . .37 D8
Patrixbourne Ave ME8 . . . .49 C2
Pattenden Gdns TN12 . . . .120 A7
Pattenden La TN12 . . . . . .138 C7
Pattens Gdns ME1 . . . . .47 E2
Pattens La ME1 . . . . .47 E1
Pattens Pl ME1 . . . . .47 D2
Patterdale Rd DA2 . . . . .27 D7
Patterson Ct DA1 . . . . .10 A2
Pattinson Point 14 E16 . . . . .1 A8
Pattison Wlk SE18 . . . . .2 C1
Paulinus Cl BR5 . . . . .38 C6
Pavement The TN30 . . . . . .173 B3
Pavilion Gdns TN13 . . . . . . .84 C3
Pavilion L Ctr The BR1 . . . .36 A7
Pavilion La ME14 . . . . .104 A8
Pavilion The 5 TN9 . . . . . .117 B1
Paxton Cl SE12 . . . . .22 C5
Paxton Rd BR1 . . . . .22 A1
Payne's La ME15 . . . . .107 B7
Paynes Cotts TN13 . . . . . . .68 D1
Peace Cotts ME15 . . . . . . .121 D7
Peace St SE18 . . . . .6 A8
Peach Croft DA11 . . . . .29 E4
Peach Hall TN10 . . . . .117 C6
Peacock Mews 7 ME16 . . .91 E4
Peacock Rise ME5 . . . . .62 A4
Peacock St DA12 . . . . .30 C8
Peal Cl ME3 . . . . .34 E5
Pear Tree Ave ME20 . . . . . .75 D1
Pear Tree Cl Bexley DA8 . . . .8 D6
  Cranbrook TN17 . . . . . . .169 D3
  Swanley BR8 . . . . .39 D7
Pear Tree La
  Gillingham ME7 . . . . .62 E7
  Maidstone ME15 . . . . . . .107 B6
Pear Tree Pl ME3 . . . . .32 B3
Pear Tree Row ME7 . . . . . .108 B5
Pear Tree Wlk ME9 . . . . . . .65 A5
Peareswood Rd DA8 . . . . . . .8 F6
Pearl Cl E6 . . . . .2 A8
Pearse Pl TN3 . . . . .166 B5
Pearson Way DA1 . . . . .26 F6
Pearson's Green Rd
  TN12 . . . . .136 F3
Pearson's Green Rd
  TN12 . . . . .136 D5
Peartree Cotts ME8 . . . . . . .64 B8
Peartree La DA2,ME3 . . . . .32 A2
Peartree Way SE10 . . . . .1 A2
Pease Hill TN15 . . . . .56 F4
Peasley La TN17 . . . . .167 D6
Peat Way ME3 . . . . .20 E6
Peatfield Cl DA15 . . . . .23 E5
Peckham Cl ME2 . . . . .47 C8
Peckham Ct TN12 . . . . .119 F8
Peckham House 6 BR5 . . . .38 D1
Peckham Hurst Rd TN11 .102 F2

Peel Rd BR6 . . . . .51 C5
Peel St ME14 . . . . .92 A6
Peel Yates Ho 12 SE18 . . . . .1 E2
Peens La ME17 . . . . .123 C7
Pegasus Ct DA12 . . . . .30 C5
Peggoty Cl ME3 . . . . .32 B3
Pegley Gdns SE12 . . . . . . .22 A6
Pegwell St SE18 . . . . .6 E7
Pelham Cotts DA5 . . . . .25 B7
Pelham Prim Sch DA7 . . . . .8 A4
Pelham Rd Bexley DA7 . . . . .8 A4
  Gravesend DA11 . . . . .30 A8
Pelham St DA11 . . . . .29 F7
Pelham Terr DA11 . . . . .29 F8
Pelican Cl ME2 . . . . .46 C6
Pelican Ct ME18 . . . . .104 F7
Pell Cl TN5 . . . . .175 A6
Pellipar Gdns SE18 . . . . .1 F1
Pellipar Rd SE18 . . . . .1 F1
Pells La TN15 . . . . .71 A7
Pemberton Gdns BR8 . . . . .39 E7
Pemberton Sq 4 ME2 . . . .47 C8
Pemble Cl TN12 . . . . .135 A7
Pembroke ME4 . . . . .48 B8
Pembroke Cl DA10 . . . . .4 D2
Pembroke Ct ME4 . . . . .48 A4
Pembroke Gdns ME8 . . . . . .63 E4
Pembroke Par DA8 . . . . .4 C1
Pembroke Pl DA4 . . . . .41 A5
Pembroke Rd Bromley BR1 .36 D7
  Coxheath ME17 . . . . .106 C3
  Erith DA8 . . . . .4 D2
  Newham E6 . . . . .1 F8
  Sevenoaks TN13 . . . . .84 B2
  Tonbridge TN9 . . . . .117 A1
Pembroke Rise ME4 . . . . . .48 A7
Pembury Cl TN2 . . . . .150 D7
Pembury Cres DA14 . . . . . .24 E6
Pembury Cty Prim Sch
  TN2 . . . . .150 D8
Pembury Gdns ME16 . . . . . .91 D3
Pembury Gr TN2 . . . . .133 C8
Pembury Grange TN2 . . . .150 A6
Pembury Hall Rd
  TN11,TN2 . . . . .134 C3
Pembury Hospl TN2 . . . . .150 B7
Pembury Rd Erith DA7 . . . . .7 E8
  Pembury TN11 . . . . .134 A2
  Royal Tunbridge Wells TN2 .149 E4
  Tonbridge TN11,TN9 . . . .133 D7
Pembury Vineyard* TN2 .134 F1
Pembury
  Walks TN11,TN2 . . . . . . .134 C2
Pembury Way ME8 . . . . . . .49 E2
Pen Way TN10 . . . . .117 E5
Pencroft Dr DA1 . . . . .26 C8
Penda Rd DA8 . . . . .8 B7
Pendant Ct BR6 . . . . .52 A5
Pendennis Rd
  Orpington BR6 . . . . .52 C8
  Sevenoaks TN13 . . . . .84 B4
Penderel Mews TN30 . . . .183 B8
Pendlebury Ho SE18 . . . . . . .5 E6
Pendragon Rd BR1,SE12 . .22 A5
Pendragon Sec Sch BR1 . .22 A5
Pendrell St SE18 . . . . .6 D8
Pendrill Pl TN5 . . . . .174 F5
Penenden DA3 . . . . .56 F8
Penenden Ct ME14 . . . . . . .92 B7
Penenden Heath Rd ME14 92 C7
Penenden St ME14 . . . . . . .92 A6
Penfold Cl Chatham ME5 . . .62 B7
  Maidstone ME15 . . . . . . .107 E5
Penfold Hill ME17 . . . . . . .109 B8
Penfold House 14 SE18 . . . .6 B8
Penfold La DA7 . . . . .24 D7
Penfold Way ME15 . . . . . .106 F6
Penfolds Cl TN10 . . . . .117 C5
Penford Gdns SE9 . . . . .5 D4
Pengarth Rd DA5 . . . . .7 D1
Penguin Cl ME2 . . . . .46 D6
Penhale Cl BR6 . . . . .52 A6
Penhall Rd SE7 . . . . .1 D2
Penhill Rd DA5 . . . . .24 C8
Penhurst Cl ME14 . . . . .92 F5
Penlee Cl TN8 . . . . .112 C2
Penmon Rd SE2 . . . . .3 A3
Penn Gdns BR7 . . . . .37 B7
Penn La DA5 . . . . .7 E1
Penn Yd TN2 . . . . .150 C6
Pennant Rd ME1 . . . . .61 C7
Penney Cl DA1 . . . . .26 D8
Pennine Way Erith DA7 . . . .8 E6
  Maidstone ME15 . . . . .93 A1
  Northfleet DA11 . . . . .29 E5
Pennine Wlk TN2 . . . . . . .149 D5
Pennington Manor 1
  TN4 . . . . .132 F2
Pennington Pl TN4 . . . . . .133 B1
Pennington Rd TN4 . . . . . .133 A2
Pennington Way SE12 . . . . .22 B6
Penny Cress Gdns ME16 . .91 C3
Pennyfields TN17 . . . . .169 D4
Pennypool La ME15 . . . . . . .90 F5
Penryn Manor 4 ME7 . . . .48 C6
Penshurst Ave DA15 . . . . . . .7 A1
Penshurst
  CE Prim Sch TN11 . . . . .131 A4
Penshurst Cl
  Gillingham ME8 . . . . .49 E2
  New Barn DA3 . . . . .43 D7
  West Kingsdown TN15 . . . .55 E4
Penshurst
  Enterprise Ctr TN11 . . . .131 C4
  Penshurst Place* TN11 . .131 B4
Penshurst Rd Bexley DA7 . . .7 F6
  Penshurst TN3,TN11 . . . .131 A5

Penshurst Rd continued
  Poundsbridge TN11, TN3 . .147 E8
Penshurst Sta TN11 . . . . . .114 F1
Penshurst Vinyard * TN11130 F5
Penshurst Way BR5 . . . . . . .38 C5
Penstocks The ME15 . . . . . .91 D2
Pensular Park Rd SE7 . . . . . .1 A2
Penton Ho 3 SE2 . . . . .3 D4
Pentstemon Dr DA10 . . . . .11 E2
Penventon Ct 8 RM18 . . . .13 A5
Pepingstraw Cl ME19 . . . . .88 D7
Pepper Cl E6 . . . . .1 F8
Pepper Hill DA11 . . . . .29 C5
Pepper Hill La DA11 . . . . . .29 C5
Pepy's Way ME2 . . . . .46 F8
Pepys Cl 4 Dartford DA1 . . .10 A3
  Northfleet DA11 . . . . .29 D5
  Tilbury RM18 . . . . .13 C6
Pepys Cres E16 . . . . .1 A5
Pepys Rise BR6 . . . . .37 F1
Perch La TN3 . . . . .151 D1
Percival Rd BR6 . . . . .51 B8
Percy Rd DA7 . . . . .7 E5
Percy St 8 RM17 . . . . .12 C8
Percy Terr TN4 . . . . .149 A6
Peregrine Ct DA16 . . . . .6 F6
Peregrine Dr ME19 . . . . . . .89 A2
Peridot St E6 . . . . .1 E8
Perie Row 9 ME7 . . . . .48 A6
Perimeter Rd ME20 . . . . . . .75 C3
Periton Rd SE9 . . . . .5 D3
Perkins Cl DA9 . . . . .10 F2
Perpins Rd SE9 . . . . .6 E1
Perran Cl DA3 . . . . .42 F5
Perry Gr DA1 . . . . .10 A3
Perry Hall Cl BR6 . . . . .38 A2
Perry Hall Prim Sch BR6 . .37 F3
Perry Hall Rd BR6 . . . . .38 A2
Perry Hill ME3 . . . . .16 C1
Perry Ho DA14 . . . . .24 A3
Perry St Chatham ME4 . . . . .47 E3
  Chislehurst BR7 . . . . .23 E2
  Crayford DA1 . . . . .8 E4
  Maidstone ME14 . . . . .91 F6
  Northfleet DA11 . . . . .29 F7
Perry Street Gdns BR7 . . . .23 E2
Perryfield St ME14 . . . . .91 F6
Perrys La BR6,TN14 . . . . . .67 C6
Perth House 4 RM18 . . . . .13 A5
Pescot Ave DA3 . . . . .43 B6
Pested Bars Rd ME17 . . . .107 D5
Peter St 5 DA12 . . . . .30 B8
Peterborough Gdns ME2 . .46 C6
Peters Cl DA16 . . . . .6 E5
Petersfield TN2 . . . . .150 E7
Petersham Dr BR5 . . . . .38 A6
Petersham Gdns BR5 . . . . .37 F7
Peterstone Rd SE2 . . . . .3 B1
Petham Court Cotts BR8 . .39 F4
Petham Gn ME8 . . . . .49 C2
Petlands ME17 . . . . .107 D5
Petrie House 3 SE18 . . . . . .6 A8
Pett Lane ME9 . . . . .80 B7
Pett St SE18 . . . . .1 E2
Petten Cl BR5 . . . . .38 D1
Petten Gr BR5 . . . . .38 D1
Petteridge La TN12 . . . . . .151 F7
Pettits Row TN12 . . . . .137 D8
Pettman Cres SE28,SE18 . . .2 D3
Petts Wood Rd BR5 . . . . . . .37 D4
Petts Wood Sta BR5 . . . . . .37 C4
Petworth Rd DA6 . . . . .8 A2
Peverel E6 . . . . .2 A7
Peverel Dr ME14 . . . . .93 A5
Peverel Gn ME8 . . . . .63 D4
Peverill Ct 15 DA2 . . . . . . .10 B1
Pheasant Cl E16 . . . . .1 B7
Pheasant La ME15 . . . . . . .107 B8
Pheasant Rd ME4 . . . . .48 C2
Phelps Cl TN15 . . . . .55 E4
Philimore Cl SE18 . . . . .2 E1
Philipot Almshouse SE9 . . . .5 F1
Philipot Path SE9 . . . . .5 F1
Philippa Gdns SE9 . . . . .5 D2
Phillip Ave BR8 . . . . .39 D5
Phillips Cl DA1 . . . . .9 B1
Phillips Ct ME8 . . . . .49 B2
Philpots La TN11 . . . . .115 E6
Philpott's Cross TN18 . . . .178 E2
Phineas Pett Rd SE9 . . . . . . .5 E4
Phipps Ho 1 SE7 . . . . .1 B1
Phoenix Cotts ME18 . . . . .104 D6
Phoenix Dr Orpington BR2 . .50 D7
  Wateringbury ME18 . . . . .104 E7
Phoenix Ind Est ME2 . . . . .47 D7
Phoenix Pk ME15 . . . . .107 F4
Phoenix Pl DA1 . . . . .26 D8
Phoenix Rd ME5 . . . . .62 B2
Phoenix Yard Cotts ME18 . .89 F1
Picardy Manorway DA17 . . .4 B3
Picardy Rd DA17 . . . . .4 A2
Picardy St DA17 . . . . .4 A3
Piccadilly The 4 ME5 . . . . .48 B3
Pickering Ct 20 DA2 . . . . . .10 B1
Pickering Ho 4 SE18 . . . . . .2 A2
Pickering St ME15 . . . . . . .107 B6
Pickford Cl DA7 . . . . .7 E5
Pickford La DA7 . . . . .7 E5
Pickford Rd DA7 . . . . .7 E4
Pickforde La TN5 . . . . .176 D1
Pickhill Oast TN30 . . . . . . .183 B4
Pickhurst La ME2 . . . . .36 A1
Pickle's Way ME3 . . . . .16 A6
Pickmoss La TN14 . . . . .69 A3
Pickwick Cres ME1 . . . . . . .47 C3
Pickwick Ct SE9 . . . . .22 F7
Pickwick Gdns DA11 . . . . . .29 D5
Pickwick House DA11 . . . . .29 D5

Pickwick Way BR7 . . . . . . .23 C2
Piedmont Rd SE18 . . . . .2 D1
Pier Approach Rd ME7 . .48 D7
Pier Par 3 E16 . . . . .2 A5
Pier Pl ME7 . . . . .34 A3
Pier Rd Erith DA8 . . . . .8 F8
Gillingham ME7 . . . . .48 E7
Newham E16 . . . . .2 A4
Northfleet DA11 . . . . .12 F1
Swanscombe DA9 . . . . . . .11 B3
Pier Rd Ind Est ME7 . . . .48 D7
Pier Way SE28 . . . . .2 D3
Pierce Mill La TN11 . . . . .119 C6
Piermont Pl BR1 . . . . .36 F7
Pigdown La TN8 . . . . .129 D4
Piggott's Cross TN8 . . . . .113 D7
Pigsdean Rd DA13 . . . . . . .45 B2
Pike Cl BR1 . . . . .22 B3
Pikefields ME8 . . . . .49 C2
Pikefish La TN12,ME18 . . .120 F2
Pikey La ME19 . . . . .89 E5
Pile La TN12 . . . . .140 A5
Pilgrim's Way Cotts TN15 .70 A2
Greenwich SE3 . . . . .5 A6
Pilgrims Ct Dartford DA1 . . .10 A2
Pilgrims Lakes ME17 . . . .110 E6
Pilgrims Rd
Upper Halling ME2 . . . . . . .59 F6
Wouldham ME1 . . . . .60 D1
Pilgrims View
Maidstone,Sandling ME14 . .76 E3
Swanscombe DA9 . . . . . . .11 C1
Pilgrims Way Boxley ME14 .77 E3
Broad Street ME14,ME17 . .94 C6
Cuxton ME2 . . . . .46 C3
Dartford DA1 . . . . .27 B8
Detling ME14 . . . . .78 B1
Eccles ME20 . . . . .76 B6
Hollingbourne ME17 . . . . . .94 F3
Lenham ME17 . . . . .111 B7
Otford TN14 . . . . .68 E3
Upper Halling
ME2,ME6,ME19 . . . . .59 D3
Vigo Village ME19 . . . . . . .73 B7
Wrotham TN15 . . . . .72 A3
Wrotham TN15 . . . . .72 C4
Pilgrims Way E TN14 . . . .69 D3
Pilgrims Way W
Otford TN13,TN14 . . . . . . .68 D3
Otford TN14 . . . . .68 F3
Pilgrims' Rd DA10 . . . . . . .11 E7
Pilgrims' Way TN15,TN14 . .70 C5
Pilkington Rd BR6 . . . . . . .51 C8
Pillar Box La TN11 . . . . . .102 D5
Pillar Box Rd TN15 . . . . . .85 E5
Pilot Rd ME1 . . . . .61 C8
Pilots Pl DA12 . . . . .13 C1
Pimp's Court Cotts ME15 106 E6
Pimp's Court Farm Ctr
ME15 . . . . .106 E6
Pimpernel Cl ME14 . . . . . .93 B4
Pimpernel Way ME5 . . . . .61 E4
Pinchbeck Rd BR6 . . . . . . .51 F4
Pincott Rd DA6 . . . . .8 A3
Pincroft Wood DA3 . . . . . .43 C6
Pine Ave DA12 . . . . .30 D7
Pine Cl Larkfield ME20 . . . .75 A2
Swanley BR8 . . . . .39 F5
Pine Cotts ME14 . . . . .91 E8
Pine Glade BR6 . . . . .50 F6
Pine Gr Edenbridge TN8 . . .112 B2
Gillingham ME7 . . . . .63 A5
Maidstone ME14 . . . . .92 B6
Pine Ho 5 ME14 . . . . .92 B4
Pine House 3 ME5 . . . . . .61 F5
Pine Lodge ME16 . . . . .91 C3
Pine Pl ME15 . . . . .91 E1
Pine Rd ME2 . . . . .46 F6
Pine Ridge TN10 . . . . .117 B6
Pine Rise DA13 . . . . .44 A3
Pine View TN15 . . . . .87 C7
Pine Tree La TN15 . . . . . . .86 A2
Pinecrest Gdns BR6 . . . . . .51 B6
Pinecroft DA16 . . . . .7 A7
Pinecroft Wood DA3 . . . . .43 C6
Pinehurst Chislehurst BR7 . .23 B7
Sevenoaks TN14 . . . . .84 E6
Pinehurst Wlk 4 BR6 . . . .37 D1
Pineneedle La TN13 . . . . . .84 B4
Pines Rd BR1 . . . . .36 F1
Pinesfield La ME19 . . . . . .73 B6
Pinewood BR7 . . . . .23 A2
Pinewood Ave
Sevenoaks TN13 . . . . .84 C6
Sidcup DA15 . . . . .23 E7
Pinewood Cl Orpington BR6 37 D1
Paddock Wood TN12 . . . . .135 F6
Pinewood Ct TN4 . . . . . . .133 A1
Pinewood Dr Chatham ME5 77 D8
Orpington BR6 . . . . .51 E5
Pinewood Gdns TN4 . . . . .133 A1
Pinewood Rd Bromley BR2 .36 A5
Erith SE2 . . . . .7 D8
Royal Tunbridge Wells TN2 .149 D5
Pinkham TN12 . . . . .120 A5
Pinkham Gdns TN12 . . . .120 A6
Pinks Hill BR8 . . . . .39 E4
Pinnacle Hill DA7 . . . . .8 B3
Pinnacle Hill N DA7 . . . . . .8 B3
Pinnacles The ME4 . . . . . .34 C1
Pinnell Rd SE9 . . . . .5 D3
Pinnock La TN12 . . . . . . .139 E1
Pinnock's Ave DA11 . . . . . .30 B7
Pintail Cl Grain ME3 . . . . . .21 B6
Newham E6 . . . . .1 E8
Pintails The ME4 . . . . .34 B1
Pinto Way SE3 . . . . .5 B3
Pinton Hill TN5 . . . . .176 B3

Pioneer Way BR8 . . . . .39 E6
Piper's Green Rd TN16 . . . .97 B7
Pipers Cl TN5 . . . . .175 A4
Pipers La TN16 . . . . .97 A8
Pippenhall SE9 . . . . .6 B1
Pippin Cl ME17 . . . . .106 B2
Pippin Croft ME7 . . . . .63 A6
Pippin Rd TN12 . . . . .119 F6
Pippin Way ME19 . . . . .89 A2
Pippins The DA13 . . . . .44 A3
Pirbright Cl ME5 . . . . .62 D2
Pirie St E16 . . . . .1 B5
Pirrip Cl DA12 . . . . .30 F6
Pit La TN8 . . . . .112 C4
Pitfield DA3 . . . . .42 F5
Pitfield Cres SE28 . . . . .3 A5
Pitfield Dr DA13 . . . . .57 F7
Pitfold Rd SE12 . . . . .5 A1
Pitt Rd Langley Heath ME17 109 A2
Maidstone ME16 . . . . .91 B1
Orpington BR6 . . . . .51 C6
Pittlesden TN30 . . . . .183 A7
Pittlesden Pl 1 TN30 . . . .183 A7
Pittsmead Ave BR2 . . . . . .36 A2
Pittswood Cotts TN11 . . . .118 A8
Pix's La TN17 . . . . .182 A3
Pixot Hill TN12 . . . . .136 B2
Pizien Well Rd ME18 . . . .104 B7
Place Farm Ave BR6 . . . . . .37 D1
Place La ME9 . . . . .64 D4
Plain Rd TN12 . . . . .138 C4
Plain The TN17 . . . . .167 E8
Plains Ave ME15 . . . . .92 C1
Plaistow Gr BR1 . . . . .22 B1
Plaistow La BR1 . . . . .36 C8
Plaistow Sq DA11 . . . . . . .29 D8
Plane Rd ME3 . . . . .34 E3
Plane Tree Ho SE7 . . . . . . .1 D1
Plane Wlk TN10 . . . . .117 C7
Plantagenet Ho SE18 . . . . .1 F3
Plantation Cl DA9 . . . . . . .10 F1
Plantation Dr BR5 . . . . . . .38 D1
Plantation La ME3 . . . . . . .93 A3
Plantation Rd Erith DA8 . . . .9 A6
Gillingham ME7 . . . . .49 A6
Hextable BR8 . . . . .26 A2
Plantation The SE3 . . . . . . .5 A5
Plat The TN8 . . . . .112 D1
Platt CE Prim Sch TN15 . .87 C7
Platt Comm TN15 . . . . . . .87 C7
Platt House La TN15 . . . . . .72 C6
Platt Ind Est TN15 . . . . . . .87 C8
Platt The Frant TN3 . . . . . .163 B1
Sutton Valence ME17 . . . .124 E7
Platt's Heath Prim Sch
ME17 . . . . .110 F2
Platters The ME8 . . . . .63 C7
Plaxdale Green Rd TN15 . .71 D7
Plaxtol Cl BR1 . . . . .36 C8
Plaxtol La TN15,TN11 . . . .101 D8
Plaxtol Prim Sch TN15 . . .101 E7
Plaxtol Rd DA8 . . . . .8 A7
Playground Cl ME9 . . . . . .65 B6
Playstool Rd ME9 . . . . . . .65 A6
Pleasance Rd BR5 . . . . . . .38 B6
Pleasant Row 10 ME7 . . . .48 A6
Pleasant View DA8 . . . . . . .4 E1
Pleasant View Pl BR6 . . . .51 C5
Pleasaunce Ct SE9 . . . . . . .5 F3
Pleasure House Rd ME7 125 A8
Plewis Ho ME7 . . . . .48 E7
Plomley Cl ME8 . . . . .63 D4
Plough Cotts ME17 . . . . . .108 E2
Plough Hill TN15 . . . . .86 F4
Plough Wents Rd ME17 . .108 B2
Plough Wlk TN8 . . . . .112 C3
Ploughmans Way
Chatham ME5 . . . . .62 A1
Gillingham ME8 . . . . .63 E6
Plover Cl Chatham ME5 . . . .62 D1
Marlpit Hill TN8 . . . . .112 C3
Plover Rd ME20 . . . . .74 F2
Plowenders Cl ME19 . . . . .73 D2
Pluckley Cl ME8 . . . . .49 C3
Pluckley Rd TN27 . . . . . . .143 D2
Plug La DA13 . . . . .58 D5
Plum La SE18 . . . . .6 C7
Plum Tree Cotts TN18 . . . .184 E8
Plum Tree Rd ME9 . . . . . . .79 B8
Plumcroft Prim Sch SE18 . .6 C8
Plumey Feather Cotts
TN3 . . . . .160 E3
Plummer La TN30 . . . . . . .182 F6
Plummers Croft TN13 . . . .83 E6
Plumpton Wlk 9 ME15 . . .107 F6
Plumstead Common Rd
SE18 . . . . .6 C8
Plumstead High St SE18,SE2 2 E1
Plumstead Manor Sch
SE18 . . . . .6 D8
Plumstead Rd SE18 . . . . . . .2 C1
Plumstead Sta SE18 . . . . . .2 D2
Plumtree Gr ME7 . . . . .63 A4
Plumtree Rd TN27 . . . . . . .140 F7
Plumtrees ME16 . . . . .91 A2
Plymouth Dr TN13 . . . . . . .84 C3
Plymouth Pk TN13 . . . . . . .84 C3
Plymouth Rd Bromley BR1 . .36 B8
Newham E16 . . . . .1 A8
Plympton Cl 8 DA17 . . . . . .3 E3
Plymstock Rd DA16 . . . . . . .7 C7
Poachers Cl ME5 . . . . .62 C5
Pochard Cl ME4 . . . . .34 B1
Pococks Bank TN13 . . . . .113 C3
Podkin Wood ME5 . . . . . . .76 F8
Pointer Cl SE28 . . . . .3 D7
Pointer Sch The SE3 . . . . . .5 A7
Polebrook Rd SE3 . . . . .5 C4

Polegate Cotts RM17 . . . .11 E8
Polesden Rd TN2 . . . . . . .149 D2
Polhill TN13,TN14 . . . . . . .68 C4
Polhill Dr ME5 . . . . .61 F2
Police Station Rd ME19 . .89 C8
Pollard Cl E16 . . . . .1 A5
Pollard Ct ME7 . . . . .48 C5
Pollard Wlk DA14 . . . . . . .24 C2
Polley Cl TN12 . . . . .150 D7
Pollyhaugh DA4 . . . . .54 E7
Polperro Cl BR6 . . . . .37 F3
Polthorne Gr SE18 . . . . .2 D2
Pond Cl SE3 . . . . .5 A5
Pond Farm Rd
Hucking ME17 . . . . .79 D1
Oad Street ME9 . . . . .65 F1
Pond La TN15 . . . . .85 E2
Pond Path BR7 . . . . .23 B2
Pondfield La DA12 . . . . . . .31 E1
Pondfield Rd BR6 . . . . .51 B7
Pondwood Rise BR6 . . . . .37 E2
Pontefract Rd BR1 . . . . . . .22 A3
Pontoise Cl TN13 . . . . .83 F5
Pook La TN27 . . . . .158 D3
Poona Rd TN1 . . . . .149 B2
Pootings Rd TN8 . . . . .112 E7
Pope Dr TN12 . . . . .139 E4
Pope House La TN30 . . . . .173 B4
Pope Rd BR2 . . . . .36 D4
Pope St ME15 . . . . .91 C2
Pope Street Ct SE9 . . . . . .22 F7
Popes Cott TN17 . . . . .166 F2
Popes Wood ME14 . . . . . . .92 F6
Poplar Ave
Gravesend DA12 . . . . .30 C4
Orpington BR6 . . . . .51 B8
Poplar Cl ME3 . . . . .34 E3
Poplar Field TN30 . . . . . . .189 D6
Poplar Gr ME16 . . . . .91 C5
Poplar Mount DA17 . . . . . . .4 C2
Poplar Pl SE28 . . . . .3 C6
Poplar Rd Rochester ME2 . .46 E5
Wittersham TN30 . . . . .189 D4
Poplar Wlk DA13 . . . . .44 B3
Poplars Cl DA3 . . . . .43 C6
Poplars The DA12 . . . . . . .30 E8
Poplicans Rd ME2 . . . . . . .46 B3
Poppy Cl Gillingham ME7 . .48 C5
Maidstone ME16 . . . . .91 D3
Popular Cl ME2 . . . . .46 F5
Porchester Cl Hartley DA3 . .42 F5
Maidstone ME15 . . . . .107 A6
Porchfield Cl DA12 . . . . . . .30 C6
Porcupine Cl SE9 . . . . .22 E6
Porrington Cl BR7 . . . . .37 A8
Port Ave DA9 . . . . .11 B1
Port Cl Chatham ME5 . . . . .62 B3
Maidstone ME14 . . . . .93 A5
Port Hill ME6 . . . . .67 B7
Port Rise ME4 . . . . .47 F3
Port Victoria Rd ME3 . . . . .21 C4
Porter Cl RM20 . . . . .11 C8
Porter Rd E6 . . . . .1 F7
Porters Cl TN12 . . . . .151 F6
Porters Wlk ME17 . . . . . . .108 E4
Porters Wood TN12 . . . . . .151 E6
Porteus Ct DA1 . . . . .26 D6
Porthkerry Ave DA16 . . . . . .7 A3
Portland Ave
Gravesend DA12 . . . . .30 B6
Sidcup DA15 . . . . .7 A1
Portland Cres SE9 . . . . . . .22 E6
Portland Rd Bromley BR1 . .22 C3
Chislehurst SE9 . . . . .22 E6
Gillingham ME7 . . . . .48 E6
Gravesend DA12 . . . . .30 B7
Northfleet DA11 . . . . .12 D1
Wouldham ME1 . . . . .60 C4
Portland St 1 ME4 . . . . . .48 B2
Portland Villas DA12 . . . . .30 B7
Portman Pl 1 ME4 . . . . . .48 A4
Portman Cl Bexley DA7 . . . .7 E4
Dartford DA5 . . . . .25 E7
Portman Pk TN15 . . . . . . .117 C3
Portobello Par TN15 . . . . . .56 A2
Portree Mews ME7 . . . . . . .48 E3
Portsdown Cl ME16 . . . . . .91 B2
Portsea Rd ME18 . . . . .13 C6
Portsmouth Cl ME2 . . . . . .46 D6
Portsmouth Mews E16 . . . .1 B5
Portway Gdns SE18 . . . . . . .5 D7
Portway Rd ME3 . . . . .33 B7
Post Barn Rd ME4 . . . . . . .47 F2
Post Office Rd 12 TN18 . .178 F2
Postern La TN9,TN11 . . . .117 E1
Postley Commercial Ctr
ME15 . . . . .92 A2
Postley Rd ME15 . . . . .92 A1
Postmill Dr ME15 . . . . .91 F1
Potash La TN15 . . . . .87 C6
Potter's La ME18 . . . . .179 A6
Pottery Rd Coldblow DA5 . .25 C6
Hoo St Werburgh ME3 . . . .34 D5
Potyn Ho ME1 . . . . .47 C4
Poulters Wood BR2 . . . . . .50 D5
Pound Bank Cl TN15 . . . . .55 F2
Pound Cl BR6 . . . . .51 D8
Pound Court Dr BR6 . . . . . .51 D8
Pound Ho TN11 . . . . .118 E8
Pound La Halstead TN14 . . .67 D4
Sevenoaks TN13 . . . . .84 C3
Pound Park Rd SE7 . . . . . . .1 D2
Pound Pl SE9 . . . . .6 A1
Pound Rd TN12 . . . . .119 F6
Poundfield Rd TN18 . . . . .186 B5

Poundsbridge Hill
TN11,TN3 . . . . .147 D7
Poundsbridge La TN11 . .131 D2
Pounsley Rd TN13 . . . . . . .83 E6
Pout Rd ME6 . . . . .74 F7
Powder Mill La
Dartford DA1 . . . . .26 F6
Leigh TN11 . . . . .116 A1
Royal Tunbridge Wells TN4 .149 B8
Tonbridge TN11 . . . . .116 E2
Powdermill Ho TN4 . . . . .149 C8
Powell Ave DA2 . . . . .27 C6
Powell Cl ME20 . . . . .76 A3
Powerscroft Rd DA14 . . . .24 C2
Powis Cl ME9 . . . . .2 A1
Powlett Rd ME2 . . . . .33 C1
Powster Rd BR1 . . . . .22 B3
Powys Cl DA7 . . . . .7 D8
Poynder Rd ME18 . . . . . . .13 B6
Poynings Rd BR6 . . . . .52 C8
Poyntell Cres BR7 . . . . . . .37 D8
Poyntell Rd TN12 . . . . . . .139 F4
Pragnell Rd SE12 . . . . .22 B6
Prall's La TN12 . . . . .135 C2
Pratling St ME20 . . . . .76 C4
Pratt's Bottom
Prim Sch TN14 . . . . .67 C8
Premier Par ME20 . . . . . . .75 E1
Prentiss Ct SE7 . . . . .1 D2
Prescott Ave BR5 . . . . .37 B3
Presentation Ho 8 DA12 . .30 B8
Prestbury Sq SE9 . . . . . . .22 F4
Preston Ave ME7 . . . . .48 E1
Preston Ct DA14 . . . . .23 F4
Preston Dr DA7 . . . . .7 D6
Preston Hall Hospl ME20 . .75 F1
Preston Ho 1 SE18 . . . . . . .2 A2
Preston Rd Northfleet DA11 .29 E7
Tonbridge TN9 . . . . .117 A1
Prestons Rd BR2 . . . . .50 A8
Prestwood Cl SE18 . . . . . . .7 A7
Pretoria Ho 4 Erith DA8 . . . .8 E7
8 Maidstone ME15 . . . . .107 E5
Pretoria Rd Chatham ME4 . .47 F2
Gillingham ME7 . . . . .48 B7
Prettymans La TN8 . . . . . .112 F4
Pridmore Rd ME6 . . . . .74 F8
Priest's Wlk DA12 . . . . . . .31 A6
Priestdale Ct ME4 . . . . . . .47 E3
Priestfield Rd ME7 . . . . . . .48 E5
Priestfield Stad
(Gillingham FC) ME7 . . . .48 E5
Priestfields ME1 . . . . .47 B3
Priestlands Park Rd BR5 . .23 F5
Priestley Dr Lunsford ME20 .74 F4
Tonbridge TN10 . . . . .117 E7
Priestwood Rd DA13 . . . . .58 C5
Primrose Ave ME8 . . . . . . .63 B5
Primrose Cl ME14 . . . . . . .61 E7
Primrose Dr ME20 . . . . . . .75 D1
Primrose Ho 10 ME15 . . . .107 E7
Primrose Rd ME2 . . . . .59 E5
Primrose Terr DA12 . . . . . .30 C7
Primrose Wlk TN12 . . . . . .136 A5
Prince Arthur Rd ME7 . . . .48 B6
Prince Charles Ave
Chatham ME5 . . . . .62 B4
Sutton at Hone DA4 . . . . . .41 D7
Prince Charles Ho DA4 . . .41 E7
Prince Consort Dr BR7 . . .37 D8
Prince Henry Rd SE7 . . . . . .5 D7
Prince Imperial Rd
Chislehurst BR7 . . . . .23 B1
Woolwich SE18 . . . . .6 A6
Prince John Rd SE9 . . . . . .5 E2
Prince Of Wales Rd
Greenwich SE3 . . . . .5 A6
Newham E16 . . . . .1 C7
Prince Regent La E16 . . . . .1 C7
Prince Regent Sta E16 . . . .1 C6
Prince Rupert Rd SE9 . . . . .5 F3
Prince's Plain BR2 . . . . . . .36 E1
Prince's Plain
Prim Sch BR2 . . . . .36 E2
Prince's St Rochester ME1 . .47 C4
Royal Tunbridge Wells TN2 .149 C3
Princes Ave Chatham ME5 . .62 B5
Dartford DA2 . . . . .27 B7
Orpington BR5 . . . . .37 E4
Princes Cl DA14 . . . . .24 D5
Princes Rd
Dartford DA1,DA2 . . . . . . .26 D7
Gravesend DA12 . . . . .30 C5
Hextable BR8 . . . . .26 A2
Princes St Bexley DA7 . . . . .7 E4
Gravesend DA11 . . . . .13 B1
Maidstone ME14 . . . . .92 A5
Princes View DA1 . . . . . . .27 A7
Princes Way ME14 . . . . . . .78 A1
Princess Alice Way SE28 . .2 D4
Princess Margaret Rd
RM18 . . . . .14 D7
Princess Mary Ave ME4 . .48 B7
Princess Par BR6 . . . . .51 A7
Prinys Dr ME8 . . . . .63 C4
Priolo Rd SE7 . . . . .1 C1
Prior's Way TN8 . . . . .145 A6
Priorsdean Cl ME16 . . . . . .90 E1
Priorsford Ave BR5 . . . . . .38 B5
Priory Ave BR5 . . . . .37 F3
Priory Cl Bromley BR7 . . . . .36 F8
Dartford DA1 . . . . .9 E1
East Farleigh ME15 . . . . . .106 B8
Priory Ct 3 Dartford DA1 . . .9 D1

Priory Ct continued
Gillingham ME8 . . . . .49 A2
Priory Ctr The DA1 . . . . . .26 E8
Priory Dr SE2 . . . . .3 D1
Priory Fields DA1 . . . . .54 F8
Priory Gate 4 ME14 . . . . .92 A5
Priory Gdns Dartford DA1 . . .9 D2
Orpington BR6* 38 B2
Priory Gr Aylesford ME20 . .75 D1
Tonbridge TN9 . . . . .133 B8
Priory Hill DA1 . . . . .9 D1
Priory Ho 3 SE7 . . . . .5 C8
Priory La DA4 . . . . .40 F1
Priory Leas SE9 . . . . .22 E7
Priory Mews DA2 . . . . .27 C8
Priory Pl DA1 . . . . .9 D1
Priory Rd Dartford DA1 . . . . .9 D1
Gillingham ME8 . . . . .49 A2
Maidstone ME15 . . . . .92 A3
Rochester ME2 . . . . .47 A6
Tonbridge TN9 . . . . .133 C8
Priory Sch The BR5 . . . . . .38 C1
Priory St TN9 . . . . .133 B8
Priory Way TN30 . . . . .183 C7
Priory Wlk TN9 . . . . .133 B8
Pristling La TN12 . . . . . . .155 B8
Pritchard Ct ME7 . . . . .48 C3
Progress Est The ME15 . .108 A4
Prospect Ave ME2 . . . . . . .47 B8
Prospect Cl DA17 . . . . .4 A2
Prospect Cotts
Lamberhurst TN3 . . . . .166 A3
Pratt's Bottom BR6 . . . . . .52 C3
Prospect Gr DA12 . . . . . . .30 D8
Prospect Pk TN4 . . . . .132 F5
Prospect Pl Bromley BR2 . .36 B6
Collier Street TN12 . . . . . .121 C2
Dartford DA1 . . . . .9 E1
Gravesend DA12 . . . . .30 D8
Grays RM17 . . . . .12 B8
Maidstone ME16 . . . . .91 E3
Prospect Rd
Royal Tunbridge Wells TN2 .149 C3
Royal Tunbridge
Wells,Southborough TN4 . .132 F1
Sevenoaks TN13 . . . . .84 C4
Prospect Row
Chatham ME4 . . . . .48 A3
Gillingham ME7 . . . . .48 A6
Prospect Vale SE18 . . . . . . .1 E2
Prospero Ho 7 DA17 . . . . . .4 A1
Provender Way ME7 . . . . . .48 C5
Providence Chapel TN12 138 C6
Providence Cotts
Groombridge TN3 . . . . . . .161 C7
Higham ME3 . . . . .32 B2
Providence La ME1 . . . . . .47 C5
Providence Pl TN27 . . . . .141 A7
Providence St DA9 . . . . . . .11 A2
Prudhoe Ct 27 DA2 . . . . . .10 B1
Pudding La Maidstone ME14 91 F4
Seal TN15 . . . . .84 F5
Pudding Rd ME8 . . . . .63 F8
Puddingcake La TN17 . . . .182 C5
Puddledock La
Hextable BR8,DA2 . . . . . . .25 F2
Ide Hill TN16 . . . . .97 A3
Puffin Rd ME3 . . . . .21 B5
Pullington Cotts TN17 . . . .180 E6
Pullman Mews SE12 . . . . . .5 B5
Pullman Pl SE9 . . . . .5 E2
Pump Cl ME19 . . . . .74 D1
Pump La ME7,ME8 . . . . . .49 D3
Punch Croft DA3 . . . . .56 E7
Purbeck Rd ME4 . . . . .47 E2
Purcell Ave TN10 . . . . . . .117 F6
Purfleet By-Pass RM19 . . .10 D8
Purland Rd SE28,SE18 . . . .2 F4
Purneys Rd SE9 . . . . .5 D3
Purrett Rd SE18 . . . . .2 F1
Purser Way ME7 . . . . .48 C7
Putlands L Ctr TN12 . . . .136 A5
Puttenden Rd TN11 . . . . .101 F3
Pym Orch TN16 . . . . .82 C3
Pynham Cl SE2 . . . . .3 B3
Pyrus Cl ME5 . . . . .77 A8

Q

Quadrant The DA7 . . . . .7 D7
Quaggy Wlk SE3 . . . . .5 A3
Quaker Cl TN13 . . . . .84 D4
Quaker Dr TN17 . . . . .169 D6
Quaker La TN17 . . . . .169 D6
Quaker's Hall La TN13 . . . .84 C5
Quakers Cl DA3 . . . . .42 E6
Quantock Cl TN2 . . . . .149 D5
Quantock Rd DA1 . . . . .8 E5
Quarries The ME17 . . . . . .107 C4
Quarry Bank TN9 . . . . .133 A4
Quarry Cotts TN5 . . . . . . .174 D7
Quarry Hill TN15 . . . . .84 C5
Quarry Hill Par 3 TN9 . . .133 B8
Quarry Hill Rd
Borough Green TN15 . . . . .86 F6
Tonbridge TN9 . . . . .133 B8
Quarry Rd Maidstone ME15 .92 A2
Royal Tunbridge Wells TN1 .149 B5
Quarry Rise TN9 . . . . .133 A4
Quarry Sq ME14 . . . . .92 A5
Quarry Wood Ind Est
ME20 . . . . .90 E8
Quay La DA9 . . . . .11 B3

Quayside ME4 . . . . .48 B8
Quebec Ave TN16 . . . . .81 D1
Quebec Cotts **9** TN16 . . . . .81 D1
Quebec Rd RM18 . . . . .13 A5
Quebec Sq **10** TN16 . . . . . .81 D1
Queen Anne Ave BR2 . . . .36 A6
Queen Anne Gate DA7 . . . .7 D4
Queen Anne Rd ME14 . . . . .92 B4
Queen Borough Gdns BR7 23 D2
Queen Elizabeth Military
  Hospl The SE18 . . . . .5 E7
Queen Elizabeth
  Sq ME15 . . . . .107 D6
Queen Mary's Hospl DA14 24 A2
Queen Mother Ct The
  ME1 . . . . .47 B4
  Chatham ME4 . . . . .48 A4
  Erith DA8 . . . . .8 E8
  Gravesend DA12 . . . . . . .13 B1
  Paddock Wood TN12 . . . .136 D7
  Rochester ME1 . . . . .47 C4
  Sandhurst TN18 . . . . . . .186 B5
Queen's Ave
  Maidstone ME16 . . . . . . .91 D5
  Snodland ME6 . . . . .75 A8
Queen's Dr TN14 . . . . .84 C7
Queen's Farm Rd DA12 . . .31 E7
Queen's Gdns TN4 . . . . . .149 B6
Queen's Mews **12** TN18 . .179 A2
Queen's Pas BR7 . . . . .23 B2
Queen's Rd Bexley DA16 . . .7 B5
  Bromley BR1 . . . . .36 A7
  Chatham ME5 . . . . .48 D1
  Chislehurst BR7 . . . . .23 B2
  Gillingham ME7 . . . . .48 C4
  Hawkhurst TN18 . . . . . . .179 A2
  Maidstone ME16 . . . . . . .91 C4
  Royal Tunbridge Wells TN4 149 B6
  Snodland ME6 . . . . .75 A8
Queendown Ave ME8 . . . . .63 D5
Queens Cotts TN5 . . . . . .174 E6
Queens Ct Edenbridge TN8 112 D1
  11 Hawkhurst TN18 . . . .179 A2
  1 Sidcup DA14 . . . . . . .24 A4
Queens Gate Gdns BR7 . . .37 D8
Queens Gdns DA2 . . . . . . .27 B7
Queens Ho ME16 . . . . .91 B3
Queens Rd Erith DA8 . . . . . .8 E8
  Gravesend DA12 . . . . . . .30 C5
Queens Way ME14 . . . . . . .78 A1
Queenscroft Rd SE9 . . . . . .5 D1
Queensland Ho **2** E16 . . . .2 A5
Queensway
  Allhallows-on-Sea ME3 . . .19 D9
  Hayes BR2,BR5 . . . . .50 A6
  Orpington BR5 . . . . .37 C3
Queenswood Rd
  Kit's Coty ME20 . . . . .76 D7
  Sidcup DA15 . . . . .6 F1
Quern The ME15 . . . . .91 E1
Quernmore Cl BR1 . . . . . . .22 A2
Quernmore Rd BR1 . . . . . .22 A2
Quested Way ME17 . . . . . .110 C6
Quickrells Ave ME3 . . . . . .16 B5
Quickthorn Cres ME5 . . . . .61 E5
Quiet Nook BR2 . . . . .50 D7
Quilter Gdns BR5 . . . . .38 C1
Quilter Rd BR5 . . . . .38 D1
Quilter St SE18 . . . . .2 F1
Quincewood Gdns TN10 .117 D7
Quinion Cl ME5 . . . . .77 A8
Quinnell St ME8 . . . . .49 E1
Quixote Cres ME2 . . . . . . .33 B1

R

Rabbits Rd DA4 . . . . .41 E7
Rablus Pl DA4 . . . . .40 F3
Racefield Cl DA12 . . . . . . .31 E1
Rackham Cl DA16 . . . . .7 B5
Radfield Way DA15 . . . . . .23 D8
Radland Rd E16 . . . . .1 A7
Radleigh Gdns ME1 . . . . . .47 E1
Radley Ho **18** SE2 . . . . . . .3 D4
Radnor Ave DA16 . . . . .7 B2
Radnor Rd BR7 . . . . .23 E2
Radnor Cres SE18 . . . . .7 A7
Raeburn Ave DA1 . . . . .9 B2
Raeburn Cl TN10 . . . . . . .117 E6
Raeburn Pl DA10 . . . . .11 E2
Raeburn Rd DA15 . . . . .6 E1
Rafford Way BR1 . . . . .36 B6
Raggatt Pl ME15 . . . . .92 B2
Ragge Way TN15 . . . . .84 F7
Raggleswood BR7 . . . . . . .37 A8
Raglan Ct SE12 . . . . .5 A2
Raglan Prim Sch BR2 . . . .36 D5
Raglan Rd Bromley BR2 . . .36 C5
  Erith DA17 . . . . .3 F2
  Woolwich SE18 . . . . .2 C1
Ragstone Ct ME20 . . . . . . .90 C8
Ragstone Rd ME15 . . . . . .93 A2
Railway App TN9 . . . . . . .133 B8
Railway Cotts
  Cowden TN8 . . . . .145 D8
  Marden TN12 . . . . .138 D6
Railway Pl Erith DA17 . . . . .4 A3
  19 Gravesend DA12 . . . .13 B1
Railway Sidings The DA13 .44 B4
Railway St Chatham ME4 . . .47 F4
  Gillingham ME7 . . . . .48 D6
  Northfleet DA11 . . . . .12 A2
Railway St Ind Pk ME7 . . .48 D6

Railway Terr TN16 . . . . . . .81 D1
Rainham Cl
  Maidstone ME15 . . . . . . .92 A1
  Sidcup SE9 . . . . .6 E1
Rainham Mark Gram Sch
  ME8 . . . . .49 D2
Rainham Rd ME5 . . . . .48 C3
Rainham Sch for Girls
  ME8 . . . . .63 C8
Rainham Sh Ctr ME8 . . . . .63 F8
Rainham Sta ME8 . . . . . . .49 F1
Rainton Rd SE7 . . . . .1 A1
Raleigh Cl Chatham ME5 . .62 A6
  Erith DA8 . . . . .8 F8
Raleigh Mews **6** BR6 . . . .51 F5
Ramac Ind Est SE7 . . . . . . .1 B1
Ramac Way SE7 . . . . .1 B1
Ramillies Cl ME5 . . . . .62 A6
Ramillies Rd DA15 . . . . .7 A1
Rammell Mews TN17 . . . .169 D4
Rampion Cl ME14 . . . . .92 E5
Ramsden Jun & Inf Sch
  BR5 . . . . .38 C2
Ramsden La TN17 . . . . . .180 F4
Ramsden Rd Erith DA8 . . . .8 D7
  Orpington BR5,BR6 . . . . .38 B1
Ramsgate Cl E16 . . . . .1 B5
Ramslye Cotts TN3 . . . . . .162 D8
Ramslye Rd TN3 . . . . .162 E8
Ramus Wood Ave BR6 . . . .51 E5
Rance Ho **11** SE18 . . . . . . .1 E2
Rancliffe Gdns SE9 . . . . . . .5 E3
Randall Cl DA8 . . . . .8 C8
Randall Hill Rd TN15 . . . . .71 F3
Randall Rd ME4 . . . . .47 E1
Randall St ME14 . . . . .91 F6
Randalls Row ME15 . . . . .106 F5
Randle's La TN14 . . . . .67 D5
Randolph App E16 . . . . .1 C1
Randolph Cl DA7 . . . . .8 C4
Randolph Cotts ME2 . . . . .33 B1
Randolph Ho ME7 . . . . . . .48 C5
Ranelagh Gdns DA11 . . . . .29 F8
Range Rd DA12 . . . . .30 E8
Rangefield Rd BR1 . . . . . . .22 A3
Rangeworth Pl DA15 . . . . .23 F5
Rankine Rd TN2 . . . . .149 D7
Ranleigh Gdns DA7 . . . . . . .7 F7
Ranmore Path BR5 . . . . . . .38 A5
Ranscombe Cl ME2 . . . . . .46 D5
Ranscombe Farm
  Cotts ME2 . . . . .46 C4
Ransom Rd **1** SE7 . . . . . . .1 C1
Ranters La TN17 . . . . .167 C7
Ranters Oak TN17 . . . . . .181 B4
Ranworth Rd DA7,DA8 . . . .8 E5
Raphael Ave RM18 . . . . . . .13 B7
Raphael Ct TN11 . . . . .116 E7
Raphael Rd DA12 . . . . .30 D8
Rashleigh Way DA4 . . . . . .41 C5
Ratcliffe Cl SE12 . . . . .22 A8
Ratcliffe Highway
  High Halstow ME3 . . . . . .18 D5
  Hoo St Werburgh ME3 . . .34 C7
Rathmore Rd
  Gravesend DA11 . . . . . . .30 B8
  Greenwich SE7 . . . . .1 B1
Raven Cl ME20 . . . . .75 A1
Raven's Hoe DA14 . . . . . . .24 A3
Ravensbourne Coll of
  Design &
  Communication BR7 . . . .22 F3
Ravensbourne Ct **28** BR5 .38 D1
Ravensbourne Rd
  Bromley BR1 . . . . .36 A6
  Crayford DA1 . . . . .9 A4
Ravensbourne Sch BR2 . . .36 B4
Ravensbury Rd BR5 . . . . . .38 A5
Ravenscourt Rd BR5 . . . . .38 B7
Ravenscroft **5** E16 . . . . . . .1 A8
Ravenscroft Cres SE9 . . . . .22 F5
Ravenscroft Rd E16 . . . . . . .1 A8
Ravenshill BR7 . . . . .37 B8
Ravensleigh Gdns BR1 . . .22 B3
Ravensquay Bsns Ctr BR5 38 B4
Ravenswood DA5 . . . . .24 E7
Ravenswood Ave
  Rochester ME2 . . . . .33 B1
  Royal Tunbridge Wells TN2 149 D6
Ravensworth Rd SE9 . . . . .22 F4
Ravine Gr SE18 . . . . .6 E8
Rawdon Rd ME15 . . . . .92 A3
Rawlings Cl **3** BR6 . . . . . .51 F5
Rawsthorne Cl E16 . . . . .1 F5
Ray Lamb Way DA8 . . . . . . .9 B7
Rayfield Cl Bromley BR2 . . .36 E3
  Snodland ME2 . . . . .60 A1
Rayford Cl DA1 . . . . .9 C2
Rayleas Cl SE18 . . . . .6 B6
Rayleigh Cl ME16 . . . . .91 D7
Rayleigh Ho **2** ME15 . . . .107 D8
Rayleigh Rd E16 . . . . .1 B5
Raymer Rd ME14 . . . . .92 B8
Raymere Gdns SE18 . . . . . .6 E7
Raymond Postgate Ct **5**
  SE28 . . . . .3 B6
Raynehurst Jun & Inf Sch
  DA12 . . . . .30 F5
Rayners Ct DA11 . . . . .12 B1
Raynham Villas TN12 . . . .122 A4

Rays Hill DA4 . . . . .41 C4
Read Way DA12 . . . . .30 E3
Reader's Bridge Rd TN30 172 E4
Reading House **4** ME15 .107 F5
Readscroft Rd ME8 . . . . . .63 D5
Rebecca Ct DA14 . . . . .24 B4
Recreation Ave ME6 . . . . . .75 A8
Recreation Cl ME14 . . . . . .92 B6
Recreation Ground Rd
  TN30 . . . . .183 B7
Rectory Dr TN3 . . . . .132 D3
Rectory Cl Crayford DA1 . . .8 E3
  Sidcup DA14 . . . . .24 B4
  Snodland ME6 . . . . .75 A8
  Wouldham ME1 . . . . .60 C5
Rectory Dr TN3 . . . . .132 D3
Rectory Field Cres SE7 . . . .5 C7
Rectory Fields TN17 . . . . .169 D5
Rectory Grange ME1 . . . . .47 C2
Rectory La Brasted TN16 . .82 C3
  Harrietsham ME17 . . . . .110 F5
  Ightham TN15 . . . . .86 C5
  Maidstone ME16 . . . . . . .91 A1
  Sevenoaks TN13 . . . . . . .84 C1
  Sidcup DA14 . . . . .24 C4
  Sutton Valence ME17 . . .124 C5
  Sutton Valence ME17 . . .124 F7
Rectory La N ME19 . . . . . . .74 F1
Rectory La S ME19 . . . . . . .74 E1
Rectory Meadow DA13 . . . .29 A3
Rectory Paddock Sch BR5 38 C7
Rectory Park Rd TN12 . . .153 A3
Rectory Pl SE18 . . . . .2 A2
Rectory Rd Cliffe ME3 . . . .16 A3
  3 Grays RM17 . . . . . . .12 D8
  New Ash Green TN15 . . . .57 C5
  Orpington BR2 . . . . .50 D3
  Swanscombe DA10 . . . . .28 E8
  Tilbury RM18 . . . . .13 D8
Reculver Wlk ME15 . . . . .107 F7
Red Barracks Rd **4** SE18 . .1 F2
Red Cedars Rd BR6 . . . . . .37 E2
Red Hill Chislehurst BR7 . .23 B3
  Red Hill ME18 . . . . .89 F1
Red Hill Prim Sch BR7 . . .23 B3
Red House Gdns ME18 . . .104 C3
Red House La DA6 . . . . .7 E3
Red Lion Cl BR5 . . . . .38 C3
Red Lion La SE18 . . . . .6 A6
Red Lion Pl SE18 . . . . .6 A6
Red Lodge Cres DA5 . . . . .25 E5
Red Lodge Rd DA5 . . . . . . .25 D5
Red Oak TN18 . . . . .184 E8
Red Oast Cotts TN5 . . . . .177 C3
Red Robin Cotts ME9 . . . . .65 B6
Red St DA13 . . . . .29 B2
Redbank ME19 . . . . .74 E2
Redbridge Cl ME5 . . . . . . .62 C4
Redcliffe La ME14 . . . . . . .92 B7
Redding Cl DA2 . . . . .27 E6
Redding Ho SE18 . . . . .1 E3
Reddy Rd DA8 . . . . .8 F8
Rede Court Rd ME2 . . . . . .46 E8
Rede Wood Rd ME16 . . . . .90 F3
Redfern Ave ME7 . . . . .48 E5
Redfern Ho ME7 . . . . .59 F5
Redgate Dr BR2 . . . . .50 B8
Redhill Rd DA3 . . . . .56 F6
Redhill Wood DA3 . . . . . . .57 A7
Redland Shaw ME4 . . . . . .47 E1
Redlands Rd TN13 . . . . . . .83 F3
Redleaf Cl Erith DA17 . . . . .8 A8
  Royal Tunbridge Wells TN2 149 D6
Redmans La BR6,TN14 . . . .53 E4
Redpoll Way **2** SE2 . . . . . .3 D3
Redpoll Wlk TN12 . . . . . .136 A5
Redruth Manor **3** ME7 . .48 C6
Redsells Cl ME15 . . . . .93 A1
Redshank Rd ME4 . . . . . . .34 B1
Redstart Cl E6 . . . . .1 E8
Redvers Rd ME4 . . . . .48 A2
Redwall La ME15, ME17 . .122 C6
Redwell La TN15 . . . . .86 B4
Redwing Cl ME20 . . . . .75 A2
Redwing Path SE28 . . . . . . .2 D4
Redwing Rd ME5 . . . . .62 B7
Redwings La TN2 . . . . . . .134 C2
Redwood Cl Chatham ME5 .62 B2
  Sidcup DA15 . . . . .24 A7
Redwood Ct DA1 . . . . .10 A1
Redwood Pk TN12 . . . . . .135 A5
Reed Ave BR6 . . . . .51 E7
Reed Cl Eltham SE12 . . . . . .5 A2
  Newham E16 . . . . .1 A8
Reed Court Cotts TN12 . .122 A5
Reed Court Farm Trail*
  TN12 . . . . .122 A5
Reed St ME3 . . . . .16 B6
Reedham Cres ME3 . . . . . .33 C7
Reeds Cotts TN17 . . . . . .170 A8
Reeds La TN11 . . . . .101 E5
Reeves Cl TN12 . . . . .139 E4
Reeves Cres DA9 . . . . .39 D6
Reeves Ct Ditton ME19 . . . .75 A1
  Fordcombe TN3 . . . . . . .147 B5
Reeves Rd SE18 . . . . .6 B8
Reeves Terr TN5 . . . . .176 E1
Reform Rd ME4 . . . . .48 B2
Regal Ho BR2 . . . . .36 A4
Regency Cl Gillingham ME8 .63 C3
  West Kingsdown TN15 . . .55 E4
Regency Hall **18** TN2 . . .149 A2
Regency Ho TN2 . . . . .149 B2
Regency Way DA7 . . . . .7 D4
Regent Dr ME15 . . . . .107 A8
Regent Pl TN2 . . . . .149 D3
Regent Rd ME7 . . . . .48 C4

Regent Sq DA17 . . . . .4 B2
Regent St TN17 . . . . .181 E4
Regent's Pl SE3 . . . . .5 A5
Regents Ct **2** DA11 . . . . .13 B1
Regents Dr BR2 . . . . .50 D5
Regina Ct TN4 . . . . .148 F6
Reginald Ave ME2 . . . . . . .46 C3
Reginald Rd ME16 . . . . . . .91 E3
Reginald St SE18 . . . . .2 E2
Reigate Rd BR1,SE12 . . . . .22 A5
Reinden Gr **1** ME15 . . . . .92 F1
Rembrandt Cl TN10 . . . . .117 E6
Rembrandt Dr DA11 . . . . . .29 E5
Remington Rd E6 . . . . .1 E7
Rendlebury Ho **12** SE18 . . .1 F2
Renfrew Cl E6 . . . . .2 A6
Rennets Cl SE9 . . . . .6 E2
Rennets Wood Ho SE9 . . . .6 D2
Rennets Wood Rd SE9 . . . .6 D2
Renown Rd ME5 . . . . .62 C2
Renshaw Cl **7** DA17 . . . . . .7 F8
Renton Dr BR5 . . . . .38 D2
Repository Rd SE18 . . . . . . .1 F1
Repton Rd BR6 . . . . .52 A6
Repton Way ME5 . . . . .61 F4
Resolution Cl ME5 . . . . . . .62 A6
Resolution Wlk SE18 . . . . . .1 F3
Restharrow Rd ME14 . . . . .92 E4
Restharrow Way ME4 . . . . .34 C1
Restons Cres SE9 . . . . .6 E1
Retreat The Grays RM17 . .12 B8
  Orpington BR6 . . . . .52 B4
Revell Rise SE18 . . . . .6 F8
Revenge Rd ME5 . . . . .77 C8
Revenue Rd **8** RM17 . . . .12 D8
Reviley Ct BR1 . . . . .37 A6
Reynard Cl **7** SE28 . . . . . . .3 A6
Reynolds Cl TN10 . . . . . . .117 E6
Reynolds Fields ME3 . . . . .32 C6
Reynolds La TN4 . . . . .148 F6
Reynolds Pl SE3 . . . . .5 B7
Rhode St ME4 . . . . .48 A4
Rhodes Ho **5** ME5 . . . . . .48 C2
Rhodewood Cl ME15 . . . . .93 A1
Rhododendron Ave DA13 .58 A3
Ribblesdale Rd DA2 . . . . . .27 C7
Ribston Cl BR2 . . . . .36 F1
Ribston Gdns TN12 . . . . .135 F7
Ricardo Path **5** SE28 . . . . .3 C5
Rice Par BR5 . . . . .37 D4
Richard Cl SE18 . . . . .1 E2
Richard House Dr E16 . . . . .1 E7
Richard St Chatham ME4 . .47 F4
  Rochester ME1 . . . . .47 C3
Richard's Cl TN11 . . . . . . .114 F2
Richardson Cl DA9 . . . . . . .11 A2
Richardson Rd TN4 . . . . . .149 A5
Richborough Cl BR5 . . . . . .38 D5
Richborough Drive ME2 . .33 A1
Richings House BR5 . . . . . .38 A8
Richmer Rd DA8 . . . . .9 A7
Richmond Cl Chatham ME5 62 B4
  Upper Upnor ME2 . . . . . .33 F1
Richmond Ct Lewisham BR1 22 B1
  Sevenoaks TN13 . . . . . . .84 B4
Richmond Cty Inf Sch ME7 48 C6
Richmond Pl
  Royal Tunbridge Wells TN2 149 B1
  SE18 . . . . .2 C2
Richmond Rd
  Gillingham ME7 . . . . .48 C7
  1 Grays RM17 . . . . . . .12 C8
Richmond Way ME15 . . . .107 A8
Richmount Gdns SE3 . . . . .5 A4
Rickyard Path SE9 . . . . .5 E3
Riddlesdale Ave TN4 . . . .149 A5
Riddons Rd SE12 . . . . .22 C4
Rideout St SE18 . . . . .1 F2
Rider Cl DA15 . . . . .6 E1
Ridge Ave DA1 . . . . .8 F1
Ridge Cl SE28 . . . . .2 D4
Ridge La DA13 . . . . .58 A2
Ridge Meadow
  Cty Prim Sch ME5 . . . . . .61 F6
Ridge The
  Groombridge TN3 . . . . . .161 A6
  Orpington BR6 . . . . .51 D8
  Sidcup DA14 . . . . .24 F8
Ridge View Sch TN10 . . . .117 D5
Ridge Way Crayford DA1 . . .8 F1
  Marlpit Hill TN8 . . . . . . .112 D4
Ridgebrook Rd SE3 . . . . . . .5 D4
Ridgecroft Cl DA5 . . . . . . .25 C7
Ridgelands TN3 . . . . .132 C4
Ridgeway Dartford DA2 . . .27 E3
  Hayes BR2 . . . . .50 A8
  Hurst Green TN19 . . . . . .184 A3
  Pembury TN2 . . . . .150 D7
  The Moor TN18 . . . . . . .184 E8
Ridgeway Ave DA12 . . . . . .30 B5
Ridgeway Bglws DA12 . . . .31 F1
Ridgeway Cres
  Orpington BR6 . . . . .51 E7
  Tonbridge TN10 . . . . . . .117 D4
Ridgeway Crescent
  Gdns BR6 . . . . .51 E7
Ridgeway Dr BR1 . . . . .22 B4
Ridgeway E DA15 . . . . .6 F2
Ridgeway The
  Chatham ME4 . . . . .61 E7
  Gillingham ME7 . . . . .48 C7
  Shorne DA12 . . . . .31 E1
  Tonbridge TN10 . . . . . . .117 D4
Ridgeway W DA15 . . . . .6 E2
Ridgewood DA3 . . . . .43 C7
Ridgway ME16 . . . . .91 B2
Ridgwell Rd E16 . . . . .1 C8
Ridgy Field Cl TN15 . . . . . .72 A2

Riding La TN11 . . . . .100 D2
Riding Pk TN11 . . . . .116 D7
Ridings The
  Paddock Wood TN12 . . .136 A7
  Royal Tunbridge Wells TN2 149 F6
Ridley Ct BR6 . . . . .51 C6
Ridley Rd Bexley DA16 . . . .7 B6
  Bromley BR2 . . . . .36 A6
  Rochester ME1 . . . . .47 B4
Riefield Rd SE9 . . . . .6 C2
Riggs Way TN15 . . . . .71 F3
Ring Cl BR1 . . . . .22 B1
Ringden Ave TN12 . . . . . .135 F6
Ringer's Ct BR1 . . . . .36 A6
Ringer's Rd BR1 . . . . .36 A6
Ringle Gn TN18 . . . . .186 C5
Ringlestone Cres ME14 . . .91 F8
Ringlestone Rd ME17 . . . . .95 D4
Ringlet Cl E16 . . . . .1 B8
Ringlet Rd ME4 . . . . .34 C2
Ringmer Way BR1 . . . . .36 F4
Rings Hill TN11 . . . . .116 B4
Ringshall Rd BR5 . . . . .38 B4
Ringwood Ave BR6 . . . . . . .52 C1
Ringwood Cl ME8 . . . . .63 D8
Ringwood Rd ME15 . . . . .107 C8
Ripley Cl BR1 . . . . .36 F4
Ripley Rd Erith DA17 . . . . . .4 A2
  Newham E16 . . . . .1 C7
Ripon Cl ME8 . . . . .49 D3
Ripon Rd SE18 . . . . .6 B8
Rippersley Rd DA16 . . . . . . .7 A6
Rippolson Rd SE18 . . . . . . .2 F1
Risden La TN18 . . . . .185 D7
Rise The Crayford DA1 . . . .8 F3
  Gillingham ME4 . . . . .48 A7
  Gillingham, Hempstead ME7 63 A3
  Gravesend DA12 . . . . . . .30 E4
  Rochester ME1 . . . . .47 D3
  Sevenoaks TN13 . . . . . . .99 C2
  Sidcup DA5 . . . . .24 C8
Risedale Rd DA7 . . . . .8 C4
Riseden Rd TN5 . . . . .174 C1
Ritch Rd ME6 . . . . .74 E8
Ritter St SE18 . . . . .6 A8
River Bank Cl **8** ME15 . . .92 B4
River Cl ME15 . . . . .106 A7
River Cotts BR5 . . . . .38 C7
River Ct TN13 . . . . .83 E5
River Dr ME2 . . . . .46 F7
River Lawn Rd TN9 . . . . . .117 B1
River Park View BR6 . . . . . .38 B2
River Rd IG11 . . . . .3 A8
River St **6** ME7 . . . . .48 A6
River View **6** Dartford DA1 .10 A3
  Greenwich SE7 . . . . .1 C3
  Maidstone ME15 . . . . . . .91 F2
River View Cl **6** ME4 . . . .47 F3
River Way ME20 . . . . .75 B4
River Wlk TN9 . . . . .117 B1
Riverbank Rd BR1 . . . . . . .22 A5
Riverdale Est TN9 . . . . . . .133 D8
Riverdale Rd Erith DA8 . . . .4 C1
  Sidcup DA5 . . . . .7 F1
  Woolwich SE18 . . . . .2 F1
Riverhead Cl ME16 . . . . . . .91 D6
Riverhead Cty Prim Sch
  TN13 . . . . .83 F5
Riverhead Mews TN13 . . . .83 E4
Riverhill TN15 . . . . .99 E4
Riverhill Cotts TN15 . . . . .99 E5
Riverhill House Gdns*
  TN15 . . . . .99 E5
Riverhope Mans SE18 . . . . .1 E3
Rivers Cl ME18 . . . . .104 E7
Rivers Wlk ME17 . . . . .111 C5
Riversdale DA11 . . . . .29 E5
Riverside Edenbridge TN8 .112 C1
  Eynsford DA4 . . . . .54 D8
  Greenwich SE7 . . . . .1 B3
Riverside Cl BR5 . . . . .38 C7
Riverside Cotts TN14 . . . . .53 F1
Riverside Ct
  2 Orpington BR5 . . . . . .38 C4
  Tonbridge TN9 . . . . .117 C1
Riverside Ctry Pk* ME7 . . .49 D5
Riverside East Rd ME4 . . . .34 C1
Riverside Ind Est DA1 . . . . .9 E2
Riverside Rd DA14 . . . . . . .24 E6
Riverside Ret Pk TN14 . . . .84 C8
Riverside Way DA1 . . . . . . .9 E2
Riverston Sch SE12 . . . . . . .5 A2
Riverview Inf Sch DA12 . . .30 E4
Riverview Jun Sch DA12 . .30 E4
Riverview Rd DA9 . . . . .11 A2
Riverwood La BR7 . . . . . . .37 D8
Rixon Ho SE18 . . . . .6 B8
Roach St ME2 . . . . .47 A7
Roan Ct ME2 . . . . .46 F8
Robert Napier Sch The
  ME7 . . . . .48 E3
Robert St Newham E16 . . . .2 B5
  Woolwich SE18 . . . . .2 D2
Roberton Dr BR1 . . . . .36 C8
Roberts Cl Eltham SE9 . . . .23 D7
  8 Orpington BR5 . . . . .38 C4
Roberts Ho SE18 . . . . .5 E6
Roberts Mews BR6 . . . . . .38 A1
Roberts Orchard Rd ME16 .90 F3
Roberts Rd Erith DA17 . . . .4 A1
  Gillingham ME8 . . . . .63 E8
  Snodland ME6 . . . . .74 F8
Robertson House SE18 . . . .5 F6
Robin Cres E6 . . . . .1 D8
Robin Ct ME1 . . . . .47 D4
Robin Hill Dr BR7 . . . . . . .22 E2

Robin Hood Gn BR5 . . . . . .38 A4
Robin Hood La Bexley DA6 . .7 E2
Chatham ME5 . . . . .61 D1
Robin Hood Lane (Lower)
ME5 . . . . .61 F2
Robin Hood Lane (Upper)
ME5 . . . . .61 E1
Robin House 5 ME16 . . . . .91 E4
Robin Way BR5 . . . . .38 B6
Robina Cl DA6 . . . . .7 D3
Robina Ct BR8 . . . . .40 A5
Robinia Ave DA11 . . . . .29 D8
Robins Ave ME17 . . . . .111 C6
Robins Cl ME17 . . . . .111 C4
Robins Ct Lewisham SE12 . .22 C5
Maidstone ME14 . . . . .92 B7
Robins Gr BR4 . . . . .50 A7
Robinwood Dr TN15 . . . . . .84 F8
Robson Cl E6 . . . . .1 E7
Robson Dr Aylesford ME20 .75 D2
Hoo St Werburgh ME3 . . . .34 D6
Robson Ho SE18 . . . . .6 A7
Robyn Cotts TN26 . . . . . . .173 E8
Robyns Croft 6 DA11 . . . . .29 E5
Robyns Way
Edenbridge TN8 . . . . .128 D8
Sevenoaks TN13 . . . . .83 F5
Rocfort Rd ME6 . . . . .75 A8
Rochdale Rd TN1 . . . . .149 C5
Rochdale Rd
Royal Tunbridge Wells TN1 .149 C6
Woolwich SE2 . . . . .3 B2
Rochester Airport
ME1,ME5 . . . . .61 C6
Rochester Ave Bromley BR1 36 B7
Rochester ME1 . . . . .47 C4
Rochester Castle★ ME1 . . .47 C6
Rochester Cath★ ME1 . . . .47 C6
Rochester Cl 1 DA16 . . . . . .7 B1
Rochester Cres ME3 . . . . . .34 D6
Rochester Ct ME2 . . . . .47 E8
Rochester Dr DA5 . . . . .8 A1
Rochester Gate ME1 . . . . . .47 D5
Rochester Gram
Sch for Girls ME1 . . . . . . .47 C2
Rochester Ho 1 ME15 . . .107 D7
Rochester Mathematical
Sch The ME1 . . . . .47 C1
Rochester Rd Burham ME1 .60 E2
Chalk DA12 . . . . .31 B6
Chatham ME1,ME5 . . . . . . .61 C6
Dartford DA1 . . . . .27 A8
Pratling Street ME20 . . . . .76 B4
Rochester ME2 . . . . .46 D4
Tonbridge TN10 . . . . .117 D4
Rochester St ME1 . . . . .47 E3
Rochester Sta ME1 . . . . . . .47 D5
Rochester Way
Dartford DA1 . . . . .25 F8
Eltham SE9 . . . . .6 B4
Eltham,Kidbrooke SE3,SE9 . .5 D4
Rock Ave ME7 . . . . .48 C3
Rock Cotts TN3 . . . . .163 B1
Rock Farm Oasthouse
ME18 . . . . .104 C6
Rock Hill BR6 . . . . .53 B4
Rock Hill Rd TN27 . . . . . . .127 E2
Rock Rd
Borough Green TN15 . . . . .86 F7
Maidstone ME14 . . . . .92 A6
Rock Villa Rd TN1 . . . . . . .149 A4
Rockdale TN13 . . . . .84 B2
Rockdale Rd TN13 . . . . . . .84 C2
Rockliffe Manor
Prim Sch SE18 . . . . .2 F1
Rockmount Rd SE18 . . . . . . .2 F1
Rocks Cl ME19 . . . . .90 A6
Rocks Hill TN17 . . . . .156 A4
Rocks Rd The ME19 . . . . . .90 B6
Rocky Hill ME16 . . . . .91 E4
Rocky Hill Terr 2 ME16 . . .91 E4
Rodeo Cl DA8 . . . . .9 B6
Roding Rd E6 . . . . .2 B8
Rodmell Rd TN2 . . . . .149 A4
Rodney Ave TN10 . . . . . . .117 E4
Rodney Gdns BR4 . . . . .50 A7
Rodway Rd BR1 . . . . .36 B8
Roebourne Way E16 . . . . . . .2 A5
Roebuck Rd ME1 . . . . .47 C5
Roedean Cl BR6 . . . . .52 B6
Roedean Rd TN2 . . . . .149 A4
Roehampton Cl DA12 . . . . .30 E8
Roehampton Dr BR7 . . . . . .23 C2
Roethorne Gdns TN30 . . .183 B8
Roffen Rd ME1 . . . . .47 C2
Rogers Ct BR8 . . . . .40 A5
Rogers Rough Rd TN17 . . .167 B2
Rogers Wood La DA3 . . . . .56 B6
Rogersmead TN30 . . . . . . .183 A7
Rogley Hill TN27 . . . . .171 B6
Rogues Hill TN11 . . . . .131 C3
Rokesby Cl DA16 . . . . .6 D5
Rolinsden Way BR2 . . . . . . .50 D6
Rollesby Way SE28 . . . . .3 C7
Rolleston Ave BR5 . . . . .37 B3
Rolleston Cl BR5 . . . . .37 B2
Rollo Rd BR8 . . . . .25 F1
Rolvenden Ave ME8 . . . . . .49 C3
Rolvenden Gdns BR1 . . . . .22 D1
Rolvenden Hill TN17 . . . . .182 C5
Rolvenden Prim Sch
TN17 . . . . .181 D6
Rolvenden Rd
Rochester ME2 . . . . .33 C2
Tenterden TN30 . . . . .182 E7
Rolvenden Sta TN30 . . . . .182 D6
Roman Cl ME5 . . . . .61 D1
Roman Hts ME14 . . . . .92 C6

Roman Rd Edenbridge TN8 128 D5
Northfleet DA11 . . . . .29 C5
Snodland ME6 . . . . .74 F8
Roman Sq SE28 . . . . .3 A5
Roman Villa Rd DA2,DA4 . .27 C2
Roman Way Crayford DA1 . .8 D2
Rochester ME2 . . . . .46 F4
Romany Ct ME5 . . . . .48 D1
Romany Rd ME8 . . . . .49 C2
Romany Rise ME5 . . . . .37 C1
Romden Rd
Biddenden Green TN27 . . .143 D1
Haffenden Quarter TN27 . .159 A3
Rome Terr ME4 . . . . .47 F4
Romero Sq SE3 . . . . .5 C5
Romford Rd TN2,TN12 . . .150 F7
Romney Br ME1 . . . . .22 D1
Romney Cl ME14 . . . . .93 A3
Romney Dr BR1 . . . . .22 D1
Romney Gdns DA7 . . . . .7 F6
Romney Pl ME15 . . . . .92 A4
Romney Rd Chatham ME5 . .62 B5
Northfleet DA11 . . . . .29 E5
Woolwich SE18 . . . . .2 A2
Romney Way TN10 . . . . . . .117 D5
Romsey Cl Orpington BR6 . .51 C6
Rochester ME2 . . . . .46 E8
Ron Green Ct DA8 . . . . .8 D8
Ronald House SE3 . . . . .5 C5
Ronalds Rd BR1 . . . . .36 A8
Ronaldstone Rd DA15 . . . . .6 E1
Ronfearn Ave BR5 . . . . .38 D4
Ronver Rd SE12 . . . . .22 A7
Roodlands La TN8 . . . . . . .113 D6
Rook La ME9 . . . . .65 F6
Rookdean TN13 . . . . .83 C5
Rookery Cres ME3 . . . . .16 B6
Rookery Ct RM20 . . . . .11 A8
Rookery Dr BR7 . . . . .37 A8
Rookery Gdns BR5 . . . . .38 C4
Rookery Hill ME6 . . . . .74 F8
Rookery La BR2 . . . . .36 B3
Rookery Lodge ME3 . . . . . . .16 C5
Rookery Rd BR6 . . . . .51 A1
Rookery View 4 RM17 . . . .12 D8
Rookesley Rd BR5 . . . . .38 D3
Rookley Cl TN2 . . . . .149 D2
Rooks Hill TN15 . . . . .100 D6
Roopers TN3 . . . . .148 A7
Roosevelt Ave ME5 . . . . . . .62 A8
Rope Wlk ME4 . . . . .47 F5
Rope Wlk The TN18 . . . . . .186 B5
Rope Yard Rails SE18 . . . . . .2 B3
Ropemakers Ct ME4 . . . . . .48 A1
Roper Cl ME8 . . . . .63 C3
Roper St 1 SE9 . . . . .6 A1
Roper's Gate TN2 . . . . . . .148 E1
Roper's Green La ME3 . . . . .18 B2
Roper's La ME3 . . . . .34 F8
Ropery Bsns Pk SE7 . . . . . . .1 C2
Ropewalk TN17 . . . . .169 C5
Rose Ave DA12 . . . . .30 E2
Rose Bruford Coll DA15 . . .24 B7
Rose Cotts ME2 . . . . .46 B8
Rose Ct ME17 . . . . .106 D1
Rose Dale BR6 . . . . .51 B8
Rose Hill Ho TN1 . . . . .149 A3
Rose Hill Sch TN4 . . . . . . .148 C5
Rose St Northfleet DA11 . . .12 B1
Rochester ME1 . . . . .47 D3
Tonbridge TN9 . . . . .133 C8
Rose Terr ME19 . . . . .88 D7
Rose Way SE12 . . . . .5 A2
Rose Yd ME14 . . . . .92 A4
Roseacre Gdns ME14 . . . . .93 A3
Roseacre Jun Sch ME14 . . .93 A4
Roseacre La ME14 . . . . .93 A4
Rosebank Gdns DA16 . . . . . .7 B4
Rosebank Gdns DA11 . . . . .29 E7
Rosebank Wlk 13 SE18 . . . .1 C6
Roseberry Gdns
Dartford DA1 . . . . .26 C8
Orpington BR6 . . . . .51 E7
Rosebery Ave DA15 . . . . . .23 E8
Rosebery Ct DA11 . . . . .29 F7
Rosebery Rd Chatham ME4 .47 E2
Gillingham ME7 . . . . .48 D7
Grays RM17 . . . . .11 E8
Rosecroft Cl BR5 . . . . .38 C3
Rosedale Cl Dartford DA2 . .27 B8
Woolwich SE2 . . . . .3 B3
Rosedene Cl DA1 . . . . .26 C8
Rosefield Sevenoaks TN13 .84 A3
Rosefield 15 Sidcup DA14 . . .24 A4
Rosegarth DA13 . . . . .43 E8
Rosehill Wlk TN1 . . . . .149 A3
Roseholme ME16 . . . . .91 D2
Roselare Cl TN16 . . . . .81 D1
Roseleigh Ave ME15 . . . . . .91 C5
Rosemary Cl 4 ME5 . . . . . .61 F4
Rosemary Ct ME1 . . . . .47 D4
Rosemary La
Culverstone Green TN15 . . .57 D3
Headcorn TN27 . . . . .142 F5
Kilndown TN5 . . . . .177 A5
Rosemary Rd Bexley DA16 . .6 F6
East Malling ME19 . . . . . . .74 F1
Maidstone ME15 . . . . .93 A3
Rosemount Cl ME15 . . . . .106 F4
Rosemount Ct ME2 . . . . . . .33 A1
Rosemount Dr BR1 . . . . . . .36 F5
Rosenheath Cl BR6 . . . . . . .52 C3
Rosetta Prim Sch E16 . . . . .1 B8
Roseveare Rd SE12 . . . . . . .22 C4
Rosewood DA2 . . . . .25 E4
Rosewood Cl DA14 . . . . . . .24 C5
Rosewood Ct BR1 . . . . .36 D8
Rosher Ho DA11 . . . . .12 F1

Rosherville
CE Prim Sch DA11 . . . . . . .12 E1
Rosherville Way DA11 . . . . .12 E1
Roslin Way BR1 . . . . .22 A3
Ross Ct ME5 . . . . .27 F1
Ross House SE18 . . . . .5 E6
Ross Rd DA1 . . . . .9 A1
Ross St ME1 . . . . .47 D4
Ross Way SE9 . . . . .5 E4
Rossdale TN2 . . . . .149 D5
Rosse Mews SE3 . . . . .5 B6
Rossell Rd RM18 . . . . .12 F5
Rossland Cl DA6 . . . . .8 B2
Rosslyn Gn ME16 . . . . .91 B5
Rossmore DA14 . . . . .24 A3
Rother Cl 2 BR5 . . . . .38 D1
Rother Rd TN10 . . . . .117 C5
Rother Vale ME5 . . . . .62 C3
Rothermere Cl TN17 . . . . .180 E6
Rothesay Ct 6 SE12 . . . . . .22 B5
Rothley Cl TN30 . . . . .183 B8
Rouge La DA12 . . . . .30 B7
Roughetts Rd ME19 . . . . . .73 F3
Roughway La TN11 . . . . . . .102 C2
Round Ash Way DA3 . . . . . .42 E3
Round Green Cotts TN17 154 F4
Round St DA12,DA13 . . . . .44 D5
Round Wood Cl ME5 . . . . . .62 A1
Roundel Way TN12 . . . . . .138 D5
Roundhay ME15 . . . . .74 E1
Roundhill Rd TN2 . . . . . . .149 D1
Roundlyn Gdns BR5 . . . . . .38 B5
Roundtable Rd BR1 . . . . . . .22 A5
Roundwell ME14 . . . . .93 D3
Roundwood BR7 . . . . .37 B7
Routh St E6 . . . . .1 F8
Rover Rd ME5 . . . . .62 B2
Row The DA3 . . . . .56 F8
Rowan Ave Aylesford ME20 .75 E1
Longfield DA3 . . . . .42 D7
Meopham Sta DA13 . . . . . .44 B3
Paddock Wood TN12 . . . . .135 F5
Rowan Cres DA1 . . . . .26 C7
Rowan Ct 2 SE12 . . . . .22 A8
Rowan Ho 4 Chatham ME5 .61 F5
Sidcup DA14 . . . . .23 F5
Rowan Lea ME5 . . . . .48 B1
Rowan Rd Bexley DA7 . . . . . .7 E4
Swanley BR8 . . . . .39 D6
Rowan Shaw TN10 . . . . . . .117 D6
Rowan Tree Rd TN2 . . . . . .148 E1
Rowan Wlk Chatham ME4 . .47 E3
Orpington BR2 . . . . .50 F7
Rowanwood Ave DA15 . . . .24 A7
Rowbrocke Cl ME8 . . . . . . .63 D3
Rowdow La TN14,TN15 . . .69 E5
Rowe Pl ME20 . . . . .75 F6
Rowenden Vineyard★
TN17 . . . . .181 B2
Rowfield 6 TN8 . . . . .112 D3
Rowhill Cotts DA2 . . . . .25 E2
Rowhill Rd DA2 . . . . .26 A3
Rowhill Sch DA2 . . . . .26 C4
Rowland Ave ME7 . . . . .48 E2
Rowland Cl ME7 . . . . .48 E2
Rowlatt Cl DA2 . . . . .26 C4
Rowlatt Rd DA2 . . . . .26 C5
Rowley Ave DA15 . . . . .24 B8
Rowley Hill TN2 . . . . .134 D1
Rowmarsh Cl DA11 . . . . . . .29 D4
Rowntree Path 1 SE28 . . . . .3 B5
Rowton Rd SE18 . . . . .6 C7
Rowzill Rd BR8 . . . . .25 F2
Royal Albert Sta 4 E16 . . . . .1 E6
Royal Albert Way
Newham E16 . . . . .1 E6
Newham,Cyprus E6 . . . . .2 A6
Royal Ave TN9 . . . . .133 D8
Royal Chase TN4,TN1 . . . .148 F4
Royal Cl BR6 . . . . .51 B6
Royal Ct SE9 . . . . .5 F1
Royal Docks Com Sch E16 . .1 C7
Royal Docks Rd E6 . . . . .2 B7
Royal Eagle Cl ME2 . . . . . .47 E7
Royal Engineers Mus★ME7 48 B6
Royal Engineers' Rd ME14 91 F7
Royal Oak Rd DA6 . . . . .8 A3
Royal Par BR7 . . . . .23 C1
Royal Parade Mews BR7 . .23 C1
Royal Park Prim Sch DA14 24 E5
Royal Pier Rd DA12 . . . . . .13 C1
Royal Rd Hawley DA2 . . . . .27 A3
Newham E16 . . . . .1 D7
Sidcup DA14 . . . . .24 D5
Royal Sovereign Ave ME4 .48 B7
Royal Star Arc 6 ME14 . . . .91 F4
Royal Tunbridge Wells
Bsns Pk TN2 . . . . .133 D1
Royal Victoria Place
Sh Ctr TN1 . . . . .149 B4
Royal Victoria Sta E16 . . . . .1 C1
Royal West Kent Ave
TN10 . . . . .117 D4
Roydene Rd SE18 . . . . .2 E1
Roydon Hall★ TN12 . . . . .103 F4
Roydon Hall Rd TN12 . . . .103 F4
Royston Rd Crayford DA1 . . .8 F1
Maidstone ME15 . . . . .93 A3
Roystons Cl ME8 . . . . .49 F2
Royton Ave ME17 . . . . . . .111 D5
Rubin Pl ME19 . . . . .89 B3
Ruck La TN12 . . . . .152 E3
Ruckinge Way ME8 . . . . . . .49 C3
Ruddstreet Cl SE18 . . . . .2 C2
Rudge Cl ME5 . . . . .62 D2
Rudland Rd DA7 . . . . .8 B4
Ruegg House 5 SE18 . . . . . .6 A8
Ruffet Cl TN2 . . . . .148 E1

Ruffets Wood DA12 . . . . . .30 C2
Rugby Cl ME5 . . . . .61 F4
Ruggles Cl ME23 . . . . .17 E3
Rumania Wlk DA12 . . . . . . .30 F5
Rumstead La ME17,ME9 . . .79 D4
Rumstead Rd ME9 . . . . .79 E4
Rumwood Ct ME17 . . . . . .108 B5
Runciman Cl BR6 . . . . .52 C1
Runham La ME17 . . . . .110 C1
Running Horse Rndbt The
ME14 . . . . .76 E1
Runnymede Ct ME14 . . . . . .27 C7
Runnymede Gdns ME15 . .107 A8
Rural Vale DA11 . . . . .29 E8
Ruscombe Cl TN4 . . . . .132 F2
Rush Cl ME5 . . . . .62 A3
Rushbrook Rd SE9 . . . . .23 C6
Rushdean Rd ME2 . . . . .46 D5
Rushdene SE2 . . . . .3 D3
Rushet Rd BR5 . . . . .38 A7
Rushetts TN3 . . . . .147 F4
Rushetts Rd TN15 . . . . .55 E3
Rusheymead Ho 6 SE18 . . . .2 F1
Rushford Cl TN27 . . . . .141 D5
Rushgrove St SE18 . . . . .1 F2
Rushley Cl BR2 . . . . .50 E6
Rushlye Cl TN3 . . . . .163 F5
Rushmead Dr ME15 . . . . .107 A7
Rushmore Cl BR1 . . . . .36 F5
Rushmore Ct 8 ME14 . . . . .93 A3
Rushmore Hill BR6,TN14 . .67 D6
Rushymead TN15 . . . . .70 A1
Ruskin Ave DA16 . . . . .7 A5
Ruskin Cl ME19 . . . . .89 F8
Ruskin Ct SE9 . . . . .5 F1
Ruskin Dr Bexley DA16 . . . . .7 A5
Orpington BR6 . . . . .51 E7
Ruskin Gr Bexley DA16 . . . . .7 A5
Dartford DA1 . . . . .10 A2
Ruskin Rd DA17 . . . . .4 A2
Ruskin Wlk BR2 . . . . .36 F3
Rusland Ave BR6 . . . . .51 D7
Russell Cl Bexley DA7 . . . . . .8 A3
Crayford DA1 . . . . .9 A3
Greenwich SE7 . . . . .5 C7
Russell Ct ME4 . . . . .48 B3
Russell House Sch TN14 . . .69 C3
Russell Pl DA4 . . . . .41 C5
Russell Rd Gravesend DA12 13 D1
Kit's Coty ME20 . . . . .76 D7
Newham E16 . . . . .1 B7
Tilbury RM18 . . . . .12 F6
Russell Sq DA3 . . . . .42 D6
Russell Terr DA3 . . . . .41 C5
Russells Ave ME8 . . . . .64 A8
Russells Yd TN17 . . . . .169 D4
Russet Cl ME17 . . . . .106 C3
Russet Ct ME17 . . . . .106 C3
Russet House RM17 . . . . . .12 C7
Russet Way ME19 . . . . .88 F2
Russets The
Maidstone ME16 . . . . .91 B5
Meopham Sta DA13 . . . . . .44 B3
Russett Cl Ditton ME20 . . . .90 E8
Orpington BR6 . . . . .52 B5
Russett Rd TN12 . . . . .119 F6
Russett Way BR8 . . . . .39 D8
Rusthall Grange TN4 . . . . .148 D4
Rusthall High St TN4 . . . . .148 C4
Rusthall Pk TN4 . . . . .148 C4
Rusthall Rd TN4 . . . . .148 D4
Ruston Rd SE18 . . . . .1 E3
Rustwick TN4 . . . . .148 E1
Ruth House ME16 . . . . .91 E5
Rutherford Way TN10 . . . .117 D7
Rutherglen Rd SE2 . . . . .7 A8
Ruthin Rd SE3 . . . . .5 A8
Rutland Ave DA15 . . . . .24 A8
Rutland Cl Dartford DA1 . . .26 D8
Sidcup DA5 . . . . .24 D7
Rutland Ct Chislehurst BR7 .37 A8
Sidcup SE9 . . . . .23 C6
Rutland Gate DA17 . . . . .4 B1
Rutland Ho 10 SE18 . . . . . . .1 F2
Rutland Pl ME8 . . . . .63 C3
Rutland Way
Maidstone ME15 . . . . .107 E8
Orpington BR5 . . . . .38 C3
Ruxley Cl DA14 . . . . .24 E2
Ruxley Cnr DA14 . . . . .24 E2
Ruxley Corner Ind Est
DA14 . . . . .24 D2
Ruxley Ct 1 BR1 . . . . .36 C7
Ruxley Manor Prim Sch
SE9 . . . . .23 A4
Ruxton Cl BR8 . . . . .39 E6
Ruxton Ct 5 BR8 . . . . .39 E6
Ryan Cl SE3 . . . . .5 C3
Ryan Dr ME15 . . . . .93 A2
Ryarsh Cres BR6 . . . . .51 E6
Ryarsh La ME19 . . . . .74 B1
Ryarsh Prim Sch ME19 . . . .74 A4
Ryarsh Rd ME19 . . . . .74 B5
Rycaut Cl ME8 . . . . .63 D2
Rycroft La TN14 . . . . .98 E5
Rydal Cl TN4 . . . . .148 E5
Rydal Dr Bexley DA7 . . . . . . .8 A6
Royal Tunbridge Wells TN4 148 E5
Ryde Cl ME5 . . . . .62 B8
Rydens Ho SE9 . . . . .22 C5
Ryder Cl BR1 . . . . .22 B3
Ryders TN3 . . . . .148 A3
Rydons Cl SE9 . . . . .5 E4
Rye Cl DA5 . . . . .8 B1
Rye Cres BR5 . . . . .38 D1
Rye Field 25 BR5 . . . . .38 D1
Rye La Otford TN14 . . . . . . .69 A2
Sevenoaks TN13,TN14 . . . .83 F7

Rye Rd Four Throws TN18 . .185 D8
TN18 . . . . .179 B1
Rye Wood Cotts TN14 . . . . .83 F7
Ryecault Cl 4 ME16 . . . . . .91 E3
Ryecroft Gravesend DA12 . .30 E3
New Barn DA3 . . . . .43 D5
Ryecroft Rd Orpington BR5 .37 D3
Otford TN14 . . . . .69 C3
Ryedale Cl TN13 . . . . .83 E6
Ryegrass Cl ME5 . . . . .62 C6
Ryelands Cres SE12 . . . . . . .5 C1
Rymers Cl TN2 . . . . .149 D5
Rymill St E16 . . . . .2 A5
Rysted La TN16 . . . . .81 D1

S

Sabre Ct ME7 . . . . .49 A1
Sackville Ave BR2 . . . . .36 A1
Sackville Cl TN13 . . . . .84 B5
Sackville Rd DA2 . . . . .26 E6
Sackville Sch TN11 . . . . . .116 C6
Sacred Heart Sch TN5 . . . .174 D5
Saddington St ME12 . . . . . .30 C8
Saddler's Pk DA4 . . . . .54 D7
Saddlers Cl ME14 . . . . .92 E5
Sadlers Cl ME5 . . . . .61 D2
Saffron Way 1 ME5 . . . . . . .61 F5
Sage Cl 7 E6 . . . . .1 F8
Sage Rd ME1 . . . . .47 B3
Saigasso Cl E16 . . . . .1 D7
Sailfield Ct ME4 . . . . .47 F7
Sailmakers Ct 5 ME4 . . . . .48 B2
Saints Hill TN11 . . . . .147 A8
SS Peter & Paul
RC Prim Sch BR5 . . . . . . .37 E7
St Aidan's Way DA12 . . . . .30 E5
St Alban's Cl DA12 . . . . . . .30 D5
St Alban's Gdns DA12 . . . . .30 D5
St Alban's Rd DA1 . . . . .9 F1
St Alban's Rd Inf Sch DA1 . .9 F1
St Albans Cl ME7 . . . . .48 C1
St Albans Rd ME2 . . . . .46 D6
St Alfege Rd SE7 . . . . .5 D8
St Andrew Rd ME7 . . . . .48 D7
St Andrew's Cl ME16 . . . . . .91 A2
St Andrew's Ct 4 BR8 . . . . .39 E6
St Andrew's Rd
10 Gravesend DA12 . . . . . .30 B8
Maidstone ME16 . . . . .91 A3
Tilbury RM18 . . . . .12 E5
St Andrew's Wlk ME3 . . . . .19 D8
St Andrews CE TN12 . . . . .136 A6
St Andrews Ct
24 Gravesend DA12 . . . . . .13 B1
Royal Tunbridge Wells TN4 .133 A1
St Andrews Dr BR5 . . . . . . .38 A2
St Andrews Mews SE3 . . . . .5 A7
St Andrews Park Rd TN4 133 A1
St Andrews Rd
Paddock Wood TN12 . . . . .136 A6
Sidcup DA14 . . . . .24 D5
St Ann's Green La TN12 . .138 D7
St Anselm's
RC Prim Sch DA1 . . . . . . .10 A2
St Anthony's Ct BR6 . . . . . .51 B8
St Aubyns Cl BR6 . . . . .51 F7
St Aubyns Gdns BR6 . . . . . .51 F8
St Audrey Ave DA7 . . . . .8 A5
St Augustine Ho 1 TN9 . . .133 B8
St Augustine of
Canterbury RC
Prim Sch ME8 . . . . .63 D3
St Augustine's Ave BR2 . . .36 A2
St Augustine's
Jun & Inf Schs DA17 . . . . .3 F2
St Augustine's RC
Prim Sch TN4 . . . . .149 A2
St Augustine's Rd DA17 . . . .3 F2
St Barnabas CE
Prim Sch TN1 . . . . .149 B5
St Barnabas Cl
Gillingham ME7 . . . . .48 D3
Maidstone ME16 . . . . .91 C8
St Barnabas' Cl TN1 . . . . .149 B5
St Bartholomew's Hospl
ME1 . . . . .47 E4
St Bartholomew's La 4
ME1 . . . . .47 E4
St Bartholomew's Terr
ME1 . . . . .47 E4
St Bartholomews RC
Prim Sch BR8 . . . . .39 E6
St Benedict Rd ME6 . . . . . .74 F8
St Benedict's Ave DA12 . . .30 E6
St Benedicts RC
Prim Sch ME5 . . . . .62 C2
St Benets Ct TN30 . . . . . . .183 B8
St Benets Way TN30 . . . . .183 B8
St Benjamins Dr BR6 . . . . .52 C2
St Bernards Dr TN10 . . . . .117 C6
St Blaise Ave BR1 . . . . .36 B7
St Boltophs Ct TN13 . . . . . .84 B3
St Botolph's Ave ME13 . . . .84 A3
St Botolph's CE Prim
Sch DA11 . . . . .29 D8
St Botolph's Rd TN13 . . . . .84 B3
St Brelade's Ct TN8 . . . . . .112 A3
St Brides Cl DA18 . . . . .3 D1
St Catherine's Hospl ME1 .47 D4
St Catherine's RC Sch for
Girls DA6 . . . . .8 B2

St Chad's Dr DA12 . . . . . . .30 E5
St Chad's Rd RM18 . . . . . . .13 A7
St Chad's Sch RM18 . . . . . .13 A6
St Christopher's (Trng
  Coll, Dr Barnardo's
  Home) TN2 . . . . .149 D4
St Clement's Ave RM20 . . .11 B8
St Clement's Ho ME1 . . . . .47 D5
St Clement's Rd RM20 . .11 C7
St Clements Cl DA11 . . . . .29 F5
St Clements Ct RM17 . . . . .11 E8
St Clere Hill Rd TN15 . . . . .70 F7
St Columba's Cl DA12 . . . .30 E5
St Columba's
  RC Boys Sch DA6 . . . . . . .8 B2
St David's Bridge TN17 .169 D4
St David's Cres DA12 . . . .30 D4
St David's Rd
  Allhallows ME3 . . . . .19 D8
  Hextable BR8 . . . . .25 F1
  Royal Tunbridge Wells TN4 .149 B6
St Domingo Ho SE18 . . . . .1 F8
St Dunstan's Dr DA12 . . . .30 E5
St Dunstans Wlk TN17 . .169 D4
St Edith's Rd TN15 . . . . . .70 A2
St Edmund's Cotts TN15 .56 A2
St Edmund's Ct TN15 . . . .56 A2
St Edmunds Cl DA18 . . . . .3 D4
St Edmunds Rd DA1 . . . . .10 A3
St Faith's La ME14 . . . . . .93 B4
St Faith's St ME14 . . . . . .91 F4
St Fidelis RC Prim Sch DA8 8 C8
St Fidelis' Rd DA8 . . . . . . .4 D1
St Francis Ave DA12 . . . . .30 E4
St Francis Cl
  Maidstone ME14 . . . . .92 B7
  Orpington BR6 . . . . .37 E3
St Francis RC Prim Sch
  Maidstone ME14 . . . . .92 A5
  Maidstone, Penenden
  Heath ME14 . . . . .92 B7
St Francis Rd DA13 . . . . .58 B3
St Francis Sch ME14 . . . . .92 B7
St Francis' Rd DA8 . . . . . .4 D2
St George's Bickley CE
  Prim Sch BR1 . . . . .36 D7
St George's CE Prim Sch
  TN15 . . . . .71 F3
St George's CE Sch DA11 .30 A6
St George's Cres DA12 . . .30 D4
St George's Ct TN15 . . . . .71 F3
St George's Ctr DA11 . . . .13 B1
St George's Pk TN2 . . . .162 F8
St George's Rd
  Gillingham ME7 . . . . .48 C6
  Sevenoaks TN13 . . . . .84 B5
  Sidcup DA14 . . . . .24 D2
St George's Sch TN2 . . .150 A5
St George's Sq ME16 . . . .91 E3
St George's Wlk ME3 . . . .19 D8
St Georges Cl SE28 . . . . . .3 D7
St Georges Mews TN9 133 B8
St Georges Rd Bromley BR1 36 F6
  Orpington BR5 . . . . .37 D3
  Swanley BR8 . . . . .39 F5
St Georges Rd W BR1 . . .36 E7
St Georges Sq DA3 . . . . .42 E6
St German's Pl SE3 . . . . . .5 A6
St Giles Cl BR6 . . . . .51 D5
St Gregory's Catholic
  Comp Sch TN4 . . . . .149 A7
St Gregory's Cres DA12 . .30 E6
St Gregory's Ct DA12 . . . .30 E6
St Helens CE Prim Sch
  ME3 . . . . .16 B5
St Helens Cotts ME15 . .105 E8
St Helens La ME15 . . . . .105 E8
St Helens Rd Cliffe ME3 . .16 B5
  [7] Erith DA18 . . . . .3 D4
St Helier's Cl ME16 . . . . .91 B2
St Hilda's Way DA12 . . . . .30 E5
St Hildas TN15 . . . . .101 F8
St James Cl
  East Malling ME19 . . . . . . .89 F8
  Grain ME3 . . . . .21 B6
St James Ct SE3 . . . . .5 B6
St James Oaks DA11 . . . .30 A8
St James Pl DA1 . . . . .9 D1
St James RC Prim Sch
  BR5 . . . . .37 B4
St James Rd ME3 . . . . . . .21 B5
St James Sq DA3 . . . . . . .42 E6
St James Terr ME4 . . . . . .52 C2
St James Way DA14 . . . . .24 E3
St James' CE Inf Sch
  TN2 . . . . .149 C4
St James' CE Jun Sch
  TN2 . . . . .149 C4
St James' Inf Sch ME19 . .89 F4
St James' La DA9 . . . . . . .27 E8
St James' Pk TN1 . . . . . .149 C5
St James' Prim Sch ME3 . .21 B6
St James' Rd TN1 . . . . . .149 C5
St James's Ave DA11 . . . .30 A8
St James's Cl SE18 . . . . . .2 B2
St James's Ct TN1 . . . . .149 B4
St James's Rd
  Gravesend DA11 . . . . .13 A1
  Sevenoaks TN13 . . . . .84 B5
St James's St DA11 . . . . .13 A1
St Joachim's RC Sch E16 . .1 C7
St John Fisher
  Catholic Sch ME4 . . . . . .47 E3
St John Fisher RC
  Lower Sch ME4 . . . . .47 F2

St John Fisher RC
  Prim Sch DA18 . . . . .3 E3
St John's CE Inf Sch ME4 .47 E3
St John's CE Prim Sch
  Maidstone ME14 . . . . .92 E4
  Royal Tunbridge Wells TN4 .149 A5
  Sevenoaks TN13 . . . . .84 D4
St John's Cl ME3 . . . . . . .32 C4
St John's Ct TN13 . . . . . .84 C5
St John's Hill TN13,TN14 .84 C5
St John's La DA3 . . . . . . .42 F3
St John's Par [4] DA14 . . .24 B4
St John's Pk Greenwich SE3 .5 A7
  Royal Tunbridge Wells TN4 .149 A8
St John's RC
  Comp Sch DA12 . . . . . . .30 D7
St John's RC
  Prim Sch DA12 . . . . .30 E7
St John's Rd Bexley DA16 . .7 B4
  Dartford DA1 . . . . .27 C8
  Erith DA8 . . . . .4 D1
  Gillingham ME7 . . . . .48 C3
  Gravesend DA12 . . . . .30 D8
  Higham ME3 . . . . .32 C4
  Newham ME4 . . . . .1 A7
  Orpington BR5 . . . . .37 C5
  Royal Tunbridge Wells TN4 .149 A6
  Sevenoaks TN13 . . . . .84 C5
  Sidcup DA14 . . . . .24 B4
St John's Terr SE18 . . . . . .6 D8
St Johns CE
  Prim Sch TN4 . . . . .149 B8
St Johns Ct DA8 . . . . .4 D1
St Johns Rd ME8 . . . . . . .34 D6
St Johns Way ME1 . . . . . .47 A2
St Joseph's RC Prim Sch
  Bromley BR1 . . . . .22 B1
  Crayford DA1 . . . . .8 E3
  Northfleet DA11 . . . . .29 D8
St Josephs Cl BR6 . . . . . .51 F6
St Josephs Ct [4] SE12 . .22 B5
St Josephs Prep Sch
  DA12 . . . . .30 C6
St Justin Cl BR5 . . . . .38 D6
St Katherine's La ME6 . . .74 F7
St Katherine's Prim Sch
  ME6 . . . . .74 F7
St Katherines Cotts DA12 .31 E3
St Katherines Rd DA18 . . .3 D4
St Keverne Rd SE9 . . . . . .22 E4
St Kilda Rd BR6 . . . . .37 F1
St Laurence Ave ME16 . . .91 C8
St Laurence Ct BR5 . . . . .38 D6
St Lawrence Ave TN4 . . .132 D3
St Lawrence CE
  Prim Sch TN15 . . . . .85 E3
St Leonard's St ME19 . . . .89 B7
St Leonards Ave ME4 . . . .47 F2
St Leonards Cl
  [4] Bexley DA16 . . . . .7 A4
  Grays RM17 . . . . .11 F8
St Leonards Rd ME16 . . . .91 C8
St Leonards Rise BR6 . . . .51 E6
St Luke's Ave ME14 . . . . .92 B5
St Luke's CE Inf Sch TN4 149 C7
St Luke's Rd
  Maidstone ME14 . . . . .92 B5
  Royal Tunbridge Wells TN4 .149 B6
St Luke's Way ME3 . . . . . .19 D8
St Lukes Cl Dartford DA2 . .27 E3
  Swanley BR8 . . . . .39 D7
St Lukes Cotts BR8 . . . . .39 D7
St Margaret Clitherow
  RC Prim Sch
  Tonbridge TN10 . . . . . . .117 B6
  Woolwich SE28 . . . . .3 B5
St Margaret's at Troy
  Town CE Prim Sch ME1 .47 D5
St Margaret's Banks ME1 .47 D5
St Margaret's
  CE Jun Sch ME8 . . . . . . .63 E8
St Margaret's
  CE Prim Sch SE18 . . . . . .2 C1
St Margaret's Cl DA2 . . . .27 D6
St Margaret's Cres ME23 .17 E3
St Margaret's Ct ME23 . . .17 E3
St Margaret's Gr SE30 . . .18 C8
St Margaret's Inf Sch ME8 63 E8
St Margaret's Mews ME1 .47 C5
St Margaret's Rd
  Northfleet DA11 . . . . .29 E7
  Sutton at Hone DA2,DA4 . . .27 E7
St Margaret's St ME1 . . . .47 C5
St Margaret's Terr SE18 . . .2 C1
St Margarets Ave DA15 . . .23 D5
St Margarets
  CE Prim Sch TN12 . . . .121 D1
St Margarets Cl
  Maidstone ME16 . . . . .91 B2
  Orpington BR6 . . . . .52 B6
St Margarets Ct ME8 . . . .63 C5
St Margarets Villas TN12 .137 D8
St Mark's Ave DA11 . . . . .29 F8
St Mark's CE Prim Sch
  Bromley BR2 . . . . .36 B6
St Mark's Rd Bromley BR2 .36 B6
  Royal Tunbridge Wells TN4 .148 D1
St Marks
  CE Prim Sch ME20 . . . . .75 F6
St Marks Ct ME20 . . . . . .75 F6
St Marks Ho ME7 . . . . . . .48 C5
St Marks Ind Est E16 . . . . .1 D5
St Martin's Cl ME14 . . . . .78 A1
St Martin's Dr DA4 . . . . . .54 D7
St Martin's Rd DA1 . . . . . .9 F1
  [11] Erith DA18 . . . . .3 D4
  Newington ME9 . . . . .65 C7

St Martins Mdw TN16 . . . .82 C4
St Mary & St Joseph's
  RC Sch DA14 . . . . .24 A3
St Mary Cray
  Prim Sch BR5 . . . . .38 C3
St Mary Cray Sta BR5 . . .38 B5
St Mary St SE18 . . . . .2 A2
St Mary's ME3 . . . . .18 D5
St Mary's Abbey ME19 . . .89 C8
St Mary's CE (VA)
  Prim Sch BR8 . . . . .39 E5
St Mary's Church Rd TN14 82 F2
St Mary's Cl
  Gravesend DA12 . . . . .30 C6
  Grays RM17 . . . . .12 D8
  Laddingford ME18 . . . . . .120 E4
  Platt TN15 . . . . .87 C7
  St Paul's Cray BR5 . . . . . .38 C7
  Ticehurst TN5 . . . . .176 D1
St Mary's Ct
  [5] Westerham TN16 . . . . .81 D1
  Woolwich DA17 . . . . .3 D2
St Mary's
  Cty Prim Sch ME2 . . . . . .47 B7
St Mary's Dr TN13 . . . . . .83 E4
St Mary's Gdns ME4 . . . . .48 B7
St Mary's Island
  CE Prim Sch ME4 . . . . . .34 B2
St Mary's La
  Speldhurst TN3 . . . . .148 A8
  Ticehurst TN5 . . . . .176 D1
St Mary's Pl [11] Eltham SE9 . . .6 A1
  Newington ME9 . . . . .65 C7
St Mary's RC Prim Sch
  Eltham SE9 . . . . .6 A2
  Gillingham ME7 . . . . .48 D6
  Tilbury RM18 . . . . .12 F5
St Mary's Rd Coldblow DA5 .25 C7
  Gillingham ME7 . . . . .48 C6
  Rochester ME2 . . . . .47 B7
  Stone DA9 . . . . .10 E2
  Swanley BR8 . . . . .39 E5
  Tonbridge TN9 . . . . .133 B7
  Wrotham TN15 . . . . .72 A2
St Mary's View ME9 . . . . .65 C7
St Mary's Wlk ME1 . . . . . .60 F1
St Marys Ct SE7 . . . . .5 D7
St Marys Way DA3 . . . . . .42 E6
St Matthew's
  CE Inf Sch ME1 . . . . .47 A2
St Matthew's Cl ME9 . . . .65 C7
St Matthew's High
  Brooms CE PrimSch
  TN4 . . . . .149 B8
St Matthew's Way ME3 . .19 D8
St Matthews Dr
  Bromley BR1 . . . . .36 F6
  Rochester ME1 . . . . .47 A2
St Merryn Cl SE18 . . . . . . .6 D7
St Michael's
  CE Jun Sch ME16 . . . . . .91 E3
St Michael's CE Prim Sch
  Maidstone ME16 . . . . .91 E3
  Tenterden TN30 . . . . .173 A3
St Michael's Cl
  Chatham ME4 . . . . .47 F3
  Erith DA18 . . . . .3 D4
St Michael's Ct [5] ME4 . . .47 B8
St Michael's
  Cty Prim Sch TN7 . . . . .160 B5
St Michael's East
  Wickham
  CE Prim Sch DA16 . . . . . . .7 C6
St Michael's
  RC Prim Sch ME4 . . . . . .47 F3
St Michael's Rd
  Bexley DA16 . . . . .7 B4
  Maidstone ME16 . . . . .91 D3
  Royal Tunbridge Wells TN4 .149 B7
St Michael's Rise DA16 . . .7 B6
St Michael's Terr TN30 . .173 B3
St Michaels Cl Bromley BR1 36 E6
  [4] Newham E16 . . . . .1 D8
  Pratling Street ME20 . . . . .76 C3
St Michaels Ct TN11 . . . .116 E7
St Michaels Dr TN14 . . . .69 E3
St Mildred's Cl [4] TN30 . .183 A7
St Mildreds Rd [5] SE12 . .22 A8
St Nicholas
  CE Cty Inf Sch ME2 . . . .47 A7
St Nicholas Ct SE18 . . . . . .2 F1
St Nicholas Dr TN13 . . . . .84 C1
St Nicholas Gdns ME2 . . .46 F8
St Nicholas Rd SE18 . . . . .2 F2
St Nicolas La BR7 . . . . . . .36 E8
St Olave's Sch BR6 . . . . .52 B2
St Olaves Prep Sch SE9 . .23 B6
St Patrick's Gdns DA12 . . .30 D5
St Patrick's
  RC Prim Sch SE18 . . . . . .2 D2
St Paul's
  CE Prim Sch BR8 . . . . . .40 B8
St Paul's CE Inf Sch TN4 148 B4
  Rochester ME2 . . . . .46 D5
  Swanscombe DA10 . . . . . .28 E8
St Paul's Cray Rd BR5,BR7 37 D8
St Paul's Ct TN4 . . . . . . .148 C4
St Paul's RC Sch SE7 . . . . .7 A8
St Paul's Rd DA8 . . . . .8 C7
St Paul's Sq BR2 . . . . . . .36 A7
St Paul's St TN4 . . . . . . .148 C4
St Paul's Wood Hill BR5 . .37 F7
St Paulinus CE Prim
  Sch DA1 . . . . .8 E3
St Paulinus Ct DA1 . . . . . .8 E3
St Pauls CE Jun Sch TN4 148 B4
St Pauls Cl TN10 . . . . . .117 D5

St Pauls Cray
  CE Prim Sch BR5 . . . . . .38 D6
St Pauls Inf Sch ME14 . . .92 A7
St Peter Chanel
  RC Prim Sch DA14 . . . . .24 C3
St Peter St ME1 . . . . .47 D4
St Peter's Bridge ME14 . .91 F4
St Peter's CE Prim Sch
  Aylesford ME20 . . . . .76 A3
  Royal Tunbridge Wells TN2 .149 C3
St Peter's Cl DA10 . . . . . .28 F8
St Peter's Cty Inf Sch ME1 147 C3
St Peter's Path ME1 . . . . .47 D5
St Peter's
  RC Prim Sch SE18 . . . . . .2 B1
St Peter's St TN2 . . . . . .149 C3
St Peters
  Chislehurst BR7 . . . . .23 D1
  Ditton ME20 . . . . .75 B1
St Peters La BR5 . . . . . . .38 A7
St Peters Pl ME20 . . . . . .75 F6
St Peters Rd ME20 . . . . . .75 B1
St Peters Row TN3 . . . . .147 A5
St Peters St ME16 . . . . . .91 F4
St Philip's Ave ME15 . . . .92 B2
St Philips Ct TN2 . . . . . .149 D6
St Philomena's
  RC Prim Sch SE18 . . . . .38 C2
St Quentin Rd DA16 . . . . . .6 F4
St Ronan's Cl ME15 . . . .107 C7
St Ronan's Sch TN18 . . .179 D2
St Saviours Rd ME15 . . .107 D6
St Simon Stock Sch ME16 91 C4
St Stephen's Cl ME9 . . . .65 C7
St Stephen's
  Cty Prim Sch TN9 . . . . .133 D8
St Stephen's
  RC Prim Sch DA16 . . . . . .7 A5
St Stephen's Sq ME15 . . .91 E2
St Stephen's St TN9 . . . .133 B8
St Stephens Ct TN1 . . . .149 B5
St Stephens Mews ME1 . .61 E8
St Thomas Ct DA5 . . . . . .25 A8
St Thomas More RC
  Prim Sch Bexley DA7 . . . . .7 F5
  Eltham SE9 . . . . .5 E4
  ME5 . . . . .62 A5
St Thomas More
  RC Sec Sch SE9 . . . . .6 A1
St Thomas of Canterbury
  Prim Sch ME8 . . . . .49 B2
St Thomas
  RC Prim Sch TN13 . . . . .84 B2
  Newham E16 . . . . .1 A7
  Northfleet DA11 . . . . .29 E6
St Thomas' CE
  Prim Sch TN3 . . . . .161 C6
St Thomas' Dr BR5 . . . . .37 C1
St Thomas' RC
  Prim Sch RM17 . . . . .12 C8
St Thomas's
  Almshouses DA11 . . . . . .30 B7
St Thomas's Ave DA11 . . .30 B7
St Thomas's Pl [10] RM17 . .12 C8
St Thomas-a-Becket RC
  Prim Sch SE2 . . . . .3 A3
St Timothy's Mews [3] BR1 .36 B8
St Vincents Ave DA1 . . . .10 A2
St Vincents La ME19 . . . .73 A2
St Vincents RC
  Prim Sch SE9 . . . . .22 E4
St Vincents St [4] SE18 . .22 E4
St Welcume's Way ME17 .110 E6
St Werburgh Ct ME3 . . . .34 D5
St Werburgh Ct ME3 . . . .34 D5
St William of Perth RC
  Prim Sch ME1 . . . . .47 B2
St William's Way ME1 . . .47 D2
Sala House SE3 . . . . .5 B3
Salcote Rd DA12 . . . . . . .30 E3
Salem Pl DA11 . . . . .29 D8
Salem St ME15 . . . . .92 A3
Salisbury Ave
  Gillingham ME8 . . . . .63 D8
  Swanley BR8 . . . . .40 A5
Salisbury Cl TN10 . . . . . .117 D5
Salisbury Ho [5] ME15 . .107 D7
Salisbury Mews BR2 . . . .36 E4
Salisbury Rd Bromley BR2 .36 E4
  Chatham ME4 . . . . .48 A3
  Dartford DA2 . . . . .27 C7
  Gravesend DA11 . . . . .29 F7
  [2] Grays RM17 . . . . .12 C8
  Kit's Coty ME20 . . . . .76 D7
  Maidstone ME14 . . . . .92 A6
  Royal Tunbridge Wells,
  High Brooms TN4 . . . . . .149 C8
  Royal Tunbridge Wells,
  Langton Green TN3 . . . . .147 F3
  Sidcup DA5 . . . . .25 A7
  Tonbridge TN10 . . . . . . .117 D4
Salix Rd ME17 . . . . .12 D8
Sallows Shaw DA13 . . . . .44 C4
Sally Port ME7 . . . . .48 A6
Sally Port Gdns ME7 . . . .48 B6
Salmon Rd Dartford DA1 . . .9 F4
  Erith DA8 . . . . .4 A1
Salomons Rd Newham E13 . .1 C8
  Royal Tunbridge Wells TN4 .148 C4
Salt La ME3 . . . . .15 F4
Salt's Ave ME15 . . . . . . .106 F3
Saltash Rd DA16 . . . . .7 C6
Salter's Cross SE18 . . . .105 A1
Saltford Cl DA8 . . . . .4 E1
Saltings Rd ME6 . . . . .75 A7

Saltley Cl E6 . . . . .1 E7
Salts La ME15 . . . . .107 A4
Saltwood Cl BR6 . . . . . . .52 C6
Saltwood Rd ME15 . . . . .91 F1
Sam Bartram Cl SE7 . . . . .1 C1
Samara Cl ME5 . . . . .62 A1
Samphire Cl ME14 . . . . . .92 E4
Samphire Ct RM17 . . . . . .12 E8
Samphire Way ME4 . . . . .34 A2
Sampson Cl DA17 . . . . . . .3 D3
Samson Ho SE18 . . . . .2 C2
Samuel Palmer Ct BR6 . .38 A2
Samuel St SE18 . . . . .1 F2
Sanctuary Cl DA1 . . . . . . .9 D1
Sanctuary Rd ME8 . . . . . .49 A3
Sanctuary The DA5 . . . . . .7 D1
Sand La TN17 . . . . .156 F4
Sand Rd TN3 . . . . .166 A4
Sandalwood House DA15 .23 C5
Sandbach Pl SE18 . . . . . . .2 C1
Sandbanks Hill DA2 . . . . .28 B2
Sandbourne Dr ME14 . . . .76 F1
Sandby Gn SE9 . . . . .5 E4
Sandcliff Rd DA8 . . . . .4 D1
Sanderling Ct SE28 . . . . . .3 C6
Sanderson Way TN9 . . . .117 E1
Sandersons Ave TN14 . . .53 B1
Sanderstead Rd BR5 . . . .38 B3
Sandfield Rd TN11 . . . . .147 A7
Sandford Rd
  Bexley DA7,DA6 . . . . .7 E4
  Bromley BR2 . . . . .36 A5
Sandgate Ct ME8 . . . . . . .63 F4
Sandgate Rd DA16 . . . . . .7 C7
Sandham Point SE18 . . . . .2 B2
Sandhill La ME3 . . . . .32 D6
Sandhurst Ave TN2 . . . .150 E6
Sandhurst Cl
  Gillingham ME8 . . . . .49 C3
  Royal Tunbridge Wells TN2 .149 C6
  Sandhurst TN18 . . . . . . .186 A4
Sandhurst Cross TN12 . .140 F1
Sandhurst
  Cty Prim Sch TN18 . . . .186 C6
Sandhurst Ho TN2 . . . . .149 D5
Sandhurst La TN17 . . . . .181 B2
Sandhurst Pk TN2 . . . . .149 C6
Sandhurst Rd Bexley DA5 . .7 D2
  Orpington BR6 . . . . .52 A6
  Royal Tunbridge Wells TN2 .149 D6
  Sidcup DA15 . . . . .24 A5
  Tilbury RM18 . . . . .13 C5
Sandhurst
  Vineyards* TN18 . . . . . .186 E5
Sandilands TN13 . . . . . . .83 D5
Sandling Ct ME14 . . . . . .92 B7
Sandling La ME14 . . . . . .92 A8
Sandling Prim Sch ME14 .92 B8
Sandling Rd
  Maidstone ME14 . . . . .91 F6
  Maidstone,Ringlestone ME14 .91 F7
Sandling Rise SE9 . . . . . .23 A5
Sandling Way ME4 . . . . . .34 B1
Sandown Cl TN2 . . . . . . .149 F6
Sandown Court
  Com Coll TN2 . . . . .149 F5
Sandown Dr ME8 . . . . . . .63 D7
Sandown Gr TN2 . . . . . .149 F6
Sandown Pk TN2 . . . . . .149 F6
Sandown Rd
  Gravesend DA12 . . . . .30 C2
  New Town ME19 . . . . .89 B8
Sandpiper Dr DA8 . . . . . . .9 B7
Sandpiper Rd ME5 . . . . . .62 D2
Sandpiper Way BR5 . . . . .38 D6
Sandpipers The DA12 . . . .30 D6
Sandpit Pl SE7 . . . . .1 E1
Sandpit Rd DA1 . . . . .9 C3
Sandringham Cl ME19 . . .89 A1
Sandringham Dr DA16 . . . .6 E5
Sandringham Ho ME1 . . .47 B4
Sandringham Rd
  Bromley BR1 . . . . .22 A3
  Gillingham ME8 . . . . .63 E3
Sandrock Ho TN2 . . . . . .149 D4
Sandrock Rd TN2 . . . . . .149 C4
Sandrook Villas TN18 . . .178 F3
Sandstone Rd SE12 . . . . .22 B6
Sandstone Rise ME5 . . . .77 C8
Sandtoft Rd SE7 . . . . .5 B8
Sandway Path [6] BR5 . . .38 C5
Sandway Rd Lenham ME17 110 F4
  Orpington BR5 . . . . .38 C5
Sandy Bank Rd DA12 . . . .30 B7
Sandy Bury BR6 . . . . .51 D7
Sandy Dell ME7 . . . . .63 A3
Sandy Hill Ave SE18 . . . . .2 B1
Sandy Hill La SE18 . . . . . .2 B2
Sandy Hill Rd SE18 . . . . . .2 B1
Sandy La Bean DA13,DA2 . . .28 D5
  Ightham TN15 . . . . .86 B3
  Maidstone,Harbourland ME14
  ME14 . . . . .92 C8
  Maidstone,Penenden
  Heath ME14 . . . . .92 C7
  Maidstone,Ware Street ME14 92 B8
  New Town ME19 . . . . .74 A1
  Orpington BR6 . . . . .38 A2
  Sevenoaks TN13 . . . . .84 C4
  Snodland ME6,ME19 . . . . .74 E6
  St Paul's Cray BR5 . . . . . .38 D8
  Tenterden TN30 . . . . . . .183 B7
  Tilbury RM18 . . . . .13 B8
  West Thurrock RM20 . . . . .11 B8
  Westerham TN16 . . . . .81 D2
  Wrotham Heath TN15,ME19 . .72 F1
Sandy Mount ME14 . . . . .93 B5

Sandy Ridge
Borough Green TN15 . . . . . .87 A7
Chislehurst BR7 . . . . .23 A2
Sandycroft SE2 . . . . .7 A8
Sandycroft Rd ME2 . . . . . . .32 F1
Santana House SE18 . . . . .6 B7
Santer Rd TN18 . . . . .184 E8
Sapho Pk DA12 . . . . .30 F4
Saphora Cl BR6 . . . . .51 D5
Sappers Wlk ME7 . . . . .48 C5
Sapphire Cl E6 . . . . .2 A7
Sara Cres DA9 . . . . .11 B3
Sara House 1 DA8 . . . . .8 E7
Sara Pk DA12 . . . . .30 E4
Sara Turnbull Ho 3 SE18 . . .1 F7
Saracen Cl ME7 . . . . .49 A1
Saracen Fields ME5 . . . . . . .77 C8
Sarafand Ho ME1 . . . . .47 B4
Sark Wlk E16 . . . . .1 B7
Sarsen Hts ME5 . . . . .61 F1
Sarsens Cl DA3 . . . . .44 F6
Sassoon Cl ME20 . . . . .75 A4
Satanita Cl E16 . . . . .1 D7
Saunder's Cross TN14 . . . . .53 B2
Saunders Cl DA11 . . . . .29 E6
Saunders Rd
Royal Tunbridge Wells TN4 . .148 E1
Woolwich SE18 . . . . .2 F1
Saunders St Gillingham ME7 48 C6
7 Rochester ME4 . . . . .47 F3
Saunders Way Dartford DA1 26 F6
Woolwich SE28 . . . . .3 B6
Savage Gdns E6 . . . . .1 F7
Savage Rd ME5 . . . . .62 B3
Savill Ho E16 . . . . .2 B5
Saville Rd E16 . . . . .1 E5
Savoy Rd DA1 . . . . .9 D2
Sawyers Ct ME4 . . . . .48 B2
Saxby Wood TN11 . . . . . . .115 F1
Saxbys Rd TN15 . . . . .85 D5
Saxon Cl Kings Hill ME19 . . .88 F2
Northfleet DA11 . . . . .29 C5
Otford TN14 . . . . .68 F2
Rochester ME2 . . . . .32 F1
Saxon Pl Horton Kirby DA4 . .41 C4
Rochester ME2 . . . . .46 F5
Saxon Rd Bromley BR1 . . . . .22 A1
Hawley DA2 . . . . .26 E4
Saxon Wlk DA14 . . . . .24 C2
Saxons Dr ME14 . . . . .92 B7
Saxton St ME7 . . . . .48 C5
Saxville Rd BR5 . . . . .38 B6
Sayer Cl DA9 . . . . .11 A2
Sayers La 6 TN30 . . . . . . .183 A4
Sayes Court Rd BR5 . . . . . . .38 B5
Scabharbour Rd TN14 . . . . .99 C1
Scadbury Gdns BR5 . . . . . . .38 A7
Scadbury Park
Nature Reserve* BR7 . . . . .23 F2
Scads Hill Cl BR6 . . . . .37 F3
Scarborough La ME1 . . . . . .60 D7
Scarlet Cl BR5 . . . . .38 B5
Scarlett Cl ME5 . . . . .62 C5
Scarsbrook Rd SE3 . . . . .5 D4
Schofield Wlk SE18 . . . . .5 A7
Scholars Rise ME2 . . . . .46 D7
Scholey Cl ME2 . . . . .60 B4
School App TN15 . . . . .86 F7
School Ave ME7 . . . . .48 C4
School Cl DA13 . . . . .44 A2
School Cotts
Crockenhill BR8 . . . . .39 D3
Sidcup DA14 . . . . .24 C3
School Cres DA1 . . . . .8 F3
School Field TN8 . . . . .112 C2
School Hill TN3 . . . . .166 B6
School House La TN12 . . . .153 E7
School La Bean DA2 . . . . . . .28 C5
Bexley DA16 . . . . .7 B4
Chestnut Street ME9 . . . . . .65 F4
Hadlow TN11 . . . . .118 E8
Hextable BR8 . . . . .26 B1
Higham ME3 . . . . .32 C5
Horton Kirby DA3,DA4 . . . . .41 E4
Knockmill TN15 . . . . .70 F8
Maidstone ME15 . . . . .92 E1
Newington ME9 . . . . .65 B7
Platt's Heath ME17 . . . . . .110 F2
Plaxtol TN11,TN15 . . . . . .101 E6
Seal TN15 . . . . .84 F6
Sutton Valence ME17 . . . .124 E7
Trottiscliffe ME19 . . . . .73 A5
Vigo Village DA13 . . . . .58 A2
Wouldham ME1 . . . . .60 D5
School Rd Chislehurst BR7 . .23 C1
Gravesend DA12 . . . . .30 C5
School Rise TN2 . . . . .148 F1
School Terr 6 TN18 . . . . .178 F2
School Villas ME18 . . . . . .104 D5
Schoolfield Rd RM20 . . . . . .11 A8
Schooner Ct DA2 . . . . .10 C3
Schriber Mews ME7 . . . . . . .48 D5
Scilla Ct 10 RM17 . . . . .12 D8
Scimitar Cl ME7 . . . . .49 A1
Scords La TN16 . . . . .97 C4
Scotby Ave ME5 . . . . .62 B4
Scotland La DA12 . . . . .30 E4
Scott Ave ME8 . . . . .64 A8
Scott Cl ME20 . . . . .90 C8
Scott Cres DA8 . . . . .8 F6
Scott Ho 4 DA17 . . . . .3 F1

Scott Rd Gravesend DA12 . .30 D3
Tonbridge TN9 . . . . .132 F8
Scott St ME14 . . . . .91 F6
Scott Wilkie Prim Sch E16 . .1 C7
Scott's Terr ME4 . . . . .47 F3
Scotteswood Ave ME4 . . . . .47 F2
Scotts Ho DA16 . . . . .7 C8
Scotts Park Prim Sch BR1 36 C6
Scotts Pas 11 SE18 . . . . . . .2 B1
Scotts Rd BR1 . . . . .22 A1
Scotts Way
Royal Tunbridge Wells TN2 .162 E8
Sevenoaks TN13 . . . . .83 E5
Scoulding Rd E16 . . . . .1 A7
Scragged Oak Rd
Detling ME14 . . . . .78 C5
Hucking ME17 . . . . .79 C1
Scratchers La DA3 . . . . .55 E7
Scratton Fields DA12 . . . . . .44 D4
Scrubbs La ME4 . . . . .91 D4
Scudders Hill DA3 . . . . .42 C3
Scudebrook Rd TN10 . . . . .117 A3
Seabrooke Rise ME17 . . . . .12 B8
Seacourt Rd SE2 . . . . .3 D4
Seaford Ct ME1 . . . . .47 B5
Seagull Rd ME2 . . . . .46 D6
Seal CE Prim Sch TN15 . . .84 F7
Seal Dr TN15 . . . . .84 F6
Seal Hollow Rd TN15 . . . . .84 D4
Seal Rd TN13 ,TN14 ,TN15 . .84 C6
Sealand Ct ME1 . . . . .47 B5
Seamew Ct ME2 . . . . .46 C7
Searles Dr E6 . . . . .2 B8
Seaton Rd Bexley DA16 . . . .7 C7
Dartford DA1 . . . . .26 A8
Gillingham ME7 . . . . .48 E3
Seaview ME3 . . . . .21 B5
Seaview Rd ME3 . . . . .21 B5
Second Ave Chatham ME4 . .48 C1
Gillingham ME7 . . . . .48 E3
West Thurrock RM20 . . . . . .11 A8
Secretan Rd ME1 . . . . .47 B1
Sedcombe Cl DA14 . . . . . . .24 C4
Sedge Cres ME5 . . . . .61 E4
Sedgebrook Rd SE3 . . . . .5 D4
Sedgemere Rd SE2 . . . . .3 C3
Sedley DA13 . . . . .29 A2
Sedley Cl Aylesford ME20 . .75 F2
Cliffe Woods ME3 . . . . .33 C7
Gillingham ME8 . . . . .63 C3
Sedley's CE Prim Sch
DA13 . . . . .29 A3
Sefton Cl BR5 . . . . .37 F5
Sefton Rd BR5 . . . . .37 F5
Sejant House 4 RM17 . . . .12 B8
Selah Dr BR8 . . . . .39 C8
Selborne Ave DA5 . . . . .24 E7
Selborne Rd DA14 . . . . .24 B4
Selbourne Rd ME7 . . . . .48 D7
Selbourne Wlk ME15 . . . . .107 F6
Selby Cl Chislehurst BR7 . . .23 A2
18 Newham E6 . . . . .1 E8
Selby Rd Maidstone ME15 .107 F4
Newham E6 . . . . .1 E8
Selkirk Dr DA8 . . . . .8 E6
Sellbourne Pk TN3 . . . . . .163 C4
Sellinge Gn ME8 . . . . .49 C3
Sellwood Ct DA1 . . . . .27 B7
Selsey Cres DA16 . . . . .7 D6
Selstead Ct ME8 . . . . .49 C2
Selwyn Cres DA16 . . . . .7 B3
Selwyn Pl 1 BR5 . . . . . . .38 B6
Selwyn Rd RM18 . . . . .12 F5
Semple Gdns ME4 . . . . .47 E3
Senacre La ME15 . . . . .107 E6
Senacre Sq ME15 . . . . . . .107 F7
Senacre Tech Coll ME15 .107 D6
Senacre Wood Prim Sch
ME15 . . . . .107 F7
Senator Wlk SE28 . . . . .2 D3
Sencler Ho SE2 . . . . .3 D1
Sencler House SE2 . . . . .7 D8
Senlac Pl TN3 . . . . .161 C7
Senlac Rd SE12 . . . . .22 B7
Sennen Wlk SE9 . . . . .22 E5
Sennocke Ct TN13 . . . . . . .84 B2
Sequoia Gdns BR6 . . . . .37 F2
Sermon Dr BR8 . . . . .39 C6
Serpentine Ct TN13 . . . . . .84 D5
Serpentine Rd TN13 . . . . . .84 D4
Serviden Dr BR1 . . . . .36 D8
Sessions House Sq ME14 . .91 F5
Setford Rd ME4 . . . . .62 C6
Settington Ave ME5 . . . . . . .48 C1
Seven Acres
Crockenhill BR8 . . . . .39 D3
New Ash Green DA3 . . . . . . .56 F7
Seven Mile La
Kings Hill TN15,ME18 . . . . .88 A3
Mereworth TN11,TN12 . . . .103 E3
Wrotham Heath TN15 . . . . . .87 F7
Seven Wents TN15 . . . . . . .84 D8
Sevenoaks Bsns Ctr TN14 .84 C6
Sevenoaks By-Pass
TN13,TN14 . . . . .98 F7
Sevenoaks
Cty Prim Sch TN13 . . . . . .84 B5
Sevenoaks Hospl
Sevenoaks TN13 . . . . .84 B2
Sevenoaks,St John's TN13 . .84 C6
Sevenoaks Prep Sch TN15 85 A1
Sevenoaks Rd
Borough Green TN15 . . . . . .86 F7
Ightham TN15 . . . . .86 B4
Orpington BR6 . . . . .51 F6
Otford TN14 . . . . .69 B3
Pratt's Bottom BR6,TN14 . .52 C2

Sevenoaks Sch TN13 . . . . . .84 C1
Sevenoaks Sta TN13 . . . . . .84 A3
Sevenoaks Way BR5 . . . . . .38 C7
Sevenoaks Wildfowl
Reserve* TN14 . . . . .84 A7
Severn Cl TN10 . . . . .117 C5
Severn Rd ME5 . . . . .62 C5
Sevington Pk ME15 . . . . . .106 F6
Sewell Rd SE28 . . . . .3 B4
Sextant Pk ME2 . . . . .47 E6
Sexton Rd RM18 . . . . .12 F6
Seymour Dr BR2 . . . . .36 F1
Seymour Rd
1 Chatham ME5 . . . . . . .48 B3
Gillingham ME8 . . . . .64 C8
Northfleet DA11 . . . . .29 F6
Tilbury RM18 . . . . .12 F6
Seymour St SE18 . . . . .2 C3
Seymour Wlk DA10 . . . . . . .28 E8
Shacklands Rd TN14 . . . . . .53 D1
Shackleton Cl ME5 . . . . . . .62 B6
Shades The ME2 . . . . .46 C7
Shaftesbury Cl ME19 . . . . . .74 F1
Shaftesbury Ct 3 SE28 . . . .3 C5
Shaftesbury Dr ME8 . . . . . .91 C4
Shaftesbury La DA1 . . . . . . .10 B3
Shaftesbury Rd ME4 . . . . .149 A5
Shaftsbury Ct E6 . . . . .2 A7
Shakespeare Ho 1 DA17 . . .7 F1
Shakespeare Rd Bexley DA7 . .7 E6
Dartford DA1 . . . . .10 B3
Gillingham ME7 . . . . .48 C3
Tonbridge TN9 . . . . .132 F8
Shalder Ho ME7 . . . . .48 D7
Shalford Rd ME6 . . . . .51 C6
Shallons Rd SE9 . . . . .23 B4
Shambles The TN13 . . . . . .84 C2
Shamel Bsns Ctr ME2 . . . . .47 C7
Shamley Rd ME5 . . . . .62 C6
Shamrock Rd DA12 . . . . . . .30 F8
Shandon Cl TN2 . . . . .149 C4
Shanklin Cl ME5 . . . . .62 C8
Shannon Ct BR6 . . . . .38 A2
Sharfleet Dr ME2 . . . . .46 B7
Sharland Rd DA12 . . . . .30 C6
Sharman Ct DA14 . . . . .24 A4
Sharnal La ME6 . . . . .75 A7
Sharnal St ME3 . . . . .18 A2
Sharnbrooke Cl DA16 . . . . . .7 C4
Sharon Cres ME5 . . . . .61 C4
Sharon Ct 10 DA14 . . . . . . .24 B4
Sharp Way DA1 . . . . .9 F4
Sharp's Field TN27 . . . . . .141 E5
Sharps Gn ME8 . . . . .49 D5
Sharsted Way
Gillingham ME7 . . . . .63 A3
Maidstone ME15 . . . . .93 B5
Shaw Cl Cliffe Woods ME3 . .33 B8
Woolwich SE28 . . . . .3 B5
Shaw Cres RM18 . . . . .13 B6
Shaw Ho 6 Erith DA17 . . . . .3 F1
5 Newham E16 . . . . .2 A5
Shaw The TN2 . . . . .149 C2
Shawbrooke Rd SE9 . . . . . . .5 D3
Shawcroft Sch BR5 . . . . . . .38 E4
Shawfield Pk BR1 . . . . .36 D7
Shaws Way ME1 . . . . .47 C3
Shawstead Rd ME7,ME7 . . .62 D5
Sheafe Dr TN17 . . . . .169 C5
Sheal's Cres ME15 . . . . . . .92 A2
Sheals Ct ME15 . . . . .92 A2
Shearers Cl ME14 . . . . .92 E4
Shears Cl DA2 . . . . .26 C6
Shears Green Ct DA11 . . . . .30 A6
Shears Green Inf Sch
DA11 . . . . .29 F5
Shears Green Jun Sch
DA11 . . . . .29 F5
Shearwater
Maidstone ME16 . . . . .91 B5
New Barn DA3 . . . . .43 B6
Shearwater Cl ME2 . . . . . . .46 C7
Shearwood Cres DA1 . . . . . . .9 A4
Sheen Rd BR5 . . . . .37 F5
Sheepcote La BR5,BR8 . . . .38 F4
Sheephurst La TN12 . . . . .137 C5
Sheerness Harbour Est
ME12 . . . . .21 F3
Sheerwater Rd E16 . . . . .1 D8
Sheet Hill TN15 . . . . .86 D2
Sheffield Rd 4 TN4 . . . . . .132 F2
Sheilings The TN15 . . . . . . .84 F7
Shelbury Ct DA14 . . . . .24 A5
Shelden Dr ME8 . . . . .63 F8
Shelden Bsns Ctr ME2 . . . .47 D8
Sheldon Cl SE12 . . . . .5 B2
Sheldon Rd DA7 . . . . .7 F6
Sheldon Way ME20 . . . . . . .75 B3
Sheldrake Cl E16 . . . . .1 F5
Sheldwich Terr BR2 . . . . . . .36 E3
Shell Cl BR2 . . . . .36 E3
Shellbank La DA2 . . . . .28 A4
Shelldrake Cl ME3 . . . . .21 B5
Shelley Cl BR6 . . . . .51 E7
Shelley Dr DA16 . . . . .6 E6
Shelley Ho DA1 . . . . .8 E2
Shelley Pl RM18 . . . . .13 B6
Shelley Rd ME16 . . . . .91 C2
Shelleys La TN14 . . . . .67 A3
Shelton Cl TN10 . . . . .117 C5
Shenden Cl TN13 . . . . .99 C7
Shenden Way TN13 . . . . . . .99 C7
Shenfield Ho SE18 . . . . .5 D7
Shenley Gr ME14 . . . . .76 F2
Shenley Rd DA1 . . . . .27 A8

Shenstone Sch DA1 . . . . . . .8 D3
Shepherd St DA11 . . . . .29 D8
Shepherds Cl BR6 . . . . .51 F7
Shepherds Gate ME7 . . . . . .62 F5
Shepherds Gate Dr ME14 . .92 A8
Shepherds Gn BR7 . . . . . . .23 D1
Shepherds La ME1 . . . . .26 B8
Shepherds Leas SE9 . . . . . . .6 D3
Shepherds Way
Langley Heath ME17 . . . . .108 E4
Lower Stoke ME3 . . . . .19 C4
Shepherds Wlk ME7 . . . . . .149 D4
Shepherdsgrove
La RH19 . . . . .144 A4
Shepperton Cl ME5 . . . . . . .62 C4
Shepperton Rd BR5 . . . . . . .37 C3
Sheppey Cl DA8 . . . . .9 B7
Sheppey Rd ME15 . . . . . . .107 A7
Sheppey Ho 1 BR1 . . . . . .22 B7
Sheppey Pl DA12 . . . . .30 B8
Shepway Ct ME15 . . . . . . .107 C8
Shepway Inf Sch ME15 . . .107 E8
Shepway Jun Sch ME15 . .107 E8
Sherard Mans SE9 . . . . .5 F2
Sherard Rd SE9 . . . . .5 E2
Sheraton Ct ME5 . . . . .61 F1
Sherborne Rd BR5 . . . . .37 F7
Sherbourne Cl
Royal Tunbridge Wells TN2 .149 D2
West Kingsdown TN15 . . . . .55 E4
Sherbourne Dr
Maidstone ME16 . . . . .91 B2
Rochester ME2 . . . . .33 A1
Sherbrooke Cl DA7 . . . . .8 A3
Sherenden La TN12 . . . . . .154 D8
Sherenden Pk TN11 . . . . . .119 A5
Sherenden Rd TN11 . . . . . .134 C7
Sherfield Rd ME17 . . . . .12 B8
Sheridan Cl Chatham ME5 . .62 C7
Maidstone ME14 . . . . .91 E8
Swanley BR8 . . . . .39 F6
Sheridan Cres BR7 . . . . . . .37 B7
Sheridan Ct DA1 . . . . .10 A3
Sheridan Lodge 1 BR2 . . .36 C5
Sheridan Rd Bexley DA7 . . . .7 E4
Erith DA17 . . . . .4 A2
Sheriff Dr ME5 . . . . .62 A2
Sheringham Cl ME16 . . . . . .91 D7
Sheringham Ho 5 ME15 .107 D8
Sherington Prim Sch SE7 . .5 B8
Sherington Rd SE7 . . . . .5 B8
Sherlies Ave BR6 . . . . .51 E8
Sherman Cl ME7 . . . . .49 B1
Sherman Ct 4 BR1 . . . . . .36 B8
Sherman Rd BR1 . . . . .36 A8
Shernden La TN8 . . . . .128 C4
Shernold Sch ME16 . . . . . . .91 D5
Shernolds ME15 . . . . .107 B7
Sherway Cl TN27 . . . . .141 D6
Sherway Rd TN27 . . . . .142 D6
Sherwin Knight
Jun & Inf Sch ME2 . . . . . .46 E5
Sherwood Ave ME5 . . . . . . .62 A2
Sherwood Cl DA5 . . . . .7 C1
Sherwood Ho ME8 . . . . .7 B3
Sherwood Park Ave DA15 . . .7 B1
Sherwood Park Cty
Prim Sch TN2 . . . . .149 D6
Sherwood Park
Prim Sch DA15 . . . . .7 D1
Sherwood Pl TN3 . . . . . . .147 E3
Sherwood Rd Bexley DA16 . .6 E4
Royal Tunbridge Wells TN2 .149 C5
Sherwood Way TN2 . . . . . .149 D6
Shieldhall St SE2 . . . . .3 C2
Shieling The DA13 . . . . .57 F1
Shillingheld Cl ME14 . . . . . .92 F5
Shinecroft TN14 . . . . .69 A3
Shingle Barn La ME15 . . . .105 C3
Shinglewell Rd DA8 . . . . .8 A7
Ship La BR8,DA4 . . . . .40 E8
Sutton at Hone BR8,DA4 . . .40 E8
Shipbourne
Prim Sch TN11 . . . . .101 C4
Shipbourne Rd
Shipbourne TN11 . . . . . . .101 D2
Tonbridge TN10 . . . . .117 C5
Shipley Ct ME14 . . . . .92 A4
Shipley Hills Rd DA13 . . . . .43 E1
Shipman Rd E16 . . . . .1 C7
Shipwrights Ave ME4 . . . . . .48 B2
Shire Ct SE2 . . . . .3 C3
Shire La Farthing Street BR6 51 C3
Orpington BR6 . . . . .51 E5
Shirebrook Rd SE3 . . . . .5 D4
Shirehall Rd DA2 . . . . .26 E4
Shires The TN12 . . . . .136 A7
Shirley Ave Chatham ME5 . .61 D5
Sidcup DA5 . . . . .24 D7
Shirley Cl Chalk DA12 . . . . .31 B6
Dartford DA1 . . . . .9 C3
Shirley Ct ME15 . . . . .107 C5
Shirley Gdns TN4 . . . . .148 C5
Shirley Gr TN4 . . . . .148 C5
Shirley House Dr SE7 . . . . . .5 C7
Shirley Rd DA15 . . . . .23 C5
Shirley Way ME15 . . . . .93 A3
Sholden Gdns BR5 . . . . .38 C4
Sholden Rd ME2 . . . . .33 C1
Shooters Hill SE18 . . . . .6 A6
Shooters Hill Rd SE18,SE3 . .5 D6
Shore The Northfleet DA11 . .12 A6
Northfleet, Rosherville DA11 .12 F1
Shoreham Aircraft Mus*
TN14 . . . . .68 F8
Shoreham Cl DA5 . . . . .24 D7
Shoreham
Cty Prim Sch TN14 . . . . . .68 F8

San–Sil 223

Shoreham Ho TN14 . . . . . . .69 A8
Shoreham La
Badgers Mount TN14 . . . . . .68 A7
Chelsfield BR6 . . . . .53 A3
Sevenoaks TN13 . . . . .83 F4
Tenterden TN30 . . . . .173 A3
Shoreham Pl TN14 . . . . .69 A7
Shoreham Rd Otford TN14 . .69 B5
St Paul's Cray BR5 . . . . . . .38 B7
Shoreham Sta TN14 . . . . . .69 B8
Shoreham Way BR2 . . . . . . .36 A3
Shoreham Wlk ME15 . . . . .107 F7
Shorehill La TN15 . . . . .69 F4
Shoreland Ct ME1 . . . . .47 B5
Shorne CE Prim Sch DA12 31 E3
Shorne Ct Orpington BR5 . . .38 D5
3 Sidcup DA15 . . . . .7 B1
Shorne Ifield Rd DA12 . . . . .31 C2
Shorne Wood (Ctry Pk)*
DA12 . . . . .31 C1
Shornefield Cl BR1 . . . . . . .37 A6
Short Path SE18 . . . . .6 B8
Short St 3 ME4 . . . . .48 B3
Shortlands DA17 . . . . .3 F3
Shortlands Gn ME15 . . . . .107 F5
Shorts Way ME1 . . . . .47 A3
Shortway SE9 . . . . .5 A4
Shottenden Rd ME7 . . . . . .48 D7
Shottery Cl SE9 . . . . .22 E5
Showfields Rd TN2 . . . . . .148 F1
Shrapnel Cl SE18 . . . . .5 E7
Shrapnel Rd SE9 . . . . .5 F4
Shrewsbury La SE18 . . . . . . .6 B6
Shroffold Rd BR1 . . . . .22 A5
Shropshire Terr 1 ME15 .107 E7
Shrubbery Rd
Gravesend DA12 . . . . .30 C7
Sutton at Hone DA4 . . . . . .41 D8
Shrubcote TN30 . . . . .183 C7
Shrublands Ct
Royal Tunbridge Wells TN2 .149 C4
1 Tonbridge TN9 . . . . . . .117 C2
Shrubsall Cl SE9 . . . . .22 E7
Shrubsole Dr ME14 . . . . . . .76 F3
Shurland Ave BR8 . . . . .39 D7
Shurlock Dr BR6 . . . . .51 C6
Shuttle Cl Biddenden TN27 158 A2
Sidcup DA15 . . . . .23 F8
Shuttle Rd DA1 . . . . .9 A4
Shuttlemead DA5 . . . . .24 F8
Sibley Cl DA6 . . . . .7 E2
Sibthorpe Rd SE12 . . . . . . .22 C8
Sidcup By Pass Rd
Sidcup DA14 . . . . .23 F3
St Paul's Cray BR5,BR7,DA14 .24 B1
Sidcup Hill DA14 . . . . .24 B3
Sidcup Hill Gdns DA14 . . . .24 C3
Sidcup Hill Prim Sch
DA14 . . . . .24 B3
Sidcup Pl DA14 . . . . .24 A3
Sidcup Rd SE12,SE9 . . . . . .22 D7
Sidcup Sta DA15 . . . . .24 A6
Sidewood Rd SE9 . . . . .23 D7
Sidmouth Ct DA1 . . . . .9 D7
Sidmouth Rd Bexley DA16 . . .7 C7
Orpington BR5 . . . . .38 B5
Sidney Cl TN2 . . . . .162 F8
Sidney Gdns TN14 . . . . . . .69 C2
Sidney House SE18 . . . . .6 A8
Sidney Rd Gillingham ME7 . .48 C7
Rochester ME1 . . . . .47 A2
Sidney St ME16 . . . . .91 C2
Siebert Rd SE3 . . . . .5 A8
Siedle House 9 SE18 . . . . . .6 A8
Siemens Rd 1 SE18 . . . . . .1 D3
Silchester Ct ME14 . . . . . . .92 C7
Silecroft Rd DA7 . . . . .8 A6
Silk Cl SE12 . . . . .5 A1
Silk Mills Cl TN13 . . . . .84 C6
Silver Bank ME5 . . . . .62 A6
Silver Birch Ave
Dartford DA2 . . . . .25 E4
Woolwich SE28 . . . . .3 A5
Silver Birch Cl
Dartford DA2 . . . . .25 E4
Woolwich SE28 . . . . .3 A5
Silver Birches ME5 . . . . . . .62 A3
Silver Cl TN9 . . . . .133 B6
Silver Hill Chatham ME4 . . .47 F3
Hurst Green TN19 . . . . . . .184 B1
Rochester ME1 . . . . .46 F2
Tenterden TN30 . . . . .173 B1
Silver Hill Gdns 4 ME4 . . .47 F3
Silver Rd DA12 . . . . .30 E6
Silver Spring Cl DA8 . . . . . . .8 B8
Silver St ME9 . . . . .80 F5
Silver Tree ME5 . . . . .62 B6
Silverdale Hartley DA3 . . . . .42 F5
Maidstone ME16 . . . . .91 A2
Silverdale Dr
Chislehurst SE9 . . . . .22 E6
Gillingham ME8 . . . . .63 F7
Silverdale La
Royal Tunbridge Wells TN4 .149 A6
Sandhurst TN18 . . . . .185 F5
Silverdale Rd Bexley DA7 . . .8 B5
Orpington BR5 . . . . .37 C5
Royal Tunbridge Wells TN4 .149 B6
St Paul's Cray BR5 . . . . . . .38 A6
Silverden Cotts TN18 . . . . .185 F4
Silverhurst Dr TN10 . . . . . .117 C2
Silverland St E16 . . . . .1 F5
Silverlocke Rd RM17 . . . . . .12 D8
Silverspot Cl ME8 . . . . .63 F7
Silversted La TN16 . . . . . . .81 D6
Silverstone Ct 9 BR1 . . . . .36 C7
Silvertown Sta E16 . . . . .1 E5

Silvertown Way E16 . . . . .1 A5
Silverweed Rd ME5 . . . . . .61 F4
Silwood Cl TN2 . . . . .149 E7
Simmonds Ct TN4 . . . . . .148 B4
Simmonds Dr DA3 . . . . . . .43 A4
Simmonds La ME15 . . . . .108 B6
Simmons Rd SE18 . . . . .2 B1
Simnel Rd SE12 . . . . .22 B8
Simon Ct 5 SE28 . . . . .3 B5
Simone Cl BR1 . . . . .36 D8
Simpson Rd ME6 . . . . .75 A6
Simpson's Cotts BR2 . . . . .50 C7
Simpson's Rd BR1,BR2 . . .36 A6
Sinclair Cl ME8 . . . . .63 E5
Sinclair Way DA2 . . . . .27 D4
Singapore Dr ME7 . . . . . . .48 B5
Single St TN16 . . . . .66 B4
Single's Cross TN14 . . . . . .67 D4
Single's Cross La TN14 . . . .67 C5
Singlewell Prim Sch DA12 30 D2
Singlewell Rd DA11 . . . . . . .30 B4
Sinkertweazel TN17 . . . . .169 C2
Sir David's Pk TN4 . . . . . .132 E1
Sir Evelyn Rd ME7 . . . . . . .47 B1
Sir John Hawkins Way
ME4 . . . . .47 F4
Sir Martin Bowes Ho 11
SE18 . . . . .2 A2
Sir Thomas Longley Rd
ME2 . . . . .47 E6
Sirdar Strand DA12 . . . . . .30 F3
Siskin Gdns TN12 . . . . . .136 A5
Siskin Wlk ME20 . . . . .74 F2
Sissinghurst Castle Gdns*
TN17 . . . . .156 D1
Sissinghurst CE
Prim Sch TN17 . . . . . .170 B8
Sissinghurst Dr ME16 . . . .91 B4
Sissinghurst Rd
Biddenden TN27 . . . . . . .157 C2
Sissinghurst TN17,TN27 . .170 D8
Sittingbourne Rd
Maidstone,Detling ME14 . . .92 E8
Maidstone,Penenden
Heath ME14 . . . . .92 B6
Siward Rd BR2 . . . . .36 C6
Six Bells La TN13 . . . . .84 C1
Six Fields Path TN30 . . . .183 A7
Sixpenny Cl TN8 . . . . .128 C8
Skeet Hill La BR5,BR6 . . . .52 E8
Skeffington St SE18 . . . . . . .2 C3
Skeynes Rd TN8 . . . . .112 B1
Skibbs La BR5,BR6 . . . . . . .52 E7
Skinner Gdns TN17 . . . . .170 A8
Skinner St Chatham ME4 . . .47 F3
Gillingham ME7 . . . . .48 C5
Skinner Street Prim Sch
ME7 . . . . .48 C6
Skinner's Way ME17 . . . . .108 E4
Skinners Cl ME20 . . . . .76 A6
Skinners La TN8 . . . . .112 D2
Skinners' Sch The TN4 . . .149 A6
Skinney La DA4 . . . . .41 D6
Skippers Cl DA9 . . . . .11 B2
Skua Ct ME2 . . . . .46 C7
Skye Cl ME15 . . . . .107 A7
Slade Cl ME5 . . . . .62 B2
Slade Gdns DA8 . . . . .8 F6
Slade Green Inf Sch DA8 . . .9 A7
Slade Green Jun Sch DA8 . .9 A7
Slade Green Rd DA8 . . . . . .9 B7
Slade Green Sta DA8 . . . . . .9 A6
Slade Prim Sch TN9 . . . . .117 B2
Slade The
Lamberhurst TN3 . . . . . . .166 A3
Tonbridge TN9 . . . . .117 B2
Woolwich SE18 . . . . .6 E8
Sladebrook Rd SE3 . . . . . . .5 D4
Sladedale Rd SE18 . . . . . . .2 E1
Slades Dr BR7 . . . . .23 C4
Slaney Rd TN12 . . . . .139 F4
Slater Cl 6 SE18 . . . . .2 A2
Slaters TN8 . . . . .113 F2
Slatin Rd ME2 . . . . .47 B8
Sleeches Cross TN3 . . . . .163 B2
Sleepers Stile Rd TN5 . . . .165 B1
Slicketts Hill ME4 . . . . .48 A4
Slip Mill La TN18 . . . . . . .178 E2
Slip The TN16 . . . . .81 C1
Slipway Rd ME12 . . . . .21 F3
Sloane Gdns BR6 . . . . .51 C7
Sloane Sq DA3 . . . . .42 E6
Slocum Cl SE28 . . . . .3 C6
Small Bridge Cotts TN17 .153 B2
Small Bridge Rd
TN12,TN17 . . . . .153 B2
Small Grains DA3 . . . . .56 B7
Small Hythe Cl ME15 . . . . .93 B2
Small Hythe Rd TN30 . . . .183 C3
Small Profits ME15,ME18 .105 A4
Smallhythe Place
(Mus)* TN30 . . . . .189 C8
Smallhythe Rd TN30 . . . .183 A6
Smarden Bsns Est TN27 . .158 D7
Smarden Cl 8 DA17 . . . . . .4 A1
Smarden Gr SE9 . . . . .22 F4
Smarden Prim Sch TN27 143 A1
Smarden Rd
East End TN27 . . . . .142 B4
Lashenden TN27 . . . . .158 B6
Smarts Cotts ME14 . . . . . . .93 C4
Smarts Hill TN11 . . . . .131 A1
Smarts Rd DA12 . . . . .30 C6
Smetham Gdns ME2 . . . . . .33 B1
Smith Rd ME5 . . . . .62 B3

Smith St ME2 . . . . .47 A6
Smith's Hill ME15 . . . . . .105 C5
Smithers Cl TN11 . . . . . . .102 E1
Smithers Ct TN12 . . . . . . .120 A7
Smithers La TN12 . . . . . . .120 A7
Smithfield Rd ME3 . . . . . . .21 C5
Smithies Rd SE2 . . . . .3 B2
Smiths La TN8 . . . . .96 C2
Smiths Orch ME9 . . . . .80 F5
Smithy Field 7 TN8 . . . . .112 D3
Smithy The TN5 . . . . .174 A3
Smugglers TN18 . . . . .179 A1
Smugglers Wharf DA9 . . . .11 B2
Smythe Cl TN4 . . . . .132 E3
Smythe Rd DA4 . . . . .41 A8
Snag La TN14 . . . . .66 D7
Snape La TN5 . . . . .174 F5
Snape View TN5 . . . . .174 F4
Snelling Ave DA11 . . . . . . .29 F6
Snipe Cl Erith DA8 . . . . .9 B7
Pembury TN2 . . . . .150 E8
Snipe Ct ME2 . . . . .46 C7
Snoad La TN12 . . . . .155 A8
Snodhurst Ave ME5 . . . . . .61 E5
Snodland CE Prim Sch
ME6 . . . . .74 F8
Snodland Rd ME19 . . . . . . .74 D7
Snodland Sta ME6 . . . . . . .75 B8
Snodlands CE ME6 . . . . . . .51 A1
Snoll Hatch Rd TN12 . . . .119 F5
Snow Ho ME7 . . . . .48 E7
Snowdon Ave ME14 . . . . . .92 B5
Snowdon Cl ME5 . . . . .62 B7
Snowdon Par ME14 . . . . . .92 C5
Snughorne La TN27 . . . . .158 D8
Sole Fields TN13 . . . . .99 C8
Sole La DA12,DA13 . . . . . .44 D4
Sole Street Sta DA13 . . . . .44 D4
Solefield Sch TN13 . . . . . . .99 C8
Solefields Rd TN13 . . . . . . .99 C8
Solent Gdns ME5 . . . . .62 B8
Soleoak Dr TN13 . . . . .99 B8
Solomon Rd Rainham ME8 . .64 A1
Rainham ME8 . . . . .64 A1
Solomons Rd ME4 . . . . . . .47 F4
Somerden Rd BR5 . . . . . . .38 D2
Somerfield Cl ME16 . . . . . .91 D5
Somerfield Hospl The
ME16 . . . . .91 E5
Somerfield La ME16 . . . . . .91 D4
Somerfield Rd ME16 . . . . . .91 D4
Somerhill Ave ME15 . . . . . .24 B8
Somerhill Rd Bexley DA16 . . .7 B5
Tonbridge TN9 . . . . .133 D8
Somerset Ave DA16 . . . . . . .6 F3
Somerset Cl ME5 . . . . .62 A5
Somerset Rd Dartford DA1 . .26 B8
Maidstone ME15 . . . . . . .107 C8
Orpington BR6 . . . . .38 A2
Royal Tunbridge Wells TN4 .149 A6
Somerset Villas TN4 . . . . .161 C2
Somersham Rd DA7 . . . . . . .7 E5
Somertrees Ave SE12 . . . . .22 B6
Somerville Gdns TN4 . . . .148 F4
Somerville Rd DA1 . . . . .9 F1
Somner Wlk ME15 . . . . . .107 A4
Soper's La TN18 . . . . .178 D4
Sophia Rd E16 . . . . .1 B7
Sophurst La TN12 . . . . . . .151 C5
Sopurst Wood TN12 . . . . .151 D5
Sorrel Cl SE28 . . . . .3 A5
Sorrel Ct 7 RM17 . . . . . . .12 D8
Sorrel Gdns E6 . . . . .1 E8
Sorrell Cl 4 TN8 . . . . . . .112 D3
Sorrell Rd ME5 . . . . .61 F4
Sorrell Way DA11 . . . . .29 E4
Sortmill Rd ME6 . . . . .75 B7
Sounds Lodge BR8 . . . . . . .39 C3
South Ash Rd TN15 . . . . . .56 E5
South Ave ME8 . . . . .49 B2
South Aylesford Ret Pk
ME20 . . . . .90 E8
South Bank Cliffe ME3 . . . .16 B2
Staplehurst TN12 . . . . . . .139 E2
Sutton Valence ME17 . . . .124 E7
Westerham TN16 . . . . .81 D1
South Borough Prim Sch
ME15 . . . . .92 A2
South Bush La ME8 . . . . . .64 B6
South Cl DA6 . . . . .7 D3
South Cres ME17 . . . . . . .106 C4
South Ct TN4 . . . . .149 A6
South Dr BR6 . . . . .51 E5
South Eastern Rd ME2 . . . .47 C7
South Frith TN4 . . . . .133 A6
South Gipsy Rd DA16 . . . . .7 D4
South Glade The DA5 . . . . .24 F7
South Gr TN1 . . . . .149 A2
South Green La ME9 . . . . . .79 F6
South Hall Cl DA4 . . . . . . .40 F2
South Hill BR7 . . . . .22 F2
South Hill Rd DA12 . . . . . .30 C7
South Kent Ave DA11 . . . . .12 C1
South La ME17 . . . . .124 E6
South Molton Rd E16 . . . . . .1 A7
South Park Bsns
Village ME15 . . . . .92 A1
South Park Rd ME15 . . . . .92 C1
South Pk TN13 . . . . .84 B2
South Pondside Rd ME4 . . .48 A8
South Rd Erith DA8 . . . . . . .8 F7
Gillingham ME8 . . . . .48 B7
Gillingham ME4,ME7 . . . . .48 A7
Marden TN12 . . . . .138 C5
South Ridge BR2 . . . . .36 C5
South Rise Jun & Inf Sch
SE18 . . . . .2 D1
South Rise Way SE18 . . . . . .2 D2

South Row Greenwich SE3 . . .5 A5
Penshurst TN8 . . . . .130 D5
South Side Three Rd ME4 .48 C8
South St Bromley BR1 . . . . .36 A7
Gravesend DA12 . . . . .30 B8
Maidstone ME16 . . . . .90 E1
Meopham ME15 . . . . .57 F7
South Street Rd ME9 . . . . .79 C7
South Terr DA4 . . . . .40 F2
South View BR1 . . . . .36 C7
South View Cl DA5 . . . . .7 F1
South View Rd
Dartford DA2 . . . . .26 D5
Royal Tunbridge Wells TN4 .149 B8
Wadhurst TN5 . . . . .174 F6
West Thurrock RM20 . . . . .11 C8
South View Terr TN17 . . . .167 E8
Southampton Mews E16 . . .1 B5
Southborough CE
Prim Schs TN4 . . . . . . .148 F8
Southborough Ct TN4 . . . .133 A2
Southborough La BR2 . . . . .36 F4
Southborough Prim Sch
BR2 . . . . .37 A4
Southbourne BR2 . . . . .36 A2
Southbourne Gdns SE12 . . .5 B7
Southbourne Gr ME5 . . . . .62 A4
Southcroft Ave DA16 . . . . . .6 E4
Southcroft Rd BR6 . . . . . . .51 E7
Southdene TN14 . . . . .67 F6
Southend Cl SE9 . . . . .6 B1
Southend Cres SE9 . . . . . . .6 B1
Southern Pl BR8 . . . . .39 D5
Southernden Rd TN27 . . . .126 E1
Southey Mews E16 . . . . .1 A5
Southey Way 1 ME20 . . . . .74 A6
Southey Wlk RM18 . . . . . . .13 B6
Southfield Ct DA1 . . . . .9 F4
Southfield Rd
Royal Tunbridge Wells TN4 .149 A6
St Paul's Cray BR7 . . . . . . .38 A6
Southfield Shaw DA13 . . . .58 B1
Southfields Hextable BR8 . .25 F1
Rochester ME1 . . . . .47 C3
Speldhurst TN3 . . . . .148 A1
S.Wadhurst TN5 . . . . .174 F6
Southfields Rd TN15 . . . . . .55 F2
Southfields Sch DA11 . . . . .30 C3
Southfields Way TN4 . . . . .149 B8
Southfleet Ave DA3 . . . . . . .43 B7
Southfleet Rd Bean DA2 . . .28 C4
7 Northfleet DA11 . . . . . . .29 F7
Orpington BR6 . . . . .51 E6
Swanscombe DA10 . . . . . . .29 A4
Southgate TN14 . . . . .148 F3
Southgate Rd TN30 . . . . . .183 C7
Southill Rd Chatham ME4 . .47 F3
Chislehurst BR7 . . . . .22 F1
Southlake Prim Sch SE2 . . .3 D4
Southland Rd SE18 . . . . .6 F7
Southlands Ave BR6 . . . . . .51 E5
Southlands Ct BR2 . . . . . . .36 D5
Southlands Gr BR1 . . . . . . .36 E6
Southlands Rd BR1,BR2 . . .36 D5
Southlees La ME9 . . . . .79 F3
Southold Rise SE9 . . . . . . .22 F5
Southover BR1 . . . . .22 A3
Southport Rd SE18 . . . . .2 D2
Southspring DA15 . . . . .23 D8
Southview Ave RM18 . . . . .13 A6
Southview Cl BR8 . . . . .40 A5
Southview Hts RM20 . . . . .11 C8
Southwark Pl BR1 . . . . .36 F6
Southwark Rd ME2 . . . . . . .46 D6
Southway BR2 . . . . .36 A2
Southways ME17 . . . . .124 E7
Southwell Rd ME2 . . . . . . .46 D6
Southwold Rd DA5 . . . . .8 B1
Southwood ME6 . . . . .90 F2
Southwood Ave TN4 . . . . .149 A6
Southwood Cl BR1 . . . . . . .36 F5
Southwood House SE9 . . . .23 B6
Southwood Rd Eltham SE9 .23 B6
Royal Tunbridge Wells TN4 .149 A6
Woolwich SE28 . . . . .3 B5
Sovereign Bvd
Gillingham ME7 . . . . .48 F2
Gillingham,Twydall ME8 . . .49 D5
Sovereign Ct Bromley BR2 . .36 F4
Sutton at Hone DA4 . . . . . .41 B8
Sovereign Ho SE18 . . . . . . .2 A2
Sovereign Way TN9 . . . . . .117 C1
Sovereigns The ME16 . . . . .91 D4
Sovereigns Way TN12 . . . .138 C6
Sowerby Cl SE9 . . . . .5 F2
Spa Ind Est TN2 . . . . .149 E8
Spa Valley Rly* TN4 . . . . .148 E1
Spade La ME9 . . . . .64 C6
Spar Cl TN11 . . . . .102 F1
Sparepenny La DA4 . . . . . .41 B8
Sparkeswood Ave TN17 . . .181 F3
Sparkeswood Cl TN17 . . . .181 F3
Sparrow Dr BR5 . . . . .37 D1
Sparrow's Farm L Ctr SE9 .23 D8
Sparrows Green Rd TN5 . .174 F5
Sparrows La SE9 . . . . .23 C7
Spearhead Rd ME14 . . . . . .91 F7
Spearman St 8 SE18 . . . . . .6 A8
Spectrum Bsns Ctr ME2 . . .47 D8
Spectrum Bsns Est ME15 107 F4
Speedgate Hill DA3 . . . . . . .56 A8
Speedwell Ave ME5 . . . . . .61 F4
Speedwell Cl
Gillingham ME7 . . . . .48 E5
Maidstone ME14 . . . . .92 E5
5 Marlpit Hill TN8 . . . . .112 D3
Speedwell Ct RM17 . . . . . .12 E7

Spekehill SE9 . . . . .22 F5
Spekes Rd ME7 . . . . .63 B6
Speldhurst CE
Prim Sch TN3 . . . . .148 A7
Speldhurst Ct ME16 . . . . . .91 D4
Speldhurst Hill TN3 . . . . .148 B8
Speldhurst Rd Royal
Tunbridge Wells, Langton
Green TN3 . . . . .147 F4
Royal Tunbridge Wells,
Modest Corner TN3,TN4 . .148 E8
Spelmonden Rd TN12 . . . .152 F2
Spencer Cl Chatham ME5 . .62 A5
Orpington BR6 . . . . .51 F8
Spencer Ct 5 BR6 . . . . . . .51 C5
Spencer Flats ME5 . . . . . . .62 B8
Spencer Mews 6 TN1 . . . .149 A2
Spencer St ME13 . . . . .30 A8
Spencer Way ME15 . . . . . .107 E7
Spencer's Mews 4 TN1 . . .149 B4
Spenlow Dr ME5 . . . . .77 A8
Spenny La TN12 . . . . .137 B7
Speranza St SE18 . . . . .2 F1
Speyside TN10 . . . . .117 B5
Spielman Rd DA1 . . . . .9 F3
Spiers The ME7 . . . . .49 C5
Spillway The ME15 . . . . . . .91 D2
Spindle Cl SE13 . . . . .1 E8
Spindle Glade ME14 . . . . . .92 C5
Spindle House 8 DA15 . . . .24 A5
Spindles RM18 . . . . .13 A7
Spindlewood Cl ME5 . . . . . .62 B3
Spinel Cl SE18 . . . . .2 F1
Spinnaker Ct 4 ME1 . . . . .47 C1
Spinnens Acre
Jun Sch ME5 . . . . .62 C1
Spinners TN27 . . . . .158 A2
Spinners Wents TN11 . . . .102 D8
Spinney Oak BR1 . . . . .36 E7
Spinney The Chatham ME5 . .62 B1
Maidstone ME15 . . . . .92 B2
Sidcup DA14 . . . . .24 C3
Swanley BR8 . . . . .39 E7
Tonbridge TN9 . . . . .133 A7
Spinney Way TN14 . . . . . . .66 D8
Spinneys The BR1 . . . . .36 F7
Spire Cl DA12 . . . . .30 B7
Spires The Dartford DA1 . . .26 D6
Maidstone ME16 . . . . .91 D4
Rochester ME2 . . . . .46 D5
Spital St DA1 . . . . .9 D1
Spitfire Cl ME5 . . . . .62 B6
Spitfire Rd ME19 . . . . .88 F3
Spode La TN8 . . . . .145 A7
Sponden La TN18 . . . . . . .186 A7
Spongs La TN17 . . . . .156 A1
Sportsfield ME14 . . . . .92 B5
Sportsmans Cotts ME19 . . .89 A5
Spot La ME15 . . . . .93 A2
Spout La Brenchley TN12 . .152 C5
Crockham Hill TN8 . . . . . . .96 C1
Spray Hill TN3 . . . . .166 B4
Spray St SE18 . . . . .2 B2
Sprig The ME14 . . . . .93 A4
Spring Cott DA1 . . . . .26 D8
Spring Cross DA3 . . . . .57 A7
Spring Ct 17 DA15 . . . . . . .24 A5
Spring Gdns Orpington BR6 .52 B4
Royal Tunbridge Wells TN4 .148 D8
Spring Gr DA12 . . . . .30 B7
Spring Head Rd TN15 . . . . .69 C2
Spring Hill TN11, TN3 . . . .147 A7
Spring La Bidborough TN3 .132 D3
Oldbury TN15 . . . . .86 B5
Spring Lodge 3 BR6 . . . . .38 C4
Spring Shaw Rd BR5 . . . . . .38 A4
Spring Vale Bexley DA7 . . . .8 B3
Dartford DA1 . . . . .26 D8
Maidstone ME16 . . . . .91 E4
Swanscombe DA9 . . . . .11 C1
Spring Vale Cl BR8 . . . . . . .39 F8
Spring Vale N DA1 . . . . . . .26 D8
Spring Vale S DA1 . . . . . . .26 D8
Springcroft DA3 . . . . .43 A4
Springdale Cotts ME3 . . . . .33 A3
Springett
Almshouses TN18 . . . . .184 E8
Springett Cl ME20 . . . . . . .75 F6
Springett Way ME17 . . . . .106 D3
Springfield Ave
Maidstone ME14 . . . . .91 F7
Swanley BR8 . . . . .39 F5
Tenterden TN30 . . . . .173 C2
Springfield Cotts TN12 . . .152 F5
Springfield Gdns BR1 . . . . .36 F5
Springfield Gr SE7 . . . . .5 C8
Springfield Ind Est TN18 .178 F3
Springfield Rd
Bexley,Bexleyheath DA7 . . .8 B3
Bexley,Welling DA16 . . . . . .7 B4
Bromley BR1 . . . . .36 F5
Edenbridge TN8 . . . . .112 B1
Gillingham ME7 . . . . .48 E6
Groombridge TN3 . . . . . . .161 C7
Lunsford ME20 . . . . .74 F4
Royal Tunbridge Wells TN4 .132 F1
Springfield Terr 7 ME4 . . .47 F4
Springfield Wlk 3 BR6 . . . .37 D1
Springfields TN5 . . . . .176 E1
Springhead
Springhead Ent Pk DA11 . .29 C7
Springhead Rd Erith DA8 . . .8 F8
Northfleet DA11 . . . . .29 C7
Springrove Cotts TN12 . . .138 B5
Springshaw TN13 . . . . .83 D4
Springvale ME8 . . . . .63 C6
Springvale Ct Eltham SE12 . .5 A3

Springvale Ct continued
Northfleet DA11 . . . . .29 C6
Springvale Ret Pk BR5 . . . .38 C6
Springvale Way BR5 . . . . . .38 C6
Springview
Apartments TN2 . . . . . .149 D6
Springwater Cl SE18 . . . . . .6 A1
Springwell Rd TN9 . . . . . .133 B8
Springwood Cl ME16 . . . . .91 A3
Springwood Rd ME16 . . . . .91 A3
Sprivers Gdns TN12 . . . . .152 E4
Spruce Cl ME20 . . . . .75 B2
Sprucedale Cl BR8 . . . . . . .39 E7
Spur Rd BR6 . . . . .52 A8
Spurgeons Cotts ME17 . . .106 E2
Spurrell Ave DA5 . . . . .25 D4
Spurway ME14 . . . . .93 A4
Square Hill ME15 . . . . .92 B4
Square Hill Rd ME15 . . . . .92 B4
Square The Cowden TN8 . .145 B6
Hadlow TN11 . . . . .118 E8
Hunton ME15 . . . . .121 D7
Leigh TN11 . . . . .115 F1
Lenham ME17 . . . . .111 D5
Sevenoaks TN13 . . . . .83 E5
Swanley BR8 . . . . .39 D6
Wadhurst TN5 . . . . .175 A4
Squerryes Ct* TN16 . . . . . .96 C7
Squerryes Mede TN16 . . . .96 C8
Squires Cl ME2 . . . . .46 B7
Squires Field TN8 . . . . .39 F8
Squires House 3 SE18 . . . . .6 B8
Squires Way DA2 . . . . .25 D4
Squires Wood Dr BR7 . . . . .22 F1
Squirrel Way TN2 . . . . . . .149 E5
Squirrels Cl BR6 . . . . .37 E1
Stable Cl ME5 . . . . .62 C5
Stabledene Way TN2 . . . . .150 D6
Stables End BR6 . . . . .51 C7
Stace Cl TN30 . . . . .183 C8
Stacey Cl DA12 . . . . .30 E3
Stacey Rd TN10 . . . . .117 A4
Staceys St ME14 . . . . .91 F5
Stack La DA3 . . . . .42 F4
Stack Rd DA4 . . . . .41 D5
Stacklands Cl TN15 . . . . . .55 E4
Stadium Rd SE18 . . . . .5 F8
Stadium Way DA1 . . . . .8 E2
Stadler Cl ME16 . . . . .91 D7
Staffa Rd ME15 . . . . .107 A7
Stafford Cl DA9 . . . . .10 F2
Stafford Rd
Royal Tunbridge Wells TN2 .149 E4
Sidcup DA14 . . . . .23 E4
Tonbridge TN9 . . . . .117 B2
Stafford St ME7 . . . . .48 C5
Stafford Way TN13 . . . . . . .99 C8
Stag Rd Chatham ME5 . . . .62 B5
Royal Tunbridge Wells TN2 .149 D8
Stagshaw Cl ME15 . . . . . . .92 A2
Stainer House SE3 . . . . .5 C3
Stainer Rd TN10 . . . . .117 F6
Staines Wlk DA14 . . . . .24 C2
Stainmore Cl BR7 . . . . .37 D5
Stair Rd TN10 . . . . .117 F4
Stairfoot La TN13 . . . . .83 C5
Stake La ME2 . . . . .60 A6
Staleys Rd TN15 . . . . .86 F7
Stalham Ct ME7 . . . . .63 B4
Stalin Ave ME5 . . . . .62 B8
Stalisfield Pl BR1 . . . . .51 A1
Stampers The ME15 . . . . . .91 D2
Stan La ME18 . . . . .103 A7
Stanam Rd TN2 . . . . .150 E6
Stanbridge Rd TN8 . . . . . .112 B2
Stanbrook Rd
Northfleet DA11 . . . . .29 F8
Woolwich SE2 . . . . .3 B4
Standard Ind Est E16 . . . . . .1 F4
Standard Rd Bexley DA6 . . .7 E3
Erith DA17 . . . . .4 A1
Farthing Street BR6 . . . . . .51 A1
Standen Cl ME8 . . . . .63 E4
Standen St
Benenden TN17,TN18 . . . .180 D2
Royal Tunbridge Wells TN4 .149 A5
Sandhurst TN17,TN18 . . .186 E8
Standings Cross TN12 . . . .135 E1
Standish House SE3 . . . . . . .5 B3
Stane Way SE18 . . . . .5 E7
Stanford Dr ME16 . . . . .91 C3
Stanford La TN11,TN12 . . .103 C2
Stanford Way ME2 . . . . . . .46 C2
Stangate Rd Birling ME19 . .74 B8
Rochester ME2 . . . . .46 C7
Stangrove Rd TN8 . . . . . . .112 C1
Stanham Pl DA1 . . . . .9 A3
Stanham Rd DA1 . . . . .9 C2
Stanhill Cotts DA2 . . . . . . .25 D2
Stanhope Ave BR2 . . . . . . .36 A1
Stanhope Cl ME14 . . . . . . .91 E7
Stanhope Rd Bexley DA7 . . .7 E5
Rochester ME2 . . . . .47 A7
Royal Tunbridge Wells TN1 .149 C5
Sidcup DA15 . . . . .24 A4
Swanscombe DA10 . . . . . . .11 F1
Stanhope Way TN13 . . . . . .83 D5
Stanley Cl
Staplehurst TN12 . . . . . . .139 E4
Stone DA9 . . . . .10 E2
Stanley Cotts DA2 . . . . . . .27 E3
Stanley Cres DA12 . . . . . . .30 D3
Stanley Rd Bromley BR2 . . .36 C5
Chatham ME5 . . . . .62 C6
Gillingham ME7 . . . . .48 C6
Grays RM17 . . . . .12 B8
Marden TN12 . . . . .138 D5
Northfleet DA11 . . . . .29 E7

Stanley Rd *continued*
Orpington BR6 . . . .**37** F1
Royal Tunbridge Wells TN1 .**149** B5
Sidcup DA14 . . . .**24** A5
Swanscombe DA10 . . . .**11** F1
Stanley Way BR5 . . . .**38** B4
Stanmore Rd DA17 . . . .**4** C2
Stanning Ct TN10 . . . .**117** C4
Stansfeld Rd E16 . . . .**1** D7
Stansted CE
  Prim Sch TN15 . . . .**56** F1
Stansted Cl ME14 . . . .**91** D7
Stansted Cres DA5 . . . .**24** D7
Stansted Hill TN15 . . . .**57** A1
Stansted La TN15 . . . .**56** C1
Stanton Cl BR5 . . . .**38** C2
Stanton Ct 8 Bromley BR1 . .**36** C7
  5 Sidcup DA15 . . . .**24** A5
Staple Cl DA5 . . . .**25** D5
Staple Dr TN12 . . . .**139** F4
Stapleford Ct TN13 . . . .**83** F4
Staplehurst House BR5 . . .**38** C4
Staplehurst Rd
  Bogden TN12 . . . .**123** C2
  Frittenden TN12,TN17 . . . .**140** D1
  Gillingham ME8 . . . .**49** B3
Staplehurst Sch TN12 . . . .**139** E3
Staplehurst Sta TN12 . . . .**139** E5
Staplers ME14 . . . .**92** B8
Staples Ho E6 . . . .**2** A7
Staples The BR8 . . . .**40** B8
Stapleton Rd Erith DA7 . . . . .**7** F8
  Orpington BR6 . . . .**51** F7
Stapley Rd DA1 . . . .**4** A1
Star Bsns Ctr RM9 . . . .**4** D8
Star Hill Crayford DA1 . . . . . .**8** E2
  Rochester ME1 . . . .**47** D5
Star Hill Rd TN14 . . . .**68** A2
Star La Gillingham ME7 . . . . .**63** A7
  St Paul's Cray BR5,BR8 . . . .**38** E5
Star Mill Ct ME5 . . . .**48** D2
Star Mill La ME5 . . . .**48** D2
Starboard Ave DA9 . . . .**11** B1
Starling Cl DA3 . . . .**43** B6
Starnes Ct 5 ME14 . . . .**92** A5
Starr Cotts TN12 . . . .**121** C3
Starts Cl BR5 . . . .**51** A7
Starts Hill Ave BR6 . . . .**51** B6
Starts Hill Rd BR6 . . . .**51** B6
Starvecrow Cl TN11 . . . . . .**117** D8
State Farm Ave BR6 . . . . . .**51** C6
Station App
  Bexley,Barnehurst DA7 . . . . .**8** C5
  Bexley,Bexleyheath DA7 . . . . .**7** E5
  Bexley,Welling DA16 . . . .**7** A5
  Borough Green TN15 . . . . . .**86** F7
  Chislehurst BR7 . . . .**37** A7
  Chislehurst,Elmstead BR7 . . .**22** E2
  Dartford DA1 . . . .**9** E1
  Edenbridge TN8 . . . .**112** C2
  Grays RM17 . . . .**12** A8
  Greenwich SE3 . . . .**5** B4
  Halling ME2 . . . .**60** A5
  Hayes BR2 . . . .**36** A1
  Maidstone ME16 . . . .**91** F3
  Orpington BR6 . . . .**51** F8
  Orpington,Chelsfield BR6 . . .**52** B5
  Otford TN14 . . . .**69** C3
  Paddock Wood TN12 . . . . .**136** A7
  St Paul's Cray BR5 . . . .**38** B5
  Staplehurst TN12 . . . .**139** E5
  Swanley BR8 . . . .**39** E5
Station Approach Rd
  RM18 . . . .**13** A3
Station Cotts
  Gill's Green TN18 . . . .**178** F5
  Hartley TN17 . . . .**168** E2
  Horsmonden TN12 . . . . . .**153** B5
Station Cres SE3 . . . .**1** A1
Station Ct TN15 . . . .**86** F7
Station Hill Chiddingstone
  Causeway TN11 . . . .**131** A8
  Hayes BR2 . . . .**50** A8
Station Mews 3 TN30 . . . .**183** A7
Station Par DA15 . . . .**24** A6
Station Rd Aylesford ME20 . .**75** E2
  Betsham DA13 . . . .**29** A4
  Bexley DA7 . . . .**7** E4
  Borough Green TN15 . . . . . .**86** F7
  Brasted TN16 . . . .**82** B4
  Bromley BR1 . . . .**36** A8
  Cliffe ME3 . . . .**16** B3
  Crayford DA1 . . . .**8** F1
  Cuxton ME2 . . . .**46** C2
  East Farleigh ME15 . . . . . .**106** A7
  East Tilbury RM18 . . . .**14** B7
  Edenbridge TN8 . . . .**112** C2
  Erith DA17 . . . .**4** A3
  Eynsford DA4 . . . .**54** D7
  Gillingham ME8 . . . .**49** F1
  Goudhurst TN17 . . . .**167** C7
  Groombridge TN3 . . . .**161** C7
  Halstead TN14 . . . .**67** F8
  Harrietsham ME17 . . . . . .**110** D6
  Headcorn TN27 . . . .**141** D5
  Hurst Green TN19 . . . .**184** A3
  Longfield DA3 . . . .**42** E6
  Maidstone ME14 . . . .**91** F5
  Meopham Sta DA13 . . . . . .**44** A4
  Nettlestead Green ME18 . . .**104** C1
  Newington ME9 . . . .**65** B6
  Northfleet DA11 . . . .**12** B1
  Northiam TN31 . . . .**187** C1
  Orpington BR6 . . . .**51** F8
  Otford TN14 . . . .**69** C3
  Paddock Wood TN12 . . . . .**135** F7
  Rochester ME1 . . . .**47** C7
  Sevenoaks TN13 . . . .**83** E7

Station Rd *continued*
  Shoreham TN14 . . . .**69** A7
  Sidcup DA14,DA15 . . . .**24** A5
  St Paul's Cray BR5 . . . .**38** C5
  Staplehurst TN12 . . . .**139** F5
  Stone DA9 . . . .**11** A2
  Sutton at Hone DA4 . . . . . .**41** B7
  Swanley BR8 . . . .**39** E5
  Tenterden TN30 . . . .**183** A4
  Wadhurst TN5 . . . .**174** C6
  Withyham TN7 . . . .**160** B3
Station Rd N DA17 . . . .**4** B3
Station Sq BR5 . . . .**37** C4
Station St E16 . . . .**2** B5
Steadman Cl ME3 . . . .**32** C6
Stede Hill ME17 . . . .**95** F3
Stedley 17 DA14 . . . .**24** A4
Stedman Cl DA5 . . . .**25** E5
Steele Ave DA9 . . . .**11** A2
Steele St ME2 . . . .**47** A8
Steele Wlk ME2 . . . .**8** B7
Steele's La DA13 . . . .**58** A6
Steellands Rise TN5 . . . . .**176** F1
Steep Cl BR6 . . . .**51** F4
Steerforth Cl ME1 . . . .**47** C2
Steers Pl TN11 . . . .**102** F3
Stella Cl TN12 . . . .**138** D5
Stelling Rd DA8 . . . .**8** D7
Stephen Cl BR6 . . . .**51** F7
Stephen Rd DA7 . . . .**8** D4
Stephen's La TN4 . . . .**149** B6
Stephenson Ave RM18 . . . .**13** A6
Stephenson Ho SE2 . . . .**3** D1
Stepneyford La TN17 . . . . .**181** C7
Steps Hill Rd ME9 . . . .**79** D6
Sterling Ave ME16 . . . .**91** C5
Sterling House SE3 . . . .**5** B3
Sterndale Rd DA1 . . . .**26** F8
Stevanne Ct 1 DA17 . . . .**4** A1
Stevedale Rd DA16 . . . .**7** C5
Stevens Cl
  Dartford, Joydens End DA5 . .**25** D4
  Dartford, Lane End DA2 . . . .**27** E3
  Egerton TN27 . . . .**127** F3
  Snodland ME6 . . . .**75** A8
Stevens Rd ME20 . . . .**75** F6
Stevenson Cl Dartford DA8 . . .**9** B7
  Maidstone ME15 . . . .**91** F3
Stevenson Way ME20 . . . . .**74** F4
Stewart Cl ME3 . . . .**33** F6
Stewart Ho ME3 . . . .**33** F6
Stewart Rd TN4 . . . .**149** C7
Steyning Gr SE9 . . . .**22** F4
Steynton Ave DA5 . . . .**24** D6
Stickens La ME19 . . . .**89** E7
Stickfast La TN27 . . . .**125** D3
Stickland Rd 2 DA17 . . . .**4** A2
Stilebridge La
  Underling Green ME17 . . . .**123** A5
  Underling Green TN12 . . . .**122** E3
Stiles Cl Bromley BR2 . . . . . .**36** F3
  Erith DA8 . . . .**4** B1
Still La TN4 . . . .**149** C7
Stirling Cl Gillingham ME8 . .**63** E4
  Rochester ME1 . . . .**47** A3
Stirling Dr BR6 . . . .**52** B5
Stirling Ho 5 SE18 . . . .**2** B1
Stirling Rd ME19 . . . .**88** F3
Stisted Way TN27 . . . .**127** F3
Stock La DA2 . . . .**26** C4
Stockbury Dr ME16 . . . .**91** D7
Stockbury House 7 BR5 . . .**38** D1
Stockenbury TN12 . . . .**119** F6
Stockett La ME15 . . . .**106** D6
Stockfield 1 TN8 . . . .**112** D3
Stockland Green Rd TN11 . .**148** B8
Stocks Green Prim Sch
  TN11 . . . .**116** E5
Stocks Green Rd TN11 . . . .**116** C5
Stocks Rd TN30 . . . .**189** F3
Stockton Cl ME14 . . . .**92** B8
Stockwell Cl BR1 . . . .**36** B7
Stofield Gdns SE9 . . . .**22** D5
Stoke Com Sch ME3 . . . . . .**19** C5
Stoke Rd Allhallows ME3 . . . .**19** C7
  Hoo St Werburgh ME3 . . . . .**34** F6
  Kingsnorth ME3 . . . .**35** C8
  Lower Stoke ME3 . . . .**18** E1
Stokesay Ct 14 DA2 . . . .**10** B1
Stone Cotts TN3 . . . .**165** F4
Stone Court La TN2 . . . . . .**150** E8
Stone Cross Rd TN5 . . . . . .**175** A4
Stone Crossing Sta DA9 . . .**10** E2
Stone Ct DA8 . . . .**4** F1
Stone Hill Rd TN27 . . . .**127** F2
Stone House Hospl DA2 . . .**10** C1
Stone Lake Ind Pk SE7 . . . . .**1** C2
Stone Lake Ret Pk SE7 . . . . .**1** C2
Stone Lodge Farm Park*
  DA2 . . . .**10** D1
Stone Pit La TN18 . . . .**186** E5
Stone Place Rd DA9 . . . .**10** E2
Stone Rd BR2 . . . .**36** A5
Stone Row TN3 . . . .**147** B5
Stone Row Cotts TN3 . . . . .**147** B5
Stone St Cranbrook TN17 . . .**169** D5
  Gravesend DA11 . . . .**13** B1
  Royal Tunbridge Wells TN1 . .**85** E2
Stone Street Rd TN15 . . . . .**85** E2
Stone Wood DA2 . . . .**28** C5
Stone, St Mary's CE
  Prim Sch DA9 . . . .**27** C8
Stoneacre* ME15 . . . .**108** B7
Stoneacre Cl ME8 . . . .**63** D6
Stoneacre Ct ME15 . . . .**92** A1
Stoneacre La ME15 . . . .**108** B7
Stonebridge Green Rd
  TN27 . . . .**127** F4

Stonebridge Rd DA11 . . . . .**12** B2
Stonechat Sq 6 E6 . . . .**1** E8
Stonecroft SE9 . . . .**23** A8
Stonecroft Rd DA8 . . . .**8** C7
Stonecrop Cl ME4 . . . .**34** C1
Stonecross Lea ME5 . . . . . .**48** C1
Stonefield Cl DA7 . . . .**8** A4
Stonefield Way SE7 . . . .**5** D7
Stonegate Cl BR5 . . . .**38** C6
Stonegate Rd TN5 . . . .**175** C1
Stonehorse Ct ME3 . . . .**33** A3
Stonehorse La ME2 . . . .**33** A2
Stonehouse Cnr RM19 . . . .**10** E8
Stonehouse La
  Pratt's Bottom TN14 . . . . . .**52** E1
  Purfleet RM19 . . . .**10** E8
Stonehouse Rd BR6,TN14 . .**52** D1
Stoneings La TN14 . . . .**81** F8
Stoneness Rd RM20 . . . .**11** C7
Stones Cross Rd BR8 . . . . . .**39** C4
Stonestile Rd TN27 . . . .**141** A7
Stonewall E6 . . . .**2** A8
Stonewall Park Rd TN3 . . . .**147** F3
Stonewood Cl TN4 . . . .**149** A8
Stonewood Rd DA8 . . . .**4** E1
Stoney Alley SE18 . . . .**6** A5
Stoney Bank ME7 . . . .**48** F1
Stony Cnr DA13 . . . .**43** E6
Stony La ME1 . . . .**61** C5
Stonyfield TN8 . . . .**112** D3
Stopford Rd ME7 . . . .**48** D4
Store Rd E16 . . . .**2** A4
Storehouse Wharf ME12 . . .**21** F3
Storey Prim Sch E16 . . . .**2** B5
Storey St E16 . . . .**2** A4
Stornaway Strand DA12 . . .**30** F4
Stour 4 Orpington BR2 . . . . .**50** C6
  Rochester ME2 . . . .**46** F7
  Tonbridge TN10 . . . .**117** B5
Stour Ct 22 BR5 . . . .**38** D1
Stour Rd DA1 . . . .**9** A4
Stowe Rd BR6 . . . .**52** B6
Stowting Rd BR6 . . . .**51** E6
Strait Rd E6 . . . .**1** F6
Strand Approach Rd ME7 . .**48** E7
Strand Cl DA13 . . . .**44** A3
Strand Rdbt The ME7 . . . . .**48** E7
Strandfield Cl SE18 . . . .**2** E1
Stratfield Ho SE12 . . . .**22** A6
Stratford Ave ME6 . . . .**63** D8
Stratford House Ave BR1 . .**36** E6
Stratford La 2 ME6 . . . .**63** D8
Stratford Rd ME19 . . . .**89** A8
Stratford St TN1 . . . .**149** C5
Strathaven Rd SE12 . . . .**5** B1
Stratheden Par SE3 . . . .**5** A7
Stratheden Rd SE3 . . . .**5** A7
Stratton Cl DA7 . . . .**7** E4
Stratton Rd DA7 . . . .**7** E4
Stratton Terr TN16 . . . .**96** C8
Straw Mill Hill ME15 . . . . . .**91** E1
Strawberry Cl TN2 . . . .**162** E7
Strawberry Fields BR8 . . . .**39** E7
Strawberry Vale TN9 . . . . .**117** C5
Stream La TN18 . . . .**185** B7
Stream Lane Cotts TN18 . .**185** A7
Stream Pit La TN18 . . . .**186** B5
Stream Side TN10 . . . .**117** D6
Stream The ME20 . . . .**75** C1
Stream Way DA17 . . . .**8** A8
Streamdale SE2 . . . .**7** B8
Streamside ME20 . . . .**75** B1
Streamside Cl BR2 . . . .**36** A5
Streatfield TN8 . . . .**112** D1
Streatfield Ho TN16 . . . .**81** D1
Street End Rd ME5 . . . .**48** B1
Street Farm Cotts ME3 . . . .**34** F6
Street The Ash TN15 . . . .**56** E5
  Benenden TN17 . . . .**180** D6
  Boxley ME14 . . . .**77** C3
  Bredhurst ME7 . . . .**63** B1
  Cobham DA12 . . . .**44** F6
  Detling ME14 . . . .**78** A1
  Egerton TN27 . . . .**127** F3
  Fenn Street ME3 . . . .**18** A3
  Frittenden TN17 . . . .**156** E7
  Hartlip ME9 . . . .**64** D5
  High Halstow ME23 . . . .**17** E3
  Horton Kirby DA4 . . . .**41** C5
  Ightham TN15 . . . .**86** D6
  Maidstone ME14 . . . .**93** C4
  Meopham DA13 . . . .**44** A1
  Mereworth ME18 . . . .**103** D8
  Plaxtol TN15 . . . .**101** F7
  Ryarsh ME19 . . . .**73** F4
  Shorne DA12 . . . .**31** E3
  Silver Street ME9 . . . .**80** F5
  Sissinghurst TN17 . . . .**170** B8
  Teston ME18 . . . .**105** A7
  Trottiscliffe ME19 . . . .**73** A5
  Ulcombe ME17 . . . .**125** F7
  Upper Halling ME2 . . . .**59** E5
  Wittersham TN30 . . . .**189** D3
  Wormshill ME9 . . . .**95** F7
Streetfield ME17 . . . .**125** F7
Streetfield Mews SE3 . . . . . .**5** A4
Streetfield Rd ME8 . . . .**49** F1
Strettit Gdns TN12 . . . .**119** F5
Strickland Ave DA1 . . . .**9** F4
Strickland Way 4 BR6 . . . . .**51** F6
Strongbow Cres SE9 . . . .**5** F2
Strongbow Rd SE9 . . . .**5** F2
Strood Sta ME2 . . . .**47** C7
Strover St ME7 . . . .**48** C7
Struttons Ave DA11 . . . .**29** F6
Stuart Ave BR2 . . . .**36** A1
Stuart Cl Hextable BR8 . . . . .**26** A1
  Maidstone ME14 . . . .**92** C6

Stuart Cl *continued*
  Royal Tunbridge Wells TN2 . .**162** F1
Stuart Evans Cl SE18 . . . .**7** C4
Stuart Mantle Way DA8 . . . .**8** E7
Stuart Rd Bexley DA16 . . . . . .**7** B6
  Gillingham ME7 . . . .**48** D3
  Gravesend DA11 . . . .**13** A1
Stubbs Hill BR6,TN14 . . . . .**67** C6
Stubbygrove Cotts TN3 . . .**163** E4
Studland Cl DA15 . . . .**23** F5
Studley Cres DA3 . . . .**43** C7
Studley Ct DA14 . . . .**24** B3
Stumble Hill TN11 . . . .**101** C5
Sturdee Ave ME7 . . . .**48** E4
Sturdee Cotts ME3 . . . .**35** A6
Sturges Field BR7 . . . .**23** D2
Sturla Rd ME4 . . . .**48** A3
Sturmer Ct ME19 . . . .**89** A2
Sturry Way ME8 . . . .**49** F1
Styants Bottom Rd TN15 . .**85** F5
Style Cl ME8 . . . .**63** E4
Styles Cl TN8 . . . .**113** B5
Styles Cotts TN8 . . . .**113** B5
Sudbury E6 . . . .**2** A7
Sudbury Cres BR1 . . . .**22** A3
Suffolk Ave ME8 . . . .**49** F1
  Gravesend DA12 . . . .**13** D1
Suffolk Rd Dartford DA1 . . . . .**9** E1
  Maidstone ME15 . . . .**107** D8
  Sidcup DA14 . . . .**24** C2
Suffolk Way TN13 . . . .**84** C2
Sullivan Ave E16 . . . .**1** D8
Sullivan Cl DA1 . . . .**26** C8
Sullivan Rd Tilbury RM18 . . .**13** A6
  Tonbridge TN10 . . . .**117** E5
Sultan Rd ME5 . . . .**62** C2
Summer Cl DA8 . . . .**8** F5
Summer Hill BR7 . . . .**37** A7
Summerfield
  7 Bromley BR1 . . . .**36** B8
  Marden TN17 . . . .**158** F1
Summerfield St 9 SE12 . . . .**22** A8
Summerhill Ave TN4 . . . . . .**132** F1
Summerhill Cl BR6 . . . .**51** E7
Summerhill Rd
  Bogden TN12 . . . .**123** C1
  Dartford DA1 . . . .**26** D8
Summerhouse Dr DA2,DA5 .**25** D4
Summerlands Lodge BR6 . .**51** A6
Summerton Way SE28 . . . . . .**3** D7
Summervale Rd TN2,TN4 . .**148** E1
Sumner Cl Orpington BR6 . . .**51** C6
  Rolvenden TN17 . . . .**181** F3
Sun Ct DA8 . . . .**8** F5
Sun Hill DA3 . . . .**56** A8
Sun La Gravesend DA12 . . . . .**30** C6
  Greenwich SE3 . . . .**5** B7
Sun Rd DA10 . . . .**11** F1
Sun Terr ME5 . . . .**62** B4
Sunburst Cl TN12 . . . .**138** D5
Sunbury St SE18 . . . .**1** F3
Sunderland Cl ME1 . . . .**47** A3
Sunderland Dr ME8 . . . .**64** A8
Sunderland Ho 3 ME7 . . . . .**48** C7
Sundew Ct 8 RM17 . . . .**12** D8
Sundorne Rd SE7 . . . .**1** C1
Sundridge & Brasted CE
  Prim Sch TN14 . . . .**82** E2
Sundridge Ave Bexley DA16 .**6** D4
  Bromley BR1 . . . .**36** D8
Sundridge Cl DA1 . . . .**10** A1
Sundridge Ct 9 BR1 . . . .**22** B1
Sundridge Dr ME5 . . . .**62** B4
Sundridge Hill Cuxton ME2 . .**46** C3
  Halstead TN14 . . . .**67** C1
Sundridge La TN14 . . . .**67** C2
Sundridge Park Sta BR1 . . . .**22** B1
Sundridge Rd TN14 . . . .**83** B8
Sunfields Pl SE3 . . . .**5** B7
Sunhill Ct TN2 . . . .**150** C6
Sunland Ave DA6 . . . .**7** E3
Sunningdale Cl
  Gillingham ME8 . . . .**63** D6
  Woolwich SE28 . . . .**3** F7
Sunningdale Ct ME15 . . . . . .**92** B4
Sunningdale Dr ME8 . . . .**63** D6
Sunningdale Rd BR1,BR2 . . .**36** E4
Sunninghill DA11 . . . .**29** E6
Sunnybank TN5 . . . .**177** E3
Sunnydale BR6 . . . .**51** A8
Sunnydale Rd SE12 . . . .**5** B2
Sunnyfield Rd BR7 . . . .**38** A6
Sunnyfields Cl ME8 . . . .**63** E8
Sunnymead Ave ME7 . . . . . .**48** E5
Sunnyside TN8 . . . .**112** B3
Sunnyside Rd TN4 . . . .**148** C4
Sunray Ave BR2 . . . .**36** F3
Sunset Cl DA8 . . . .**9** B7
Sunset Rd SE28 . . . .**3** A5
Sunshine Cl 1 ME8 . . . .**63** F8
Superabbey Est ME20 . . . . .**76** B2
Superior Dr 2 BR6 . . . .**51** F4
Surlingham Cl SE28 . . . .**3** D6
Surrenden Rd TN12 . . . .**139** E3
Surrey Cl TN2 . . . .**162** F8
Surrey Rd ME15 . . . .**107** D8
Susan Rd SE3 . . . .**5** B5
Susan Wood BR7 . . . .**37** A8
Sussex Cl TN2 . . . .**149** C1
Sussex Dr ME5 . . . .**62** A4
Sussex Mews ME7 . . . .**149** A2
Sussex Rd Dartford DA1 . . . . .**27** A3
  Erith DA8 . . . .**8** D7
  Maidstone ME15 . . . .**107** D8
  Orpington BR5 . . . .**38** C3
  Sidcup DA14 . . . .**24** B3
  Tonbridge TN9 . . . .**133** A8

Sussex Road
  Cty Prim Sch TN9 . . . . . .**133** A8
Sutcliffe Rd Bexley DA16 . . . .**7** C5
  Woolwich SE18 . . . .**6** E8
Sutherland Ave Bexley DA16 .**6** E3
  Orpington BR5 . . . .**37** F4
Sutherland Cl DA12 . . . .**31** B6
Sutherland Gdns ME8 . . . . .**63** E6
Sutherland House SE7 . . . . . .**5** F6
Sutherland Rd Erith DA17 . . . .**4** A3
  Royal Tunbridge Wells TN1 . .**149** B3
Sutlej Rd SE7 . . . .**5** C7
Sutton at Hone CE
  Prim Sch DA4 . . . .**27** A1
Sutton Cl ME8 . . . .**64** A8
Sutton Ct TN12 . . . .**138** C5
Sutton Forge TN12 . . . .**138** D5
Sutton Rd
  Langley Heath ME17 . . . . . .**108** C5
  Maidstone ME15 . . . .**107** D6
Sutton St SE14 . . . .**93** D4
Sutton Valence
  Prim Sch ME17 . . . .**124** E7
Sutton Valence Sch
  ME17 . . . .**124** E7
Swadelands Cl ME17 . . . . . .**111** C5
Swadelands Sch ME17 . . . .**111** C5
Swaffield Rd TN13 . . . .**84** C5
Swain Cl ME2 . . . .**46** F8
Swain Rd Gillingham ME8 . . .**63** B6
  Tenterden TN30 . . . .**173** D3
Swaisland Rd DA1 . . . .**9** B1
Swaislands Dr DA1 . . . .**8** F2
Swale Rd Crayford DA1 . . . . . .**9** A3
  Rochester ME2 . . . .**46** C7
Swaledale Rd DA2 . . . .**27** C7
Swallow Cl Erith DA8 . . . .**8** E6
  Stone DA9 . . . .**10** F2
Swallow Ct 3 SE12 . . . .**22** A8
Swallow Dr TN2 . . . .**149** F6
Swallow House 4 ME16 . . . .**91** E4
Swallow Rd ME20 . . . .**74** F2
Swallow Rise ME5 . . . .**62** A5
Swallow St E6 . . . .**1** E8
Swallowfield Rd SE7 . . . .**1** B1
Swallowfields 2 DA11 . . . . .**29** E5
Swallowtail Cl BR5 . . . .**38** D5
Swan Apartments 12
  ME15 . . . .**107** E5
Swan App E6 . . . .**1** E8
Swan Bsns Pk DA1 . . . .**9** C3
Swan Cl BR5 . . . .**38** A6
Swan Cotts TN30 . . . .**189** D3
Swan La Brandfold TN17 . . . .**153** F3
  Dartford DA1 . . . .**25** F8
  Marlpit Hill TN8 . . . .**112** C4
Swan Rd SE18 . . . .**1** D3
Swan Ridge TN8 . . . .**112** D4
Swan St West Malling ME19 . .**89** C8
  Wittersham TN30 . . . .**189** C3
Swan Valley ComSch
  DA10 . . . .**28** F8
Swanbridge Rd DA7 . . . .**8** B6
Swanland Dr TN9 . . . .**132** F7
Swanley Ctr BR8 . . . .**39** E6
Swanley La BR8 . . . .**39** F6
Swanley New Barn Rly*
  BR8 . . . .**39** E8
Swanley Rd DA16 . . . .**7** C6
Swanley Sch BR8 . . . .**39** E6
Swanley Sta BR8 . . . .**39** D5
Swanley Village Rd BR8 . . . .**40** B8
Swanmead Way TN9 . . . . .**117** D2
Swanscombe Bsns Ctr
  DA10 . . . .**11** E2
Swanscombe
  House 1 BR5 . . . .**38** B7
Swanscombe
  Inf Sch DA10 . . . .**28** F8
Swanscombe St DA10 . . . . .**11** F1
Swanscombe Sta DA10 . . . .**11** F2
Swansea Cl E16 . . . .**2** C6
Swanton Rd Erith DA8 . . . . . .**8** B7
  Mereworth ME18 . . . .**103** A8
Swanzy Rd TN14 . . . .**84** C7
Sward Rd BR5 . . . .**38** A3
Swattenden La TN17 . . . . . .**169** B1
Swaylands Rd DA17 . . . .**8** A8
Sweeps Hill Cl TN2 . . . .**150** D7
Sweeps La BR5 . . . .**38** D5
Sweetings La TN3,TN5 . . . . .**165** D1
Sweetlands La TN12 . . . . . .**140** A5
Sweets La ME19 . . . .**90** A4
Swetenham Wlk SE18 . . . . . .**2** C1
Sweyn Pl SE3 . . . .**5** A5
Sweyne Jun Sch The
  DA10 . . . .**28** F8
Sweyne Rd DA10 . . . .**11** E1
Swift Cl ME20 . . . .**75** A2
Swift Cres ME5 . . . .**62** C6
Swift House 6 ME16 . . . .**91** E4
Swift's View TN17 . . . .**169** D6
Swiller's La DA12 . . . .**31** E3
Swinburne Gdns RM18 . . . . .**13** B5
Swingate Ave ME3 . . . .**16** B6
Swingate Cl ME5 . . . .**62** B2
Swingate Inf Sch ME5 . . . . .**62** C1
Swingate La SE18 . . . .**6** F7
Swingfield Ct BR2 . . . .**36** D4
Swinton Ave ME3 . . . .**33** F5
Swires Shaw BR2 . . . .**50** D6
Swithland Gdns SE9 . . . .**23** A4
Syamore Mews DA8 . . . .**4** D1
Sycamor Ct DA8 . . . .**4** D1

Sycamore Ave DA15 . . . . . .6 F1
Sycamore Cl Eltham SE9 . . . . . .5 E1
Gravesend DA12 . . . . .30 D8
Tilbury RM18 . . . . .13 A5
Sycamore Cotts TN2 . . . . . .150 C6
Sycamore Cres ME16 . . . . . .91 C5
Sycamore Ct DA9 . . . . .27 E8
Sycamore Dr
Aylesford ME20 . . . . .75 E1
Swanley BR8 . . . . .39 E7
Sycamore Gdns TN12 . . . . .135 F5
Sycamore Lodge BR6 . . . . . .52 A8
Sycamore Rd Dartford DA1 . .26 D7
Rochester ME2 . . . . .46 C5
Sychem La TN12 . . . . .135 A6
Sychem Pl TN12 . . . . .135 A6
Sydenham Cotts SE12 . . . . . .22 C6
Sydney Bexley DA6 . . . . .7 D3
Chatham ME4 . . . . .48 A3
Erith SE2 . . . . .3 D3
Sidcup DA14 . . . . .23 E4
Tilbury RM18 . . . . .13 A5
Sydney St SE18 . . . . .2 C3
Sydney Terr TN18 . . . . . . .178 F3
Sylewood Cl ME1 . . . . .61 B8
Sylvan Glade ME5 . . . . .77 A8
Sylvan Rd ME8 . . . . .63 C8
Sylvan Wlk BR1 . . . . .36 F6
Sylvester Ave BR7 . . . . .22 F2
Sylvestre Cl ME2 . . . . .60 A4
Sylvestres TN13 . . . . .83 E6
Symonds Cl TN15 . . . . .55 E5
Symonds La ME18 . . . . . . .120 F6
Symonds Rd ME3 . . . . .16 A4
Symons Ave ME4 . . . . .48 A2
Syon Lodge 11 SE12 . . . . . . .22 A8
Syringa Ct 9 RM17 . . . . . . .12 D8

T

Tabor Ct TN12 . . . . .153 A6
Tadburn Gn ME5 . . . . .62 B4
Taddington Wood La ME5 .61 E2
Tadley Ct Chatham ME1 . . . . .47 B1
Gillingham ME7 . . . . .48 F6
Tail Race The ME15 . . . . . . .91 E2
Tainter Rd TN11 . . . . .102 E1
Talbot Pk TN2 . . . . .149 D5
Talbot Rd Maidstone ME16 . .91 C6
The Moor TN18 . . . . .184 F8
Tall Trees Cl ME17 . . . . . . .109 D2
Tallents Cl DA4 . . . . .27 B1
Tallis Cl E16 . . . . .1 B7
Tallis Gr SE7 . . . . .5 B8
Tamar Dr ME2 . . . . .46 F7
Tamar Rd TN10 . . . . .117 B5
Tamar St SE7 . . . . .1 B2
Tamarind Cl ME7 . . . . .63 A4
Tamesis Strand DA12 . . . . . .30 E3
Tan Yard La DA5 . . . . .25 A8
Tandridge Dr BR6 . . . . .37 D1
Tandridge Pl 2 BR6 . . . . . . .37 D1
Tangier La TN3 . . . . .163 B6
Tangleberry Cl BR1 . . . . .36 F5
Tanglewood Cl ME8 . . . . . . .63 C6
Tanglewood Ct BR5 . . . . . . .38 C6
Tangmere Cl ME7 . . . . .48 F5
Tanker Hill ME8 . . . . .63 D6
Tanners Mead TN8 . . . . . . .112 C1
Tannery Rd TN9 . . . . .117 C1
Tansy Cl E6 . . . . .2 A7
Tanyard Rolvenden TN17 . . .181 E4
Sandhurst TN18 . . . . .186 B5
Tanyard Cotts DA12 . . . . . . .31 E1
Tanyard Hill DA12 . . . . .31 E2
Tanyard La TN4 . . . . .132 F1
Tanyard The TN17 . . . . . . .169 D4
Tapsell's La TN5 . . . . .174 D5
Tarbutts TN17 . . . . .169 D4
Target Bsns Ctr ME15 . . . . .107 F4
Tarland Ho TN2 . . . . .149 D3
Tarling Rd DA14 . . . . .24 B5
Tarnwood Pk SE9 . . . . .22 F7
Tarragon Rd ME16 . . . . .91 B3
Tasker Cl ME15 . . . . .93 B3
Tasman Wlk E16 . . . . .1 D7
Tasmania House RM18 . . . . .13 A6
Tassell Cl ME19 . . . . .75 A1
Tate Rd E16 . . . . .1 F5
Tates TN18 . . . . .179 A1
Tates Orch DA3 . . . . .42 F3
Tatler Cl ME5 . . . . .62 D2
Tatsfield Cl ME8 . . . . .49 A2
Tatsfield La TN16 . . . . .81 A6
Tattersall Cl SE9 . . . . .5 E2
Tattershall Ct 22 DA2 . . . . . .10 B1
Tattlebury La TN17 . . . . . . .153 F1
Tattlebury Rd TN27 . . . . . .141 D5
Taunton Bexley DA7 . . . . .8 D5
Maidstone ME15 . . . . .107 F4
Taunton Rd DA1 . . . . .12 A2
Taunton Vale DA12 . . . . .30 D5
Tavern Cl TN15 . . . . .86 F7
Tavern Cotts TN15 . . . . .85 A3
Taverners Rd ME8 . . . . .63 C7
Tavistock Cl Chatham ME5 . .61 F1
Gillingham ME8 . . . . .63 C7
Tavistock Rd Bexley DA16 . . .7 C6
2 Bromley BR2 . . . . .36 A5
Tavy Bridge SE2 . . . . .3 C4
Tawney Rd SE28 . . . . .3 B6
Tay Cl ME5 . . . . .62 B5
Taylor Cl
Harrietsham ME17 . . . . . .110 D6

Taylor Cl continued
3 Orpington BR6 . . . . .51 F6
Taylor Ct TN2 . . . . .149 C7
Taylor Rd ME6 . . . . .74 F8
Taylor Row DA2 . . . . .26 C5
Taylor St SE18 . . . . .149 A8
Taylor's Bldgs SE18 . . . . .2 B2
Taylor's La Higham ME3 . . . .32 B5
Rochester ME2 . . . . .47 B7
Taylors Cl DA14 . . . . .23 F4
Taylors La ME19 . . . . .72 F6
Tea Garden La TN3, TN4 . . .148 C2
Teal Ave BR5 . . . . .38 D5
Teal Cl Grain ME3 . . . . .21 B5
Newham E1 . . . . .1 D8
Teapot La ME20 . . . . .75 E1
Teasaucer Hill ME15 . . . . . .106 F8
Teasel Cl ME14 . . . . .92 F4
Teasel Rd ME5 . . . . .61 F4
Teasels TN27 . . . . .158 A1
Teasley Mead TN3 . . . . .146 C4
Tebbs Way TN15 . . . . .86 C3
Tedder Ave ME5 . . . . .62 A7
Tedder Rd TN4 . . . . .149 B7
Teesdale Rd DA2 . . . . .27 C7
Teeswater Ct SE2 . . . . .3 D3
Teignmouth Rd DA16 . . . . . . .7 C5
Teise Cl TN2 . . . . .149 D2
Telegraph Hill ME3 . . . . . . .32 C3
Telemann Sq SE3 . . . . .5 A4
Telford Ho 2 Erith DA17 . . .4 A3
1 Maidstone ME14 . . . . .92 A6
Telford Rd SE9 . . . . .23 D6
Tellson Ave SE18 . . . . .5 E6
Telscombe Cl BR6 . . . . .51 E8
Telston La TN14 . . . . .68 F2
Temeraire Manor 2 ME7 . .48 A6
Tempest Rd ME19 . . . . .88 F3
Templar Dr Erith SE28 . . . . . .3 D7
Gravesend DA11 . . . . .30 A3
Templars Ct 11 TN8 . . . . . .112 D3
Temple Cl SE28 . . . . .2 C3
Temple Gdns ME2 . . . . .47 A6
Temple Hill DA1 . . . . .9 F2
Temple Hill Cty Prim Sch
DA1 . . . . .10 A2
Temple Hill Sq DA1 . . . . .9 F2
Temple Manor* ME2 . . . . . .61 C8
Temple Sch ME2 . . . . .33 B2
Temple Way ME19 . . . . .74 F1
Templemore DA14 . . . . .24 B3
Tenby Rd DA16 . . . . .7 D6
Tenney House RM17 . . . . . . .12 B7
Tennyson Ave ME3 . . . . .33 B7
Tennyson Cl DA16 . . . . .6 F6
Tennyson Ho 2 DA17 . . . . . .3 F1
Tennyson Rd Dartford DA1 . .10 A2
Gillingham ME7 . . . . .48 C3
Tennyson Wlk
Northfleet DA11 . . . . .29 D5
Tilbury RM18 . . . . .13 B5
Tensing Ave DA11 . . . . .29 E5
Tent Peg La BR5 . . . . .37 C4
Tenterden & District
Mus* TN30 . . . . .183 A7
Tenterden CE Jun Sch
TN30 . . . . .183 B7
Tenterden Cl SE9 . . . . .22 F7
Tenterden Inf Sch TN30 . .183 B7
Tenterden Rd
Biddenden TN27 . . . . .172 B7
Chatham ME5 . . . . .62 B5
Fosten Green TN27 . . . . . . .171 F4
Tenterden TN17 . . . . .182 A5
Tenterden Sta
TN30 . . . . .183 A8
Tenterden Vineyard*
TN30 . . . . .183 C1
Tenzing Ct SE9 . . . . .22 E6
Terence Cl Chatham ME4 . . .48 A2
Gravesend DA12 . . . . .30 F6
Terence Ct 6 DA17 . . . . .7 F8
Terminus Rd ME16 . . . . .91 A2
Tern Cres ME2 . . . . .46 C6
Terrace Rd ME16 . . . . .91 E3
Terrace St DA12 . . . . .13 B1
Terrace The 28
Gravesend DA12 . . . . .13 B1
Rochester ME1 . . . . .47 C5
Sevenoaks TN13 . . . . .83 D5
Terraces The DA2 . . . . .27 C8
Terry Wlk ME19 . . . . .74 E2
Terry's Lodge Rd TN15 . . . .71 C6
Teston House ME14 . . . . . . .105 A7
Teston La ME15,ME18 . . . . .105 C7
Teston Rd Kings Hill ME19 . .89 B5
Offham ME19 . . . . .88 C7
Red Hill ME18 . . . . .89 E2
West Malling ME19 . . . . .89 A6
Tetty Way BR1,BR2 . . . . .36 A7
Teviot Cl DA16 . . . . .7 B6
Tewson Rd SE18 . . . . .2 E1
Teynham Gn
Gillingham ME8 . . . . .49 A4
Hayes BR2 . . . . .36 A4
Teynham House SE9 . . . . .6 D1
Thackeray Ave RM18 . . . . . .13 B6
Thackeray Rd ME20 . . . . .74 F3
Thames Ave Gillingham ME8 63 E8
High Halstow ME23 . . . . . . .17 E4
Thames Barrier
Visitor Ctr* SE18 . . . . .1 D3
Thames Gate DA10 . . . . .11 E1
Thames Rd Crayford DA1 . . . .9 A4
Grays RM17 . . . . .12 B7
Newham E16 . . . . .1 D5
Tonbridge TN10 . . . . .117 C5
Thames Road Ind Est E16 . .1 D4

Thames Terr ME3 . . . . .16 B6
Thames View ME3 . . . . .33 C7
Thames View Cotts ME3 . . .32 D3
Thames View Inf Sch ME8 49 D2
Thames View Jun Sch
ME8 . . . . .49 D2
Thames Way
Gravesend DA11 . . . . .13 A1
Northfleet DA11 . . . . .29 E7
Thamesbank Pl SE28 . . . . . . .3 C7
Thameside
Cty Inf & Jun Schs RM17 12 C8
Thameside Ind Est E16 . . . . .1 D4
Thamesmead Com Coll
DA18 . . . . .3 E4
Thamesmere Dr SE28 . . . . . .3 A6
Thamesview Sch DA12 . . . . .30 F5
Thanet Dr BR2 . . . . .50 D7
Thanet Ho 6 DA11 . . . . .29 F7
Thanet House 7 ME15 . . . .107 F5
Thanet Rd Erith DA8 . . . . . . .8 E7
Sidcup DA5 . . . . .25 A8
Thanington Ct SE9 . . . . .6 E1
Thatch Barn Rd TN27 . . . . .141 D6
Thatcher Ct DA1 . . . . .26 D8
Thatcher Rd TN12 . . . . .139 E4
Thatchers La ME3 . . . . .16 B5
Thatchers The ME16 . . . . . . .91 B5
Thaxted Rd SE9 . . . . .23 C6
Theatre Sq 7 TN30 . . . . . . .183 A7
Thelma Cl DA12 . . . . .30 F3
Thelma Gdns SE3 . . . . .5 E6
Theobalds TN18 . . . . .178 F2
Theobalds St TN15 . . . . .70 A1
Theodore Cl TN2 . . . . .149 E7
Theodore Pl ME7 . . . . .48 C5
Thicketts TN13 . . . . .84 C4
Third Ave Chatham ME5 . . . . .48 C1
Gillingham ME7 . . . . .48 F4
West Thurrock RM20 . . . . . .11 A8
Third St TN3 . . . . .147 F3
Thirlemere Cl ME16 . . . . . . .91 D8
Thirlmere Cl
Gillingham ME7 . . . . .49 A5
Rochester ME2 . . . . .33 C1
Thirlmere Rd Bexley DA7 . . .8 C6
Royal Tunbridge Wells TN4 .148 F5
Thirsk House 6 ME15 . . . .107 F6
Thirza Rd DA1 . . . . .9 F1
Thistle Ct DA1 . . . . .27 B7
Thistle Rd DA12 . . . . .30 E8
Thistlebank ME5 . . . . .62 A3
Thistlebrook SE2 . . . . .3 C4
Thistledown
Gravesend DA12 . . . . .30 D2
Maidstone ME14 . . . . .92 F4
Thistledown Cl ME7 . . . . . . .63 A4
Thistlemead BR7 . . . . .37 B7
Thomas Aveling Sch The
ME1 . . . . .61 C8
Thomas Cotts DA13 . . . . .29 B1
Thomas Cribb Mews E6 . . . .2 A7
Thomas Dinwiddy Rd
SE12 . . . . .22 B6
Thomas Dr DA12 . . . . .30 D6
Thomas Dunk
Almshouses 13 TN18 . . . .179 A2
Thomas St Rochester ME1 . .47 C3
Royal Tunbridge Wells TN4 .149 A5
Woolwich SE18 . . . . .2 B2
Thomas Tallis Sch SE3 . . . . .5 B4
Thomas Wyatt Way TN15 . .71 F3
Thompson Cl ME8 . . . . .64 A8
Thomson Cl ME6 . . . . .60 A1
Thong La Basted TN15 . . . . . .86 F5
Maidstone DA12 . . . . .31 A2
Thorn Cl Bromley BR2 . . . . . .37 A3
Chatham ME5 . . . . .61 D1
Thorn Rd TN12 . . . . .138 E4
Thorn's Mdw TN16 . . . . . . .82 C4
Thorndale BR7 . . . . .22 F1
Thorndale Cl ME5 . . . . .61 D4
Thornden Ct TN17 . . . . .188 A8
Thornden La TN17 . . . . .182 A1
Thorndike Cl ME1 . . . . .61 F8
Thorndon Cl BR5 . . . . .37 F7
Thorndon Rd BR5 . . . . .37 F7
Thorndyke Way TN15 . . . . . .71 F3
Thorne Cl Erith DA8 . . . . .8 B8
Newham E16 . . . . .1 A7
Thornet Wood Rd BR1 . . . .37 A6
Thorney Croft ME17 . . . . . .109 D2
Thornfield Gdns TN2 . . . . .149 F5
Thornham Rd ME8 . . . . .49 C3
Thornhill Ave SE18 . . . . .6 E7
Thornhill Pl ME14 . . . . .92 A6
Thornton Dene DA14 . . . . . .24 A3
Thornton Rd Bromley BR1 . .22 A3
Erith DA17 . . . . .4 B2
Thorntree Rd SE7 . . . . .1 D1
Thorntree Sch SE7 . . . . .1 D1
Thorold Rd ME5 . . . . .48 B3
Thorpe Ave TN10 . . . . .117 C5
Thorpe Cl BR6 . . . . .51 E8
Thorpe Wlk ME8 . . . . .63 D3
Thorpe Works TN4 . . . . . . .148 F8
Thrale Way ME8 . . . . .63 E4
Three Corners DA7 . . . . .8 B5
Three Elm La TN11 . . . . . . .118 D5
Three Gates Rd DA3 . . . . . . .42 A2
Three Oaks La TN5 . . . . . . .174 D7
Thresher Field TN8 . . . . . . .130 A6
Threshers Dr ME14 . . . . .92 E5
Thrift The DA2 . . . . .28 C5
Throckmorten Rd E16 . . . . . .1 B7
Throwley Cl SE2 . . . . .3 C3
Thrush Cl ME5 . . . . .62 B7
Thunderer Rd RM9 . . . . .3 F8

Thurnham CE Inf Sch
ME14 . . . . .93 A4
Thurnham House 6 BR5 . .38 D1
Thurnham La ME14 . . . . .93 C7
Thurrock Bsns Ctr RM20 . .10 F8
Thurrock Ent Ctr RM17 . . .12 A8
Thurrock Park Way RM17 . .12 D7
Thursland Rd DA14 . . . . .24 E3
Thursley Rd SE9 . . . . .22 F5
Thurston Dr ME2 . . . . .46 D7
Thurstone Ct ME14 . . . . .91 F6
Thwaite Cl DA8 . . . . .8 C8
Thyer Cl BR6 . . . . .51 C6
Tibbs Court La TN12 . . . . . .152 A6
Ticehurst Cl BR5 . . . . .24 A1
Tichborne Cl ME16 . . . . .91 C6
Tickford Cl SE2 . . . . .3 C4
Tidal Basin Rd E16 . . . . .1 A6
Tidebrook Ct 4 BR5 . . . . . . .38 C5
Tideside Ct SE18 . . . . .1 F7
Tideway The ME1 . . . . .61 C8
Tidford Rd DA16 . . . . .6 F5
Tiger La ME2 . . . . .36 B5
Tilbrook Rd SE3 . . . . .5 D4
Tilbury Cl BR5 . . . . .38 B7
Tilbury Fort* RM18 . . . . . . .13 C3
Tilbury Manor
Cty Inf Sch RM18 . . . . . . .13 B7
Tilbury Manor
Cty Jun Sch RM18 . . . . . .13 B7
Tilbury Town Sta RM18 . . . .12 F5
Tilden Cl TN26 . . . . .173 D7
Tilden Gill Rd TN30 . . . . . .183 C7
Tilden La TN12 . . . . .122 C3
Tilden Rd ME17,TN27 . . . . .125 E2
Tile Farm Rd BR6 . . . . .51 D7
Tile Fields ME17 . . . . .94 D2
Tile Kiln La Coldblow ME5 . .25 C6
Dartford DA2,DA5 . . . . .25 F5
Tilebarn Cnr TN10 . . . . .117 E4
Tilehurst Point 2 SE2 . . . . . .3 C4
Tilghman Way ME6 . . . . .60 B1
Till Ave DA4 . . . . .40 F2
Tillingbourne Gn BR5 . . . . .38 A5
Tillmans TN15 . . . . .87 A7
Tillmans Mead DA4 . . . . .41 A2
Tilsden La TN17 . . . . .169 E3
Tilt Yard App SE9 . . . . .5 F1
Tilton Rd TN15 . . . . .86 F7
Timber Bank DA13 . . . . .72 F8
Timber Cl BR7 . . . . .37 A7
Timber Ct RM17 . . . . .12 A8
Timber Tops ME5 . . . . .77 D8
Timberbank ME5 . . . . .62 A6
Timbercroft Jun Sch SE18 . .6 E7
Timbercroft La SE18 . . . . .6 E7
Timothy Cl DA6 . . . . .7 E3
Timothy Ho DA18 . . . . .3 E4
Tinker Pot La TN15 . . . . .70 D6
Tinker's Alley ME4 . . . . .47 F7
Tinkerpot Rise TN15 . . . . . . .70 C5
Tinkers La TN5 . . . . .176 E3
Tintagel Gdns ME2 . . . . .46 F7
Tintagel Manor 6 ME7 . . . .48 C6
Tintagel Rd BR5 . . . . .38 C1
Tintern Rd ME16 . . . . .91 D7
Tippens Cl TN17 . . . . .169 D4
Titan Rd RM17 . . . . .12 B8
Titchfield Cl 5 ME15 . . . . .107 F6
Titchfield Rd ME15 . . . . . . .107 F6
Tithe Yd ME17 . . . . .111 D5
Titmuss Ave SE28 . . . . .3 B6
Tiverton Dr SE9 . . . . .23 C7
Tivoli Gdns Gravesend DA12 30 B7
Woolwich SE18 . . . . .1 E2
Tobruk Way ME5 . . . . .61 F6
Toby Gdns TN11 . . . . .118 E8
Tockwith Ct TN13 . . . . .84 C4
Toddington Cres ME5 . . . . . .61 D1
Tolcairn Ct 2 DA17 . . . . .4 A1
Tolgate La ME2 . . . . .47 B7
Tolgate Way ME14 . . . . .76 E4
Tolhurst Rd TN12 . . . . .135 A2
Tollgate Mews TN15 . . . . . . .87 A8
Tollgate Pl TN27 . . . . .141 E5
Tollgate Rd Dartford DA2 . . .27 D8
Newham E6 . . . . .1 E8
Tolsey Mead TN15 . . . . .87 A8
Tom Coombs Cl SE9 . . . . . . .5 E3
Tom Cribb Rd SE28 . . . . .2 D3
Tom Jenkinson Rd E16 . . . . .1 A5
Tom Joyce Cl ME6 . . . . .74 F7
Tomlin Cl Snodland ME6 . . . .74 F7
Staplehurst TN12 . . . . .139 E4
Tonbridge By-Pass
Tonbridge TN11,TN9,TN4,TN14,TN15
TN11,TN9,TN4,TN14,TN15 . .116 B5
Tonbridge TN4,TN9,TN11 . .133 C6
Tonbridge
Chambers TN9 . . . . .133 B8
Tonbridge Cottage Hospl
TN11 . . . . .133 C6
Tonbridge Ct ME16 . . . . .91 D3
Tonbridge Gram Sch
for Girls TN9 . . . . .133 C7
Tonbridge Ho ME2 . . . . .33 C1
Tonbridge Rd
Hadlow TN11 . . . . .118 C7
Ightham TN15 . . . . .86 C3
Little Mill TN11,TN12 . . . . .119 D4
Maidstone ME16 . . . . .90 E1
Pembury TN2, TN11 . . . . . .150 A7
Sevenoaks TN13,TN15 . . . . .99 D7
Tonbridge TN11 . . . . .116 E5
Wateringbury ME18 . . . . . .104 C8
Tonbridge Sch TN10 . . . . .117 C3
Tonbridge Sta TN9 . . . . . . .117 B1

Tong La TN12 . . . . .152 B2
Tong Rd TN12,TN3 . . . . . . .152 A4
Tongswood Dr TN18 . . . . . .179 C1
Tooley St DA11 . . . . .29 C8
Top Dartford Rd BR8,DA2 . .26 A2
Topcliffe Dr BR6 . . . . .51 D6
Topley Dr ME23 . . . . .17 E3
Topley St SE9 . . . . .5 D3
Tor Rd DA16 . . . . .7 C6
Torbay Rd TN12 . . . . .120 B5
Torbrook Cl DA5 . . . . .7 E1
Tormount Rd SE18 . . . . .6 E8
Toronto Rd Gillingham ME7 . .48 E4
Tilbury RM18 . . . . .13 A5
Torrens Wlk DA12 . . . . .30 E3
Torrington Cl ME18 . . . . . . .103 D8
Torver Way BR6 . . . . .51 D7
Totnes Rd DA16 . . . . .7 C7
Tovil Gn ME15 . . . . .91 E2
Tovil Green Bsns Pk ME15 91 E1
Tovil Hill ME15 . . . . .91 E2
Tovil Rd ME15 . . . . .91 F2
Tovil, St Stephen's
CE Inf Sch ME15 . . . . .91 E2
Tower Cl Gravesend DA12 . . .30 E3
Orpington BR6 . . . . .51 F7
Tower Croft DA4 . . . . .54 E8
Tower Gdns ME14 . . . . .93 B4
Tower Hill ME19 . . . . .88 D7
Tower Ind Est TN15 . . . . . . .71 D5
Tower La ME14 . . . . .93 B4
Tower Park Rd DA1 . . . . .8 F2
Tower Rd Bexley DA7 . . . . . . .8 A3
Dartford DA1 . . . . .9 C1
Erith DA17 . . . . .4 C2
Orpington BR6 . . . . .51 F7
Tower Ret Pk DA1 . . . . .8 F2
Tower View ME19 . . . . .89 B3
Towerfields BR2 . . . . .50 E6
Towers Wood DA4 . . . . .41 D8
Town Acres TN10 . . . . .117 C4
Town Hill
Lamberhurst TN3 . . . . .166 A4
West Malling ME19 . . . . .74 C1
Town Hill Cl ME19 . . . . .74 C1
Town Lock Ho 3 TN9 . . . .117 C2
Town Meadow TN17 . . . . . .169 D4
Town Pier 4 DA11 . . . . .13 B1
Town Rd ME3 . . . . .33 A6
Town Sq DA8 . . . . .8 E8
Town Square Cres DA9 . . . . .27 F8
Town Station Cotts TN8 . . .112 D1
Towncourt Cres BR5 . . . . . . .37 D5
Towncourt La BR5 . . . . .37 D2
Townfield Cnr DA12 . . . . . . .30 D7
Townland Cl TN27 . . . . .158 A2
Townlands Rd TN5 . . . . .174 F4
Townley
Gram Sch for Girls DA5 . .7 F1
Townley Rd DA6 . . . . .7 F2
Townsend Rd
Snodland ME6 . . . . .74 F8
Woolwich SE18 . . . . .2 B3
Townsend Sq ME19 . . . . .89 A2
Townshend Cl DA14 . . . . . . .24 C2
Townshend Ho 14 SE18 . . . .1 F2
Townshend Rd BR7 . . . . .23 B3
Toy's Hill TN16,TN8 . . . . . . .97 C3
Toynbec Ct BR7 . . . . .23 B4
Tracies The ME9 . . . . .65 C6
Trader Rd E6 . . . . .2 B7
Tradescant Dr DA13 . . . . . . .44 B3
Trafalgar Rd Dartford DA1 . .26 E6
Gravesend DA12 . . . . .30 A8
Wouldham ME1 . . . . .60 C4
Trafalgar St ME7 . . . . .48 C5
Tramways ME5 . . . . .48 C2
Tranquil Rise DA8 . . . . .4 E1
Transfesa Rd TN12 . . . . . . .136 A7
Transmere Cl BR5 . . . . .37 C3
Transmere Rd BR5 . . . . .37 C3
Transom Ho 3 ME1 . . . . . . .47 C1
Trapfield Cl ME14 . . . . .93 C4
Trapfield La ME14 . . . . .93 C4
Trapham Rd ME16 . . . . .91 D5
Travers Gdns ME9 . . . . .80 F5
Travertine Rd ME5 . . . . .62 B1
Trebble Rd DA10 . . . . .11 E1
Trebilco Cl TN12 . . . . .149 D7
Tredegar Rd DA2 . . . . .26 A5
Tredwell Cl BR2 . . . . .36 E5
Tree La TN15 . . . . .101 E8
Tree Rd E16 . . . . .1 C7
Treetops Gravesend DA12 . . .30 B4
Kemsing TN15 . . . . .70 A2
Tonbridge TN9 . . . . .133 B7
Treetops Cl SE2 . . . . .3 E1
Treewall Gdns BR1 . . . . .22 B4
Trefoil Ho Erith DA18 . . . . . . .3 E4
Grays RM17 . . . . .12 B7
Tregony Rd BR6 . . . . .51 F6
Trelawn Cres ME5 . . . . .62 B2
Trellyn Cl ME5 . . . . .90 F2
Trench Rd TN10 . . . . .117 C6
Trenear Cl BR6 . . . . .52 A6
Trent Rd ME5 . . . . .62 B5
Trentham Dr BR5 . . . . .38 A5
Trenton Cl ME16 . . . . .91 B7
Trevale Rd ME1 . . . . .47 B1
Trevelyan Cl DA1 . . . . .9 F3
Trevereux Hill RH8 . . . . .96 A3
Trevino Dr ME5 . . . . .61 F2
Trevithick Dr DA1 . . . . .9 F3
Trevor Cl BR2 . . . . .36 A2
Trevor Dr ME16 . . . . .91 C5
Trewin Cl ME20 . . . . .75 D2
Trewsbury Ho 2 SE2 . . . . . . .3 D4
Triangle Ct E16 . . . . .1 C8

Triangle The DA15 . . . . .24 A8
Trident Cl ME2 . . . . .47 E7
Trinity Cl Orpington BR2 . . .36 E1
Royal Tunbridge Wells TN2 .149 D4
Trinity Ct Aylesford ME20 . . .76 A3
Dartford DA1 . . . . .27 B7
Eltham SE9 . . . . .6 B1
Trinity Gdns DA1 . . . . .9 D1
Trinity Pl DA1 . . . . .7 F3
Trinity Rd Gillingham ME7 . .48 C6
Gravesend DA12 . . . . .30 C8
Trinity Sch,Belvedere DA17 4 C2
Trinity St 12 E16 . . . . .1 A8
Tristan Gdns TN4 . . . . .148 D4
Triumph Rd E6 . . . . .1 F7
Trivett Cl DA9 . . . . .11 A2
Trolling Down Hill DA2 . . .27 C6
Troodos Hill ME14 . . . . .91 F8
Troon Cl SE28 . . . . .3 D7
Trosley Ave DA11 . . . . .30 B6
Trosley Country Park
Visitor Ctr* DA13 . . . . . . .72 E7
Trosley Ctry Pk*
ME19,DA13 . . . . .73 A7
Trosley Rd DA17 . . . . .8 A8
Trottiscliffe CE
Prim Sch ME19 . . . . .73 A5
Trottiscliffe Rd ME19 . . . . .73 D3
Trotts La TN16 . . . . .96 C8
Trotwood Cl ME5 . . . . .77 A8
Troughton Rd SE7 . . . . .1 B1
Troutbeck Ho ME20 . . . . . . .75 C1
Troy Ct 6 SE18 . . . . .2 B2
Troys Mead ME17 . . . . .94 D2
Trubridge Rd ME3 . . . . .34 E5
Truro Cl ME8 . . . . .49 D3
Truro Rd DA12 . . . . .30 D5
Truro Wlk TN10 . . . . .117 D5
Trusedale Rd E6 . . . . .1 F7
Trycewell La TN15 . . . . .86 D6
Tuam St SE18 . . . . .6 D8
Tubbenden Cl BR6 . . . . .51 E7
Tubbenden Dr BR6 . . . . . . .51 D6
Tubbenden
Inf & Jun Sch BR6 . . . . . .51 D6
Tubbenden La BR6 . . . . .51 E7
Tubbenden La S BR6 . . . . . .51 D6
Tubs Hill TN13 . . . . .84 B3
Tubs Hill Par TN13 . . . . .84 A3
Tudeley La Tonbridge TN9 .133 D7
Tonbridge,
Tudeley TN11,TN9 . . . . .134 B8
Tudor Ave ME14 . . . . .92 B6
Tudor Cl Bromley BR7 . . . . .36 F8
Dartford DA1 . . . . .9 B1
Northfleet DA11 . . . . .29 E7
Tudor Cres TN14 . . . . .69 D3
Tudor Ct Crockenhill BR8 . . .39 C2
Royal Tunbridge Wells TN2 .148 E1
Sidcup DA14 . . . . .24 A5
Tudor Dr TN14 . . . . .69 C3
Tudor Gr Chattenden ME3 . . .33 F4
Gillingham ME8 . . . . .63 F8
Tudor Par SE9 . . . . .5 E3
Tudor Way BR5 . . . . .37 D3
Tudor Wlk DA5 . . . . .7 E1
Tudway Rd SE3 . . . . .5 C3
Tufa Cl ME5 . . . . .62 B1
Tuff Cotts ME3 . . . . .19 C3
Tufnail Rd DA1 . . . . .9 F1
Tufton Rd ME8 . . . . .49 F1
Tufton St ME14 . . . . .92 A4
Tugboat St SE28 . . . . .2 E4
Tugmutton Cl BR6 . . . . .51 B6
Tulip Cl 5 E6 . . . . .1 F8
Tulip Tree Cl TN9 . . . . .133 B8
Tumblefield Est TN15 . . . . .71 F8
Tumblefield Rd TN15 . . . . . .71 F7
Tumblers Hill ME17 . . . . . .124 F7
Tunbridge Wells Gram
Sch for Boys TN4 . . . . . .149 A7
Tunbridge Wells Gram
Sch for Girls TN4 . . . . . .149 A6
Tunbridge Wells
Ind Hospl The TN3 . . . .147 B3
Tunbridge Wells Mus*
TN1 . . . . .149 B4
Tunbridge Wells
Trade Pk TN2 . . . . .149 D8
Tunbridge Wells West
Sta TN3 . . . . .148 F1
Tunbury Ave ME5 . . . . .61 F1
Tunbury Ave S ME5 . . . . . . .61 F1
Tunbury Cty Prim Sch
ME5 . . . . .61 F1
Tunnan Leys E6 . . . . .2 A7
Tunnel Ave 1 SE10 . . . . .1 A1
Tunnel Cotts RM20 . . . . . . .11 A8
Tunnel Est RM20 . . . . .10 F8
Tunnel Rd TN1 . . . . .149 B4
Tunstall Cl BR6 . . . . .51 E6
Tunstock Way DA17 . . . . . . .3 E3
Tupman Cl ME1 . . . . .47 B4
Turgis Cl ME12 . . . . .108 E4
Turks Hall Pl ME2 . . . . .59 E5
Turley Cotts TN3 . . . . .148 A8
Turnberry Way BR6 . . . . . . .37 D1
Turnbull Cl DA9 . . . . .27 E8
Turnden Rd TN17 . . . . .169 A3
Turner Ave TN17 . . . . .169 D3
Turner Ct DA1 . . . . .9 F2
Turner Ho Gravesend DA12 .30 C6
5 Greenwich SE7 . . . . .5 B8
Turner Rd Bean DA2 . . . . . . .28 B5
Tonbridge TN10 . . . . .117 C5
Turner St ME3 . . . . .16 B5
Turners Ave TN30 . . . . . . .183 B8

Turners Gdns TN13 . . . . . . .99 C7
Turners Green La TN5 . . . .174 F6
Turners Green Rd TN5 . . . .174 F6
Turners Pl DA4 . . . . .41 C8
Turnpike Ct DA6 . . . . .7 D3
Turnpike Dr BR6 . . . . .52 D2
Turnpike La RM18 . . . . .13 D8
Turnstone DA3 . . . . .43 A7
Turnstone Rd ME5 . . . . .62 C1
Turnstones The DA12 . . . . .30 D6
Turpin La DA8 . . . . .9 A8
Turpington Cl BR2 . . . . .36 E2
Turpington La BR2 . . . . . . .36 E3
Turton Road 5 SE18 . . . . . .2 A2
Tuscan Dr ME5 . . . . .62 C1
Tuscan Rd SE18 . . . . .2 D1
Tutsham Way TN12 . . . . . .135 F6
Tuxford Rd TN4 . . . . .148 B5
Tweed Rd TN10 . . . . .117 C5
Tweedy Rd BR1 . . . . .36 A8
Twigg Cl DA8 . . . . .8 E7
Twisden Rd ME19 . . . . .89 F8
Twiss Ho 6 SE18 . . . . .2 D1
Twistleton Ct DA1 . . . . .9 D1
Twitton La TN14 . . . . .68 E3
Twitton Meadows TN14 . . .68 E3
Two Gates Hill ME3 . . . . . . .32 F5
Twydall Ent Ctr ME8 . . . . .49 C4
Twydall Gn ME8 . . . . .49 B3
Twydall Inf Sch ME8 . . . . . .49 B2
Twydall Jun Sch ME8 . . . . .49 B2
Twydall La ME8 . . . . .49 B2
Twyford Ct ME14 . . . . .92 D6
Twyford Rd TN11 . . . . .102 E1
Twysden Cotts TN18 . . . . .186 A4
Tydeman Rd ME15 . . . . .92 F2
Tye La BR6 . . . . .51 C5
Tyeshurst Cl SE2 . . . . .3 E1
Tyland Barn Wildlife
Conservation Ctr* ME14 .76 E3
Tyland La ME14 . . . . .76 F3
Tyler Cl ME19 . . . . .89 F8
Tyler Dr ME8 . . . . .63 E4
Tyler Gr DA1 . . . . .9 F3
Tylers Green Rd BR8 . . . . . .39 C2
Tylney Rd BR1 . . . . .36 D7
Tyndall Rd DA16 . . . . .6 F4
Tyne Cl ME5 . . . . .62 C5
Tyne Rd TN10 . . . . .117 B5
Tynedale Cl DA2 . . . . .27 D7
Tynemouth Cl E6 . . . . .2 B7
Typhoon Rd ME19 . . . . .88 F3
Tyron Way DA14 . . . . .23 F3
Tyrrell Ave DA16 . . . . .7 A3
Tyrrells Hall Cl RM17 . . . . .12 D8
Tyrwhitt-Drake
Mus of Carriages* ME15 .92 A3

U

Uckfield La TN8 . . . . .129 D4
Udall Cotts DA15 . . . . .23 E5
Ufton Cl ME15 . . . . .92 E1
Ulcombe CE
Prim Sch ME17 . . . . . . .125 F6
Ulcombe Hill ME17 . . . . . .109 F1
Ulcombe Rd
Headcorn TN27 . . . . .141 C6
Langley Heath ME17 . . . .108 E3
Ullswater Ho 5 ME15 . . . .107 E7
Underdown Ave ME4 . . . . . .47 F1
Underhill Jun Sch to
Sutton Valence ME17 . . .124 C7
Underlyn Ind Est TN12 . . .122 F2
Underlyn La TN12 . . . . . . .122 D1
Underriver House Rd
TN15 . . . . .100 D5
Underwood ME19 . . . . .88 D7
Underwood Cl ME15 . . . . . .91 F2
Underwood The SE9 . . . . . .22 F6
Unicorn Wlk DA9 . . . . .10 F2
Unicumes La ME16 . . . . . . .91 C2
Union Pk ME15 . . . . .107 F4
Union Pl ME4 . . . . .48 A4
Union Rd BR2 . . . . .36 D4
Union Sq 18 TN2 . . . . .149 A2
Union St Chatham ME4 . . . .48 A3
Flimwell TN5 . . . . .177 B3
Maidstone ME14 . . . . .92 A5
Rochester ME1 . . . . .47 C5
Unity Way SE18 . . . . .1 D3
Univ of East London E16 . . .2 A6
Univ of Greenwich
Gillingham ME4 . . . . .48 B8
Woolwich SE18 . . . . .2 A2
Univ of Greenwich
(Dartford Campus) DA1 .26 C6
Univ of Greenwich
(Riverside Ho
Annexe) SE18 . . . . .2 A2
Univ of Greenwich
(Southwold Site) SE9 . . . .6 C2
Univ of Greenwich Avery
Hill Campus SE9 . . . . .6 C1
Univ of Greenwich Avery
Hill Campus
Southwood Site SE9 . . . .23 D8
University Gdns DA5 . . . . . .24 F8
University Pl DA8 . . . . .8 E7
University Way Dartford DA1 9 E4
Woolwich SE18 . . . . .2 B6
Unwin Cl ME20 . . . . .76 A3
Upbury Manor High Sch
ME7 . . . . .48 B4
Upbury Way ME4 . . . . .48 A4
Upchat Rd ME2,ME3 . . . . . .33 F3
Updale Rd DA14 . . . . .23 F4

Upland Inf Sch DA7 . . . . .7 F4
Upland Jun Sch DA7 . . . . . . .7 F4
Upland Rd DA7 . . . . .7 F4
Uplands Cl Rochester ME2 .46 D6
Sevenoaks TN13 . . . . .83 F4
Uplands Com Coll TN5 . . .175 A4
Uplands Rd ME8 . . . . .38 B1
Uplands Way TN13 . . . . . . .83 F4
Upnor Castle* ME2 . . . . . . .33 F2
Upnor Ho ME2 . . . . .107 E8
Upnor Rd Rochester ME2 . . .47 D8
Upper Upnor ME2 . . . . .34 A5
Upper Abbey Rd DA17 . . . . .4 A2
Upper Austin Lodge Rd
DA4 . . . . .54 D4
Upper Ave DA13 . . . . .43 E8
Upper Barn Hill ME15 . . . .105 E3
Upper Britton Pl ME7 . . . . .48 B5
Upper Bush Rd ME2 . . . . . .45 D7
Upper Church Hill DA9 . . . .10 E2
Upper Cumberland Wlk
TN1 . . . . .149 B1
Upper Dunstan Rd TN4 . . .149 B6
Upper East Rd ME4 . . . . . . .48 B8
Upper Fant Rd ME16 . . . . . .91 D2
Upper Green La TN11 . . . .101 D5
Upper Green Rd TN11 . . . .101 D5
Upper Grosvenor Rd
TN1,TN4 . . . . .149 B6
Upper Grove Rd DA17 . . . . .7 B8
Upper Hayesden La
TN11,TN9 . . . . .132 E6
Upper Holly Hill Rd DA17 . .4 B1
Upper Hunton Hill ME15 .106 A3
Upper Luton Rd ME5 . . . . .48 C2
Upper Mill ME8 . . . . .104 D8
Upper Nellington TN3 . . . .148 B4
Upper Park Rd
Bromley BR1 . . . . .36 C8
Erith DA17 . . . . .4 B2
Upper Platts TN5 . . . . .176 F1
Upper Profit TN3 . . . . .148 A3
Upper Rd ME5 . . . . .92 B2
Upper Sheridan Rd DA17 . . .4 A2
Upper Spring La TN15 . . . . .86 B5
Upper St
Hollingbourne ME17 . . . . .94 E3
Leeds ME17 . . . . .108 F5
Royal Tunbridge Wells TN4 .148 D4
Upper Stephens TN3 . . . . .148 A3
Upper Stone St ME15 . . . . .92 A3
Upper Street N DA3 . . . . . . .56 F8
Upper Street S DA3 . . . . . . .56 F8
Upper Wickham La DA16 . . .7 B6
Upperton Rd DA14 . . . . . . .23 F3
Upton Cl DA5 . . . . .7 F1
Upton Day Hospl DA6 . . . . .7 E3
Upton Quarry TN3 . . . . . . .147 F3
Upton Rd Bexley DA6 . . . . . .7 E2
Woolwich SE18 . . . . .6 C8
Upton Rd S DA5 . . . . .7 F1
Upton Villas 4 DA6 . . . . . . .7 E3
Uptons TN27 . . . . .141 C6
Upwood Rd SE12 . . . . .5 A1
Uridge Cres TN10 . . . . . . .117 C4
Uridge Rd TN10 . . . . .117 C4
Urquhart Cl ME5 . . . . .62 A5
Ursula Lodges DA14 . . . . . .24 B3
Usborne Cl TN12 . . . . .139 E3

V

Vale Ave
Royal Tunbridge Wells TN1 .149 A3
Royal Tunbridge
Wells,Southborough TN4 .132 F1
Vale Cl BR6 . . . . .51 A6
Vale Cotts ME9 . . . . .80 A8
Vale Ct TN4 . . . . .133 A2
Vale Dr ME5 . . . . .61 E6
Vale Rd Bromley BR1 . . . . . .37 A7
Dartford DA1 . . . . .26 B7
Hawkhurst TN18 . . . . .178 F3
Maidstone ME15 . . . . .106 E4
Northfleet DA11 . . . . .29 E7
Royal Tunbridge Wells TN1 .149 A3
Royal Tunbridge
Wells,Southborough TN4 .132 F1
Tonbridge TN9 . . . . .117 C1
Vale Rise TN9 . . . . .133 B8
Vale The ME9 . . . . .80 A8
Valence Ho ME15 . . . . .107 C7
Valence Rd DA8 . . . . .8 D7
Valence Sch TN16 . . . . .81 F1
Valence View TN17 . . . . . .156 E7
Valentine Ave DA5 . . . . .24 E7
Valentine Cl ME7 . . . . .49 A1
Valentine Dr ME23 . . . . .17 E4
Valentine Rd ME15 . . . . . . .107 E7
Valerian Cl ME5 . . . . .61 E4
Valetta Way ME1 . . . . .47 B4
Valiant Ho 5 SE7 . . . . .1 C1
Valiant Rd ME5 . . . . .62 C2
Valiant Way E6 . . . . .1 F8
Valley (Charlton Athletic
FC) The SE7 . . . . .1 C1
Valley Cl DA1 . . . . .8 F1
Valley Dr
Gravesend,Riverview
Park DA12 . . . . .30 D4
Gravesend,Singlewell DA12 .30 D3
Maidstone ME15 . . . . .106 F6
Sevenoaks TN13 . . . . .84 B1
Valley Forge Cl TN10 . . . .117 F4
Valley Gdns DA9 . . . . .11 B1
Valley Gr SE7 . . . . .1 C1
Valley L Ctr SE9 . . . . .23 C8

Valley La DA13 . . . . .58 B2
Valley Park Com Sch
ME14 . . . . .92 C4
Valley Rd Crayford DA1 . . . . .8 F1
Erith DA8 . . . . .4 D2
Fawkham Green DA3 . . . . .42 D2
Gillingham ME7 . . . . .48 E4
Royal Tunbridge Wells TN4 .148 D4
St Paul's Cray BR5 . . . . . .38 B8
Valley Rise ME5 . . . . .61 F1
Valley The ME17 . . . . .106 D3
Valley View
Royal Tunbridge Wells TN4 .133 A2
Swanscombe DA9 . . . . .11 B1
Valley View Rd ME1 . . . . . .47 B1
Valley View Terr DA4 . . . . .40 F1
Valleyside SE7 . . . . .1 D1
Valliers Wood Rd DA15 . . .23 E7
Vambery Rd SE18 . . . . .6 C8
Vanbrugh Pk SE3 . . . . .5 A7
Vanburgh Cl 2 Newham E16 1 D8
Orpington BR6 . . . . .37 E1
Vancouver Rd SE23 . . . . . . .52 A6
Vancouver Dr ME8 . . . . . . .49 C1
Vandome Cl E16 . . . . .1 B8
Vandyke Cross SE9 . . . . .5 E2
Vanessa Cl DA17 . . . . .4 A1
Vanessa Way DA5 . . . . .25 D5
Vanessa Wlk DA12 . . . . . . .30 F3
Vange Cottage Mews ME1 47 B4
Vanguard Cl E16 . . . . .1 A8
Vanity La ME17 . . . . .106 D1
Vanoc Gdns BR1 . . . . .22 A4
Vanquisher Wlk DA12 . . . . .30 F5
Varley Rd E16 . . . . .1 B7
Varnes St ME6 . . . . .75 F6
Vaughan Ave DA13 . . . . . . .43 E8
Vaughan Rd DA16 . . . . .6 F5
Vauxhall Cl DA11 . . . . .29 F8
Vauxhall Cres ME6 . . . . . . .75 A6
Vauxhall Gdns TN9 . . . . . .133 C7
Vauxhall La
Bidborough TN11,TN4 . . .133 A4
Tonbridge TN11 . . . . .133 D6
Vauxhall Pl DA1 . . . . .26 E8
Veitchil Barn BR8 . . . . .39 F8
Veles Rd SE18 . . . . .6 F4
Venmead Ct 4 DA17 . . . . . . .4 A2
Venners Cl DA7 . . . . .8 E5
Ventnor Cl ME5 . . . . .62 C8
Venture Cl DA5 . . . . .24 E8
Venture Ct SE12 . . . . .22 A8
Venus Rd SE18 . . . . .1 F3
Verdun Rd SE18 . . . . .6 F4
Veranstore
Vermont Rd TN4 . . . . .148 C4
Vernham Rd SE18 . . . . .6 C8
Vernon Cl
St Paul's Cray BR5 . . . . . .38 B6
West Kingsdown TN15 . . . .55 F7
Vernon Rd
Royal Tunbridge Wells TN1 .149 C6
Swanscombe DA10 . . . . . . .11 F1
Veroan Rd DA7 . . . . .7 E5
Verona Gdns DA12 . . . . . . .30 E4
Verona House DA8 . . . . .8 F7
Vert House RM17 . . . . .12 C7
Veryan Cl BR5 . . . . .38 C5
Vesper Ct TN27 . . . . .143 A1
Vestry Cotts New Barn DA3 .43 C5
Sevenoaks TN14 . . . . .84 C8
Vestry Rd TN14 . . . . .84 C8
Via Romana DA12 . . . . .31 B7
Viaduct Terr DA4 . . . . .41 C8
Vicarage Ave TN30 . . . . . . .173 F5
Vicarage Cl Aylesford ME20 .75 F3
Erith DA8 . . . . .8 C8
Halling ME2 . . . . .60 A5
Lower Stoke ME3 . . . . .19 A3
Vicarage Ct Chalk DA12 . . .31 A7
Newington ME9 . . . . .65 B7
Vicarage Dr DA11 . . . . .12 C1
Vicarage Hill TN16 . . . . .81 D1
Vicarage La Chalk DA12 . . .31 A6
East Farleigh ME15 . . . . . .106 B6
Hoo St Werburgh ME3 . . . .34 E4
Sevenoaks TN13 . . . . .83 D8
Vicarage Pk SE18 . . . . .2 C1
Vicarage Rd Coldblow DA5 .25 B7
Gillingham ME7 . . . . .48 C5
Halling ME2 . . . . .59 F5
Rochester ME2 . . . . .47 B8
Royal Tunbridge Wells TN4 .132 F2
Woolwich SE18 . . . . .2 C1
Yalding ME18 . . . . .105 A1
Vicarage Row ME3 . . . . .32 C4
Vicarage Sq RM17 . . . . .12 A8
Vicarage Way ME19 . . . . . .184 A3
Vicary Way ME16 . . . . .91 D5
Vickers Rd DA8 . . . . .4 D1
Victor Mills Cotts DA14 . . .25 A1
Victoria Ave 3 DA2 . . . . . . .30 B8
Victoria Bglws DA14 . . . . . .24 F1
Victoria Bsns Ctr DA16 . . . . .7 B5
Victoria Cl Chatham ME5 . . .61 D2
Edenbridge TN8 . . . . .128 C8
Victoria Cotts
Cranbrook TN17 . . . . .169 D5
Edenbridge TN8 . . . . .128 C8
Victoria Ct 6 ME16 . . . . . . .91 E4
Victoria Dock Rd E16 . . . . . .1 A7
Victoria Dr Kings Hill ME19 .88 F7
Sutton at Hone DA4 . . . . . .41 D7
Victoria Hill Rd BR8 . . . . . .40 A8
Victoria Ind Pk DA1 . . . . . . .9 E2
Victoria Rd Bexley DA6 . . . . .8 A3
Bromley BR2 . . . . .36 D4
Chatham,Luton ME4 . . . . .48 B2
Chatham,Walderslade ME5 .61 E3

Victoria Rd continued
Chislehurst BR7 . . . . .23 A3
Dartford DA1 . . . . .9 E2
Edenbridge TN8 . . . . .128 C8
Erith DA8 . . . . .8 E8
Golden Green TN11 . . . . .118 F6
Gravesend DA11 . . . . .13 B1
Royal Tunbridge Wells TN1 .149 B4
Royal Tunbridge
Wells,Modest Corner TN4 .132 E1
Sevenoaks TN13 . . . . .84 B2
Sidcup DA15 . . . . .24 A5
Victoria St Eccles ME20 . . .75 F6
Erith DA17 . . . . .3 F1
Gillingham ME7 . . . . .48 D6
Maidstone ME14 . . . . .91 E3
Rochester ME2 . . . . .47 B7
Rochester,Troy Town ME1 . .47 D5
Victoria Terr ME1 . . . . .47 A2
Victoria Way SE7 . . . . .1 B1
Victoria Wharf DA1 . . . . .9 E2
Victory Cotts TN14 . . . . . . .99 C2
Victory Manor 1 ME7 . . . . .48 A6
Victory Pk ME2 . . . . .47 E7
Victory Terr ME17 . . . . . . .124 E8
Victory Way DA2 . . . . .10 C3
Vidal Manor ME7 . . . . .48 C5
Vidgeon Ave ME3 . . . . .34 D6
View Md ME3 . . . . .33 B7
View The SE2 . . . . .3 E1
Viewfield Rd DA5 . . . . .24 C7
Viewland Rd SE18 . . . . .2 F1
Viewlands ME5 . . . . .48 C3
Viewlands Ave TN16 . . . . . .81 F7
Viewpoint Ct DA3 . . . . .42 F5
Vigilant Way DA12 . . . . . . .30 F3
Vigo Rd TN15 . . . . .72 C7
Vigo Village Sch DA13 . . . .73 A8
Viking Cl ME2 . . . . .46 F4
Viking Gdns E6 . . . . .1 E8
Viking Ho 3 SE18 . . . . .1 E1
Viking Rd DA11 . . . . .29 F8
Viking Way Erith DA8,DA17 . .4 C3
West Kingsdown TN15 . . . .55 E5
Villa Cl DA12 . . . . .31 B6
Villa Ct DA1 . . . . .26 E6
Villa Rd ME3 . . . . .32 B3
Villacourt Rd SE18,SE2 . . . . .7 A8
Village Green Rd DA1 . . . . . .9 A3
Village The SE7 . . . . .5 D8
Village View ME5 . . . . .48 C2
Villas Rd SE18 . . . . .2 C2
Vincent Cl Bromley BR2 . . .36 B5
Sidcup DA15 . . . . .23 E7
Vincent Rd Kit's Coty ME20 .76 C7
Woolwich SE18 . . . . .2 B2
Vincent St 13 E16 . . . . .1 A8
Vine Ave TN13 . . . . .84 B3
Vine Court Rd TN13 . . . . . .84 C4
Vine Ct Staplehurst TN12 . .139 F3
Wateringbury ME18 . . . . .104 D8
Vine Lodge Ct TN13 . . . . . .84 C3
Vine Rd BR6 . . . . .51 F4
Vine The TN13 . . . . .84 C3
Vine Wlk TN12 . . . . .139 E3
Vineries The ME7 . . . . .48 E5
Vines La
Hildenborough TN11 . . . .100 C1
Rochester ME1 . . . . .47 C5
Viney's Gdns TN30 . . . . . .173 C5
Vineyard La TN5 . . . . .176 C2
Vinson Cl BR6 . . . . .38 A1
Vinson Ct DA15 . . . . .24 A6
Vinters Rd ME14 . . . . .92 B4
Vintners Way ME14 . . . . . . .92 E4
Viola Ave SE2 . . . . .3 B1
Violet Cl ME5 . . . . .77 A8
Violets The TN12 . . . . .136 A5
VIP Trad Est SE7 . . . . .1 C2
Virginia Rd ME7 . . . . .48 C7
Virginia Wlk DA12 . . . . .30 E2
Viscount Dr E6 . . . . .1 F8
Vista The SE9 . . . . .22 E8
Vixen Cl ME5 . . . . .62 C6
Voce Rd SE18 . . . . .6 D7
Vogue Ct 12 BR1 . . . . .36 B8
Volante Way DA12 . . . . .30 E4
Voyagers Cl SE28 . . . . .3 C7
Vulcan Cl Chatham ME5 . . . .62 B7
Newham E6 . . . . .2 A7
Vyne The DA7 . . . . .8 A3
Vyvyan Cotts TN17 . . . . . .180 C3
Vyvyan House SE18 . . . . .6 A6

W

Wadard Terr BR8 . . . . .40 C4
Wade Ave BR5 . . . . .38 D2
Wadeville Cl DA17 . . . . .4 A1
Wadhurst Bsns Pk TN5 . . .174 B7
Wadhurst CE Prim Sch
TN5 . . . . .174 F4
Wadhurst Par TN5 . . . . . . .174 F4
Wadhurst Sta TN5 . . . . . . .174 C6
Wadlands Rd ME3 . . . . .16 B5
Waghorn Rd ME6 . . . . .75 A8
Waghorn St ME4 . . . . .48 B2
Wagon La TN12 . . . . .120 C1
Wagoners Cl ME14 . . . . . . .92 E4
Wagtail Way BR5 . . . . .38 D5
Waid Cl DA1 . . . . .9 F1
Wainhouse Cl TN8 . . . . . . .112 D3
Wainscott Prim Sch ME2 . .33 D2
Wainscott Rd ME2 . . . . .33 D2

Wainscott Wlk ME2 ....33 D3
Waite Davies Rd 8 SE12 .22 A8
Wake Rd ME1 ....61 C8
Wakefield Cl ME2 ....46 D6
Wakefield Rd DA9 ....11 C2
Wakehurst Cl ME17 .....106 B3
Wakeleys Cotts ME8 ....64 B8
Wakerly Cl 6 E6 ....1 F7
Waldair Ct E16 ....2 B4
Waldeck Rd DA1 ....10 A1
Waldegrave Rd BR1 ....36 F5
Walden Ave BR7 ....22 F4
Walden Cl DA17 ....3 F1
Walden Par BR7 ....22 F2
Walden Rd BR7 ....22 F2
Waldenhurst Rd BR5 .....38 D2
Waldens Cl BR5 ....38 D2
Waldens Rd BR5 ....38 E3
Waldens The ME17 ......109 E2
Walderslade Ctr ME5 .....62 A3
Walderslade Girls Sch
  ME5 ....61 F5
Walderslade Prim Sch
  ME5 ....62 A3
Walderslade Rd ME5 ......61 F6
Walderslade Woods ME5 .61 E2
Waldo Ind Est BR1 ....36 D6
Waldo Rd BR1 ....36 D6
Waldrist Way DA18 ....3 F4
Waldstock Rd SE28 ....3 A6
Walk The ME17 ....109 E2
Walkden Rd BR7 ....23 A3
Walker Cl Crayford DA1 ...8 F4
  Woolwich SE18 ....2 C2
Walker Pl TN15 ....86 D6
Walkhurst Cotts TN17 ...180 F7
Walkhurst Rd TN17 ......180 F7
Walkley Rd DA1 ....9 B2
Walks The ME3 ....161 C8
Wall Cl ME3 ....34 D7
Wallace Cl Erith SE28 .....3 D6
  Royal Tunbridge Wells TN2 .163 A8
Wallace Gdns DA10 ....11 E1
Wallace Rd ME1 ....61 E8
Wallace Terr TN15 ....56 E4
Waller Hill TN17 ....156 B5
Wallhouse Rd DA8 ....9 C7
Wallis Ave ME15 ....107 E5
Wallis Cl DA2 ....25 F5
Wallis Field TN3 ....161 B6
Wallis Pk DA11 ....12 B2
Walmer Cl BR6 ....51 D6
Walmer Ct 3 ME14 ....92 A5
Walmer Ho ME1 ....33 C1
Walmer Terr SE18 ....2 D2
Walmers Ave ME3 ....32 A4
Walnut Cl Chatham ME5 ...62 B8
  Eynsford DA4 ....54 D7
  Paddock Wood TN12 ....136 A6
  Yalding ME18 ....104 F1
Walnut Hill Rd DA13 ......43 E6
Walnut Tree Ave
  Dartford DA1 ....26 E6
  Maidstone ME15 ....107 A5
Walnut Tree Cl BR7 ....37 C8
Walnut Tree Ct ME20 .....75 B1
Walnut Tree La ME15 ....107 A5
Walnut Tree Rd DA8 ....4 E1
Walnut Tree Way DA13 ...44 B3
Walnut Way
  Royal Tunbridge Wells TN4 .133 D1
  Swanley BR8 ....39 D7
Walnuts Rd BR6 ....38 B1
Walnuts The BR6 ....38 A1
Walpole Cl ME19 ....74 F1
Walpole Pl SE18 ....2 B2
Walpole Rd BR2 ....36 D4
Walsham Cl SE28 ....3 D6
Walsham Rd ME5 ....61 F1
Walshaw House 2 ME14 ..92 A6
Walsingham Cl ME8 ....63 D3
Walsingham House 3
  ME14 ....92 A6
Walsingham Pk BR7 ....37 D7
Walsingham Rd BR5 ......38 B8
Walsingham Wlk DA17 .....8 A8
Walter Burke Ave ME4 ...60 C5
Walter's Farm Rd TN9 ...117 C1
Walters Green Rd TN11 .146 F6
Walters Ho ME3 ....6 A7
Walters Rd ME3 ....34 E6
Walters Yd BR1 ....36 A7
Waltham Cl Dartford DA1 ..9 A1
  Orpington BR5 ....38 D1
Waltham Rd ME8 ....49 C3
Walthamstow Hall Inf Sch
  TN13 ....84 C4
Walthamstow Hall
  Jun Sch TN13 ....84 B4
Walton Rd Sidcup DA14 ...24 C5
  Tonbridge TN10 ....117 F6
Walwyn Ave BR1 ....36 D6
Wanden La TN27 ....143 C8
Wansbury Way BR8 ....40 A5
Wanstead Cl BR1 ....36 C7
Wanstead Rd BR1 ....36 C7
Wansunt Rd DA5 ....25 C7
Warblers Cl 3 ME2 ....47 A7
Ward Cl Erith DA8 ....8 D8
  Wadhurst TN5 ....174 E5
Warde's ME18 ....104 F2
Warden Rd ME16 ....91 C4

Warden Mill Cl ME18 ....104 E7
Warden Rd ME1 ....47 C2
Wardens Field Cl 2 BR6 ..51 F4
Wardona Ct DA10 ....11 F1
Wardwell La ME9 ....65 C8
Ware St ME14 ....93 A5
Warepoint Dr SE28 ....2 D4
Warham Rd TN14 ....69 B3
Waring Cl BR6 ....52 A4
Waring Dr BR6 ....52 A4
Waring Rd DA14 ....24 C2
Warland Rd
  West Kingsdown TN15 ...55 F2
  Woolwich SE18 ....6 C7
Warlmake ME17 ....108 F1
Warlmake Est ME17 .....108 E1
Warlmake Rd ME17 ......108 C1
Warne Pl 4 DA15 ....7 B1
Warner St ME4 ....47 F3
Warnett Ct ME6 ....60 A1
Warnford Gdns ME15 ...107 A8
Warnford Rd BR6 ....51 F5
Warren Ave BR6 ....51 F5
Warren Cl DA6 ....8 A2
Warren Cotts TN11 ......131 A3
Warren Ct TN15 ....84 C3
Warren Dr BR6 ....52 B5
Warren Farm La TN3 ....162 B4
Warren Gdns BR6 ....52 A5
Warren La Hartlip ME9 ...64 C3
  Woolwich SE18 ....2 B3
Warren Rd Bexley DA6 .....8 A2
  Dartford DA1 ....26 E5
  Hayes BR2 ....50 A8
  Kit's Coty ME5 ....76 D7
  Luddesdown ME2 ....45 D3
  Northfleet DA13 ....29 B3
  Orpington BR6 ....52 C5
  Sidcup DA14 ....24 C5
Warren Ridge TN3 ......163 C3
Warren Road Prim Sch
  BR6 ....51 F6
Warren The
  Gravesend DA12 ....30 D4
  Penshurst TN11 ....131 A4
  Ticehurst TN5 ....176 E1
Warren View DA12 ....31 E2
Warren Wlk 1 SE7 ....5 C8
Warren Wood Cl BR2 .....50 A8
Warren Wood
  Cty Prim Sch
  & Language Unit ME1 ...61 C8
Warren Wood Rd ME1 ....61 C7
Warrens The DA3 ....42 F3
Warrington Rd TN12 ....136 A6
Warrior Ave DA12 ....30 C4
Warspite Rd SE18 ....1 E3
Warwall E6 ....2 B7
Warwick Cl Orpington BR6 .52 A7
  Sidcup DA5 ....24 F8
Warwick Cres ME1 ....46 F2
Warwick Gdns DA13 ......58 A8
Warwick Pk TN2 ....149 B1
Warwick Pl
  Maidstone ME16 ....91 E3
  Northfleet DA11 ....12 B2
Warwick Rd Bexley DA16 ..7 C4
  4 Royal Tunbridge
  Wells TN1 ....149 A2
  Sidcup DA14 ....24 F8
Warwick Terr SE18 ....6 D8
Washneys Rd BR6 ....67 B6
Washwell La TN5 ....174 F3
Wassall La TN17 ....187 E7
Wat Tyler Way ME15 ......92 A4
Watchgate DA2 ....27 E3
Watchmans Terr 5 ME5 ..48 C2
Water La
  Biddenden Green TN27 ..142 F2
  Four Wents TN18 ....179 B4
  Harrietsham ME17 .....110 B5
  Headcorn TN17,TN27 ...141 A4
  Hunton ME15 ....121 D6
  Kingswood ME17 ....109 F3
  6 Maidstone ME15 ......92 A4
  Maidstone,Bearsted ME14 .93 B6
  Shoreham TN14 ....68 F6
  Sidcup DA14 ....24 F6
  West Malling ME19 ......89 C8
Water Mill Way DA4 ......41 B7
Water Slippe TN11 ......102 D1
Watercress Cl TN14 ......84 C7
Watercress Dr TN14 ......84 C7
Watercroft Rd TN14 ......52 F1
Waterdale Rd SE2 ....7 A8
Waterdales DA11 ....29 D7
Waterdown Rd TN4 ......148 E1
Waterfield TN2 ....163 A7
Waterfield Cl Erith DA17 ...4 A3
  Woolwich SE28 ....3 B5
Waterfrets Cotts TN3 ...147 F5
Watergate Ho 5 SE18 .....2 A2
Waterglade Ind Pk RM20 .10 F8
Waterhead Cl DA8 ....8 E7
Waterhouse Cl E16 ....1 D8
Wateringbury
  CE Prim Sch ME18 .....104 E6
Wateringbury Cl BR5 .....38 B7
Wateringbury Rd ME19 ...89 F3
Wateringbury Sta ME18 .104 E6
Waterlakes TN8 ....128 C8
Waterloo Pl
  Cranbrook TN17 ....169 D5
  Tonbridge TN9 ....133 B8
Waterloo Rd
  Cranbrook TN17 ....169 D6
  Gillingham ME7 ....48 C4

Waterloo St
  1 Gravesend DA12 ......30 C8
  Maidstone ME15 ....92 A3
Waterlow Rd
  Maidstone ME14 ....92 A6
  Vigo Village DA13 ....72 F3
Waterman's La TN12 ....136 B3
Watermeadow Cl Erith DA8 .9 B6
  Gillingham ME7 ....62 F6
Watermill Cl
  Maidstone ME16 ....91 B5
  Rochester ME2 ....47 C8
Watermint Cl BR5 ....38 D5
Waters Cotts ME15 .....175 A4
Waters Edge ME15 ....91 F2
Waters Pl ME7 ....63 A6
Waterside DA1 ....8 F2
Waterside Ct
  Leybourne ME19 ....74 E2
  Rochester ME2 ....47 E6
Waterside La ME7 ....48 F7
Waterside Mews ME18 ..104 D6
Watersmeet Way SE28 ....3 D7
Waterton BR8 ....39 D5
Waterton Ave DA12 ......30 D8
Watery La Heaverham TN15 .85 D7
  Sidcup BR5,DA14 ....24 B2
Watford Rd E16 ....1 A8
Watkins Cl TN12 ....139 E5
Watling Ave ME5 ....48 D2
Watling House 10 SE18 ....6 A8
Watling St Bexley DA6,DA7 .8 D2
  Chatham ME5 ....48 D2
  Dartford DA1,DA2 ....27 C8
  Gravesend DA11,DA12 ...30 C2
  Northfleet DA11,DA13 ...29 C5
  Rochester ME2 ....46 D7
Watson Ave ME5 ....61 D5
Watson Cl RM20 ....11 A6
Watt Ho SE2 ....3 C1
Watt's Cross Rd TN11 ...116 B6
Watt's La BR7 ....37 C8
Watts Cl Snodland ME6 ...75 B8
  Wadhurst TN5 ....174 F4
Watts' Ave ME1 ....47 C4
Watts' St ME4 ....47 E3
Wavell Dr DA15 ....6 E1
Waveney Rd TN10 ....117 B5
Waverley Cl Bromley BR2 .36 D4
  Chatham ME5 ....62 D2
  Coxheath ME17 ....106 C3
Waverley Cres SE18 ....2 D1
Waverley Dr TN2 ....149 F6
Waverley Gdns E6 ....1 E8
Waverley Rd SE18 ....2 D1
Wayfield Cty Prim Sch
  ME5 ....62 A7
Wayfield Link SE9 ....6 D1
Wayfield Rd ME5 ....62 A7
Waylands BR8 ....39 F5
Waylands Cl TN14 ....67 E4
Wayne Cl BR6 ....51 F7
Wayne Ct ME2 ....33 D2
Wayside TN30 ....173 B2
Wayside Ave TN30 ......173 B3
Wayside Dr TN8 ....112 D3
Wayside Flats TN30 .....173 B2
Wayside Gr SE9 ....22 F4
Wayville Rd DA1 ....27 B8
Weald 1 Istead Rise DA13 .29 E1
  Maidstone ME15 ....107 C6
  Orpington BR5 ....50 E8
  Sevenoaks Weald TN14 ..99 C2
Weald
  Com Prim Sch TN14 ....99 B2
Weald Ct TN11 ....116 D6
Weald of Kent Gram
  Sch for Girls The TN9 .133 C7
Weald Rd TN13 ....99 B7
Weald The BR7 ....22 F2
Weald View
  Frittenden TN17 ....156 E6
  Paddock Wood TN12 ...136 E1
  Wadhurst TN5 ....174 F6
Weald View Rd TN9 ....133 B7
Wealden Ave TN30 .....173 B1
Wealden Cl TN11 ....116 C5
Wealden Ct 5 ME5 ....48 B3
Wealden Pl TN13 ....84 D6
Wealden Way ME20 ......90 E7
Wealdon View TN17 ....167 E8
Weardale Ave DA2 ....27 C7
Weare Rd TN4 ....149 C8
Weatherly Cl ME1 ....47 C4
Weathersfield Ct SE9 .....5 F1
Weaver Cl E6 ....2 C8
Weaver's Orch DA13 .....29 A2
Weavering Cl ME2 ....33 B2
Weavering Cotts ME14 ...92 E3
Weavering St ME14 ......92 F4
Weavers Cl Gravesend DA11 30 A7
  Staplehurst TN12 ......139 F4
Weavers La TN14 ....84 C6
Weavers The
  Biddenden TN27 ......158 A1
  Maidstone ME16 ....91 B5
Webb Cl ME3 ....34 D6
Webb Ct 6 SE28 ....3 B6
Webb's Mdw TN15 ....84 C2
Webber Cl DA8 ....9 B7
Webster Rd ME15 ....49 F1
Wedgewood Cl ME16 .....91 B5
Wedgewood Ct DA5 ......24 F8
Wedgewood Dr ME5 ......62 A7
Weeds Wood Rd ME5 .....61 F4
Week St ME14 ....92 A4
Weeks La TN27 ....158 A5

Weigall Rd SE12,SE3 ......5 A3
Weir Rd DA5 ....25 B8
Weird Wood DA3 ....43 C6
Welbeck Ave Bromley BR1 .22 A4
  Royal Tunbridge Wells TN4 .149 C8
  Sidcup DA15 ....24 A7
Welcombe Ct ME8 ....63 D8
Weld Cl TN12 ....139 F4
Weldstock Ho SE28 ....2 D3
Well Cl TN11 ....115 F1
Well Field DA3 ....42 F5
Well Hall SE9 ....5 E3
Well Hall Par SE9 ....5 F3
Well Hall Rd SE18,SE9 ....5 F3
Well Hill BR6 ....53 B5
Well Hill La BR6 ....53 B4
Well Penn Rd ME3 ....16 C3
Well Rd Maidstone ME14 ..92 A5
  Otford TN14 ....69 C3
Well St East Malling ME19 .74 E2
  Maidstone ME15,ME17 ..106 E4
Wellan Cl DA16 ....7 B2
Welland Rd TN10 ....117 B4
Wellands Cl BR1 ....36 F7
Wellbrook Rd BR6 ....51 A6
Wellcome Ave DA1 ....9 E3
Weller Ave ME1 ....47 D2
Weller Pl BR6 ....66 A8
Weller Rd TN4 ....148 C4
Wellers Cl TN16 ....96 C8
Wellesley Cl 7 SE7 ....1 C1
Welling High St DA16 .....7 B4
Welling Sch DA16 ....7 B6
Welling Sta DA16 ....7 B4
Welling Way DA16 ....6 D4
Wellingfield Ct 1 DA16 ...7 A4
Wellington Ave Sidcup DA15 .7 A1
  Woolwich SE18 ....2 D3
Wellington Cotts
  Gill's Green TN18 ......178 E4
  Meopham ME13 ....58 A7
Wellington Gdns SE7 ......1 C1
Wellington House 6
  ME15 ....107 E5
Wellington Par DA15 ......7 A2
Wellington Pl
  Maidstone ME14 ....91 F6
  Wadhurst TN5 ....174 F5
Wellington Rd Bexley DA5 ..7 C4
  Bromley BR2 ....36 C5
  Dartford DA1 ....9 C1
  Erith DA17 ....3 F1
  Gillingham ME7 ....48 C4
  Orpington BR5 ....38 C3
  Tilbury RM18 ....13 A5
Wellington St
  Gravesend DA12 ....30 C8
  Woolwich SE18 ....2 A2
Wellington Way ME19 .....88 F3
Wellingtonia Way TN8 ...112 C2
Wellmeade Dr TN13 ......99 B8
Wells Cl
  Royal Tunbridge Wells TN1 .149 A3
  Tenterden TN30 ....183 B8
  Tonbridge TN10 ....117 D4
  Westerham TN16 ....96 C4
Wells Cotts ME18 ......104 C2
Wells Ct ME2 ....46 D5
Wells Ho Bromley BR1 ...22 B3
  Royal Tunbridge Wells TN4 .148 F4
Wells Rd Bromley BR1 ....36 F7
  Rochester ME2 ....46 D5
Wellsmoor Gdns BR1 .....37 A6
Welton Cl TN9 ....132 F7
Welton Rd SE18 ....6 E7
Wemmick Cl ME1 ....61 D7
Wendover Cl ME2 ....60 B5
Wendover Ct BR2 ....36 B6
Wendover Rd
  Bromley BR1,BR2 ....36 B6
  Eltham SE9 ....5 D4
Wendover Way Bexley DA16 .7 A3
  Orpington BR6 ....38 A3
Wensley Cl SE9 ....5 F1
Wents Wood ME14 ....92 F5
Wentworth Cl
  Gravesend DA11 ....30 A3
  Hayes BR2 ....50 A8
  Orpington BR6 ....51 E5
  Woolwich SE28 ....3 D7
Wentworth Dr
  Cliffe Woods ME3 ....33 B8
  Dartford DA1 ....9 A1
  Gillingham ME8 ....63 D7
Wentworth Prim Sch DA1 .26 A8
Wenvoe Ave DA7 ....8 B5
Wernbrook St SE18 ....6 C8
Wesley Ave E16 ....1 A5
Wesley Cl Maidstone ME16 .90 F3
  St Paul's Cray BR5 ......38 C6
Wessex Dr DA8 ....8 E6
West App BR5 ....37 C4
West Borough Prim Sch
  ME16 ....91 B3
West Brow DA1 ....23 B3
West Common Rd BR2 ...50 B7
West Crescent Rd DA12 ..13 C1
West Cross TN30 ....182 F7
West Cross Gdns TN30 ..182 F7
West Ct 4 ME15 ....92 A1
West Dr
  Chartway Street ME17 ..125 B7
  Chatham ME5 ....61 D5
West End Brasted TN16 ...82 A2
  Kemsing TN15 ....70 A2
  Marden TN12 ....138 C6
West Hallowes SE9 ....22 E7
West Heath Cl DA1 ....8 F1

West Heath La TN13 ......99 B7
West Heath Rd Crayford DA1 .8 F1
  Erith SE2 ....7 D8
West Hill DA1 ....9 D1
West Hill Dr DA1 ....9 C1
West Hill Prim Sch DA1 ...9 C1
West Hill Rise DA1 ....9 D1
West Holme DA8 ....8 C6
West Kent Ave DA11 .....12 C1
West Kent Coll TN9 .....133 A7
West Kingsdown Ind Est
  TN15 ....55 F2
West Kingsdown,St
  Edmund's
  CE Prim Sch TN15 ......56 A2
West La ME3 ....21 A6
West Lodge Prep Sch
  DA14 ....24 A5
West Malling CE
  Prim Sch ME19 ....89 B8
West Malling Ind Pk ME19 73 E2
West Malling Sta ME19 ...89 D8
West Mersea Cl E16 ....1 B5
West Mill DA11 ....12 F1
West Mill Rd ME20 ....75 C4
West Park Ave TN4 ......132 F1
West Park Rd ME15 ......92 B2
West Pk SE9 ....22 E7
West Rd Gillingham ME4 ..48 A7
  Goudhurst TN17 ....167 E8
  Kildown TN17 ....166 F3
West Shaw DA3 ....42 D7
West St Bexley DA7 ....7 F4
  Bromley BR1 ....36 A7
  Erith DA8 ....4 E1
  Gillingham ME7 ....48 D6
  Gravesend DA11 ....13 B1
  Grays RM17 ....12 A8
  Harrietsham ME17 .....110 C6
  Hunton ME15 ....121 D7
  Lenham ME17 ....111 E8
  Rochester ME2 ....33 B1
  West Malling ME19 ......89 B8
  Wrotham TN15 ....71 F3
West Terr DA15 ....23 E7
West Thurrock Prim Sch
  RM20 ....11 B8
West Thurrock Way RM20 .11 B8
West View Hospl DA30 ..182 E6
West View Rd
  Crockenhill BR8 ....39 D3
  Dartford DA1 ....9 F1
  Swanley BR8 ....40 A5
West Way BR5 ....37 D4
West Wlk ME16 ....91 B3
West Wood Rd ME9 ....79 B8
West Woodside DA5 ......24 E7
Westbere House BR5 .....38 C4
Westbourne Rd DA7 ....7 E7
Westbrook Ct SE3 ....5 B6
Westbrook Dr BR5 ....38 D1
Westbrook Rd SE3 ....5 B6
Westbrook Terr TN2 ....149 D1
Westbrooke Cl ME4 ......48 A2
Westbrooke Cres DA16 ...7 C4
Westbrooke Rd Bexley DA16 .7 C4
  Sidcup DA15 ....23 D6
Westbrooke Sch DA16 .....7 D4
Westbury Ct 5 DA14 .....24 A4
Westbury Rd BR1 ....36 D8
Westbury Terr TN16 ......96 C8
Westcombe Hill SE3 ....5 A8
Westcombe Park Rd SE3 ..5 A7
Westcombe Park Sta SE3 ..1 A1
Westcott Ave DA11 ....30 A5
Westcott Cl BR1 ....36 F4
Westcourt Rd ME7 ....48 A6
Westcourt Sch DA12 .....30 E6
Westdale Rd SE18 ....6 B8
Westdean Ave SE12 ......22 C7
Wested Farm Cotts BR8 ..39 F2
Wested La BR8 ....40 A3
Westerdale Rd 5 SE10 ....1 A1
Westergate Rd Erith SE2 ..7 E8
  Rochester ME2 ....32 F1
Westerham Cl ME8 ....49 B3
Westerham Dr DA15 ....7 B1
Westerham Hill TN16 .....81 B5
Westerham Rd
  Brasted TN16 ....82 A2
  Orpington BR2 ....50 D4
  Sevenoaks TN13 ....83 C4
  Westerham TN16 ....96 A8
Westerhill Rd ME17 .....106 C1
Westerland BR7 ....23 C2
Western Ave
  Gillingham ME4 ....48 A8
  7 TN18 ....178 F2
Western Cross Cl DA9 ...11 C1
Western Rd
  Borough Green TN15 ....86 F5
  Hawkhurst TN18 ......178 F2
  Maidstone ME15 ....91 E1
  Royal Tunbridge Wells TN1 .149 C5
  Royal Tunbridge
  Wells,Southborough TN4 .133 A1
  Wadhurst TN5 ....174 F6
Western Way SE28 ....2 E4
Westfield
  New Ash Green DA3 .....56 F6
  1 Orpington BR6 ....51 C5
  Sevenoaks TN13 ....54 C5
Westfield Bsns Ctr ME2 ..47 C7
Westfield Cl DA12 ....30 C2
Westfield Cotts
  Cudham TN14 ....66 D3
  West Kingsdown TN15 ...55 F5
Westfield House TN30 ...182 F7

Westfield Rd DA7 . . . . .8 C4
Westfield Sole Rd
ME5,ME15 . . . . .77 D8
Westfield St SE18 . . . . .1 D3
Westfield Terr TN17 . . . . . .168 F1
Westgate Ct SE12 . . . . .22 A7
Westgate Prim Sch DA1 . .26 D8
Westgate Rd DA1 . . . . .9 D1
Westharold BR8 . . . . .39 D6
Westholme Ave SE12,SE9 . . .5 C2
Westhurst Dr BR7 . . . . .23 B3
Westland Ho 1 E16 . . . . .2 A1
Westland Lodge 2 BR1 . .36 C6
Westleigh Dr BR1 . . . . .36 E8
Westmarsh Cl ME15 . . . . .107 F7
Westmead ME20 . . . . .75 C4
Westminster Ind Est SE18 . .1 D3
Westmoor St SE7 . . . . .1 D4
Westmoreland Ave DA16 . . .6 E3
Westmoreland Pl 5 BR1 . .36 A6
Westmoreland Rd BR2 . . .36 A5
Westmorland Cl ME15 . . .107 C7
Westmorland Gn ME15 . . .107 C7
Westmorland Rd ME15 . . .107 C7
Westmount Ave ME4 . . . . .47 F3
Westmount Rd SE9 . . . . .6 A3
Weston Ho RM20 . . . . .10 F8
Weston Rd ME2 . . . . .47 A8
Westree Ct 7 ME16 . . . . . .91 E3
Westree Rd ME16 . . . . .91 F3
Westrise TN9 . . . . .133 A7
Westway Coxheath ME17 . .106 C3
Pembury TN2 . . . . .150 D7
Westways Marlpit Hill TN8 .112 C2
Westerham TN16 . . . . .81 C1
Westwell Cl BR5 . . . . .38 D1
Westwell Ct TN30 . . . . . . .182 F1
Westwell House TN30 . . . .182 F7
Westwood Cl BR1 . . . . .36 D6
Westwood Inf Sch DA16 . . .6 E3
Westwood Jun Sch DA16 . . .6 E3
Westwood La DA16 . . . . .6 F4
Westwood Rd
Betsham DA13 . . . . .28 E2
East Peckham TN12 . . . . . .119 E6
Maidstone ME15 . . . . .107 A7
Newham E16 . . . . .1 B5
Royal Tunbridge Wells TN4 .148 C3
Westwood Tech Coll DA16 . .6 E3
Westwood Way TN13 . . . . .83 F5
Wetheral Dr ME5 . . . . .62 B4
Wey Cl ME5 . . . . .62 C5
Weybridge Cl ME5 . . . . . . .62 C4
Weyhill Cl ME14 . . . . .92 C6
Weyman Rd SE3 . . . . .5 C6
Weymouth Cl E6 . . . . .2 B7
Wharf La ME3 . . . . .16 B6
Wharf Rd Gillingham ME7 . .48 C7
Gravesend DA12 . . . . .13 E1
Grays RM17 . . . . .11 F8
Maidstone ME15 . . . . .91 E2
Wharf Rd S RM17 . . . . .11 F8
Wharfedale Rd DA2 . . . . . .27 C7
Wharnecliffe DA9 . . . . .11 B1
Wharton Rd BR1 . . . . .36 B8
Whatcote Cotts TN15 . . . . .87 C7
Whatman ME14 . . . . .92 C6
Wheatcroft Gr ME8 . . . . . .63 F7
Wheatear Way ME4 . . . . . .62 B7
Wheatfield ME19 . . . . .74 E1
Wheatfield Cl TN17 . . . . . .169 C5
Wheatfield Dr TN17 . . . . . .169 C5
Wheatfield Lea TN17 . . . . .169 C5
Wheatfield Way TN17 . . . . .169 C5
Wheatfields Chatham ME5 .62 D2
Maidstone ME14 . . . . .92 D4
Newham E6 . . . . .2 B7
Wheatley Cl DA9 . . . . .11 A2
Wheatley Terrace Rd DA8 . .8 F8
Wheatsheaf ME15 . . . . . . .107 B8
Wheatsheaf Hill
Chelsfield TN14 . . . . .52 F2
Ide Hill TN14 . . . . .97 F4
Wheatsheaf Way TN10 . . . .117 D6
Wheelbarrow Park Est
TN12 . . . . .138 B7
Wheeler St
Headcorn TN27 . . . . .141 E5
Maidstone ME14 . . . . .92 A5
Wheeler's La ME17 . . . . . .122 E7
Wheelers The ME8 . . . . . . .63 B6
Wheelock Cl DA8 . . . . .8 B7
Wheelwrights The ME17 .110 D6
Whenman Ave DA5 . . . . . . .25 C5
Whernside SE28 . . . . .3 C6
Whetsted Rd
Five Oak Green TN12 . . . .135 C8
Whetsted TN12 . . . . .119 F1
Whetstone Rd SE3 . . . . .5 D6
Whiffen Wlk ME19 . . . . . . .75 B1
Whiffen's Ave ME4 . . . . . .47 F5
Whiffen's Ave W ME4 . . . .47 F5
Whimbrel Cl SE28 . . . . .3 C6
Whimbrel Gn ME20 . . . . . .74 F2
Whimbrel Wlk ME5 . . . . . .62 C1
Whimbrels The ME4 . . . . . .34 B1
Whinchat Rd SE28 . . . . .2 D4
Whinfell Way DA12 . . . . . .30 F4
Whinyates Rd SE9 . . . . .5 E4
Whippendell Cl BR5 . . . . . .38 B8
Whippendell Way BR5 . . . .38 B7
Whistler Rd TN10 . . . . .117 D6
Whitby Cl DA9 . . . . .11 A2
Whitby Rd SE18 . . . . .1 F2
Whitchurch Rd ME16 . . . . .91 E4
Whitcombe Cl ME5 . . . . . .62 C3

White Ave DA11 . . . . .29 F5
White Bear Pas 3 TN1 . . .149 A2
White Cottage Rd TN10 . . .117 D6
White Gates DA14 . . . . . . .24 A3
White Hart Cl TN13 . . . . . .99 C7
White Hart Par TN13 . . . . .83 E5
White Hart Rd
Orpington BR6 . . . . .38 A5
Woolwich SE18 . . . . .2 E2
White Hart Wood TN13 . . .99 C6
White Hart Yd 9 DA11 . . . .13 B1
White Hill Rd ME9,ME14 . .63 D1
White Horse Hill BR7,SE9 .23 A4
White Horse La
Harvel DA13 . . . . .58 C2
Otham Hole ME15 . . . . . . .108 A6
White Horse Rd DA13 . . . .58 L1
White House La TN14 . . . . .98 F5
White House Rd TN14 . . . .98 F5
White Lodge TN1 . . . . . . .149 C4
White Lodge Cl TN13 . . . . .84 B4
White Oak Cl 13 TN9 . . . .133 B8
White Oak Gdns DA15 . . . .23 F8
White Oak Sq 3 BR8 . . . . .39 E6
White Oak Prim Sch BR8 .39 E7
White Post Four Elms TN8 .113 A6
Hollingbourne ME17 . . . . . .95 B5
White Post Cnr TN11 . . . .101 F5
White Post Hill DA4 . . . . . .41 A2
White Post La
Culverstone Green DA13 . . .57 F2
Sole Street DA13 . . . . .44 B5
White Rd ME4 . . . . .48 A2
White Rock Ct ME16 . . . . .91 E3
White Rock Pl 6 ME16 . . .91 E3
White's La TN18 . . . . .179 B2
Whitebeam Ave BR2 . . . . .37 A3
Whitebeam Dr ME17 . . . . .106 B3
Whitebine Gdns TN12 . . . .120 A6
Whitebread La TN31 . . . . .187 D1
Whitecroft BR8 . . . . .39 E7
Whitefield Cl BR5 . . . . .38 C6
Whitefield Rd TN4 . . . . . .149 A6
Whitefriars TN13 . . . . .99 A8
Whitegate Cl TN4 . . . . . . .149 A8
Whitegate Ct ME8 . . . . . . .63 D5
Whitegates Ave TN15 . . . . .55 E4
Whitegates La TN15 . . . . .174 D8
Whitehall Dr ME17 . . . . . .109 D3
Whitehall La Erith DA8 . . . .8 F5
Grays RM17 . . . . .12 C8
Whitehall Rd
Broad Street ME14 . . . . . . .94 A4
Bromley BR2 . . . . .36 D5
Whitehaven Cl BR2 . . . . . .36 A5
Whitehead Cl DA2 . . . . . . .26 C5
Whiteheads La ME14 . . . . .93 B4
Whitehill TN15 . . . . .72 B3
Whitehill Cty Inf Sch
DA12 . . . . .30 C5
Whitehill Cty Jun Sch
DA12 . . . . .30 C5
Whitehill La DA12 . . . . .30 D5
Whitehill Par DA12 . . . . . .30 C6
Whitehill Rd Crayford DA1 . .9 A2
Gravesend DA12 . . . . .30 C6
Longfield,Whitehill DA13 . . .42 D8
Meopham DA13 . . . . .58 B7
Whitehorse Hill ME5 . . . . .48 B3
Whitehouse Cl ME4 . . . . . .34 E4
Whitehouse Cres ME1 . . . .76 A8
Whitelakes Rise ME2 . . . . .46 B3
Whitelimes TN18 . . . . . . .178 D8
Whiteoak Ct 1 BR8 . . . . . .39 E6
Whitepost La DA13 . . . . . . .73 A8
Whites Cl DA9 . . . . .11 C1
Whitewall Ctr ME2 . . . . . . .47 D8
Whitewall Rd ME2 . . . . . . .47 D7
Whitewall Way ME2 . . . . . .47 D7
Whitewebbs Way BR5 . . . .37 F8
Whitfield Rd DA7 . . . . .7 F7
Whitings Way E6 . . . . .2 A8
Whitmore St ME16 . . . . . . .91 D2
Whitney Wlk DA14 . . . . . . .24 E1
Whittaker St ME4 . . . . .48 A4
Whitworth Rd SE18 . . . . . . .6 A7
Whybourne Crest TN2 . . .149 D1
Whyman Ave ME4 . . . . . . .48 A1
Wichling Cl BR5 . . . . .38 D1
Wicken House ME16 . . . . . .91 E4
Wickenden Rd TN13 . . . . . .84 C5
Wickens Pl ME19 . . . . .89 C8
Wickets The TN14 . . . . . . .99 C2
Wickham Ct ME9 . . . . .65 B6
Wickham Common
Prim Sch BR4 . . . . .50 A6
Wickham Ct DA16 . . . . .6 E5
Wickham Field TN14 . . . . . .68 F3
Wickham Gdns TN4 . . . . .148 D5
Wickham La SE2,SE18 . . . . .7 A5
Wickham Pl ME17 . . . . . . .111 D5
Wickham St Bexley DA16 . . .7 A6
Rochester ME1 . . . . .47 D3
Wickhams Way DA3 . . . . . .42 F4
Wickhurst Rd TN14 . . . . . .98 F3
Wicks Cl SE9 . . . . .22 D4
Wicksteed Cl DA5 . . . . .25 D5
Widbury TN3 . . . . .147 F2
Widecombe Rd SE9 . . . . . .22 E5
Widgeon Cl E16 . . . . .1 B7
Widgeon Path SE28 . . . . . . .2 D3
Widgeon Rd Erith DA8 . . . . .9 B7
Rochester ME2 . . . . .46 D6
Widmore Ctr, The BR1 . . . .36 C6
Widmore Lodge Rd BR1 . .36 D7
Widmore Rd BR1 . . . . .36 C7

Wierton Hill ME17 . . . . . .123 D7
Wierton La ME17 . . . . . . .107 E1
Wierton Rd ME17 . . . . . . .123 D8
Wigmore Rd ME8 . . . . . . .63 B4
Wilberforce Ct 2 SE28 . . . .3 C5
Wilberforce Rd ME17 . . . .106 D3
Wilberforce Way DA12 . . .30 D3
Wilde Cl RM18 . . . . .13 C5
Wilde Rd DA8 . . . . .8 B7
Wilderness Rd BR7 . . . . . .23 B1
Wildernesse Ave TN15 . . . .84 E5
Wildernesse Mount N13 . .84 D5
Wildernesse Sch The
TN13 . . . . .84 E6
Wildfell Cl ME5 . . . . .77 C8
Wildman Cl ME8 . . . . .63 D3
Wildwood Cl
Kingswood ME17 . . . . . . .109 E2
Lewisham SE12 . . . . .22 A8
Wildwood Glade ME7 . . . .63 B4
Wilford Ho 8 SE18 . . . . .2 B1
Wilfred St 21 DA12 . . . . . .13 B1
Wilkinson Cl 1 DA1 . . . . . .10 A3
Wilkinson Rd E16 . . . . .1 C7
Wilks Ave DA1 . . . . .26 F6
Will Adams Ct 9 ME7 . . . .48 C6
Will Adams Rdbt ME8 . . . .48 F1
Will Adams Way ME8 . . . .48 F1
Will Crooks Gdns SE9 . . . . .5 D3
Will Thorne Pav The E16 . . .1 E7
Willenhall Rd SE18 . . . . .2 B1
Willersley Ave
Orpington BR6 . . . . .51 D7
Sidcup DA15 . . . . .23 F7
Willersley Cl DA15 . . . . . . .23 F7
Willesley Gdns TN17 . . . . .169 D6
Willett Cl BR5 . . . . .37 F5
Willett Way BR5,BR6 . . . . .37 E3
Willetts Cotts TN3 . . . . . . .146 C4
Willetts La TN3 . . . . .146 C4
William Baker Ho ME20 . . .90 F8
William Barefoot Dr SE9 . .23 A5
William Ho 4 DA12 . . . . . .30 B8
William Judge Cl TN30 . . .183 D7
William Luck Cl TN12 . . . .119 E6
William Rd ME2 . . . . .46 C2
William Smith Ho 10 DA17 . .4 A3
William St Gravesend DA12 .30 B8
Grays RM17 . . . . .12 C8
Royal Tunbridge Wells TN4 .149 A5
Willicombe Pk TN2 . . . . . .149 D4
Willington Gn ME15 . . . . .107 E2
Willington St ME15 . . . . . .92 F2
Willis Ho ME1 . . . . .47 C4
Willis Rd DA8 . . . . .4 D2
Willoughby Way SE7 . . . . . .1 B7
Willow Ave
Hoo St Werburgh ME3 . . . .34 E3
Sidcup DA15 . . . . .7 A1
Swanley BR8 . . . . .39 F5
Willow Cl Bromley BR2 . . . .36 F4
Orpington BR5 . . . . .38 B2
Sidcup DA15 . . . . .7 F1
Willow Cres
Five Oak Green TN12 . . . .135 B7
Staplehurst TN12 . . . . . . .139 F5
Willow Ct ME15 . . . . .107 A6
Willow Gr BR7 . . . . .23 B7
Willow House 2 ME5 . . . . .61 F5
Willow La
Paddock Wood TN12 . . . .136 E6
Woolwich SE18 . . . . .2 A2
Willow Lea TN10 . . . . . . .117 C7
Willow Pk TN14 . . . . .68 F2
Willow Rd Dartford DA1 . . .26 C7
Erith DA8 . . . . .9 A6
Larkfield ME20 . . . . .74 F1
Rochester ME2 . . . . .46 E6
Willow Rise ME15 . . . . . . .92 F1
Willow Terr DA4 . . . . .54 E8
Willow Tree Ct DA14 . . . . .23 F3
Willow Tree Rd TN2 . . . . .148 F1
Willow Tree Wlk BR1 . . . . .36 B8
Willow Vale BR7 . . . . .23 B2
Willow Way ME15 . . . . . . .92 B3
Willow Wents ME18 . . . . . .88 D1
Willow Wlk
Culverstone Green DA13 . . .57 F3
Orpington BR6 . . . . .51 B7
Royal Tunbridge Wells TN2 .149 E8
Willow Wood Rd DA13 . . . .57 F2
Willowbank 12 ME15 . . . . .92 B4
Willowbank Dr ME23 . . . . .17 E4
Willowby Gdns ME8 . . . . . .63 D4
Willowfields Cl 1 SE18 . . . .2 E1
Willowherb Cl ME4 . . . . . .34 C1
Willowmead ME19 . . . . . . .74 E2
Willows The Gillingham ME8 49 E2
Grays RM17 . . . . .12 D8
Newington ME9 . . . . .65 B6
Willowside ME6 . . . . .60 A1
Willrose Cres SE2 . . . . .3 B1
Willys Cotts TN8 . . . . .96 C2
Wilman Rd TN4 . . . . .149 B7
Wilmar Way TN15 . . . . . . .84 F7
Wilmecote Ct ME8 . . . . . . .63 D8
Wilmington Ave BR6 . . . . .52 B8
Wilmington Court Rd DA2 .26 A6
Wilmington
Gram Sch for Boys DA2 . .26 B5
Wilmington Hall Sch DA2 .26 B5
Wilmington Prim Sch DA2 .26 B5
Wilmington Way ME8 . . . . .49 B2
Wilmot Rd DA1 . . . . .9 B2
Wilmount St SE18 . . . . .2 B2
Wilson Ave ME1 . . . . .61 E7
Wilson Cl Maidstone ME15 107 E7
Tonbridge TN9 . . . . .116 C5

Wilson Ho 2 SE7 . . . . .5 C8
Wilson La DA4 . . . . .41 F7
Wilson Rd ME8 . . . . .49 A2
Wilson St SE18 . . . . .117 C5
Wilsons La ME15 . . . . . . .106 A5
Wilsons Way DA13 . . . . . . .57 F3
Wilton Dr ME20 . . . . .90 B8
Wilton Rd SE2 . . . . .3 C2
Wiltshire Cl Chatham ME5 .62 C8
Dartford DA2 . . . . .27 D8
Wiltshire Rd BR8 . . . . .38 A2
Wiltshire Way
Maidstone ME15 . . . . .107 E8
Royal Tunbridge Wells TN2 .149 D7
Wimborne 6 DA4 . . . . .24 B4
Wimborne Ave BR7 . . . . . .37 F6
Wimbourne Dr ME8 . . . . . .63 D7
Wimpole Cl BR2 . . . . .36 C5
Win'freds Cl TN17 . . . . . . .181 E3
Winch Cl TN17 . . . . .169 D3
Winch's Garth TN12 . . . . .139 F5
Winchcomb Gdns SE9 . . . . .5 D4
Winchelsea Ave DA7 . . . . . .7 F7
Winchelsea Rd ME5 . . . . . .62 B5
Winchester Ave ME5 . . . . .61 F4
Winchester Cl 1 E6 . . . . . . .1 F7
Winchester Cres DA12 . . . .30 D5
Winchester Gr TN13 . . . . . .84 B4
Winchester Ho
4 Maidstone ME15 . . . . . .107 D7
Woolwich SE18 . . . . .5 D7
Winchester Pl 9 ME14 . . . .92 A5
Winchester Rd Bexley DA7 . .7 D5
Hawkhurst TN18 . . . . .179 A4
Orpington BR6 . . . . .52 C6
Tonbridge TN10 . . . . .117 D5
Winchester Way ME8 . . . . .64 A8
Wincliff Rd TN9 . . . . .133 B8
Wincrofts Dr SE9 . . . . .6 D3
Windermere Cl
Dartford DA1 . . . . .26 B7
Orpington BR6 . . . . .51 B7
Windermere Dr ME8 . . . . .63 D7
Windermere Ho 4 ME15 .107 E7
Windermere Rd DA7 . . . . . .8 C5
Windhover Way DA12 . . . . .30 E4
Windmill Cl ME2 . . . . .33 B1
Windmill Cotts
Cranbrook TN17 . . . . .169 D6
Lower Stoke ME3 . . . . .19 C5
Windmill Ct
Maidstone ME17 . . . . .107 B3
Royal Tunbridge Wells TN2 .149 C3
Windmill Dr BR2 . . . . .50 C6
Windmill Hill
Hill Top TN12 . . . . .136 B1
Platt TN15 . . . . .87 D7
Pye Corner ME17 . . . . . . .126 B7
Windmill Hts ME14 . . . . . .93 B4
Windmill La
Wadhurst TN5 . . . . .174 E4
Wadhurst, Cousley
Wood TN5 . . . . .175 C8
Wrotham Heath TN15 . . . . .87 E8
Windmill La E ME19 . . . . . .89 C6
Windmill La W ME19 . . . . .89 A6
Windmill Manor ME7 . . . . .48 C4
Windmill Pk TN15 . . . . . . .87 E7
Windmill Rd
Gillingham ME7 . . . . .48 C4
Sevenoaks TN13 . . . . .99 B6
Sevenoaks Weald TN14 . . . .99 B2
Windmill Row ME17 . . . . .108 D2
Windmill St
Gravesend DA12 . . . . .30 B7
Rochester ME2 . . . . .33 B1
Royal Tunbridge Wells TN2 .149 C3
Windrush Prim Sch SE28 . . .3 B5
Windsor Ave ME4 . . . . .47 F2
Windsor Cl Chislehurst BR7 .23 B3
Maidstone ME14 . . . . .92 B6
Windsor Ct 1 BR1 . . . . . . .36 E6
Orpington BR6 . . . . .52 A4
Windsor Dr Dartford DA1 . . .9 A1
Orpington BR6 . . . . .52 A4
Windsor Hall E16 . . . . .1 B5
Windsor Rd Bexley DA6 . . . .7 E3
Gillingham ME7 . . . . .48 D5
Gravesend DA12 . . . . .30 B4
Windward Rd ME1 . . . . . . .47 C1
Windy Ridge BR1 . . . . .36 E8
Windyridge ME7 . . . . .48 E1
Winfield La TN15 . . . . .86 E3
Winford Mews ME1 . . . . . .47 A2
Wingate Rd DA14 . . . . .24 C2
Wingfield Prim Sch SE3 . . . .5 B4
Wingfield Rd DA12 . . . . . . .30 B8
Wingham Ct
Gillingham ME8 . . . . .49 C3
Maidstone ME15 . . . . .107 F7
Wingrove Dr
Maidstone ME14 . . . . .92 E5
Rochester ME2 . . . . .47 C7
Winifred Rd Dartford DA1 . . .9 B2
Erith DA8 . . . . .4 E1
Maidstone ME15 . . . . .92 F3
Winifred St E16 . . . . .1 F5
Winn Common Rd SE18 . . . .6 E1
Winn Rd SE12,SE9 . . . . . . .22 B7
Winnipeg Dr 3 BR6 . . . . . .51 F4
Winser Rd TN17 . . . . .182 A1
Winsor Prim Sch E6 . . . . . . .2 A7
Winsor Terr E6 . . . . .2 A8
Winston Cl DA10 . . . . .11 F1
Winston Ct 11 BR1 . . . . . . .36 B8
Winston Dr ME2 . . . . .33 D2
Winston Rd ME2 . . . . .46 D5
Winstone Scott Ave TN3 .147 E4
Winterborne Ave BR6 . . . .51 D7
Winterfield La ME19 . . . . . .89 C8

Wintergarden Cres DA9 . .28 A8
Wintergreen Cl
7 Newham E16 . . . . .1 E8
St Mary's Island ME4 . . . .34 C1
Winters Croft DA12 . . . . . .30 D2
Winterton Ct 8 TN16 . . . . .81 D1
Winton Ct BR8 . . . . .39 E5
Winton Rd BR6 . . . . .51 B6
Wirral Wood Cl BR7 . . . . . .23 A2
Wirrals The ME5 . . . . .62 A4
Wise Ho SE18 . . . . .6 A1
Wise's La TN15 . . . . .56 E2
Wiseacre TN3 . . . . .166 A3
Wishart Rd SE3 . . . . .5 D5
Wisley Rd BR5 . . . . .24 B1
Wistaria Cl BR6 . . . . .51 B8
Wisteria Gdns BR8 . . . . . .39 D7
Wisteria Ho 11 ME15 . . . .107 E4
Witches La TN13 . . . . .83 D4
Witham Way ME2 . . . . .46 F7
Withens Cl BR5 . . . . .38 C5
Witherston Way SE9 . . . . . .23 A5
Withyham Rd TN3 . . . . . . .161 B7
Wittersham CE
Prim Sch TN30 . . . . .189 D2
Wittersham Cl ME5 . . . . . .62 B5
Wittersham House 2 BR5 38 D1
Wittersham Rd Potman's
Heath TN17,TN30 . . . . . .188 D4
Wittersham TN30 . . . . . . .189 C5
Wittersham Road Sta
TN17 . . . . .188 D6
Wixom House SE3 . . . . .5 C3
Woburn Cl SE28 . . . . .3 D7
Woburn Ct 1 DA6 . . . . .7 E3
Wodehouse Cl ME20 . . . . .74 F4
Wodehouse Rd DA1 . . . . . .10 A3
Woldham Pl BR2 . . . . .36 C5
Woldham Rd BR2 . . . . .36 C5
Wolds Dr BR6 . . . . .51 A6
Wolfe Cl BR2 . . . . .36 A3
Wolfe Cres SE7 . . . . .1 D1
Wolfe Rd ME16 . . . . .91 B2
Wollaston Cl ME8 . . . . .63 D3
Wolseley Rd TN4 . . . . . . .149 C2
Wolsey Ct SE9 . . . . .5 F1
Wolsey Mews BR6 . . . . . . .51 F5
Wolsley Cl DA1 . . . . .8 E2
Wolvercote Rd SE2 . . . . . . .3 D4
Wombwell Gdns DA11 . . . .29 E6
Wood Cl Dartford DA5 . . . . .25 E5
Ditton ME20 . . . . .90 E8
Wood Dr Chislehurst BR7 . .22 E7
Sevenoaks TN13 . . . . .83 F1
Wood End BR8 . . . . .39 C5
Wood La Dartford DA2 . . . .27 F4
East End TN17 . . . . .171 C3
Wood Lodge Gdns BR1 . . .22 E1
Wood Lodge Grange TN13 84 C5
Wood Pl DA1 . . . . .24 A3
Wood Point 10 E16 . . . . .1 A8
Wood Retreat SE18 . . . . . . .6 D7
Wood Ride BR5 . . . . .37 E5
Wood Side Sch DA17 . . . . . .4 B2
Wood St Cuxton ME2 . . . . .46 B2
Gillingham ME7 . . . . .48 A6
6 Grays RM17 . . . . .12 C8
Newham E16 . . . . .1 B6
Royal Tunbridge Wells TN2 .149 B4
Swanley Village BR8 . . . . . .40 D8
Wood View Cl TN15 . . . . . .55 E3
Wood Way BR6 . . . . .51 A8
Woodberry Gr DA5 . . . . . .25 D5
Woodbine Rd DA15 . . . . . .23 E7
Woodbridge Dr ME15 . . . . .91 F1
Woodbrook Rd SE2 . . . . . . .7 B8
Woodbury Cl TN4 . . . . . . .149 A5
Woodbury La TN30 . . . . . .183 A7
Woodbury ParkGdns
TN4 . . . . .149 B5
Woodbury Park Rd TN4 . .149 B5
Woodbury Rd Chatham ME5 61 F1
Hawkhurst TN18 . . . . .179 A2
Woodchurch Cl
Chatham ME5 . . . . .62 B5
Sidcup DA14 . . . . .23 D5
Woodchurch Cres ME8 . . .49 C2
Woodchurch Ct 1 BR5 . . .38 C4
Woodchurch Dr BR1 . . . . .22 D1
Woodchurch House 49 C2
Woodchurch Rd TN30 . . . .183 D8
Woodclyffe Dr BR7 . . . . . .37 A7
Woodcock La
Benenden TN17 . . . . .180 E3
Grafty Green ME17 . . . . . .126 E5
Woodcocks
Headcorn TN27 . . . . .141 D5
Newham E16 . . . . .1 D8
Woodcote Dr BR6 . . . . .37 D2
Woodcroft SE9 . . . . .22 F5
Woodcut ME14 . . . . .92 A8
Woodfall Dr DA1 . . . . .8 F3
Woodfalls Ind Est SE18 . .120 D6
Woodfield Ave
Gravesend DA11 . . . . .30 B6
Tonbridge TN11 . . . . .116 E5
Woodfield Rd TN9 . . . . . . .133 B8
Woodfield Way ME3 . . . . . .33 E4
Woodfields TN13 . . . . .83 D4
Woodford House 18 SE18 . .6 B8
Woodford Rd ME16 . . . . . .91 B2
Woodgate La ME9 . . . . . . .65 C2
Woodgate Rd ME19 . . . . . .73 D4
Woodgate Way TN9,TN11 .133 C6
Woodgers Gr BR8 . . . . .39 F7

Woodget Cl E6 . . . . .1 E7
Woodhatch Cl E6 . . . . .1 E8
Woodhayes BR7 . . . . .23 B2
Woodhead Dr BR6 . . . . . . .51 E8
Woodhill SE18 . . . . .1 E2
Woodhill Pk TN2 . . . . . . .150 C6
Woodhill Prim Sch SE18 . . .1 E2
Woodhurst ME5 . . . . .61 D4
Woodhurst Ave BR5 . . . . .37 C3
Woodhurst Cl ME2 . . . . . . .46 B2
Woodhurst Rd SE2 . . . . . . .3 A2
Woodington Cl SE9 . . . . . . .6 A1
Woodknoll Dr BR7 . . . . . . .36 F8
Woodland Ave DA3 . . . . . . .42 F5
Woodland Cl
  New Barn DA3 . . . . .43 C6
  New Town ME19 . . . . . . .89 A8
  Royal Tunbridge Wells TN4 .149 C7
Woodland Dr TN8 . . . . . . .112 D3
Woodland Rd TN4 . . . . . . .149 C7
Woodland Rise TN15 . . . . .84 E4
Woodland Terr SE7 . . . . . . .1 E2
Woodland View TN30 . . . .189 E4
Woodland Way
  Bidborough TN4 . . . . .132 D3
  Erith SE2 . . . . .3 D2
  Maidstone ME14 . . . . .92 B7
  Orpington BR5 . . . . .37 C4
  Swanscombe DA9 . . . . . . .11 A3
Woodlands Bexley DA6 . . . .8 B2
  Chatham ME5 . . . . .62 A2
  Coxheath ME17 . . . . .106 B3
  Cranbrook TN17 . . . . .169 D6
  Paddock Wood TN12 . . . . .135 C4
  Pembury TN2 . . . . .150 F7
  Royal Tunbridge Wells TN4 .133 A2
  Swanley BR8 . . . . .39 E6
Woodlands Ave
  Sidcup DA15 . . . . .23 E7
  Snodland ME6 . . . . .74 F8
Woodlands Cl Bromley BR1 .36 F7
  Maidstone ME14 . . . . .92 B7
  Swanley BR8 . . . . .39 F7
  Teston ME18 . . . . .105 B8
Woodlands
  Inf & Jun Schs TN10 . .117 E6
Woodlands La DA12 . . . . . .31 E1
Woodlands Par ME20 . . . . .90 D8
Woodlands Pk DA5 . . . . . . .25 D4
Woodlands Prim Sch ME7 .48 F4
Woodlands Rd Bexley DA7 . .7 E4
  Bromley BR1 . . . . .36 F7
  Ditton ME20 . . . . .90 D8
  Gillingham ME7 . . . . .48 F4
  Orpington BR6 . . . . .52 A4
  Tonbridge TN9 . . . . .133 A7
Woodlands Rise BR8 . . . . .39 F7
Woodlands Terr BR8 . . . . .39 F7
Woodlands The BR6 . . . . . .52 B4
Woodlands View TN14 . . . .53 A1
Woodlark Rd ME4 . . . . .34 B1
Woodlea Larkfield ME19 . . .74 F2
  New Barn DA3 . . . . .43 C6
Woodleas ME16 . . . . .90 F2
Woodley Rd BR6 . . . . .52 C8
Woodman Par 4 E16 . . . . . .2 A5
Woodman St E16 . . . . .2 A5
Woodmere SE9 . . . . .22 F7
Woodmount BR8 . . . . .39 D2
Woodpecker Cl 2 TN8 . . .112 D3
Woodpecker Glade ME8 . .63 D6

Woodpecker Rd
  Larkfield ME20 . . . . .74 F1
  Woolwich SE28 . . . . .3 C6
Woodrow SE18 . . . . .1 F2
Woodrush Pl ME4 . . . . .34 B1
Woods Green Cotts TN5 .174 F7
Woodsgate Way TN2 . . . .150 B6
Woodside
  Gillingham ME8 . . . . .63 C6
  Kilndown TN17 . . . . .166 F2
  Orpington BR6 . . . . .52 B5
  Vigo Village DA13 . . . . . . .72 F8
Woodside Ave BR7 . . . . . . .23 C3
Woodside Cl Crayford DA7 . .8 D3
  Pembury TN2 . . . . .150 E6
Woodside Cres DA15 . . . . .23 E5
Woodside Dr DA2 . . . . .25 E4
Woodside Gn ME3 . . . . . . .33 B7
Woodside La DA5 . . . . .7 D1
Woodside Par DA15 . . . . . .23 E5
Woodside Rd Bromley BR1 .36 F6
  Crayford DA7 . . . . .8 D3
  Maidstone ME15 . . . . . . .107 C7
  Pembury TN2 . . . . .150 E6
  Royal Tunbridge Wells TN4 .148 D4
  Sevenoaks TN13 . . . . .84 B4
  Sidcup DA15 . . . . .23 E5
  Sundridge TN14 . . . . .82 E3
  Tonbridge TN9 . . . . .133 B7
Woodside Sch DA7 . . . . . . .8 D3
Woodstock Cl DA5 . . . . . . .24 F7
Woodstock Ct SE12 . . . . . . .5 A1
Woodstock Rd ME2 . . . . . .47 A7
Woodvale Ct BR1 . . . . .36 B7
Woodview Cl BR6 . . . . .51 C8
Woodview Cres TN11 . . . .116 F5
Woodview Rd BR8 . . . . . . .39 D7
Woodview Rise ME2 . . . . . .32 F1
Woodville SE3 . . . . .5 B6
Woodville Cl SE12 . . . . .5 A2
Woodville Gr 2 DA16 . . . . .7 A4
Woodville Pl DA12 . . . . . . .30 B8
Woodville Rd ME15 . . . . . .92 A2
Woodville St 15 SE18 . . . . . .1 E2
Woodward Terr DA9 . . . . . .10 E1
Woodyates Rd
  Lewisham SE12 . . . . .22 B8
  Lewisham SE12 . . . . .5 A1
Woolacombe Rd SE3 . . . . . .5 C5
Woolaston Cl ME15 . . . . . .91 F1
Wooldeys Rd ME8 . . . . . . .49 F2
Woolf Cl SE28 . . . . .3 B5
Woolf Wlk RM18 . . . . .13 C5
Woollett Cl DA1 . . . . .9 A3
Woollett St ME14 . . . . .92 A5
Woolley Cl TN4 . . . . .132 F1
Woolley Rd
  Maidstone ME15 . . . . . . .107 F7
  Royal Tunbridge Wells TN4 .132 F1
Woolpack Cnr TN27 . . . . .172 A7
Woolpack Cotts TN27 . . . .172 A7
Woolwich Arsenal Sta SE18 2 B2
Woolwich Church St SE18 . .1 E3
Woolwich Cl ME5 . . . . .62 A7
Woolwich Coll SE18 . . . . . .2 C2
Woolwich Coll
  (Charlton) SE7 . . . . .1 D3
Woolwich Comm SE18 . . . .6 A8
Woolwich Dockyard
  Ind Est SE18 . . . . .1 E3
Woolwich Dockyard Sta
  SE18 . . . . .1 F2
Woolwich High St SE18 . . .2 A3
Woolwich Manor Way E6 . .2 A7

Woolwich Manorway E16 . .2 B4
Woolwich Poly Sch
  (Lower) SE18 . . . . .2 B3
Woolwich Poly Sch
  (Upper) SE18 . . . . .2 B1
Woolwich Rd Bexley DA7 . .8 A4
  Erith SE2 . . . . .3 E1
  Greenwich SE10,SE7 . . . . . .1 C2
Wootton Gn ME8 . . . . .49 D3
Wootton House SE9 . . . . . . .6 D1
Wopsle Cl ME1 . . . . .61 D7
Worcester Ave ME19 . . . . .89 A2
Worcester Cl
  Istead Rise DA13 . . . . .29 F1
  Rochester ME2 . . . . .46 E8
  Swanscombe DA9 . . . . . . .11 B3
Worcester Rd ME15 . . . . .107 D7
Wordsworth Cl
  Chatham ME5 . . . . .62 C7
  Tilbury RM18 . . . . .13 C5
Wordsworth House 15 SE18 6 A8
Wordsworth Rd Bexley DA16 6 E6
  Maidstone ME14 . . . . .92 B7
Wordsworth Way
  Dartford DA1 . . . . .10 A3
  New Hythe ME20 . . . . . . .75 A4
Workhouse La ME15 . . . . .106 C4
Workhouse Rd
  Chartway Street ME17 . . . .125 A8
  Ryarsh ME19 . . . . .73 F4
World of Silk* DA1 . . . . .8 E2
Worlds End La BR6 . . . . . . .52 B3
Wormdale Hill ME9 . . . . . .65 B3
Wormdale Rd ME9 . . . . . . .65 B4
Worsenden TN27 . . . . .157 E1
Worsfold Ct ME15 . . . . . . .92 A1
Worships Hill TN13 . . . . . . .83 E4
Worth Cl BR6 . . . . .51 E6
Wotton Cl ME15 . . . . .107 E5
Wotton Gn BR5 . . . . .38 D5
Wouldham CE
  Prim Sch ME1 . . . . .60 C5
Wouldham Rd
  Grays RM17,RM20 . . . . . . .11 E8
  Rochester ME1 . . . . .46 E1
Wouldham Terr 3 BR5 . . .38 B6
Wrangleden Cl ME15 . . . .107 E5
Wrangleden Rd ME15 . . . .107 E5
Wrangling La DA13 . . . . . . .58 F3
Wrekin Rd E6 . . . . .2 A6
Wren Cl Larkfield ME20 . . . .74 F1
  St Paul's Cray BR5 . . . . . . .38 D6
Wren Ind Est ME15 . . . . . .107 F4
Wren Path SE28 . . . . .2 D4
Wren Rd DA14 . . . . .24 C5
Wren Way ME5 . . . . .62 B6
Wren Wlk RM18 . . . . .13 B7
Wrens Croft DA11 . . . . . . .29 E4
Wrens Rd ME9 . . . . .80 F6
Wricklemarsh Rd
  Greenwich SE3 . . . . .5 B6
  Greenwich SE3 . . . . .5 D6
Wright Cl Gillingham ME8 . .49 C2
  Swanscombe DA10 . . . . . .11 D1
Wrights Cl TN30 . . . . .183 A8
Wrot & Hill Ct DA4 . . . . . . .41 B8
Wrotham Hill Rd TN15 . . . .72 A6
Wrotham Rd Bexley DA16 . .7 C6
  Borough Green TN15 . . . . .87 A8
  Culverstone Green DA13 . . .57 E2
  Gravesend DA11,DA13 . . . .30 A4
  Meopham DA13 . . . . .44 A3
Wrotham Road Prim
  Sch DA11 . . . . .30 B8

Wrotham Sch TN15 . . . . . .72 A1
Wrotham Water La
  ME19,TN15 . . . . .72 E5
Wrotham Water Rd
  TN15,ME19 . . . . .72 E4
Wrottesley Rd SE18 . . . . . . .6 C8
Wroxham Rd SE28 . . . . .3 D6
Wulfred Way TN15 . . . . . . .70 B1
Wyatt Cl TN15 . . . . .86 F7
Wyatt Ho 1 ME2 . . . . .47 A7
Wyatt Pl ME2 . . . . .47 A7
Wyatt Rd DA1 . . . . .8 F4
Wyatt St ME14 . . . . .92 A4
Wyborne Prim Sch SE9 . . .23 B7
Wybourne Rise TN2 . . . . .163 B8
Wybournes La ME23 . . . . .17 C3
Wycliffe Cl DA16 . . . . .6 F6
Wycliffe Ho 5 DA11 . . . . .29 F7
Wycliffe Row DA11 . . . . . . .29 F7
Wycombe Ct SE3 . . . . .5 A7
Wydeville Manor Rd SE12 .22 B4
Wye Cl BR6 . . . . .37 F2
Wye Rd Borough Green TN15 87 A8
  Gravesend DA12 . . . . .30 D6
  Tonbridge TN10 . . . . .117 C5
Wyfold Ho 10 SE2 . . . . .3 D4
Wyke Manor Rd ME14 . . . .92 A4
Wykeham Cl DA12 . . . . . . .30 E2
Wykeham Cotts ME17 . . . .106 F2
Wykeham Ct BR7 . . . . .23 E2
Wykeham Gr ME17 . . . . . .109 A7
Wykeham St ME2 . . . . .47 B8
Wyles Rd ME4 . . . . .47 E2
Wyles St ME7 . . . . .48 C7
Wylie Ho ME3 . . . . .33 B6
Wylie Rd ME3 . . . . .34 D6
Wyncham Ave DA15 . . . . . .23 E7
Wyncroft Cl BR1 . . . . .36 F6
Wyndam Rd ME4 . . . . .47 E2
Wyndham Ave TN11 . . . . .115 F1
Wyndham Cl Leigh TN11 . .115 F1
  Orpington BR6 . . . . .37 C1
Wynford Gr BR5 . . . . .38 B6
Wynford Pl DA17 . . . . .8 A8
Wynford Way SE9 . . . . . . .22 F5
Wynn's Ave ME15 . . . . .7 A2
Wytchlings The ME17 . . . .109 D2
Wythens Wlk SE9 . . . . .6 B1
Wytherling Ct ME14 . . . . . .92 F5
Wythes Cl BR1 . . . . .36 F7
Wythes Rd E16 . . . . .1 E5
Wythfield Rd SE9 . . . . .5 F1
Wyvern Cl Dartford DA1 . . .26 C8
  Orpington BR6 . . . . .52 B7
  Snodland ME6 . . . . .75 A7
Wyvern House 3 RM17 . . .12 B8
Wyvill Cl ME8 . . . . .63 E5

Y

Yalding Cl ME2 . . . . .33 B1
Yalding Gr BR5 . . . . .38 D5
Yalding Hill ME18 . . . . . . .105 A3
Yalding Organic Gdns*
  ME18 . . . . .120 F8
Yalding St Peter & St
  Paul CE Prim Sch
  ME18 . . . . .105 A1
Yalding Sta ME18 . . . . . . .104 D1
Yantlet Dr ME2 . . . . .46 C7
Yardley Cl TN9 . . . . .117 D3
Yardley Park Rd TN9 . . . .117 D3

Yarnton Way DA17,DA18 . . . .3 E4
Yarrow Cres E6 . . . . .1 E8
Yarrow Ct ME14 . . . . .92 F5
Yarrow Rd ME5 . . . . .61 F4
Yateley St SE18 . . . . .1 D3
Yaugher La ME9 . . . . .64 C3
Ye Olde Tudor Ct BR7 . . . .23 B3
Yelsted La Chatham ME14 . .77 D7
  Yelsted ME9 . . . . .64 A1
Yelsted Rd ME9 . . . . .79 A7
Yeoman Ct E6 . . . . .2 B6
Yeoman Ct ME14 . . . . .93 B3
Yeoman Dr ME7 . . . . .48 F1
Yeoman Gdns TN12 . . . . .135 F6
Yeoman Ho ME1 . . . . .47 D4
Yeoman La ME14 . . . . .93 B4
Yeoman Pk ME15 . . . . .93 A2
Yeoman Way ME15 . . . . . . .93 A2
Yeoman's Mdws TN13 . . . .84 A1
Yeovil Cl BR6 . . . . .51 E8
Yester Dr BR7 . . . . .22 E1
Yester Pk BR7 . . . . .22 F2
Yester Rd BR7 . . . . .22 F1
Yew Rd ME3 . . . . .34 E3
Yew Tree Cl Aylesford ME20 .75 E1
  Bexley DA16 . . . . .7 A6
  Chatham ME5 . . . . .62 D1
  New Barn DA3 . . . . .43 D7
  Sevenoaks TN13 . . . . .83 D4
Yew Tree Cotts
  Groombridge TN3 . . . . . . .161 B8
  Halstead TN14 . . . . .67 F7
  Maidstone,Sandling ME14 . .76 F1
Yew Tree Green Rd
  TN12 . . . . .137 A1
Yew Tree Pl ME7 . . . . .63 B1
Yew Tree Rd TN4 . . . . . . .149 B8
Yews The DA12 . . . . .30 D7
Yoke Cl ME2 . . . . .47 B8
Yolande Gdns SE9 . . . . .5 E2
Yopps Gn TN15 . . . . .86 E1
York Ave Chatham ME5 . . . .61 F3
  Gillingham ME7 . . . . .48 C4
  Sidcup DA15 . . . . .23 F6
York Cl E6 . . . . .1 F7
York Hill ME5 . . . . .48 C2
York Par TN10 . . . . .117 C6
York Pl RM17 . . . . .12 A8
York Rd Dartford DA1 . . . . .26 F8
  Gravesend DA12 . . . . .30 C5
  Maidstone ME15 . . . . .92 C2
  Northfleet DA11 . . . . .29 D8
  Rochester ME1 . . . . .47 C3
  Royal Tunbridge Wells TN1 .149 A4
  Tonbridge TN10 . . . . .117 D5
York Rise BR6 . . . . .51 E8
York Road Jun Sch DA1 . .26 F8
York Terr DA8 . . . . .8 C6
Yorkland Ave DA16 . . . . . . .6 F3
Youens Pl ME3 . . . . .32 B3
Young Rd E16 . . . . .1 C7

Z

Zambra Way TN15 . . . . . . .84 F7
Zangwill Rd SE18,SE3 . . . . .5 D6
Zealand Ho SE18 . . . . .1 E2
Zelah Rd BR5 . . . . .38 C2
Zetland Ave ME7 . . . . .48 E2
Zillah Gdns ME8 . . . . .63 C6
Zion Pl DA12 . . . . .30 B8
Zion St TN15 . . . . .84 F6